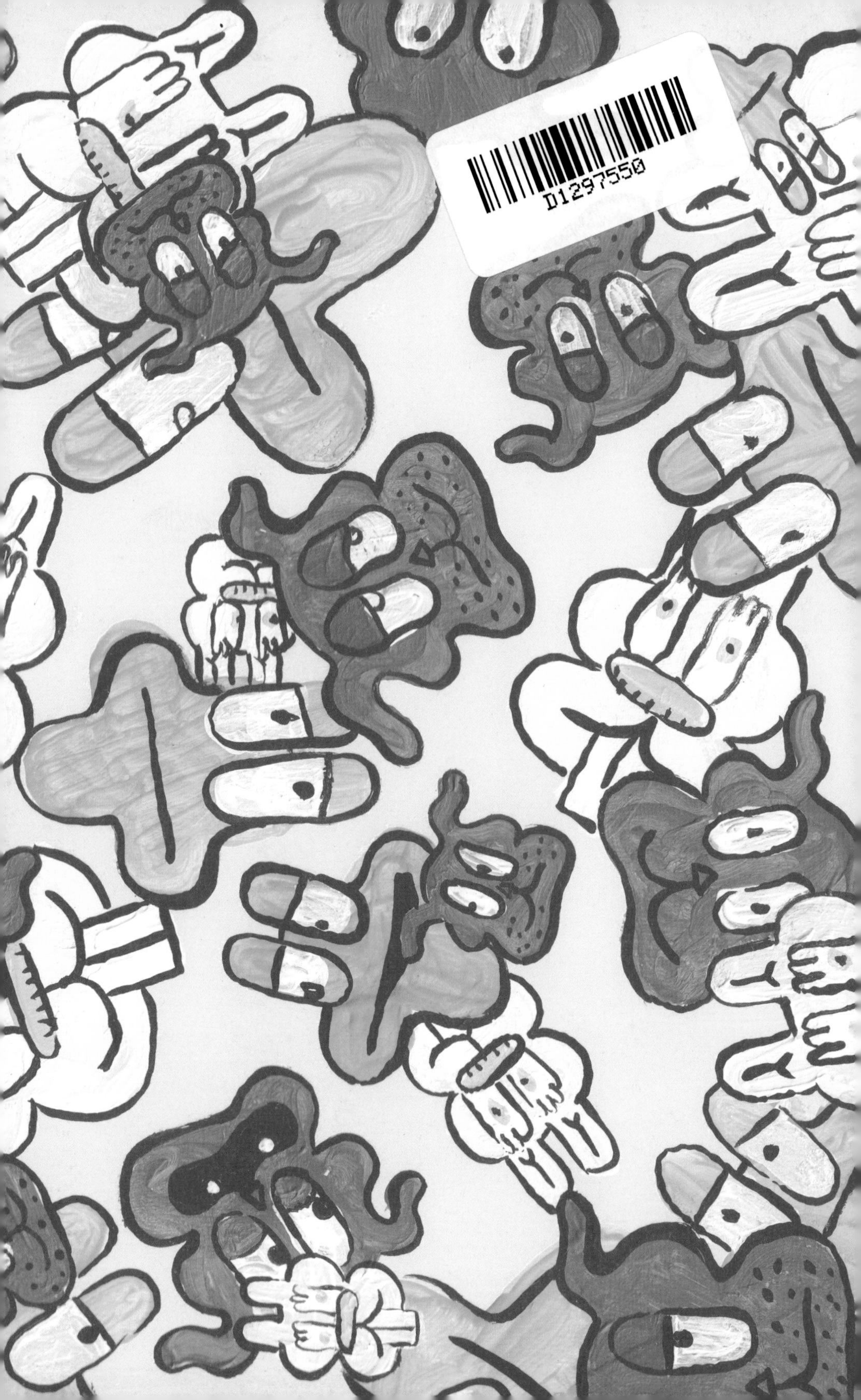

ALEX GRAHAM

Dog Biscuits

FANTAGRAPHICS

FANTAGRAPHICS BOOKS INC.
7563 Lake City Way NE
Seattle, Washington, 98115
www.fantagraphics.com

DESIGN: Graham and Covey
PRODUCTION: Paul Baresh
PROMOTION: Jacquelene Cohen
VP / ASSOCIATE PUBLISHER / EDITOR: Eric Reynolds
PRESIDENT / PUBLISHER: Gary Groth

View other comix & artworks by
Alex Graham at alexNgraham.com

ISBN 978-1-68396-552-7
Library of Congress Control Number 2021951117
First printing: June 2022
Printed in Korea

Dog Biscuits was originally a webcomic, airing up to three times daily, starting on June 17, 2020 and concluding on January 12, 2021. Each Instagram episode typically contained 6 panels (1 page) & as such the reader may observe an episodic rhythm to each page, where it either ends on a punch-line or a cliffhanger.

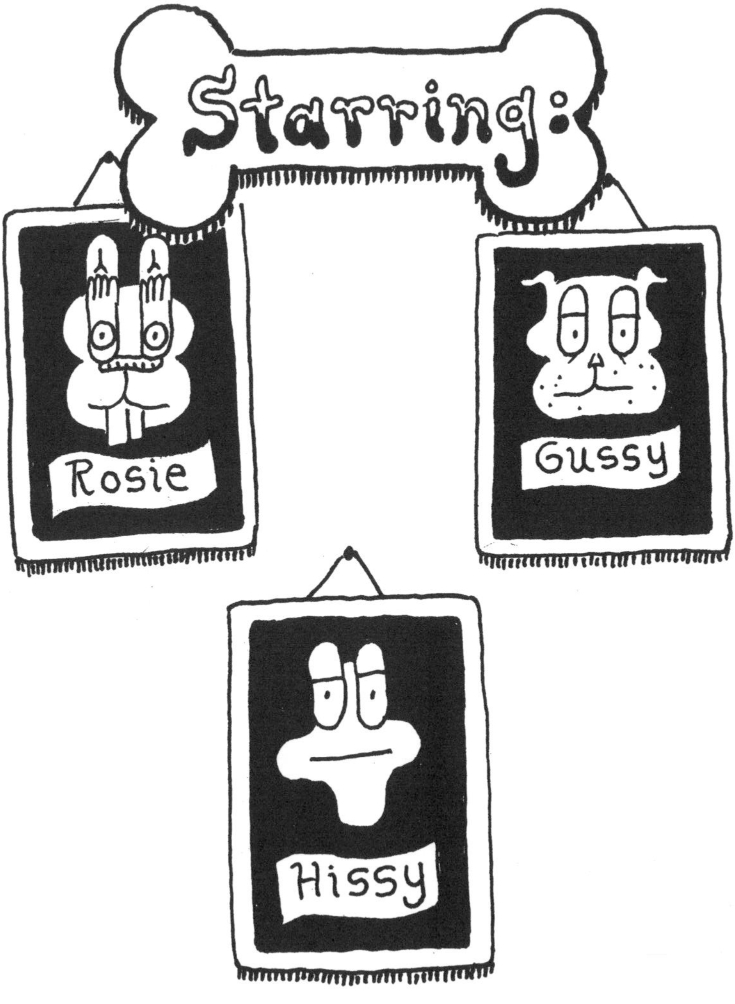
Starring:
Rosie
Gussy
Hissy

"Social Distance"

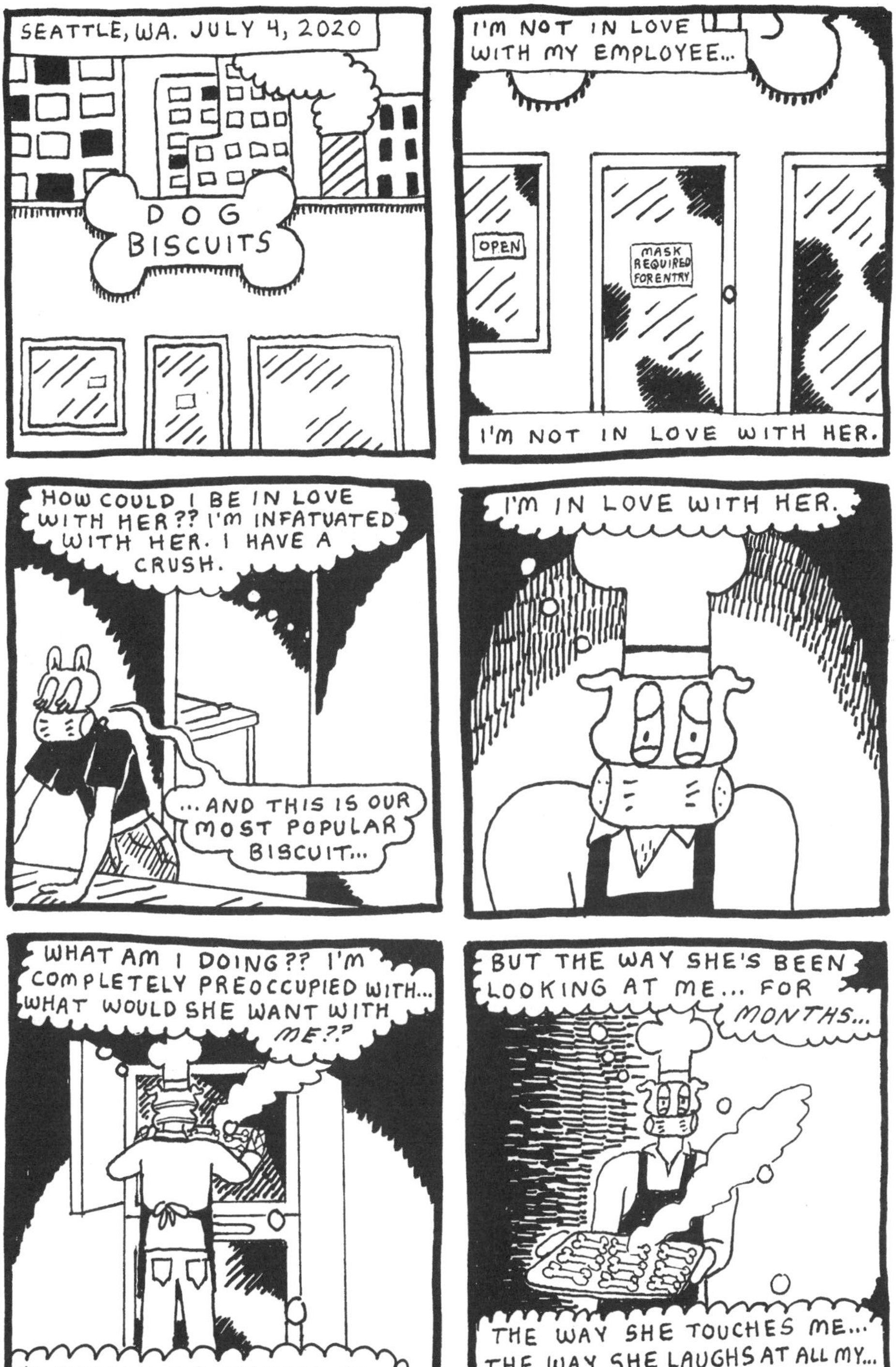
SEATTLE, WA. JULY 4, 2020
DOG BISCUITS
I'M NOT IN LOVE WITH MY EMPLOYEE...
OPEN
MASK REQUIRED FOR ENTRY
I'M NOT IN LOVE WITH HER.
HOW COULD I BE IN LOVE WITH HER?? I'M INFATUATED WITH HER. I HAVE A CRUSH.
...AND THIS IS OUR MOST POPULAR BISCUIT...
I'M IN LOVE WITH HER.
WHAT AM I DOING?? I'M COMPLETELY PREOCCUPIED WITH... WHAT WOULD SHE WANT WITH ME??
I'M JUST AN OLD, WASHED UP...
BUT THE WAY SHE'S BEEN LOOKING AT ME... FOR MONTHS...
THE WAY SHE TOUCHES ME... THE WAY SHE LAUGHS AT ALL MY...

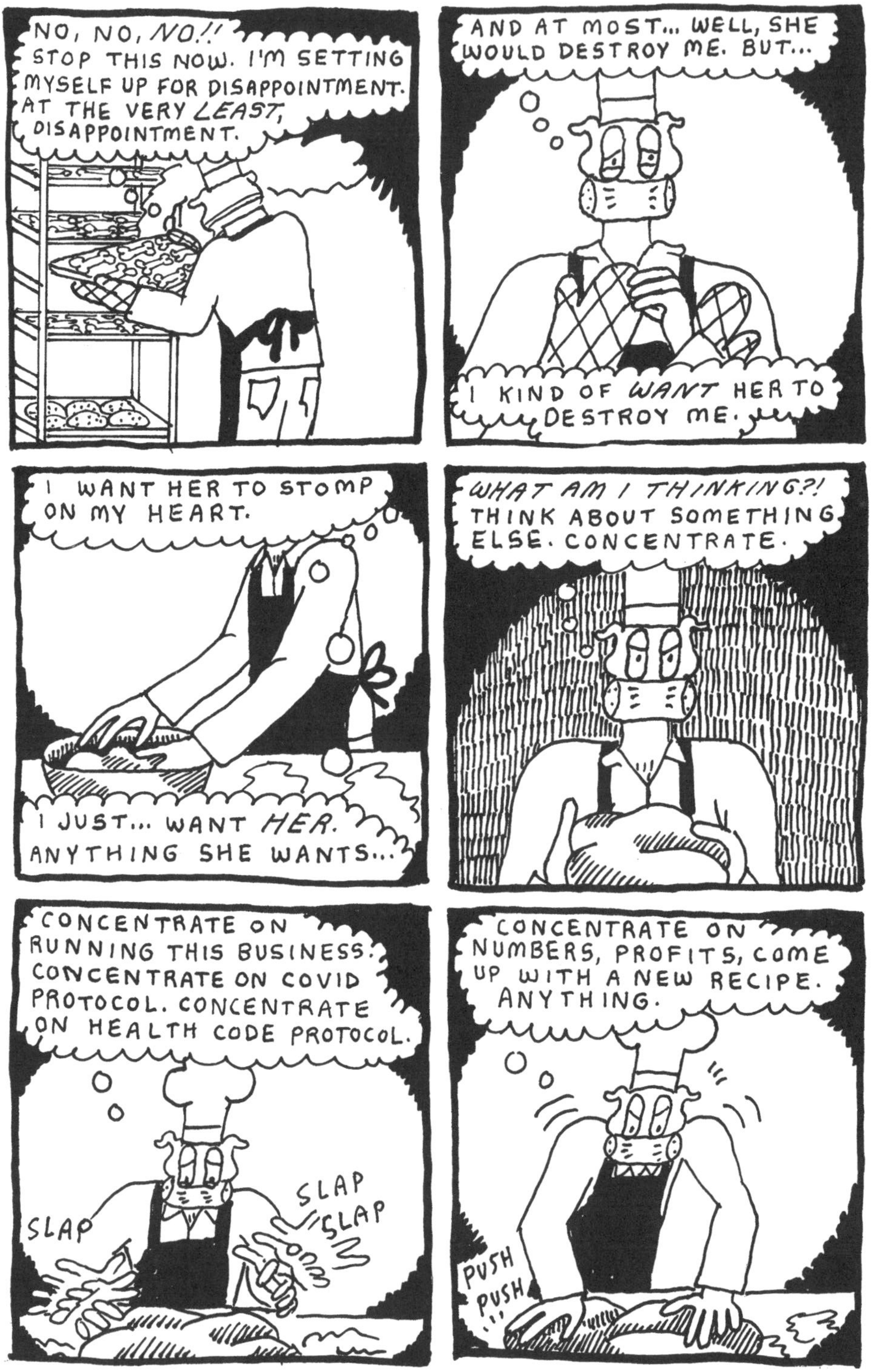
NO, NO, NO!!
STOP THIS NOW. I'M SETTING MYSELF UP FOR DISAPPOINTMENT. AT THE VERY LEAST, DISAPPOINTMENT.
AND AT MOST... WELL, SHE WOULD DESTROY ME. BUT...
I KIND OF WANT HER TO DESTROY ME.
I WANT HER TO STOMP ON MY HEART.
I JUST... WANT HER. ANYTHING SHE WANTS...
WHAT AM I THINKING?! THINK ABOUT SOMETHING ELSE. CONCENTRATE.
CONCENTRATE ON RUNNING THIS BUSINESS. CONCENTRATE ON COVID PROTOCOL. CONCENTRATE ON HEALTH CODE PROTOCOL.
SLAP
SLAP
SLAP
CONCENTRATE ON NUMBERS, PROFITS, COME UP WITH A NEW RECIPE. ANYTHING.
PUSH
PUSH

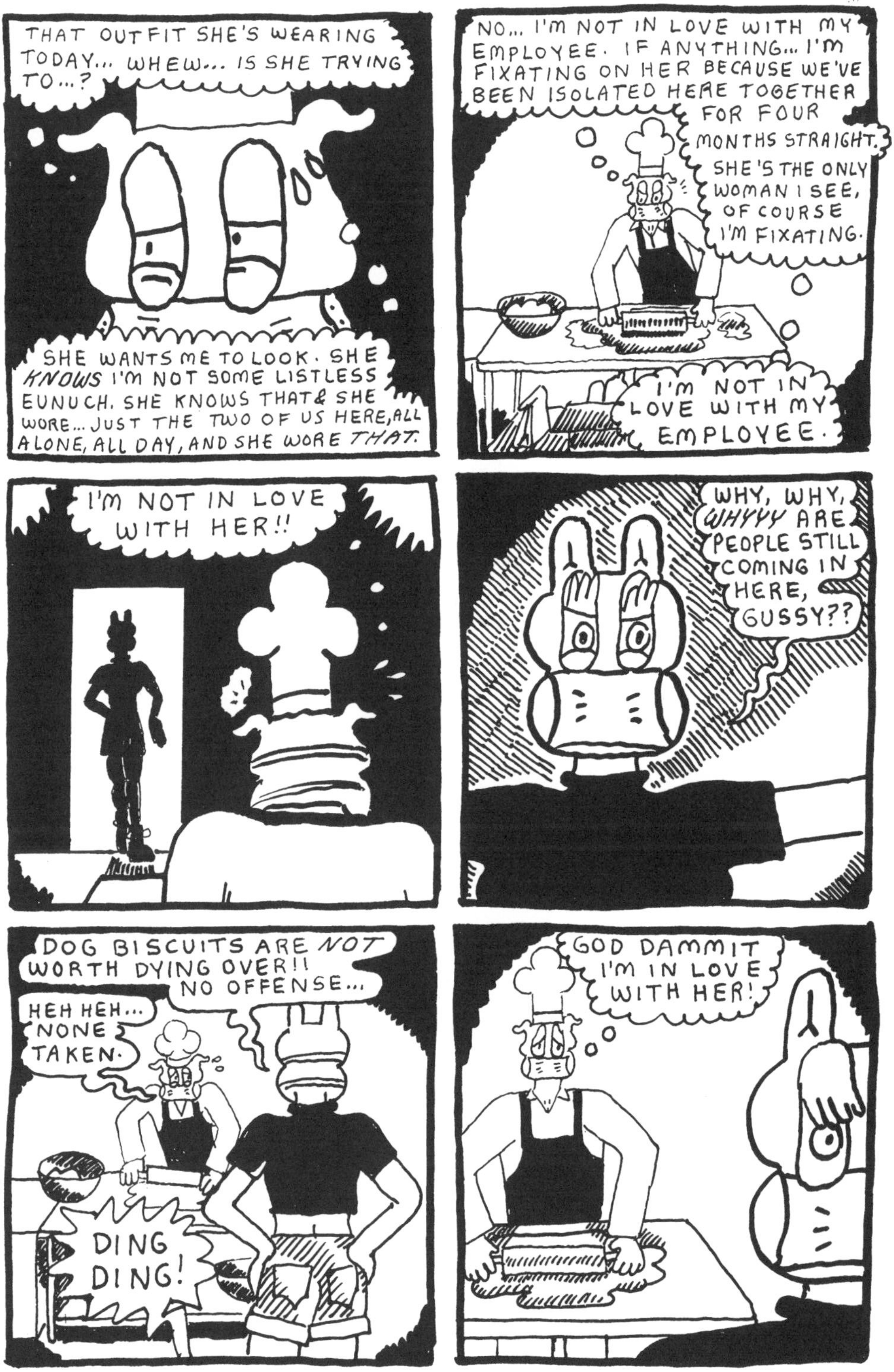
THAT OUTFIT SHE'S WEARING TODAY... WHEW... IS SHE TRYING TO...?
SHE WANTS ME TO LOOK. SHE KNOWS I'M NOT SOME LISTLESS EUNUCH. SHE KNOWS THAT & SHE WORE... JUST THE TWO OF US HERE, ALL ALONE, ALL DAY, AND SHE WORE THAT.
NO... I'M NOT IN LOVE WITH MY EMPLOYEE. IF ANYTHING... I'M FIXATING ON HER BECAUSE WE'VE BEEN ISOLATED HERE TOGETHER FOR FOUR MONTHS STRAIGHT. SHE'S THE ONLY WOMAN I SEE, OF COURSE I'M FIXATING.
I'M NOT IN LOVE WITH MY EMPLOYEE.
I'M NOT IN LOVE WITH HER!!
WHY, WHY, WHYYY ARE PEOPLE STILL COMING IN HERE, GUSSY??
DOG BISCUITS ARE NOT WORTH DYING OVER!! NO OFFENSE...
HEH HEH... NONE TAKEN.
DING DING!
GOD DAMMIT I'M IN LOVE WITH HER!

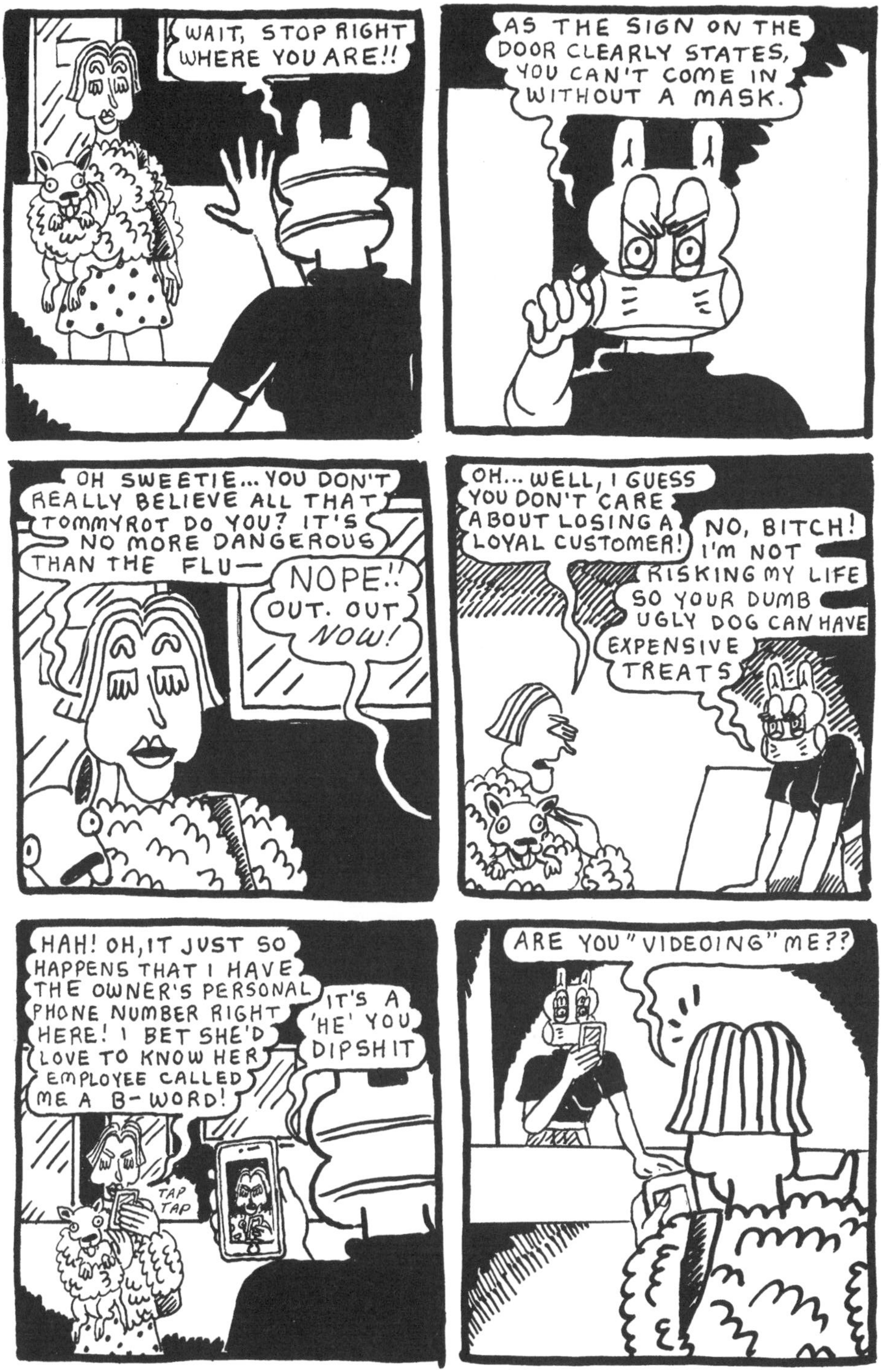
WAIT, STOP RIGHT WHERE YOU ARE!!
AS THE SIGN ON THE DOOR CLEARLY STATES, YOU CAN'T COME IN WITHOUT A MASK.
OH SWEETIE... YOU DON'T REALLY BELIEVE ALL THAT TOMMYROT DO YOU? IT'S NO MORE DANGEROUS THAN THE FLU—
NOPE!! OUT. OUT NOW!
OH... WELL, I GUESS YOU DON'T CARE ABOUT LOSING A LOYAL CUSTOMER!
NO, BITCH! I'M NOT RISKING MY LIFE SO YOUR DUMB UGLY DOG CAN HAVE EXPENSIVE TREATS
HAH! OH, IT JUST SO HAPPENS THAT I HAVE THE OWNER'S PERSONAL PHONE NUMBER RIGHT HERE! I BET SHE'D LOVE TO KNOW HER EMPLOYEE CALLED ME A B-WORD!
IT'S A 'HE' YOU DIPSHIT
TAP TAP
ARE YOU "VIDEOING" ME??

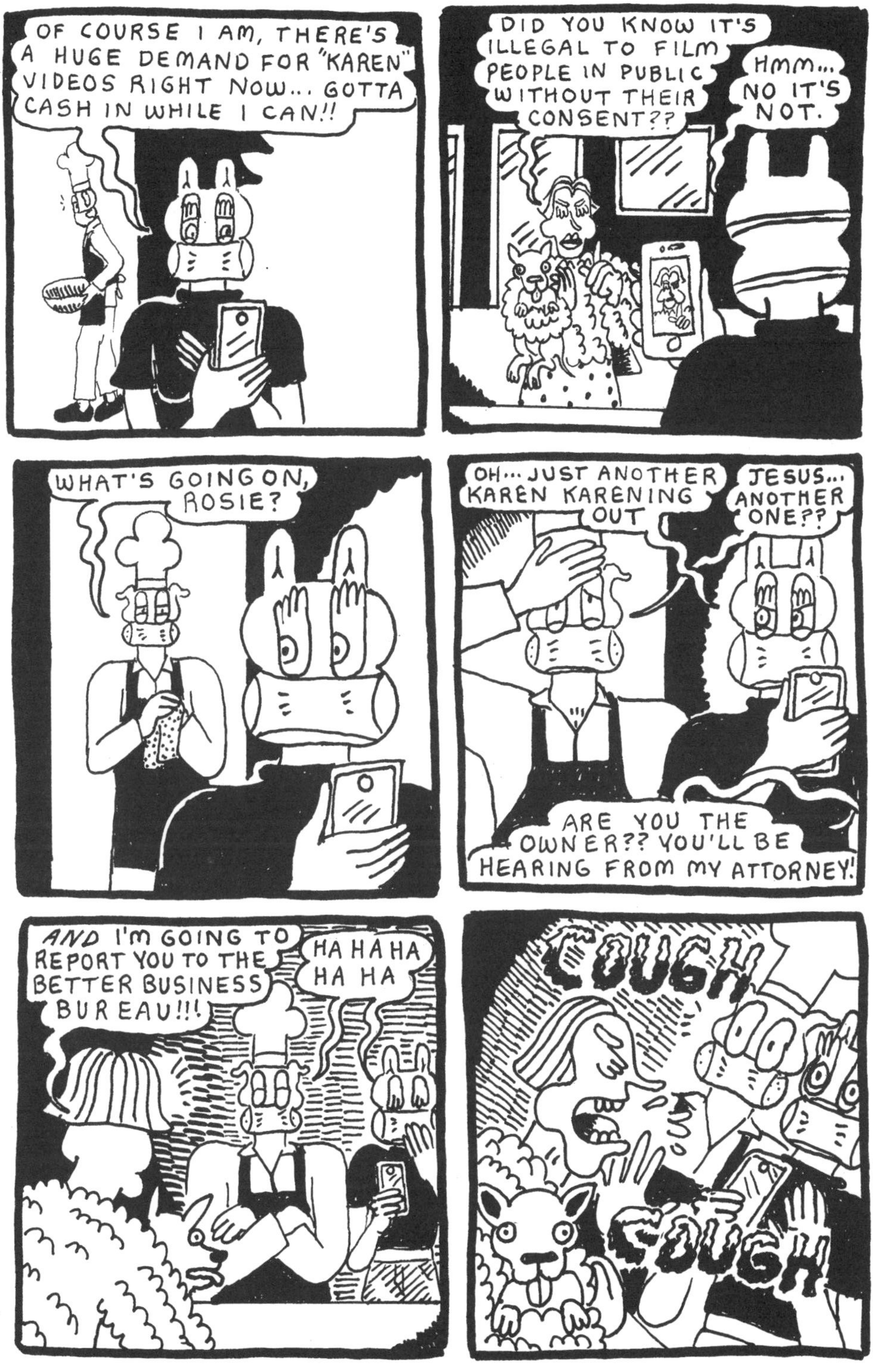
OF COURSE I AM, THERE'S A HUGE DEMAND FOR "KAREN" VIDEOS RIGHT NOW... GOTTA CASH IN WHILE I CAN!!
DID YOU KNOW IT'S ILLEGAL TO FILM PEOPLE IN PUBLIC WITHOUT THEIR CONSENT??
HMM... NO IT'S NOT.
WHAT'S GOING ON, ROSIE?
OH... JUST ANOTHER KAREN KARENING OUT
JESUS... ANOTHER ONE??
ARE YOU THE OWNER?? YOU'LL BE HEARING FROM MY ATTORNEY!
AND I'M GOING TO REPORT YOU TO THE BETTER BUSINESS BUREAU!!!
HA HA HA HA HA
COUGH
COUGH

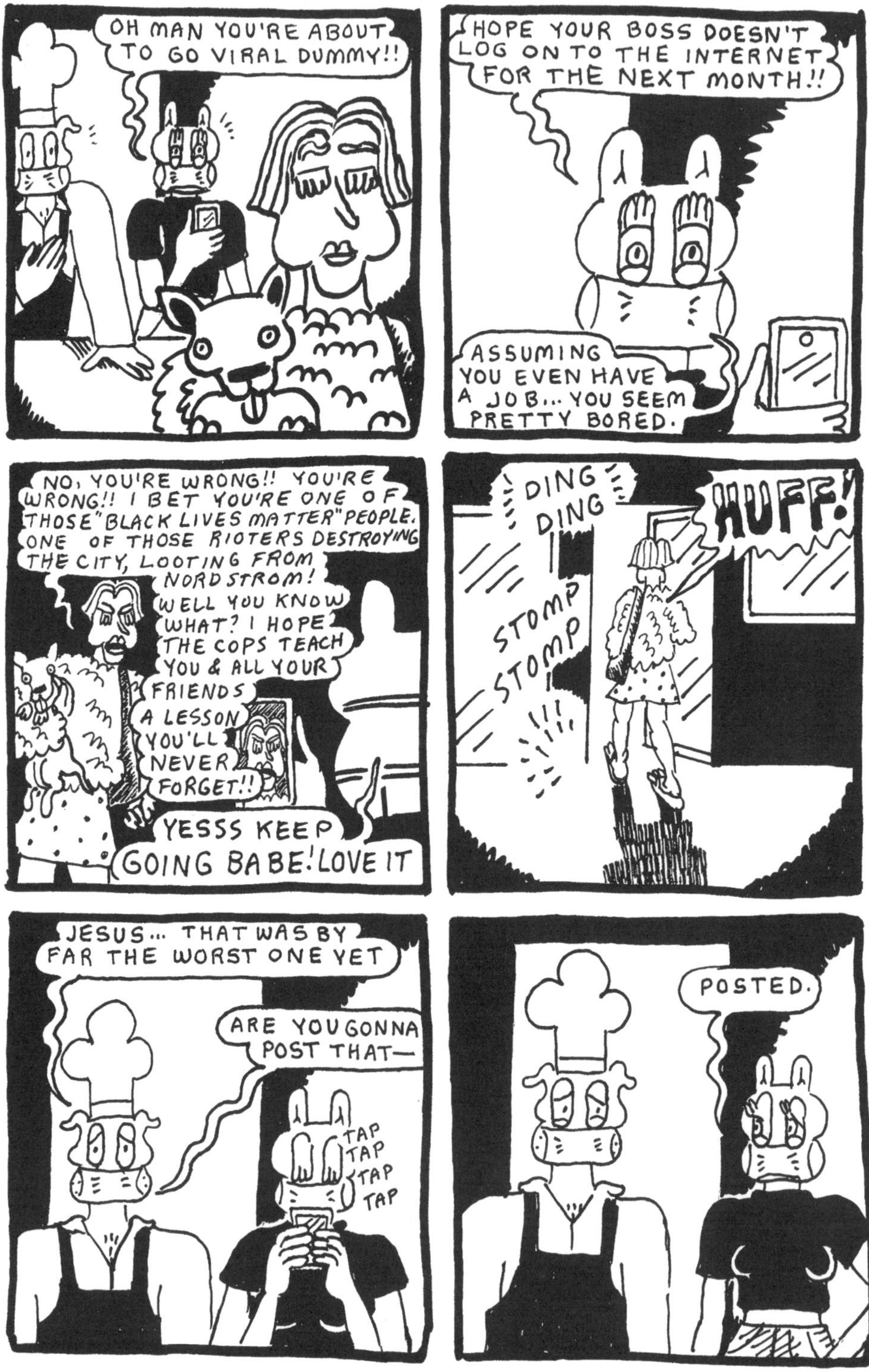
OH MAN YOU'RE ABOUT TO GO VIRAL DUMMY!!
HOPE YOUR BOSS DOESN'T LOG ON TO THE INTERNET FOR THE NEXT MONTH!!
ASSUMING YOU EVEN HAVE A JOB... YOU SEEM PRETTY BORED.
NO, YOU'RE WRONG!! YOU'RE WRONG!! I BET YOU'RE ONE OF THOSE "BLACK LIVES MATTER" PEOPLE. ONE OF THOSE RIOTERS DESTROYING THE CITY, LOOTING FROM NORDSTROM! WELL YOU KNOW WHAT? I HOPE THE COPS TEACH YOU & ALL YOUR FRIENDS A LESSON YOU'LL NEVER FORGET!!
YESSS KEEP GOING BABE! LOVE IT
DING DING
HUFF!
STOMP STOMP
JESUS... THAT WAS BY FAR THE WORST ONE YET
ARE YOU GONNA POST THAT—
TAP TAP TAP TAP
POSTED.

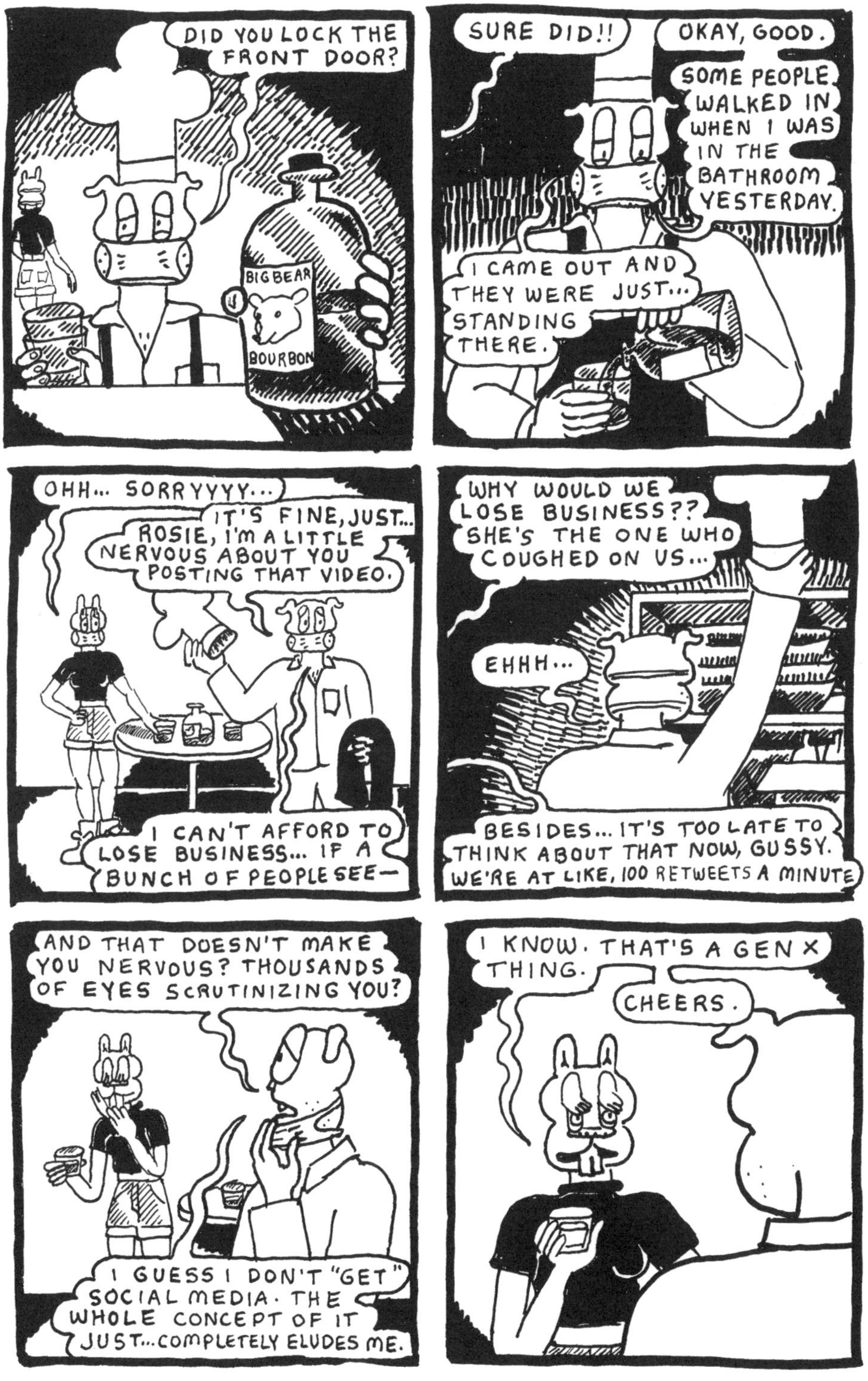
DID YOU LOCK THE FRONT DOOR?
BIG BEAR BOURBON
SURE DID!!
OKAY, GOOD.
SOME PEOPLE WALKED IN WHEN I WAS IN THE BATHROOM YESTERDAY.
I CAME OUT AND THEY WERE JUST... STANDING THERE.
OHH... SORRYYYY...
IT'S FINE, JUST... ROSIE, I'M A LITTLE NERVOUS ABOUT YOU POSTING THAT VIDEO.
I CAN'T AFFORD TO LOSE BUSINESS... IF A BUNCH OF PEOPLE SEE—
WHY WOULD WE LOSE BUSINESS?? SHE'S THE ONE WHO COUGHED ON US...
EHHH...
BESIDES... IT'S TOO LATE TO THINK ABOUT THAT NOW, GUSSY. WE'RE AT LIKE, 100 RETWEETS A MINUTE
AND THAT DOESN'T MAKE YOU NERVOUS? THOUSANDS OF EYES SCRUTINIZING YOU?
I GUESS I DON'T "GET" SOCIAL MEDIA. THE WHOLE CONCEPT OF IT JUST... COMPLETELY ELUDES ME.
I KNOW. THAT'S A GEN X THING.
CHEERS.

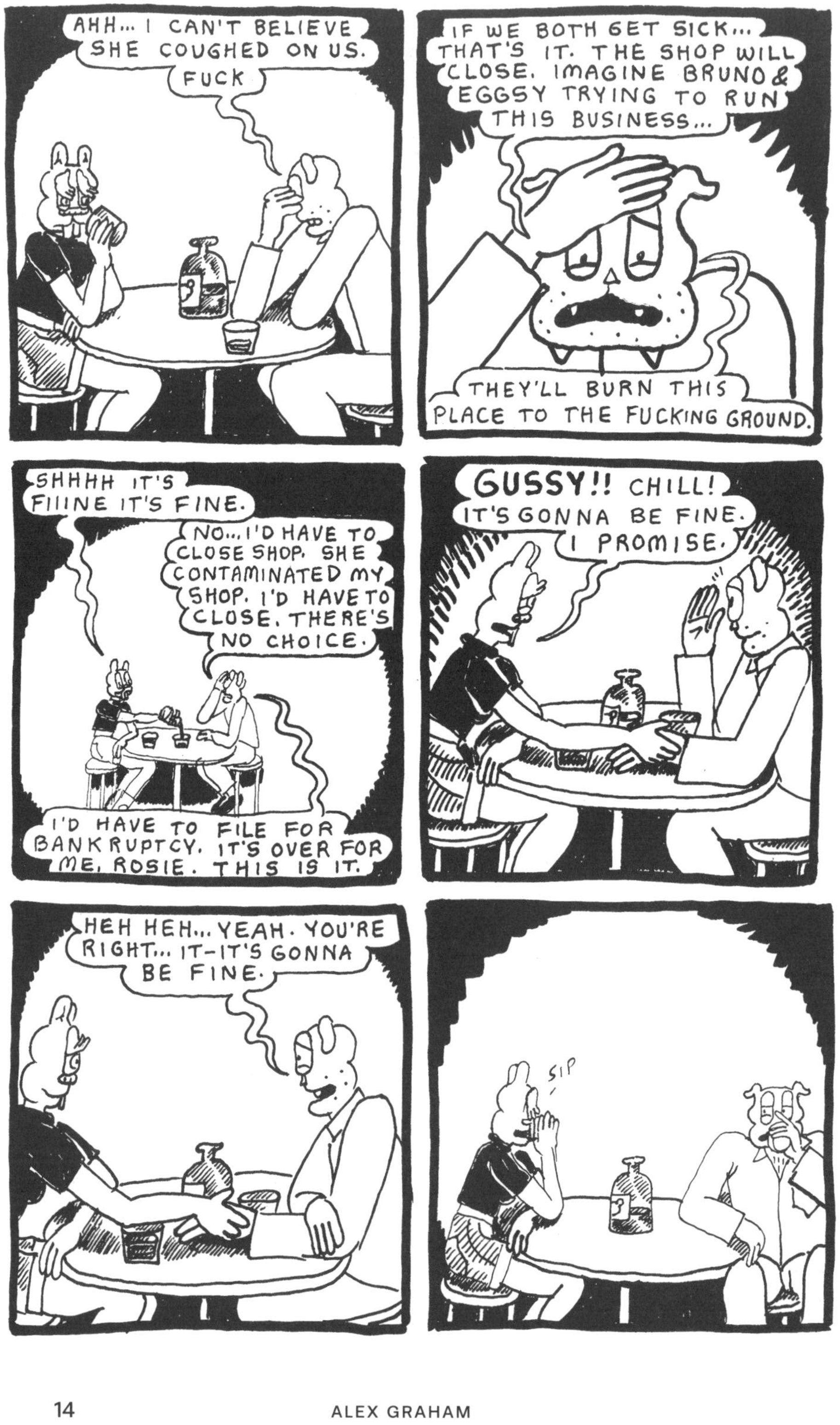
AHH... I CAN'T BELIEVE SHE COUGHED ON US.
FUCK
IF WE BOTH GET SICK... THAT'S IT. THE SHOP WILL CLOSE. IMAGINE BRUNO & EGGSY TRYING TO RUN THIS BUSINESS...
THEY'LL BURN THIS PLACE TO THE FUCKING GROUND.
SHHHH IT'S FIIINE IT'S FINE.
NO... I'D HAVE TO CLOSE SHOP. SHE CONTAMINATED MY SHOP. I'D HAVE TO CLOSE. THERE'S NO CHOICE.
I'D HAVE TO FILE FOR BANKRUPTCY. IT'S OVER FOR ME, ROSIE. THIS IS IT.
GUSSY!! CHILL! IT'S GONNA BE FINE.
I PROMISE.
HEH HEH... YEAH. YOU'RE RIGHT... IT-IT'S GONNA BE FINE.
SIP

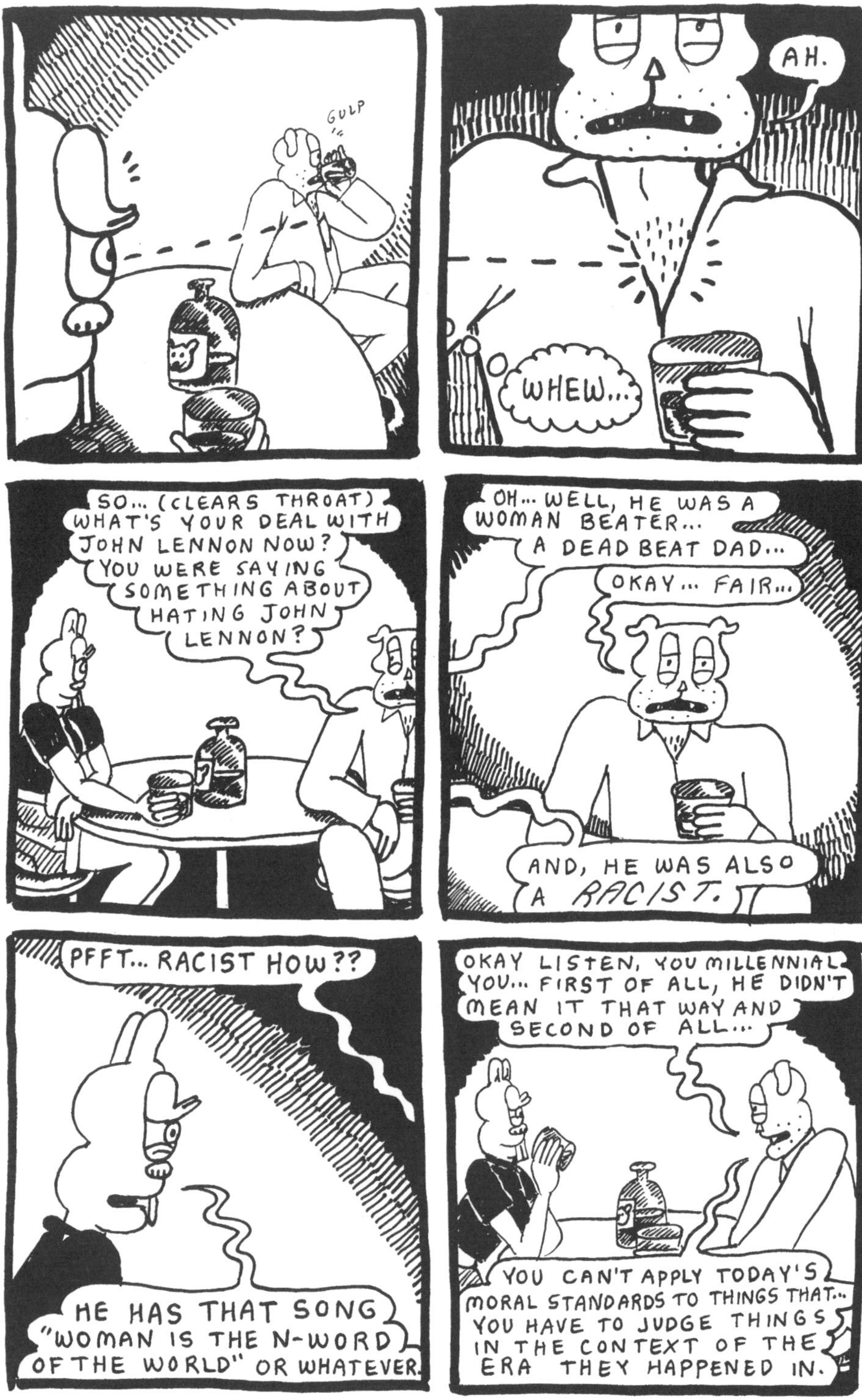
GULP
AH.
WHEW...
SO... (CLEARS THROAT) WHAT'S YOUR DEAL WITH JOHN LENNON NOW? YOU WERE SAYING SOMETHING ABOUT HATING JOHN LENNON?
OH... WELL, HE WAS A WOMAN BEATER... A DEAD BEAT DAD...
OKAY... FAIR...
AND, HE WAS ALSO A RACIST.
PFFT... RACIST HOW??
HE HAS THAT SONG "WOMAN IS THE N-WORD OF THE WORLD" OR WHATEVER.
OKAY LISTEN, YOU MILLENNIAL YOU... FIRST OF ALL, HE DIDN'T MEAN IT THAT WAY AND SECOND OF ALL...
YOU CAN'T APPLY TODAY'S MORAL STANDARDS TO THINGS THAT... YOU HAVE TO JUDGE THINGS IN THE CONTEXT OF THE ERA THEY HAPPENED IN.

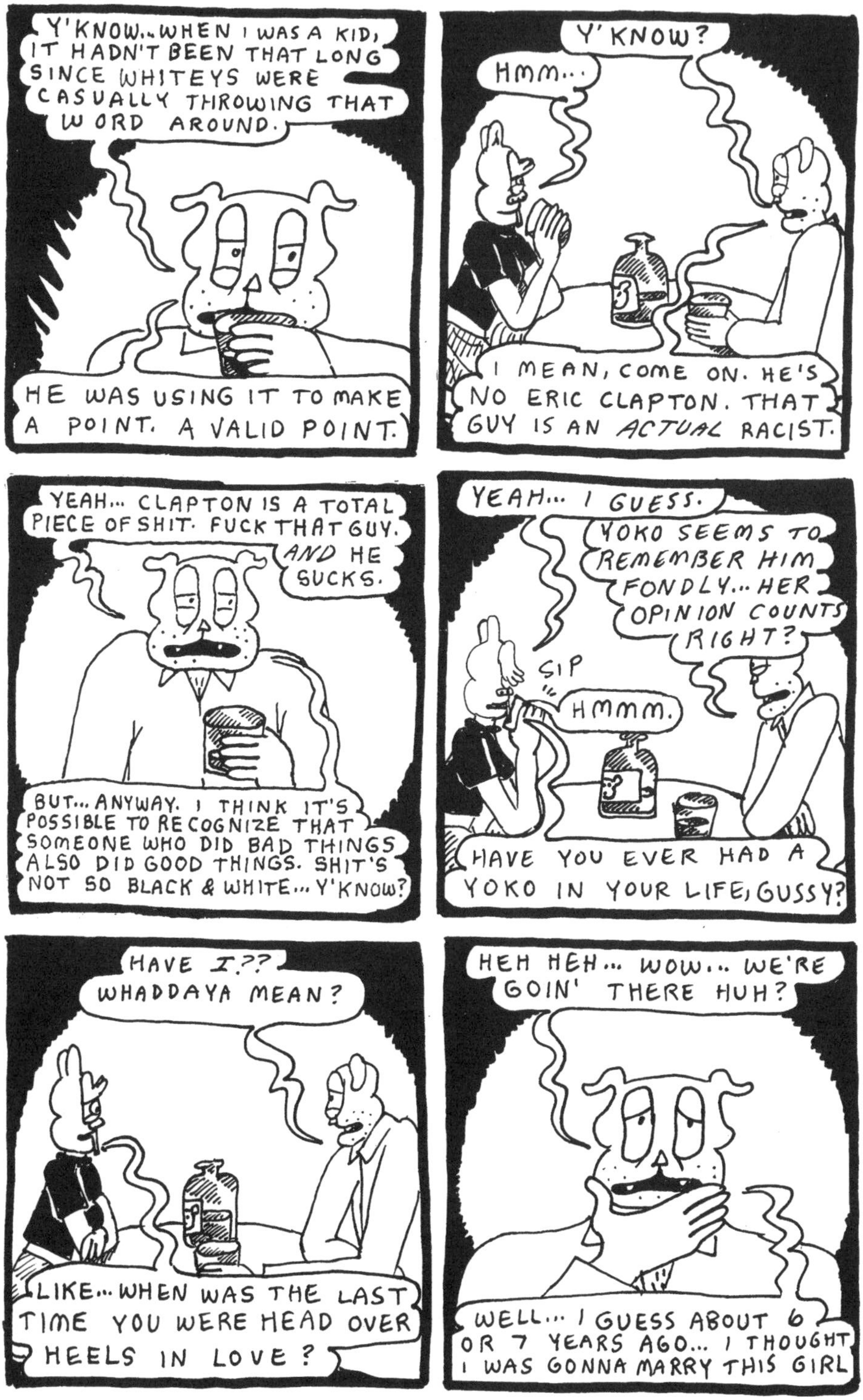
Y'KNOW.. WHEN I WAS A KID, IT HADN'T BEEN THAT LONG SINCE WHITEYS WERE CASUALLY THROWING THAT WORD AROUND.
HE WAS USING IT TO MAKE A POINT. A VALID POINT.
Y'KNOW?
HMM...
I MEAN, COME ON. HE'S NO ERIC CLAPTON. THAT GUY IS AN ACTUAL RACIST.
YEAH... CLAPTON IS A TOTAL PIECE OF SHIT. FUCK THAT GUY.
AND HE SUCKS.
BUT... ANYWAY. I THINK IT'S POSSIBLE TO RECOGNIZE THAT SOMEONE WHO DID BAD THINGS ALSO DID GOOD THINGS. SHIT'S NOT SO BLACK & WHITE... Y'KNOW?
YEAH... I GUESS.
YOKO SEEMS TO REMEMBER HIM FONDLY... HER OPINION COUNTS RIGHT?
SIP
HMMM.
HAVE YOU EVER HAD A YOKO IN YOUR LIFE, GUSSY?
HAVE I??
WHADDAYA MEAN?
LIKE... WHEN WAS THE LAST TIME YOU WERE HEAD OVER HEELS IN LOVE?
HEH HEH... WOW... WE'RE GOIN' THERE HUH?
WELL... I GUESS ABOUT 6 OR 7 YEARS AGO... I THOUGHT I WAS GONNA MARRY THIS GIRL

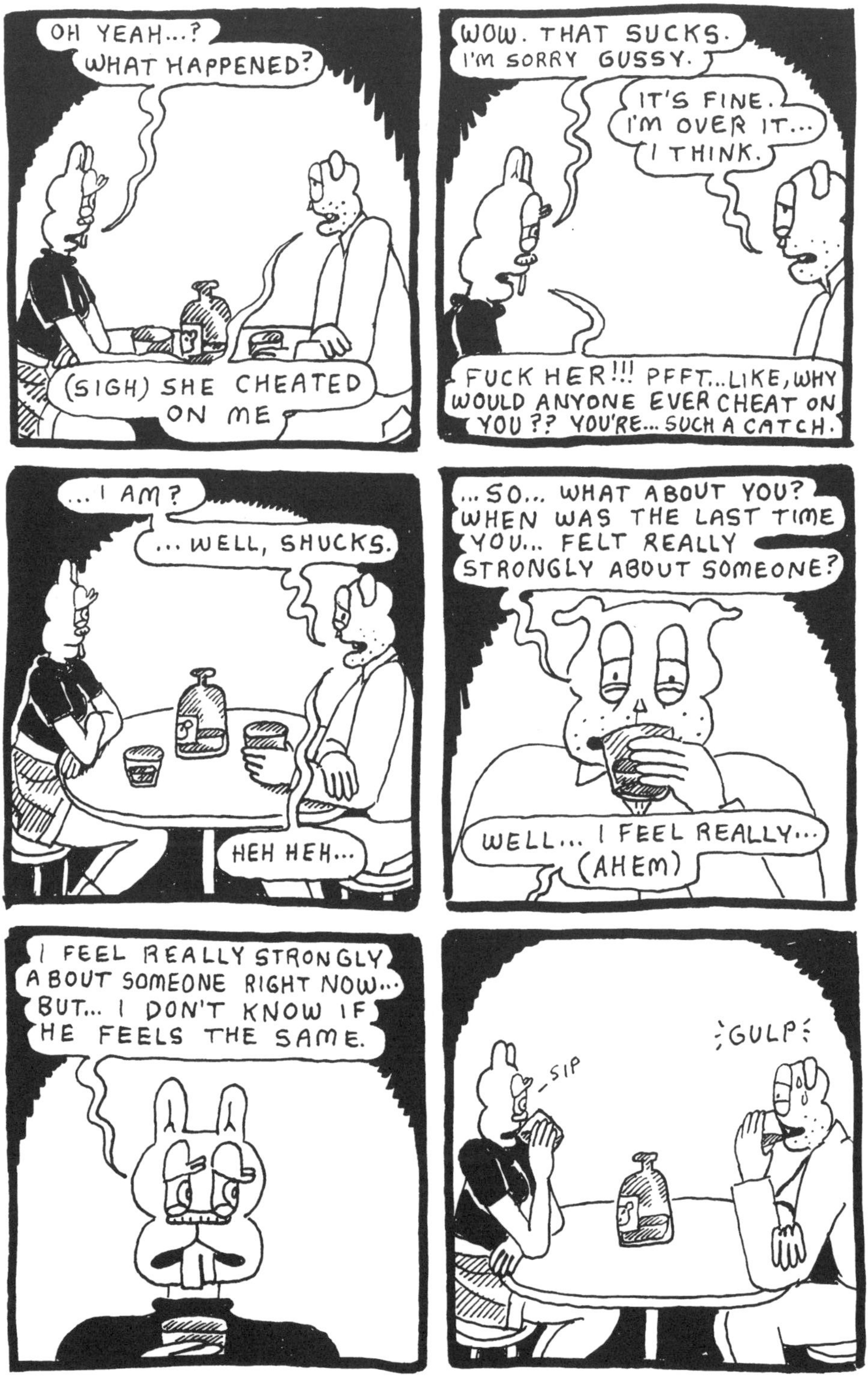
OH YEAH...?
WHAT HAPPENED?
(SIGH) SHE CHEATED ON ME
WOW. THAT SUCKS. I'M SORRY GUSSY.
IT'S FINE. I'M OVER IT... I THINK.
FUCK HER!!! PFFT...LIKE, WHY WOULD ANYONE EVER CHEAT ON YOU?? YOU'RE... SUCH A CATCH.
...I AM?
...WELL, SHUCKS.
HEH HEH...
...SO... WHAT ABOUT YOU? WHEN WAS THE LAST TIME YOU... FELT REALLY STRONGLY ABOUT SOMEONE?
WELL... I FEEL REALLY... (AHEM)
I FEEL REALLY STRONGLY ABOUT SOMEONE RIGHT NOW... BUT... I DON'T KNOW IF HE FEELS THE SAME.
SIP
GULP

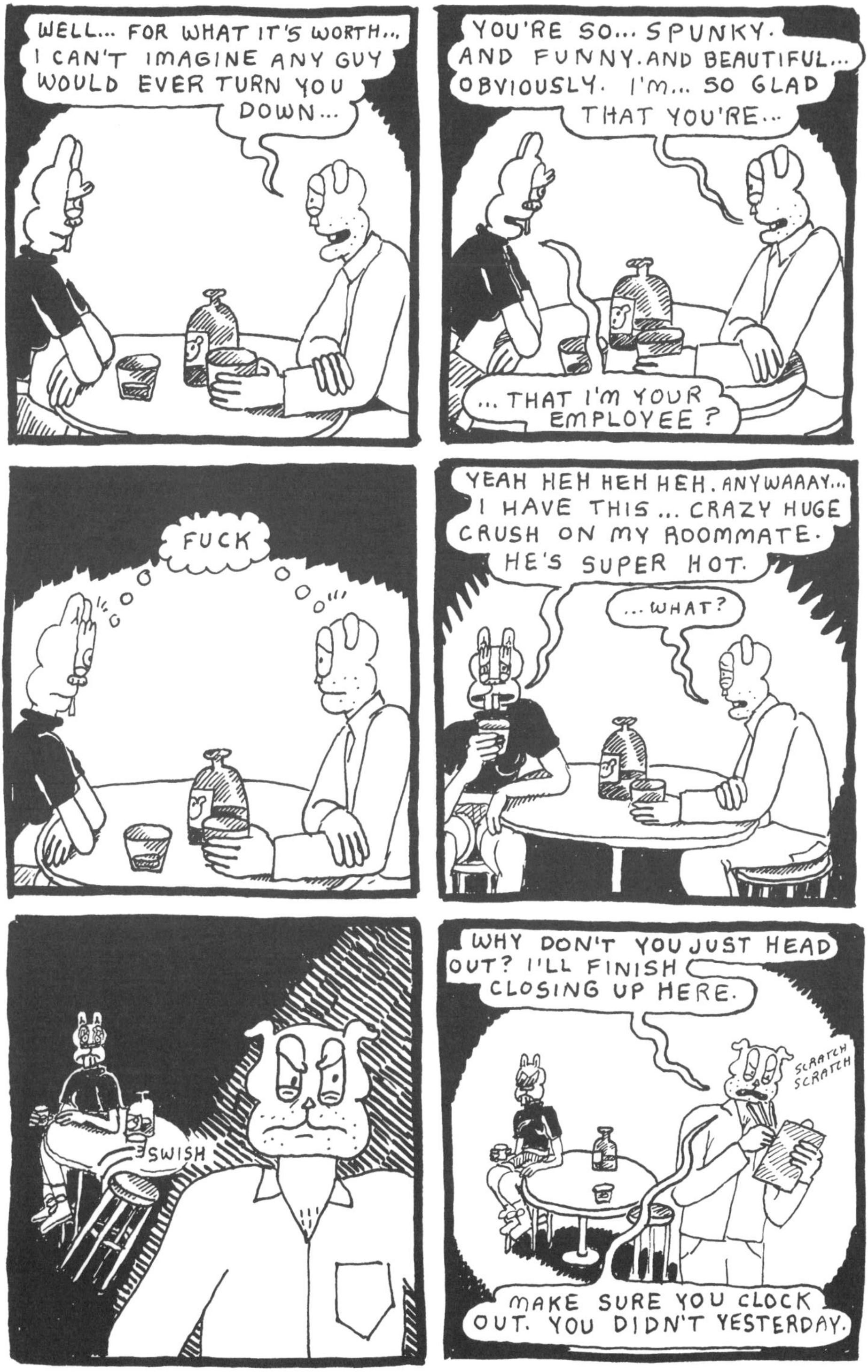
WELL... FOR WHAT IT'S WORTH... I CAN'T IMAGINE ANY GUY WOULD EVER TURN YOU DOWN...
YOU'RE SO... SPUNKY. AND FUNNY. AND BEAUTIFUL... OBVIOUSLY. I'M... SO GLAD THAT YOU'RE...
... THAT I'M YOUR EMPLOYEE?
FUCK
YEAH HEH HEH HEH. ANYWAAAY... I HAVE THIS... CRAZY HUGE CRUSH ON MY ROOMMATE. HE'S SUPER HOT.
...WHAT?
SWISH
WHY DON'T YOU JUST HEAD OUT? I'LL FINISH CLOSING UP HERE.
SCRATCH SCRATCH
MAKE SURE YOU CLOCK OUT. YOU DIDN'T YESTERDAY.

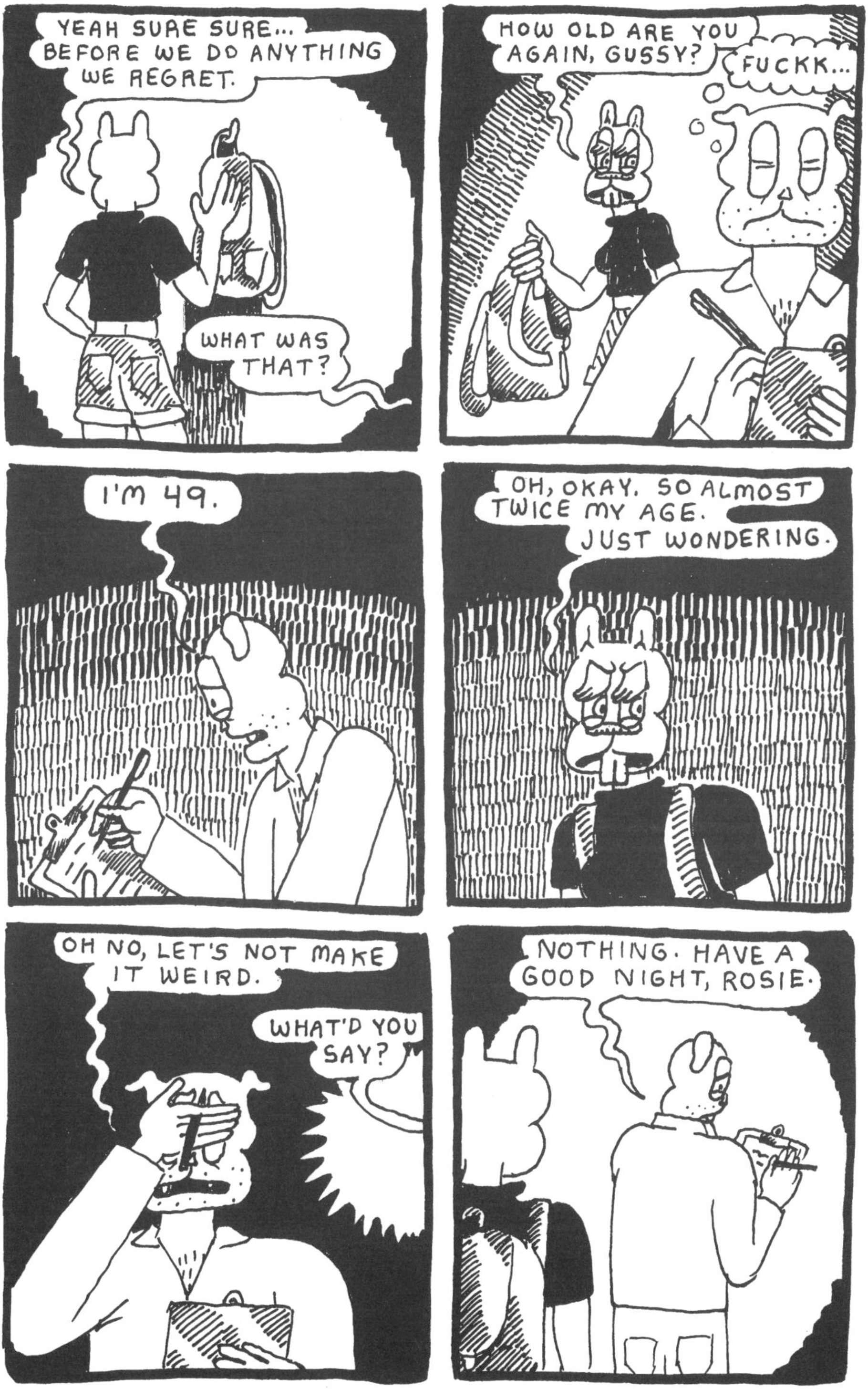
YEAH SURE SURE...
BEFORE WE DO ANYTHING
WE REGRET.
WHAT WAS
THAT?
HOW OLD ARE YOU
AGAIN, GUSSY?
FUCKK...
I'M 49.
OH, OKAY. SO ALMOST
TWICE MY AGE.
JUST WONDERING.
OH NO, LET'S NOT MAKE
IT WEIRD.
WHAT'D YOU
SAY?
NOTHING. HAVE A
GOOD NIGHT, ROSIE.

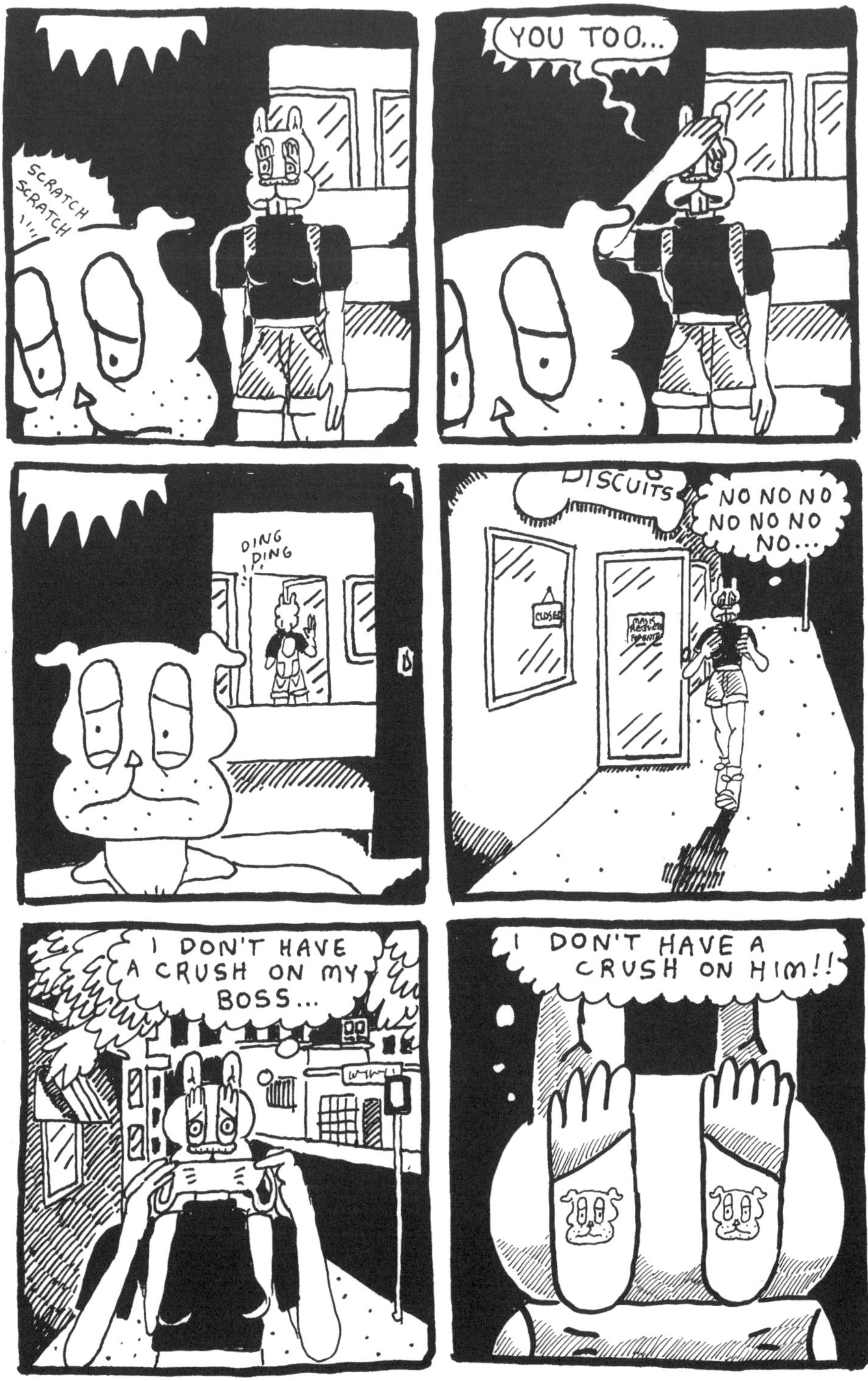
SCRATCH SCRATCH
YOU TOO...
DING DING
ISCUITS
NO NO NO NO NO NO NO...
CLOSED
I DON'T HAVE A CRUSH ON MY BOSS...
I DON'T HAVE A CRUSH ON HIM!!

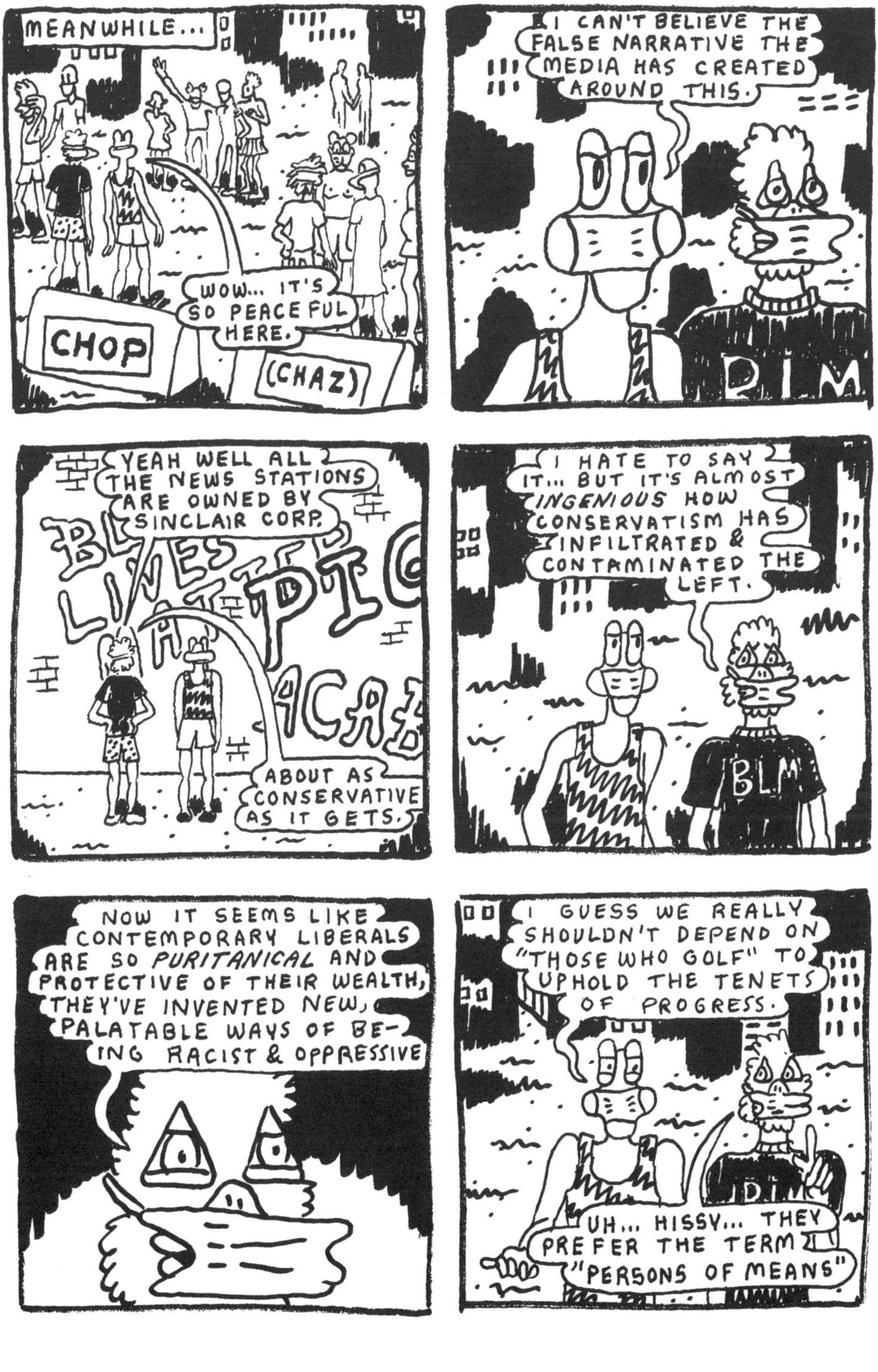
MEANWHILE...
WOW... IT'S SO PEACEFUL HERE.
CHOP
(CHAZ)
I CAN'T BELIEVE THE FALSE NARRATIVE THE MEDIA HAS CREATED AROUND THIS.
YEAH WELL ALL THE NEWS STATIONS ARE OWNED BY SINCLAIR CORP.
PIG
ACAB
ABOUT AS CONSERVATIVE AS IT GETS.
I HATE TO SAY IT... BUT IT'S ALMOST *INGENIOUS* HOW CONSERVATISM HAS INFILTRATED & CONTAMINATED THE LEFT.
BLM
NOW IT SEEMS LIKE CONTEMPORARY LIBERALS ARE SO *PURITANICAL* AND PROTECTIVE OF THEIR WEALTH, THEY'VE INVENTED NEW, PALATABLE WAYS OF BE-ING RACIST & OPPRESSIVE
I GUESS WE REALLY SHOULDN'T DEPEND ON "THOSE WHO GOLF" TO UPHOLD THE TENETS OF PROGRESS.
UH... HISSY... THEY PREFER THE TERM "PERSONS OF MEANS"

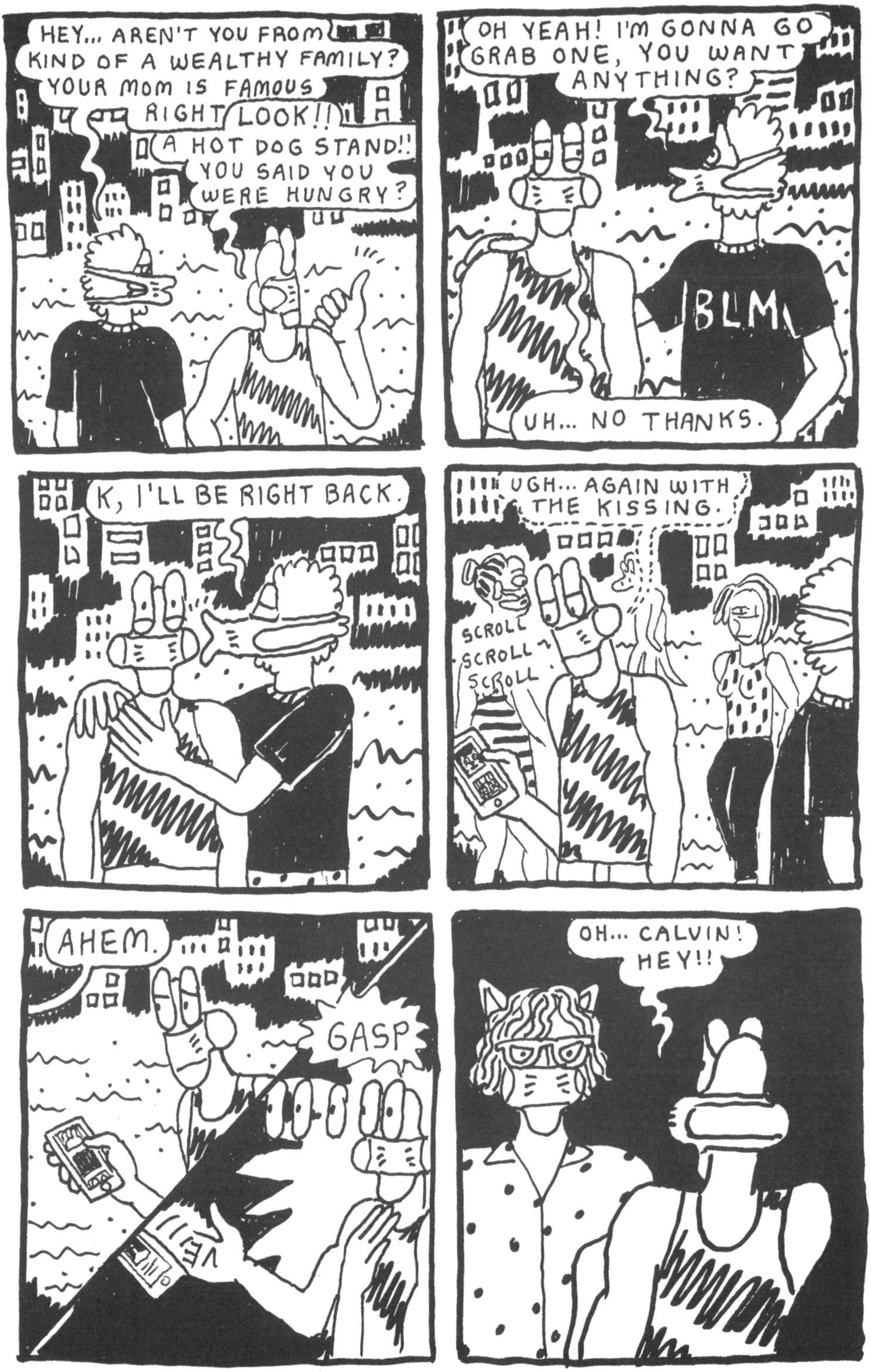
HEY... AREN'T YOU FROM KIND OF A WEALTHY FAMILY? YOUR MOM IS FAMOUS RIGHT
LOOK!! A HOT DOG STAND!! YOU SAID YOU WERE HUNGRY?
OH YEAH! I'M GONNA GO GRAB ONE, YOU WANT ANYTHING?
BLM
UH... NO THANKS.
K, I'LL BE RIGHT BACK.
UGH... AGAIN WITH THE KISSING.
SCROLL
SCROLL
SCROLL
AHEM.
GASP
OH... CALVIN! HEY!!

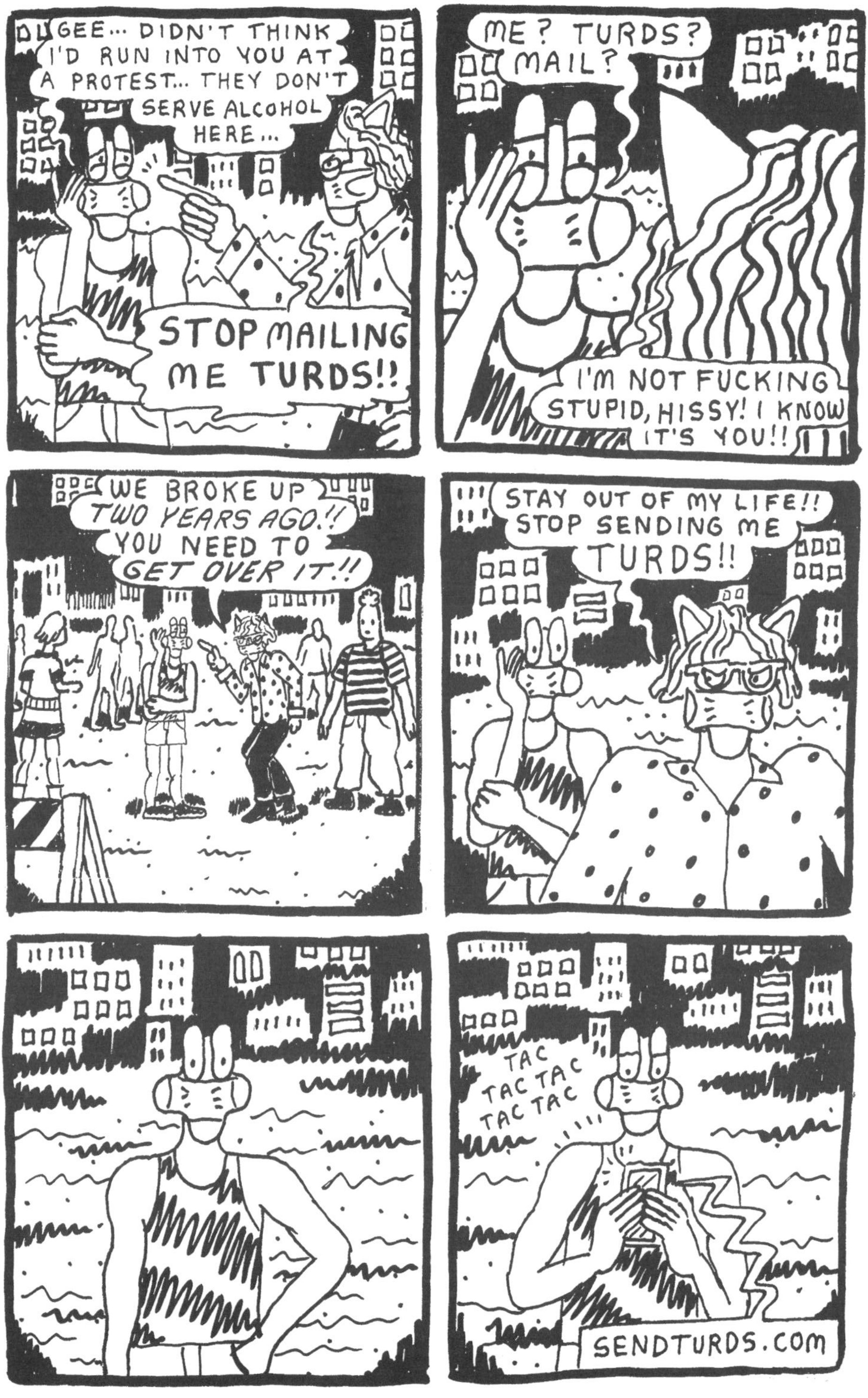
GEE... DIDN'T THINK I'D RUN INTO YOU AT A PROTEST... THEY DON'T SERVE ALCOHOL HERE...
STOP MAILING ME TURDS!!
ME? TURDS? MAIL?
I'M NOT FUCKING STUPID, HISSY! I KNOW IT'S YOU!!
WE BROKE UP TWO YEARS AGO!! YOU NEED TO GET OVER IT!!
STAY OUT OF MY LIFE!! STOP SENDING ME TURDS!!
TAC TAC TAC TAC TAC
SENDTURDS.COM

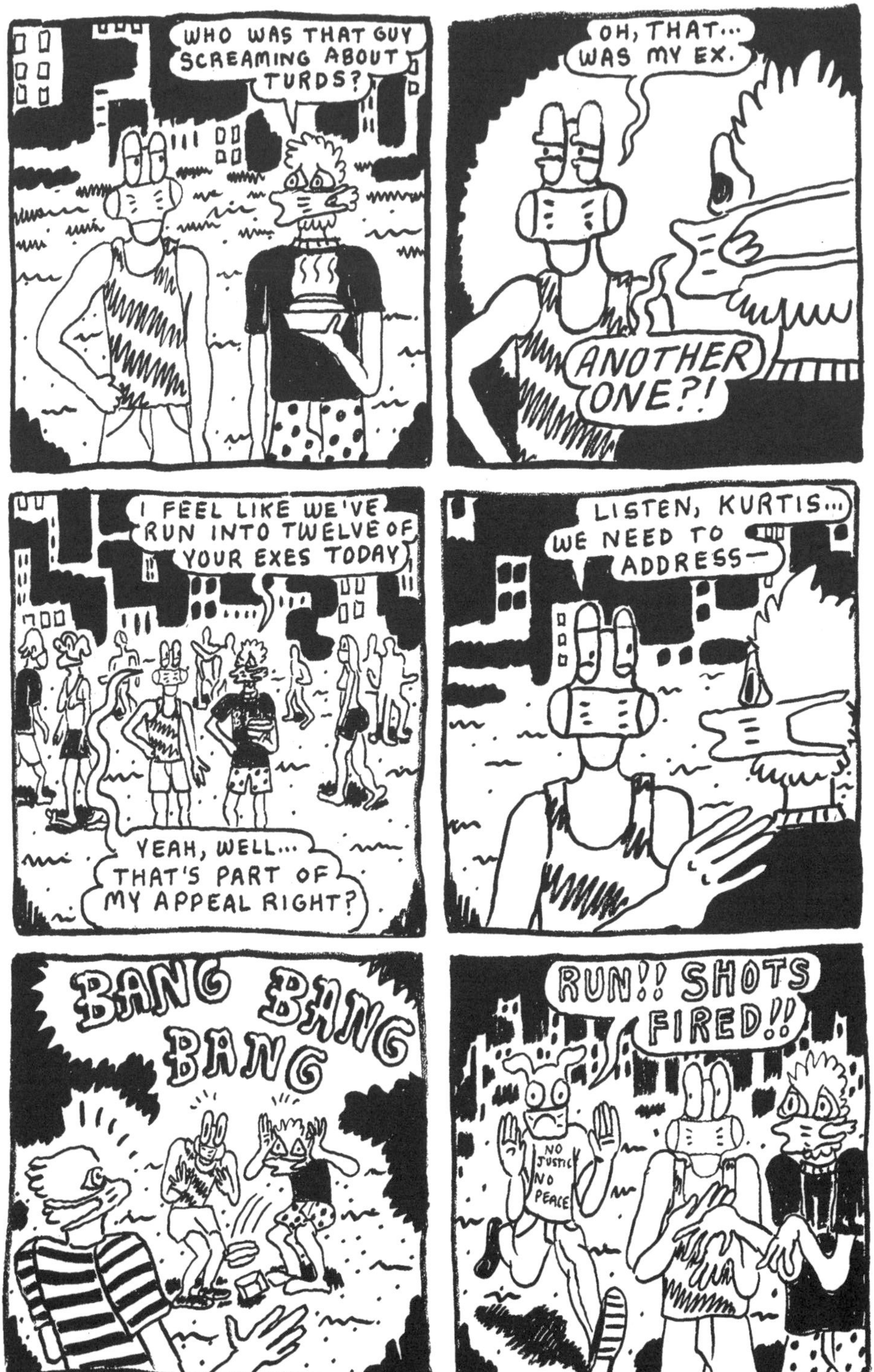
WHO WAS THAT GUY SCREAMING ABOUT TURDS?
OH, THAT... WAS MY EX.
ANOTHER ONE?!
I FEEL LIKE WE'VE RUN INTO TWELVE OF YOUR EXES TODAY
YEAH, WELL... THAT'S PART OF MY APPEAL RIGHT?
LISTEN, KURTIS... WE NEED TO ADDRESS—
BANG BANG BANG
NO JUSTICE NO PEACE
RUN!! SHOTS FIRED!!

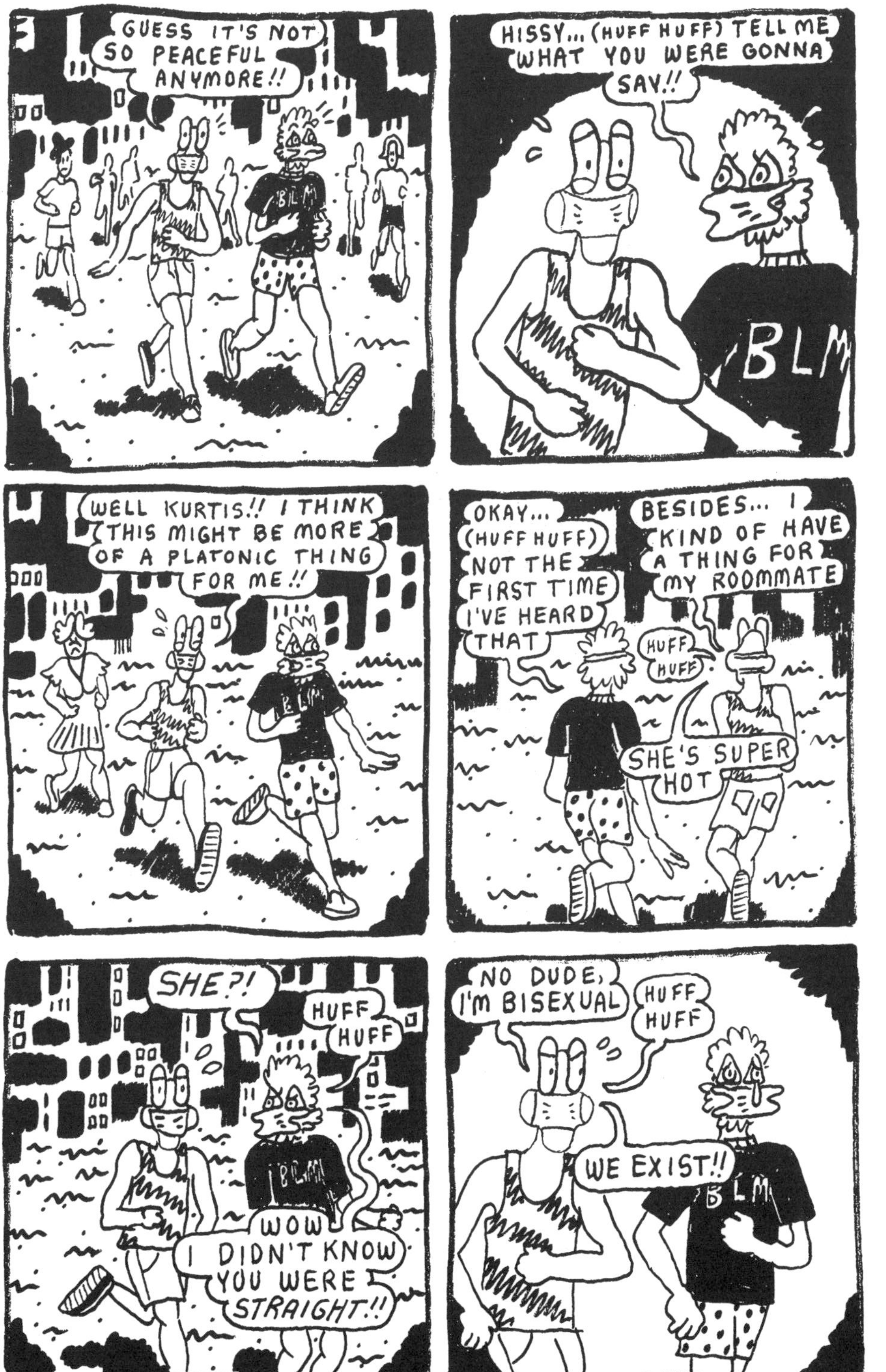
GUESS IT'S NOT SO PEACEFUL ANYMORE!!
HISSY... (HUFF HUFF) TELL ME WHAT YOU WERE GONNA SAY!!
BLM
WELL KURTIS!! I THINK THIS MIGHT BE MORE OF A PLATONIC THING FOR ME!!
OKAY... (HUFF HUFF) NOT THE FIRST TIME I'VE HEARD THAT
BESIDES... I KIND OF HAVE A THING FOR MY ROOMMATE
HUFF HUFF
SHE'S SUPER HOT
SHE?!
HUFF HUFF
WOW I DIDN'T KNOW YOU WERE STRAIGHT!!
NO DUDE, I'M BISEXUAL
HUFF HUFF
WE EXIST!!

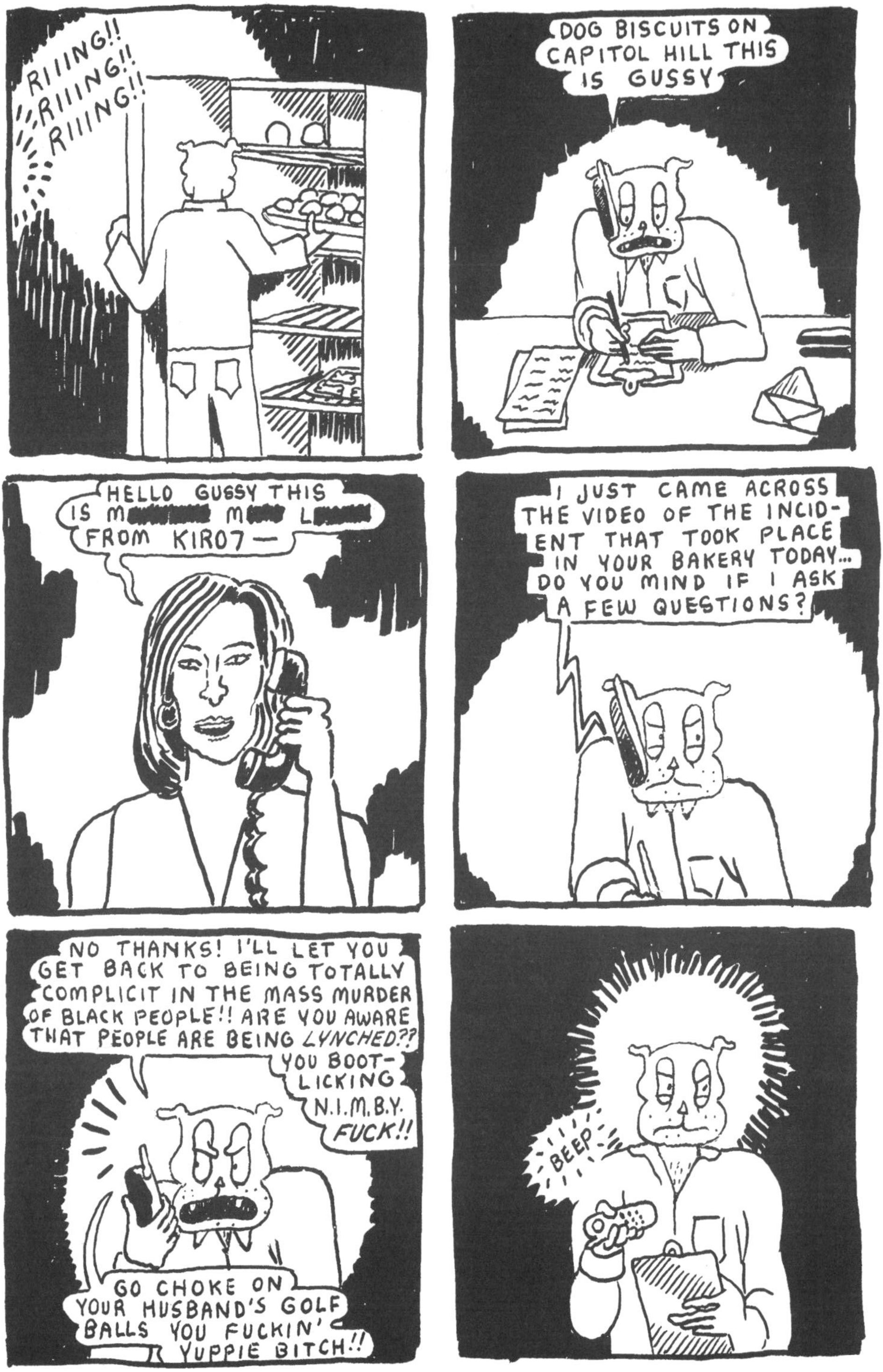
RIIING!! RIIING!! RIIING!!
DOG BISCUITS ON CAPITOL HILL THIS IS GUSSY
HELLO GUSSY THIS IS M[redacted] M[redacted] L[redacted] FROM KIRO7—
I JUST CAME ACROSS THE VIDEO OF THE INCIDENT THAT TOOK PLACE IN YOUR BAKERY TODAY... DO YOU MIND IF I ASK A FEW QUESTIONS?
NO THANKS! I'LL LET YOU GET BACK TO BEING TOTALLY COMPLICIT IN THE MASS MURDER OF BLACK PEOPLE!! ARE YOU AWARE THAT PEOPLE ARE BEING *LYNCHED*??
YOU BOOT-LICKING N.I.M.B.Y. *FUCK!!*
GO CHOKE ON YOUR HUSBAND'S GOLF BALLS YOU FUCKIN' YUPPIE BITCH!!
BEEP

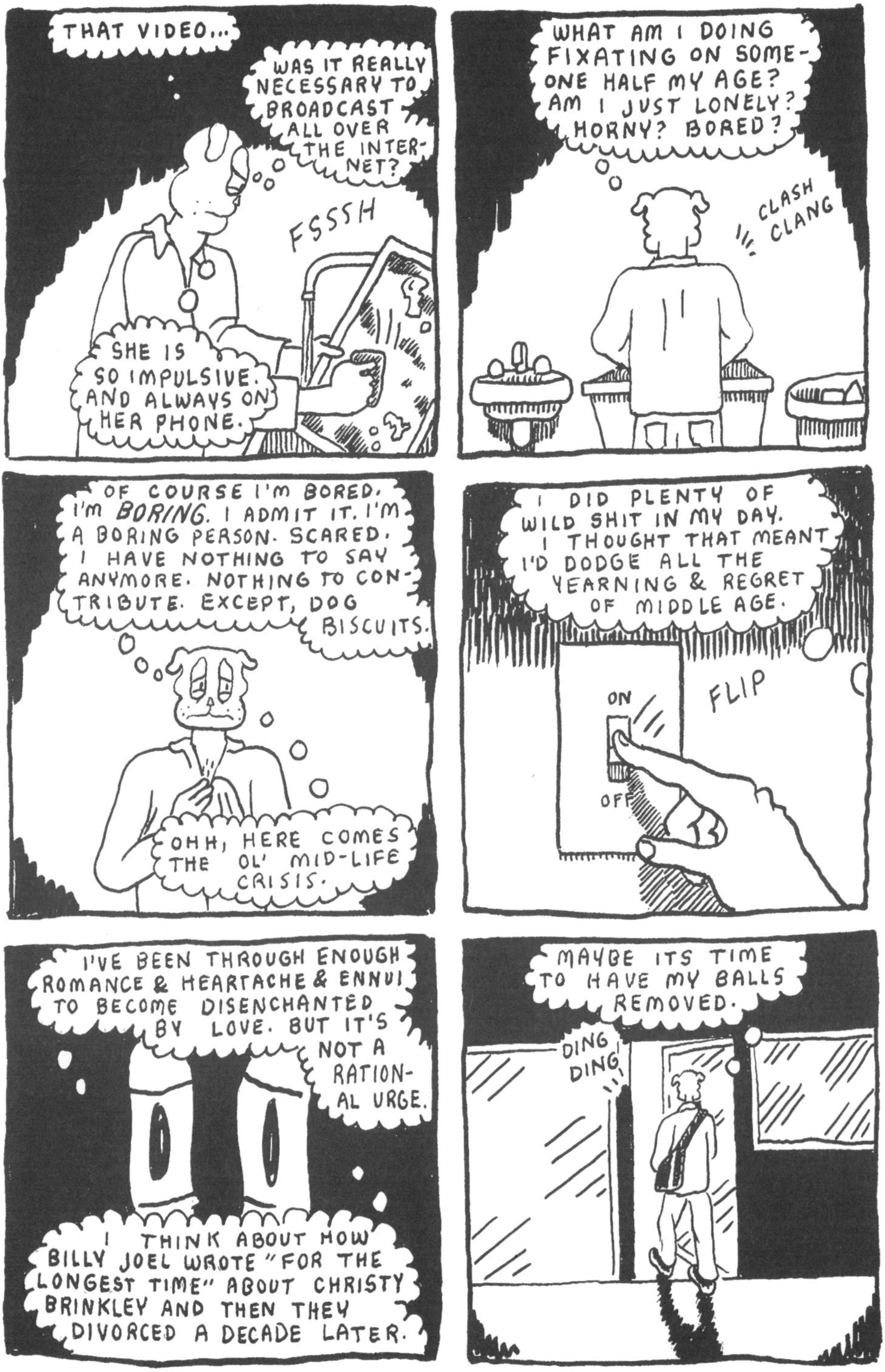
THAT VIDEO...
WAS IT REALLY NECESSARY TO BROADCAST ALL OVER THE INTER-NET?
FSSSH
SHE IS SO IMPULSIVE. AND ALWAYS ON HER PHONE.
WHAT AM I DOING FIXATING ON SOME-ONE HALF MY AGE? AM I JUST LONELY? HORNY? BORED?
CLASH CLANG
OF COURSE I'M BORED. I'M BORING. I ADMIT IT. I'M A BORING PERSON. SCARED. I HAVE NOTHING TO SAY ANYMORE. NOTHING TO CON-TRIBUTE. EXCEPT, DOG BISCUITS.
OHH, HERE COMES THE OL' MID-LIFE CRISIS.
I DID PLENTY OF WILD SHIT IN MY DAY. I THOUGHT THAT MEANT I'D DODGE ALL THE YEARNING & REGRET OF MIDDLE AGE.
ON
OFF
FLIP
I'VE BEEN THROUGH ENOUGH ROMANCE & HEARTACHE & ENNUI TO BECOME DISENCHANTED BY LOVE. BUT IT'S NOT A RATION-AL URGE.
I THINK ABOUT HOW BILLY JOEL WROTE "FOR THE LONGEST TIME" ABOUT CHRISTY BRINKLEY AND THEN THEY DIVORCED A DECADE LATER.
MAYBE ITS TIME TO HAVE MY BALLS REMOVED.
DING DING

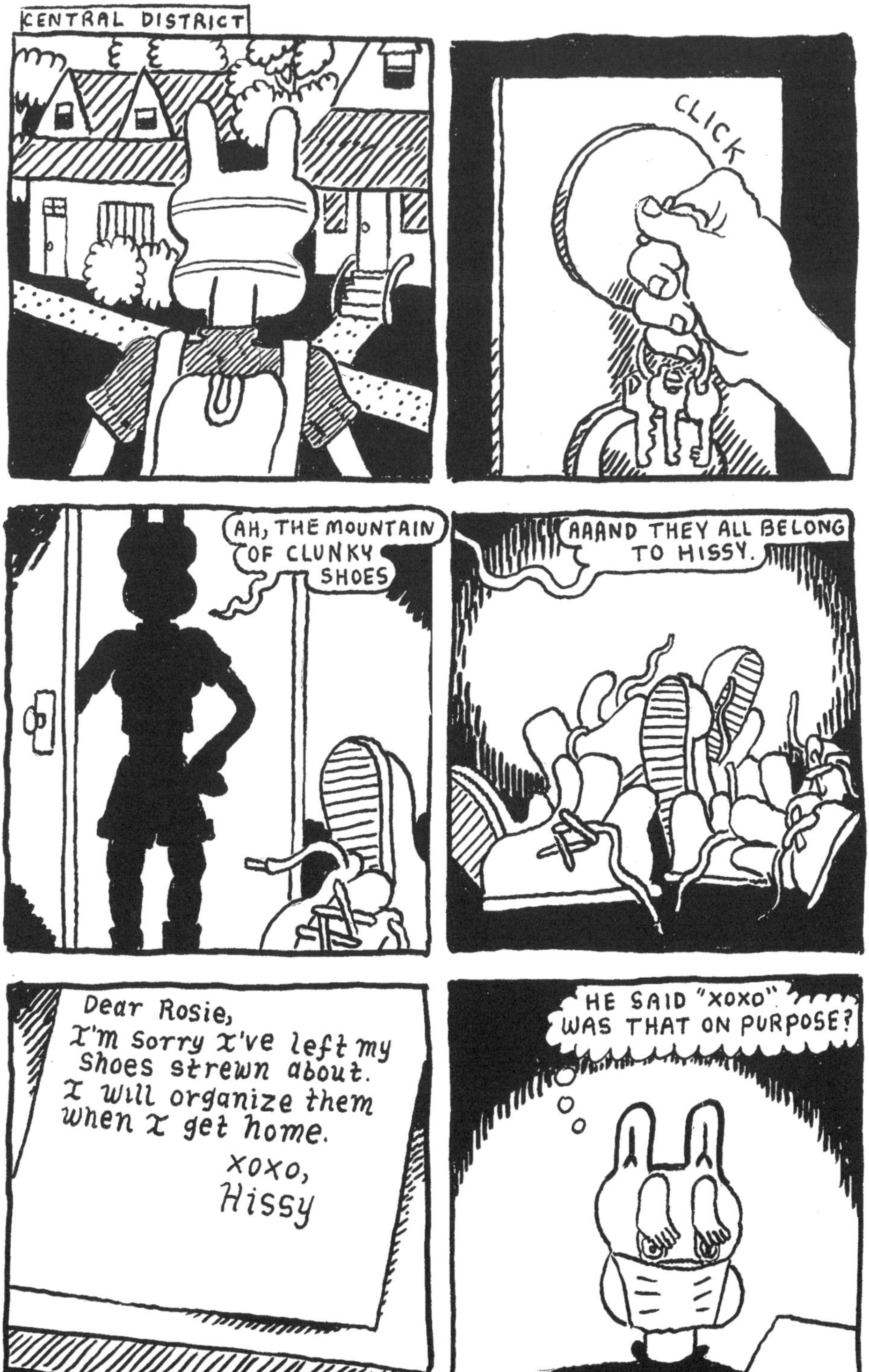
CENTRAL DISTRICT
CLICK
AH, THE MOUNTAIN OF CLUNKY SHOES
AAAND THEY ALL BELONG TO HISSY.
Dear Rosie,
I'm sorry I've left my shoes strewn about.
I will organize them when I get home.
xoxo,
Hissy
HE SAID "XOXO" WAS THAT ON PURPOSE?

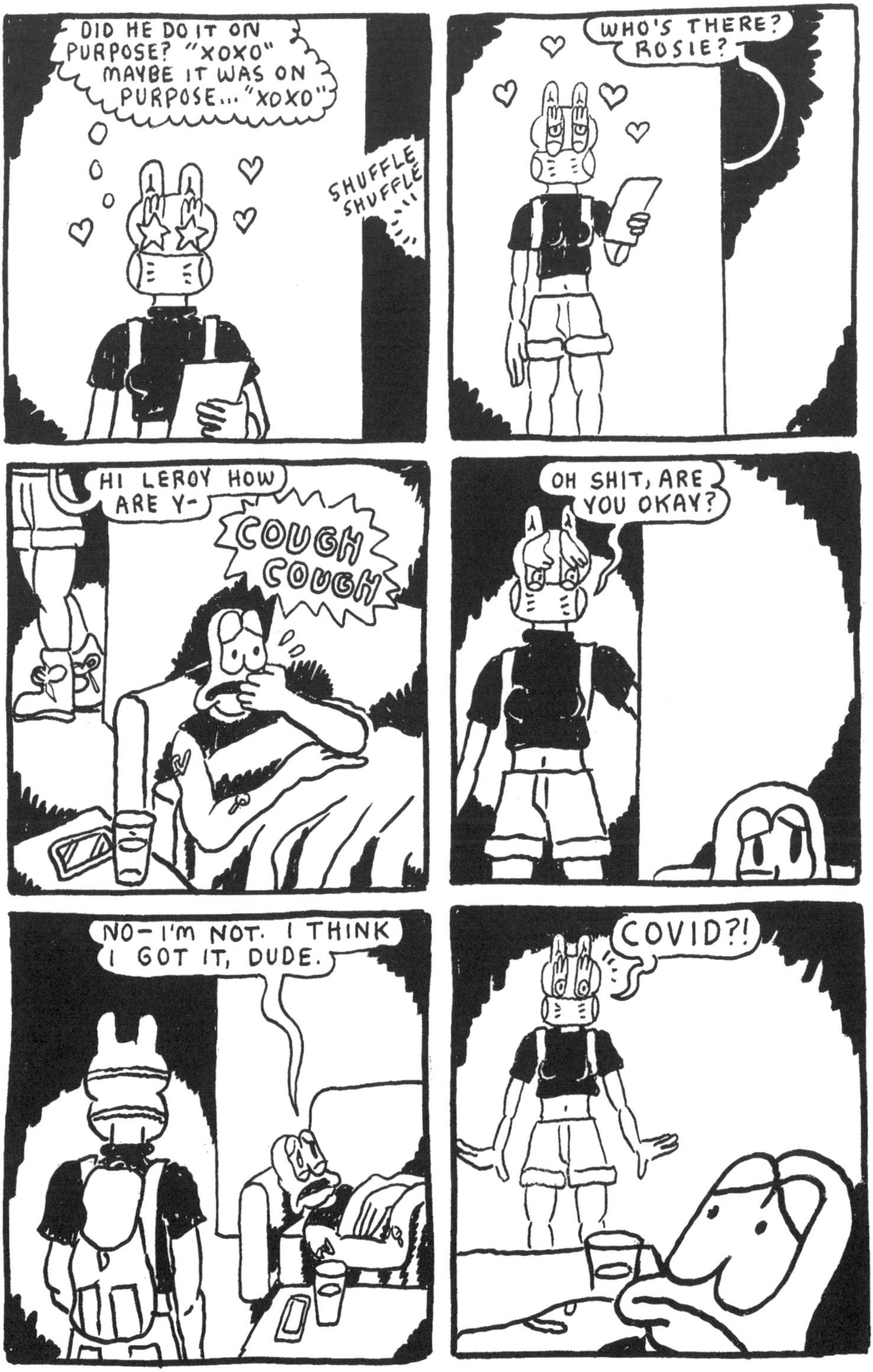
DID HE DO IT ON PURPOSE? "XOXO" MAYBE IT WAS ON PURPOSE... "XOXO"
SHUFFLE SHUFFLE
WHO'S THERE? ROSIE?
HI LEROY HOW ARE Y-
COUGH COUGH
OH SHIT, ARE YOU OKAY?
NO- I'M NOT. I THINK I GOT IT, DUDE.
COVID?!

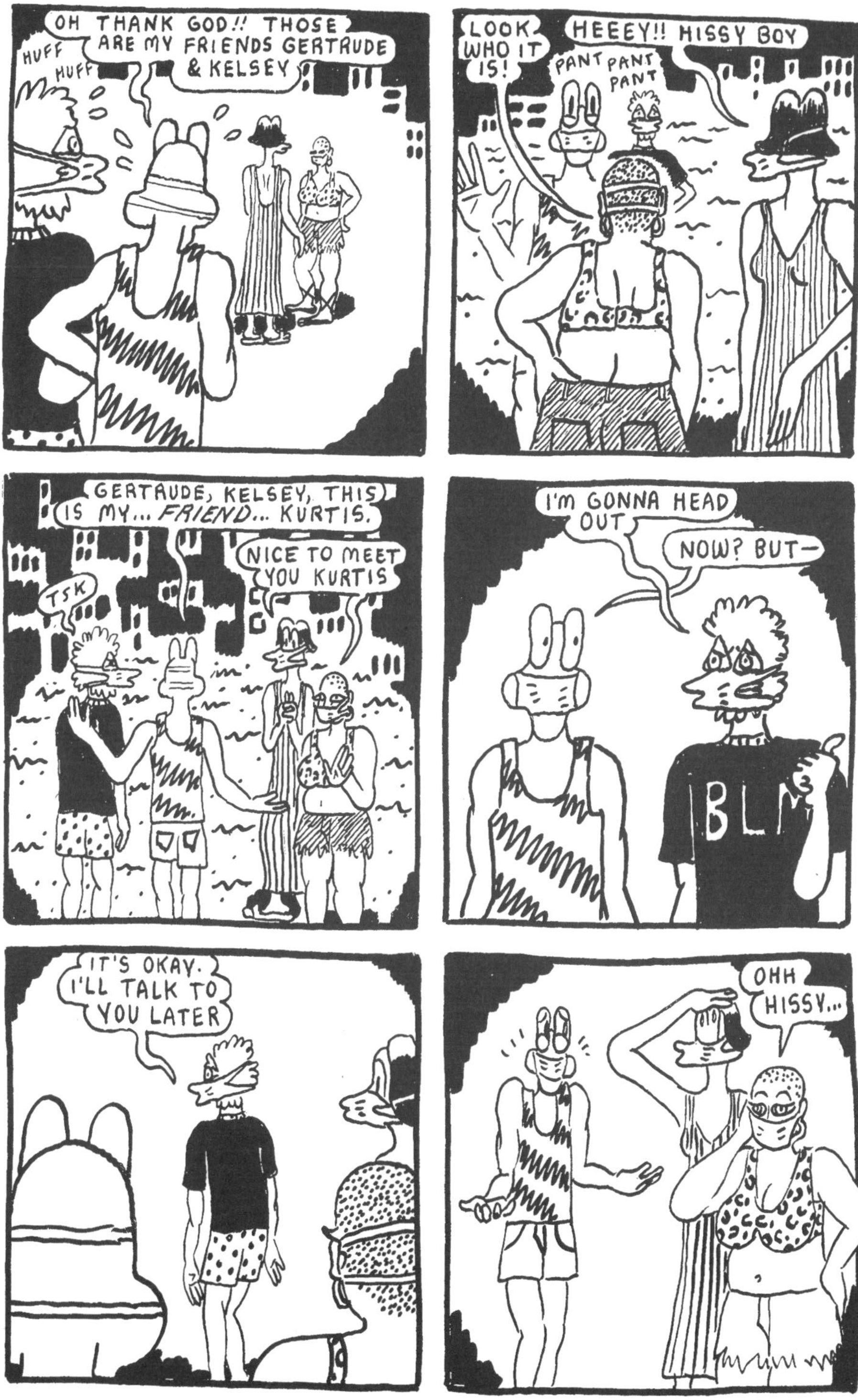
OH THANK GOD!! THOSE ARE MY FRIENDS GERTRUDE & KELSEY
HUFF HUFF
LOOK WHO IT IS!
HEEEY!! HISSY BOY
PANT PANT PANT
GERTRUDE, KELSEY, THIS IS MY... *FRIEND*... KURTIS.
TSK
NICE TO MEET YOU KURTIS
I'M GONNA HEAD OUT
NOW? BUT—
BLM
IT'S OKAY. I'LL TALK TO YOU LATER
OHH HISSY...

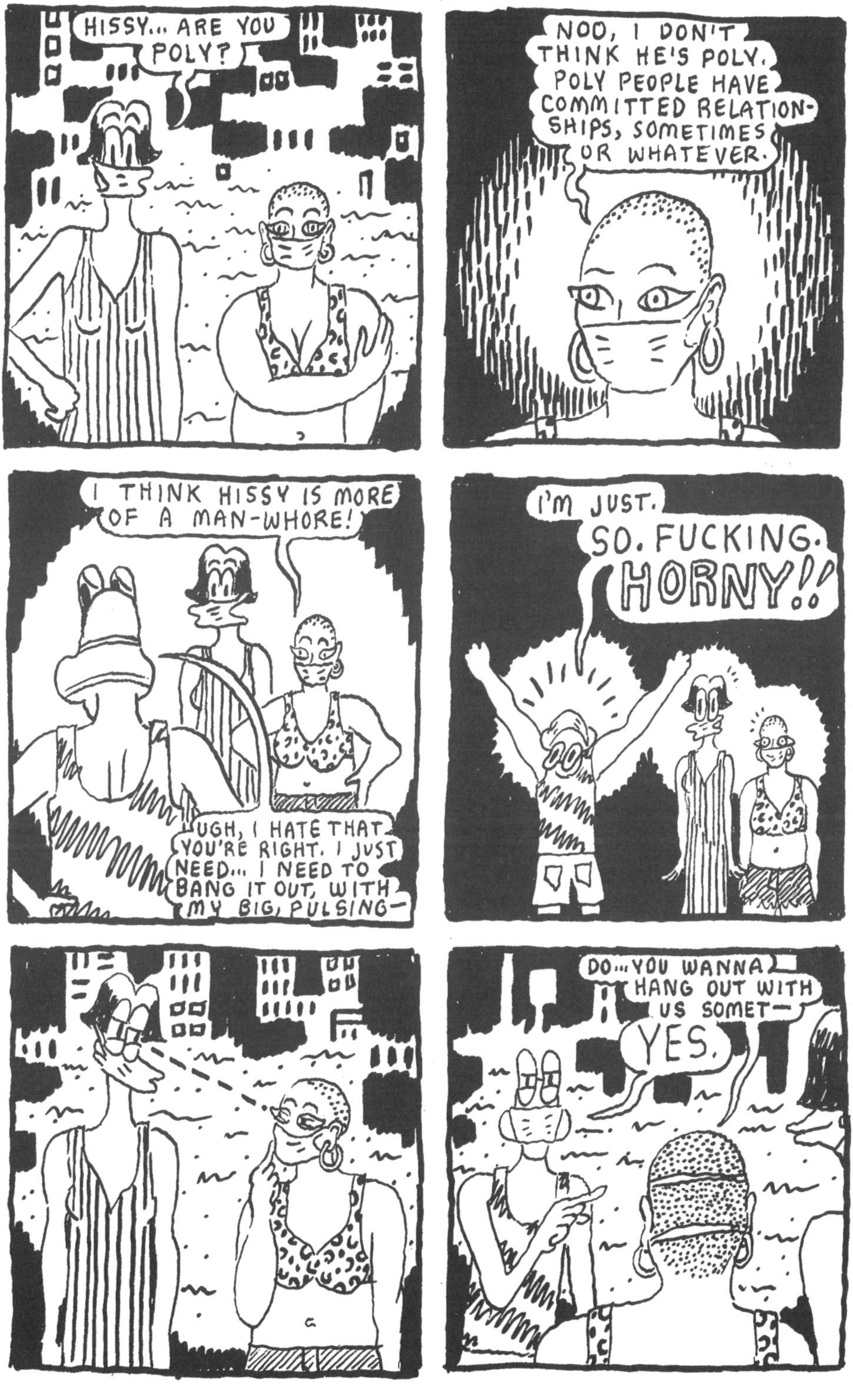
HISSY... ARE YOU POLY?
NOO, I DON'T THINK HE'S POLY. POLY PEOPLE HAVE COMMITTED RELATIONSHIPS, SOMETIMES OR WHATEVER.
I THINK HISSY IS MORE OF A MAN-WHORE!
UGH, I HATE THAT YOU'RE RIGHT. I JUST NEED... I NEED TO BANG IT OUT, WITH MY BIG, PULSING—
I'M JUST.
SO. FUCKING.
HORNY!!
DO...YOU WANNA HANG OUT WITH US SOMET—
YES.

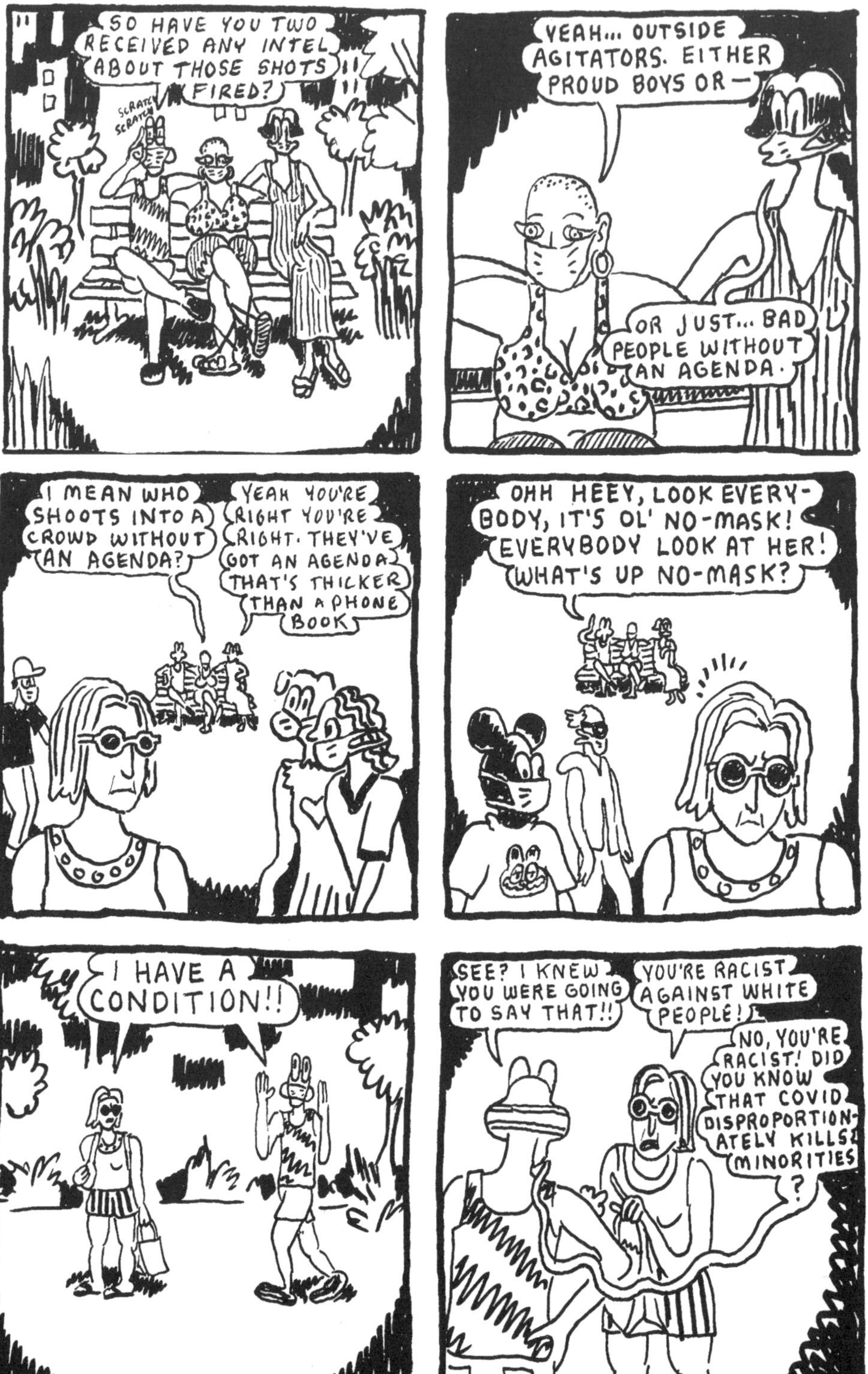
SO HAVE YOU TWO RECEIVED ANY INTEL ABOUT THOSE SHOTS FIRED?
SCRATCH SCRATCH
YEAH... OUTSIDE AGITATORS. EITHER PROUD BOYS OR—
OR JUST... BAD PEOPLE WITHOUT AN AGENDA.
I MEAN WHO SHOOTS INTO A CROWD WITHOUT AN AGENDA?
YEAH YOU'RE RIGHT YOU'RE RIGHT. THEY'VE GOT AN AGENDA THAT'S THICKER THAN A PHONE BOOK
OHH HEEY, LOOK EVERYBODY, IT'S OL' NO-MASK! EVERYBODY LOOK AT HER! WHAT'S UP NO-MASK?
I HAVE A CONDITION!!
SEE? I KNEW YOU WERE GOING TO SAY THAT!!
YOU'RE RACIST AGAINST WHITE PEOPLE!
NO, YOU'RE RACIST! DID YOU KNOW THAT COVID DISPROPORTIONATELY KILLS MINORITIES?

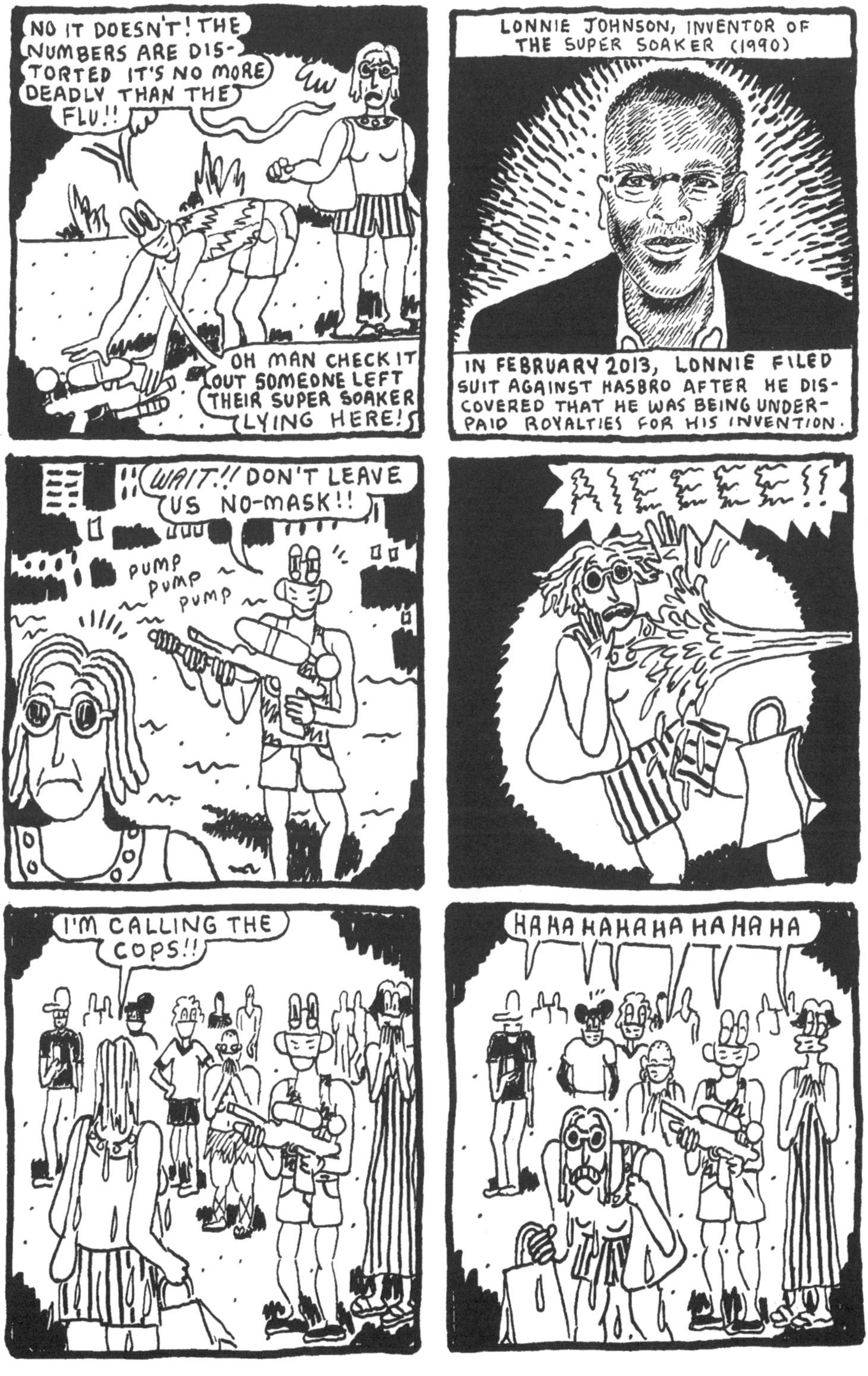
NO IT DOESN'T! THE NUMBERS ARE DISTORTED IT'S NO MORE DEADLY THAN THE FLU!!
OH MAN CHECK IT OUT SOMEONE LEFT THEIR SUPER SOAKER LYING HERE!
LONNIE JOHNSON, INVENTOR OF THE SUPER SOAKER (1990)
IN FEBRUARY 2013, LONNIE FILED SUIT AGAINST HASBRO AFTER HE DISCOVERED THAT HE WAS BEING UNDERPAID ROYALTIES FOR HIS INVENTION.
WAIT!! DON'T LEAVE US NO-MASK!!
PUMP
PUMP
PUMP
AIEEEE!!
I'M CALLING THE COPS!!
HAHA HAHAHA HA HAHA HA

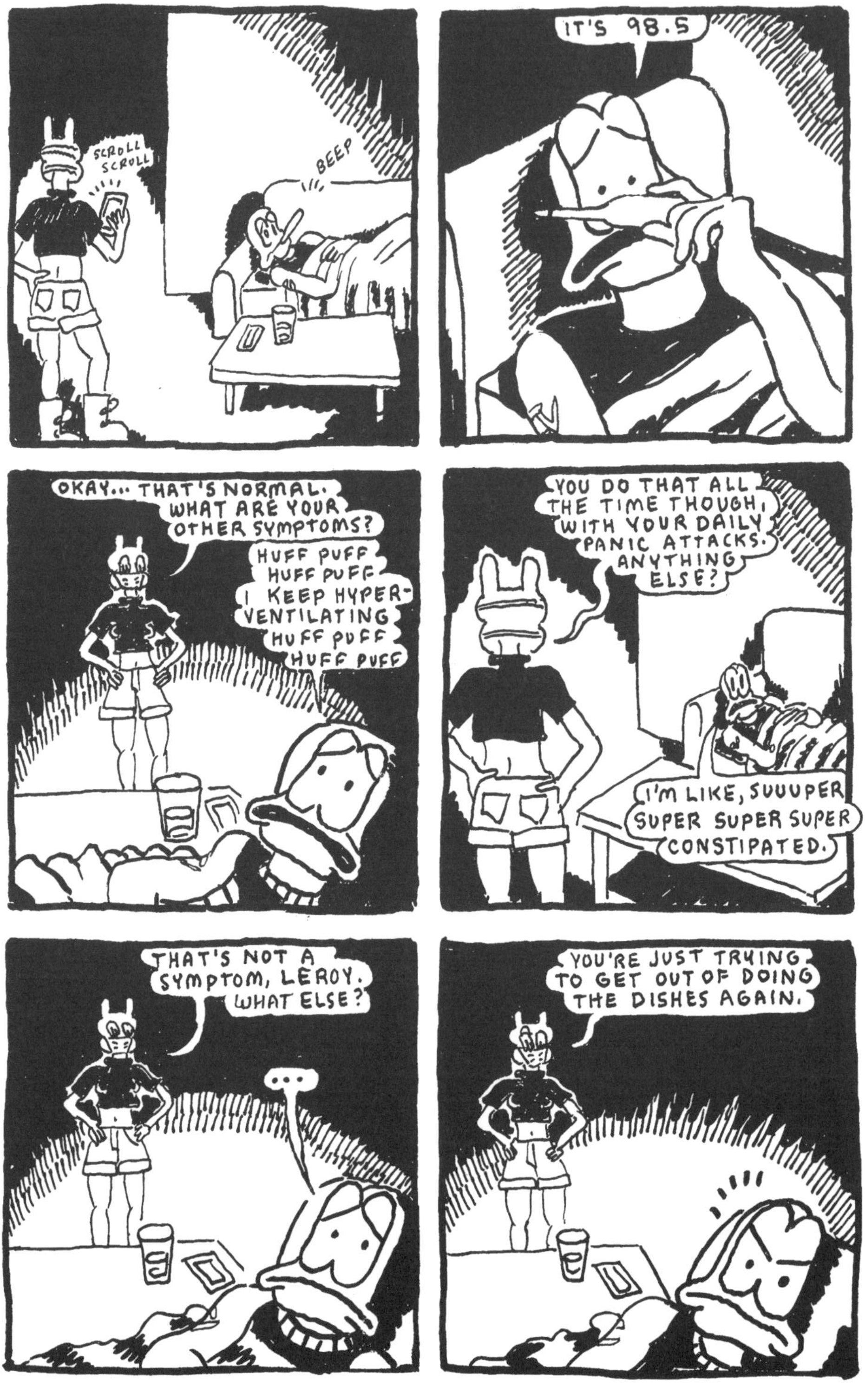
SCROLL SCROLL
BEEP
IT'S 98.5
OKAY... THAT'S NORMAL. WHAT ARE YOUR OTHER SYMPTOMS?
HUFF PUFF HUFF PUFF I KEEP HYPER-VENTILATING HUFF PUFF HUFF PUFF
YOU DO THAT ALL THE TIME THOUGH, WITH YOUR DAILY PANIC ATTACKS. ANYTHING ELSE?
I'M LIKE, SUUUPER SUPER SUPER SUPER CONSTIPATED.
THAT'S NOT A SYMPTOM, LEROY. WHAT ELSE?
...
YOU'RE JUST TRYING TO GET OUT OF DOING THE DISHES AGAIN.

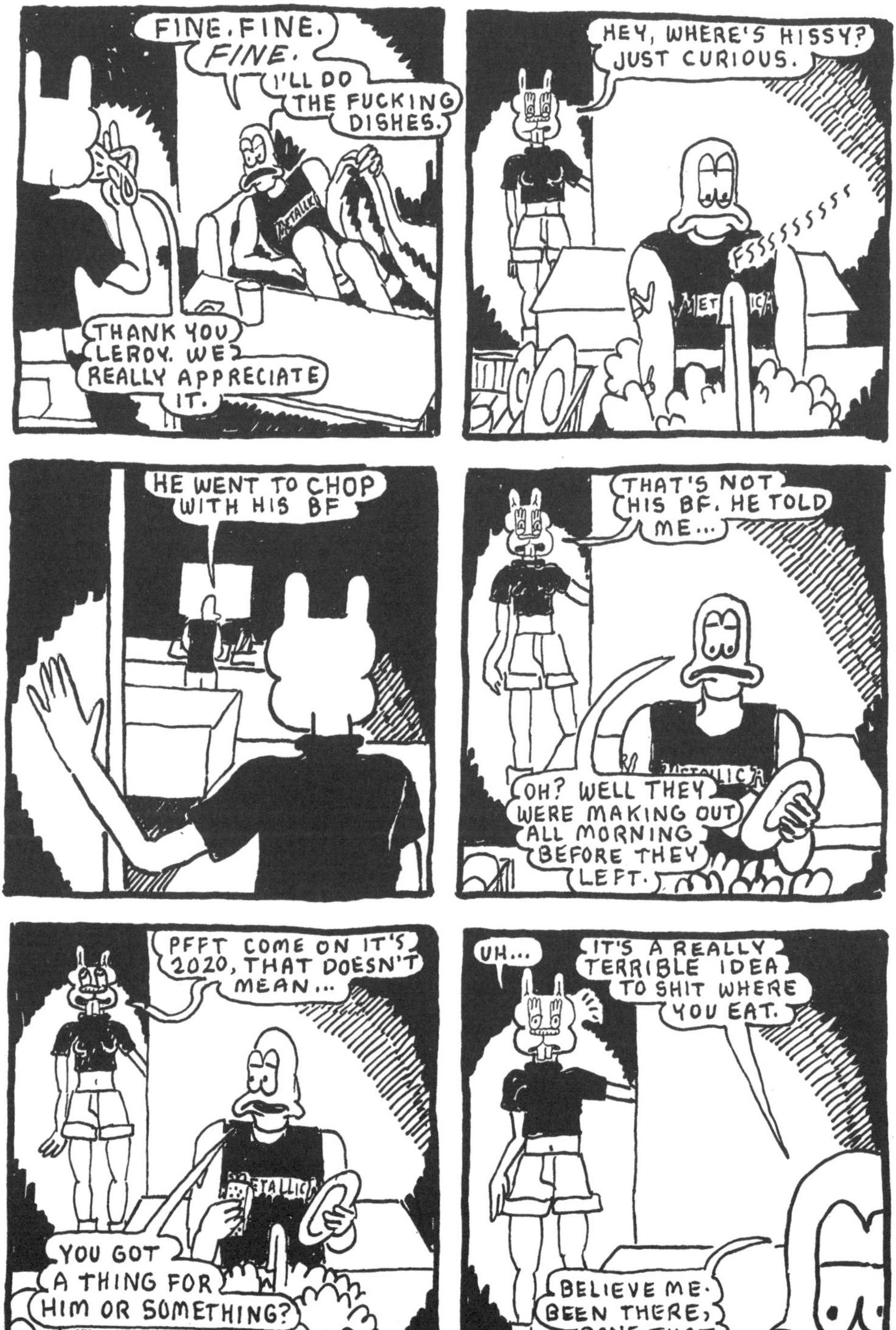
FINE. FINE. FINE.
I'LL DO THE FUCKING DISHES.
THANK YOU LEROY. WE REALLY APPRECIATE IT.
HEY, WHERE'S HISSY? JUST CURIOUS.
FSSSSSSSS
HE WENT TO CHOP WITH HIS BF
THAT'S NOT HIS BF. HE TOLD ME...
OH? WELL THEY WERE MAKING OUT ALL MORNING BEFORE THEY LEFT.
PFFT COME ON IT'S 2020, THAT DOESN'T MEAN...
YOU GOT A THING FOR HIM OR SOMETHING?
UH...
IT'S A REALLY TERRIBLE IDEA TO SHIT WHERE YOU EAT.
BELIEVE ME. BEEN THERE, DONE THAT.

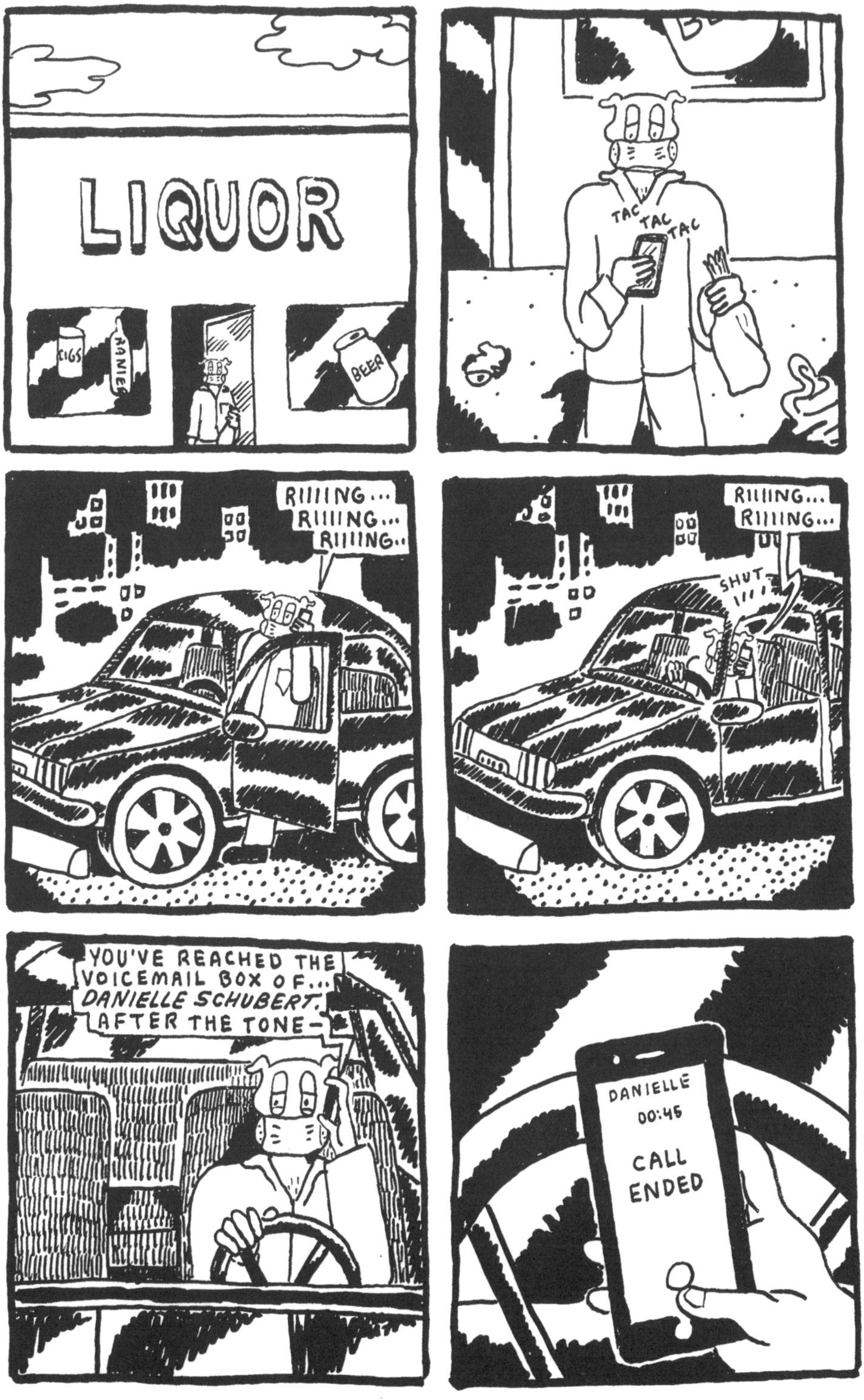
LIQUOR
CIGS
BEER
TAC TAC TAC
RIIIING... RIIIING... RIIIING..
RIIIING... RIIIING...
SHUT
YOU'VE REACHED THE VOICEMAIL BOX OF... DANIELLE SCHUBERT. AFTER THE TONE-
DANIELLE
00:45
CALL ENDED

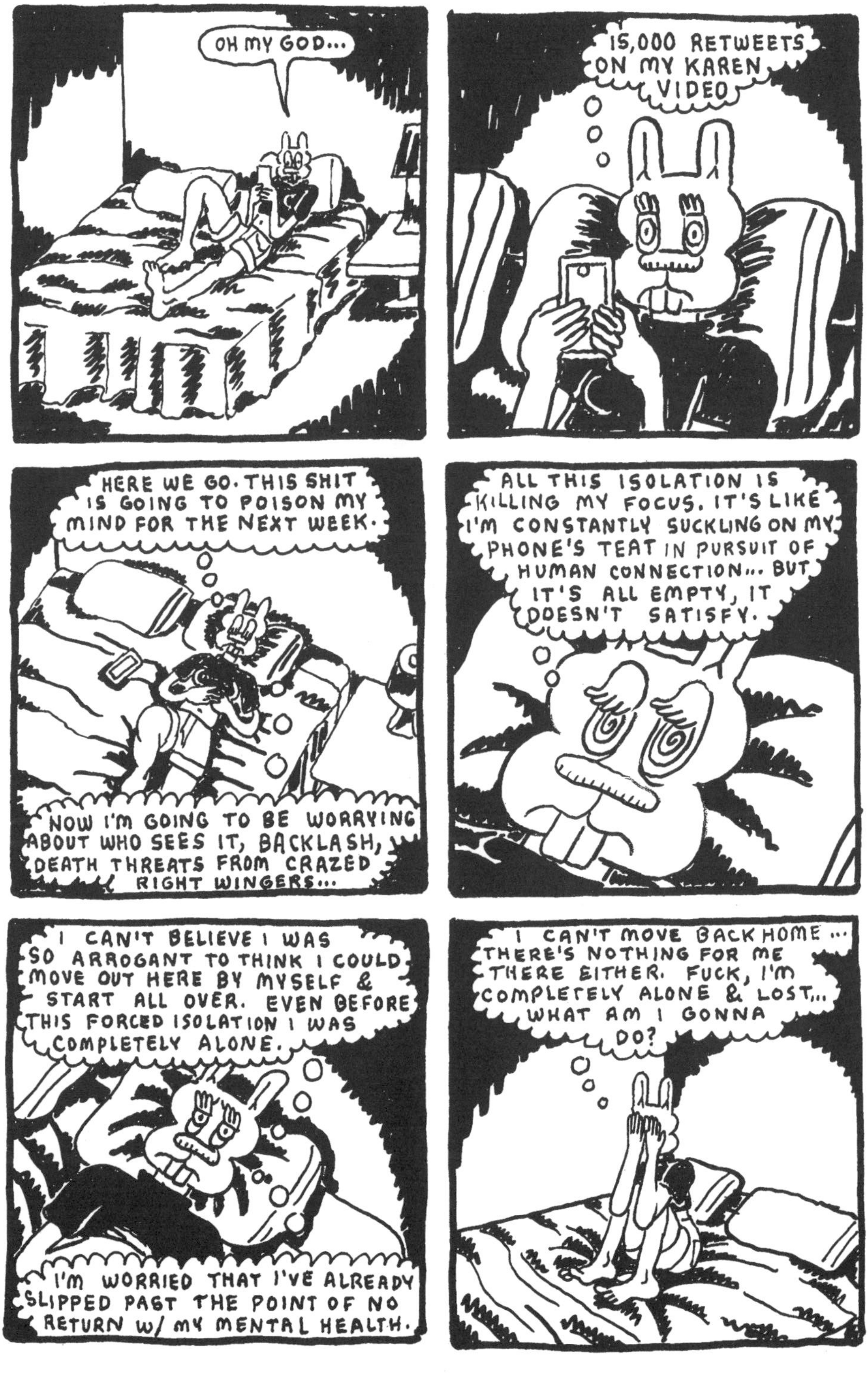
OH MY GOD...
15,000 RETWEETS ON MY KAREN VIDEO
HERE WE GO. THIS SHIT IS GOING TO POISON MY MIND FOR THE NEXT WEEK.
NOW I'M GOING TO BE WORRYING ABOUT WHO SEES IT, BACKLASH, DEATH THREATS FROM CRAZED RIGHT WINGERS...
ALL THIS ISOLATION IS KILLING MY FOCUS. IT'S LIKE I'M CONSTANTLY SUCKLING ON MY PHONE'S TEAT IN PURSUIT OF HUMAN CONNECTION... BUT IT'S ALL EMPTY, IT DOESN'T SATISFY.
I CAN'T BELIEVE I WAS SO ARROGANT TO THINK I COULD MOVE OUT HERE BY MYSELF & START ALL OVER. EVEN BEFORE THIS FORCED ISOLATION I WAS COMPLETELY ALONE.
I'M WORRIED THAT I'VE ALREADY SLIPPED PAST THE POINT OF NO RETURN W/ MY MENTAL HEALTH.
I CAN'T MOVE BACK HOME... THERE'S NOTHING FOR ME THERE EITHER. FUCK, I'M COMPLETELY ALONE & LOST... WHAT AM I GONNA DO?

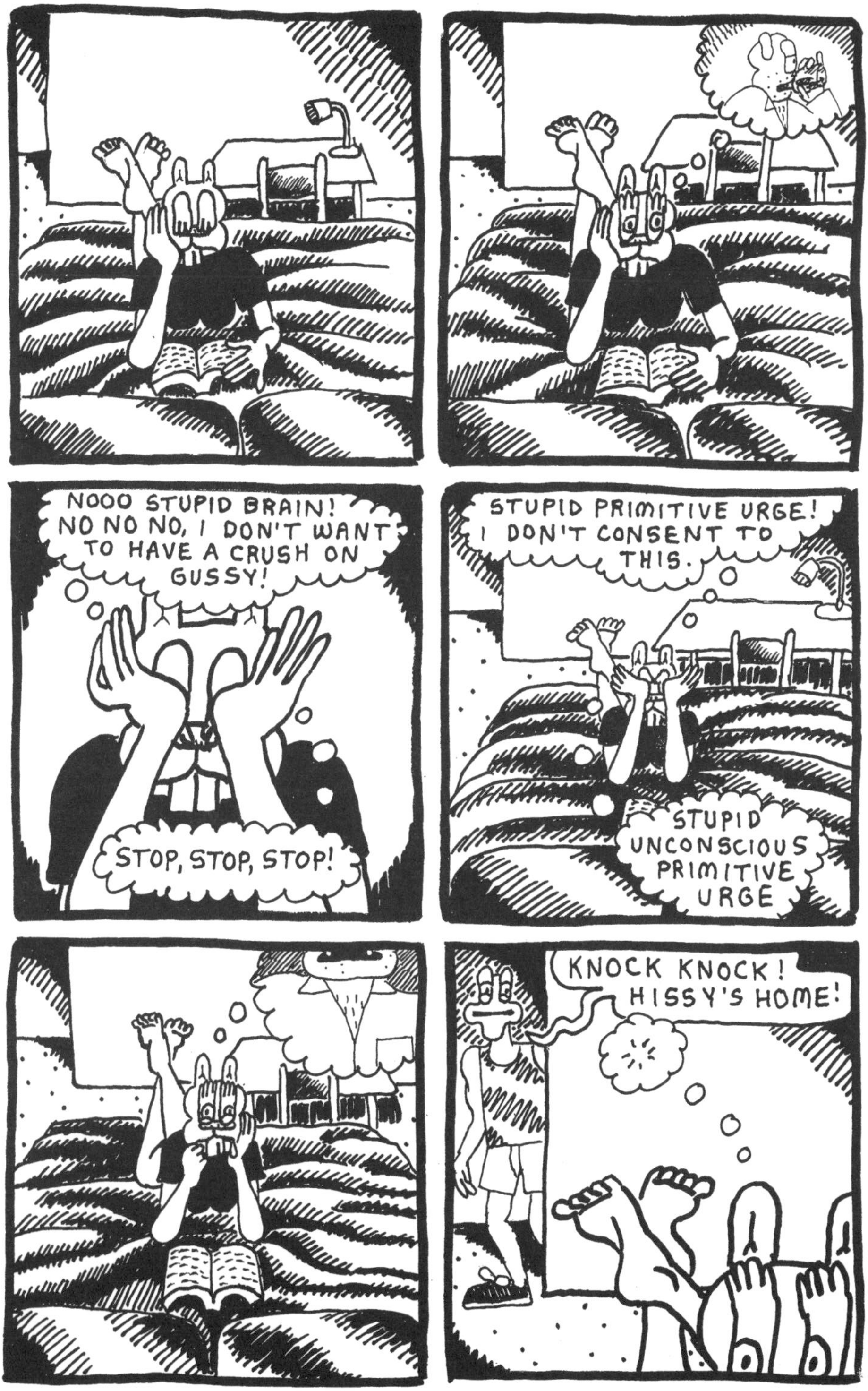
NOOO STUPID BRAIN! NO NO NO, I DON'T WANT TO HAVE A CRUSH ON GUSSY!
STOP, STOP, STOP!
STUPID PRIMITIVE URGE! I DON'T CONSENT TO THIS.
STUPID UNCONSCIOUS PRIMITIVE URGE
KNOCK KNOCK! HISSY'S HOME!

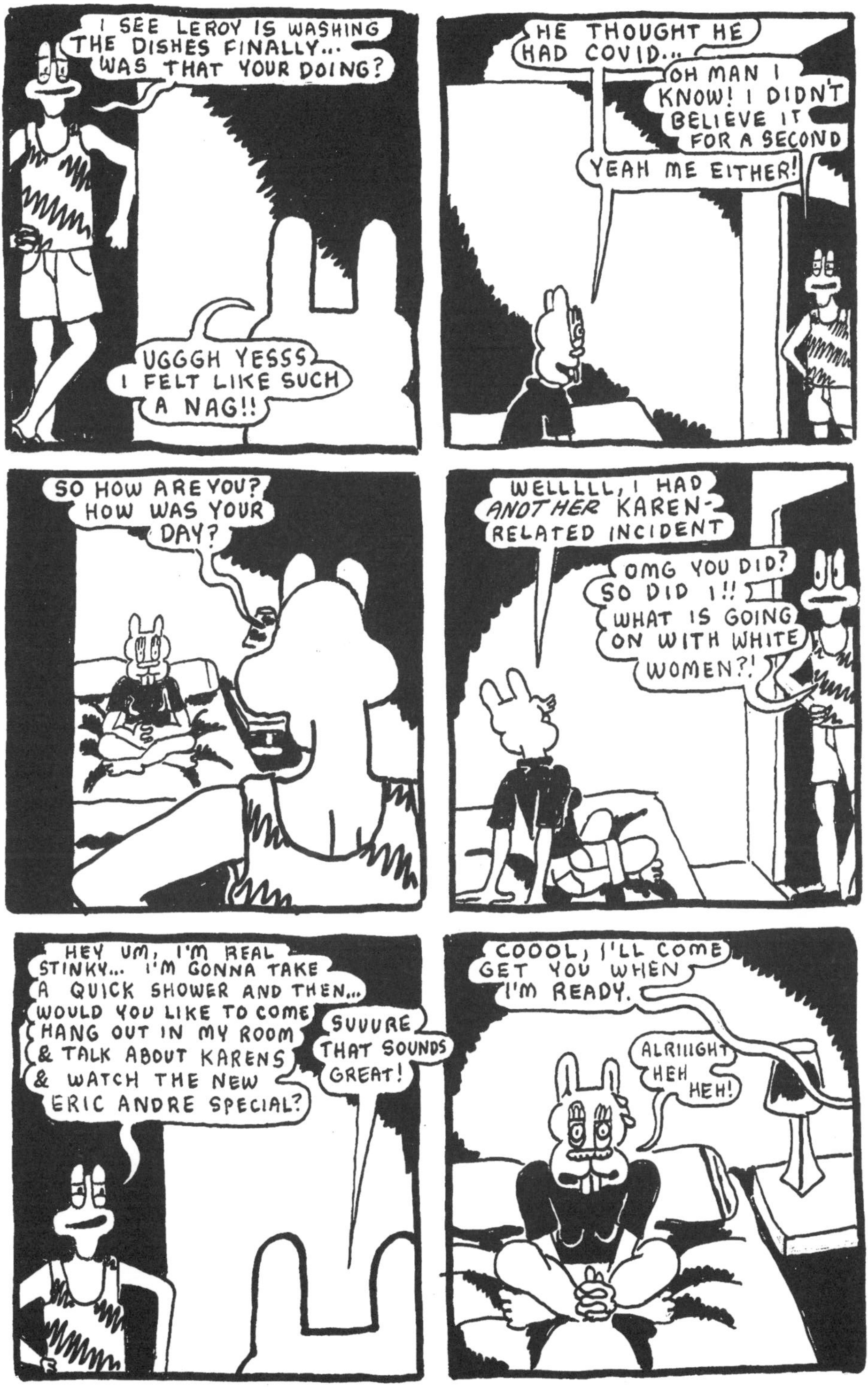
I SEE LEROY IS WASHING THE DISHES FINALLY... WAS THAT YOUR DOING?
UGGGH YESSS I FELT LIKE SUCH A NAG!!
HE THOUGHT HE HAD COVID...
OH MAN I KNOW! I DIDN'T BELIEVE IT FOR A SECOND
YEAH ME EITHER!
SO HOW ARE YOU? HOW WAS YOUR DAY?
WELLLLL, I HAD ANOTHER KAREN-RELATED INCIDENT
OMG YOU DID? SO DID I!! WHAT IS GOING ON WITH WHITE WOMEN?!
HEY UM, I'M REAL STINKY... I'M GONNA TAKE A QUICK SHOWER AND THEN... WOULD YOU LIKE TO COME HANG OUT IN MY ROOM & TALK ABOUT KARENS & WATCH THE NEW ERIC ANDRE SPECIAL?
SUUURE THAT SOUNDS GREAT!
COOOL, I'LL COME GET YOU WHEN I'M READY.
ALRIIIGHT HEH HEH!

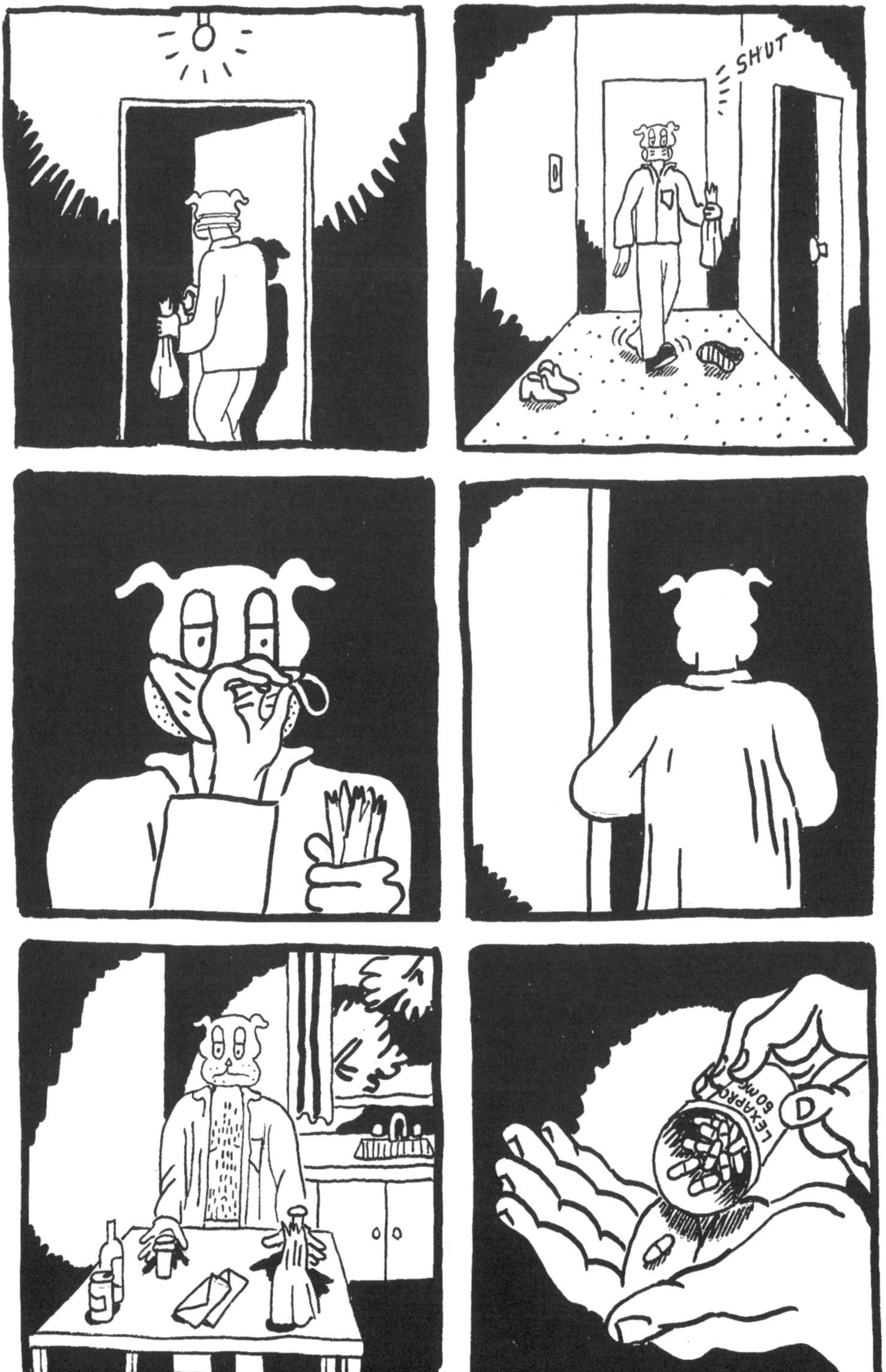
SHUT
LEXAPRO
60MG

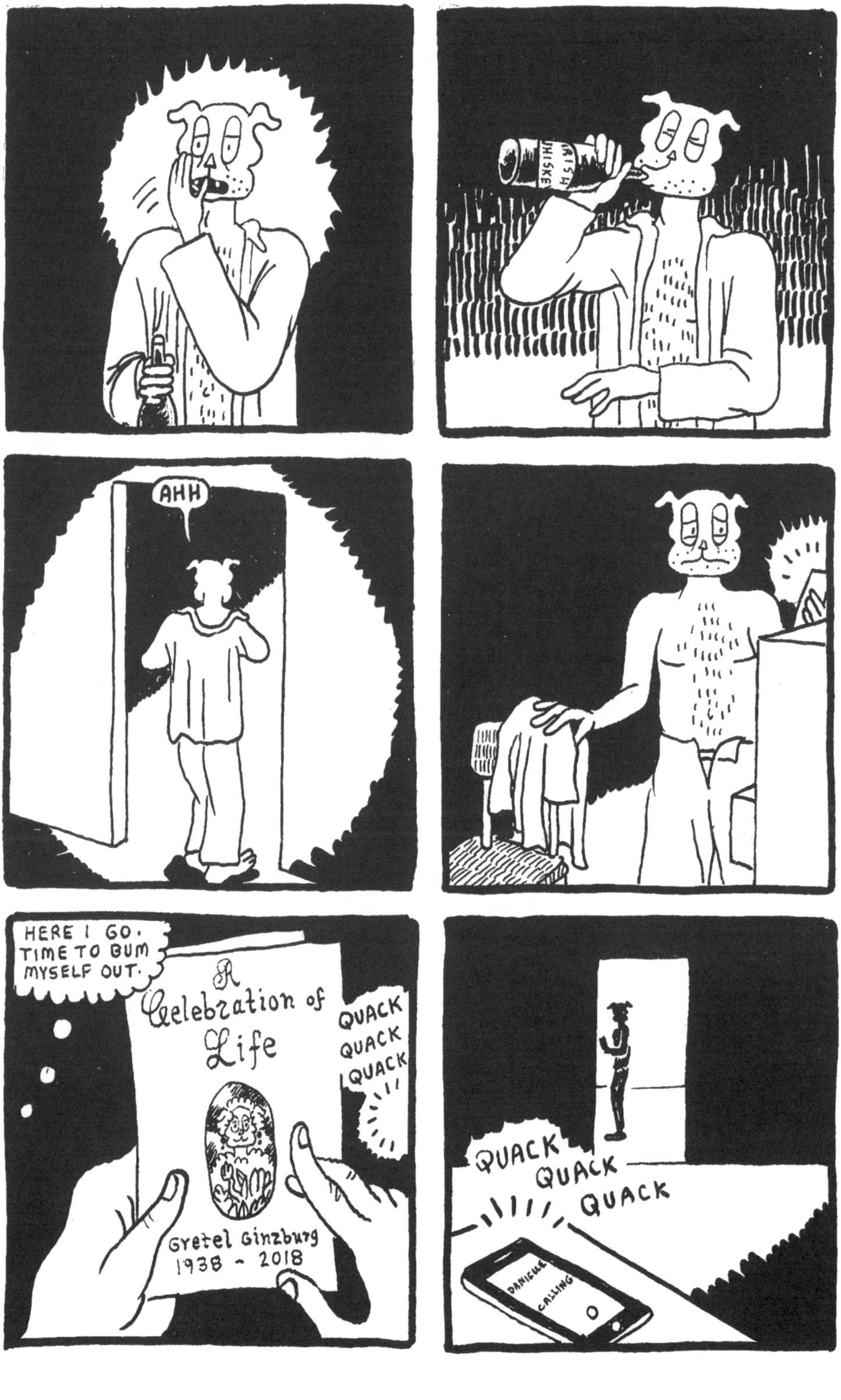

AHH
HERE I GO. TIME TO BUM MYSELF OUT.
A Celebration of Life
Gretel Ginzburg
1938 - 2018
QUACK QUACK QUACK
QUACK QUACK QUACK
DANIELLE CALLING

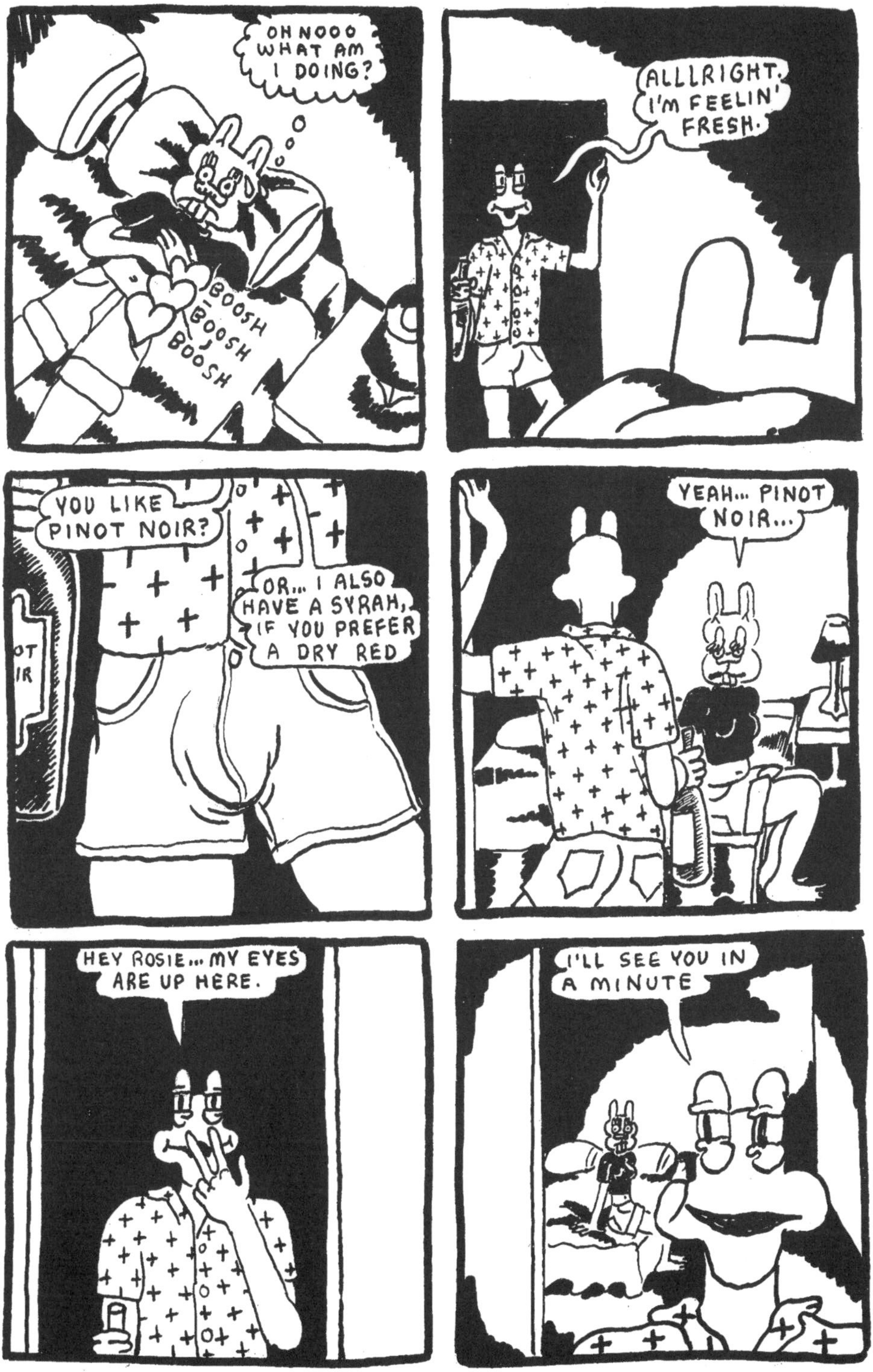
OH NOOO WHAT AM I DOING?
BOOSH BOOSH BOOSH
ALLLRIGHT. I'M FEELIN' FRESH.
YOU LIKE PINOT NOIR?
OR... I ALSO HAVE A SYRAH, IF YOU PREFER A DRY RED
YEAH... PINOT NOIR...
HEY ROSIE... MY EYES ARE UP HERE.
I'LL SEE YOU IN A MINUTE

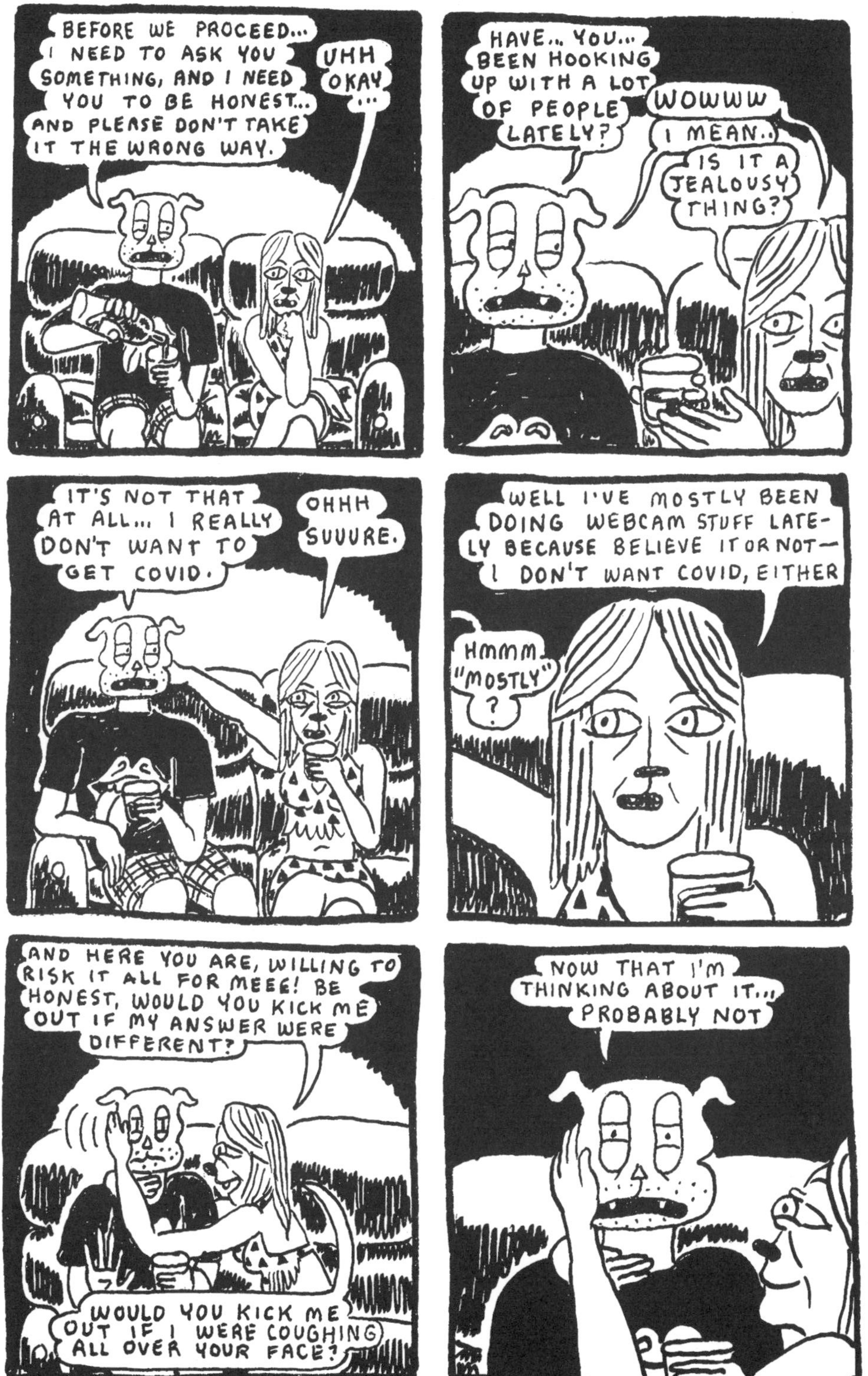
BEFORE WE PROCEED... I NEED TO ASK YOU SOMETHING, AND I NEED YOU TO BE HONEST... AND PLEASE DON'T TAKE IT THE WRONG WAY.
UHH OKAY ...
HAVE... YOU... BEEN HOOKING UP WITH A LOT OF PEOPLE LATELY?
WOWWW
I MEAN..
IS IT A JEALOUSY THING?
IT'S NOT THAT AT ALL... I REALLY DON'T WANT TO GET COVID.
OHHH SUUURE.
WELL I'VE MOSTLY BEEN DOING WEBCAM STUFF LATELY BECAUSE BELIEVE IT OR NOT— I DON'T WANT COVID, EITHER
HMMM. "MOSTLY" ?
AND HERE YOU ARE, WILLING TO RISK IT ALL FOR MEEE! BE HONEST, WOULD YOU KICK ME OUT IF MY ANSWER WERE DIFFERENT?
WOULD YOU KICK ME OUT IF I WERE COUGHING ALL OVER YOUR FACE?
NOW THAT I'M THINKING ABOUT IT... PROBABLY NOT

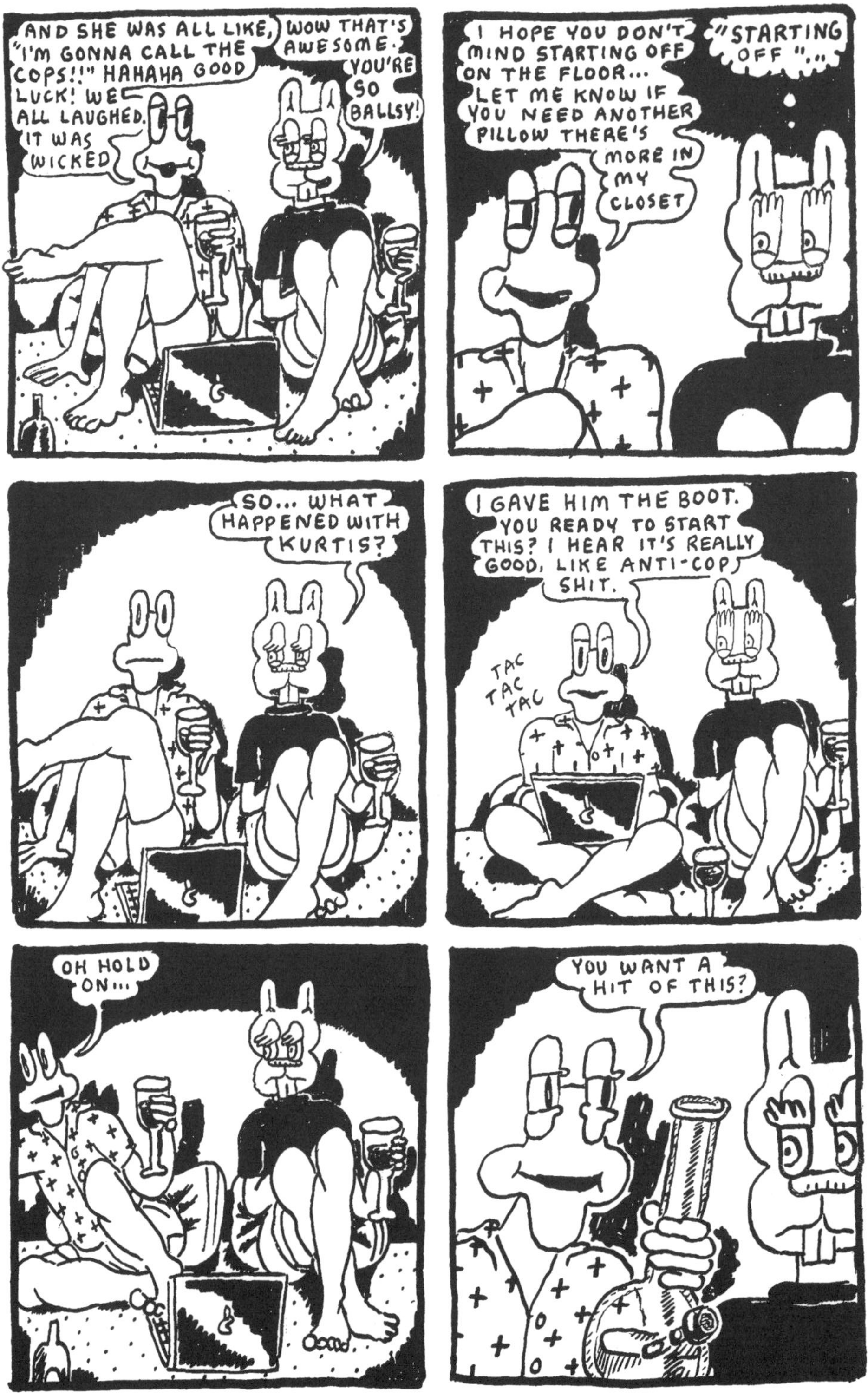
AND SHE WAS ALL LIKE, "I'M GONNA CALL THE COPS!!" HAHAHA GOOD LUCK! WE ALL LAUGHED. IT WAS WICKED
WOW THAT'S AWESOME.
YOU'RE SO BALLSY!
I HOPE YOU DON'T MIND STARTING OFF ON THE FLOOR... LET ME KNOW IF YOU NEED ANOTHER PILLOW THERE'S MORE IN MY CLOSET
"STARTING OFF"...
SO... WHAT HAPPENED WITH KURTIS?
I GAVE HIM THE BOOT. YOU READY TO START THIS? I HEAR IT'S REALLY GOOD, LIKE ANTI-COP SHIT.
TAC TAC TAC
OH HOLD ON...
YOU WANT A HIT OF THIS?

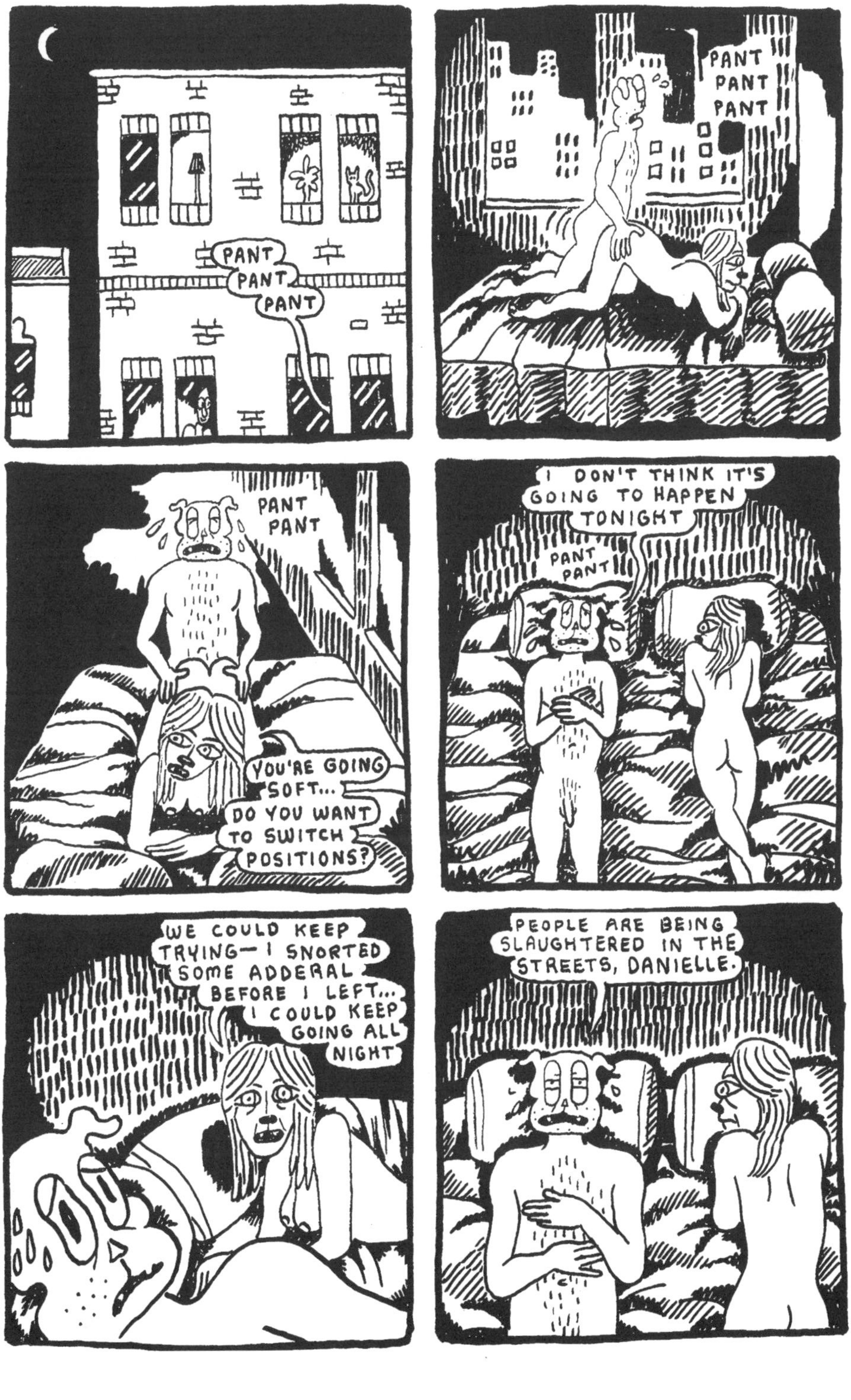
PANT
PANT
PANT
PANT
PANT
PANT
PANT
PANT
YOU'RE GOING SOFT...
DO YOU WANT TO SWITCH POSITIONS?
I DON'T THINK IT'S GOING TO HAPPEN TONIGHT
PANT PANT
WE COULD KEEP TRYING— I SNORTED SOME ADDERAL BEFORE I LEFT... I COULD KEEP GOING ALL NIGHT
PEOPLE ARE BEING SLAUGHTERED IN THE STREETS, DANIELLE.

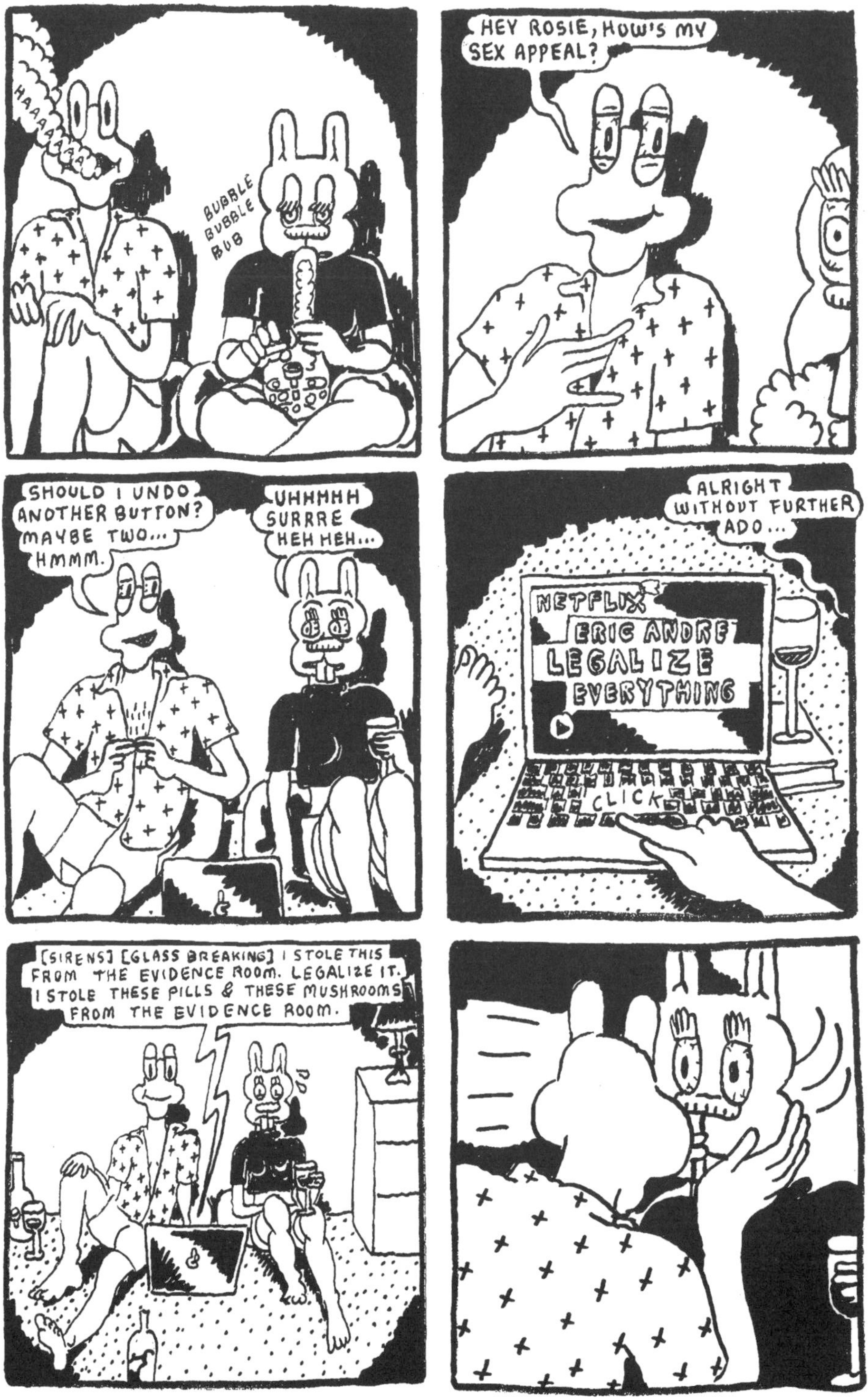
HAAAAAAAA
BUBBLE BUBBLE BUB
HEY ROSIE, HOW'S MY SEX APPEAL?
SHOULD I UNDO ANOTHER BUTTON? MAYBE TWO... HMMM.
UHHMMH SURRRE HEH HEH...
ALRIGHT WITHOUT FURTHER ADO...
NETFLIX
ERIC ANDRE LEGALIZE EVERYTHING
CLICK
[SIRENS] [GLASS BREAKING] I STOLE THIS FROM THE EVIDENCE ROOM. LEGALIZE IT. I STOLE THESE PILLS & THESE MUSHROOMS FROM THE EVIDENCE ROOM.

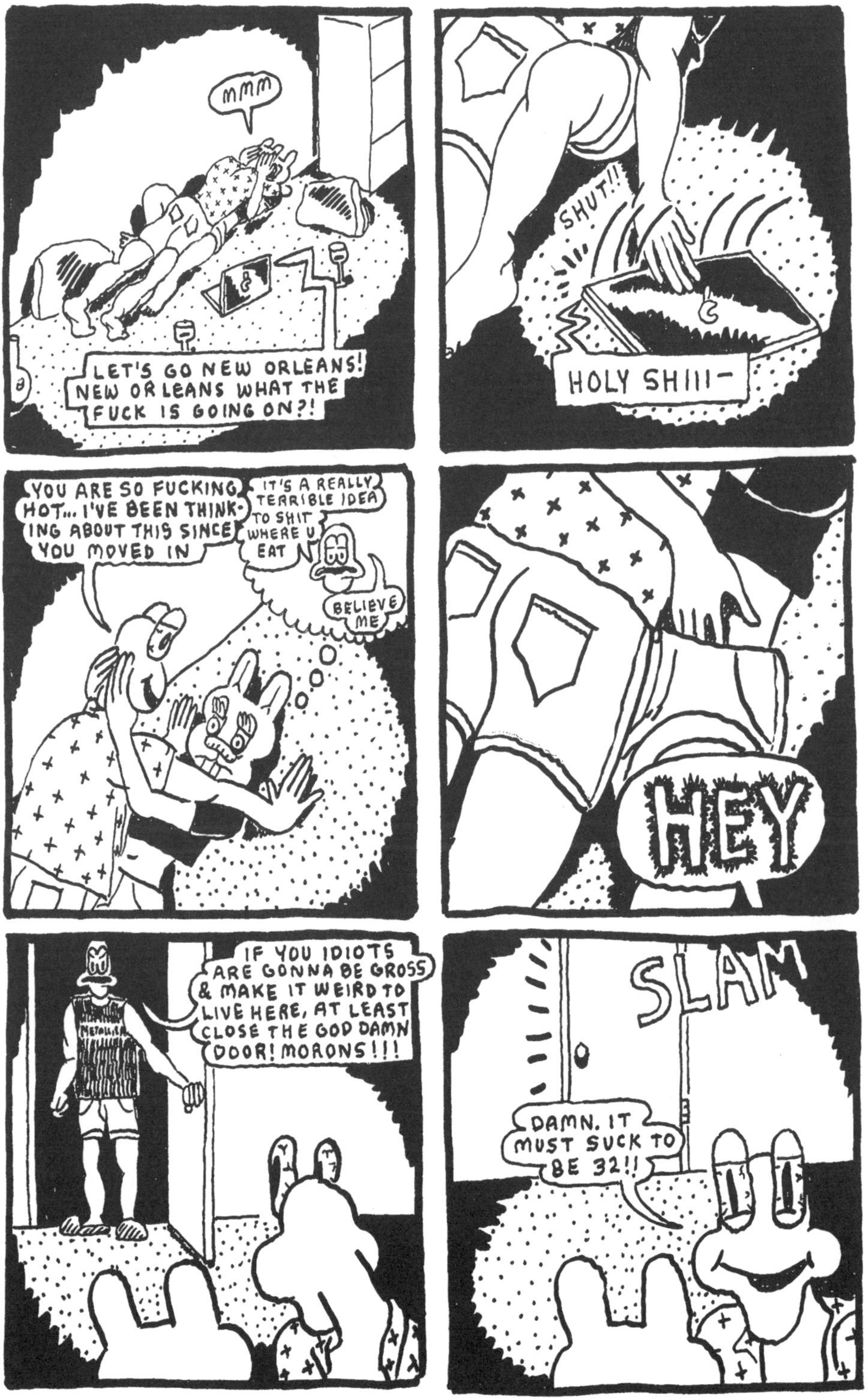
MMM
LET'S GO NEW ORLEANS! NEW ORLEANS WHAT THE FUCK IS GOING ON?!
SHUT!!
HOLY SHIII-
YOU ARE SO FUCKING HOT... I'VE BEEN THINKING ABOUT THIS SINCE YOU MOVED IN
IT'S A REALLY TERRIBLE IDEA TO SHIT WHERE U EAT
BELIEVE ME
HEY
IF YOU IDIOTS ARE GONNA BE GROSS & MAKE IT WEIRD TO LIVE HERE, AT LEAST CLOSE THE GOD DAMN DOOR! MORONS!!!
METALLICA
SLAM
DAMN. IT MUST SUCK TO BE 32!!

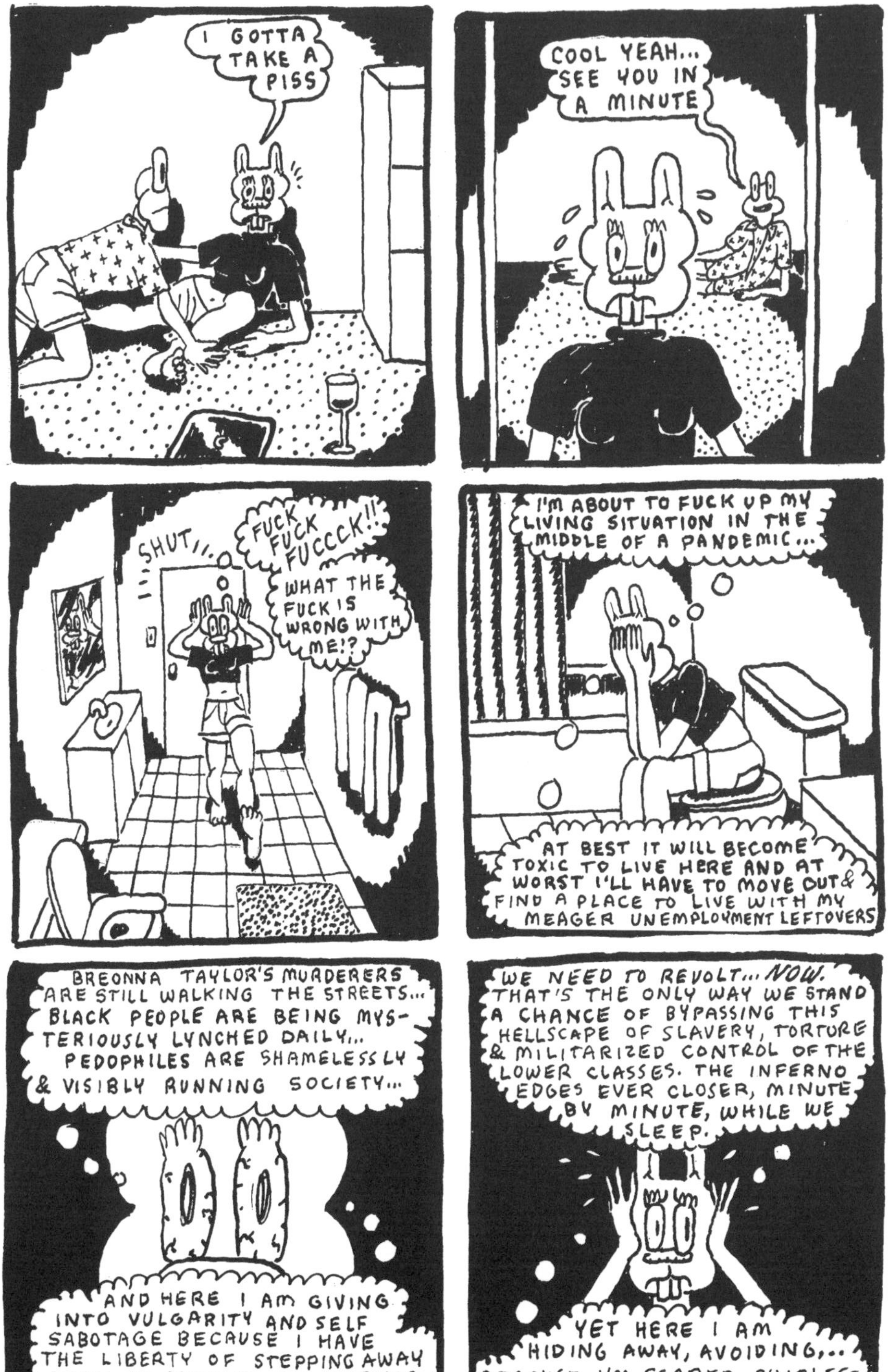
I GOTTA TAKE A PISS
COOL YEAH... SEE YOU IN A MINUTE
SHUT
FUCK FUCK FUCCCK!!
WHAT THE FUCK IS WRONG WITH ME!?
I'M ABOUT TO FUCK UP MY LIVING SITUATION IN THE MIDDLE OF A PANDEMIC...
AT BEST IT WILL BECOME TOXIC TO LIVE HERE AND AT WORST I'LL HAVE TO MOVE OUT & FIND A PLACE TO LIVE WITH MY MEAGER UNEMPLOYMENT LEFTOVERS
BREONNA TAYLOR'S MURDERERS ARE STILL WALKING THE STREETS... BLACK PEOPLE ARE BEING MYS-TERIOUSLY LYNCHED DAILY... PEDOPHILES ARE SHAMELESSLY & VISIBLY RUNNING SOCIETY...
AND HERE I AM GIVING INTO VULGARITY AND SELF SABOTAGE BECAUSE I HAVE THE LIBERTY OF STEPPING AWAY WHEN IT BECOMES TOO INTENSE.
WE NEED TO REVOLT... NOW. THAT'S THE ONLY WAY WE STAND A CHANCE OF BYPASSING THIS HELLSCAPE OF SLAVERY, TORTURE & MILITARIZED CONTROL OF THE LOWER CLASSES. THE INFERNO EDGES EVER CLOSER, MINUTE BY MINUTE, WHILE WE SLEEP.
YET HERE I AM HIDING AWAY, AVOIDING,... BECAUSE I'M SCARED SHITLESS.

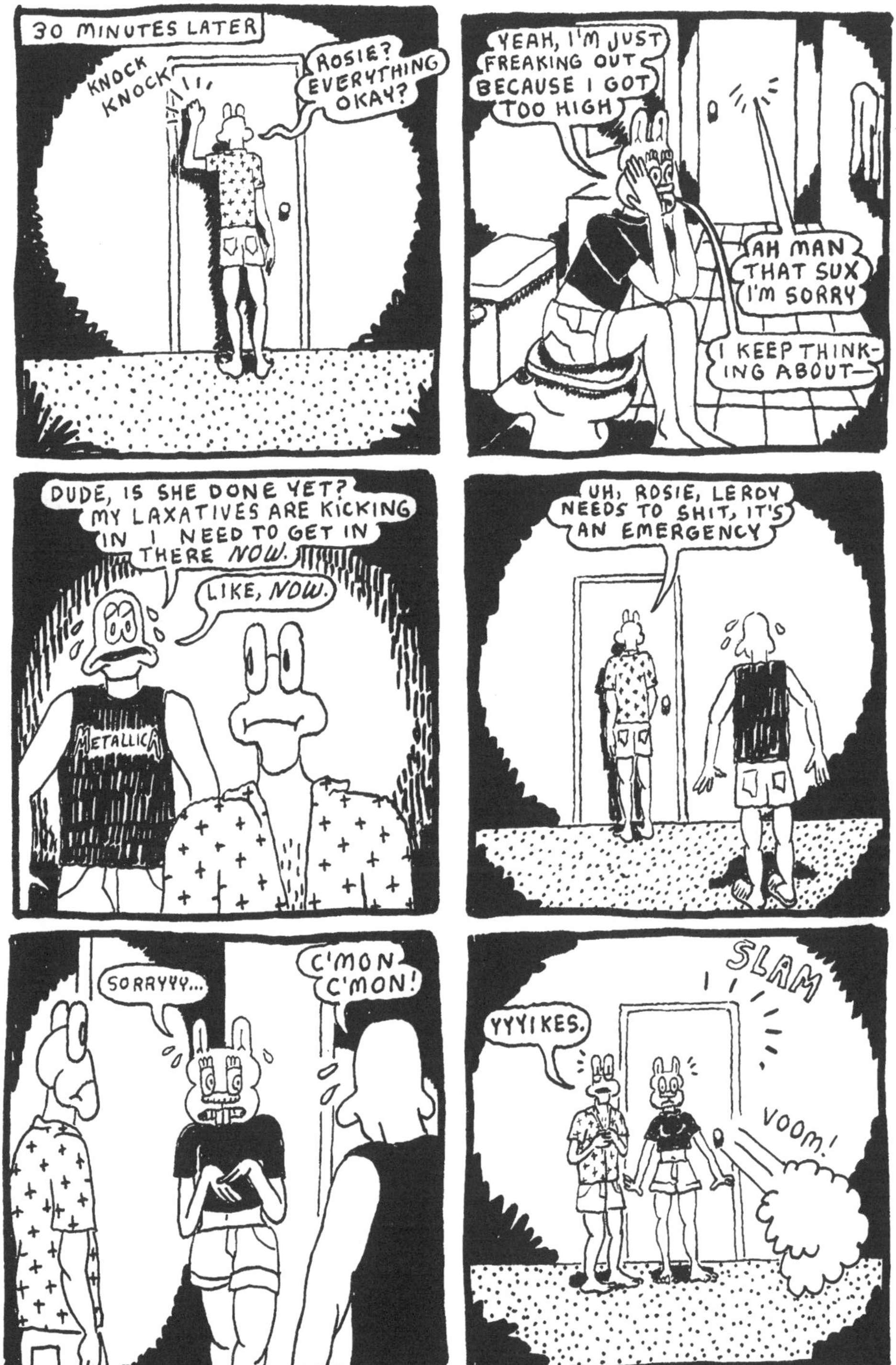
30 MINUTES LATER
KNOCK KNOCK
ROSIE? EVERYTHING OKAY?
YEAH, I'M JUST FREAKING OUT BECAUSE I GOT TOO HIGH
AH MAN THAT SUX I'M SORRY
I KEEP THINKING ABOUT—
DUDE, IS SHE DONE YET? MY LAXATIVES ARE KICKING IN I NEED TO GET IN THERE NOW.
LIKE, NOW.
METALLICA
UH, ROSIE, LEROY NEEDS TO SHIT, IT'S AN EMERGENCY
SORRYYY...
C'MON C'MON!
SLAM
YYYIKES.
VOOM!

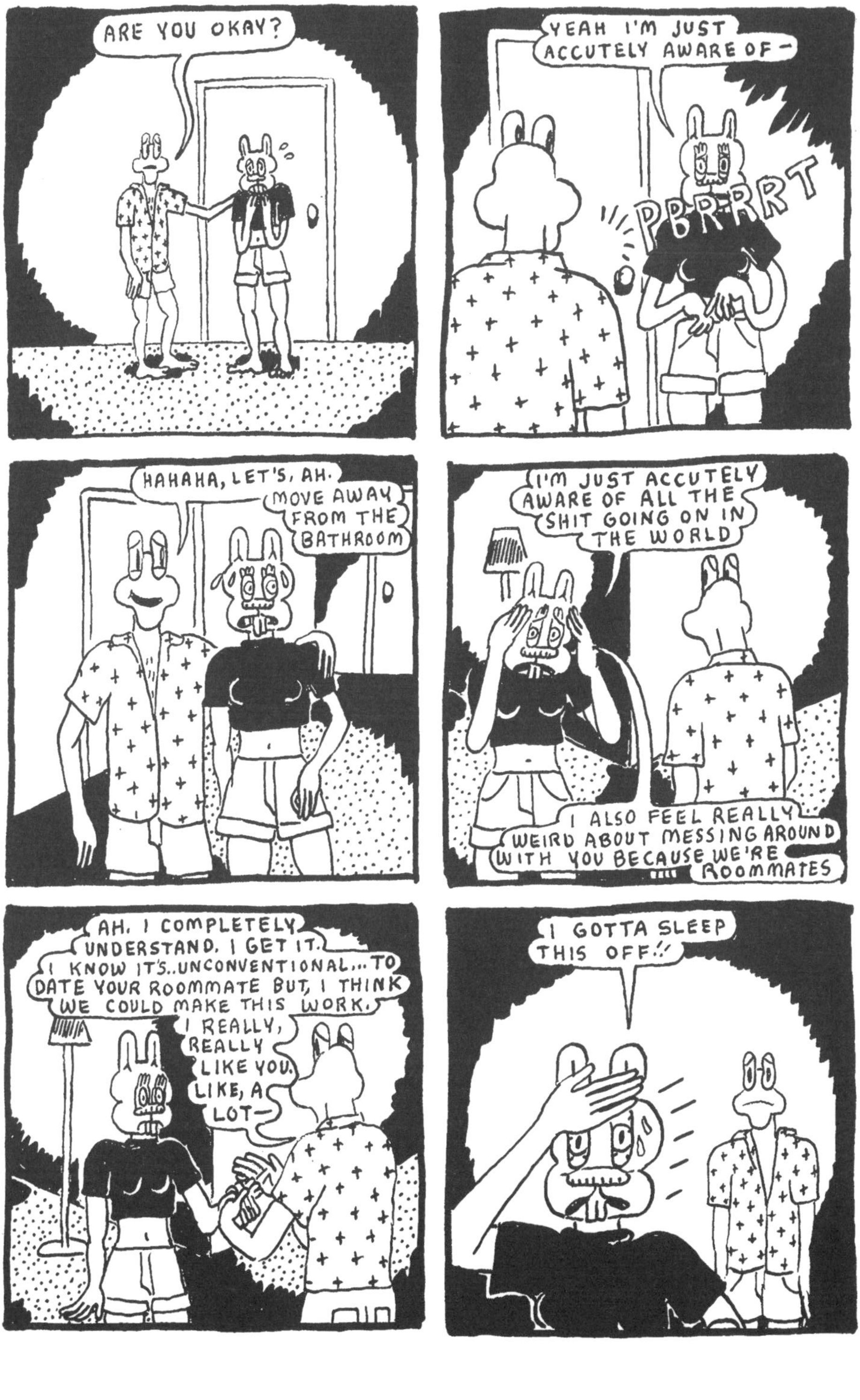
ARE YOU OKAY?
YEAH I'M JUST ACCUTELY AWARE OF–
PBRRRT
HAHAHA, LET'S, AH.
MOVE AWAY FROM THE BATHROOM
I'M JUST ACCUTELY AWARE OF ALL THE SHIT GOING ON IN THE WORLD
I ALSO FEEL REALLY WEIRD ABOUT MESSING AROUND WITH YOU BECAUSE WE'RE ROOMMATES
AH. I COMPLETELY UNDERSTAND. I GET IT. I KNOW IT'S..UNCONVENTIONAL... TO DATE YOUR ROOMMATE BUT, I THINK WE COULD MAKE THIS WORK.
I REALLY, REALLY LIKE YOU. LIKE, A LOT–
I GOTTA SLEEP THIS OFF!!

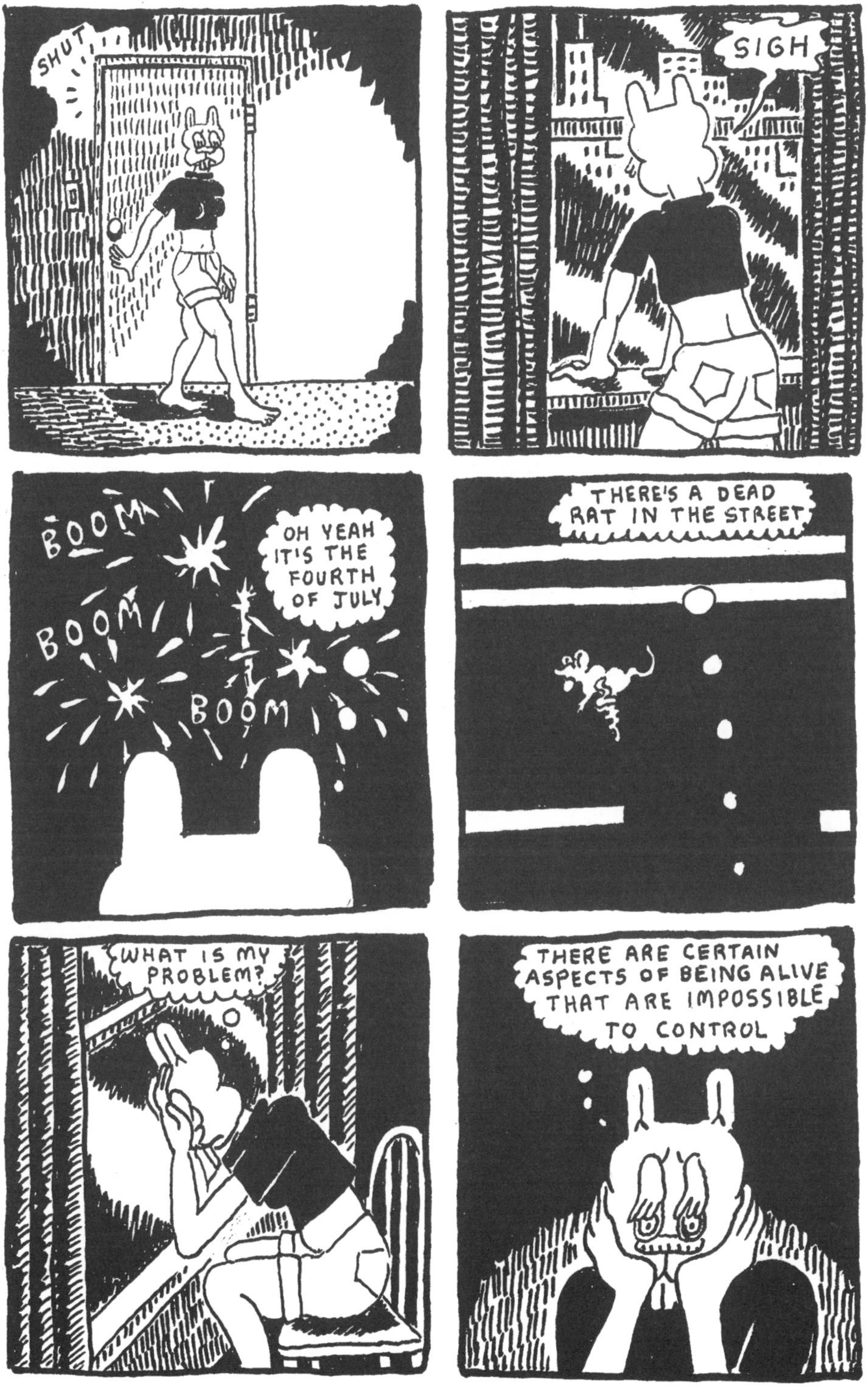
SHUT
SIGH
BOOM
BOOM
BOOM
OH YEAH IT'S THE FOURTH OF JULY
THERE'S A DEAD RAT IN THE STREET
WHAT IS MY PROBLEM?
THERE ARE CERTAIN ASPECTS OF BEING ALIVE THAT ARE IMPOSSIBLE TO CONTROL

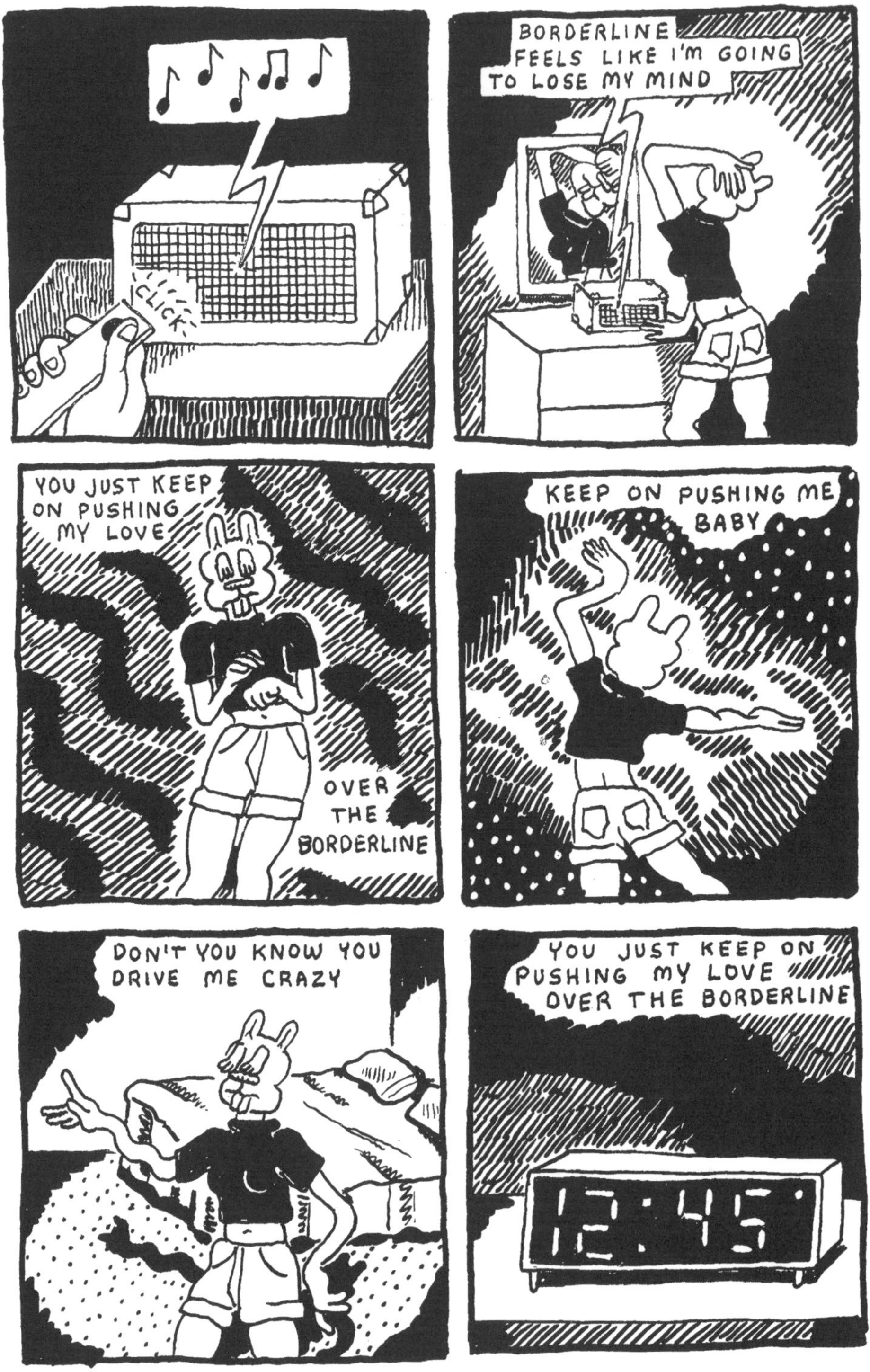
CLICK
BORDERLINE
FEELS LIKE I'M GOING
TO LOSE MY MIND
YOU JUST KEEP
ON PUSHING
MY LOVE
OVER
THE
BORDERLINE
KEEP ON PUSHING ME
BABY
DON'T YOU KNOW YOU
DRIVE ME CRAZY
YOU JUST KEEP ON
PUSHING MY LOVE
OVER THE BORDERLINE
12:45

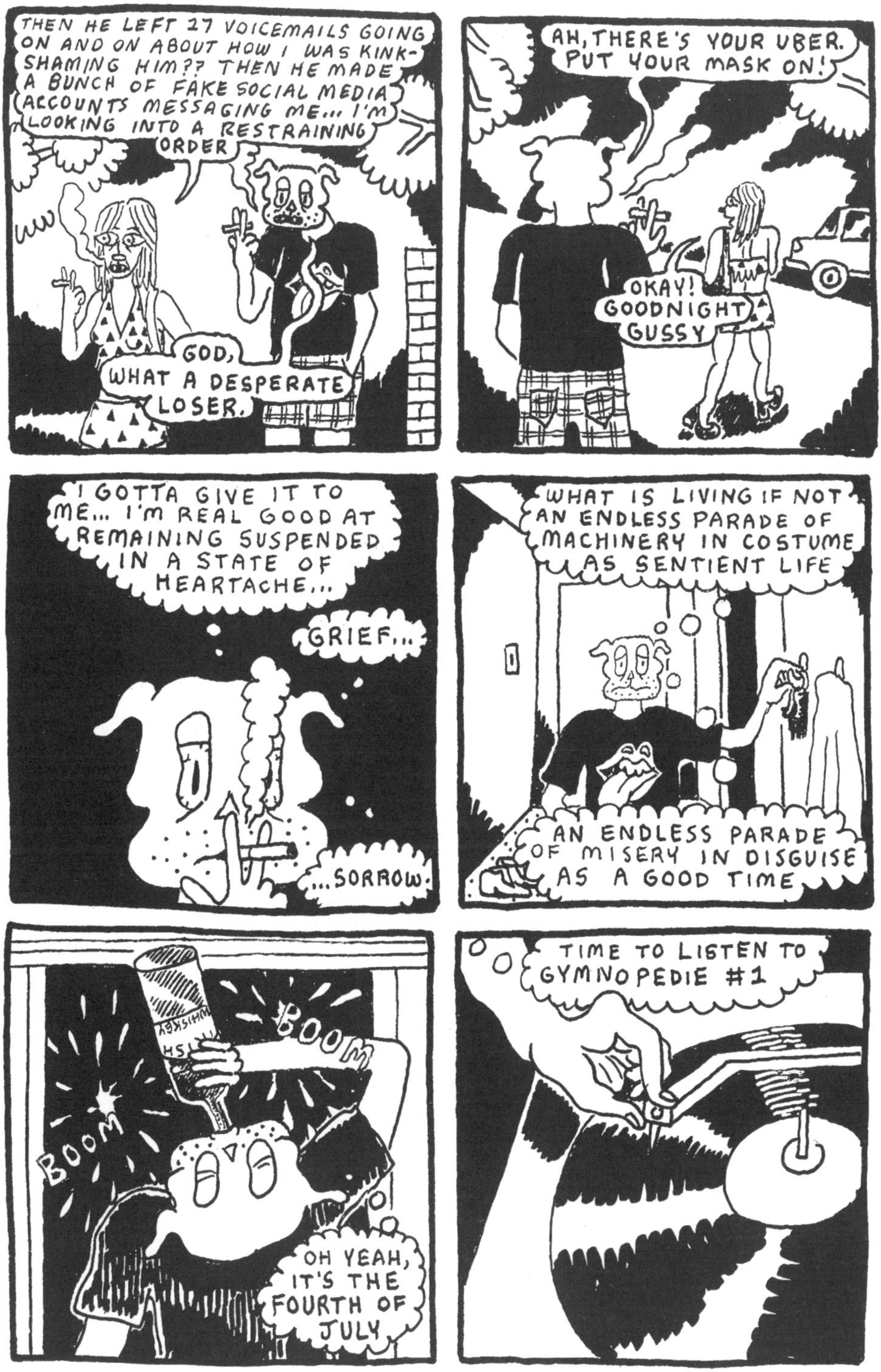
THEN HE LEFT 17 VOICEMAILS GOING ON AND ON ABOUT HOW I WAS KINK-SHAMING HIM?? THEN HE MADE A BUNCH OF FAKE SOCIAL MEDIA ACCOUNTS MESSAGING ME... I'M LOOKING INTO A RESTRAINING ORDER
GOD, WHAT A DESPERATE LOSER.
AH, THERE'S YOUR UBER. PUT YOUR MASK ON!
OKAY! GOODNIGHT GUSSY
I GOTTA GIVE IT TO ME... I'M REAL GOOD AT REMAINING SUSPENDED IN A STATE OF HEARTACHE...
GRIEF...
...SORROW.
WHAT IS LIVING IF NOT AN ENDLESS PARADE OF MACHINERY IN COSTUME AS SENTIENT LIFE
AN ENDLESS PARADE OF MISERY IN DISGUISE AS A GOOD TIME
WHISKEY
BOOM
BOOM
OH YEAH, IT'S THE FOURTH OF JULY
TIME TO LISTEN TO GYMNOPEDIE #1

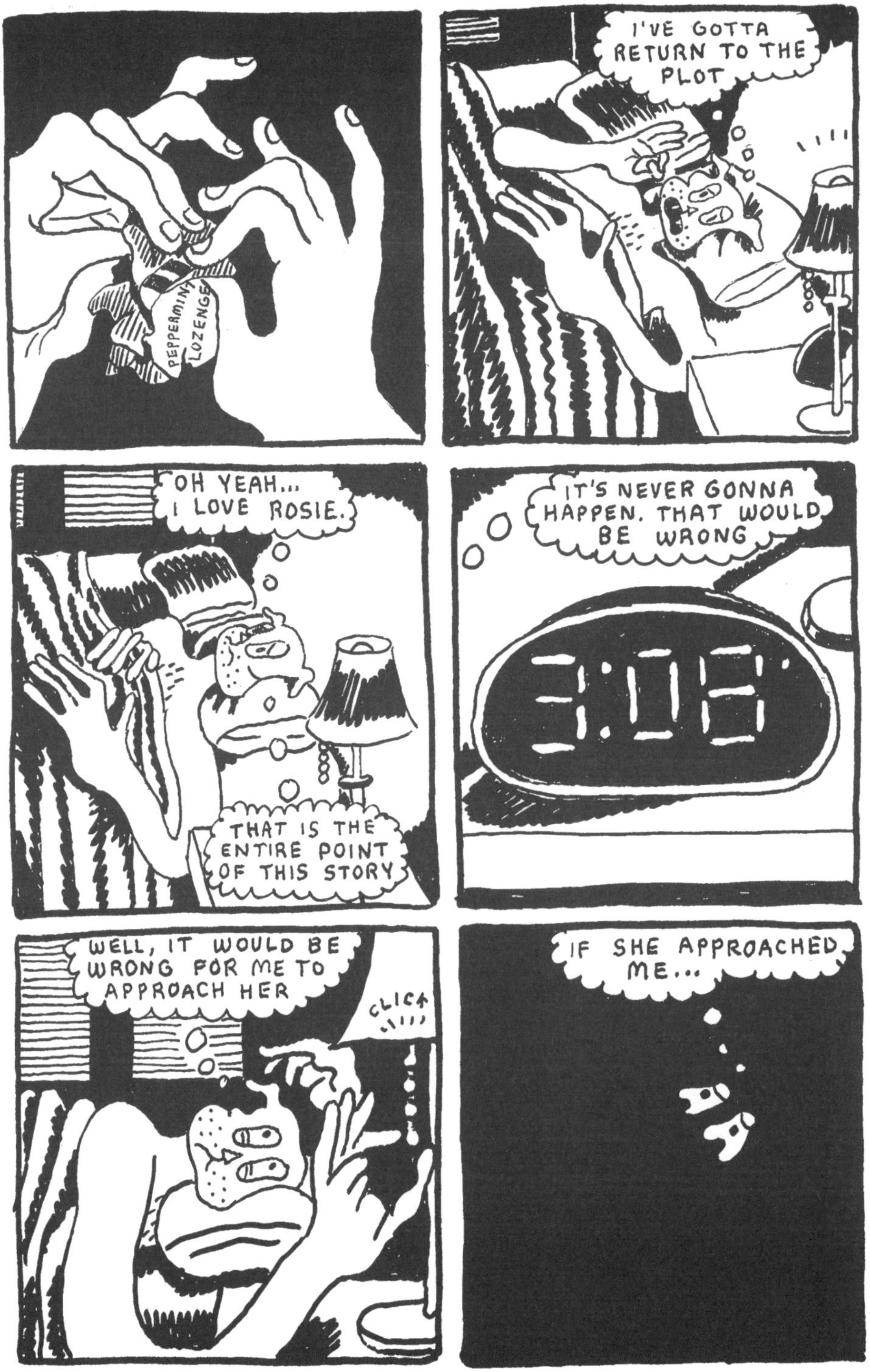
PEPPERMINT LOZENGE
I'VE GOTTA RETURN TO THE PLOT
OH YEAH... I LOVE ROSIE.
THAT IS THE ENTIRE POINT OF THIS STORY
IT'S NEVER GONNA HAPPEN. THAT WOULD BE WRONG
3:08
WELL, IT WOULD BE WRONG FOR ME TO APPROACH HER
CLICK
IF SHE APPROACHED ME...

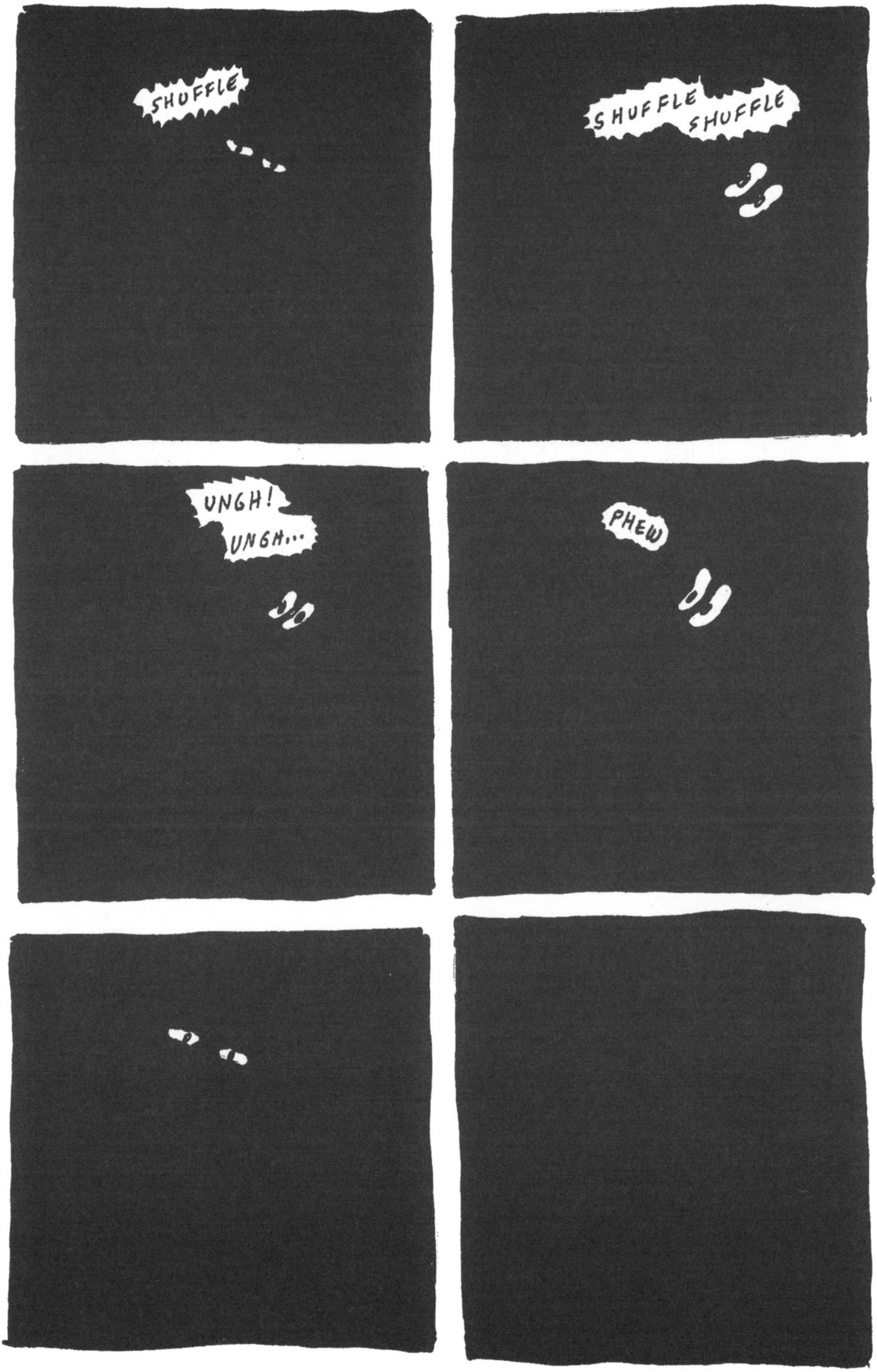
SHUFFLE
SHUFFLE SHUFFLE
UNGH! UNGH...
PHEW

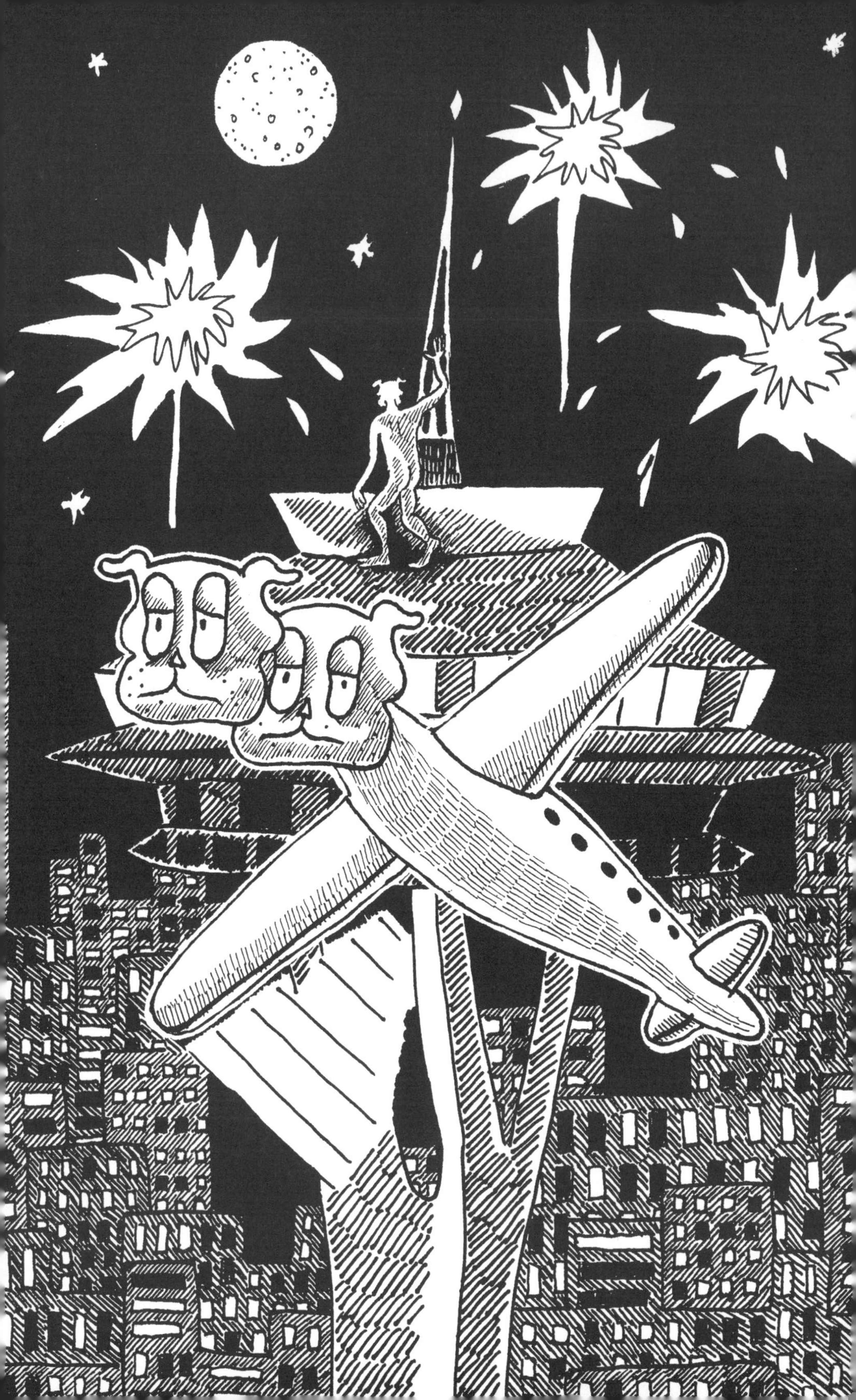

"She Knows"

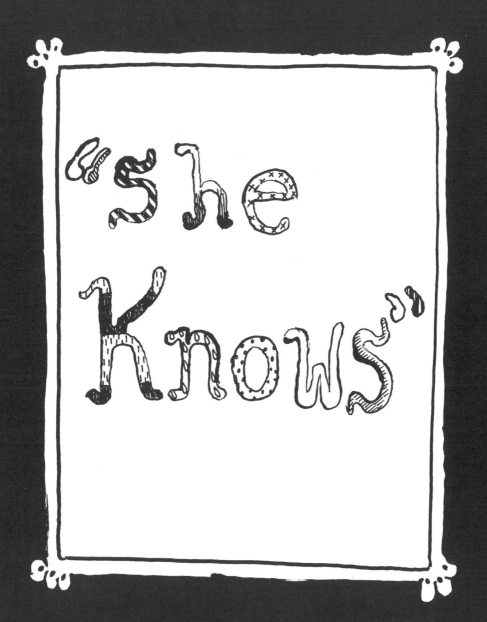

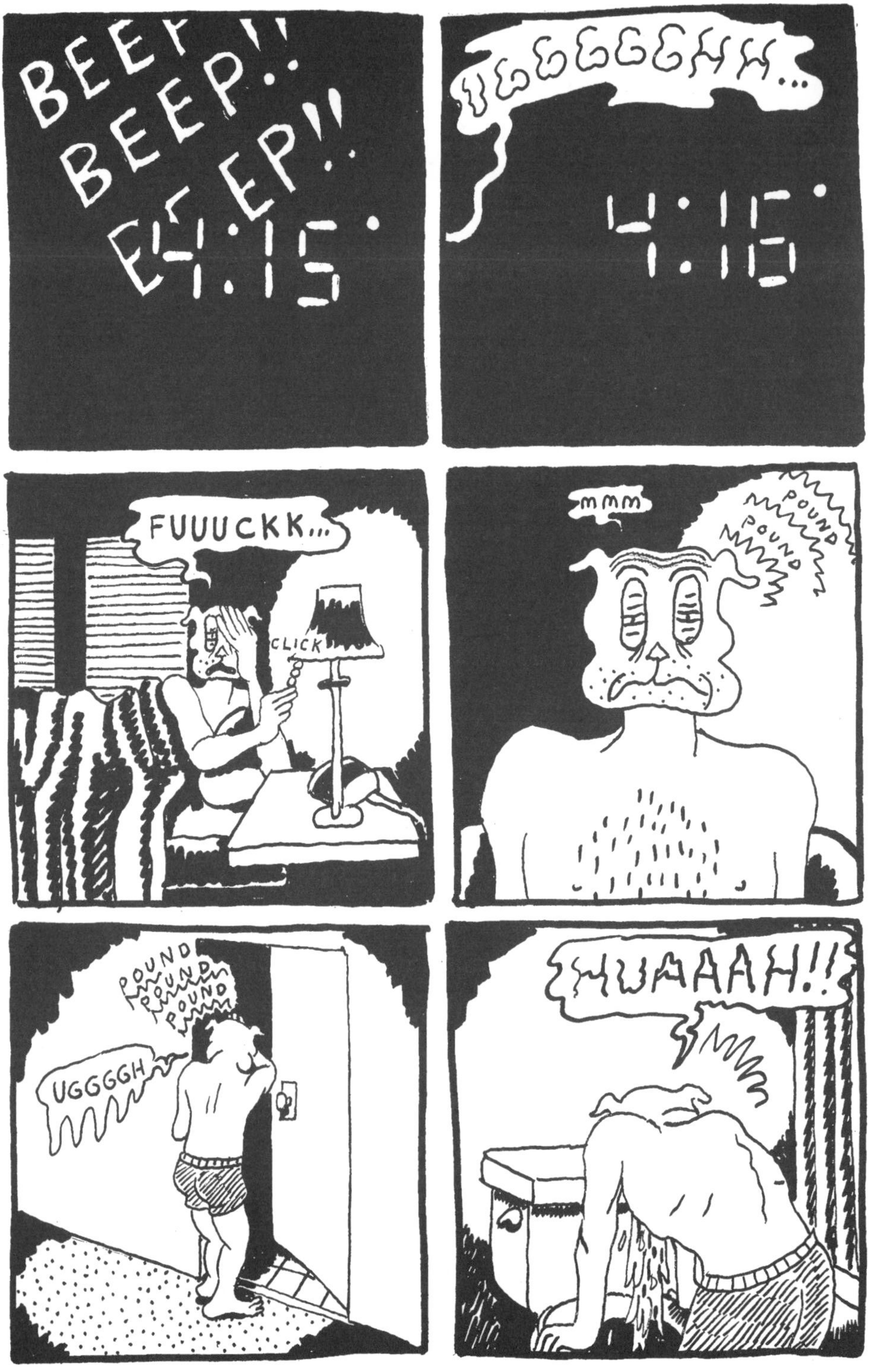
BEEP!! BEEP!! BEEP!!
4:15
UGGGGGHH...
4:16
FUUUCKK...
CLICK
mmm
POUND POUND
POUND POUND POUND
UGGGGH
HWAAAH!!

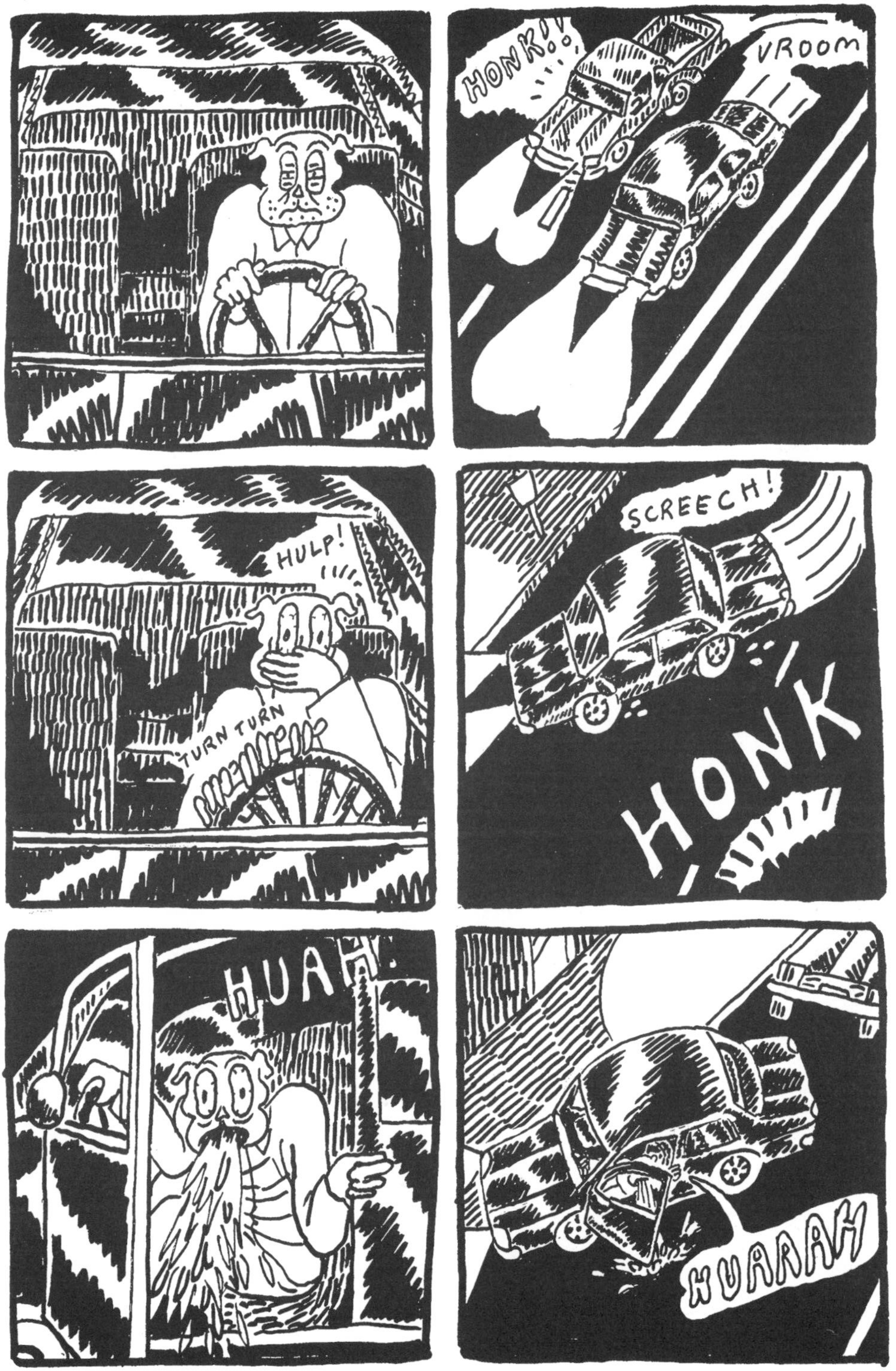
HONK!!
VROOM
HULP!
TURN TURN
SCREECH!
HONK
HUAAH
HUAAAH

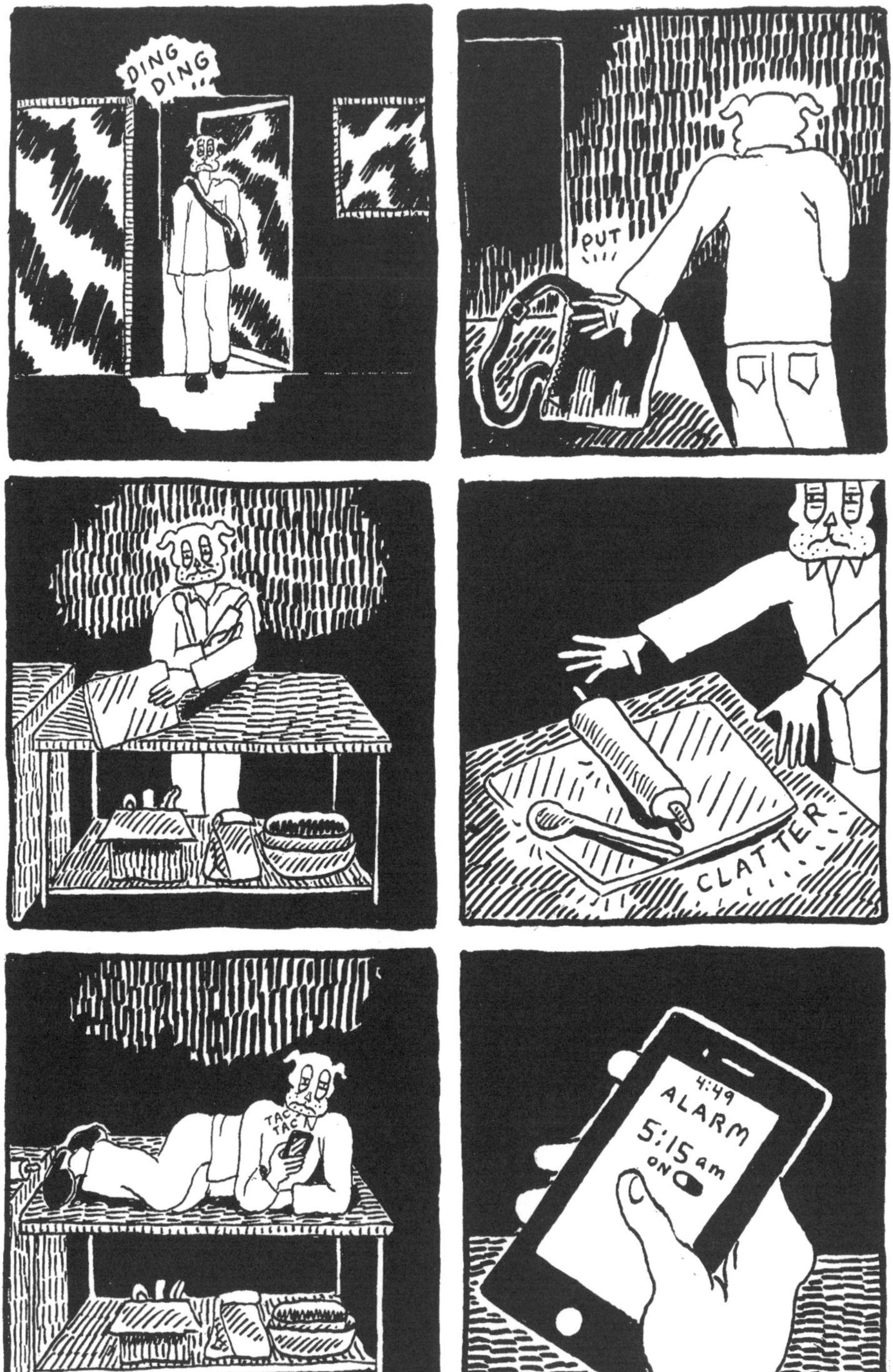
DING DING
PUT
CLATTER
TAC TAC
4:49
ALARM
5:15 am
ON

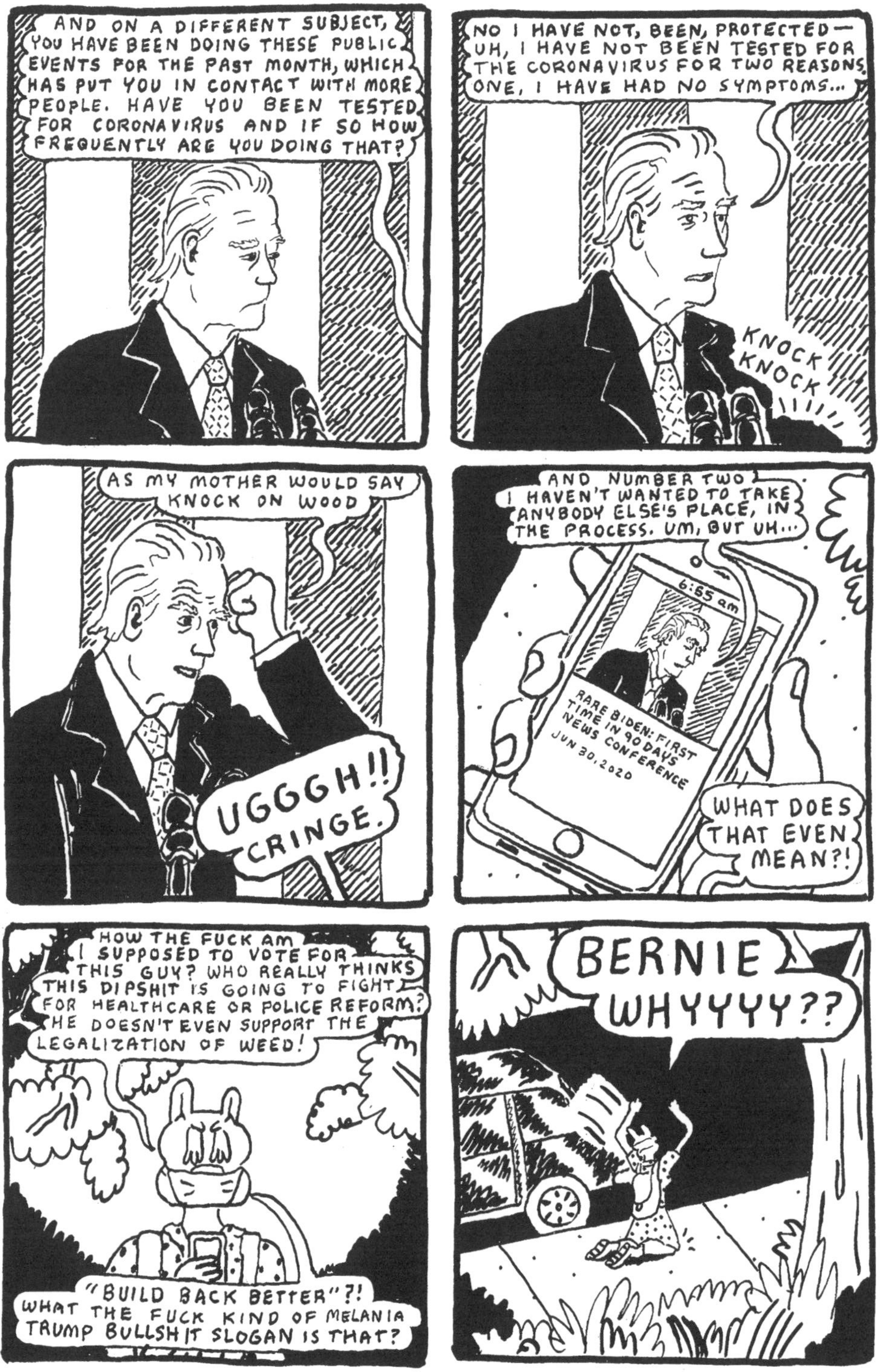
AND ON A DIFFERENT SUBJECT, YOU HAVE BEEN DOING THESE PUBLIC EVENTS FOR THE PAST MONTH, WHICH HAS PUT YOU IN CONTACT WITH MORE PEOPLE. HAVE YOU BEEN TESTED FOR CORONAVIRUS AND IF SO HOW FREQUENTLY ARE YOU DOING THAT?
NO I HAVE NOT, BEEN, PROTECTED— UH, I HAVE NOT BEEN TESTED FOR THE CORONAVIRUS FOR TWO REASONS. ONE, I HAVE HAD NO SYMPTOMS...
KNOCK KNOCK
AS MY MOTHER WOULD SAY KNOCK ON WOOD
UGGGH!! CRINGE.
AND NUMBER TWO I HAVEN'T WANTED TO TAKE ANYBODY ELSE'S PLACE, IN THE PROCESS. UM, BUT UH...
6:55 am
RARE BIDEN: FIRST TIME IN 90 DAYS NEWS CONFERENCE
JUN 30, 2020
WHAT DOES THAT EVEN MEAN?!
HOW THE FUCK AM I SUPPOSED TO VOTE FOR THIS GUY? WHO REALLY THINKS THIS DIPSHIT IS GOING TO FIGHT FOR HEALTHCARE OR POLICE REFORM? HE DOESN'T EVEN SUPPORT THE LEGALIZATION OF WEED!
"BUILD BACK BETTER"?! WHAT THE FUCK KIND OF MELANIA TRUMP BULLSHIT SLOGAN IS THAT?
BERNIE WHYYYY??

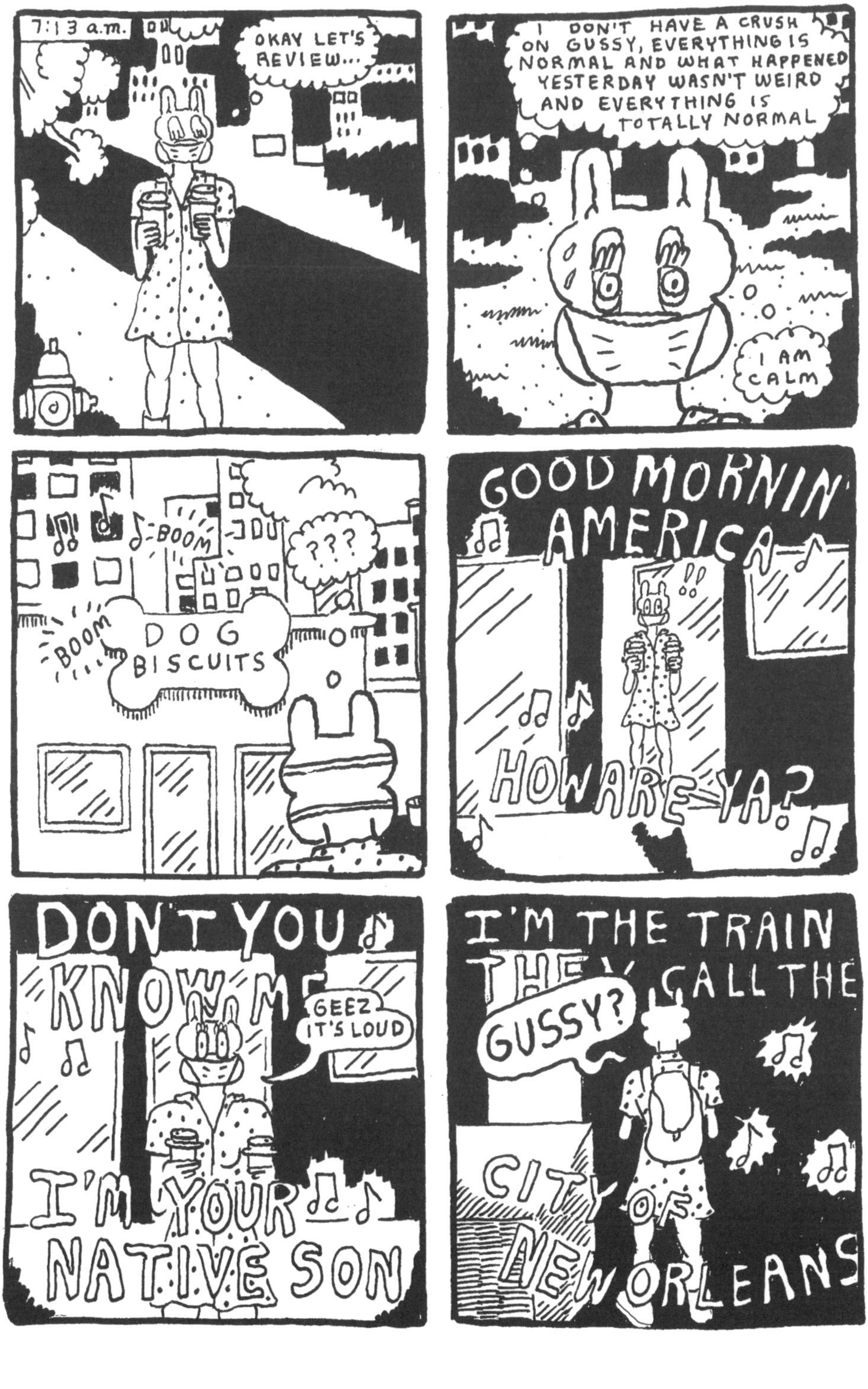
7:13 a.m.
OKAY LET'S REVIEW...
I DON'T HAVE A CRUSH ON GUSSY, EVERYTHING IS NORMAL AND WHAT HAPPENED YESTERDAY WASN'T WEIRD AND EVERYTHING IS TOTALLY NORMAL
I AM CALM
BOOM
???
BOOM
DOG BISCUITS
GOOD MORNIN' AMERICA
!!
HOW ARE YA?
DON'T YOU KNOW ME
GEEZ IT'S LOUD
I'M YOUR NATIVE SON
I'M THE TRAIN THEY CALL THE
GUSSY?
CITY OF NEW ORLEANS

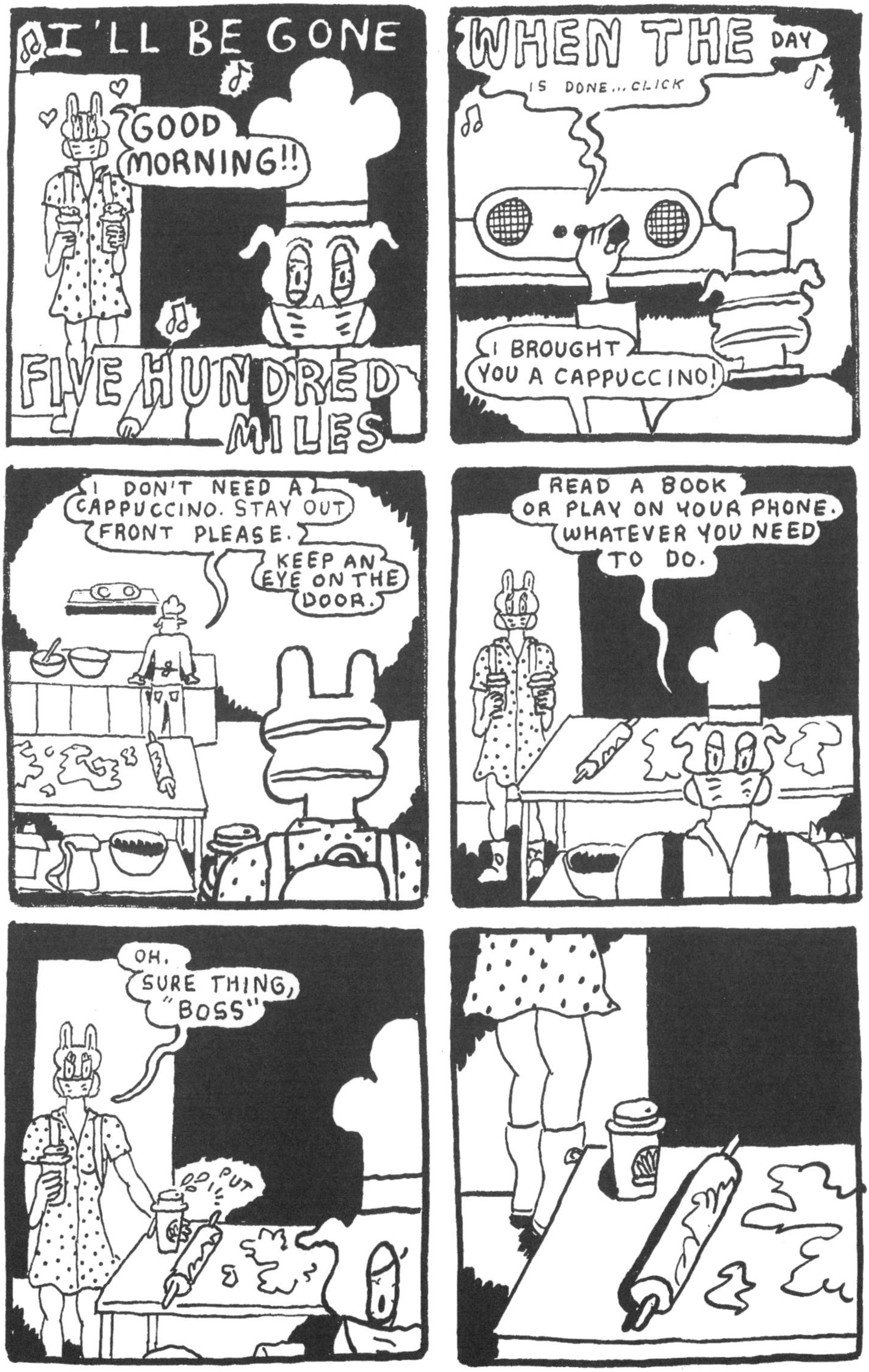
♪ I'LL BE GONE
GOOD MORNING!!
FIVE HUNDRED MILES
WHEN THE DAY
IS DONE... CLICK
I BROUGHT YOU A CAPPUCCINO!
I DON'T NEED A CAPPUCCINO. STAY OUT FRONT PLEASE.
KEEP AN EYE ON THE DOOR.
READ A BOOK OR PLAY ON YOUR PHONE. WHATEVER YOU NEED TO DO.
OH. SURE THING, "BOSS"
PUT

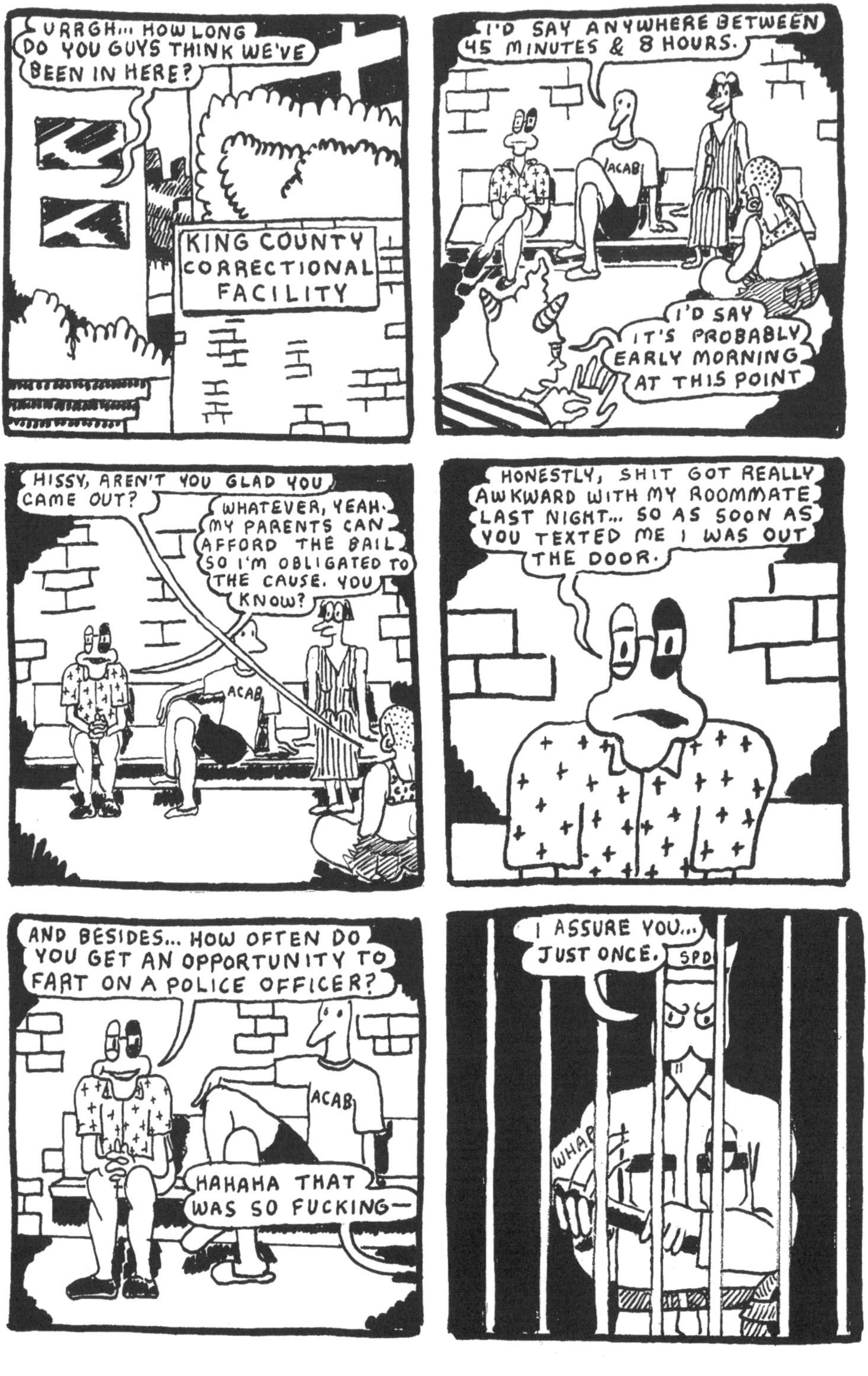
URRGH... HOW LONG DO YOU GUYS THINK WE'VE BEEN IN HERE?
KING COUNTY CORRECTIONAL FACILITY
I'D SAY ANYWHERE BETWEEN 45 MINUTES & 8 HOURS.
ACAB
I'D SAY IT'S PROBABLY EARLY MORNING AT THIS POINT
HISSY, AREN'T YOU GLAD YOU CAME OUT?
WHATEVER, YEAH. MY PARENTS CAN AFFORD THE BAIL SO I'M OBLIGATED TO THE CAUSE. YOU KNOW?
ACAB
HONESTLY, SHIT GOT REALLY AWKWARD WITH MY ROOMMATE LAST NIGHT... SO AS SOON AS YOU TEXTED ME I WAS OUT THE DOOR.
AND BESIDES... HOW OFTEN DO YOU GET AN OPPORTUNITY TO FART ON A POLICE OFFICER?
ACAB
HAHAHA THAT WAS SO FUCKING—
I ASSURE YOU... JUST ONCE.
SPD
WHAP

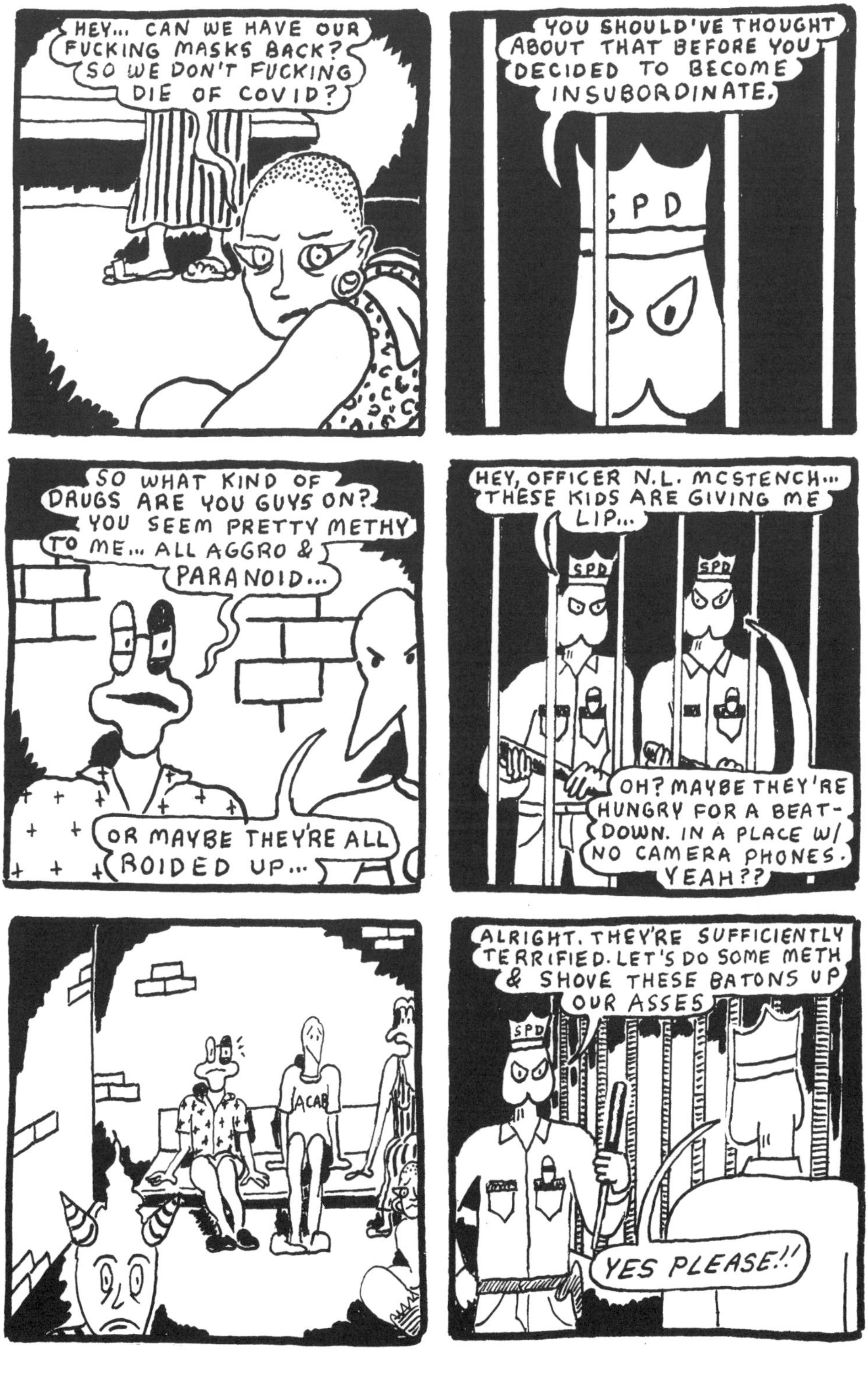
HEY... CAN WE HAVE OUR FUCKING MASKS BACK? SO WE DON'T FUCKING DIE OF COVID?
YOU SHOULD'VE THOUGHT ABOUT THAT BEFORE YOU DECIDED TO BECOME INSUBORDINATE.
SPD
SO WHAT KIND OF DRUGS ARE YOU GUYS ON? YOU SEEM PRETTY METHY TO ME... ALL AGGRO & PARANOID...
OR MAYBE THEY'RE ALL ROIDED UP...
HEY, OFFICER N.L. MCSTENCH... THESE KIDS ARE GIVING ME LIP...
SPD
SPD
OH? MAYBE THEY'RE HUNGRY FOR A BEAT-DOWN. IN A PLACE W/ NO CAMERA PHONES. YEAH??
ACAB
ALRIGHT. THEY'RE SUFFICIENTLY TERRIFIED. LET'S DO SOME METH & SHOVE THESE BATONS UP OUR ASSES
SPD
YES PLEASE!!

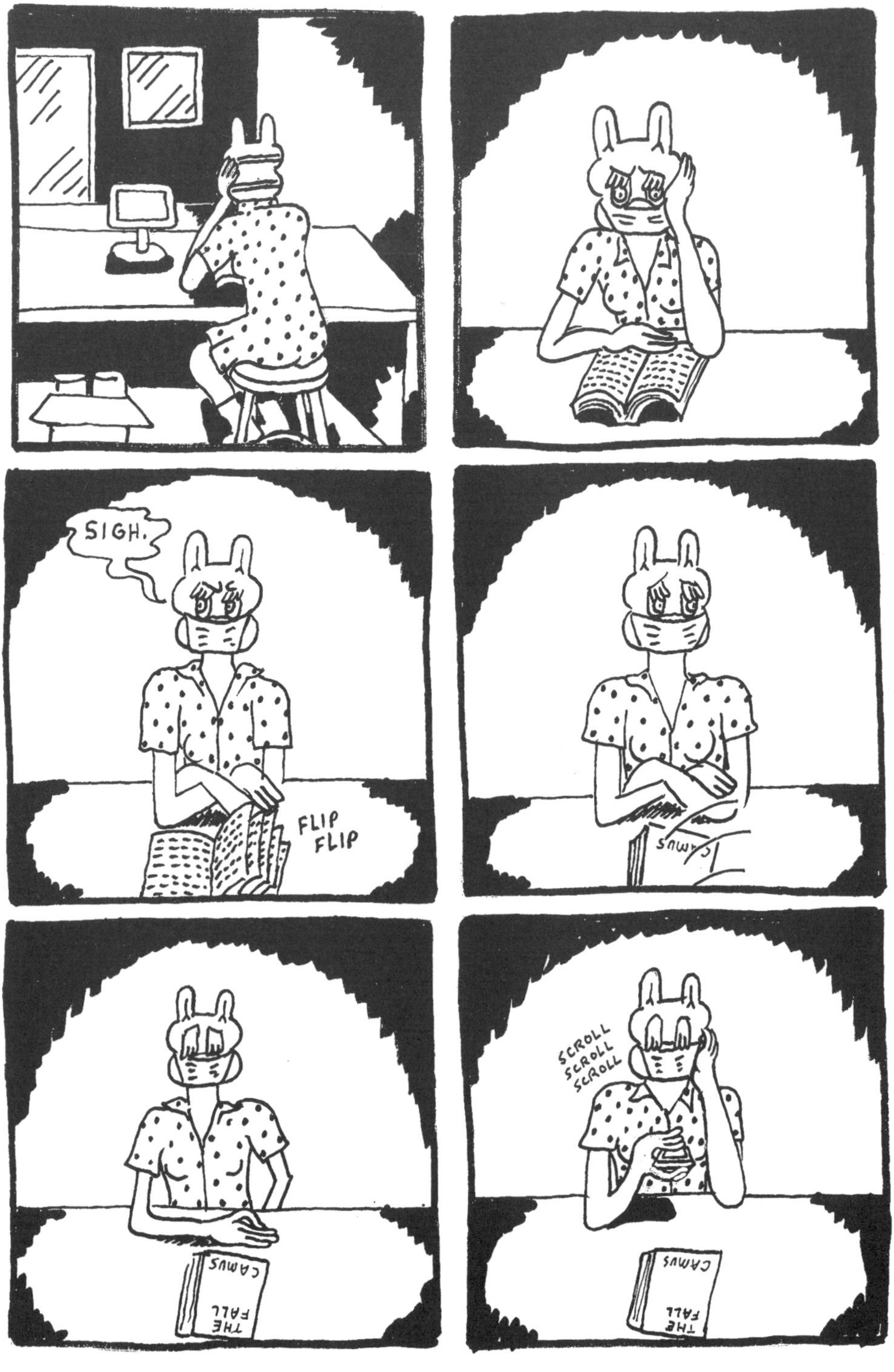
SIGH.
FLIP FLIP
CAMUS
THE FALL
CAMUS
SCROLL SCROLL SCROLL
THE FALL
CAMUS

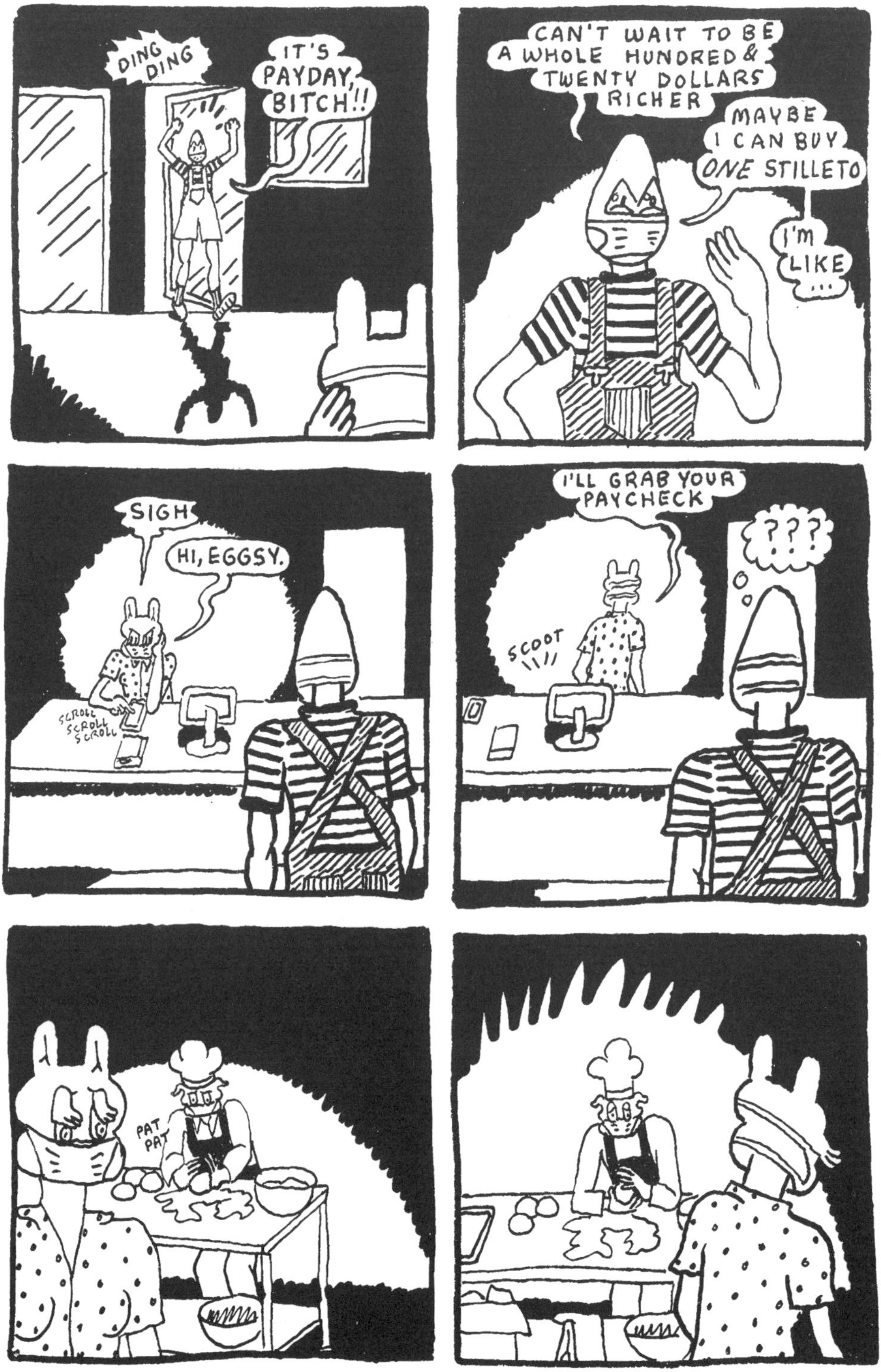
DING DING
IT'S PAYDAY, BITCH!!
CAN'T WAIT TO BE A WHOLE HUNDRED & TWENTY DOLLARS RICHER
MAYBE I CAN BUY ONE STILLETO
I'M LIKE ...
SIGH
HI, EGGSY.
SCROLL SCROLL SCROLL
I'LL GRAB YOUR PAYCHECK
???
SCOOT
PAT PAT

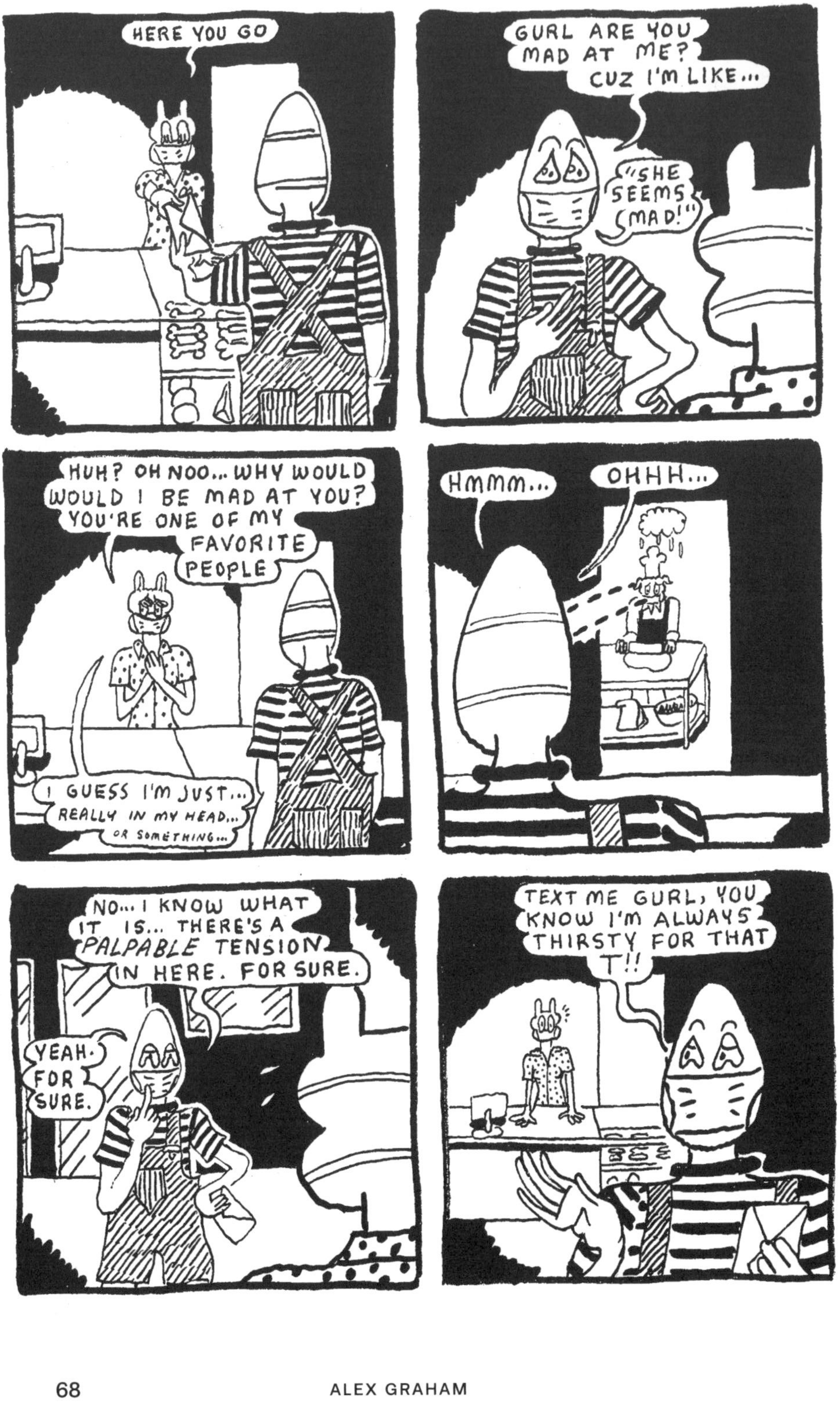
HERE YOU GO
GURL ARE YOU MAD AT ME? CUZ I'M LIKE...
"SHE SEEMS MAD!"
HUH? OH NOO... WHY WOULD WOULD I BE MAD AT YOU? YOU'RE ONE OF MY FAVORITE PEOPLE
I GUESS I'M JUST... REALLY IN MY HEAD... OR SOMETHING...
HMMM...
OHHH...
NO... I KNOW WHAT IT IS... THERE'S A PALPABLE TENSION IN HERE. FOR SURE.
YEAH. FOR SURE.
TEXT ME GURL, YOU KNOW I'M ALWAYS THIRSTY FOR THAT T!!

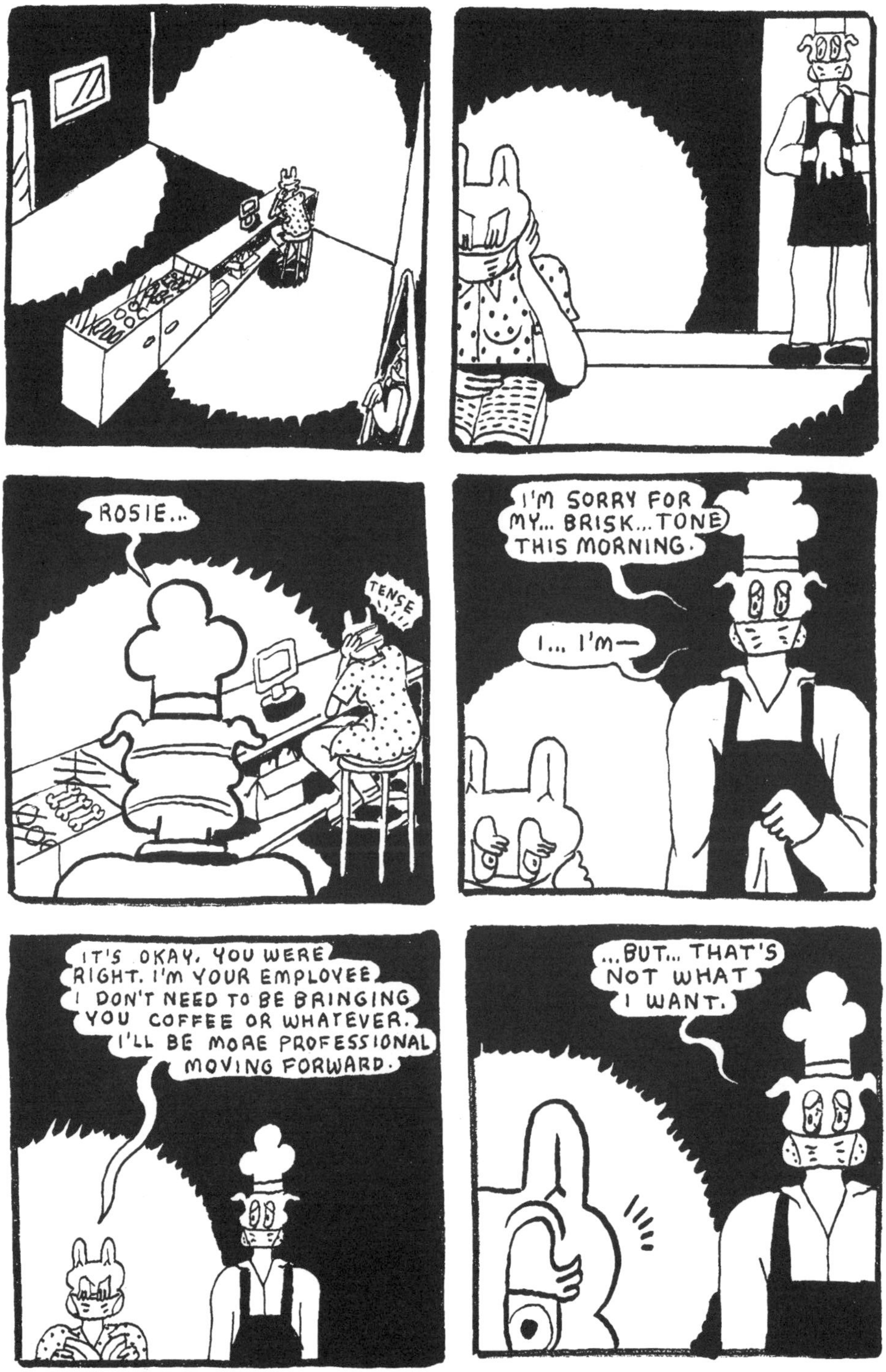
ROSIE...
TENSE
I'M SORRY FOR MY... BRISK... TONE THIS MORNING.
I... I'M—
IT'S OKAY. YOU WERE RIGHT. I'M YOUR EMPLOYEE. I DON'T NEED TO BE BRINGING YOU COFFEE OR WHATEVER. I'LL BE MORE PROFESSIONAL MOVING FORWARD.
...BUT... THAT'S NOT WHAT I WANT.

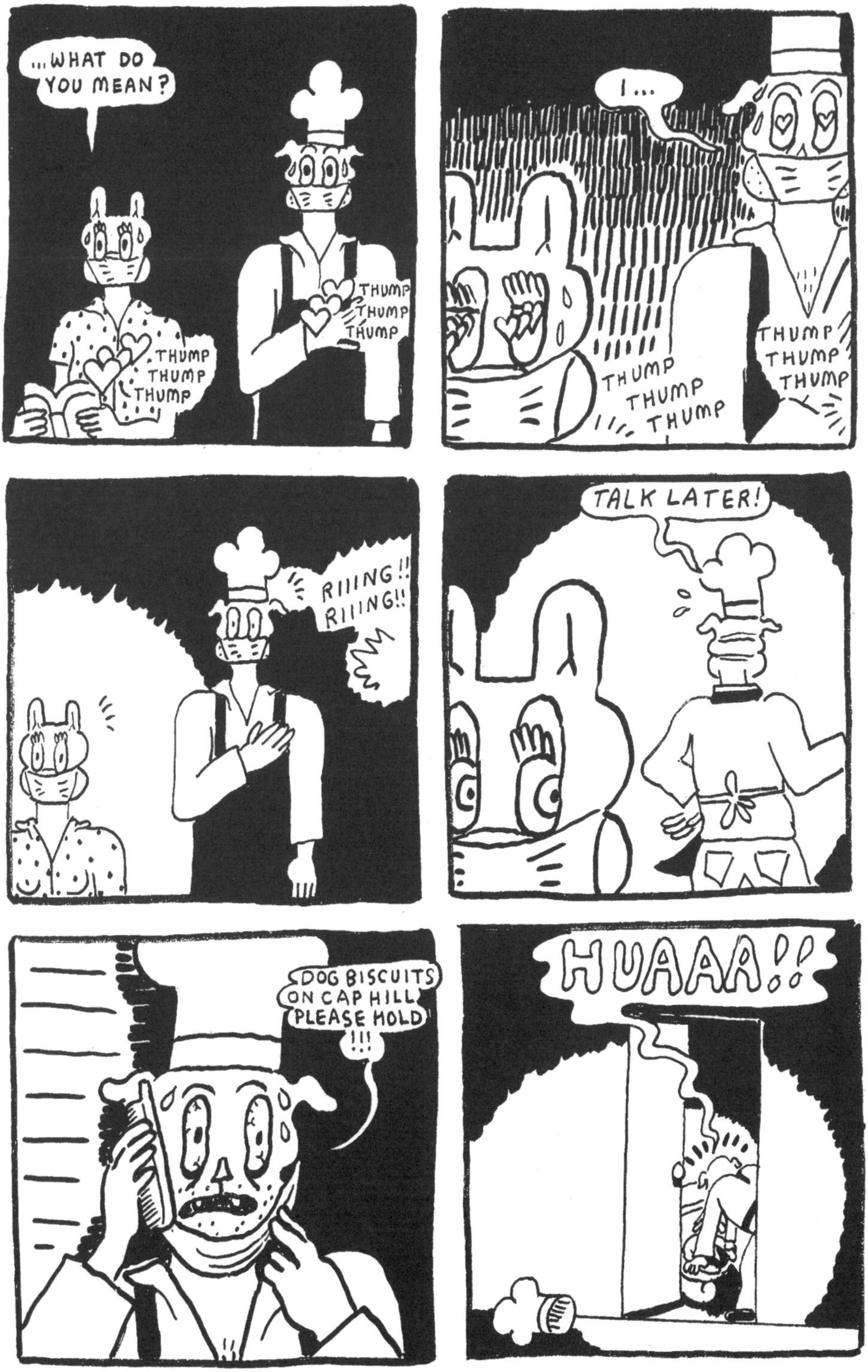
...WHAT DO YOU MEAN?
THUMP THUMP THUMP
THUMP THUMP THUMP
I...
THUMP THUMP THUMP
THUMP THUMP THUMP
RIIING!! RIIING!!
TALK LATER!
DOG BISCUITS ON CAP HILL PLEASE HOLD !!!
HUAAA!!

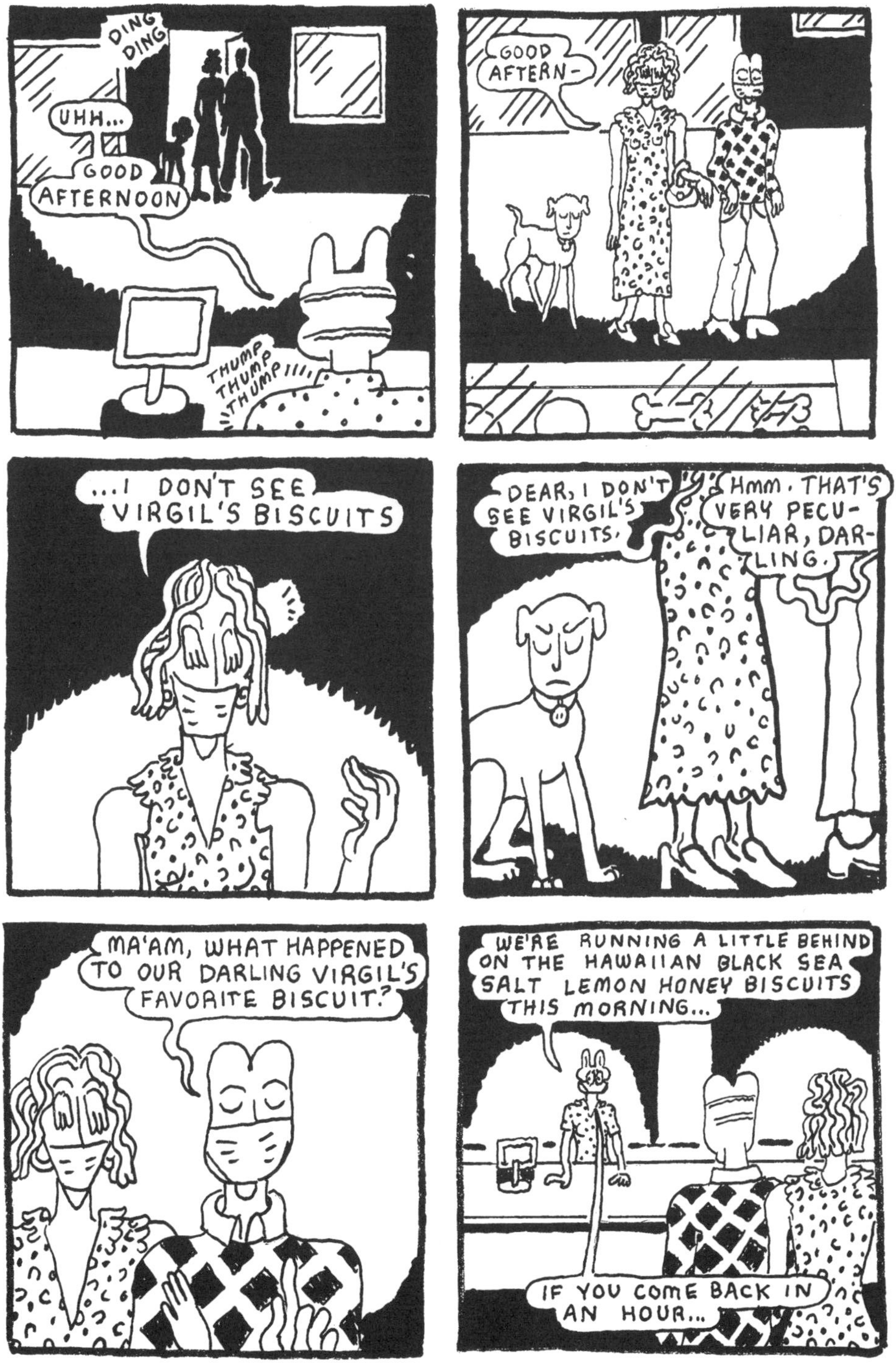
DING DING
UHH...
GOOD AFTERNOON
THUMP THUMP THUMP!!!
GOOD AFTERN-
...I DON'T SEE VIRGIL'S BISCUITS
DEAR, I DON'T SEE VIRGIL'S BISCUITS.
Hmm. THAT'S VERY PECULIAR, DARLING.
MA'AM, WHAT HAPPENED TO OUR DARLING VIRGIL'S FAVORITE BISCUIT?
WE'RE RUNNING A LITTLE BEHIND ON THE HAWAIIAN BLACK SEA SALT LEMON HONEY BISCUITS THIS MORNING...
IF YOU COME BACK IN AN HOUR...

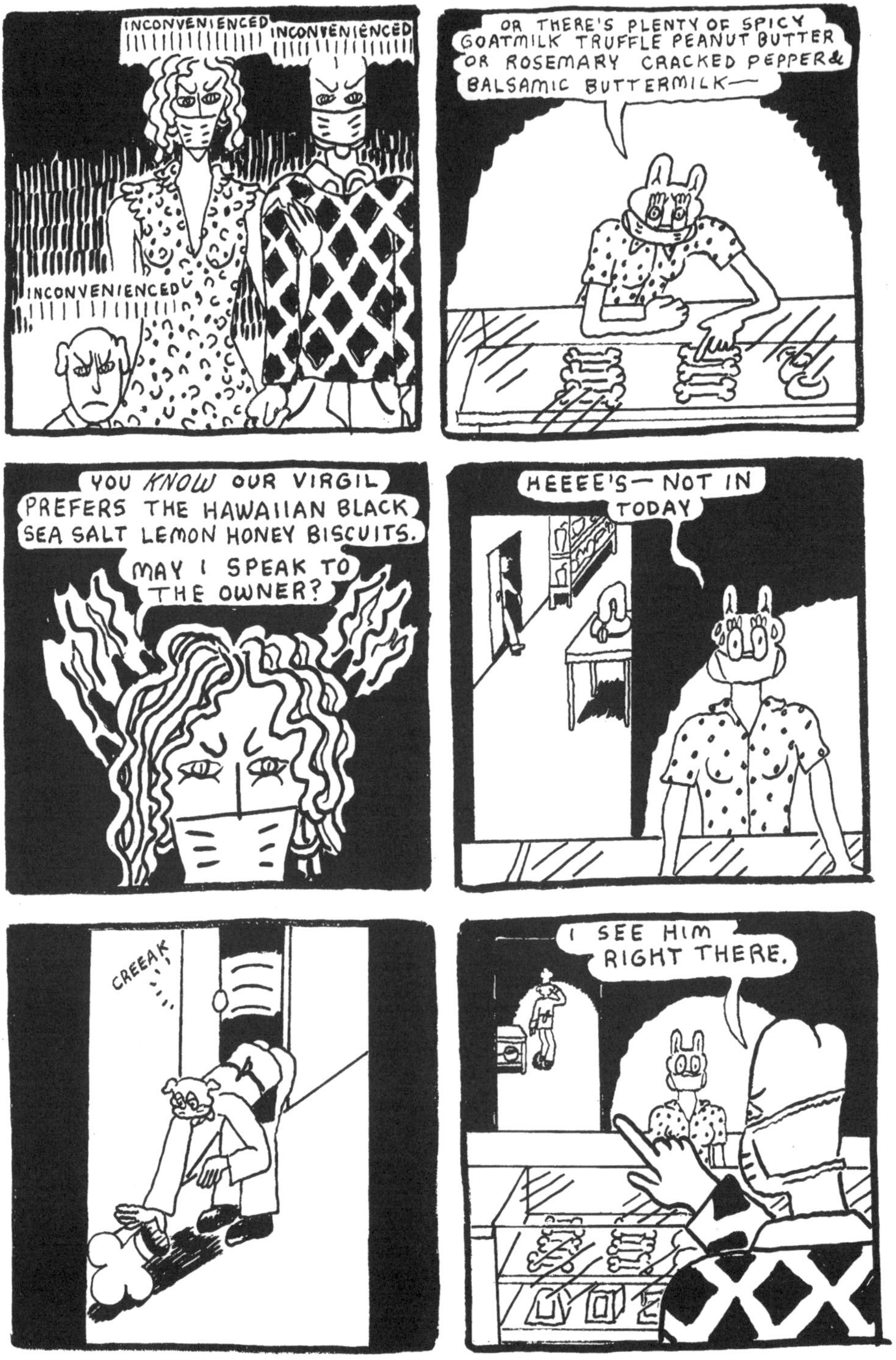
INCONVENIENCED
INCONVENIENCED
INCONVENIENCED
OR THERE'S PLENTY OF SPICY GOATMILK TRUFFLE PEANUT BUTTER OR ROSEMARY CRACKED PEPPER & BALSAMIC BUTTERMILK—
YOU *KNOW* OUR VIRGIL PREFERS THE HAWAIIAN BLACK SEA SALT LEMON HONEY BISCUITS.
MAY I SPEAK TO THE OWNER?
HEEEE'S— NOT IN TODAY
CREEAK
I SEE HIM RIGHT THERE.

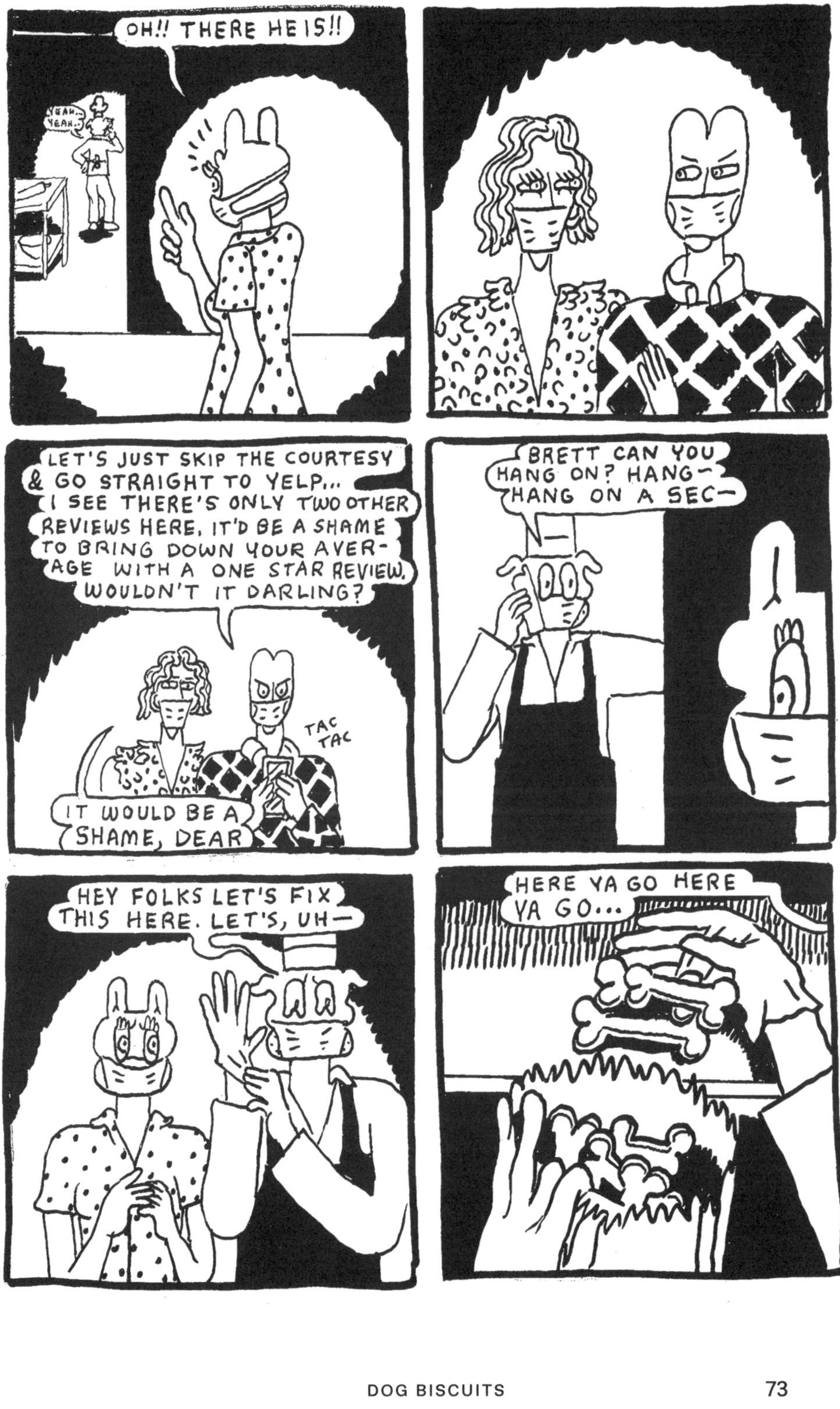
OH!! THERE HE IS!!
YEAH.. YEAH..
LET'S JUST SKIP THE COURTESY & GO STRAIGHT TO YELP... I SEE THERE'S ONLY TWO OTHER REVIEWS HERE. IT'D BE A SHAME TO BRING DOWN YOUR AVER-AGE WITH A ONE STAR REVIEW. WOULDN'T IT DARLING?
TAC TAC
IT WOULD BE A SHAME, DEAR
BRETT CAN YOU HANG ON? HANG-HANG ON A SEC—
HEY FOLKS LET'S FIX THIS HERE. LET'S, UH—
HERE YA GO HERE YA GO...

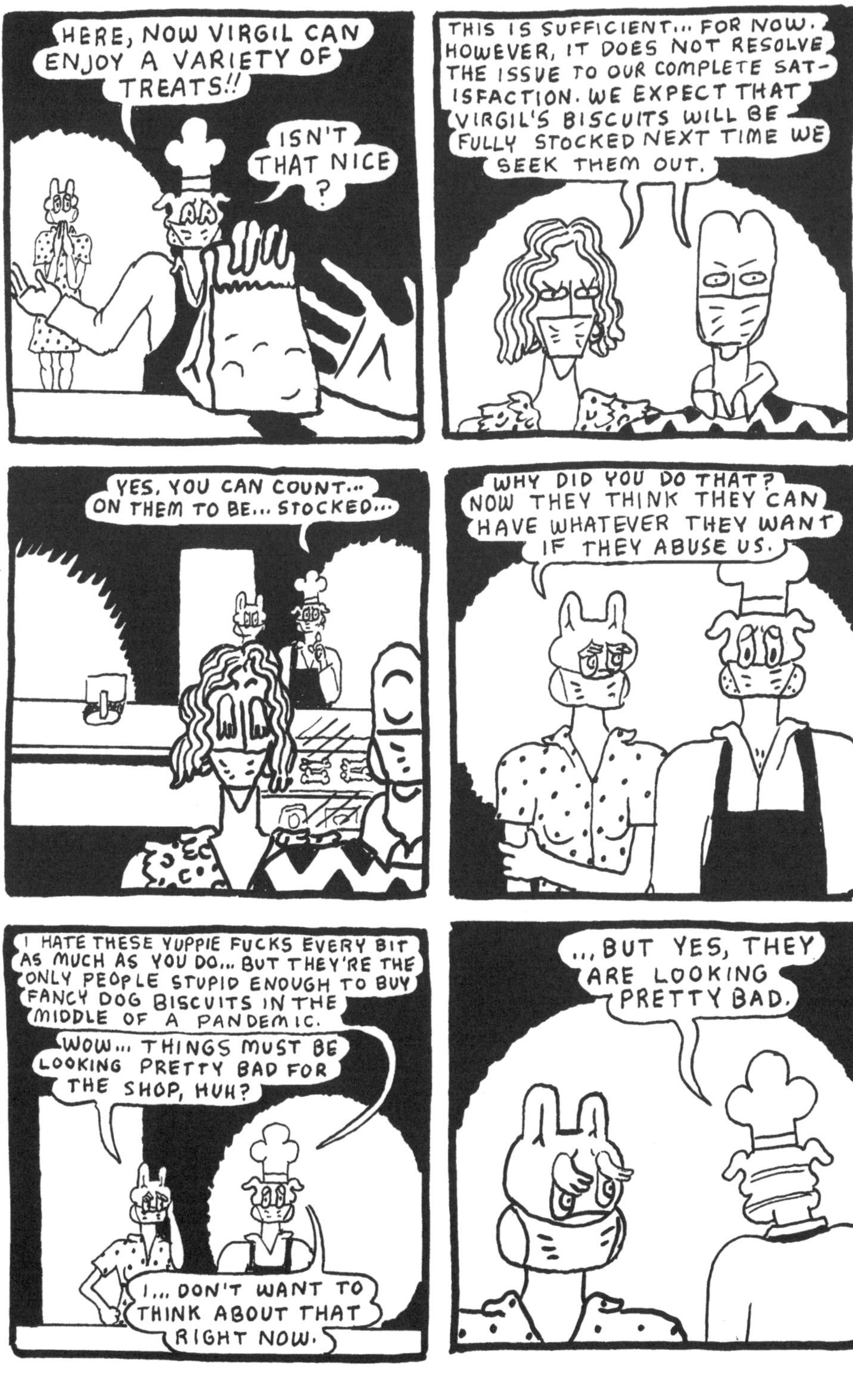
HERE, NOW VIRGIL CAN ENJOY A VARIETY OF TREATS!!
ISN'T THAT NICE ?
THIS IS SUFFICIENT... FOR NOW. HOWEVER, IT DOES NOT RESOLVE THE ISSUE TO OUR COMPLETE SATISFACTION. WE EXPECT THAT VIRGIL'S BISCUITS WILL BE FULLY STOCKED NEXT TIME WE SEEK THEM OUT.
YES. YOU CAN COUNT... ON THEM TO BE... STOCKED...
WHY DID YOU DO THAT? NOW THEY THINK THEY CAN HAVE WHATEVER THEY WANT IF THEY ABUSE US.
I HATE THESE YUPPIE FUCKS EVERY BIT AS MUCH AS YOU DO... BUT THEY'RE THE ONLY PEOPLE STUPID ENOUGH TO BUY FANCY DOG BISCUITS IN THE MIDDLE OF A PANDEMIC.
WOW... THINGS MUST BE LOOKING PRETTY BAD FOR THE SHOP, HUH?
I... DON'T WANT TO THINK ABOUT THAT RIGHT NOW.
...BUT YES, THEY ARE LOOKING PRETTY BAD.

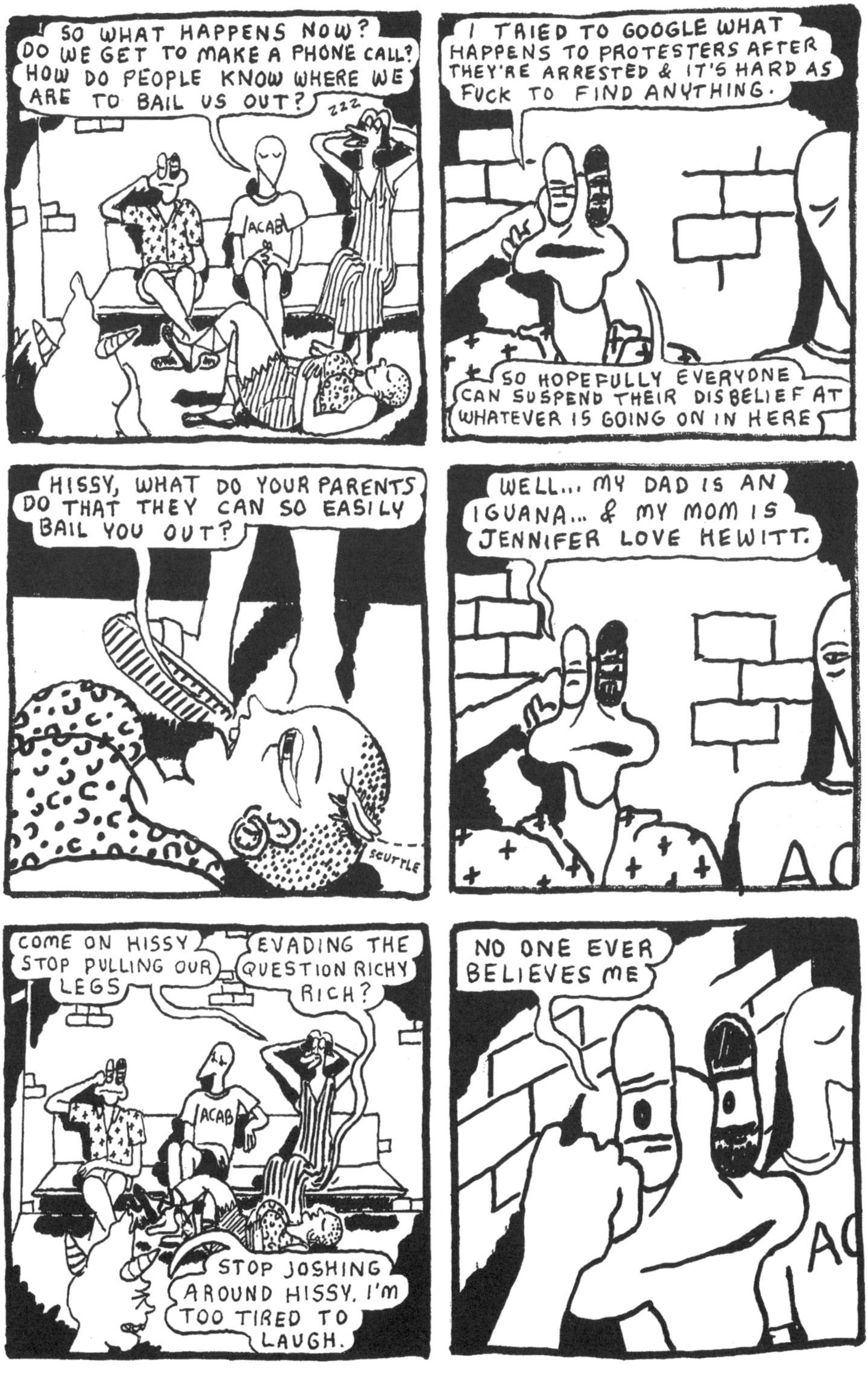
SO WHAT HAPPENS NOW? DO WE GET TO MAKE A PHONE CALL? HOW DO PEOPLE KNOW WHERE WE ARE TO BAIL US OUT?
ZZZ
I TRIED TO GOOGLE WHAT HAPPENS TO PROTESTERS AFTER THEY'RE ARRESTED & IT'S HARD AS FUCK TO FIND ANYTHING.
SO HOPEFULLY EVERYONE CAN SUSPEND THEIR DISBELIEF AT WHATEVER IS GOING ON IN HERE
HISSY, WHAT DO YOUR PARENTS DO THAT THEY CAN SO EASILY BAIL YOU OUT?
SCUTTLE
WELL... MY DAD IS AN IGUANA... & MY MOM IS JENNIFER LOVE HEWITT.
COME ON HISSY STOP PULLING OUR LEGS
EVADING THE QUESTION RICHY RICH?
STOP JOSHING AROUND HISSY. I'M TOO TIRED TO LAUGH.
NO ONE EVER BELIEVES ME

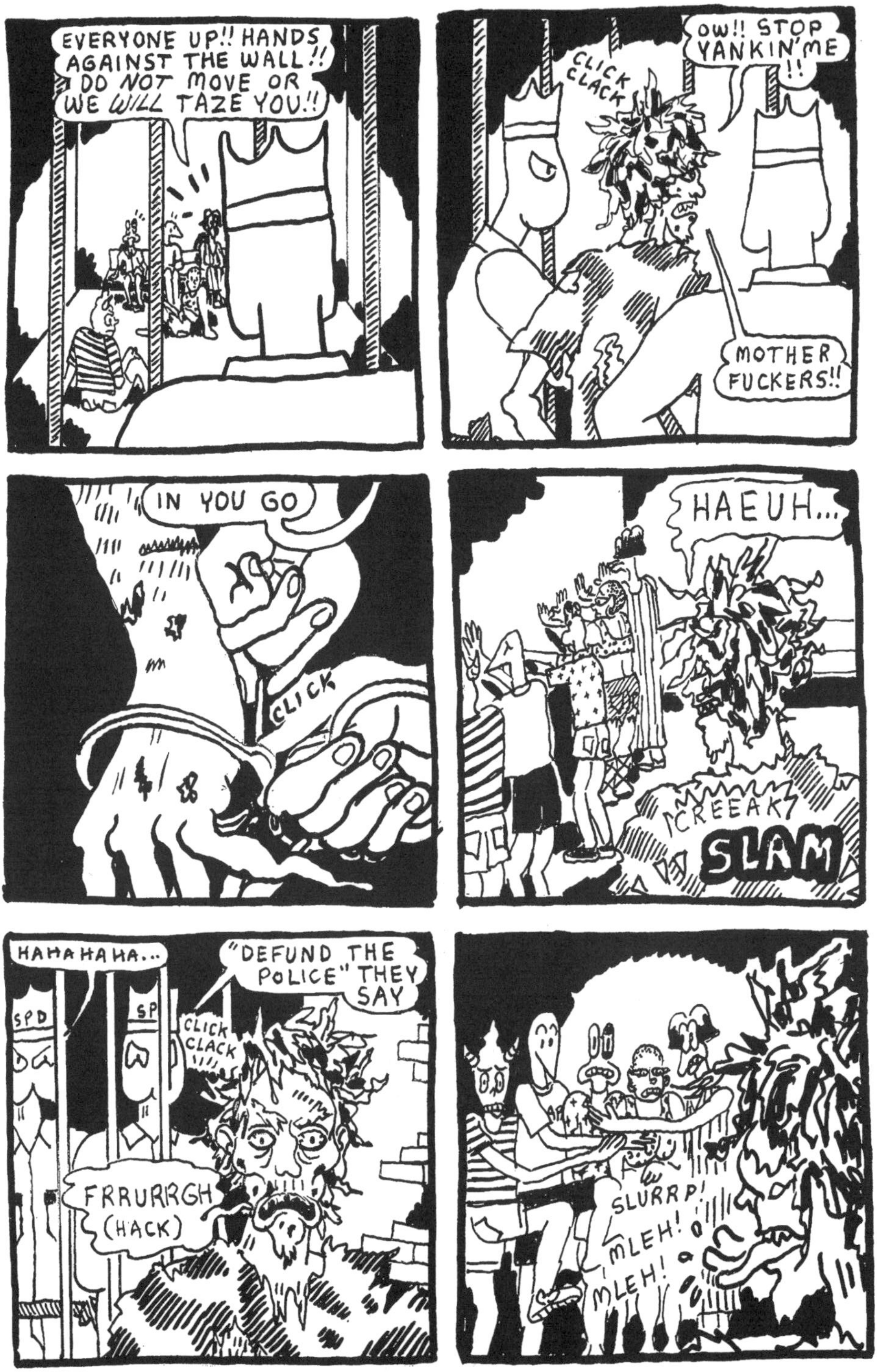
EVERYONE UP!! HANDS AGAINST THE WALL!! DO NOT MOVE OR WE WILL TAZE YOU!!
OW!! STOP YANKIN' ME !!
CLICK CLACK
MOTHER FUCKERS!!
IN YOU GO
CLICK
HAEUH...
CREEAK
SLAM
HAHAHAHA...
"DEFUND THE POLICE" THEY SAY
SPD
SP
CLICK CLACK
FRRURRGH (HACK)
SLURRP!
MLEH!
MLEH!

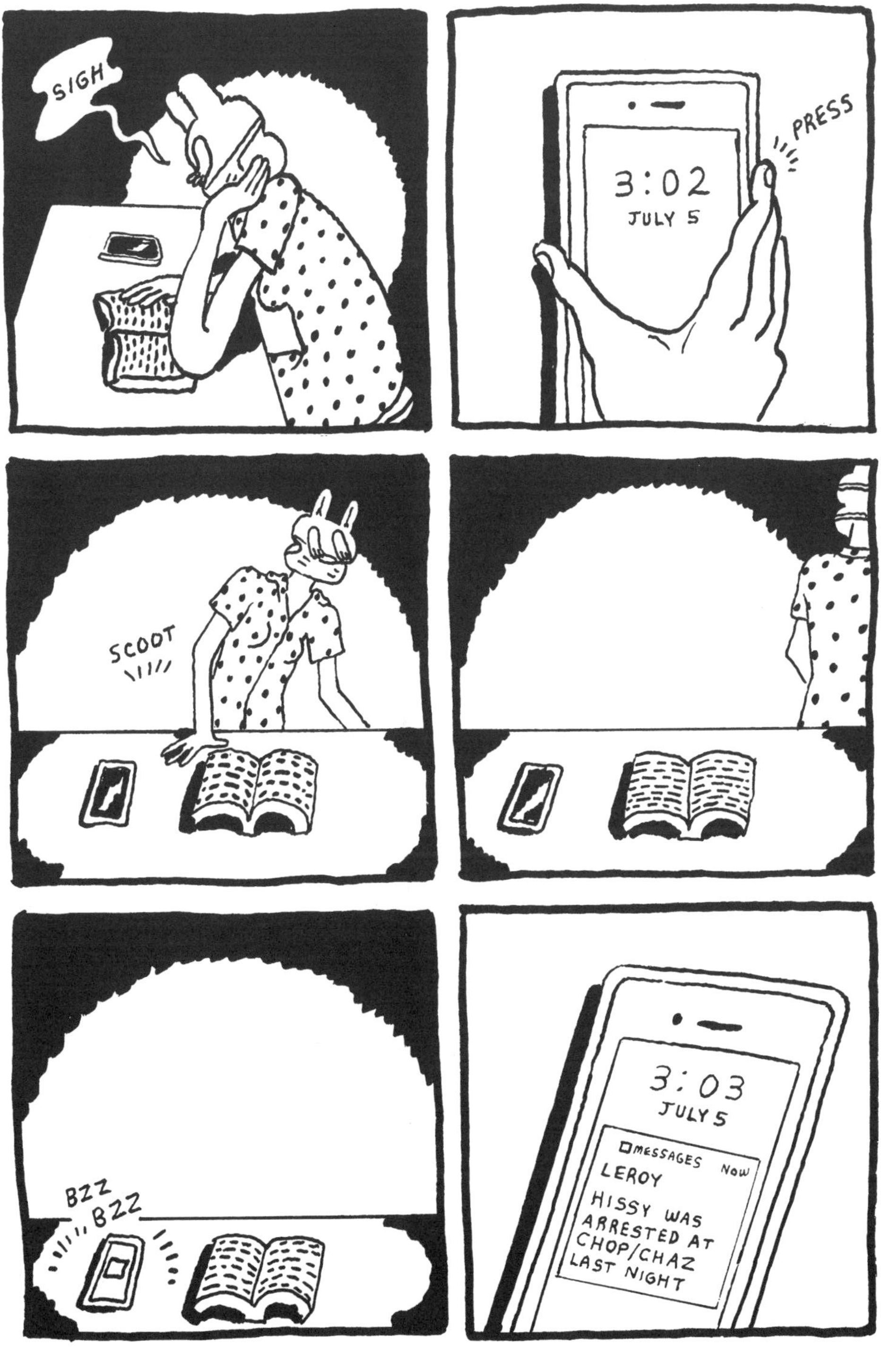
SIGH
3:02
JULY 5
PRESS
SCOOT
BZZ
BZZ
3:03
JULY 5
MESSAGES NOW
LEROY
HISSY WAS ARRESTED AT CHOP/CHAZ LAST NIGHT

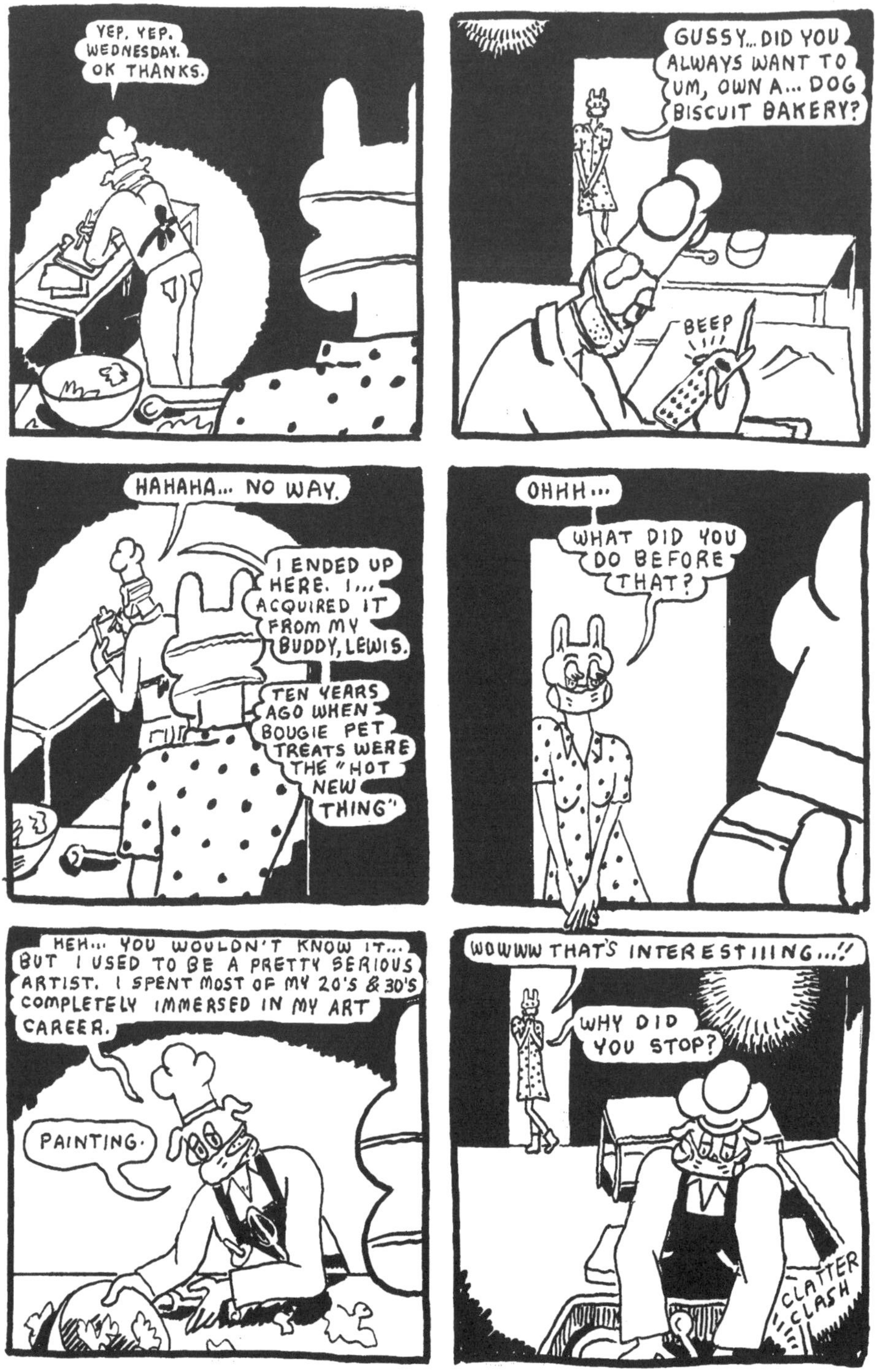
YEP. YEP. WEDNESDAY. OK THANKS.
GUSSY... DID YOU ALWAYS WANT TO UM, OWN A... DOG BISCUIT BAKERY?
BEEP
HAHAHA... NO WAY.
I ENDED UP HERE. I... ACQUIRED IT FROM MY BUDDY, LEWIS.
TEN YEARS AGO WHEN BOUGIE PET TREATS WERE THE "HOT NEW THING"
OHHH...
WHAT DID YOU DO BEFORE THAT?
HEH... YOU WOULDN'T KNOW IT... BUT I USED TO BE A PRETTY SERIOUS ARTIST. I SPENT MOST OF MY 20'S & 30'S COMPLETELY IMMERSED IN MY ART CAREER.
PAINTING.
WOWWW THAT'S INTERESTIIING...!!
WHY DID YOU STOP?
CLATTER CLASH

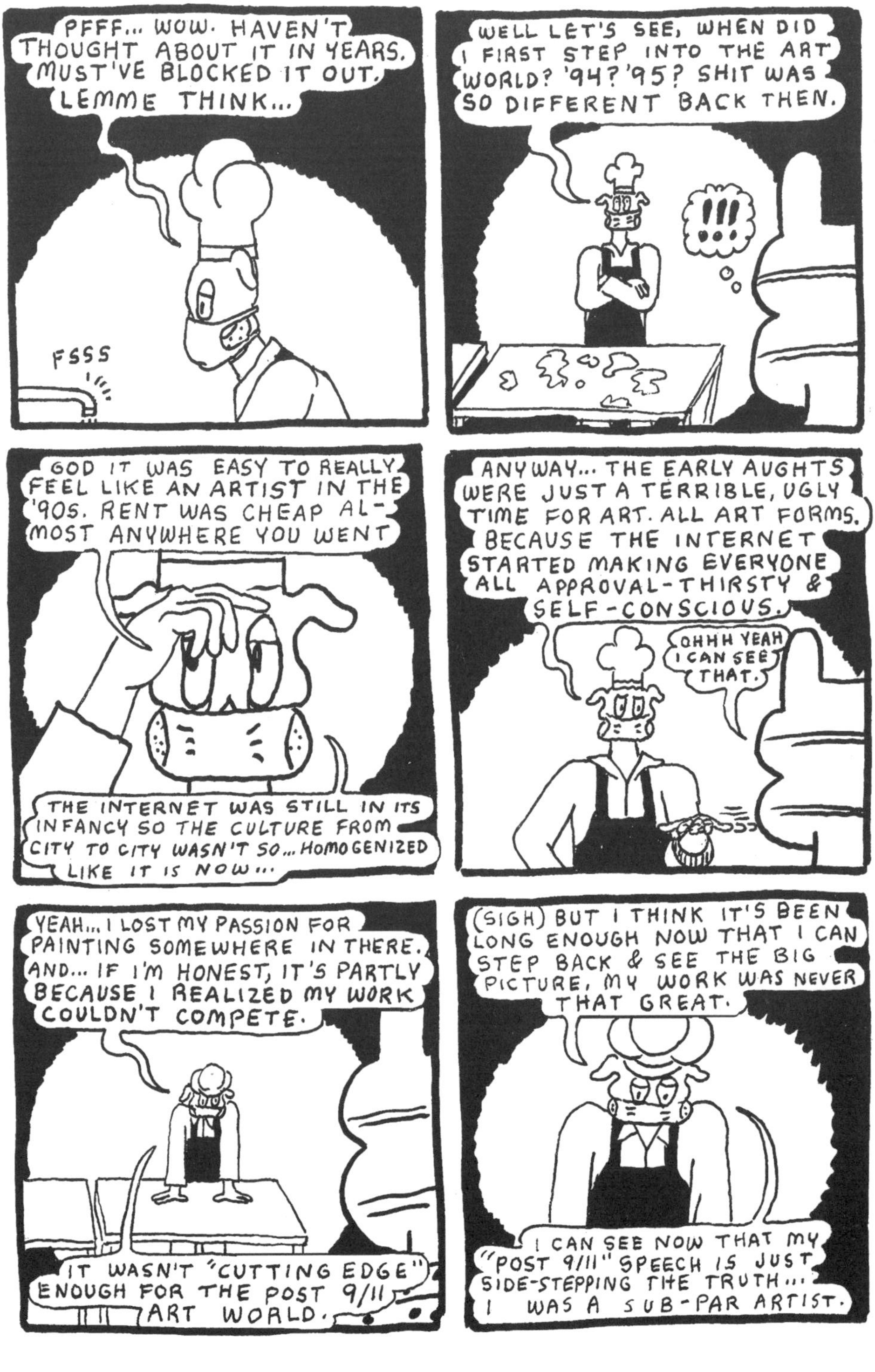
PFFF... WOW. HAVEN'T THOUGHT ABOUT IT IN YEARS. MUST'VE BLOCKED IT OUT. LEMME THINK...
FSSS
WELL LET'S SEE, WHEN DID I FIRST STEP INTO THE ART WORLD? '94? '95? SHIT WAS SO DIFFERENT BACK THEN.
!!!
GOD IT WAS EASY TO REALLY FEEL LIKE AN ARTIST IN THE '90S. RENT WAS CHEAP ALMOST ANYWHERE YOU WENT
THE INTERNET WAS STILL IN ITS INFANCY SO THE CULTURE FROM CITY TO CITY WASN'T SO... HOMOGENIZED LIKE IT IS NOW...
ANYWAY... THE EARLY AUGHTS WERE JUST A TERRIBLE, UGLY TIME FOR ART. ALL ART FORMS. BECAUSE THE INTERNET STARTED MAKING EVERYONE ALL APPROVAL-THIRSTY & SELF-CONSCIOUS.
OHHH YEAH I CAN SEE THAT.
YEAH... I LOST MY PASSION FOR PAINTING SOMEWHERE IN THERE. AND... IF I'M HONEST, IT'S PARTLY BECAUSE I REALIZED MY WORK COULDN'T COMPETE.
IT WASN'T "CUTTING EDGE" ENOUGH FOR THE POST 9/11 ART WORLD.
(SIGH) BUT I THINK IT'S BEEN LONG ENOUGH NOW THAT I CAN STEP BACK & SEE THE BIG PICTURE. MY WORK WAS NEVER THAT GREAT.
I CAN SEE NOW THAT MY "POST 9/11" SPEECH IS JUST SIDE-STEPPING THE TRUTH... I WAS A SUB-PAR ARTIST.

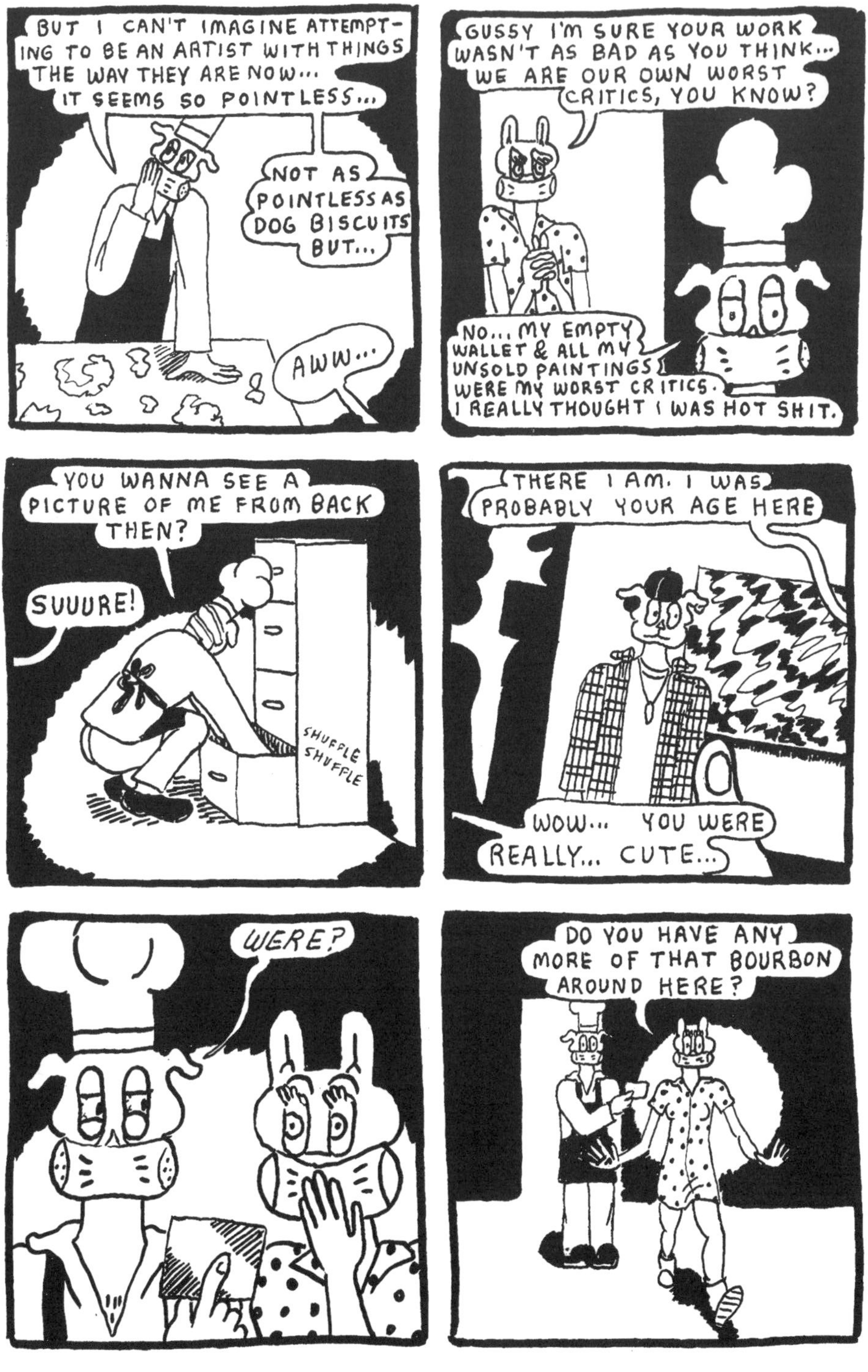
BUT I CAN'T IMAGINE ATTEMPTING TO BE AN ARTIST WITH THINGS THE WAY THEY ARE NOW... IT SEEMS SO POINTLESS...
NOT AS POINTLESS AS DOG BISCUITS BUT...
AWW...
GUSSY I'M SURE YOUR WORK WASN'T AS BAD AS YOU THINK... WE ARE OUR OWN WORST CRITICS, YOU KNOW?
NO... MY EMPTY WALLET & ALL MY UNSOLD PAINTINGS WERE MY WORST CRITICS. I REALLY THOUGHT I WAS HOT SHIT.
YOU WANNA SEE A PICTURE OF ME FROM BACK THEN?
SUUURE!
SHUFFLE SHUFFLE
THERE I AM. I WAS PROBABLY YOUR AGE HERE
WOW... YOU WERE REALLY... CUTE...
WERE?
DO YOU HAVE ANY MORE OF THAT BOURBON AROUND HERE?

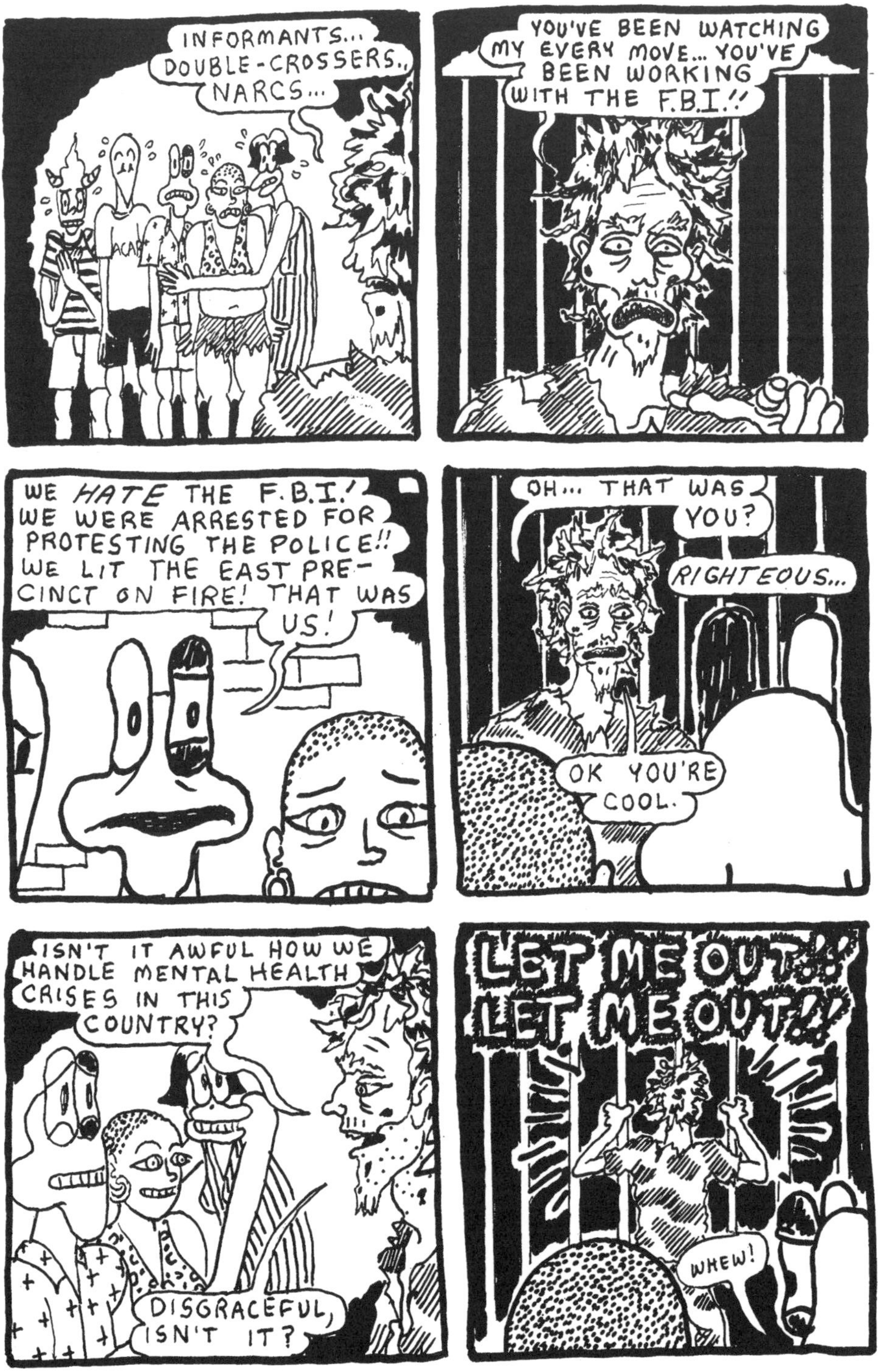
INFORMANTS... DOUBLE-CROSSERS.. NARCS...
YOU'VE BEEN WATCHING MY EVERY MOVE... YOU'VE BEEN WORKING WITH THE F.B.I.!!
WE HATE THE F.B.I.! WE WERE ARRESTED FOR PROTESTING THE POLICE!! WE LIT THE EAST PRE-CINCT ON FIRE! THAT WAS US!
OH... THAT WAS YOU?
RIGHTEOUS...
OK YOU'RE COOL.
ISN'T IT AWFUL HOW WE HANDLE MENTAL HEALTH CRISES IN THIS COUNTRY?
DISGRACEFUL, ISN'T IT?
LET ME OUT!! LET ME OUT!!
WHEW!

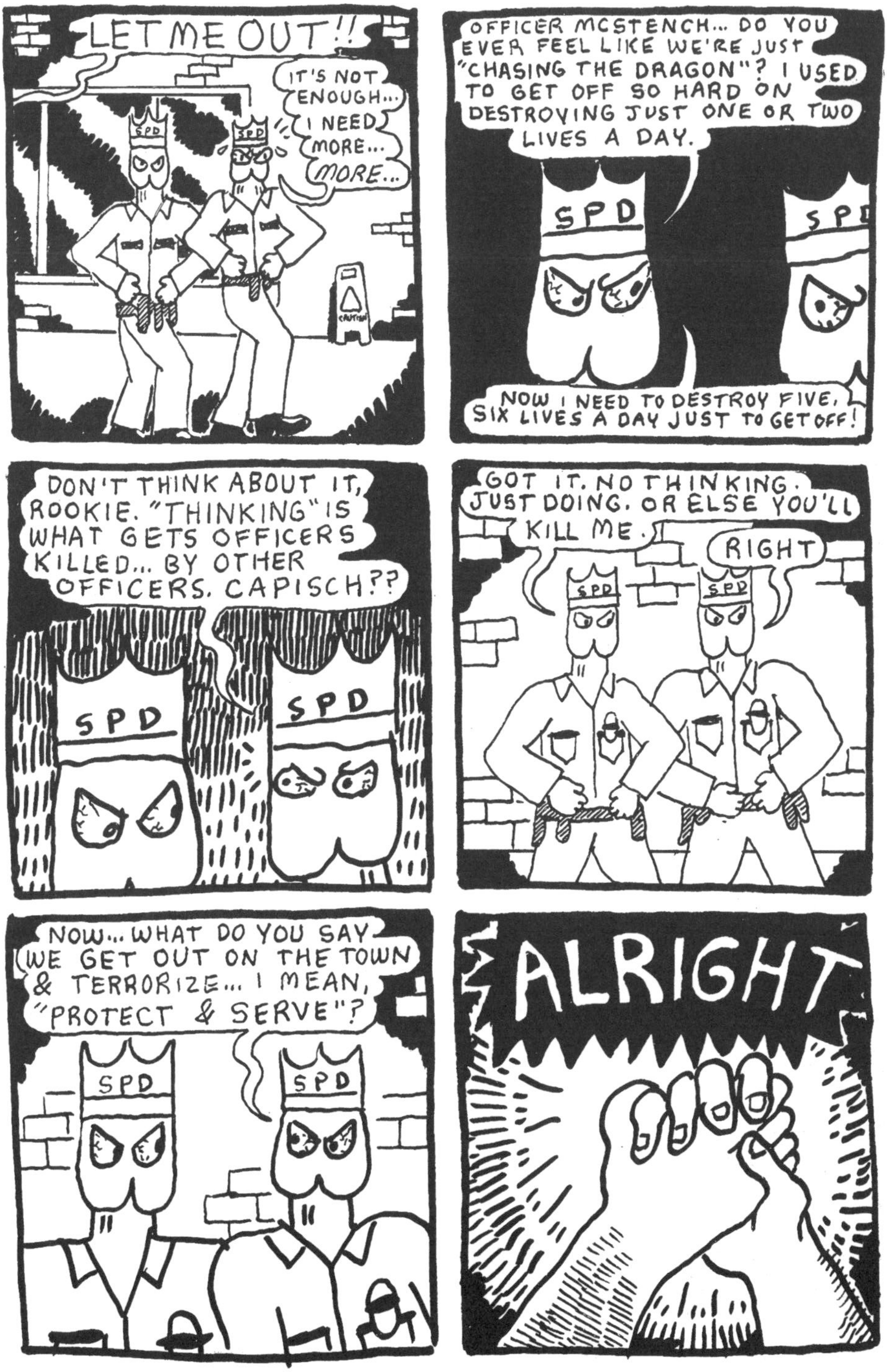
LET ME OUT!!
IT'S NOT ENOUGH... I NEED MORE... MORE...
OFFICER MCSTENCH... DO YOU EVER FEEL LIKE WE'RE JUST "CHASING THE DRAGON"? I USED TO GET OFF SO HARD ON DESTROYING JUST ONE OR TWO LIVES A DAY.
SPD
SPD
NOW I NEED TO DESTROY FIVE, SIX LIVES A DAY JUST TO GET OFF!
DON'T THINK ABOUT IT, ROOKIE. "THINKING" IS WHAT GETS OFFICERS KILLED... BY OTHER OFFICERS. CAPISCH??
SPD
SPD
GOT IT. NO THINKING. JUST DOING. OR ELSE YOU'LL KILL ME.
RIGHT
SPD
SPD
NOW... WHAT DO YOU SAY WE GET OUT ON THE TOWN & TERRORIZE... I MEAN, "PROTECT & SERVE"?
SPD
SPD
ALRIGHT

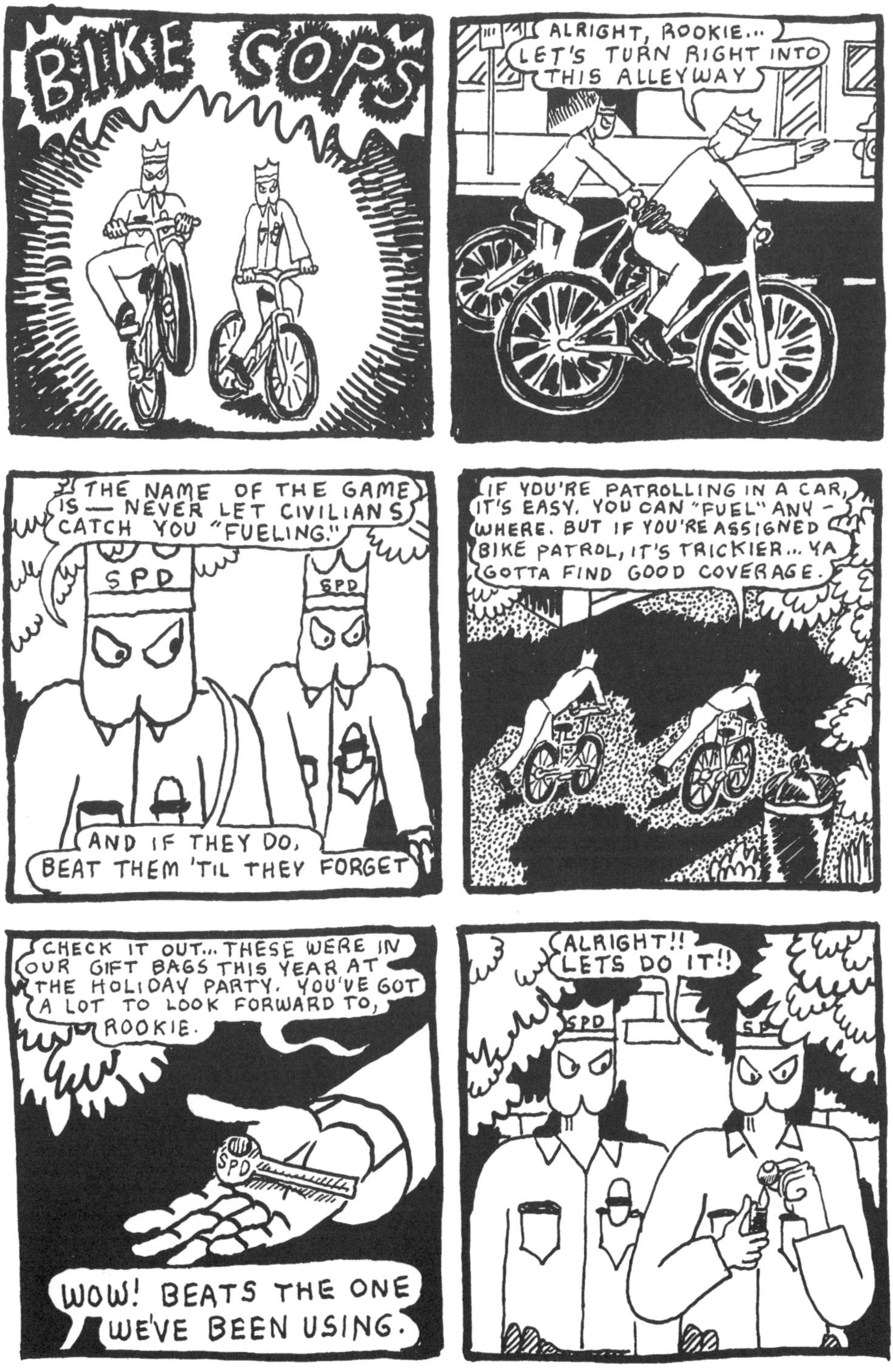
BIKE COPS
ALRIGHT, ROOKIE... LET'S TURN RIGHT INTO THIS ALLEYWAY
THE NAME OF THE GAME IS — NEVER LET CIVILIANS CATCH YOU "FUELING."
SPD
SPD
AND IF THEY DO, BEAT THEM 'TIL THEY FORGET
IF YOU'RE PATROLLING IN A CAR, IT'S EASY. YOU CAN "FUEL" ANY-WHERE. BUT IF YOU'RE ASSIGNED BIKE PATROL, IT'S TRICKIER... YA GOTTA FIND GOOD COVERAGE.
CHECK IT OUT... THESE WERE IN OUR GIFT BAGS THIS YEAR AT THE HOLIDAY PARTY. YOU'VE GOT A LOT TO LOOK FORWARD TO, ROOKIE.
SPD
WOW! BEATS THE ONE WE'VE BEEN USING.
ALRIGHT!! LETS DO IT!!
SPD

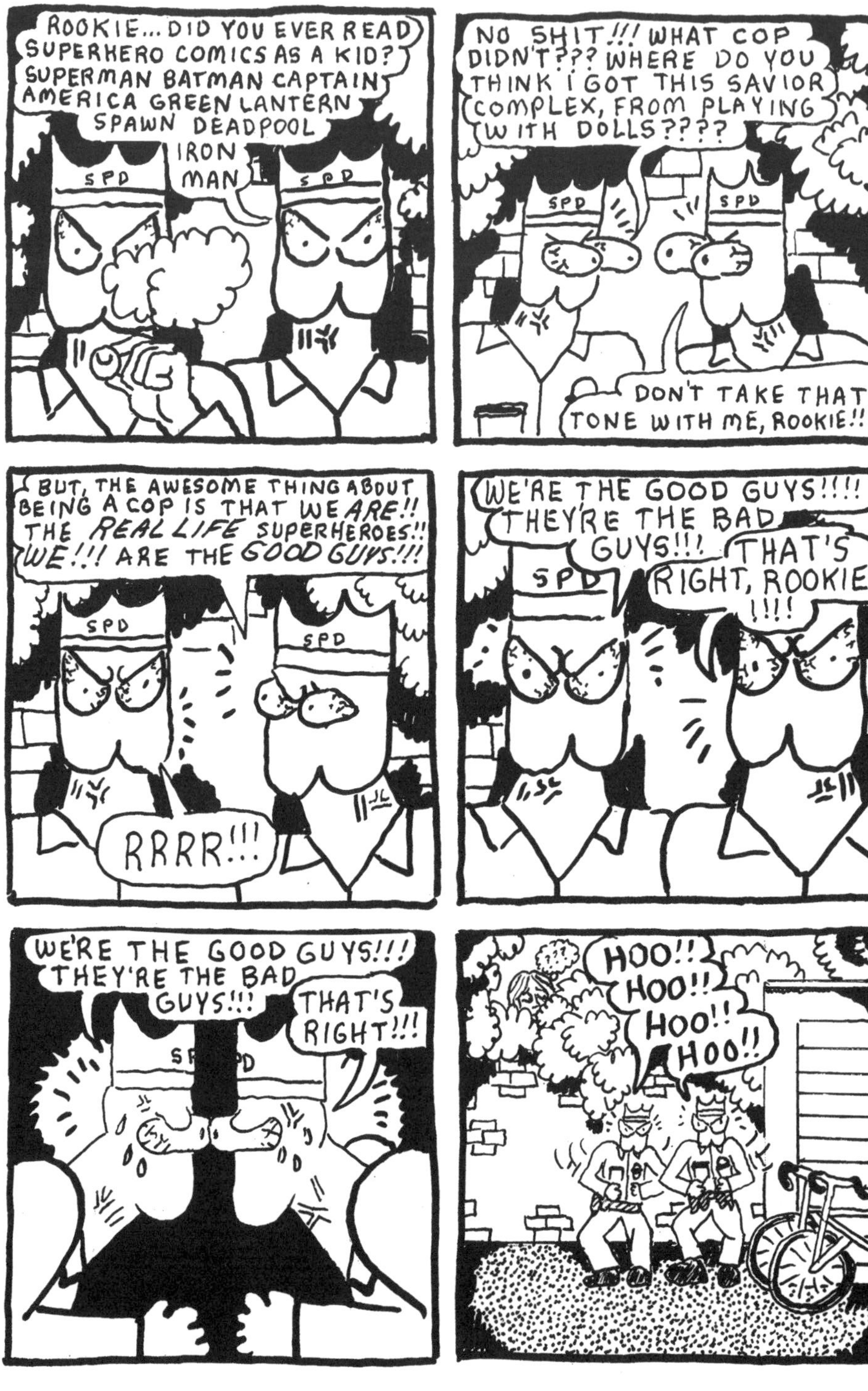
ROOKIE... DID YOU EVER READ SUPERHERO COMICS AS A KID? SUPERMAN BATMAN CAPTAIN AMERICA GREEN LANTERN SPAWN DEADPOOL
IRON MAN
SPD
SPD
NO SHIT!!! WHAT COP DIDN'T??? WHERE DO YOU THINK I GOT THIS SAVIOR COMPLEX, FROM PLAYING WITH DOLLS????
SPD
SPD
DON'T TAKE THAT TONE WITH ME, ROOKIE!!
BUT, THE AWESOME THING ABOUT BEING A COP IS THAT WE ARE!! THE REAL LIFE SUPERHEROES!! WE!!! ARE THE GOOD GUYS!!!
SPD
SPD
RRRR!!!
WE'RE THE GOOD GUYS!!!! THEY'RE THE BAD GUYS!!!
THAT'S RIGHT, ROOKIE!!!!
SPD
WE'RE THE GOOD GUYS!!! THEY'RE THE BAD GUYS!!!
THAT'S RIGHT!!!
HOO!! HOO!! HOO!! HOO!!

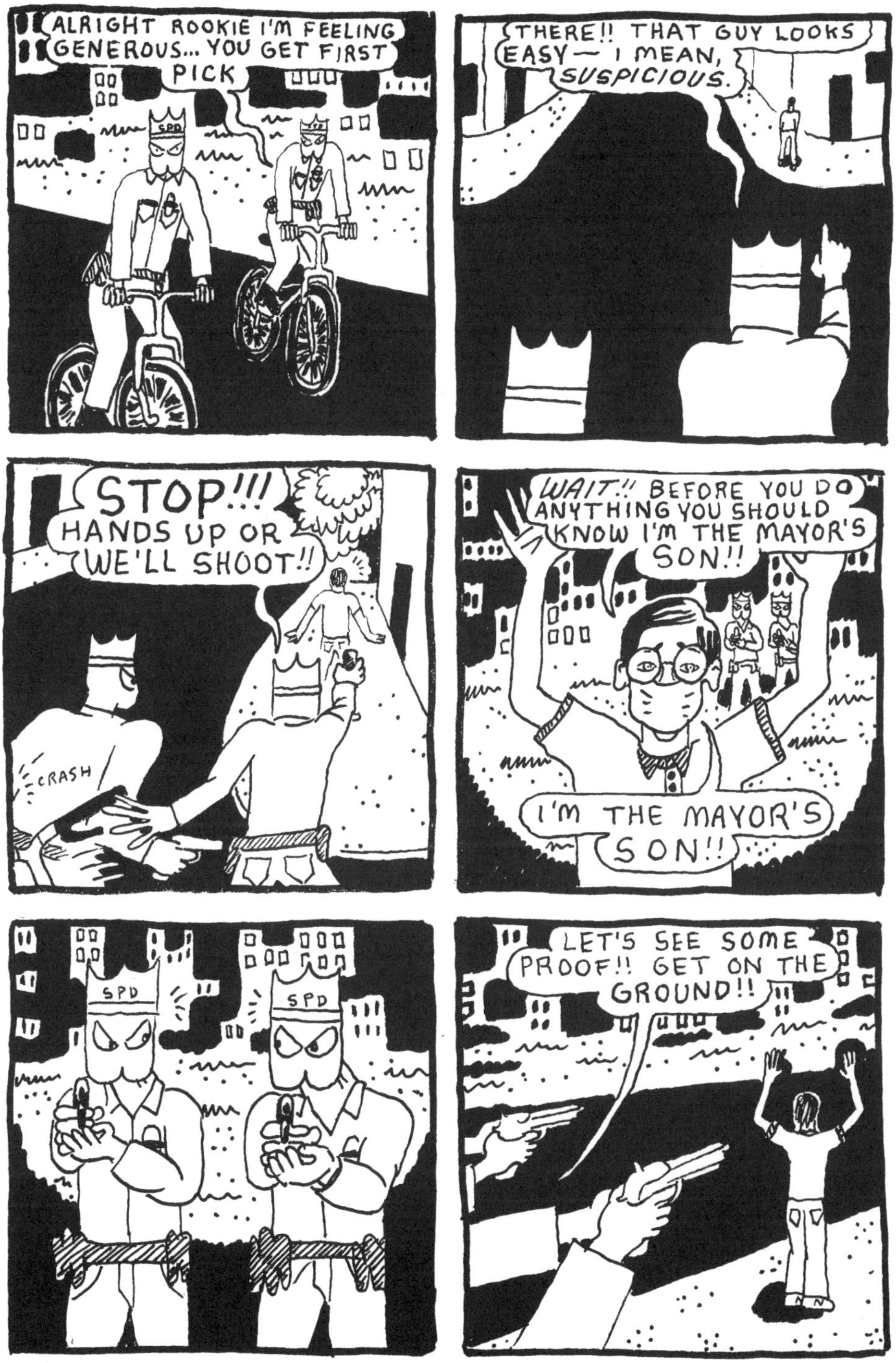
ALRIGHT ROOKIE I'M FEELING GENEROUS... YOU GET FIRST PICK
SPD
THERE!! THAT GUY LOOKS EASY — I MEAN, SUSPICIOUS.
STOP!!! HANDS UP OR WE'LL SHOOT!!
CRASH
WAIT!! BEFORE YOU DO ANYTHING YOU SHOULD KNOW I'M THE MAYOR'S SON!!
I'M THE MAYOR'S SON!!
SPD
SPD
LET'S SEE SOME PROOF!! GET ON THE GROUND!!

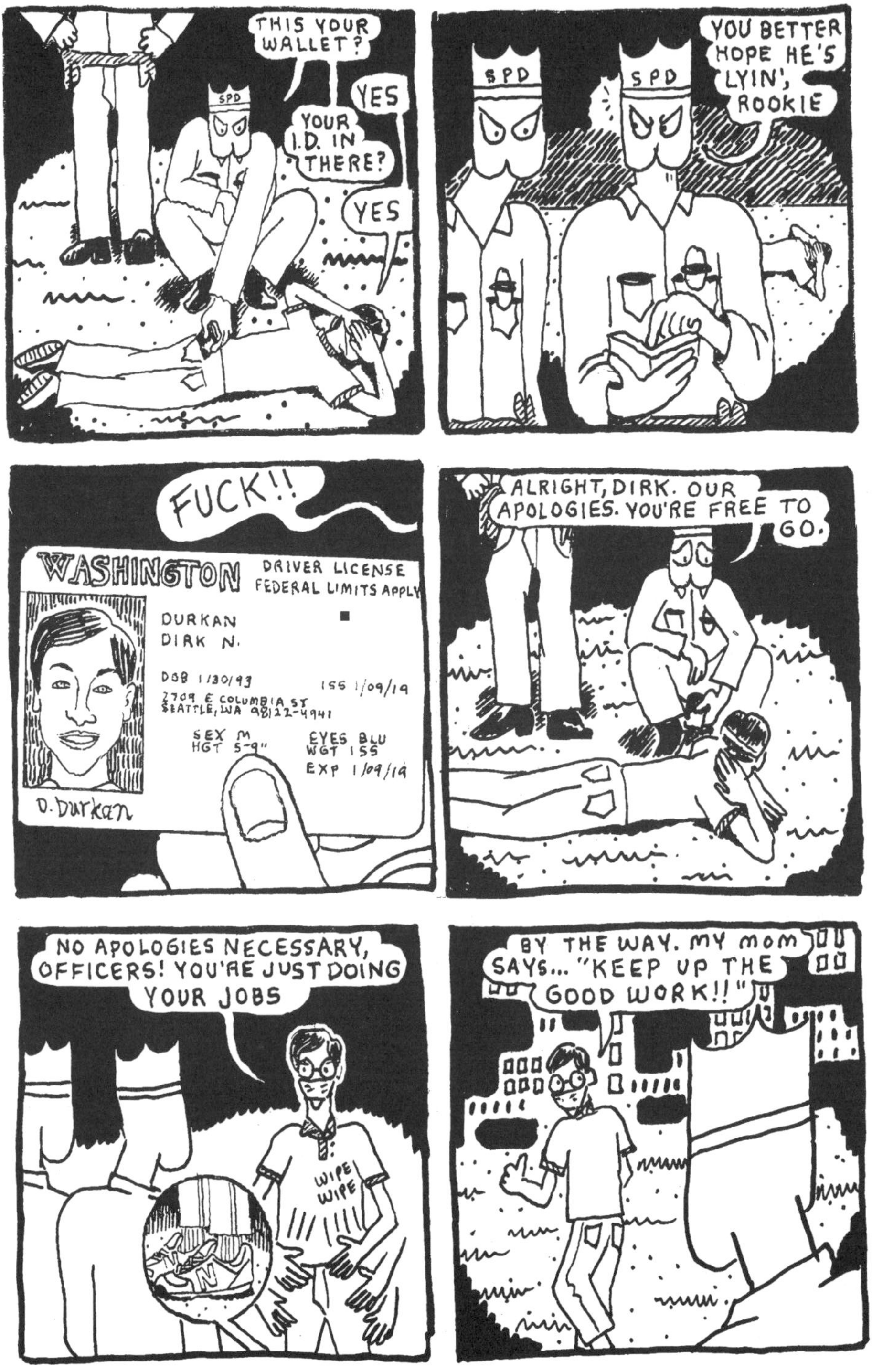
THIS YOUR WALLET?
YES
YOUR I.D. IN THERE?
YES
SPD
SPD
SPD
YOU BETTER HOPE HE'S LYIN', ROOKIE
FUCK!!
WASHINGTON
DRIVER LICENSE
FEDERAL LIMITS APPLY
DURKAN
DIRK N.
DOB 1/30/93
ISS 1/09/19
2709 E COLUMBIA ST
SEATTLE, WA 98122-4941
SEX M
HGT 5-9"
EYES BLU
WGT 155
EXP 1/09/19
D. Durkan
ALRIGHT, DIRK. OUR APOLOGIES. YOU'RE FREE TO GO.
NO APOLOGIES NECESSARY, OFFICERS! YOU'RE JUST DOING YOUR JOBS
WIPE WIPE
BY THE WAY. MY MOM SAYS... "KEEP UP THE GOOD WORK!!"

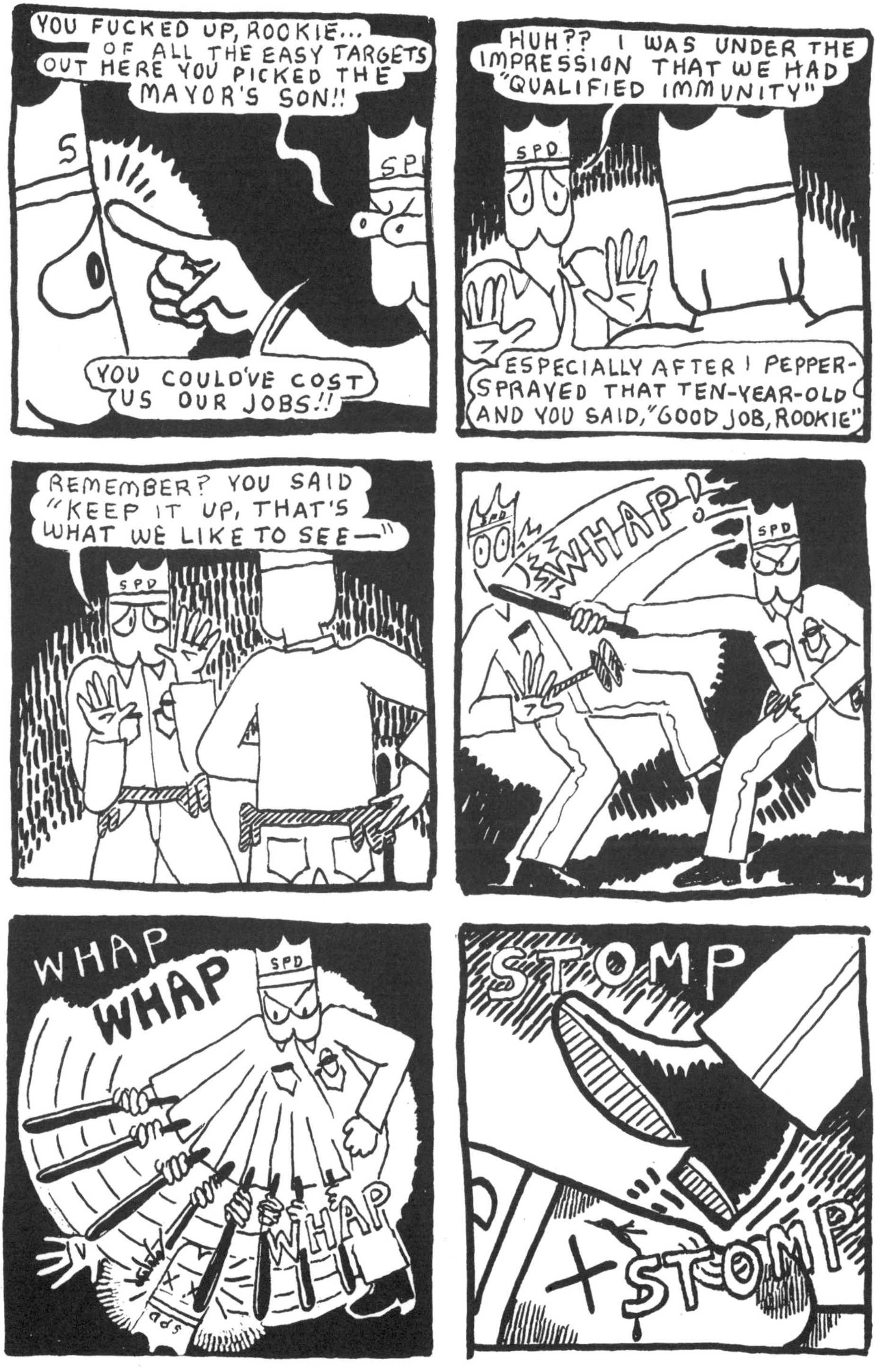
YOU FUCKED UP, ROOKIE... OF ALL THE EASY TARGETS OUT HERE YOU PICKED THE MAYOR'S SON!!
YOU COULD'VE COST US OUR JOBS!!
HUH?? I WAS UNDER THE IMPRESSION THAT WE HAD "QUALIFIED IMMUNITY"
ESPECIALLY AFTER I PEPPER-SPRAYED THAT TEN-YEAR-OLD AND YOU SAID, "GOOD JOB, ROOKIE"
REMEMBER? YOU SAID "KEEP IT UP, THAT'S WHAT WE LIKE TO SEE—"
SPD
WHAP!
WHAP
WHAP
WHAP
STOMP
STOMP

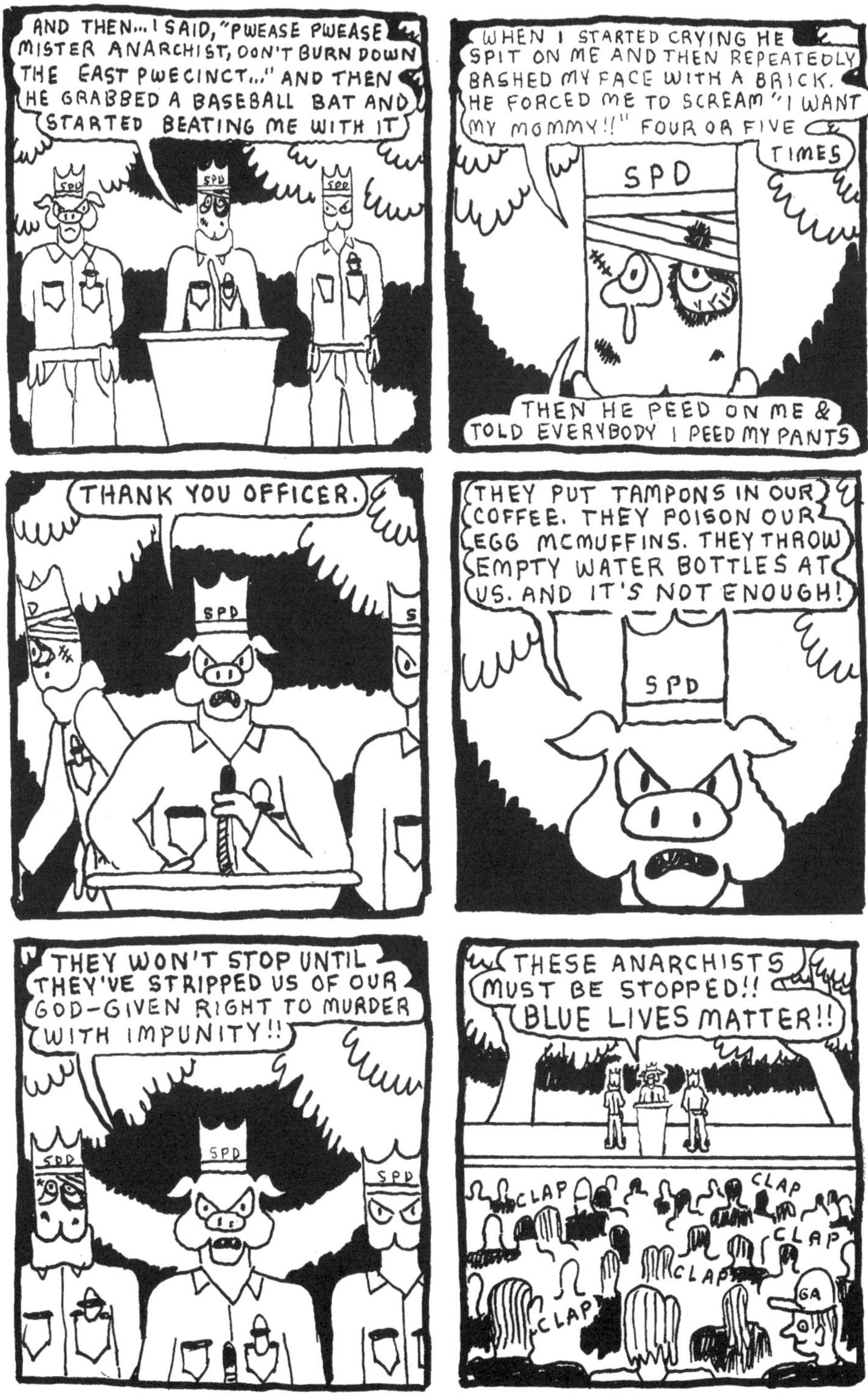
AND THEN... I SAID, "PWEASE PWEASE MISTER ANARCHIST, DON'T BURN DOWN THE EAST PWECINCT..." AND THEN HE GRABBED A BASEBALL BAT AND STARTED BEATING ME WITH IT
SPD
SPD
SPD
WHEN I STARTED CRYING HE SPIT ON ME AND THEN REPEATEDLY BASHED MY FACE WITH A BRICK. HE FORCED ME TO SCREAM "I WANT MY MOMMY!!" FOUR OR FIVE TIMES
SPD
THEN HE PEED ON ME & TOLD EVERYBODY I PEED MY PANTS
THANK YOU OFFICER.
SPD
THEY PUT TAMPONS IN OUR COFFEE. THEY POISON OUR EGG MCMUFFINS. THEY THROW EMPTY WATER BOTTLES AT US. AND IT'S NOT ENOUGH!
SPD
THEY WON'T STOP UNTIL THEY'VE STRIPPED US OF OUR GOD-GIVEN RIGHT TO MURDER WITH IMPUNITY!!
SPD
SPD
SPD
THESE ANARCHISTS MUST BE STOPPED!!
BLUE LIVES MATTER!!
CLAP
CLAP
CLAP
CLAP
CLAP
GA

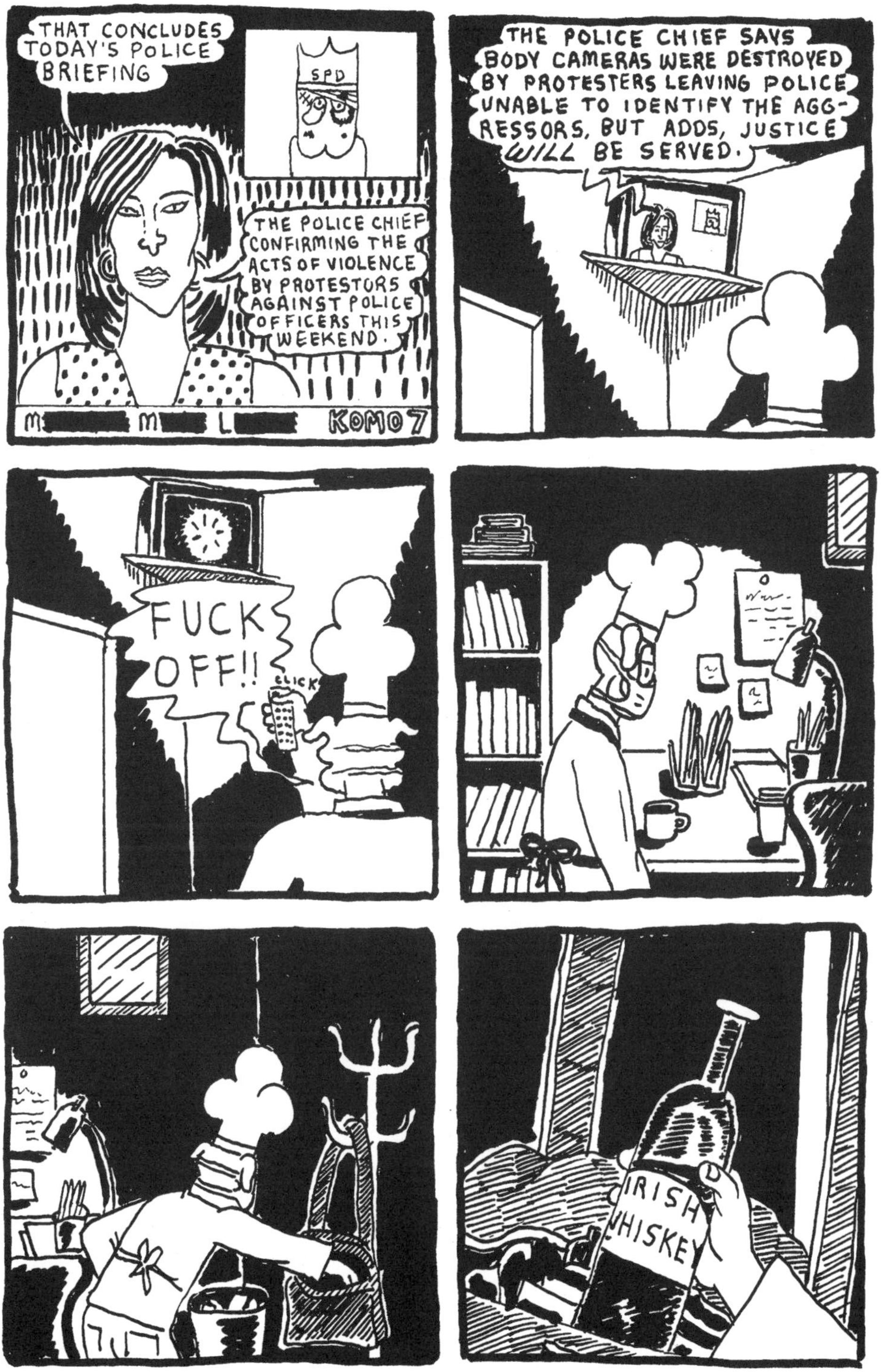
THAT CONCLUDES TODAY'S POLICE BRIEFING
SPD
THE POLICE CHIEF CONFIRMING THE ACTS OF VIOLENCE BY PROTESTORS AGAINST POLICE OFFICERS THIS WEEKEND.
M[redacted] M[redacted] L[redacted]
KOMO 7
THE POLICE CHIEF SAYS BODY CAMERAS WERE DESTROYED BY PROTESTERS LEAVING POLICE UNABLE TO IDENTIFY THE AGGRESSORS, BUT ADDS, JUSTICE WILL BE SERVED.
FUCK OFF!!
CLICK
IRISH
HISKE

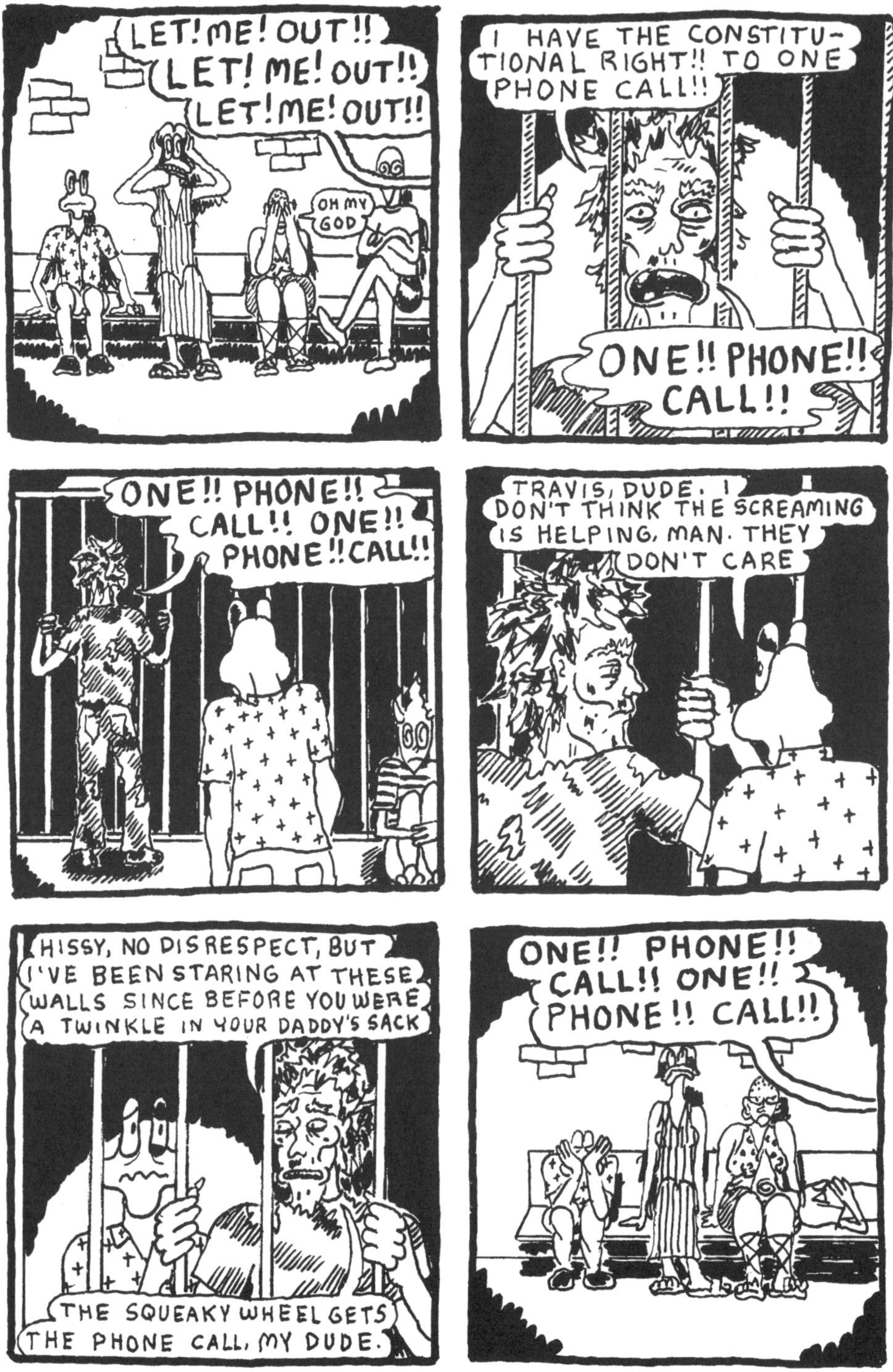
LET! ME! OUT!!
LET! ME! OUT!!
LET! ME! OUT!!
OH MY GOD
I HAVE THE CONSTITUTIONAL RIGHT!! TO ONE PHONE CALL!!
ONE!! PHONE!! CALL!!
ONE!! PHONE!! CALL!! ONE!! PHONE!! CALL!!
TRAVIS, DUDE. I DON'T THINK THE SCREAMING IS HELPING, MAN. THEY DON'T CARE
HISSY, NO DISRESPECT, BUT I'VE BEEN STARING AT THESE WALLS SINCE BEFORE YOU WERE A TWINKLE IN YOUR DADDY'S SACK
THE SQUEAKY WHEEL GETS THE PHONE CALL, MY DUDE.
ONE!! PHONE!! CALL!! ONE!! PHONE!! CALL!!

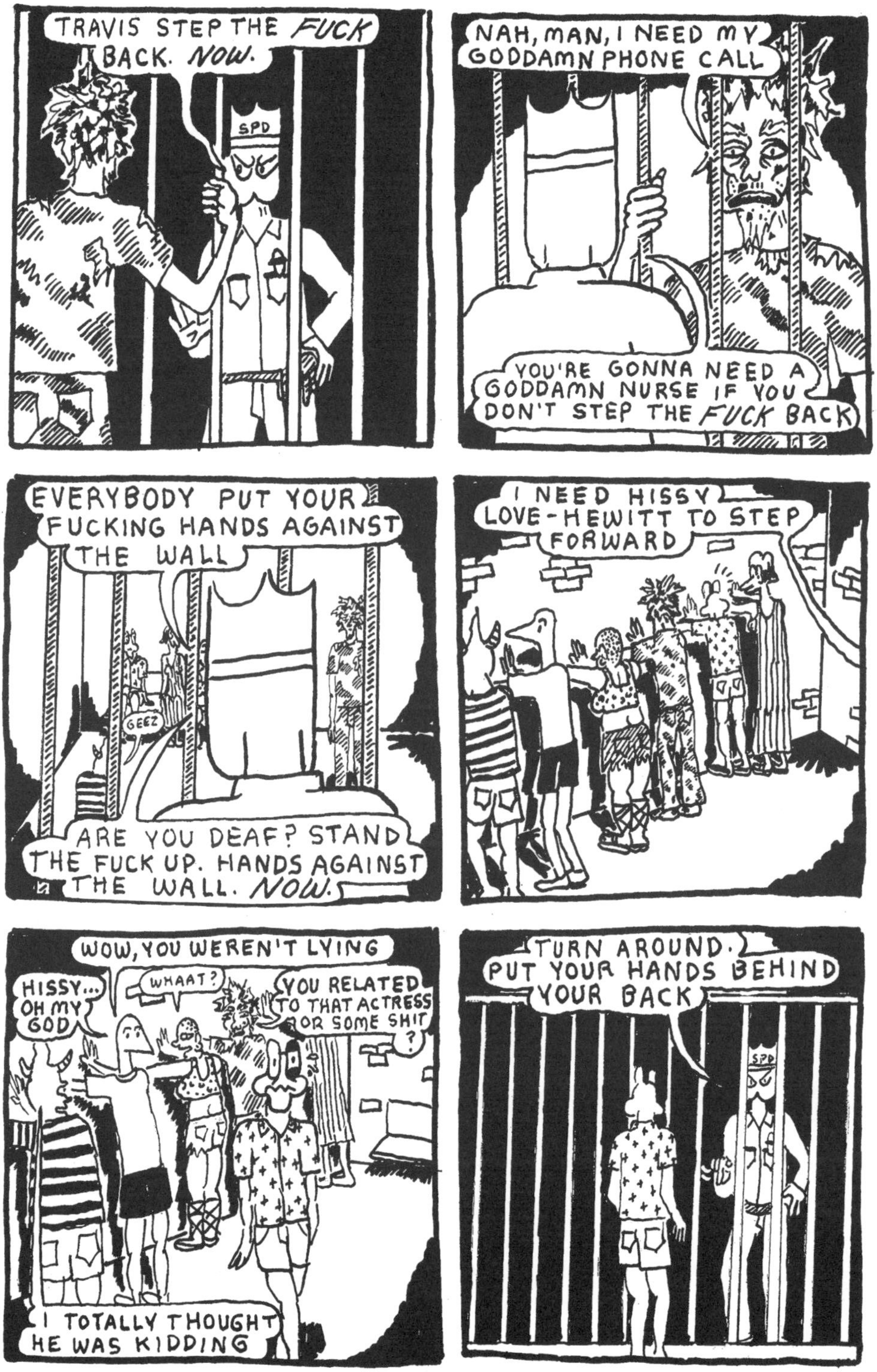
TRAVIS STEP THE FUCK BACK. NOW.
NAH, MAN, I NEED MY GODDAMN PHONE CALL
YOU'RE GONNA NEED A GODDAMN NURSE IF YOU DON'T STEP THE FUCK BACK
EVERYBODY PUT YOUR FUCKING HANDS AGAINST THE WALL
GEEZ
ARE YOU DEAF? STAND THE FUCK UP. HANDS AGAINST THE WALL. NOW.
I NEED HISSY LOVE-HEWITT TO STEP FORWARD
WOW, YOU WEREN'T LYING
HISSY... OH MY GOD
WHAAT?
YOU RELATED TO THAT ACTRESS OR SOME SHIT ?
I TOTALLY THOUGHT HE WAS KIDDING
TURN AROUND. PUT YOUR HANDS BEHIND YOUR BACK

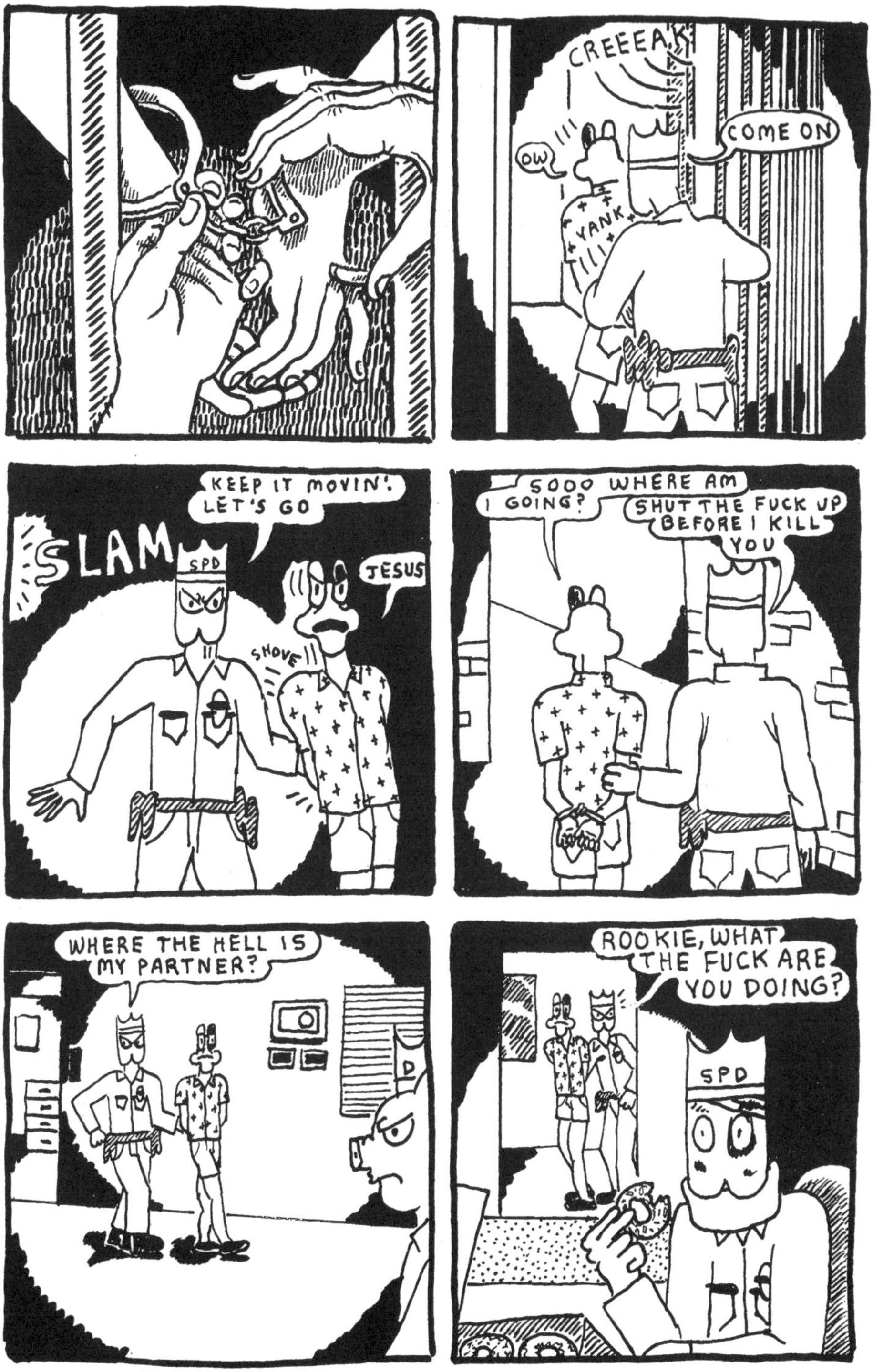
CREEEAK
OW
COME ON
YANK
KEEP IT MOVIN'. LET'S GO
SLAM
SPD
JESUS
SHOVE
SOOO WHERE AM I GOING?
SHUT THE FUCK UP BEFORE I KILL YOU
WHERE THE HELL IS MY PARTNER?
ROOKIE, WHAT THE FUCK ARE YOU DOING?
SPD

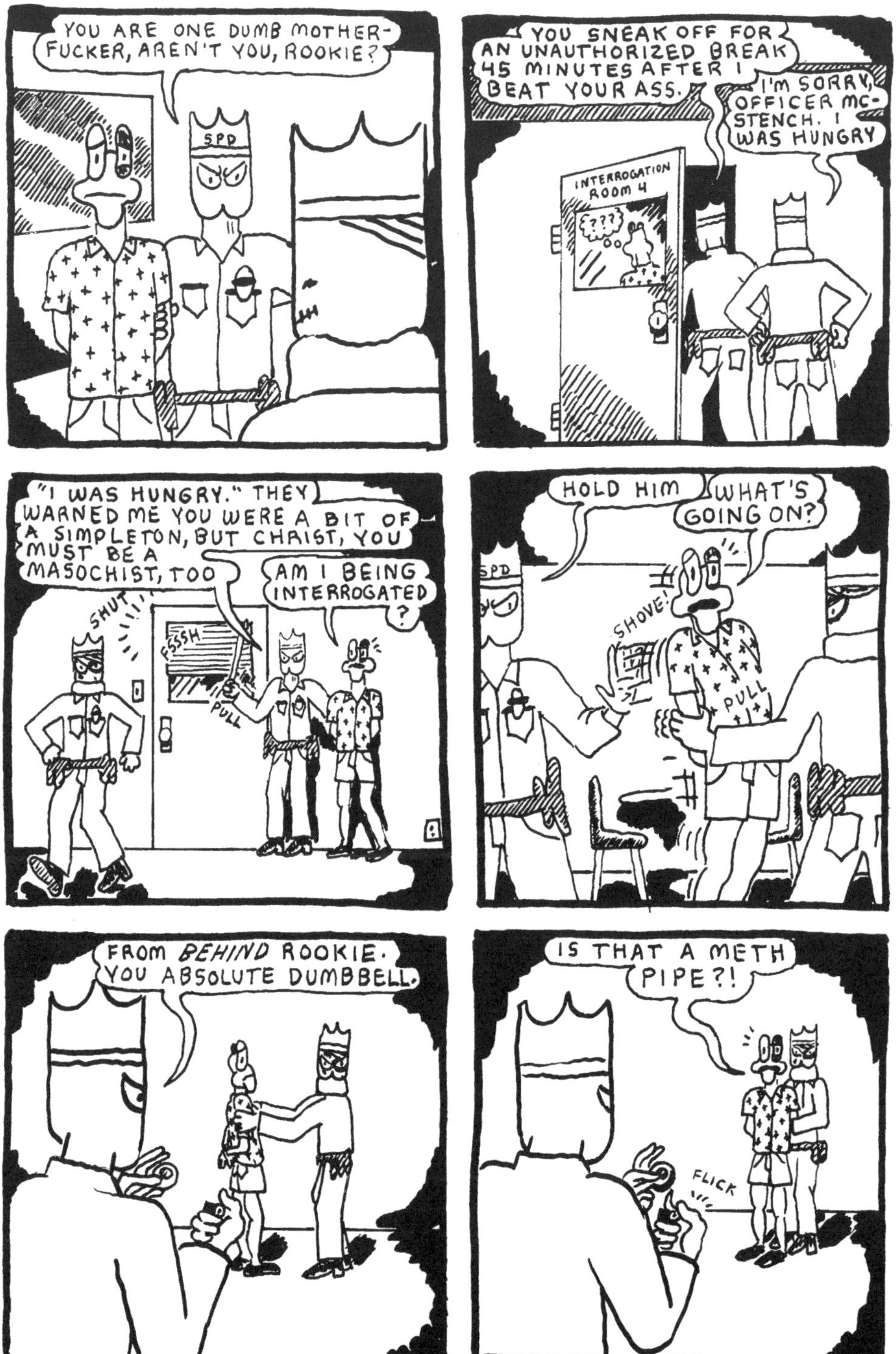
YOU ARE ONE DUMB MOTHER-FUCKER, AREN'T YOU, ROOKIE?
SPD
YOU SNEAK OFF FOR AN UNAUTHORIZED BREAK 45 MINUTES AFTER I BEAT YOUR ASS.
I'M SORRY, OFFICER MC-STENCH. I WAS HUNGRY
INTERROGATION ROOM 4
???
"I WAS HUNGRY." THEY WARNED ME YOU WERE A BIT OF A SIMPLETON, BUT CHRIST, YOU MUST BE A MASOCHIST, TOO
AM I BEING INTERROGATED?
SHUT
FSSSH
PULL
HOLD HIM
WHAT'S GOING ON?
SPD
SHOVE!
PULL
FROM *BEHIND* ROOKIE. YOU ABSOLUTE DUMBBELL.
IS THAT A METH PIPE?!
FLICK

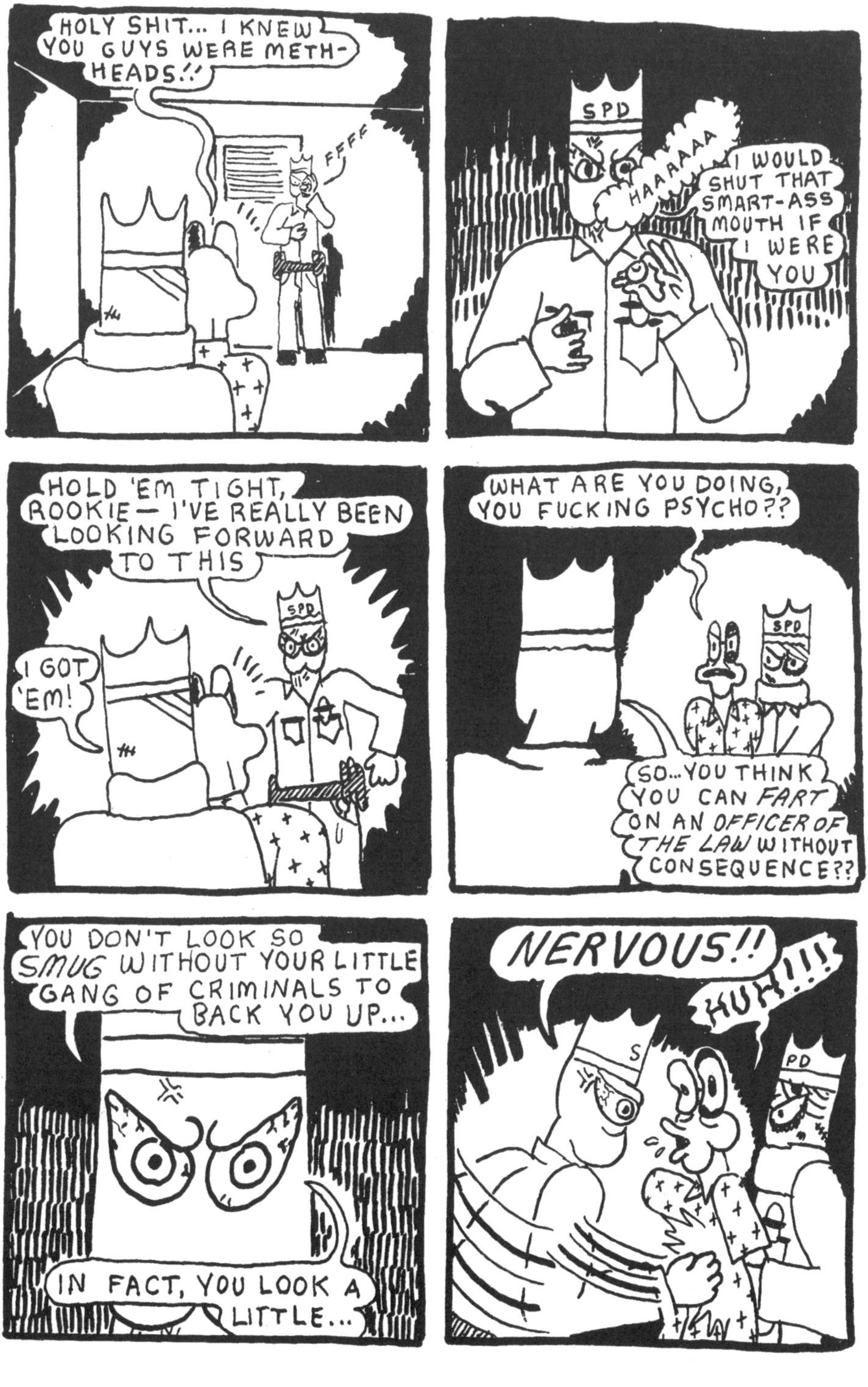
HOLY SHIT... I KNEW YOU GUYS WERE METH-HEADS!!
FFFF
HAAAAAAA
I WOULD SHUT THAT SMART-ASS MOUTH IF I WERE YOU
SPD
HOLD 'EM TIGHT, ROOKIE— I'VE REALLY BEEN LOOKING FORWARD TO THIS
I GOT 'EM!
SPD
WHAT ARE YOU DOING, YOU FUCKING PSYCHO??
SPD
SO...YOU THINK YOU CAN FART ON AN OFFICER OF THE LAW WITHOUT CONSEQUENCE??
YOU DON'T LOOK SO SMUG WITHOUT YOUR LITTLE GANG OF CRIMINALS TO BACK YOU UP...
IN FACT, YOU LOOK A LITTLE...
NERVOUS!!
HUH!!!

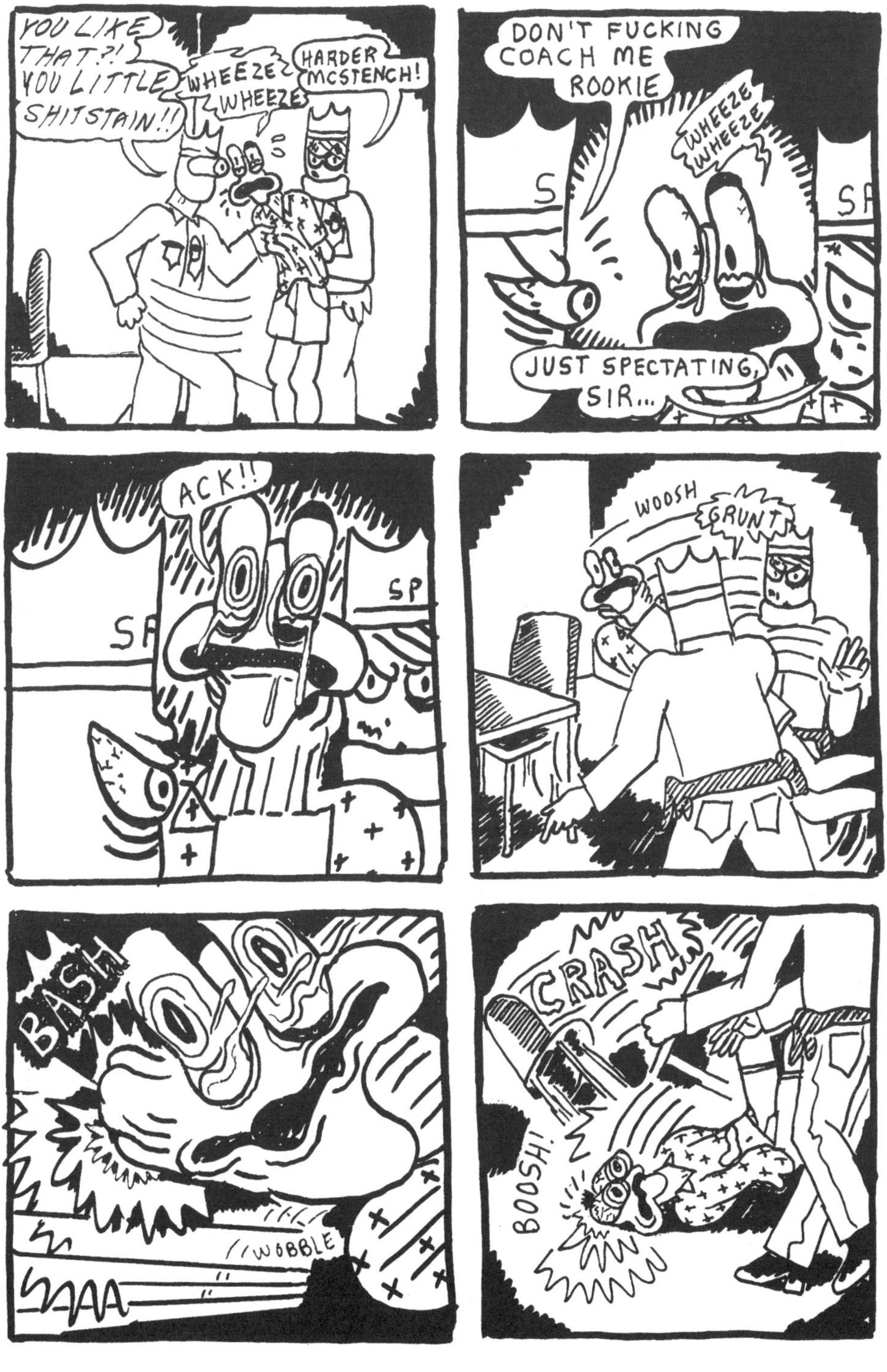

YOU LIKE THAT?! YOU LITTLE SHITSTAIN!!
WHEEZE WHEEZE
HARDER MCSTENCH!
DON'T FUCKING COACH ME ROOKIE
WHEEZE WHEEZE
JUST SPECTATING, SIR...
ACK!!
WOOSH
GRUNT
BASH
WOBBLE
CRASH
BOOSH!

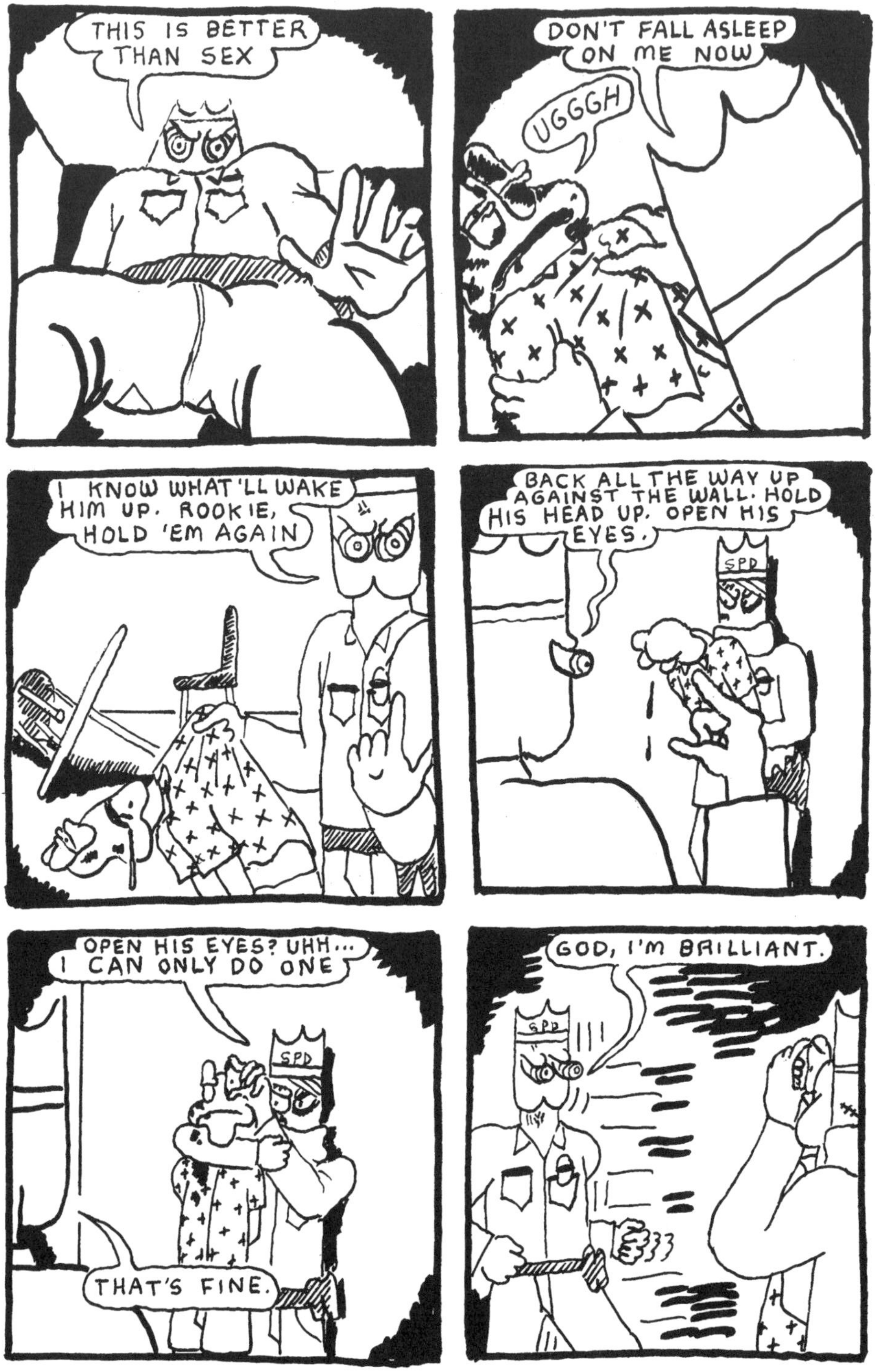
THIS IS BETTER THAN SEX
DON'T FALL ASLEEP ON ME NOW
UGGGH
I KNOW WHAT'LL WAKE HIM UP. ROOKIE, HOLD 'EM AGAIN
BACK ALL THE WAY UP AGAINST THE WALL. HOLD HIS HEAD UP. OPEN HIS EYES.
SPD
OPEN HIS EYES? UHH... I CAN ONLY DO ONE
SPD
THAT'S FINE.
GOD, I'M BRILLIANT.
SPD

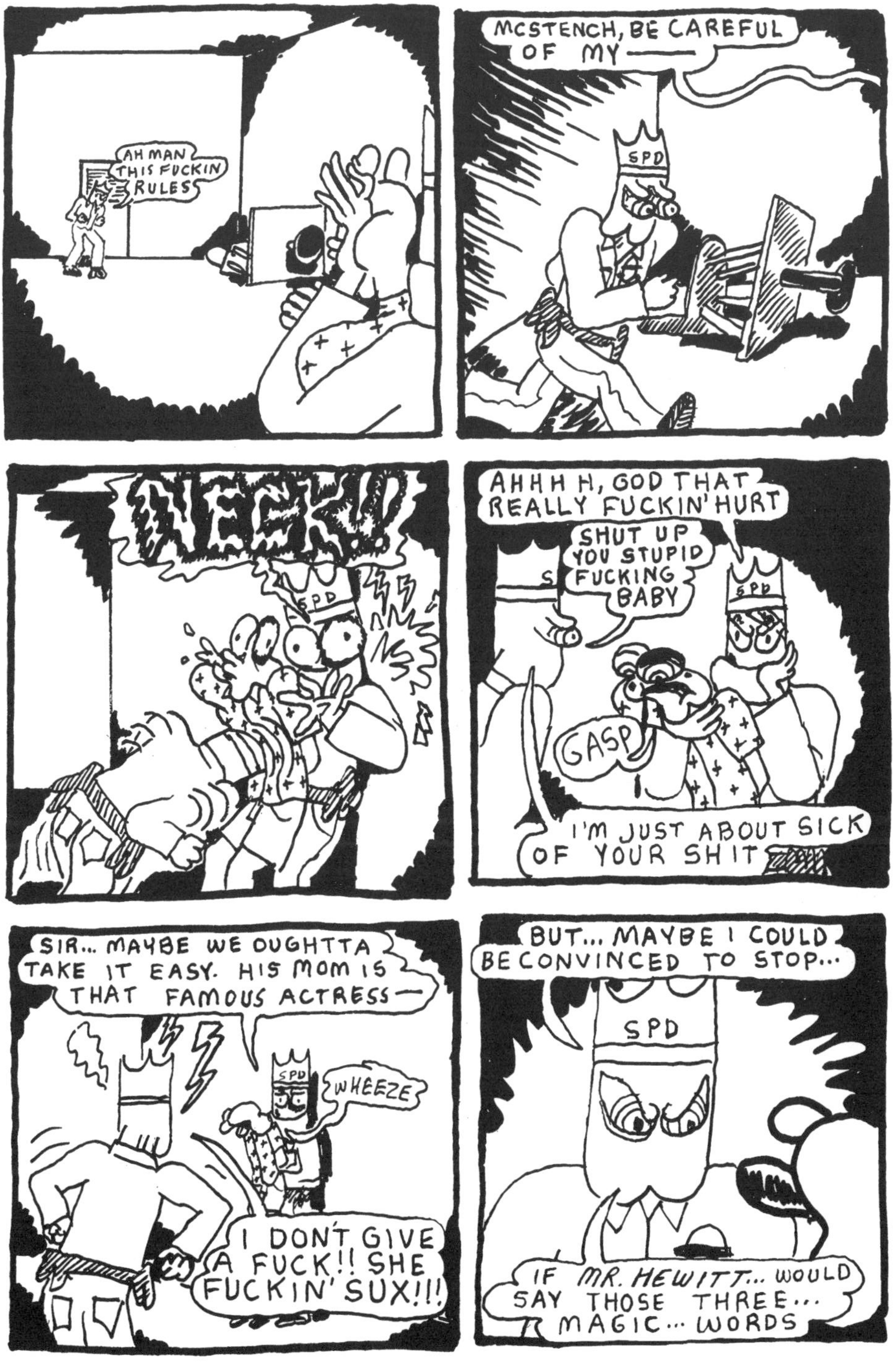
AH MAN THIS FUCKIN RULES
MCSTENCH, BE CAREFUL OF MY——
SPD
NECK!!
SPD
AHHHH, GOD THAT REALLY FUCKIN' HURT
SHUT UP YOU STUPID FUCKING BABY
SPD
GASP
I'M JUST ABOUT SICK OF YOUR SHIT
SIR... MAYBE WE OUGHTTA TAKE IT EASY. HIS MOM IS THAT FAMOUS ACTRESS—
SPD
WHEEZE
I DON'T GIVE A FUCK!! SHE FUCKIN' SUX!!!
BUT... MAYBE I COULD BE CONVINCED TO STOP...
SPD
IF MR. HEWITT... WOULD SAY THOSE THREE... MAGIC... WORDS

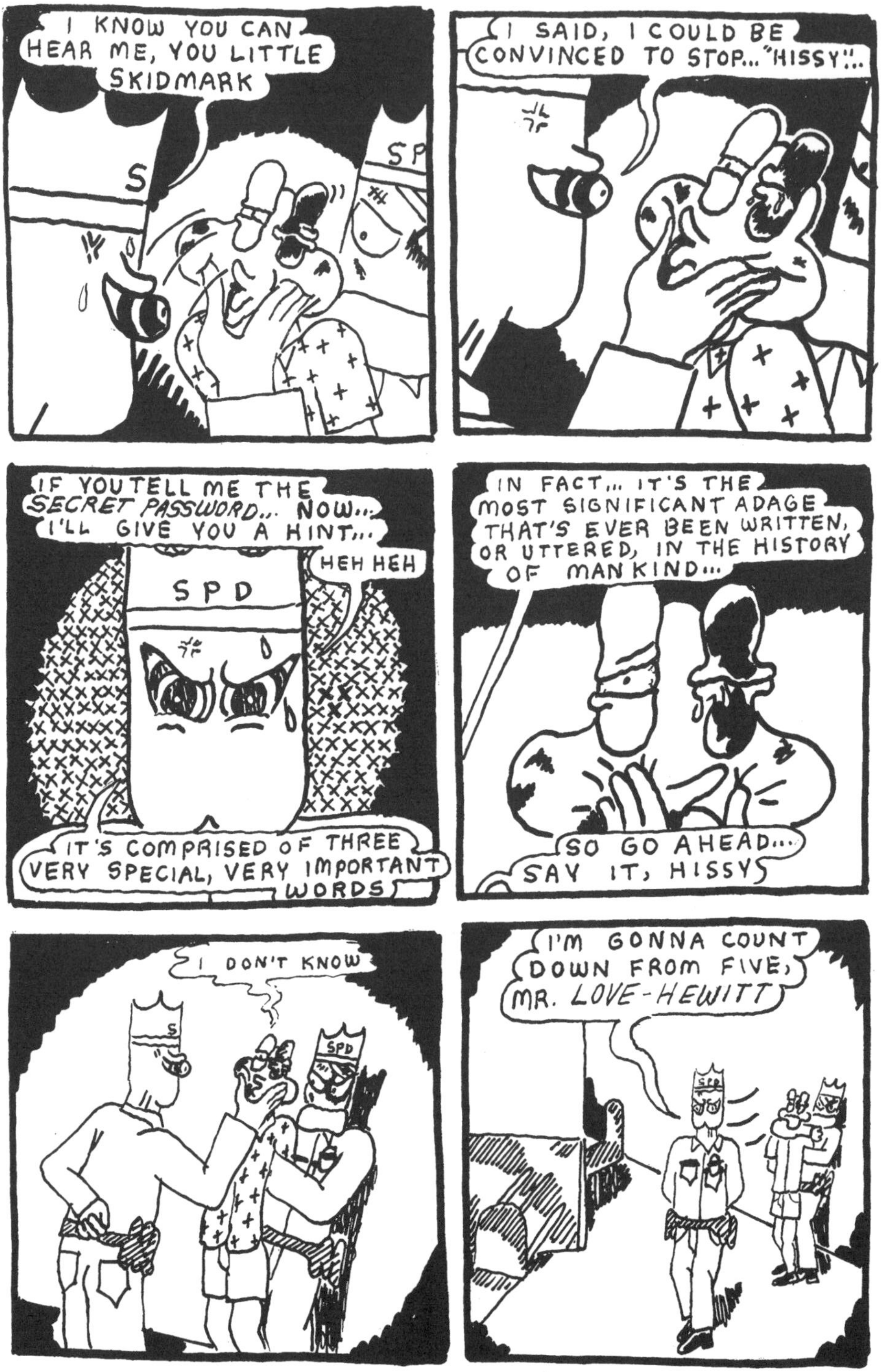
I KNOW YOU CAN HEAR ME, YOU LITTLE SKIDMARK
SPD
I SAID, I COULD BE CONVINCED TO STOP... "HISSY"...
IF YOU TELL ME THE SECRET PASSWORD... NOW... I'LL GIVE YOU A HINT...
HEH HEH
SPD
IT'S COMPRISED OF THREE VERY SPECIAL, VERY IMPORTANT WORDS
IN FACT... IT'S THE MOST SIGNIFICANT ADAGE THAT'S EVER BEEN WRITTEN, OR UTTERED, IN THE HISTORY OF MANKIND...
SO GO AHEAD... SAY IT, HISSY
I DON'T KNOW
SPD
I'M GONNA COUNT DOWN FROM FIVE, MR. LOVE-HEWITT

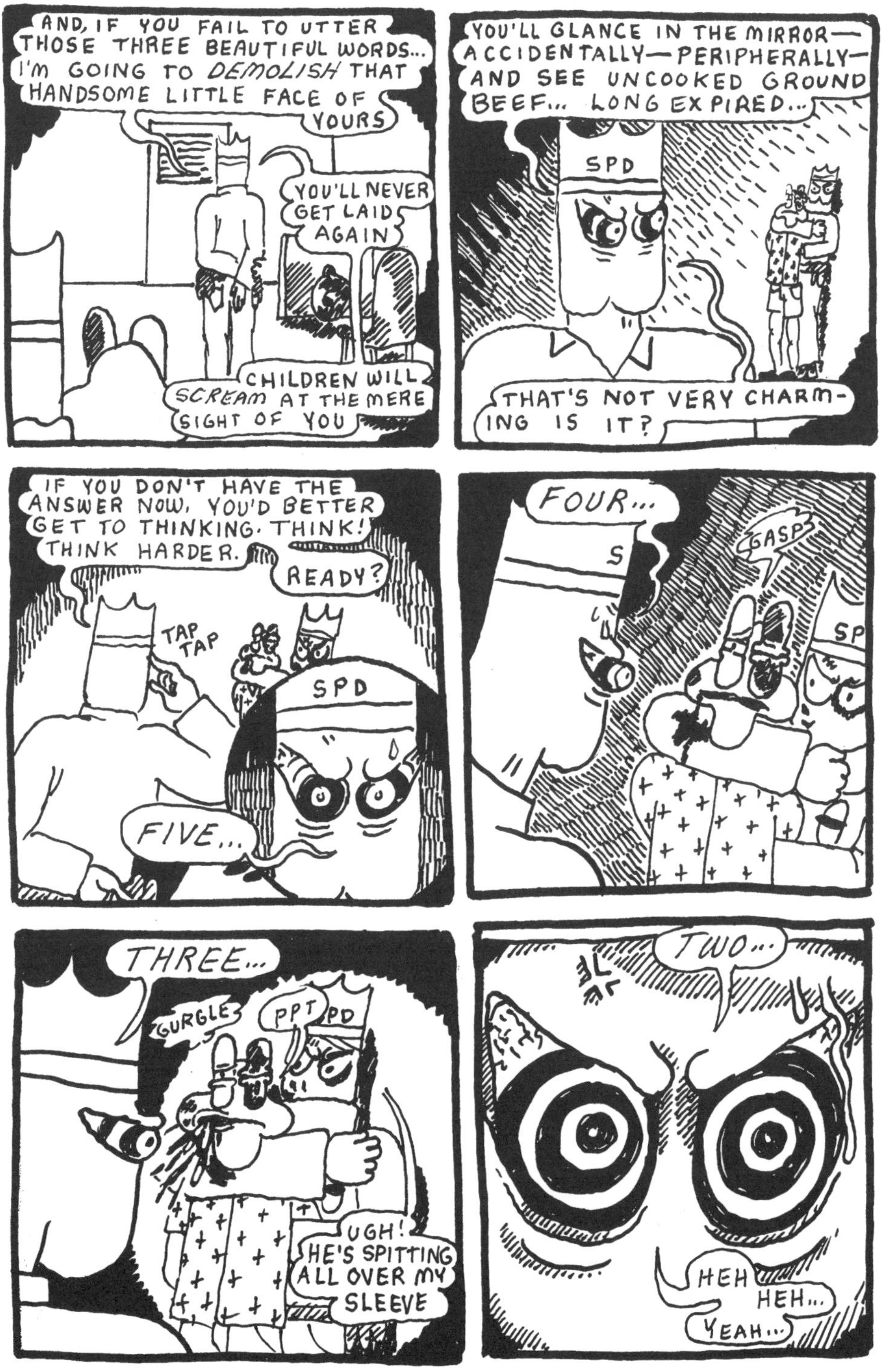
AND, IF YOU FAIL TO UTTER THOSE THREE BEAUTIFUL WORDS... I'M GOING TO DEMOLISH THAT HANDSOME LITTLE FACE OF YOURS
YOU'LL NEVER GET LAID AGAIN
CHILDREN WILL SCREAM AT THE MERE SIGHT OF YOU
YOU'LL GLANCE IN THE MIRROR— ACCIDENTALLY—PERIPHERALLY— AND SEE UNCOOKED GROUND BEEF... LONG EXPIRED...
SPD
THAT'S NOT VERY CHARMING IS IT?
IF YOU DON'T HAVE THE ANSWER NOW, YOU'D BETTER GET TO THINKING. THINK! THINK HARDER.
READY?
TAP TAP
SPD
FIVE...
FOUR...
GASP
THREE...
GURGLE
PPT
UGH! HE'S SPITTING ALL OVER MY SLEEVE
TWO...
HEH HEH... YEAH...

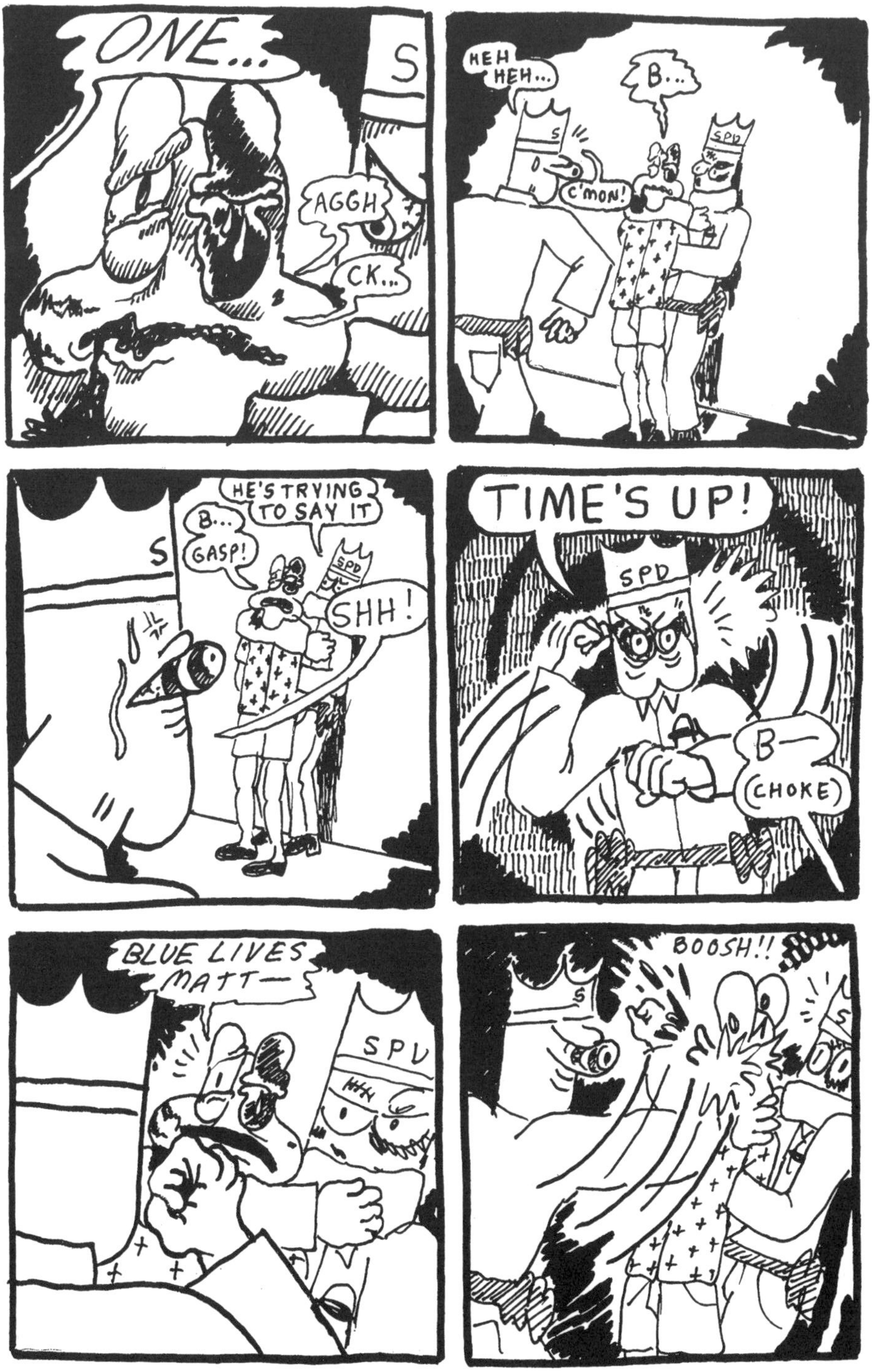
ONE...
S
AGGH
CK...
HEH HEH...
B...
S
SPD
C'MON!
HE'S TRYING TO SAY IT
B... GASP!
S
SPD
SHH!
TIME'S UP!
SPD
B—
(CHOKE)
BLUE LIVES MATT—
SPV
BOOSH!!
S
S

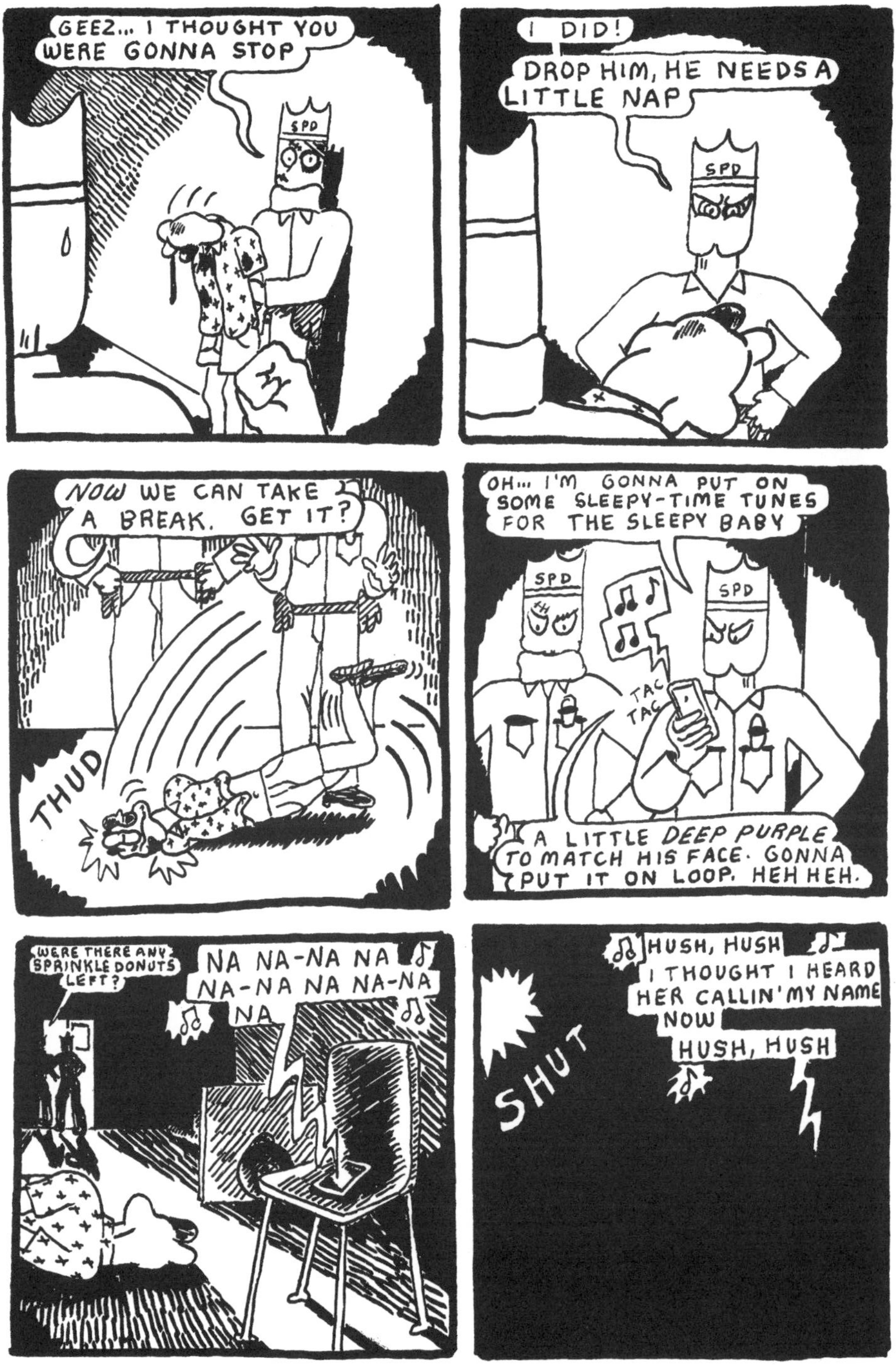
GEEZ... I THOUGHT YOU WERE GONNA STOP
SPD
I DID!
DROP HIM, HE NEEDS A LITTLE NAP
SPD
NOW WE CAN TAKE A BREAK. GET IT?
THUD
OH... I'M GONNA PUT ON SOME SLEEPY-TIME TUNES FOR THE SLEEPY BABY
SPD
SPD
TAC TAC
A LITTLE DEEP PURPLE TO MATCH HIS FACE. GONNA PUT IT ON LOOP. HEH HEH.
WERE THERE ANY SPRINKLE DONUTS LEFT?
NA NA-NA NA NA-NA NA NA-NA NA
SHUT
HUSH, HUSH
I THOUGHT I HEARD HER CALLIN' MY NAME NOW
HUSH, HUSH

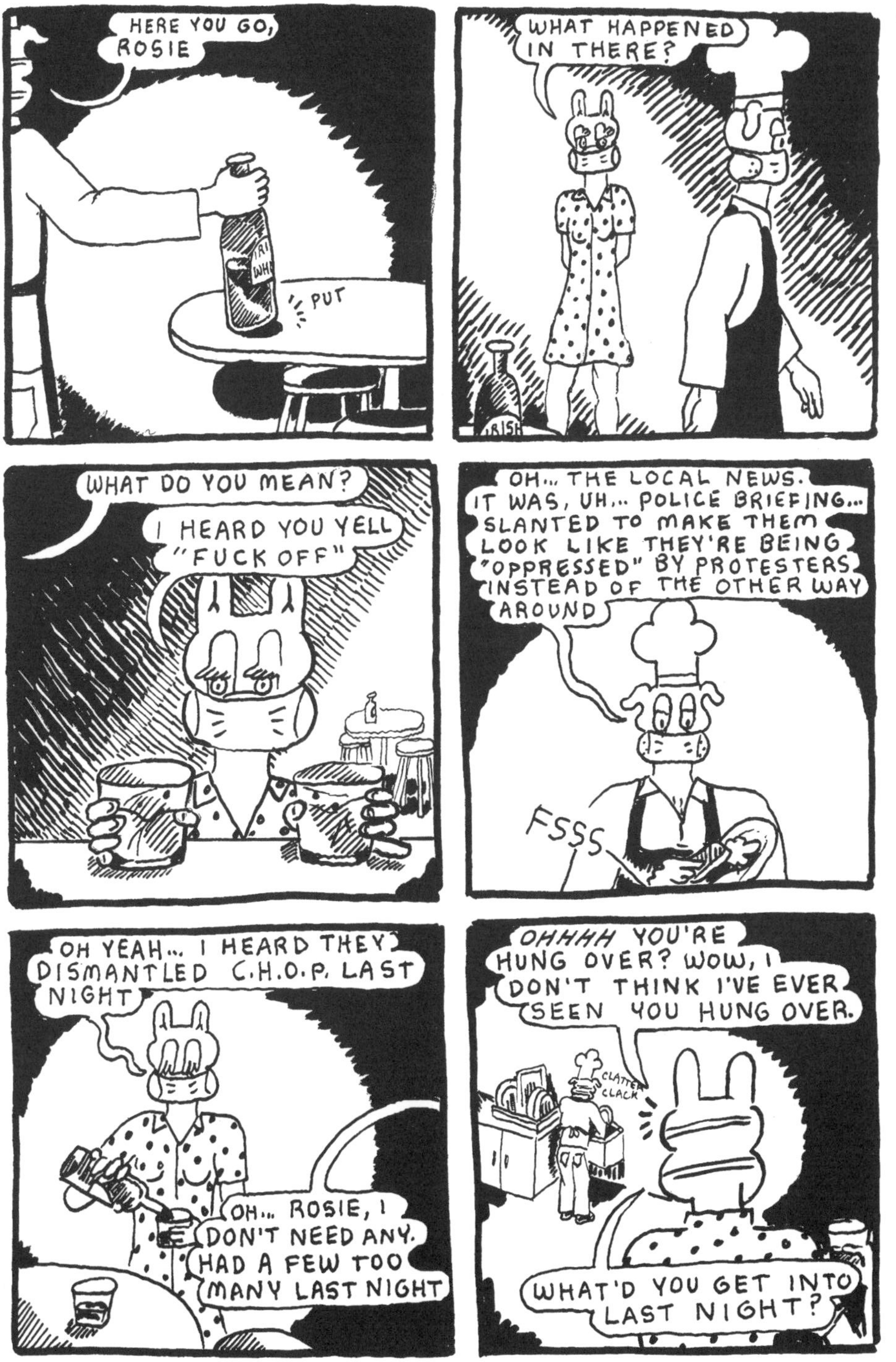
HERE YOU GO, ROSIE
PUT
WHAT HAPPENED IN THERE?
IRISH
WHAT DO YOU MEAN?
I HEARD YOU YELL "FUCK OFF"
OH... THE LOCAL NEWS. IT WAS, UH... POLICE BRIEFING... SLANTED TO MAKE THEM LOOK LIKE THEY'RE BEING "OPPRESSED" BY PROTESTERS INSTEAD OF THE OTHER WAY AROUND
FSSS
OH YEAH... I HEARD THEY DISMANTLED C.H.O.P. LAST NIGHT
OH... ROSIE, I DON'T NEED ANY. HAD A FEW TOO MANY LAST NIGHT
OHHHH YOU'RE HUNG OVER? WOW, I DON'T THINK I'VE EVER SEEN YOU HUNG OVER.
CLATTER CLACK
WHAT'D YOU GET INTO LAST NIGHT?

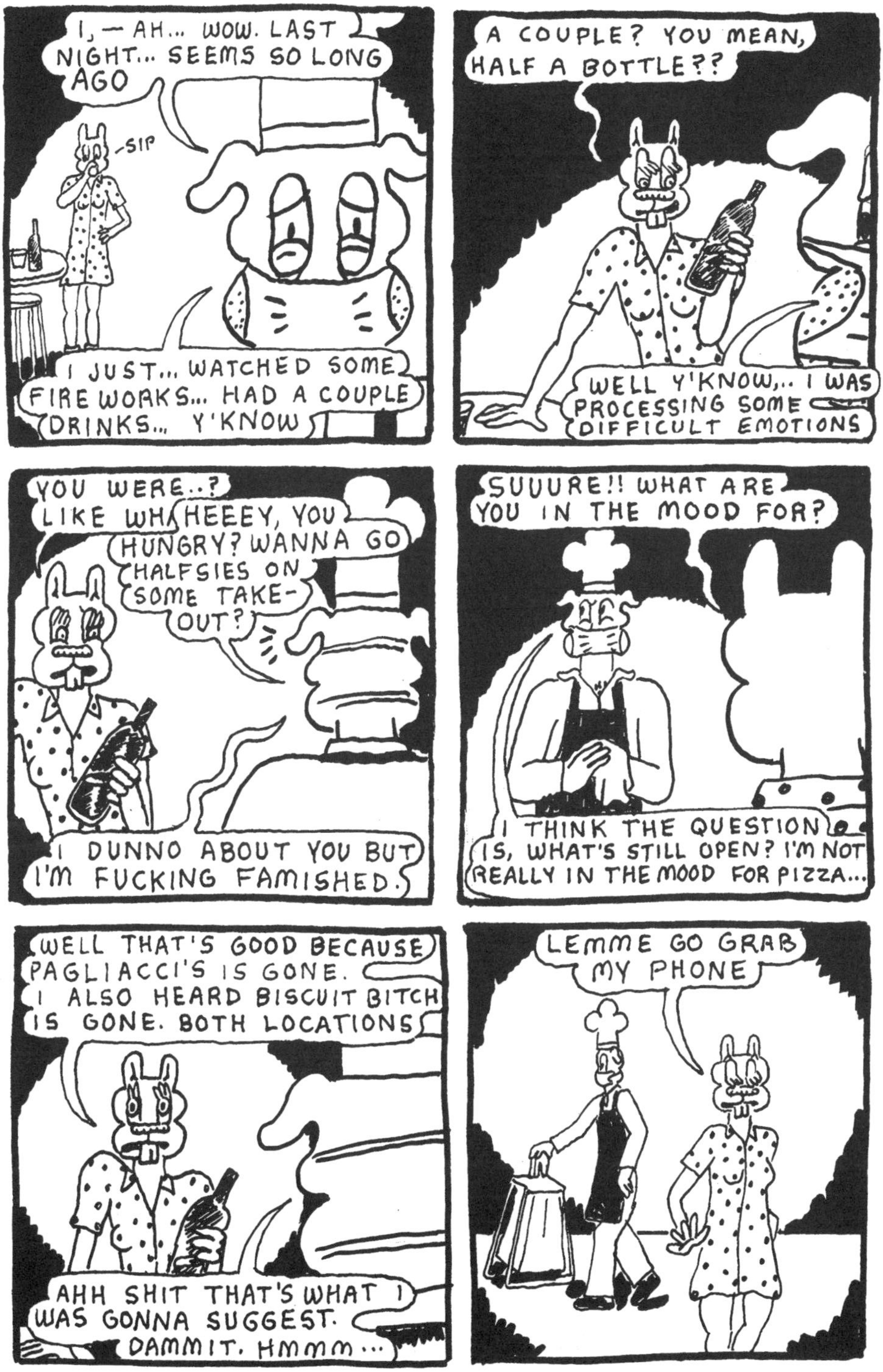
I, — AH... WOW. LAST NIGHT... SEEMS SO LONG AGO
-SIP
I JUST... WATCHED SOME FIRE WORKS... HAD A COUPLE DRINKS... Y'KNOW
A COUPLE? YOU MEAN, HALF A BOTTLE??
WELL Y'KNOW,.. I WAS PROCESSING SOME DIFFICULT EMOTIONS
YOU WERE..? LIKE WH
HEEEY, YOU HUNGRY? WANNA GO HALFSIES ON SOME TAKE-OUT?
I DUNNO ABOUT YOU BUT I'M FUCKING FAMISHED.
SUUURE!! WHAT ARE YOU IN THE MOOD FOR?
I THINK THE QUESTION IS, WHAT'S STILL OPEN? I'M NOT REALLY IN THE MOOD FOR PIZZA...
WELL THAT'S GOOD BECAUSE PAGLIACCI'S IS GONE.
I ALSO HEARD BISCUIT BITCH IS GONE. BOTH LOCATIONS
AHH SHIT THAT'S WHAT I WAS GONNA SUGGEST.
DAMMIT. HMMM...
LEMME GO GRAB MY PHONE

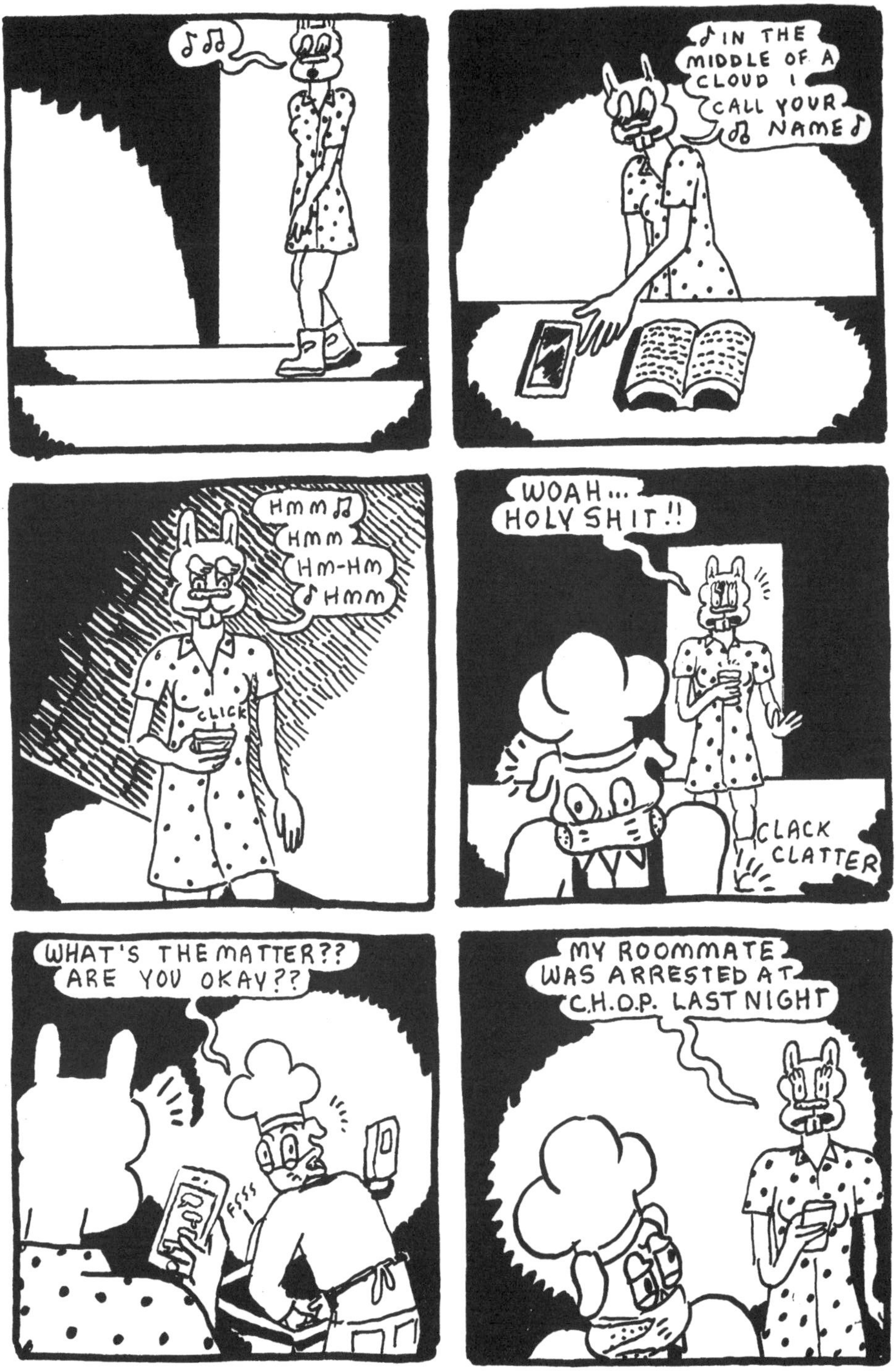
♪♫
♪ IN THE MIDDLE OF A CLOUD I CALL YOUR ♫ NAME ♪
HMM ♫ HMM HM-HM ♪ HMM
CLICK
WOAH... HOLY SHIT!!
CLACK CLATTER
WHAT'S THE MATTER?? ARE YOU OKAY??
FSSS
MY ROOMMATE WAS ARRESTED AT C.H.O.P. LAST NIGHT

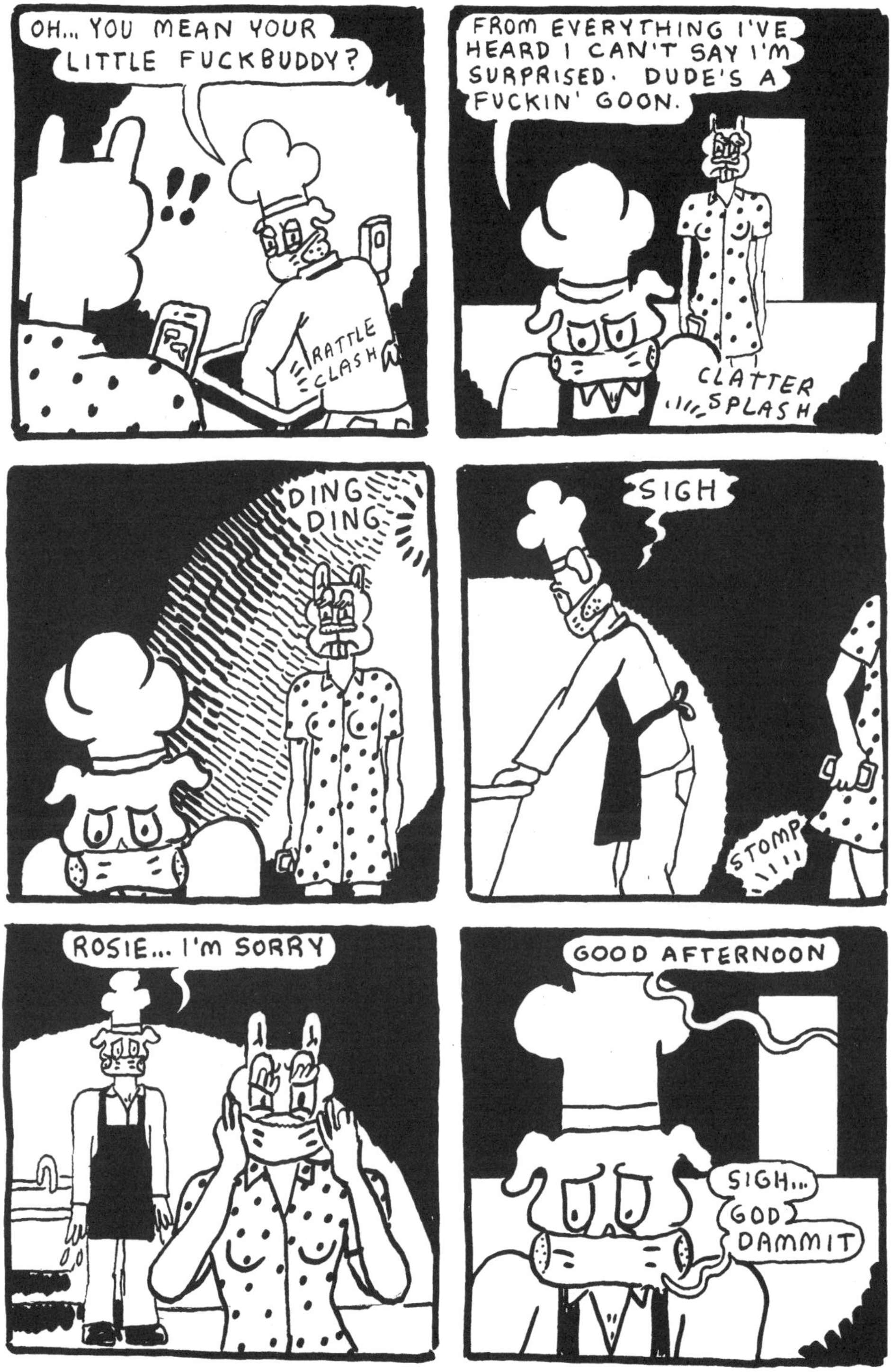
OH... YOU MEAN YOUR LITTLE FUCKBUDDY?
!!
RATTLE CLASH
FROM EVERYTHING I'VE HEARD I CAN'T SAY I'M SURPRISED. DUDE'S A FUCKIN' GOON.
CLATTER SPLASH
DING DING
SIGH
STOMP
ROSIE... I'M SORRY
GOOD AFTERNOON
SIGH...
GOD DAMMIT

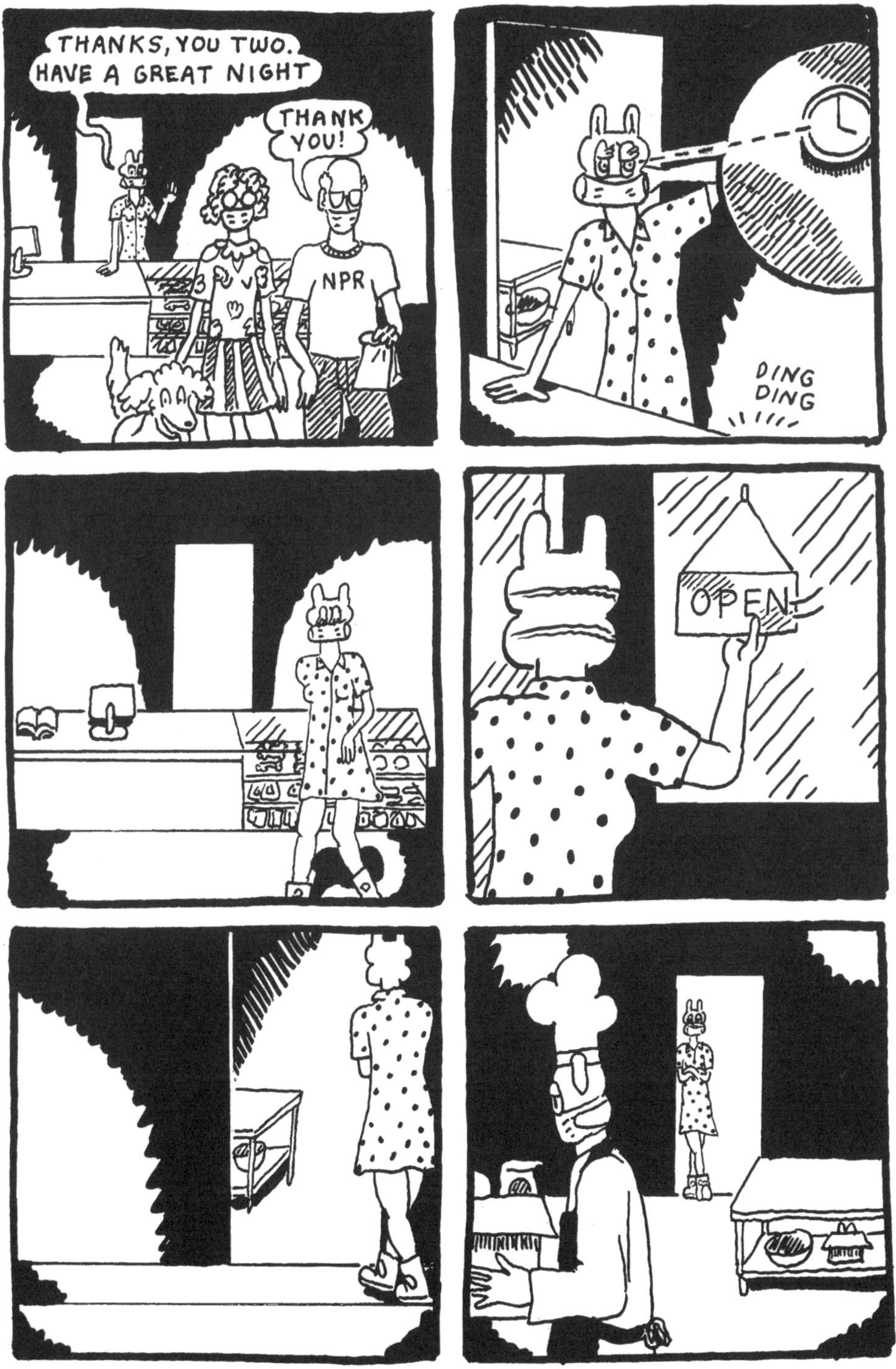
THANKS, YOU TWO. HAVE A GREAT NIGHT
THANK YOU!
NPR
DING DING
OPEN

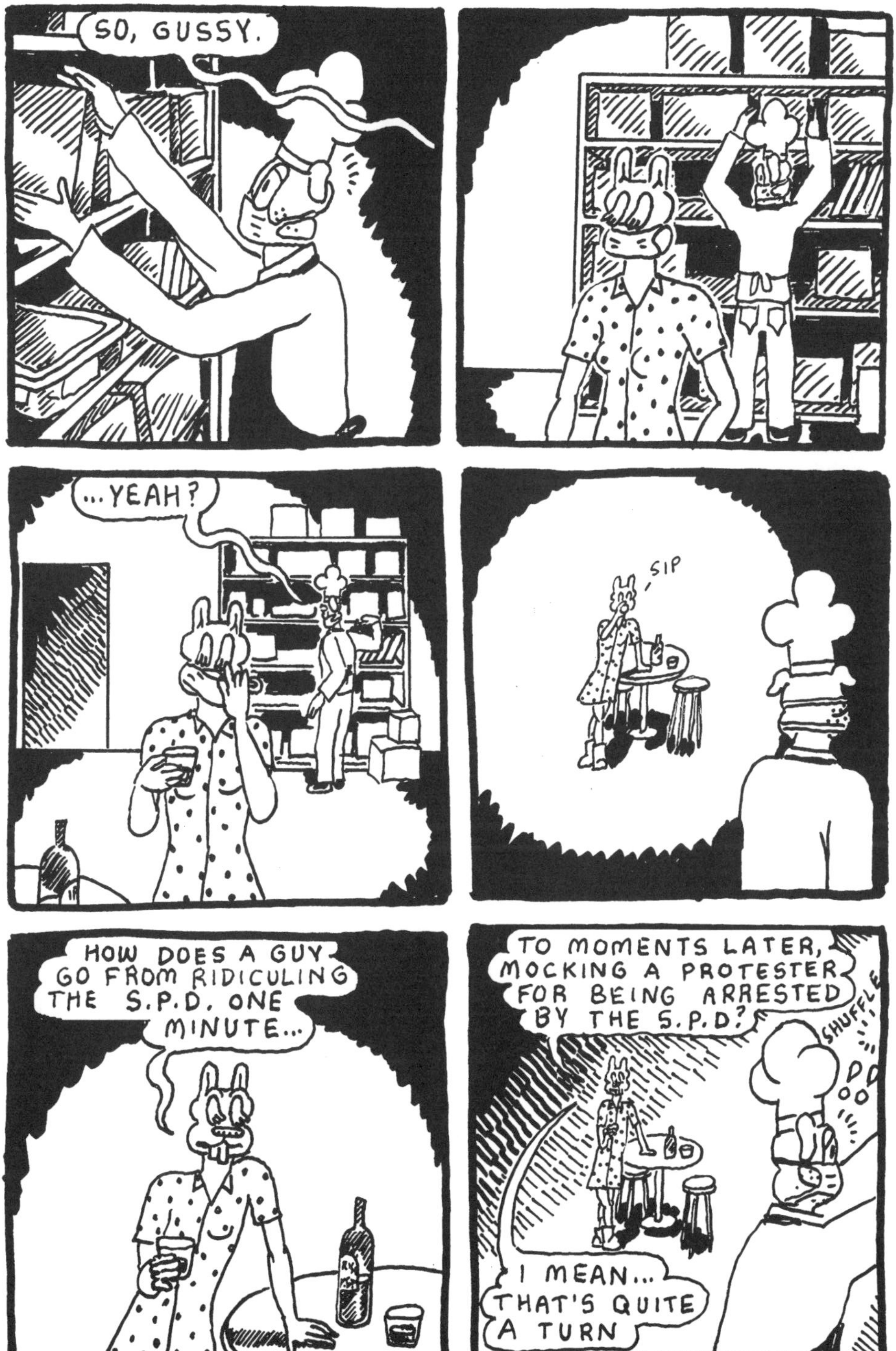
SO, GUSSY.
...YEAH?
SIP
HOW DOES A GUY GO FROM RIDICULING THE S.P.D. ONE MINUTE...
TO MOMENTS LATER, MOCKING A PROTESTER FOR BEING ARRESTED BY THE S.P.D?
SHUFFLE
I MEAN... THAT'S QUITE A TURN

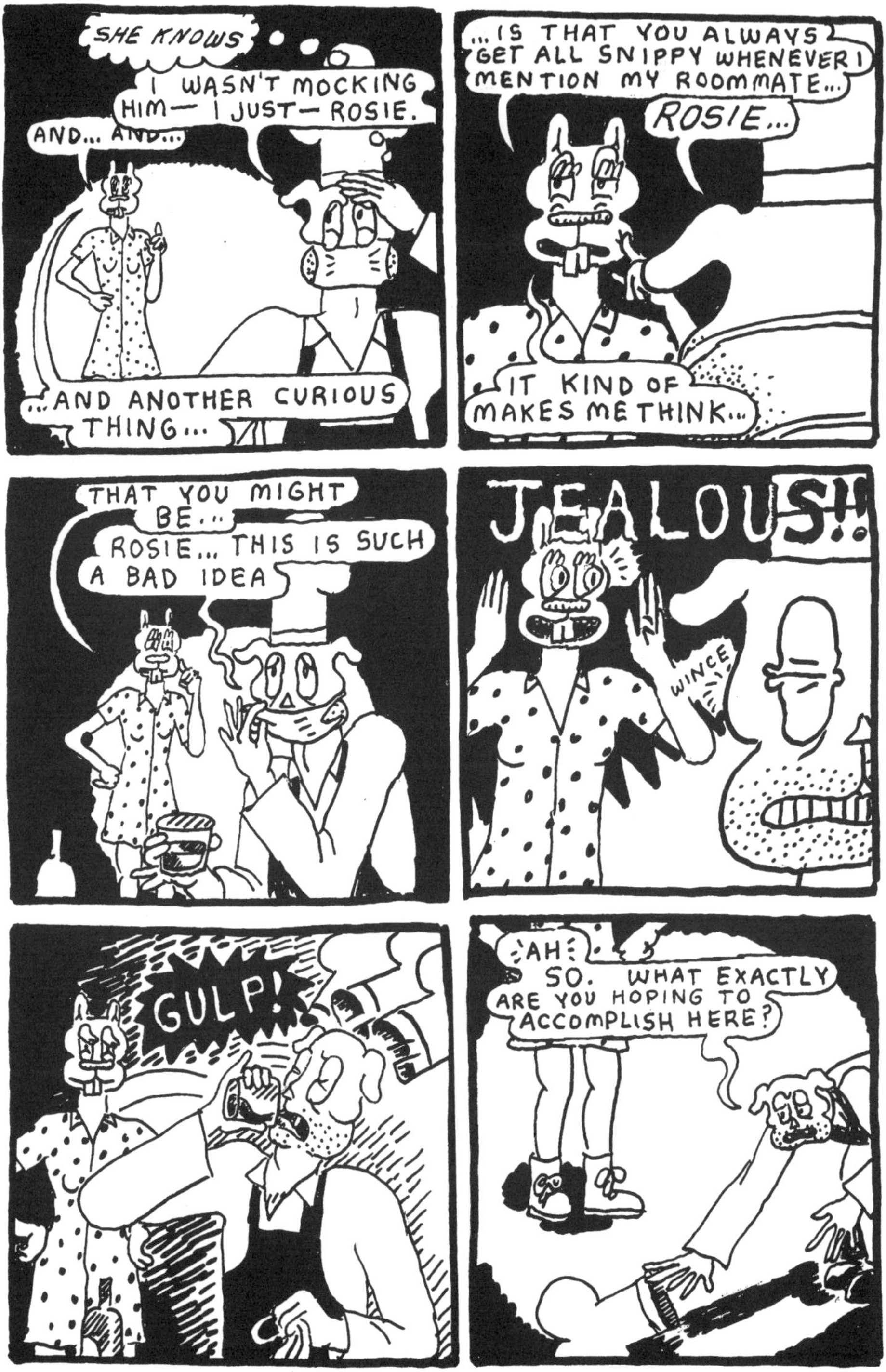
SHE KNOWS
I WASN'T MOCKING HIM— I JUST— ROSIE.
AND... AND...
...AND ANOTHER CURIOUS THING...
...IS THAT YOU ALWAYS GET ALL SNIPPY WHENEVER I MENTION MY ROOMMATE...
ROSIE...
IT KIND OF MAKES ME THINK...
THAT YOU MIGHT BE...
ROSIE... THIS IS SUCH A BAD IDEA
JEALOUS!!
WINCE
GULP!
AH
SO. WHAT EXACTLY ARE YOU HOPING TO ACCOMPLISH HERE?

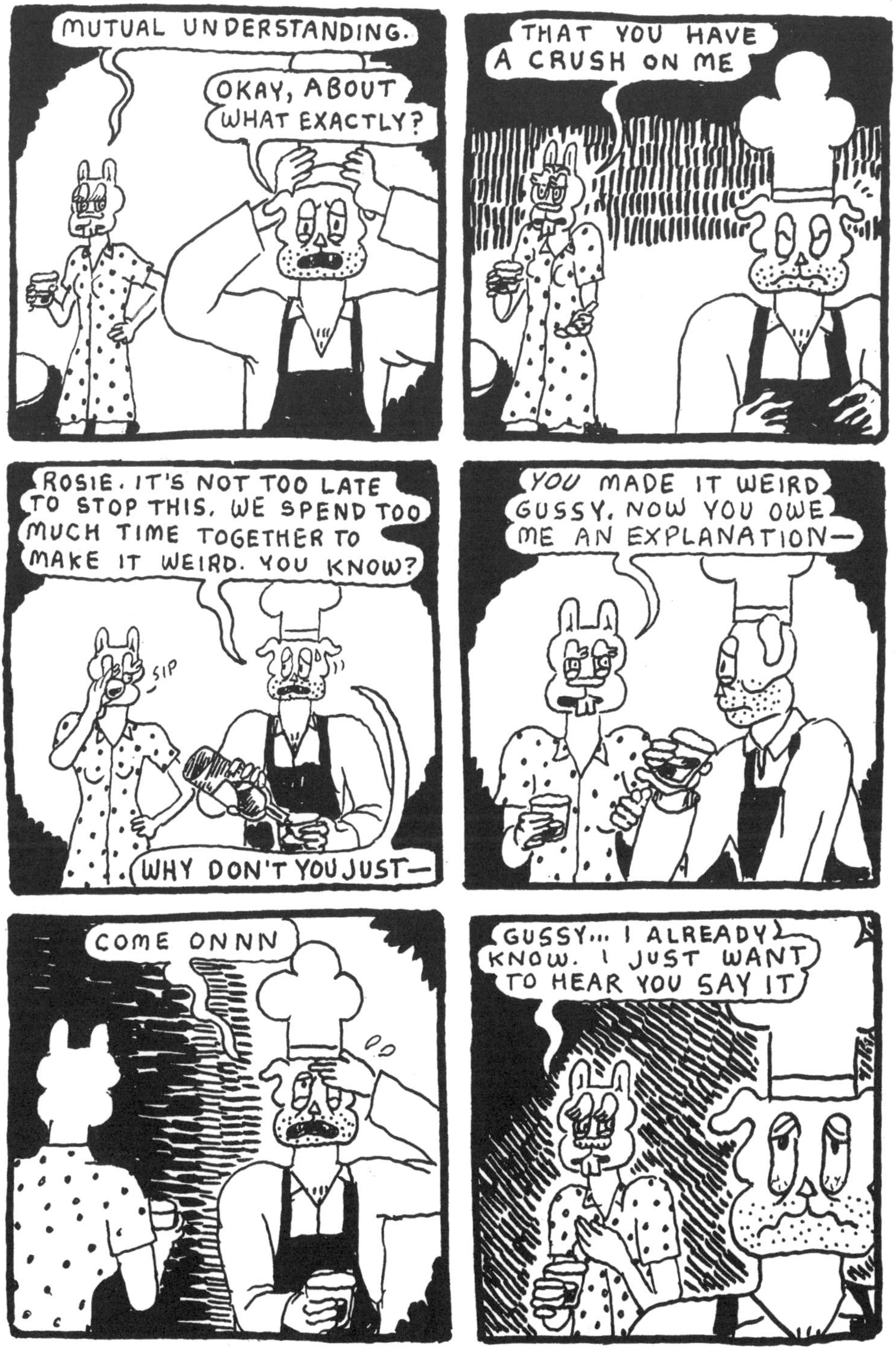
MUTUAL UNDERSTANDING.
OKAY, ABOUT WHAT EXACTLY?
THAT YOU HAVE A CRUSH ON ME
ROSIE. IT'S NOT TOO LATE TO STOP THIS. WE SPEND TOO MUCH TIME TOGETHER TO MAKE IT WEIRD. YOU KNOW?
SIP
WHY DON'T YOU JUST—
YOU MADE IT WEIRD GUSSY. NOW YOU OWE ME AN EXPLANATION—
COME ONNN
GUSSY... I ALREADY KNOW. I JUST WANT TO HEAR YOU SAY IT

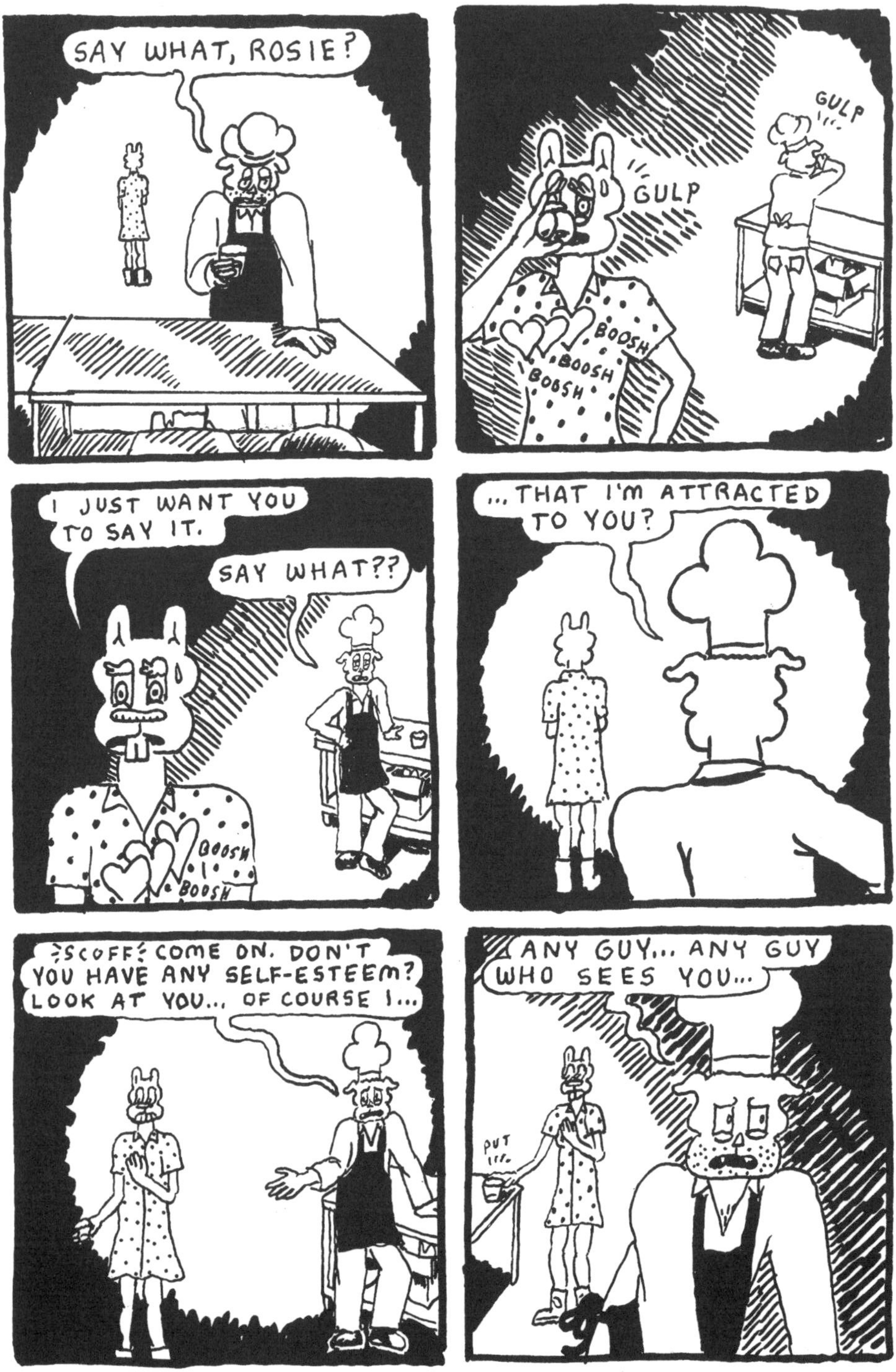

SAY WHAT, ROSIE?
GULP
GULP
BOOSH
BOOSH
BOOSH
I JUST WANT YOU TO SAY IT.
SAY WHAT??
BOOSH
BOOSH
...THAT I'M ATTRACTED TO YOU?
SCOFF COME ON. DON'T YOU HAVE ANY SELF-ESTEEM? LOOK AT YOU..., OF COURSE I...
ANY GUY... ANY GUY WHO SEES YOU...
PUT

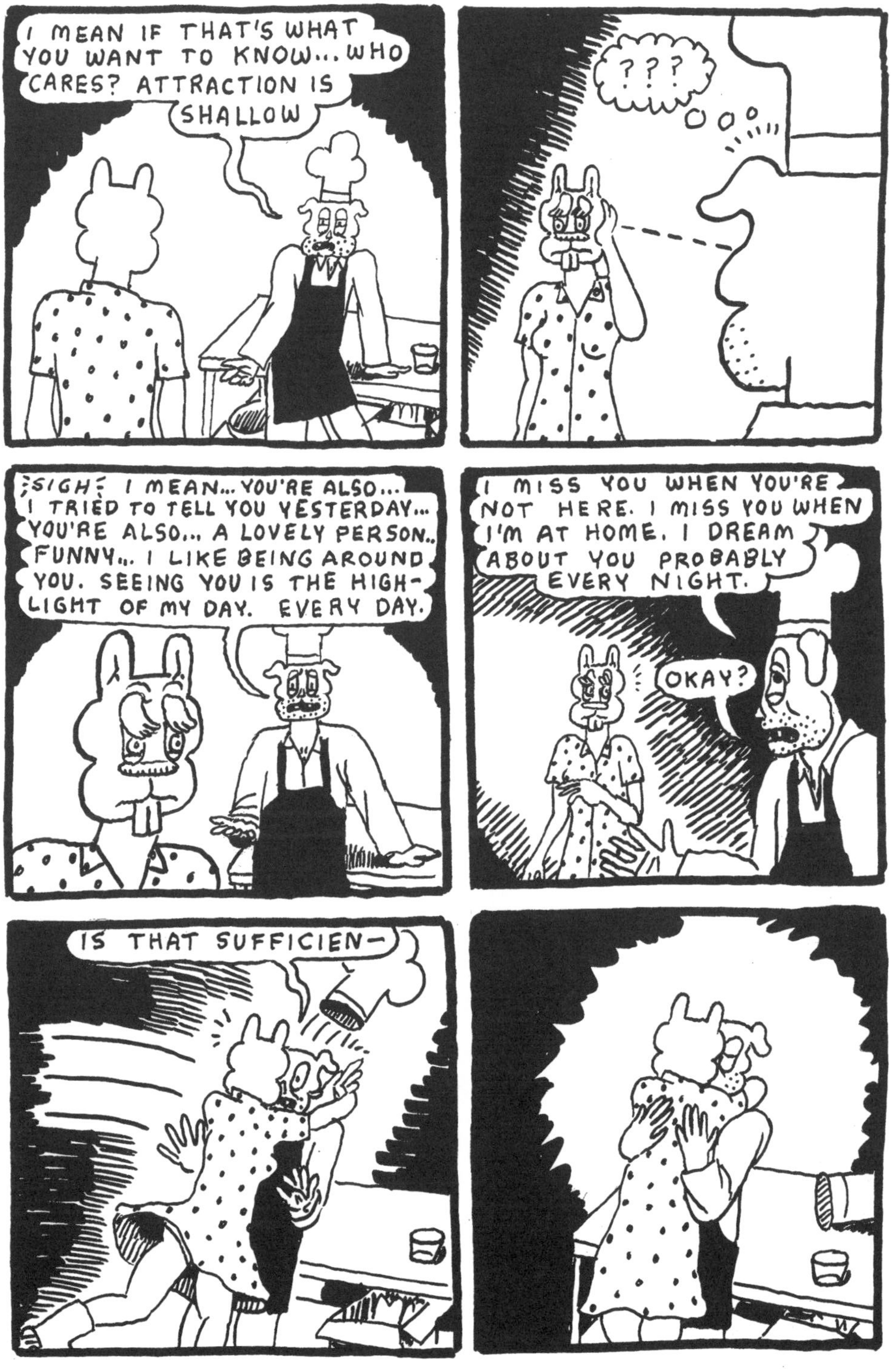
I MEAN IF THAT'S WHAT YOU WANT TO KNOW... WHO CARES? ATTRACTION IS SHALLOW
???
;SIGH; I MEAN... YOU'RE ALSO... I TRIED TO TELL YOU YESTERDAY... YOU'RE ALSO... A LOVELY PERSON.. FUNNY... I LIKE BEING AROUND YOU. SEEING YOU IS THE HIGHLIGHT OF MY DAY. EVERY DAY.
I MISS YOU WHEN YOU'RE NOT HERE. I MISS YOU WHEN I'M AT HOME. I DREAM ABOUT YOU PROBABLY EVERY NIGHT.
OKAY?
IS THAT SUFFICIEN-

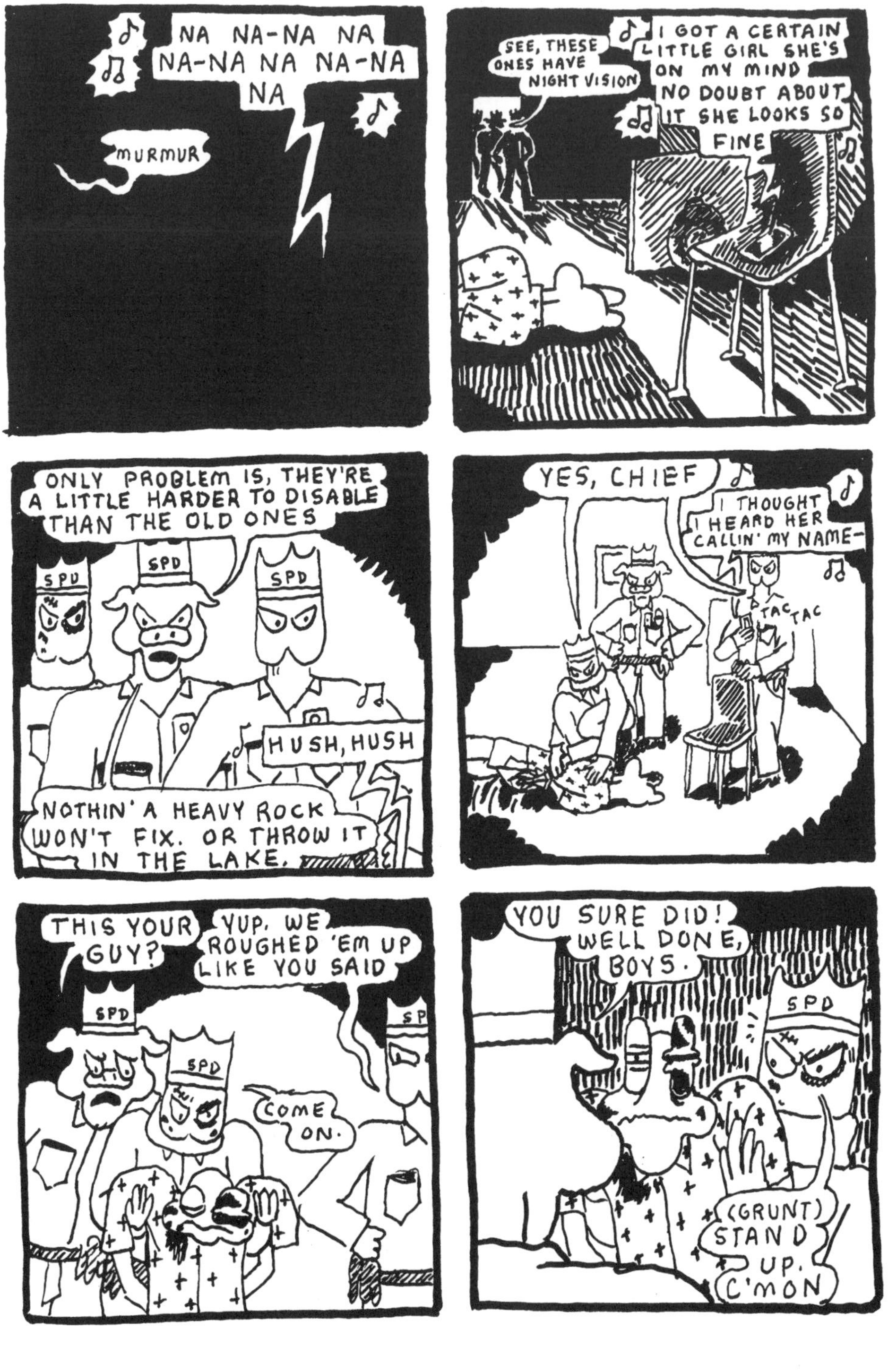
NA NA-NA NA NA-NA NA NA-NA NA
MURMUR
SEE, THESE ONES HAVE NIGHT VISION
I GOT A CERTAIN LITTLE GIRL SHE'S ON MY MIND NO DOUBT ABOUT IT SHE LOOKS SO FINE
ONLY PROBLEM IS, THEY'RE A LITTLE HARDER TO DISABLE THAN THE OLD ONES
SPD
SPD
SPD
HUSH, HUSH
NOTHIN' A HEAVY ROCK WON'T FIX. OR THROW IT IN THE LAKE.
YES, CHIEF
I THOUGHT I HEARD HER CALLIN' MY NAME-
TAC TAC
THIS YOUR GUY?
YUP. WE ROUGHED 'EM UP LIKE YOU SAID
SPD
SPD
COME ON.
YOU SURE DID! WELL DONE, BOYS.
SPD
(GRUNT) STAND UP. C'MON

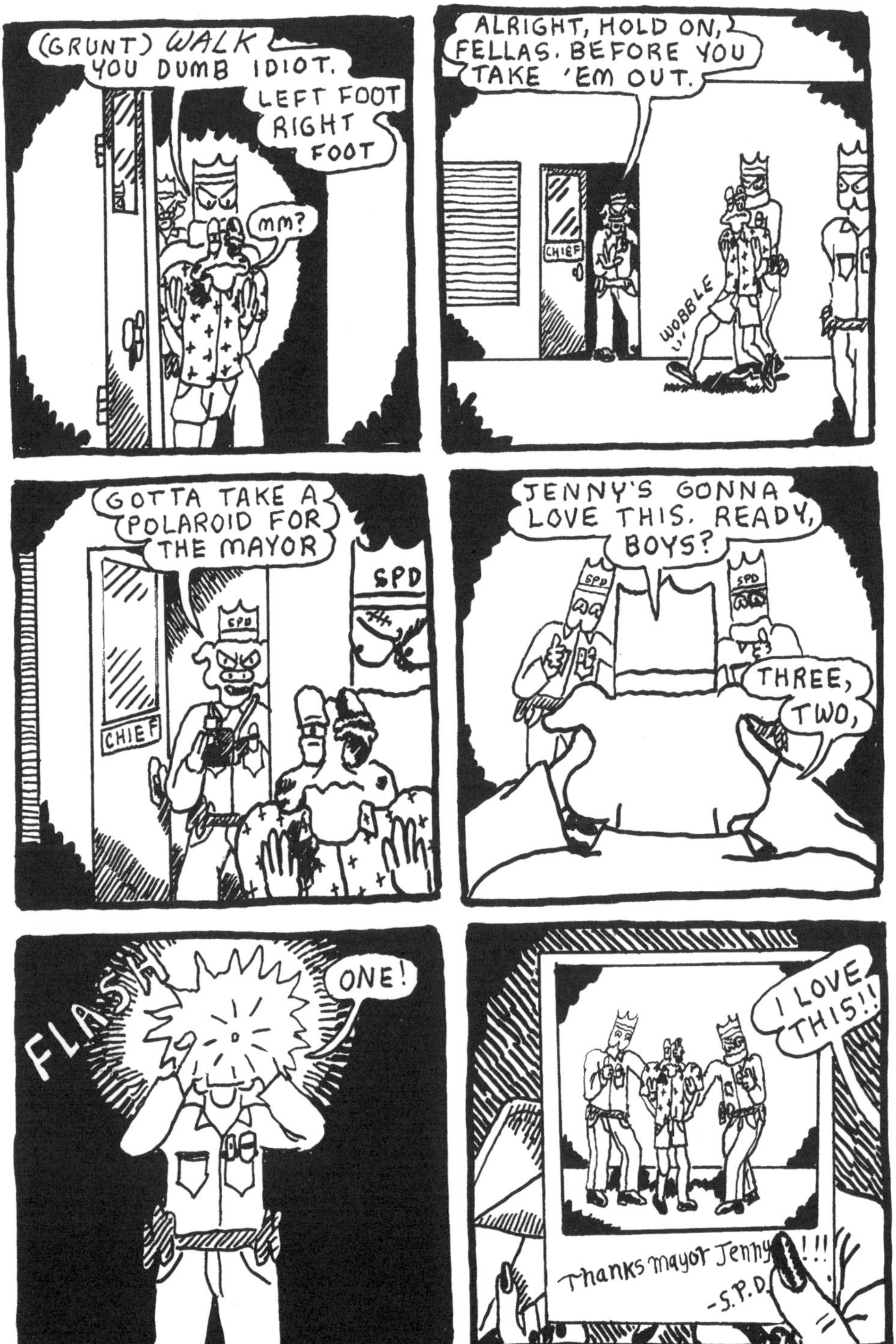
(GRUNT) WALK YOU DUMB IDIOT.
LEFT FOOT RIGHT FOOT
mm?
ALRIGHT, HOLD ON, FELLAS. BEFORE YOU TAKE 'EM OUT.
CHIEF
WOBBLE
GOTTA TAKE A POLAROID FOR THE MAYOR
SPD
CHIEF
SPD
JENNY'S GONNA LOVE THIS. READY, BOYS?
THREE, TWO,
FLASH
ONE!
I LOVE THIS!!
Thanks mayor Jenny!!!
-S.P.D.

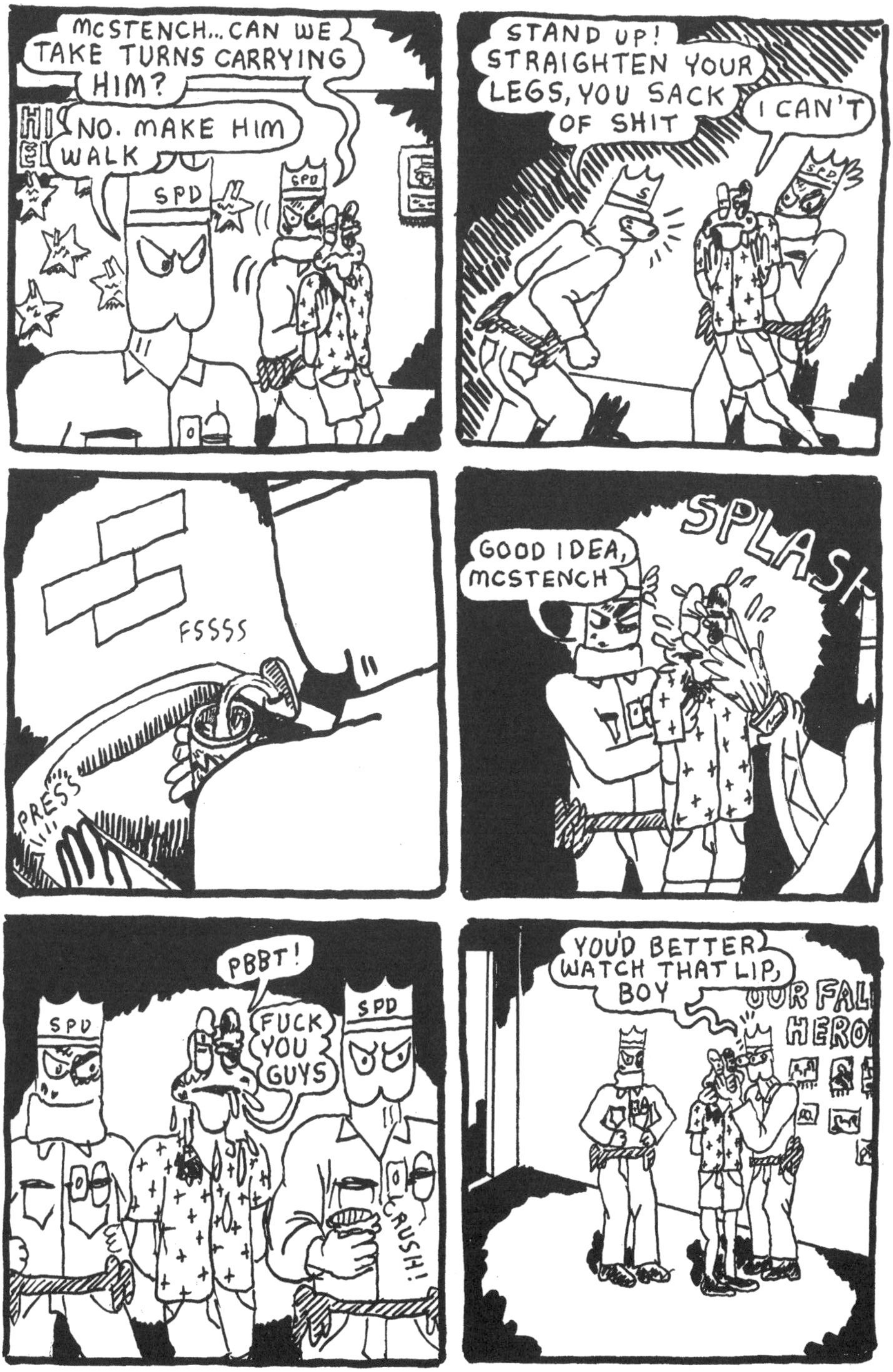
MCSTENCH... CAN WE TAKE TURNS CARRYING HIM?
NO. MAKE HIM WALK
SPD
SPD
STAND UP! STRAIGHTEN YOUR LEGS, YOU SACK OF SHIT
I CAN'T
FSSSS
PRESS
SPLASH
GOOD IDEA, MCSTENCH
PBBT!
FUCK YOU GUYS
SPD
SPD
CRUSH!
YOU'D BETTER WATCH THAT LIP, BOY

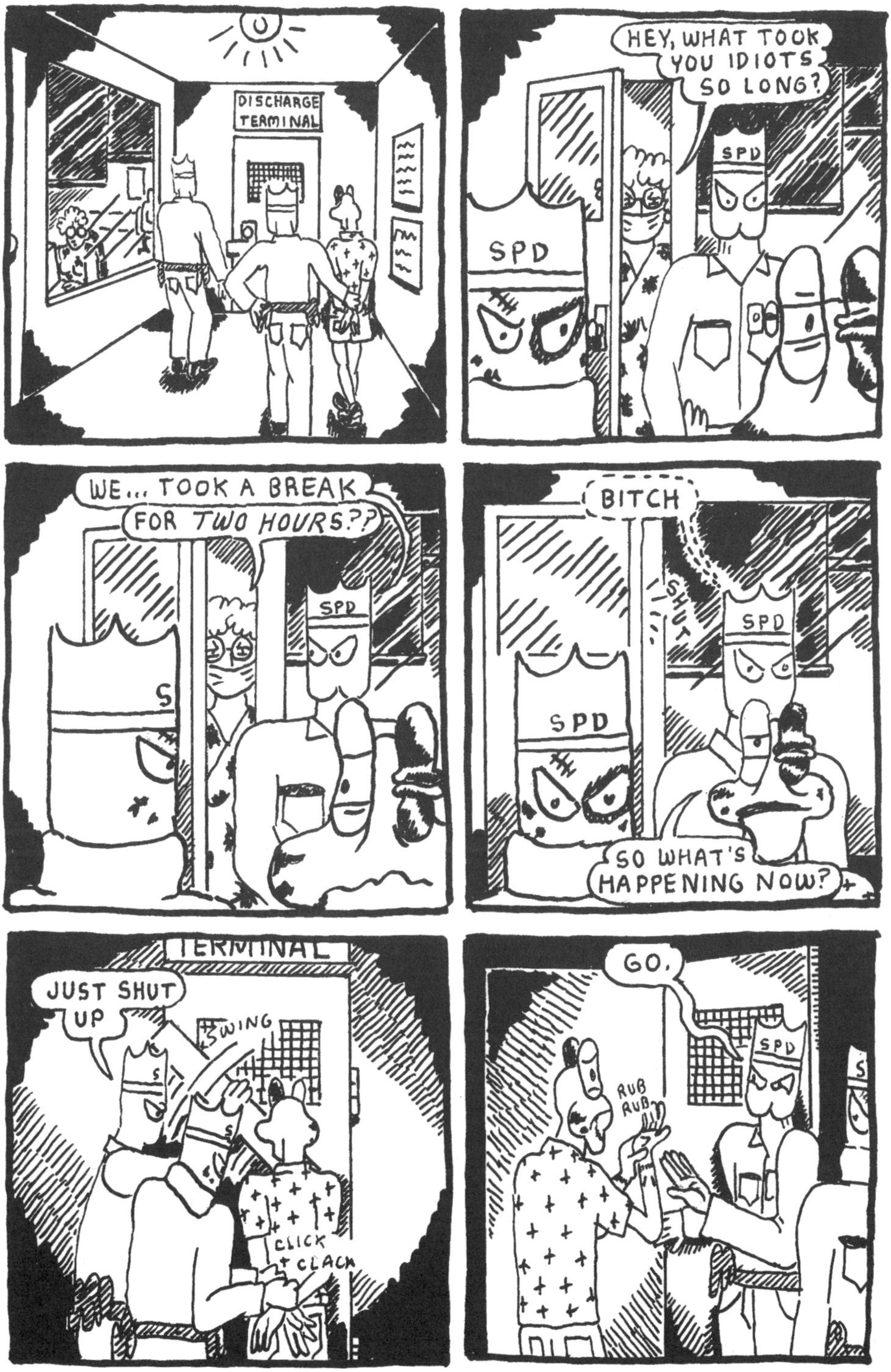
DISCHARGE TERMINAL
HEY, WHAT TOOK YOU IDIOTS SO LONG?
SPD
SPD
WE... TOOK A BREAK
FOR TWO HOURS??
SPD
BITCH
SHUT
SPD
SPD
SO WHAT'S HAPPENING NOW?
TERMINAL
JUST SHUT UP
SWING
CLICK CLACK
GO.
RUB RUB
SPD

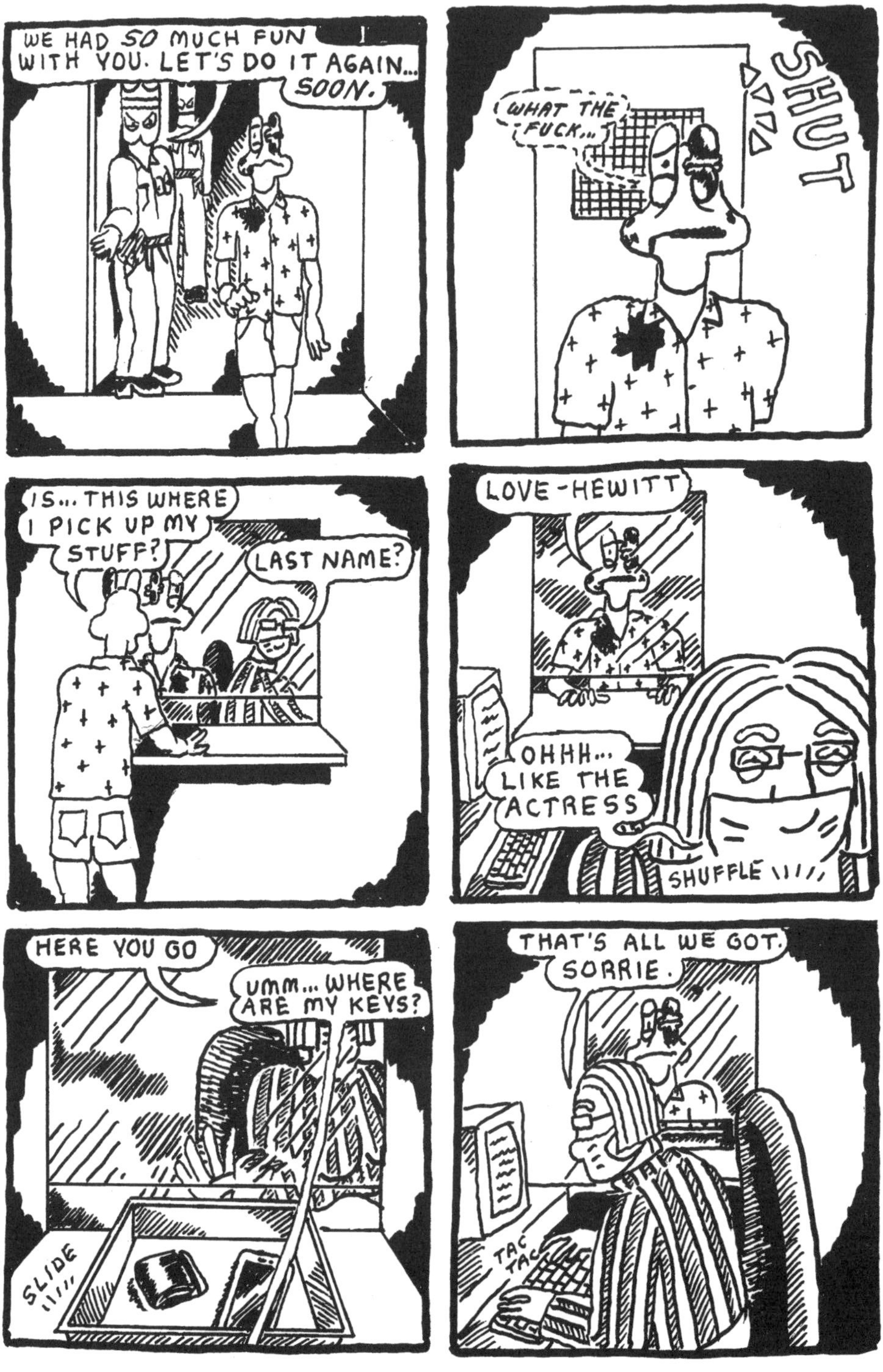
WE HAD SO MUCH FUN WITH YOU. LET'S DO IT AGAIN... SOON.
SHUT
WHAT THE FUCK...
IS... THIS WHERE I PICK UP MY STUFF?
LAST NAME?
LOVE-HEWITT
OHHH... LIKE THE ACTRESS
SHUFFLE
HERE YOU GO
UMM... WHERE ARE MY KEYS?
SLIDE
THAT'S ALL WE GOT. SORRIE.
TAC TAC

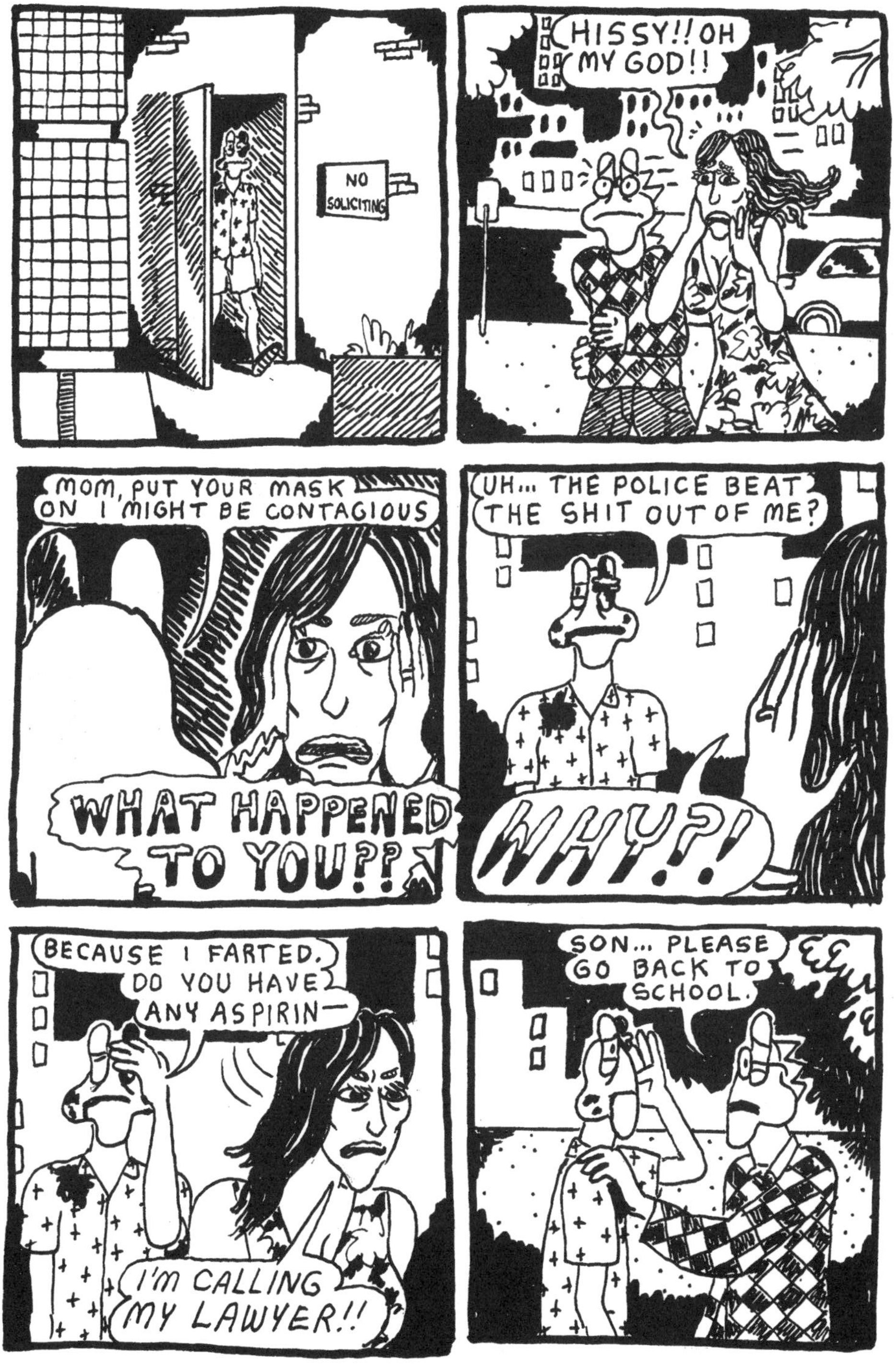
NO SOLICITING
HISSY!! OH MY GOD!!
MOM, PUT YOUR MASK ON I MIGHT BE CONTAGIOUS
WHAT HAPPENED TO YOU??
UH... THE POLICE BEAT THE SHIT OUT OF ME?
WHY?!
BECAUSE I FARTED. DO YOU HAVE ANY ASPIRIN—
I'M CALLING MY LAWYER!!
SON... PLEASE GO BACK TO SCHOOL.

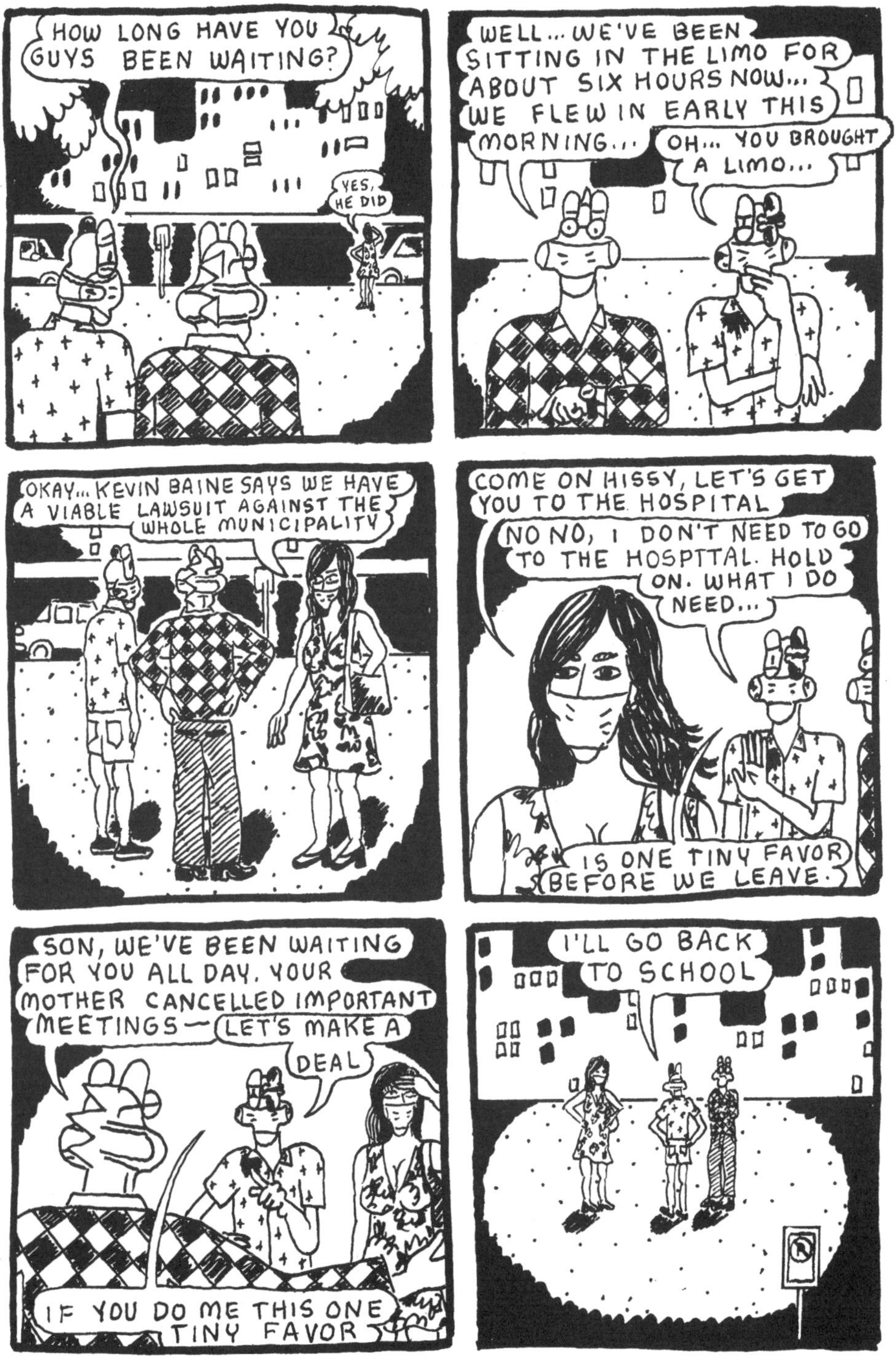
HOW LONG HAVE YOU GUYS BEEN WAITING?
YES, HE DID
WELL... WE'VE BEEN SITTING IN THE LIMO FOR ABOUT SIX HOURS NOW... WE FLEW IN EARLY THIS MORNING...
OH... YOU BROUGHT A LIMO...
OKAY... KEVIN BAINE SAYS WE HAVE A VIABLE LAWSUIT AGAINST THE WHOLE MUNICIPALITY
COME ON HISSY, LET'S GET YOU TO THE HOSPITAL
NO NO, I DON'T NEED TO GO TO THE HOSPTTAL. HOLD ON. WHAT I DO NEED...
IS ONE TINY FAVOR BEFORE WE LEAVE.
SON, WE'VE BEEN WAITING FOR YOU ALL DAY. YOUR MOTHER CANCELLED IMPORTANT MEETINGS—
LET'S MAKE A DEAL
IF YOU DO ME THIS ONE TINY FAVOR
I'LL GO BACK TO SCHOOL

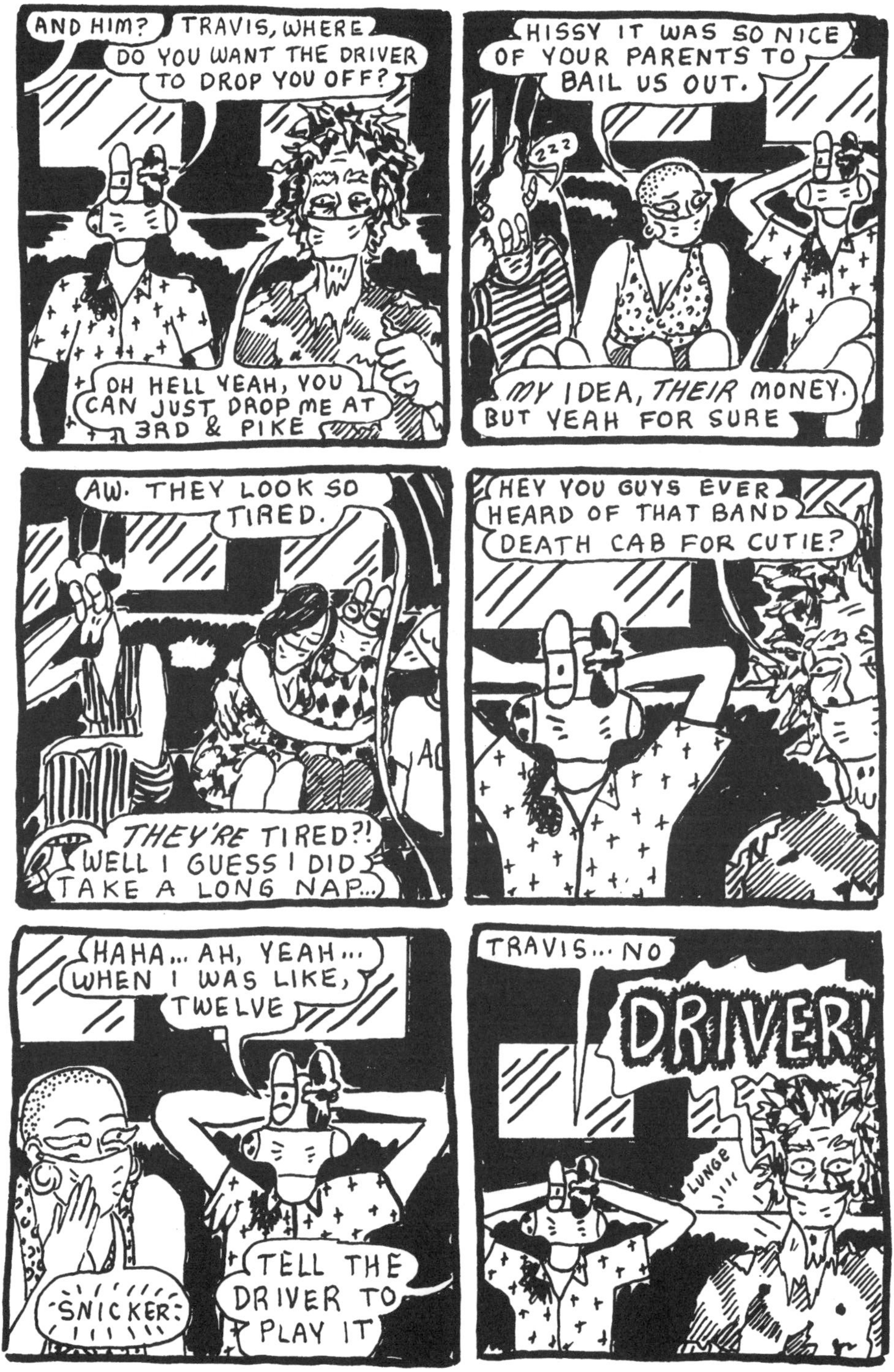
AND HIM?
TRAVIS, WHERE DO YOU WANT THE DRIVER TO DROP YOU OFF?
OH HELL YEAH, YOU CAN JUST DROP ME AT 3RD & PIKE
HISSY IT WAS SO NICE OF YOUR PARENTS TO BAIL US OUT.
ZZZ
MY IDEA, THEIR MONEY. BUT YEAH FOR SURE
AW. THEY LOOK SO TIRED.
THEY'RE TIRED?! WELL I GUESS I DID TAKE A LONG NAP...
HEY YOU GUYS EVER HEARD OF THAT BAND DEATH CAB FOR CUTIE?
HAHA... AH, YEAH... WHEN I WAS LIKE, TWELVE
SNICKER
TELL THE DRIVER TO PLAY IT
TRAVIS... NO
DRIVER!
LUNGE

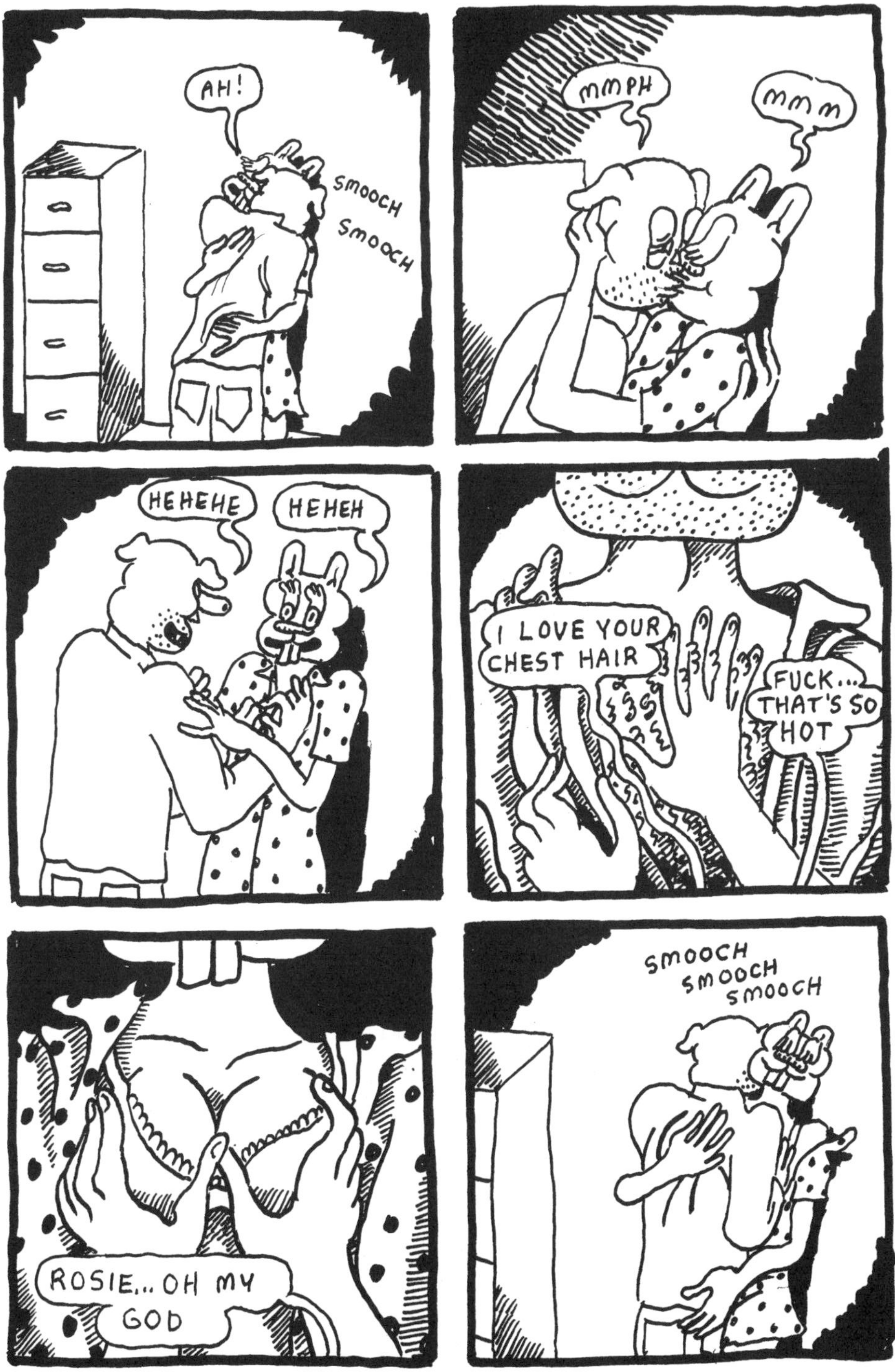
AH!
SMOOCH
SMOOCH
MMPH
MMM
HEHEHE
HEHEH
I LOVE YOUR CHEST HAIR
FUCK... THAT'S SO HOT
ROSIE... OH MY GOD
SMOOCH
SMOOCH
SMOOCH

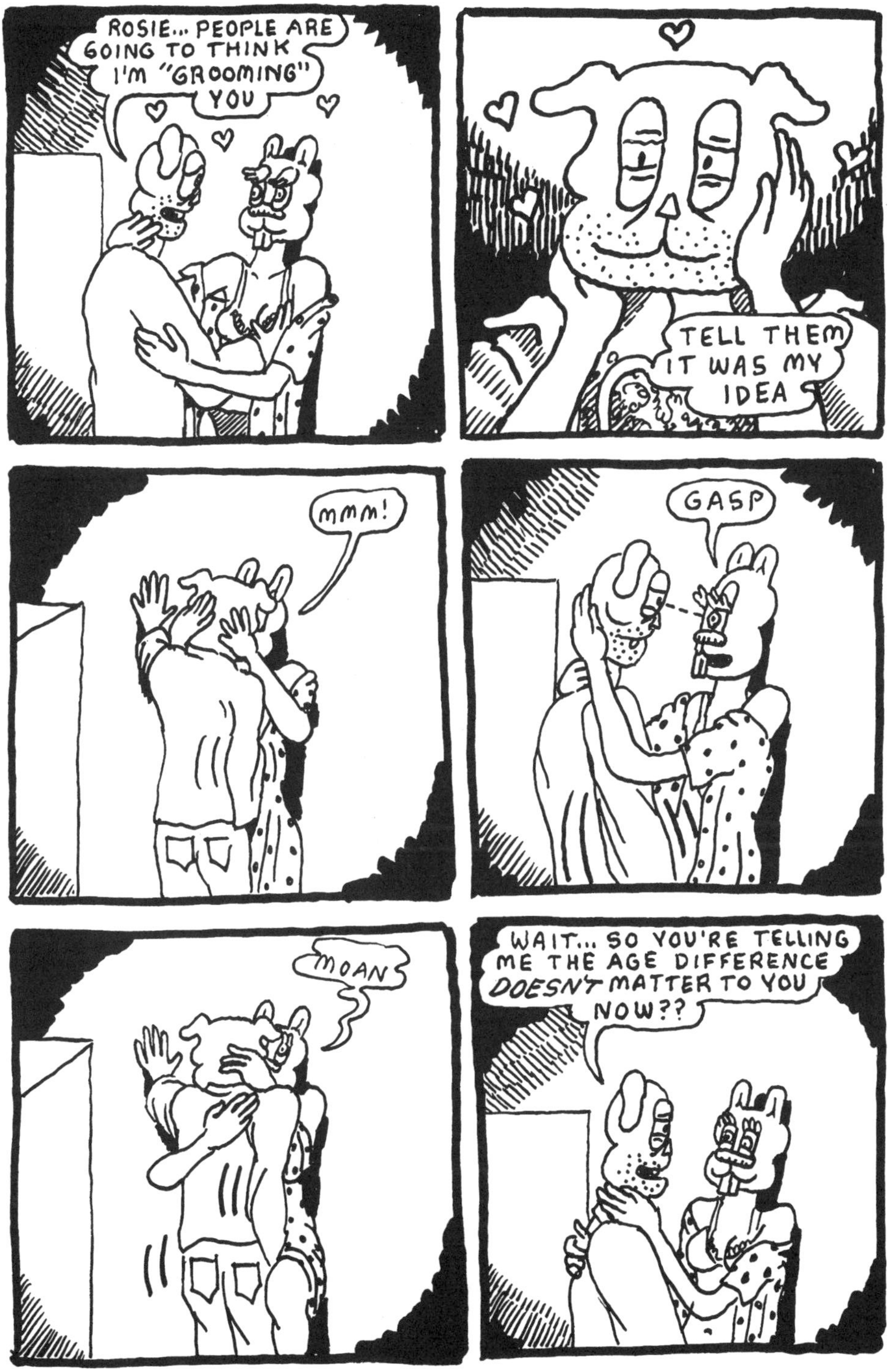
ROSIE... PEOPLE ARE GOING TO THINK I'M "GROOMING" YOU
TELL THEM IT WAS MY IDEA
MMM!
GASP
MOAN
WAIT... SO YOU'RE TELLING ME THE AGE DIFFERENCE DOESN'T MATTER TO YOU NOW??

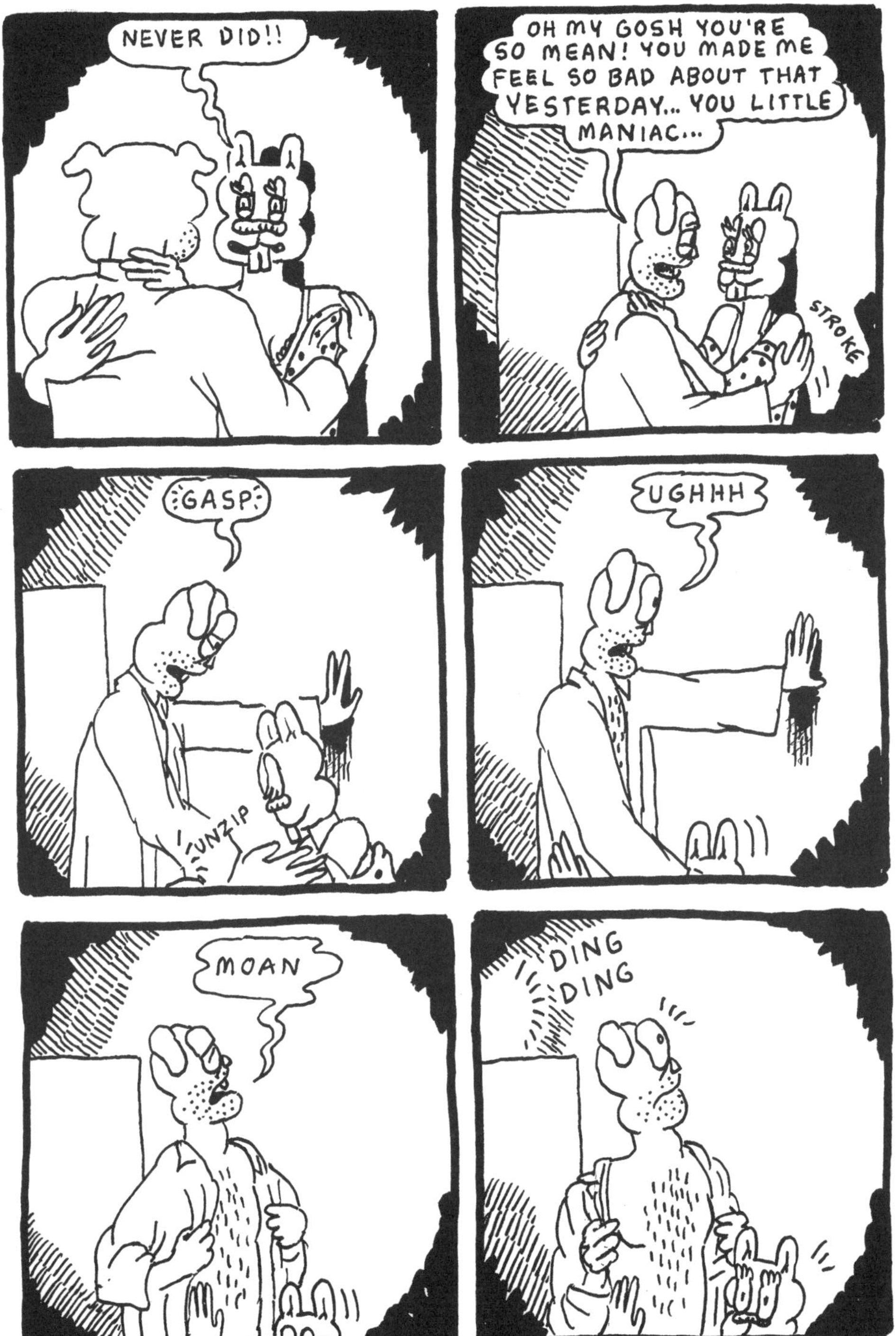
NEVER DID!!
OH MY GOSH YOU'RE SO MEAN! YOU MADE ME FEEL SO BAD ABOUT THAT YESTERDAY... YOU LITTLE MANIAC...
STROKE
GASP
UNZIP
UGHHH
MOAN
DING DING

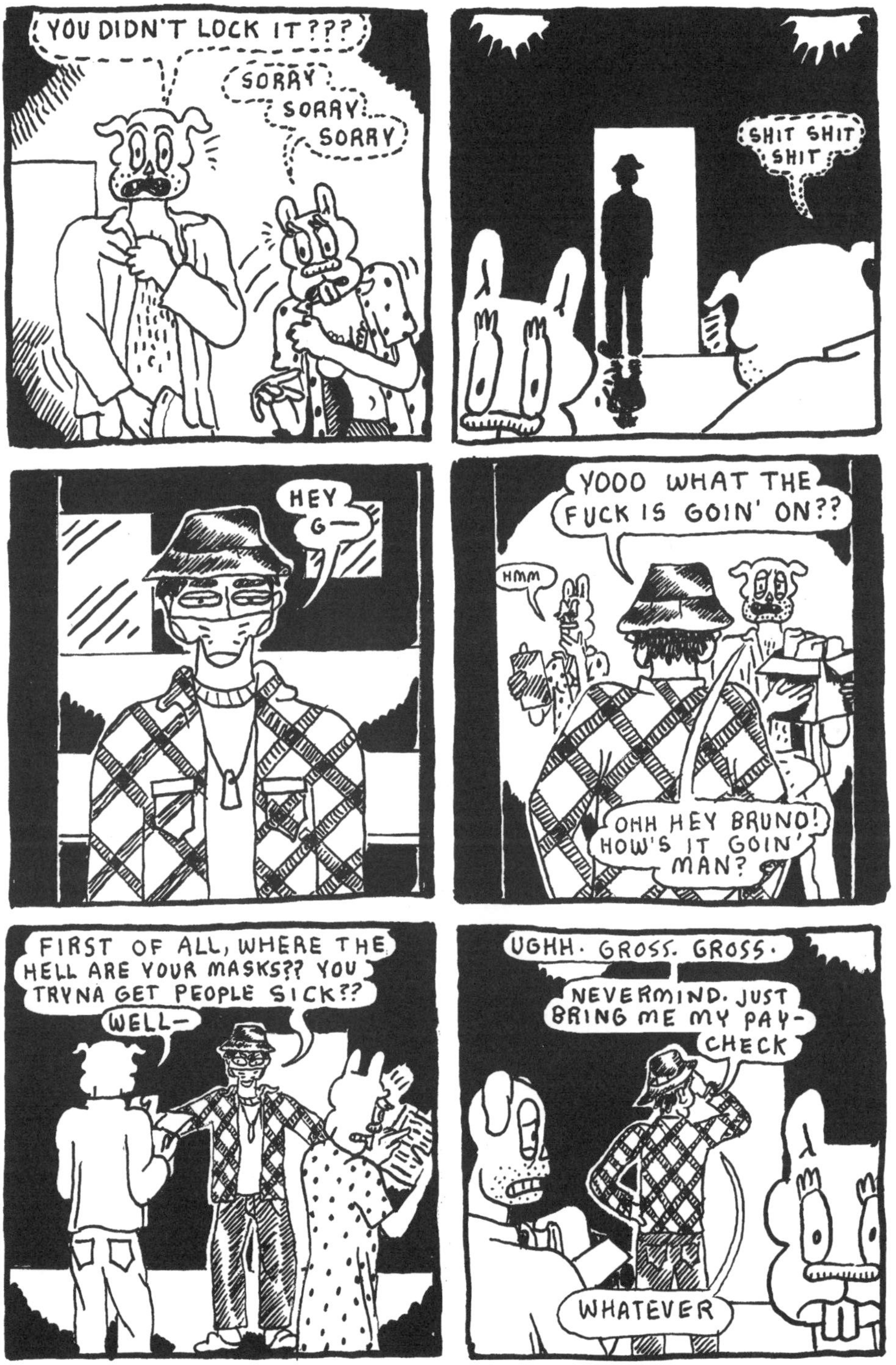
YOU DIDN'T LOCK IT???
SORRY SORRY SORRY
SHIT SHIT SHIT
HEY G—
YOOO WHAT THE FUCK IS GOIN' ON??
HMM
OHH HEY BRUNO! HOW'S IT GOIN' MAN?
FIRST OF ALL, WHERE THE HELL ARE YOUR MASKS?? YOU TRYNA GET PEOPLE SICK??
WELL—
UGHH. GROSS. GROSS.
NEVERMIND. JUST BRING ME MY PAY-CHECK
WHATEVER

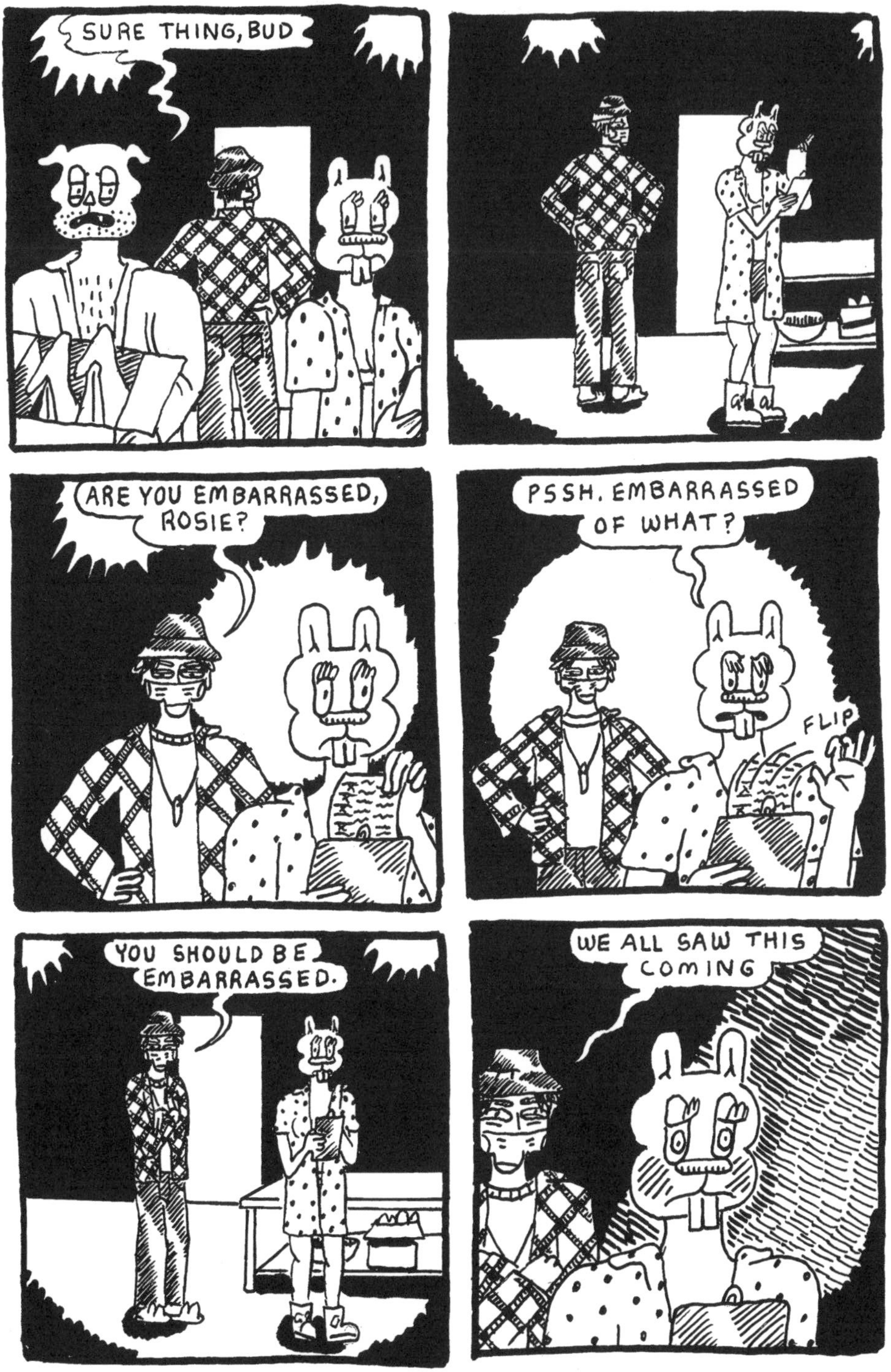
SURE THING, BUD
ARE YOU EMBARRASSED, ROSIE?
PSSH. EMBARRASSED OF WHAT?
FLIP
YOU SHOULD BE EMBARRASSED.
WE ALL SAW THIS COMING

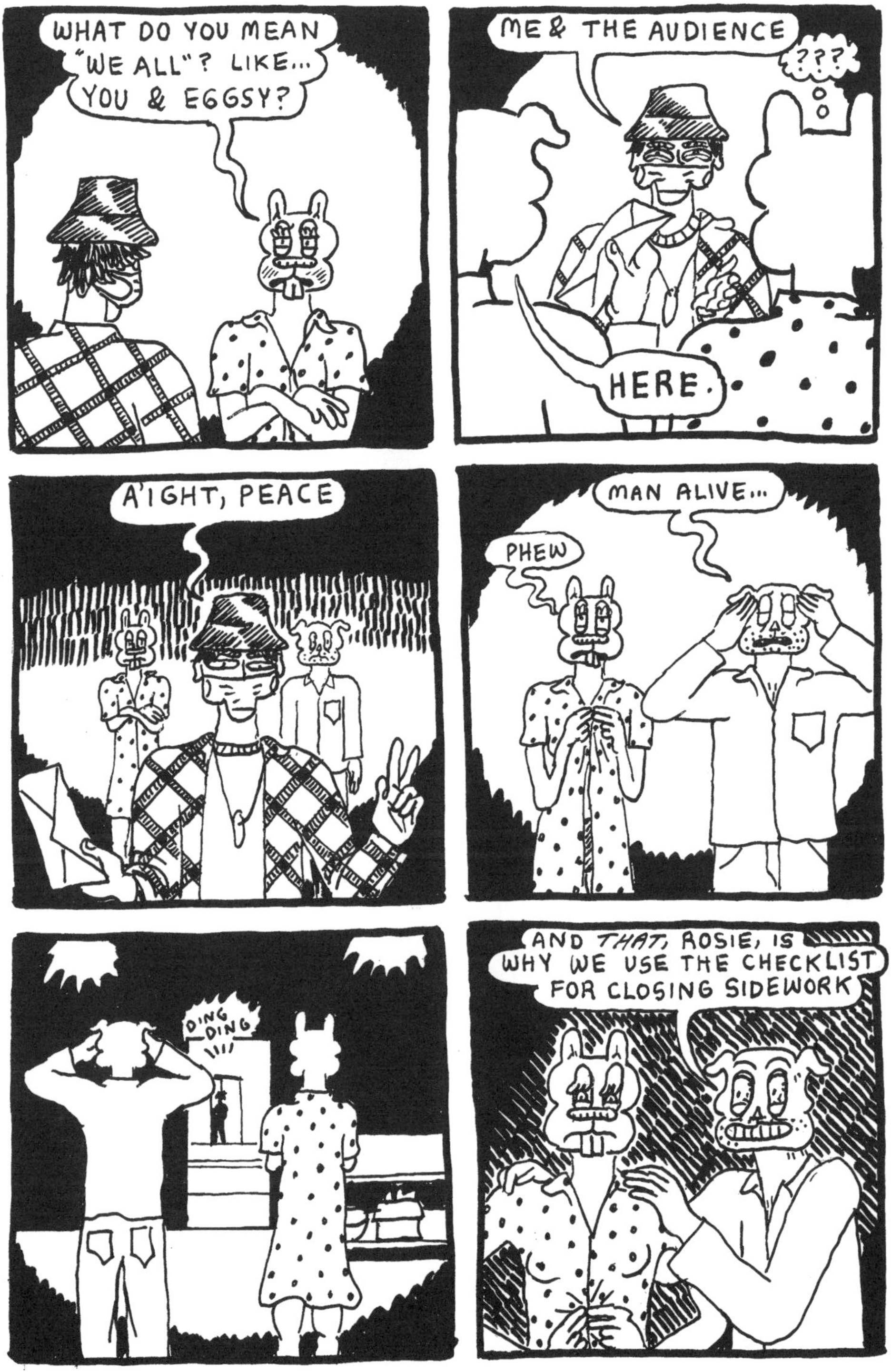
WHAT DO YOU MEAN "WE ALL"? LIKE... YOU & EGGSY?
ME & THE AUDIENCE
???
HERE.
A'IGHT, PEACE
MAN ALIVE...
PHEW
DING DING
AND THAT, ROSIE, IS WHY WE USE THE CHECKLIST FOR CLOSING SIDEWORK

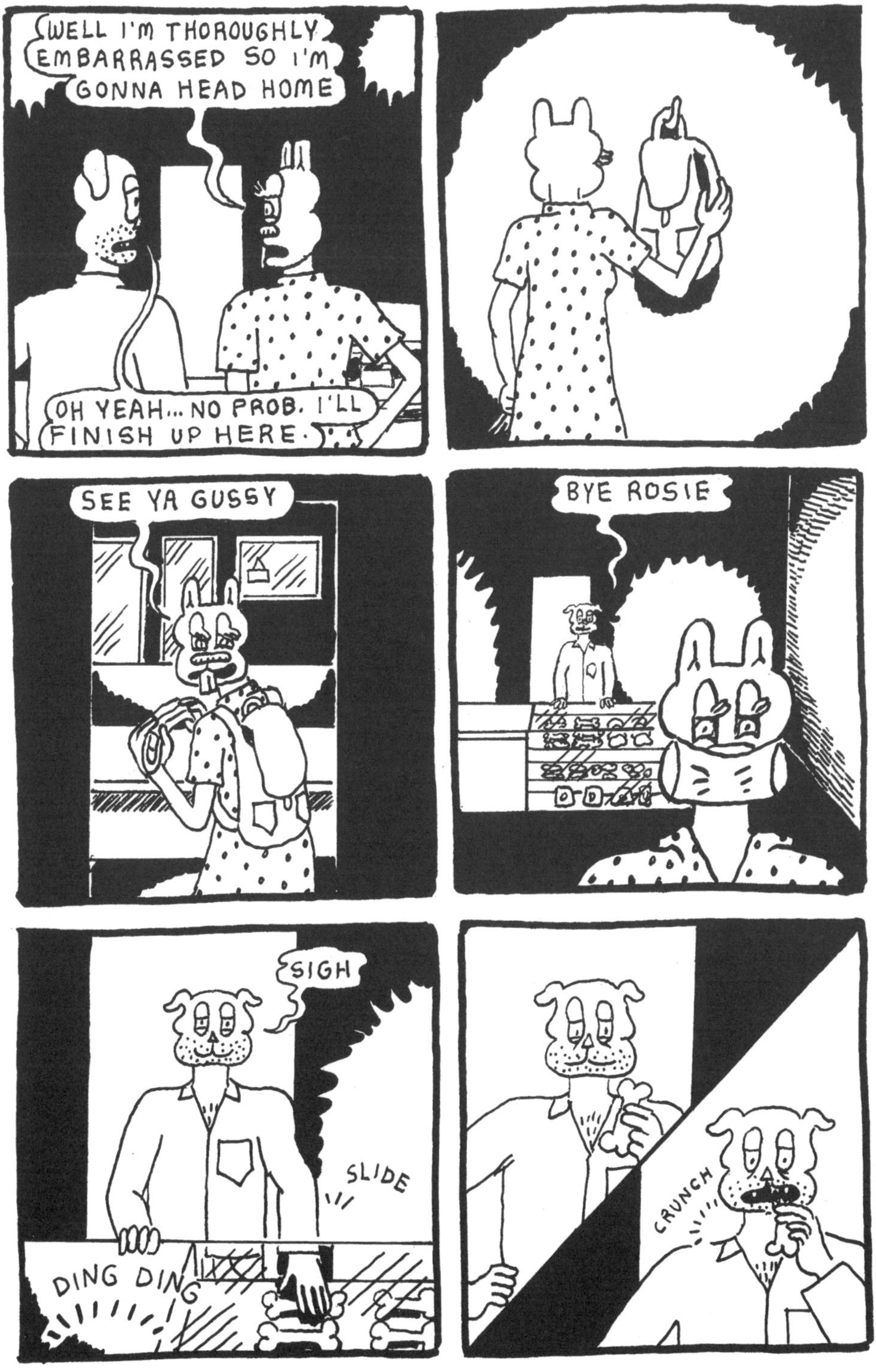
WELL I'M THOROUGHLY EMBARRASSED SO I'M GONNA HEAD HOME
OH YEAH... NO PROB. I'LL FINISH UP HERE.
SEE YA GUSSY
BYE ROSIE
SIGH
SLIDE
DING DING
CRUNCH

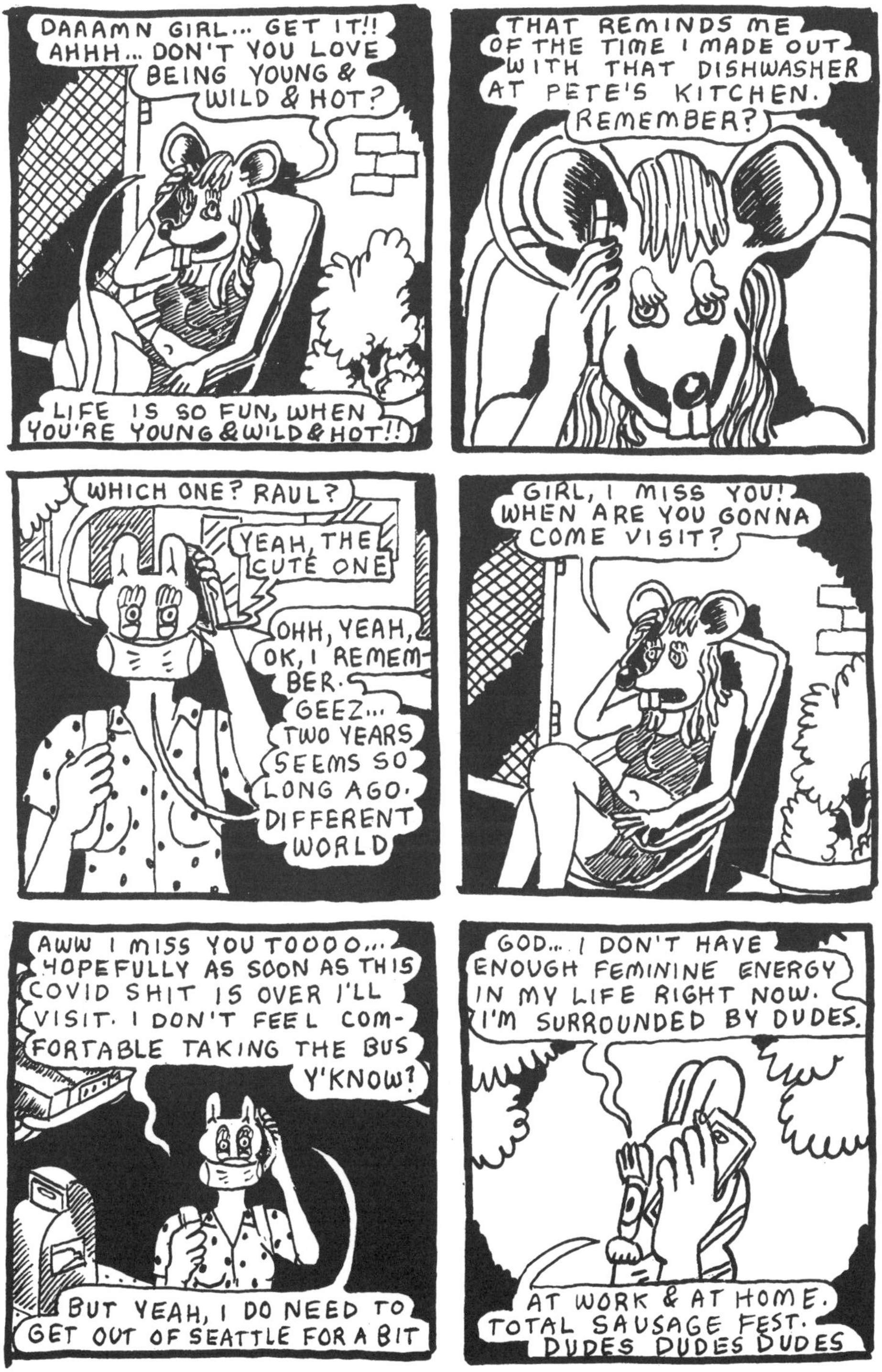
DAAAMN GIRL... GET IT!! AHHH... DON'T YOU LOVE BEING YOUNG & WILD & HOT?
LIFE IS SO FUN, WHEN YOU'RE YOUNG & WILD & HOT!!
THAT REMINDS ME OF THE TIME I MADE OUT WITH THAT DISHWASHER AT PETE'S KITCHEN. REMEMBER?
WHICH ONE? RAUL?
YEAH, THE CUTE ONE
OHH, YEAH, OK, I REMEMBER.
GEEZ... TWO YEARS SEEMS SO LONG AGO. DIFFERENT WORLD
GIRL, I MISS YOU! WHEN ARE YOU GONNA COME VISIT?
AWW I MISS YOU TOOOO... HOPEFULLY AS SOON AS THIS COVID SHIT IS OVER I'LL VISIT. I DON'T FEEL COMFORTABLE TAKING THE BUS Y'KNOW?
BUT YEAH, I DO NEED TO GET OUT OF SEATTLE FOR A BIT
GOD... I DON'T HAVE ENOUGH FEMININE ENERGY IN MY LIFE RIGHT NOW. I'M SURROUNDED BY DUDES.
AT WORK & AT HOME. TOTAL SAUSAGE FEST. DUDES DUDES DUDES

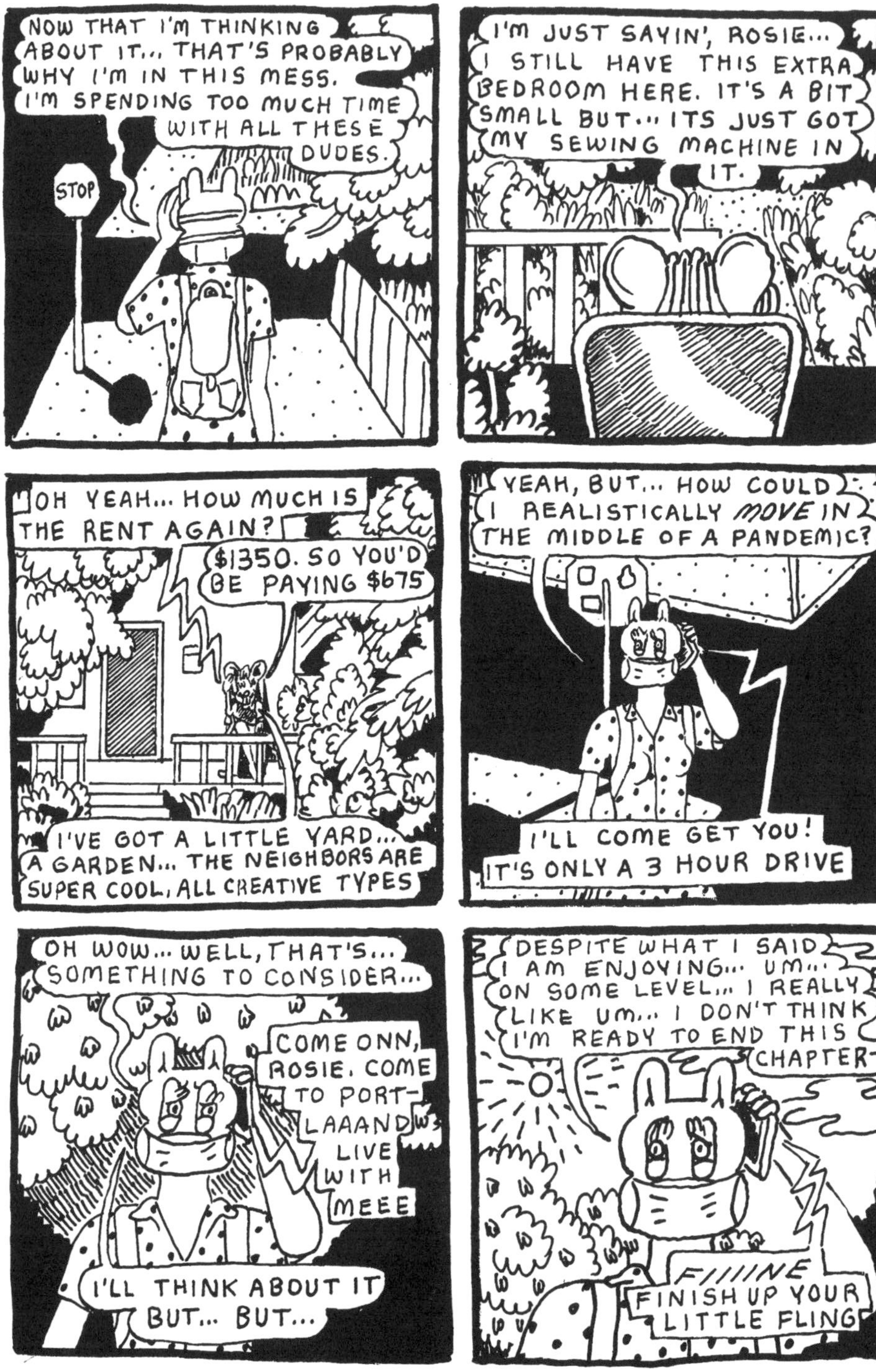
NOW THAT I'M THINKING ABOUT IT... THAT'S PROBABLY WHY I'M IN THIS MESS. I'M SPENDING TOO MUCH TIME WITH ALL THESE DUDES.
STOP
I'M JUST SAYIN', ROSIE... I STILL HAVE THIS EXTRA BEDROOM HERE. IT'S A BIT SMALL BUT... ITS JUST GOT MY SEWING MACHINE IN IT.
OH YEAH... HOW MUCH IS THE RENT AGAIN?
$1350. SO YOU'D BE PAYING $675
I'VE GOT A LITTLE YARD... A GARDEN... THE NEIGHBORS ARE SUPER COOL, ALL CREATIVE TYPES
YEAH, BUT... HOW COULD I REALISTICALLY *MOVE* IN THE MIDDLE OF A PANDEMIC?
I'LL COME GET YOU! IT'S ONLY A 3 HOUR DRIVE
OH WOW... WELL, THAT'S... SOMETHING TO CONSIDER...
COME ONN, ROSIE. COME TO PORT-LAAAND LIVE WITH MEEE
I'LL THINK ABOUT IT BUT... BUT...
DESPITE WHAT I SAID I AM ENJOYING... UM... ON SOME LEVEL... I REALLY LIKE UM... I DON'T THINK I'M READY TO END THIS CHAPTER
FIIIINE FINISH UP YOUR LITTLE FLING

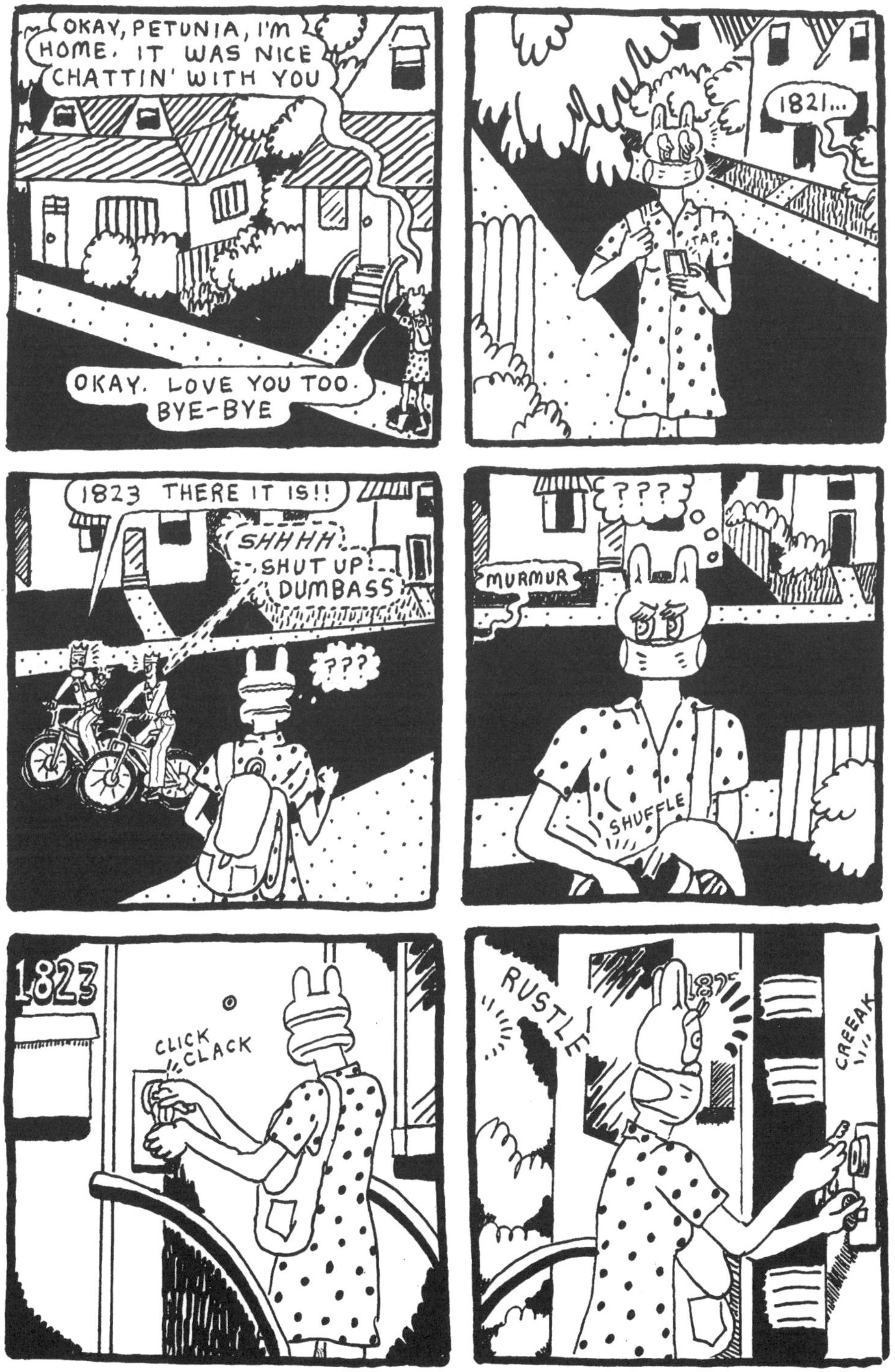
OKAY, PETUNIA, I'M HOME. IT WAS NICE CHATTIN' WITH YOU
OKAY. LOVE YOU TOO. BYE-BYE
1821...
TAP
1823 THERE IT IS!!
SHHHH SHUT UP DUMBASS
???
???
MURMUR
SHUFFLE
1823
CLICK CLACK
RUSTLE
CREEAK

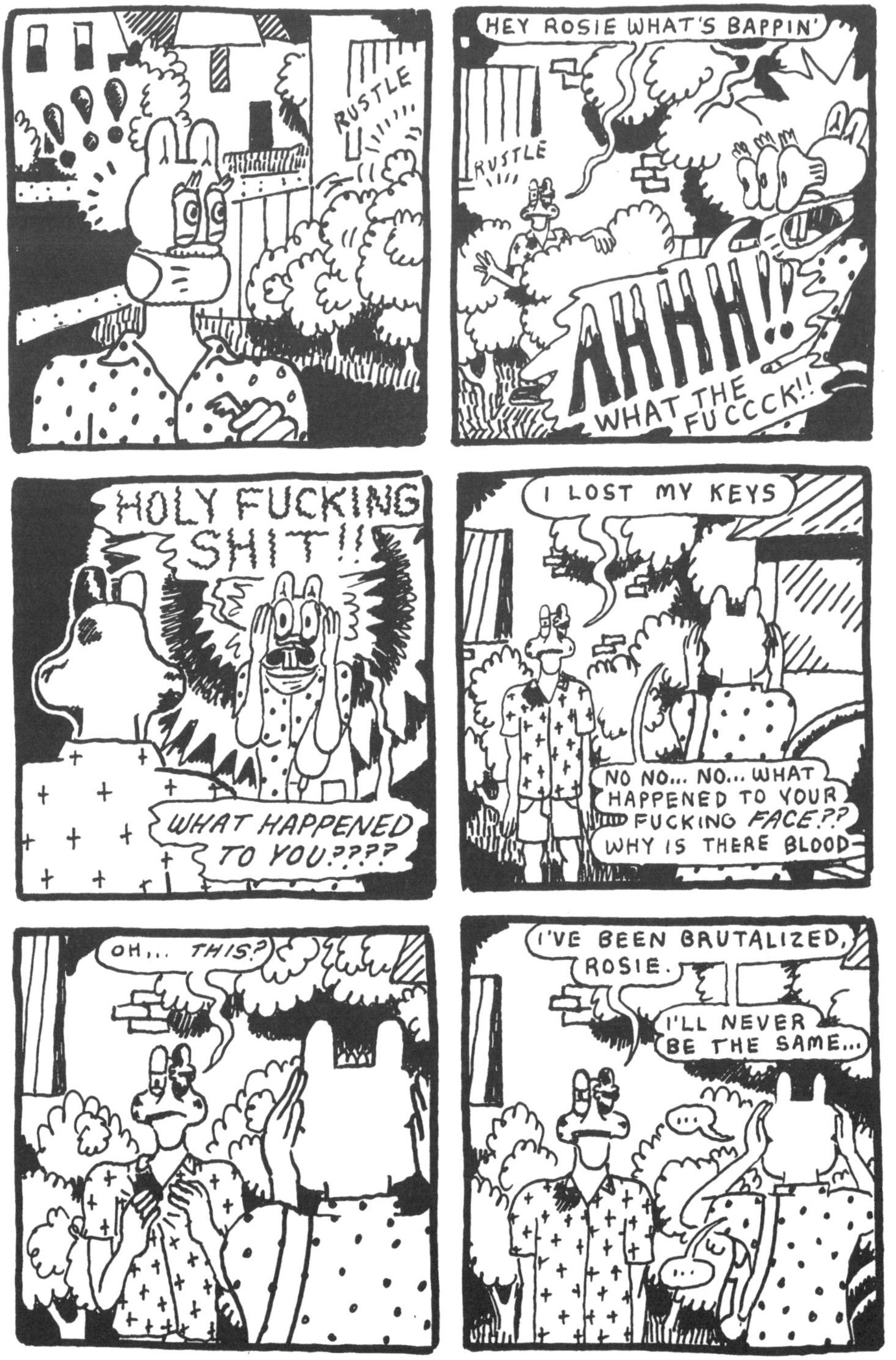
RUSTLE
HEY ROSIE WHAT'S BAPPIN'
RUSTLE
AHHH!!
WHAT THE FUCCCK!!
HOLY FUCKING SHIT!!
WHAT HAPPENED TO YOU????
I LOST MY KEYS
NO NO... NO... WHAT HAPPENED TO YOUR FUCKING FACE?? WHY IS THERE BLOOD
OH... THIS?
I'VE BEEN BRUTALIZED, ROSIE.
I'LL NEVER BE THE SAME...
...
...

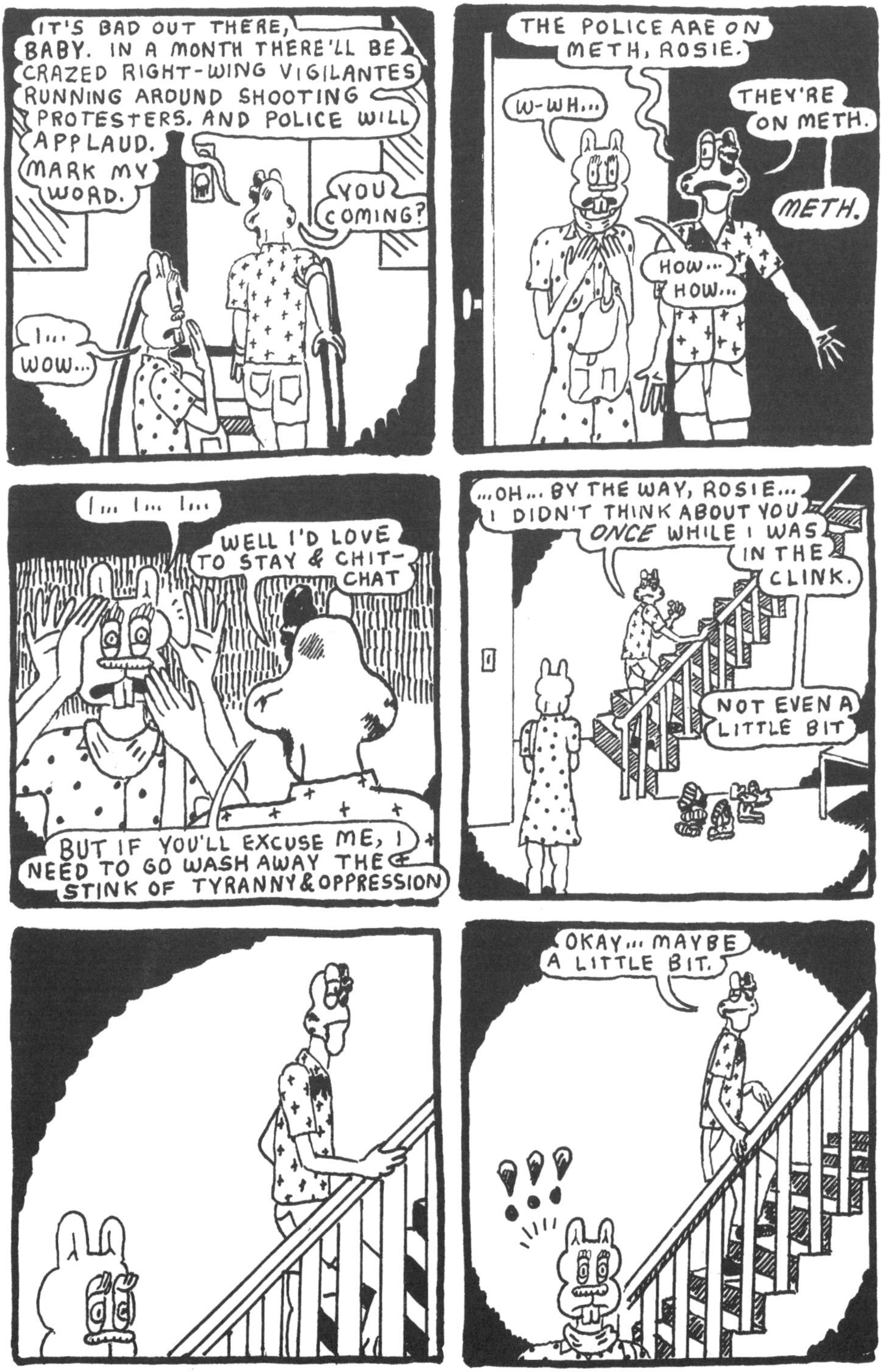
IT'S BAD OUT THERE, BABY. IN A MONTH THERE'LL BE CRAZED RIGHT-WING VIGILANTES RUNNING AROUND SHOOTING PROTESTERS. AND POLICE WILL APPLAUD.
MARK MY WORD.
YOU COMING?
I... WOW...
THE POLICE ARE ON METH, ROSIE.
W-WH...
THEY'RE ON METH.
METH.
HOW... HOW...
I... I... I...
WELL I'D LOVE TO STAY & CHIT-CHAT
BUT IF YOU'LL EXCUSE ME, I NEED TO GO WASH AWAY THE STINK OF TYRANNY & OPPRESSION
...OH... BY THE WAY, ROSIE... I DIDN'T THINK ABOUT YOU ONCE WHILE I WAS IN THE CLINK.
NOT EVEN A LITTLE BIT
OKAY... MAYBE A LITTLE BIT.

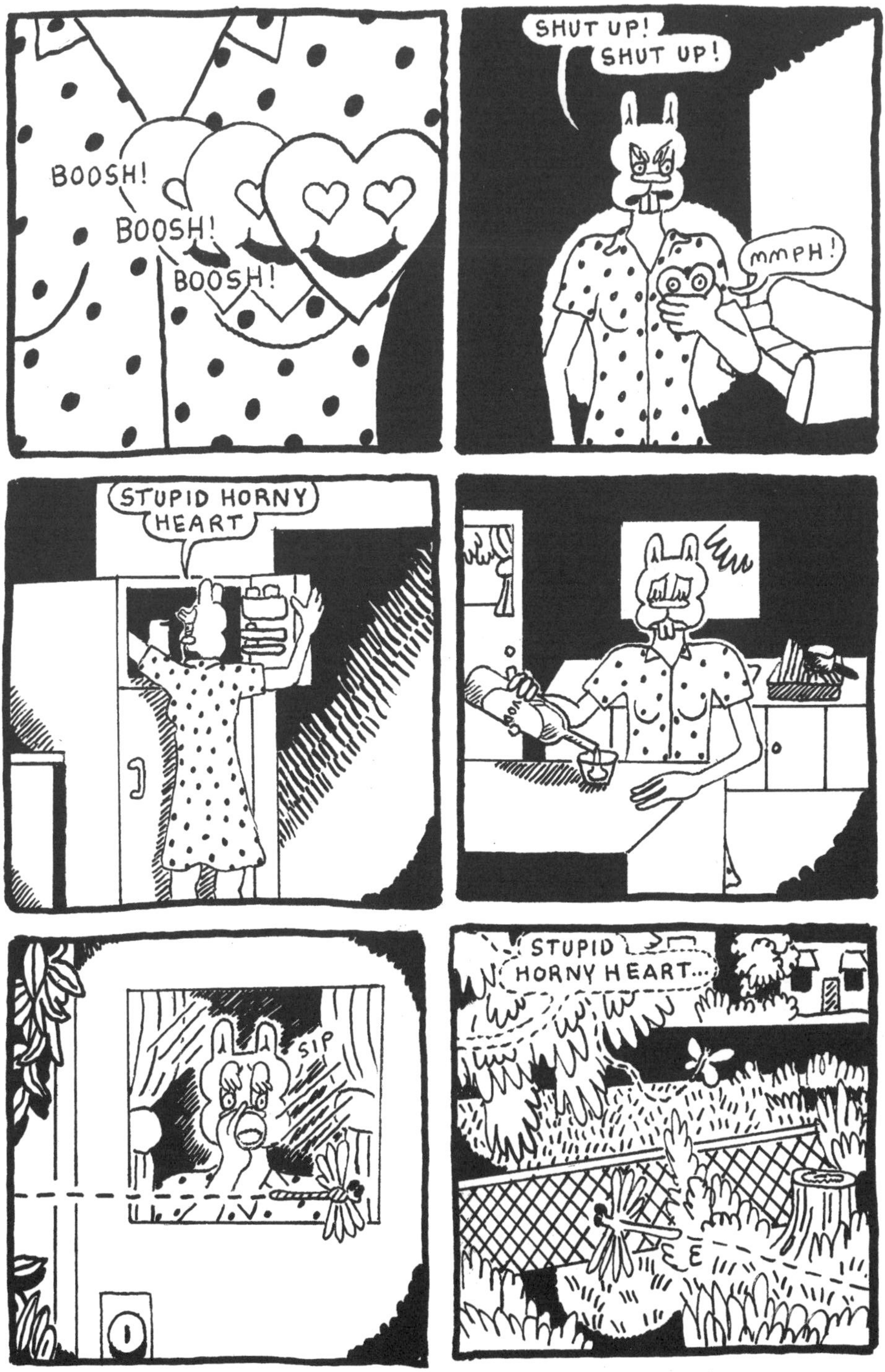
BOOSH!
BOOSH!
BOOSH!
SHUT UP!
SHUT UP!
MMPH!
STUPID HORNY HEART
SIP
STUPID HORNY HEART...
E

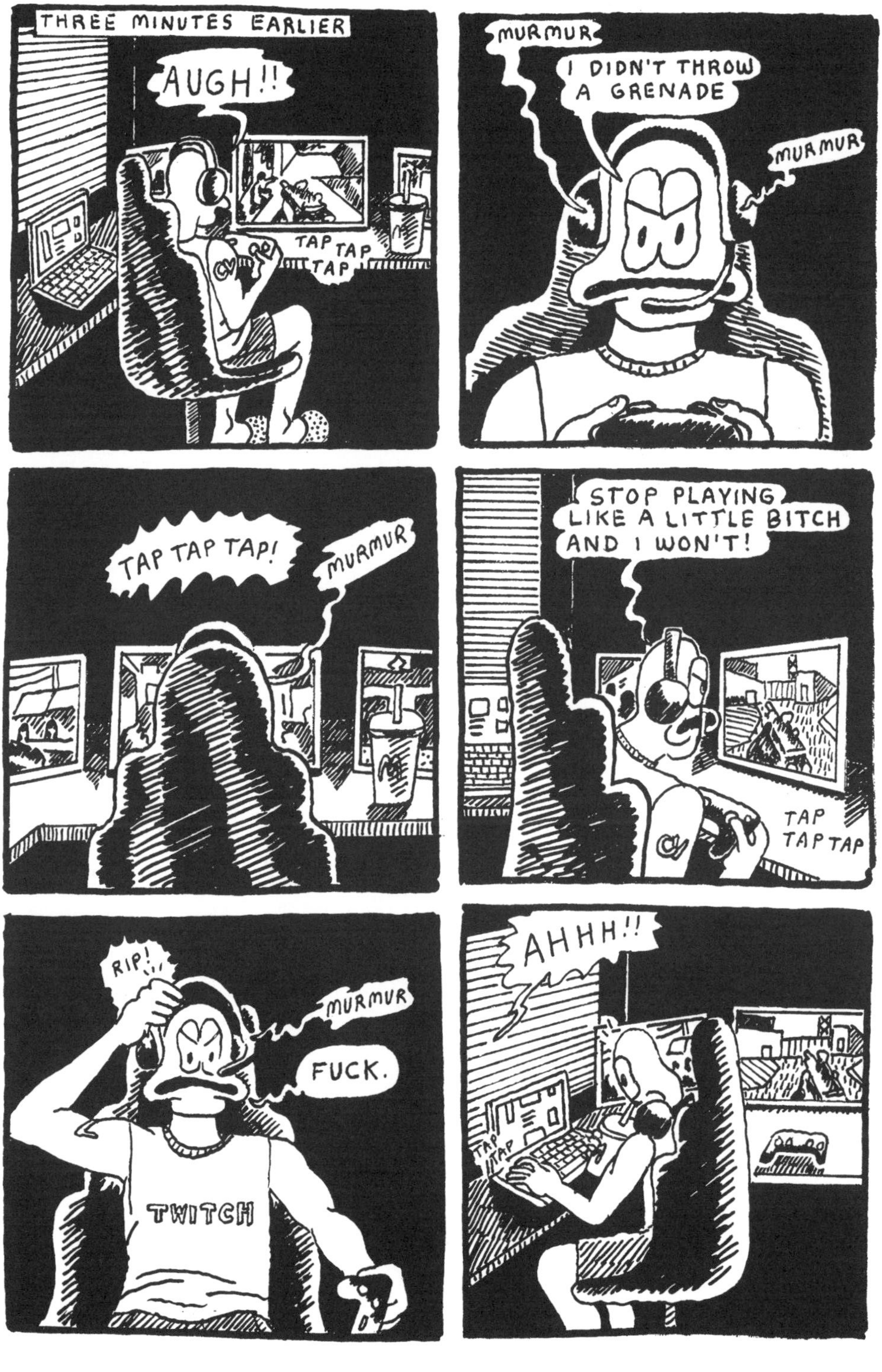
THREE MINUTES EARLIER
AUGH!!
TAP TAP TAP
MURMUR
I DIDN'T THROW A GRENADE
MURMUR
TAP TAP TAP!
MURMUR
STOP PLAYING LIKE A LITTLE BITCH AND I WON'T!
TAP TAP TAP
RIP!
MURMUR
FUCK.
TWITCH
AHHH!!
TAP TAP

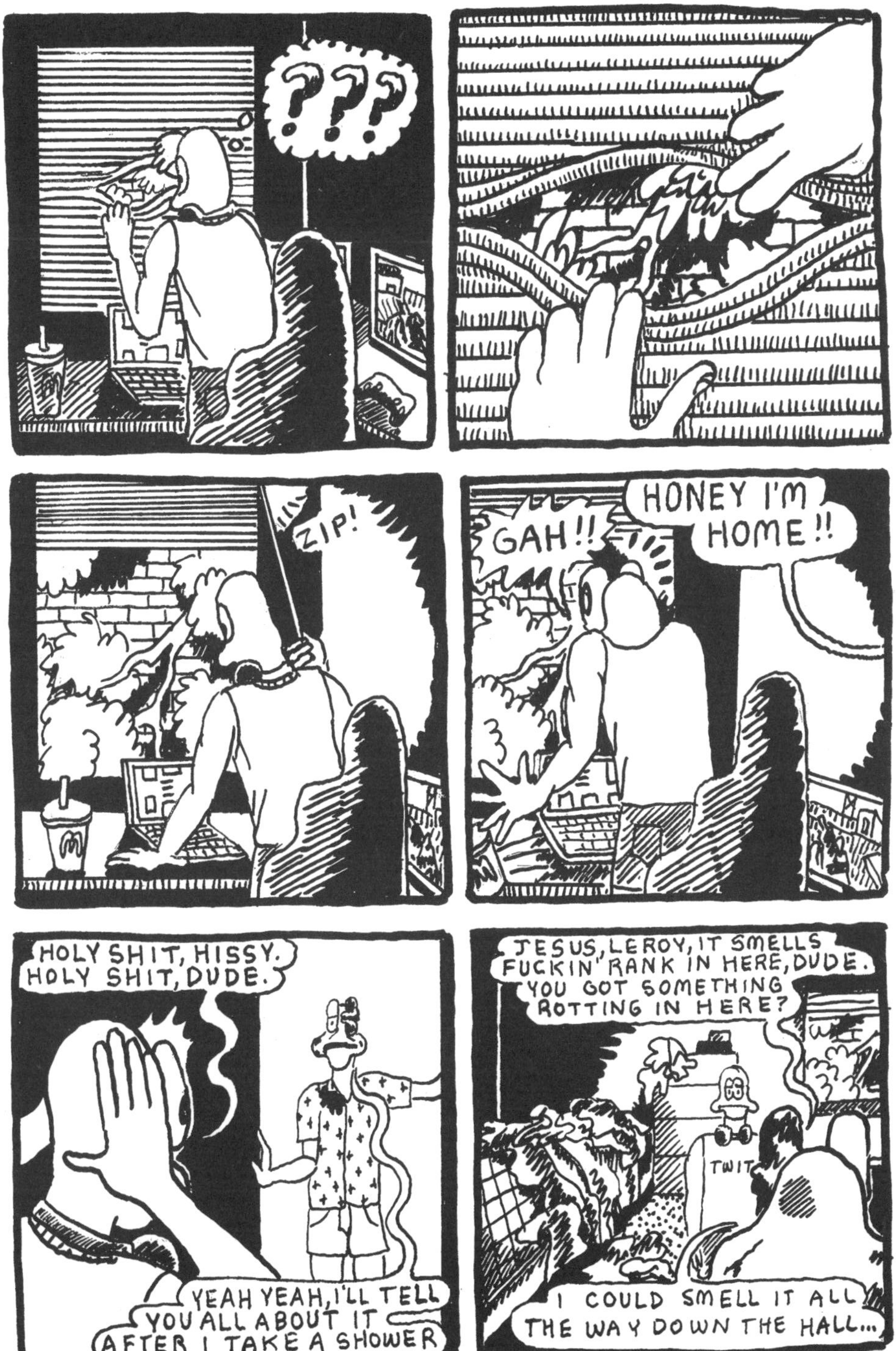
???
ZIP!
GAH!!
HONEY I'M HOME!!
HOLY SHIT, HISSY. HOLY SHIT, DUDE.
YEAH YEAH, I'LL TELL YOU ALL ABOUT IT AFTER I TAKE A SHOWER
JESUS, LEROY, IT SMELLS FUCKIN' RANK IN HERE, DUDE. YOU GOT SOMETHING ROTTING IN HERE?
TWIT
I COULD SMELL IT ALL THE WAY DOWN THE HALL...

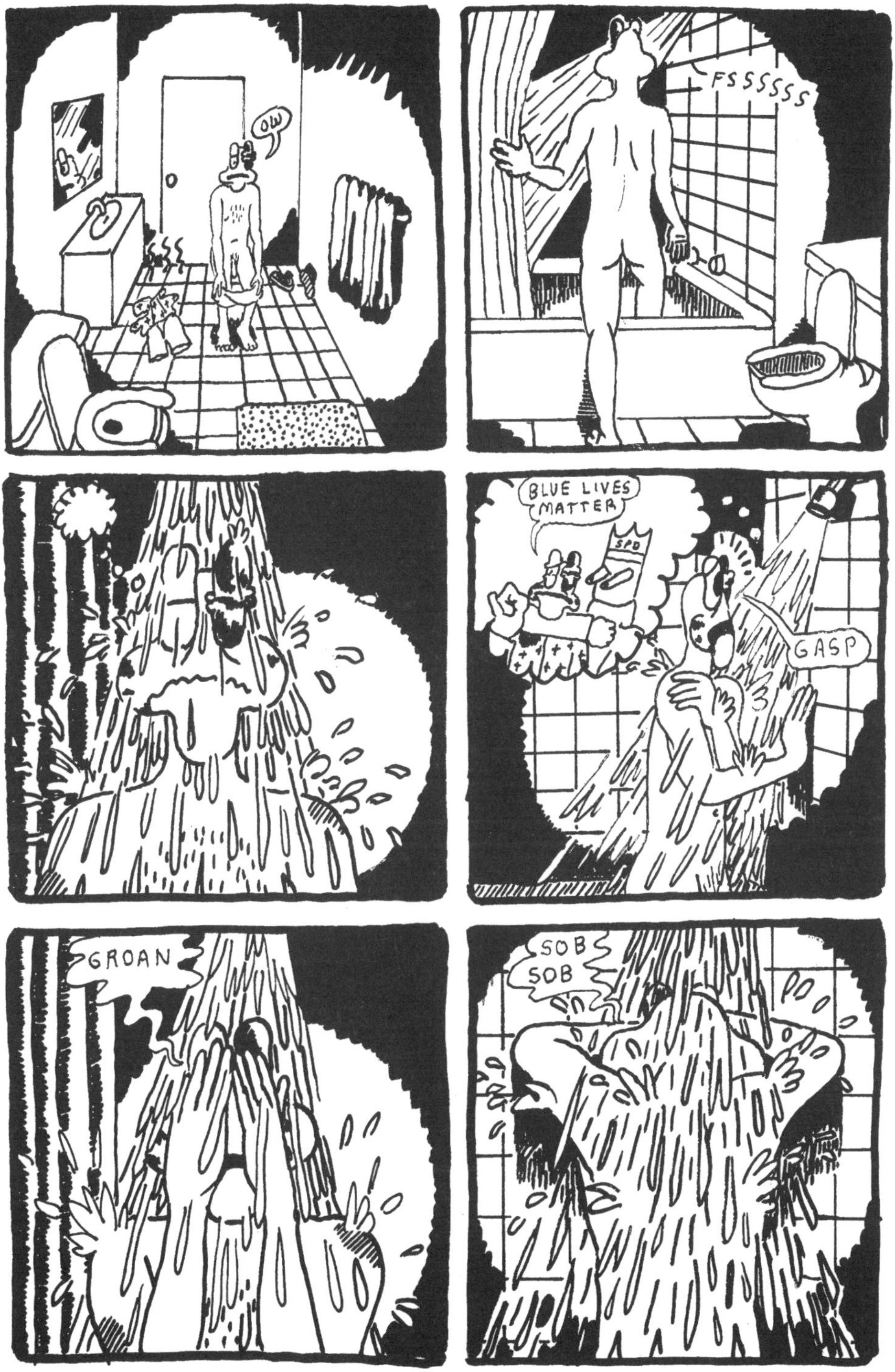
OW
FSSSSSS
BLUE LIVES MATTER
SPD
GASP
GROAN
SOB
SOB

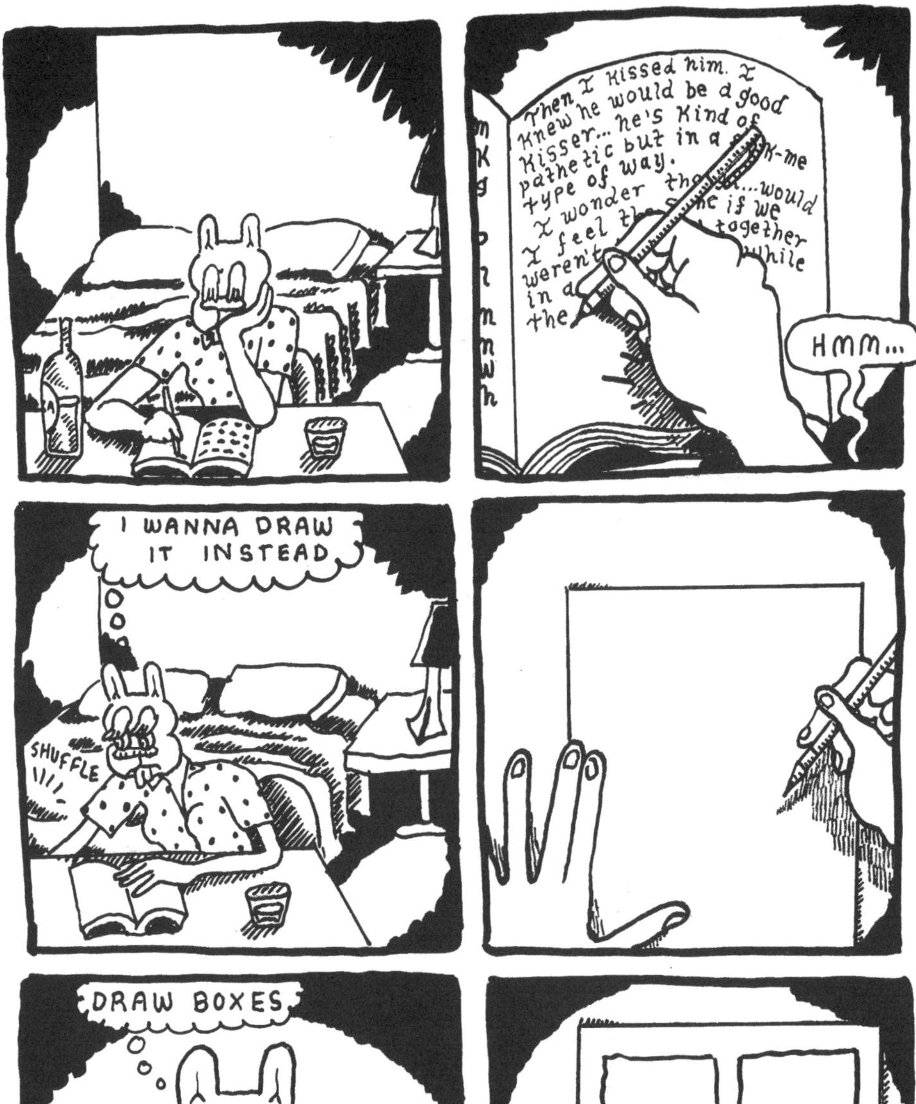

Then I kissed him. I
knew he would be a good
kisser... he's kind of
pathetic but in a
type of way.
I wonder ...would
I feel if we
weren't together
while
in a
the
HMM...
I WANNA DRAW IT INSTEAD
SHUFFLE
DRAW BOXES

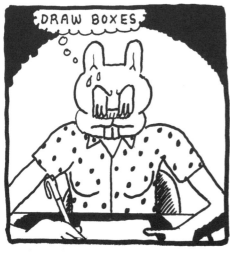

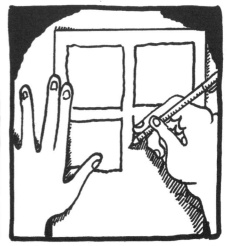

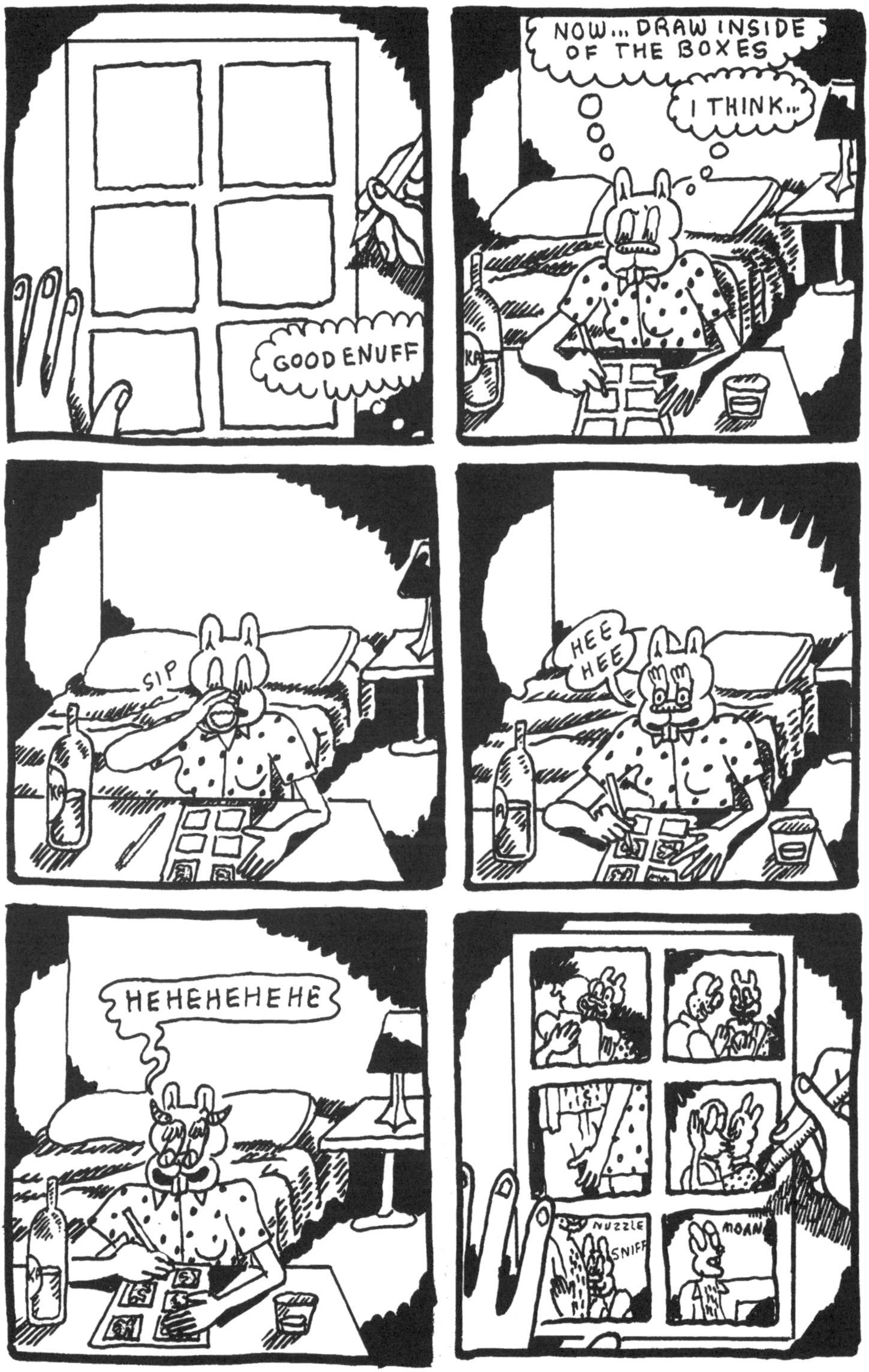
GOOD ENUFF
NOW... DRAW INSIDE OF THE BOXES
I THINK...
SIP
HEE HEE
HEHEHEHEHE
NUZZLE
SNIFF
MOAN

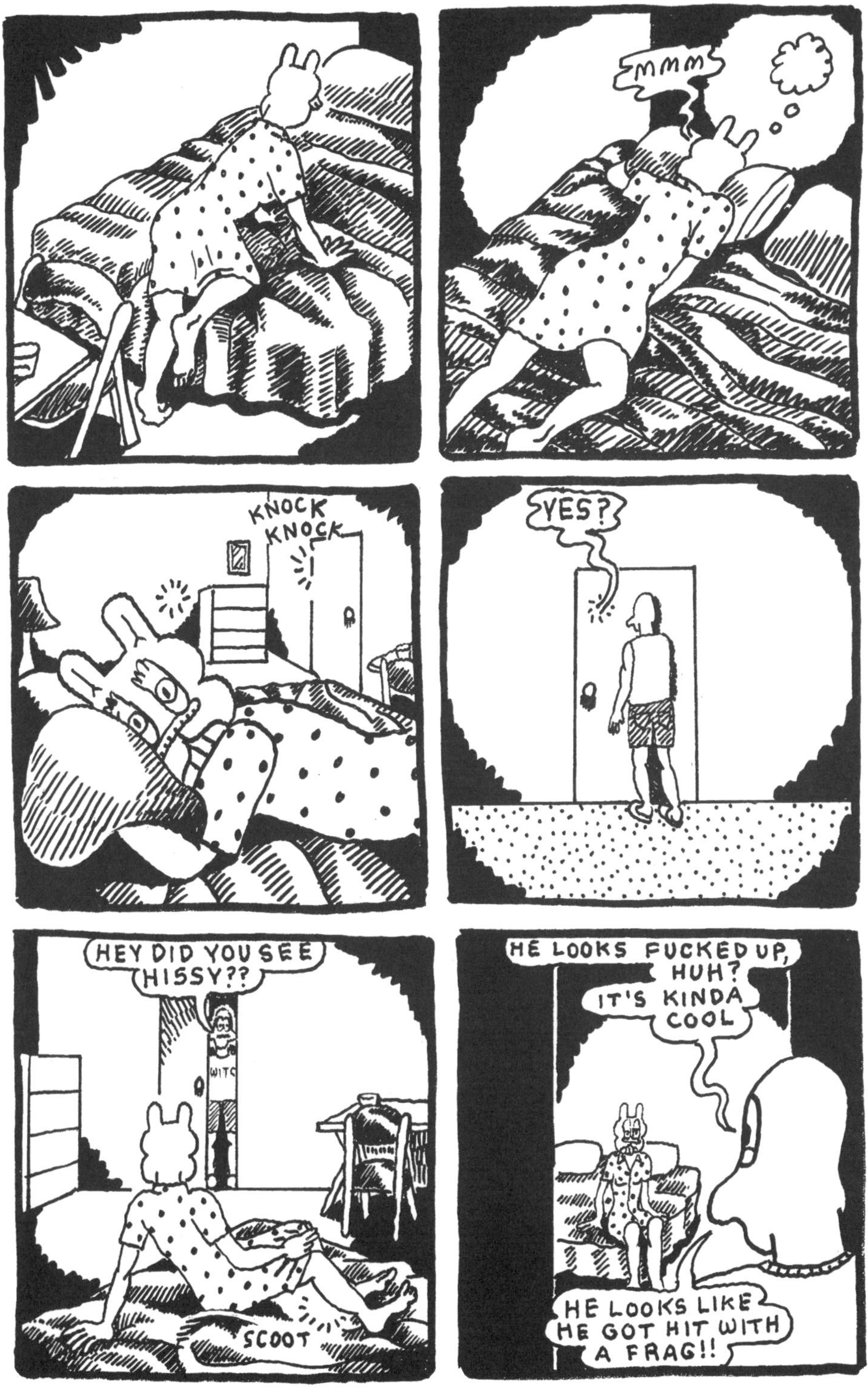
MMM
KNOCK
KNOCK
YES?
HEY DID YOU SEE HISSY??
SCOOT
HE LOOKS FUCKED UP, HUH?
IT'S KINDA COOL
HE LOOKS LIKE HE GOT HIT WITH A FRAG!!

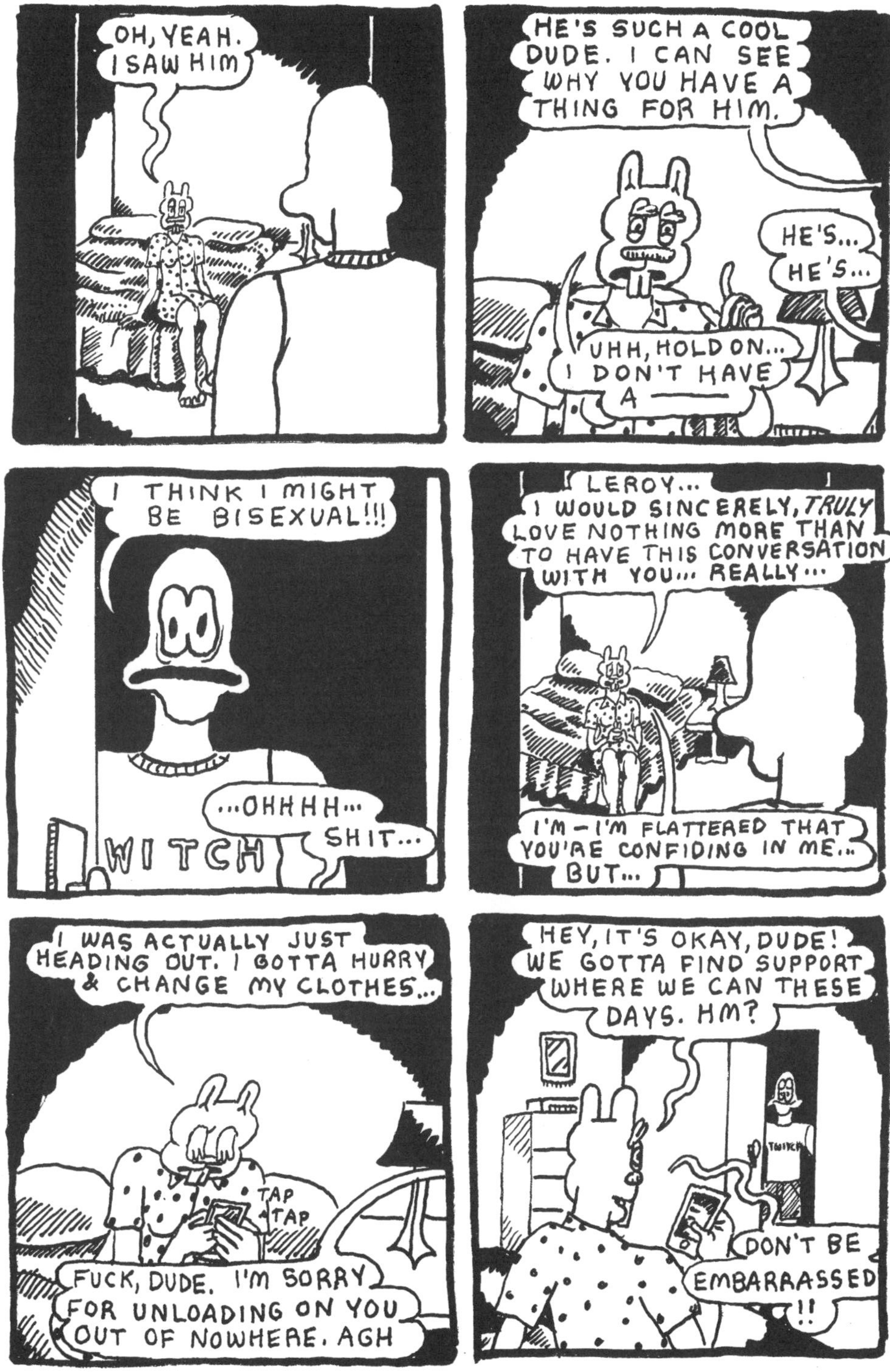
OH, YEAH. I SAW HIM
HE'S SUCH A COOL DUDE. I CAN SEE WHY YOU HAVE A THING FOR HIM.
HE'S... HE'S...
UHH, HOLD ON... I DON'T HAVE A ——
I THINK I MIGHT BE BISEXUAL!!!
...OHHHH... SHIT...
WITCH
LEROY... I WOULD SINCERELY, TRULY LOVE NOTHING MORE THAN TO HAVE THIS CONVERSATION WITH YOU... REALLY...
I'M — I'M FLATTERED THAT YOU'RE CONFIDING IN ME... BUT...
I WAS ACTUALLY JUST HEADING OUT. I GOTTA HURRY & CHANGE MY CLOTHES...
TAP TAP
FUCK, DUDE. I'M SORRY FOR UNLOADING ON YOU OUT OF NOWHERE. AGH
HEY, IT'S OKAY, DUDE! WE GOTTA FIND SUPPORT WHERE WE CAN THESE DAYS. HM?
DON'T BE EMBARRASSED!!

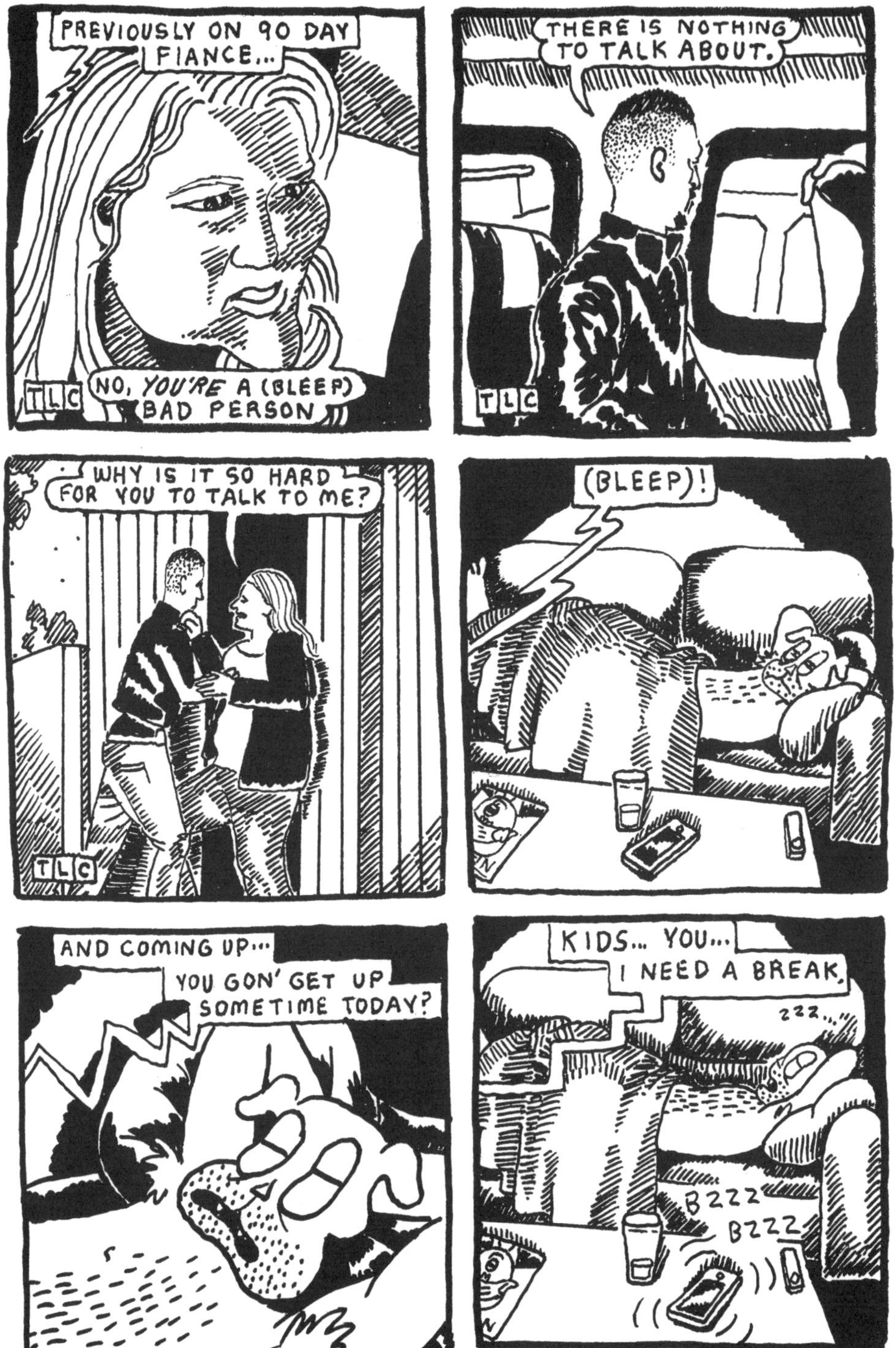
PREVIOUSLY ON 90 DAY FIANCE...
NO, YOU'RE A (BLEEP) BAD PERSON
TLC
THERE IS NOTHING TO TALK ABOUT.
TLC
WHY IS IT SO HARD FOR YOU TO TALK TO ME?
TLC
(BLEEP)!
AND COMING UP...
YOU GON' GET UP SOMETIME TODAY?
KIDS... YOU...
I NEED A BREAK.
ZZZ...
BZZZ
BZZZ

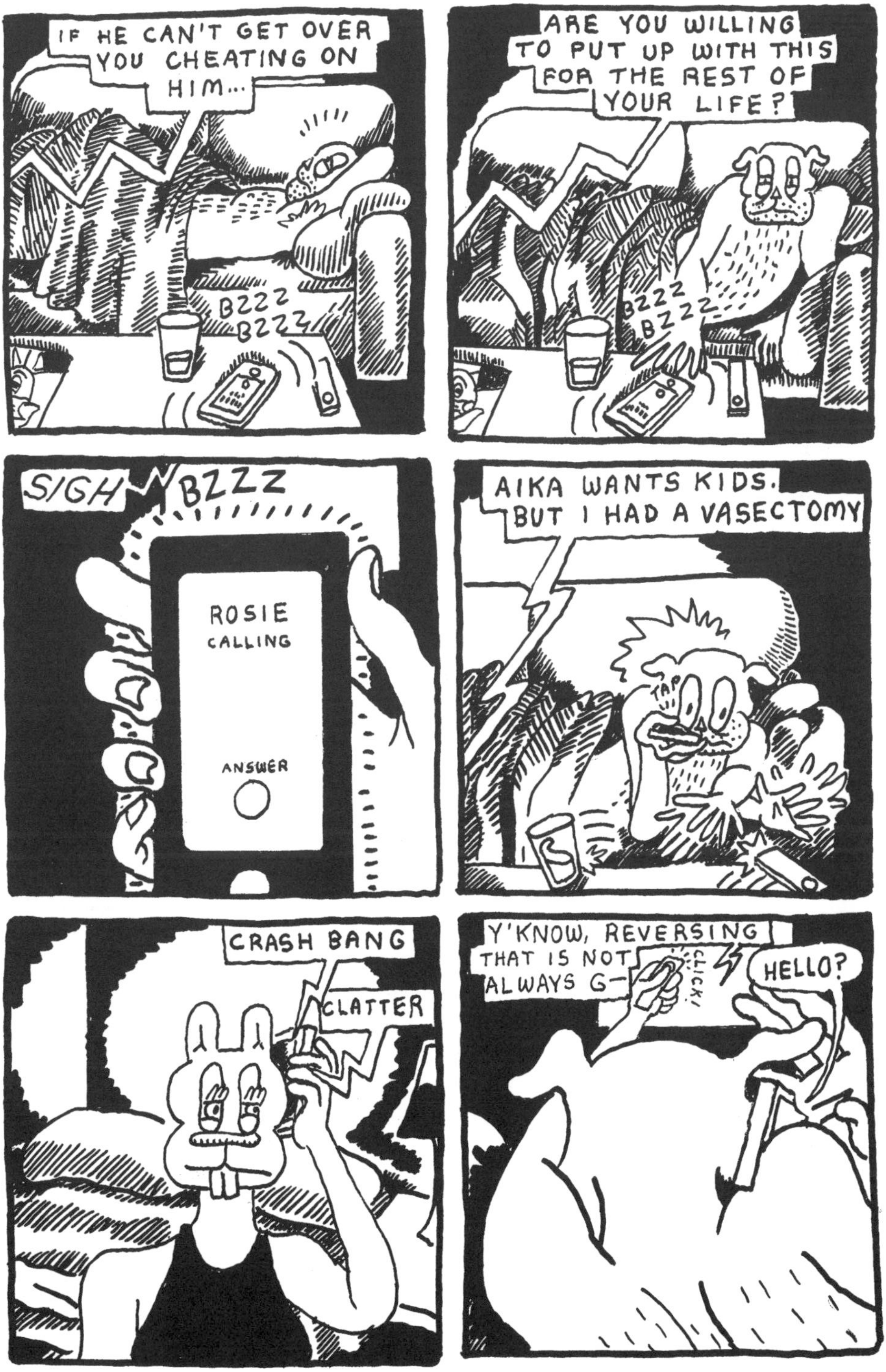
IF HE CAN'T GET OVER YOU CHEATING ON HIM...
BZZZ BZZZ
ARE YOU WILLING TO PUT UP WITH THIS FOR THE REST OF YOUR LIFE?
BZZZ BZZZ
SIGH
BZZZ
ROSIE CALLING
ANSWER
AIKA WANTS KIDS. BUT I HAD A VASECTOMY
TAP
CRASH BANG
CLATTER
Y'KNOW, REVERSING THAT IS NOT ALWAYS G—
CLICK!
HELLO?

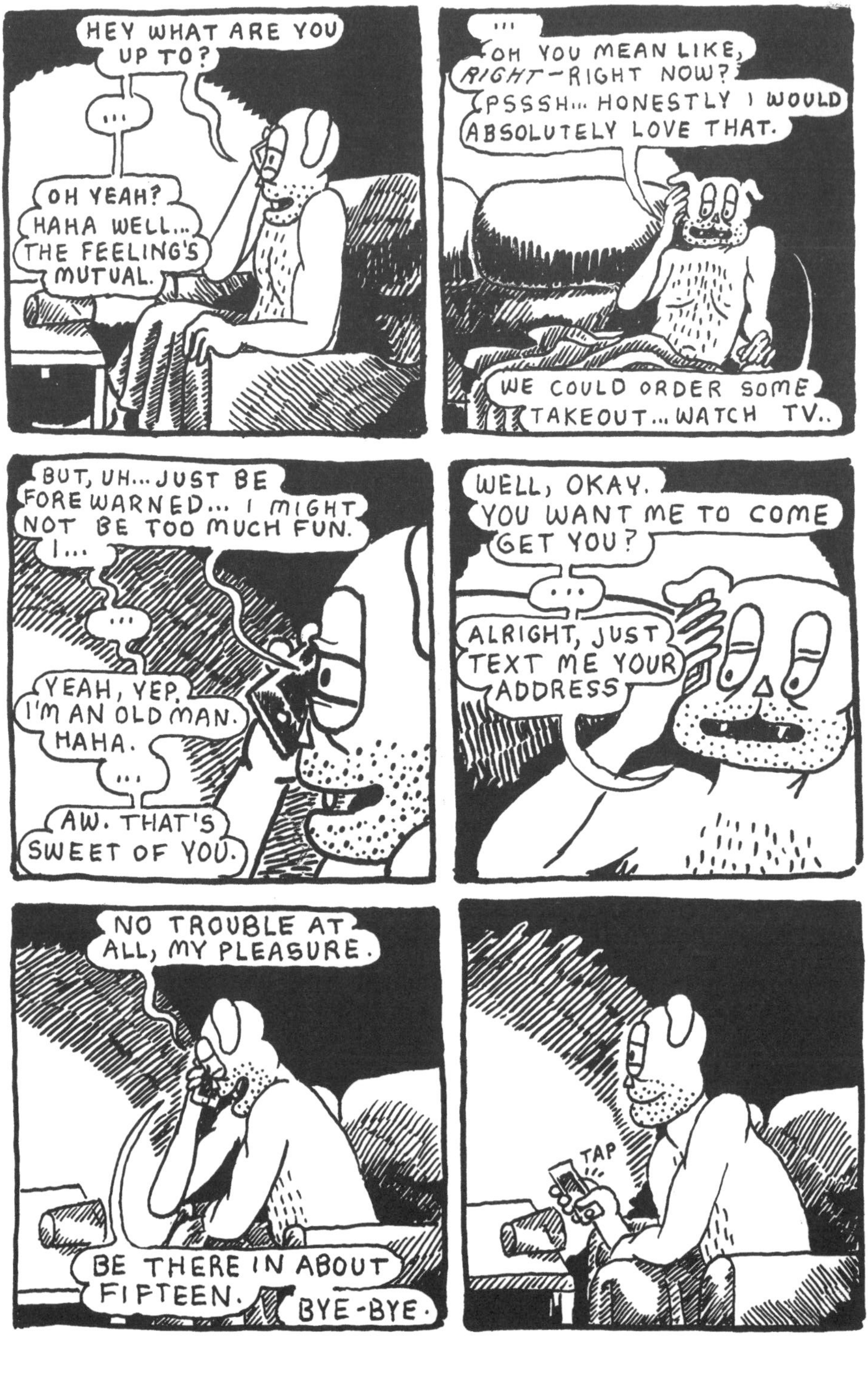
HEY WHAT ARE YOU UP TO?
...
OH YEAH? HAHA WELL... THE FEELING'S MUTUAL.
...
OH YOU MEAN LIKE, RIGHT-RIGHT NOW? PSSSH... HONESTLY I WOULD ABSOLUTELY LOVE THAT.
WE COULD ORDER SOME TAKEOUT... WATCH TV..
BUT, UH... JUST BE FOREWARNED... I MIGHT NOT BE TOO MUCH FUN. I...
...
YEAH, YEP. I'M AN OLD MAN. HAHA.
...
AW. THAT'S SWEET OF YOU.
WELL, OKAY. YOU WANT ME TO COME GET YOU?
...
ALRIGHT, JUST TEXT ME YOUR ADDRESS
NO TROUBLE AT ALL, MY PLEASURE.
BE THERE IN ABOUT FIFTEEN.
BYE-BYE.
TAP

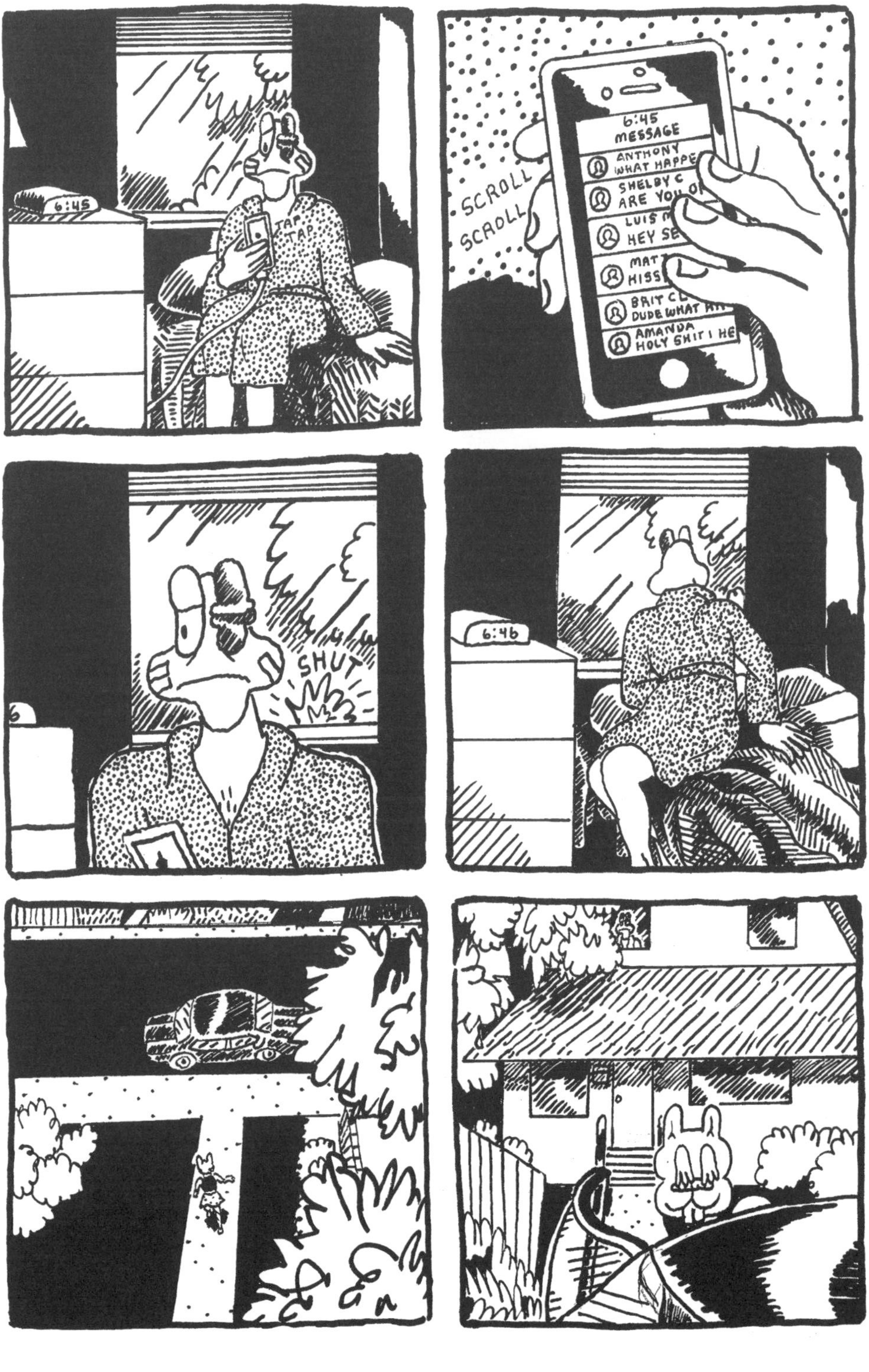
6:45
TAP TAP
6:45
MESSAGE
ANTHONY
WHAT HAPPE
SHELBY C
ARE YOU O
LUIS M
HEY SE
HISS
BRIT C
DUDE WHAT H
AMANDA
HOLY SHIT I HE
SCROLL
SCROLL
SHUT
6:46

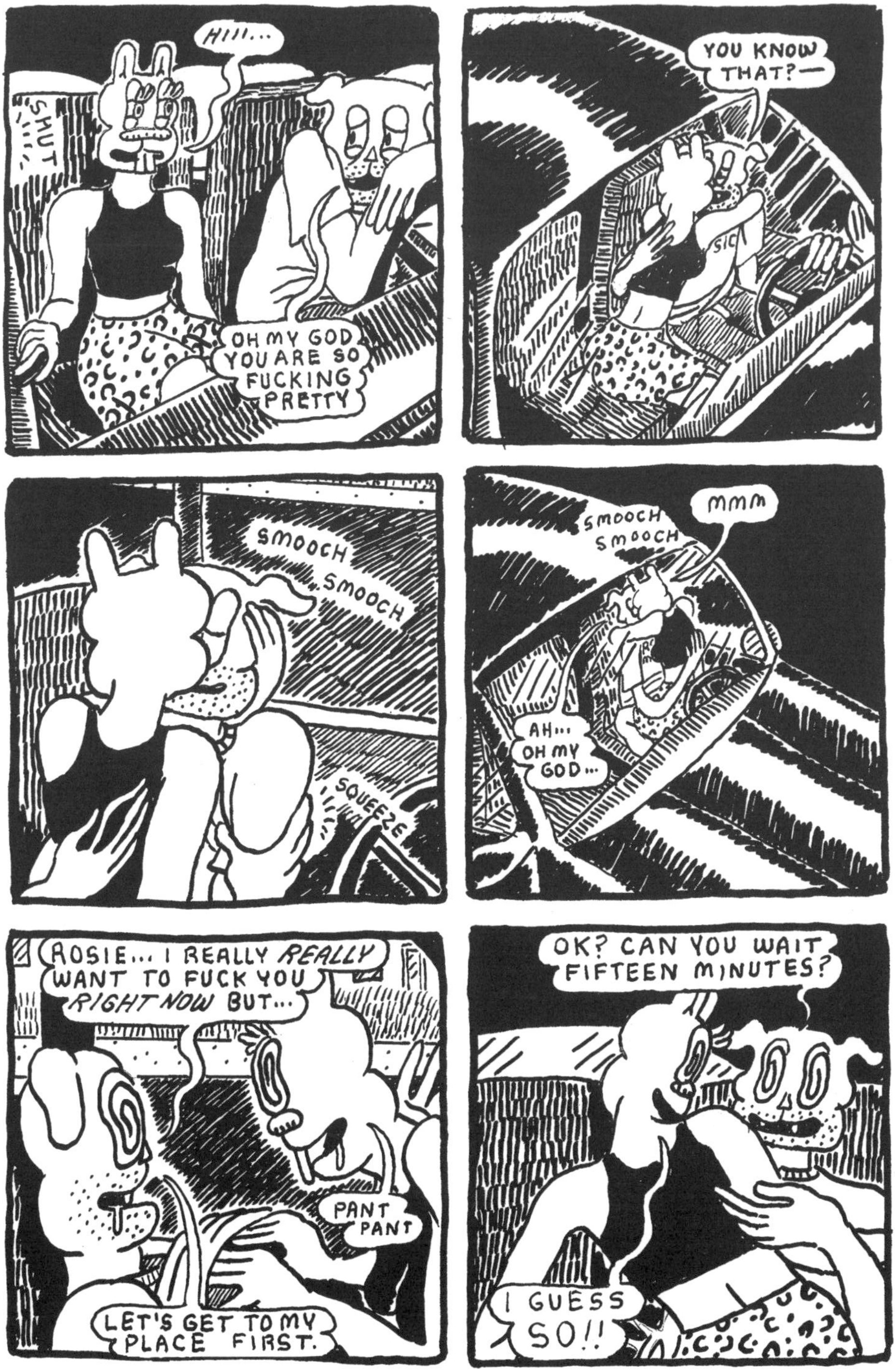
SHUT
HIII...
OH MY GOD YOU ARE SO FUCKING PRETTY
YOU KNOW THAT?—
SMOOCH SMOOCH
SQUEEZE
SMOOCH SMOOCH
MMM
AH... OH MY GOD...
ROSIE... I REALLY *REALLY* WANT TO FUCK YOU *RIGHT NOW* BUT...
PANT PANT
LET'S GET TO MY PLACE FIRST.
OK? CAN YOU WAIT FIFTEEN MINUTES?
I GUESS SO!!

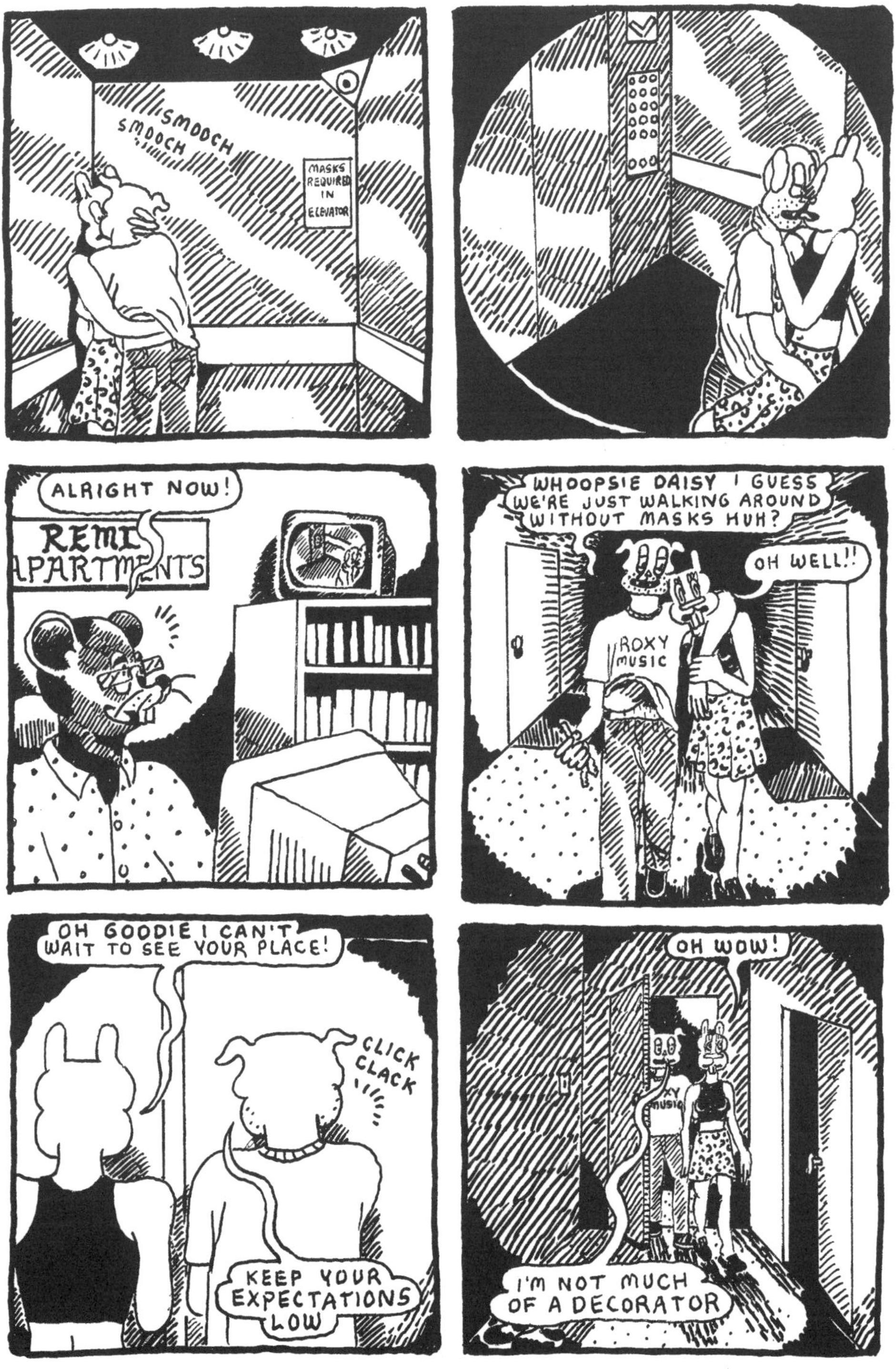
SMOOCH
SMOOCH
MASKS REQUIRED IN ELEVATOR
ALRIGHT NOW!
REMI APARTMENTS
WHOOPSIE DAISY I GUESS WE'RE JUST WALKING AROUND WITHOUT MASKS HUH?
OH WELL!!
ROXY MUSIC
OH GOODIE I CAN'T WAIT TO SEE YOUR PLACE!
CLICK CLACK
KEEP YOUR EXPECTATIONS LOW
OH WOW!
I'M NOT MUCH OF A DECORATOR

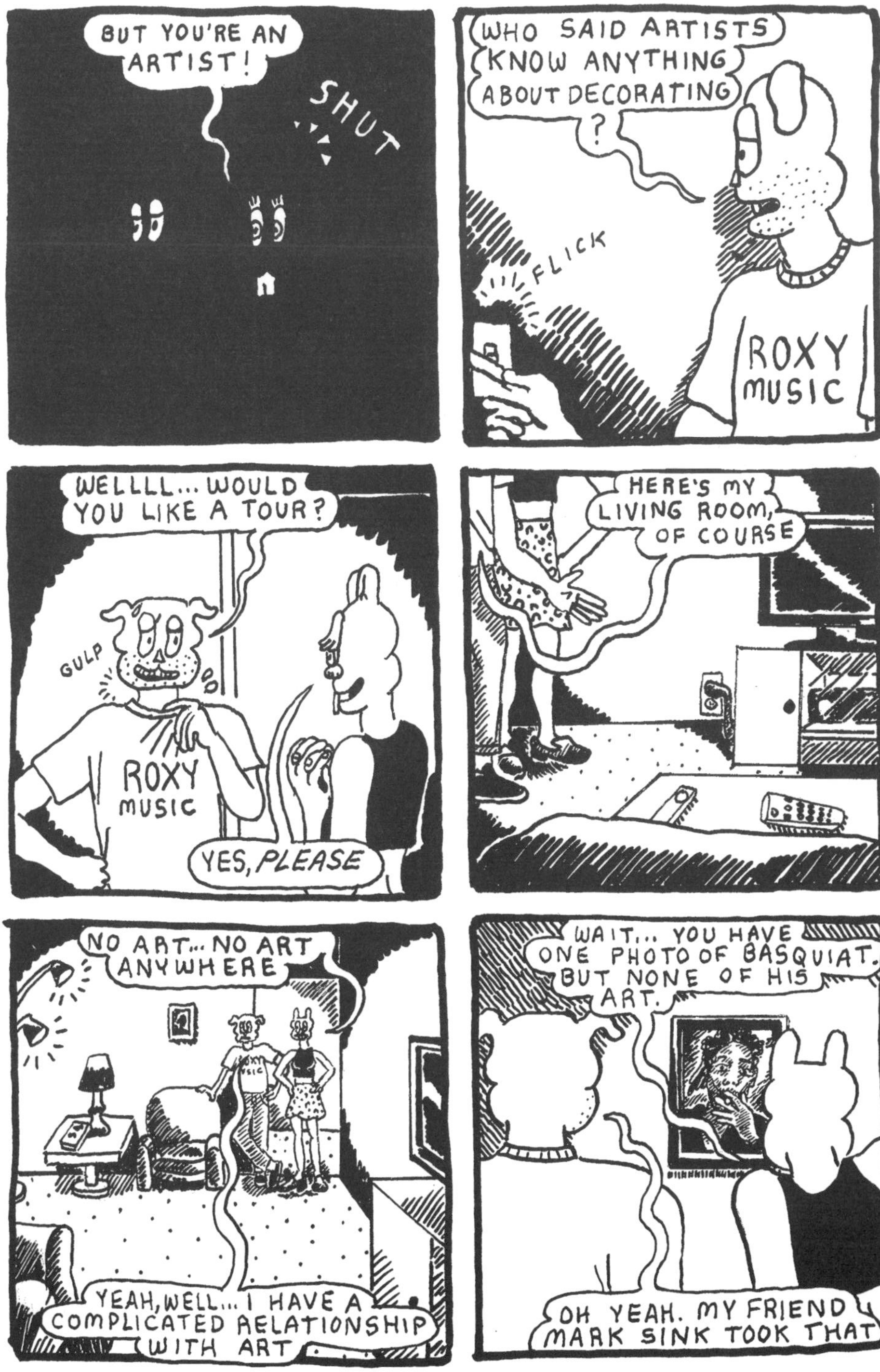
BUT YOU'RE AN ARTIST!
SHUT
WHO SAID ARTISTS KNOW ANYTHING ABOUT DECORATING ?
FLICK
ROXY MUSIC
WELLLL... WOULD YOU LIKE A TOUR?
GULP
ROXY MUSIC
YES, PLEASE
HERE'S MY LIVING ROOM, OF COURSE
NO ART... NO ART ANYWHERE
YEAH, WELL... I HAVE A COMPLICATED RELATIONSHIP WITH ART
WAIT... YOU HAVE ONE PHOTO OF BASQUIAT. BUT NONE OF HIS ART.
OH YEAH. MY FRIEND MARK SINK TOOK THAT

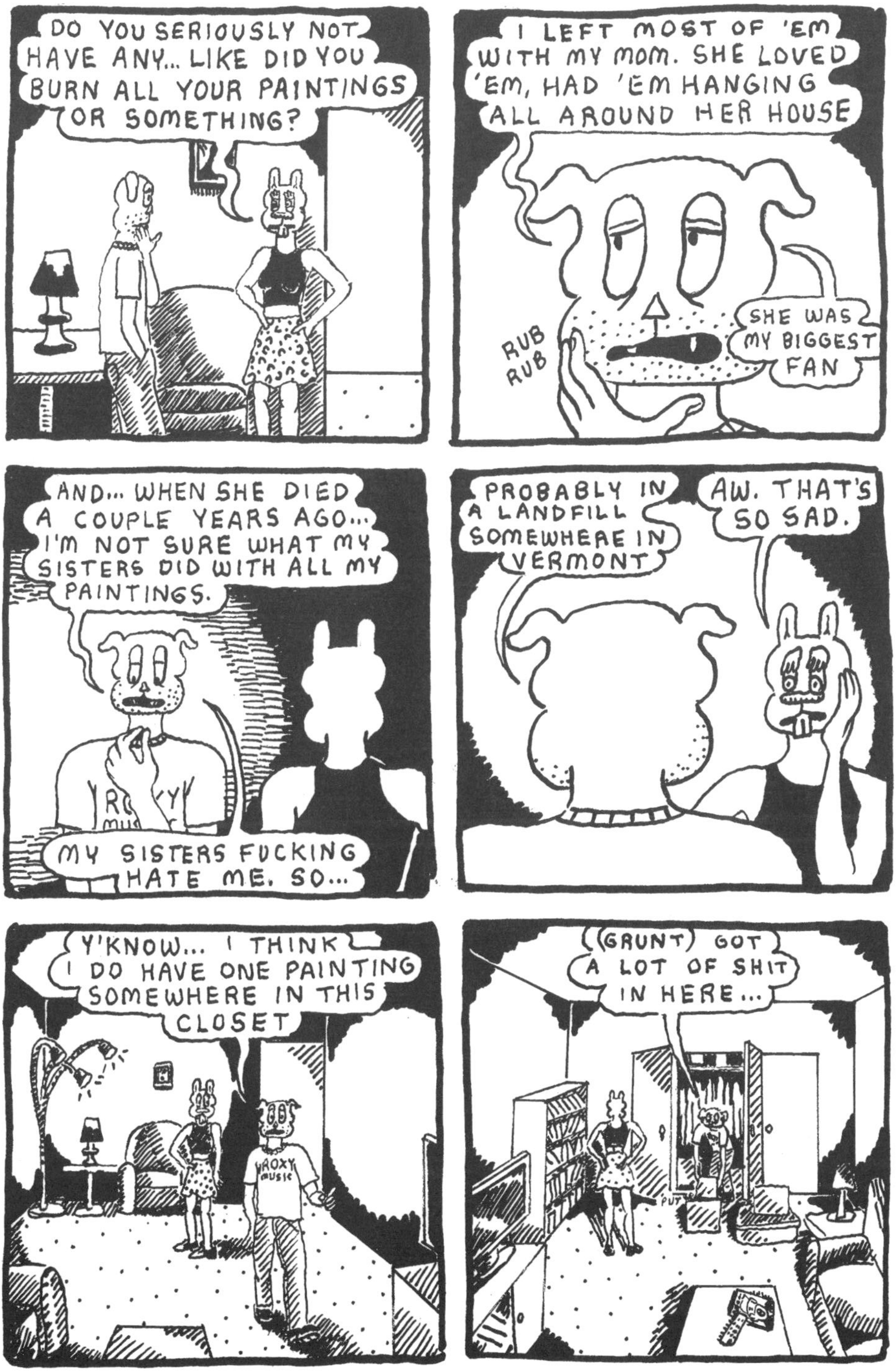
DO YOU SERIOUSLY NOT HAVE ANY... LIKE DID YOU BURN ALL YOUR PAINTINGS OR SOMETHING?
I LEFT MOST OF 'EM WITH MY MOM. SHE LOVED 'EM, HAD 'EM HANGING ALL AROUND HER HOUSE
RUB RUB
SHE WAS MY BIGGEST FAN
AND... WHEN SHE DIED A COUPLE YEARS AGO... I'M NOT SURE WHAT MY SISTERS DID WITH ALL MY PAINTINGS.
MY SISTERS FUCKING HATE ME. SO...
PROBABLY IN A LANDFILL SOMEWHERE IN VERMONT
AW. THAT'S SO SAD.
Y'KNOW... I THINK I DO HAVE ONE PAINTING SOMEWHERE IN THIS CLOSET
ROXY MUSIC
(GRUNT) GOT A LOT OF SHIT IN HERE...

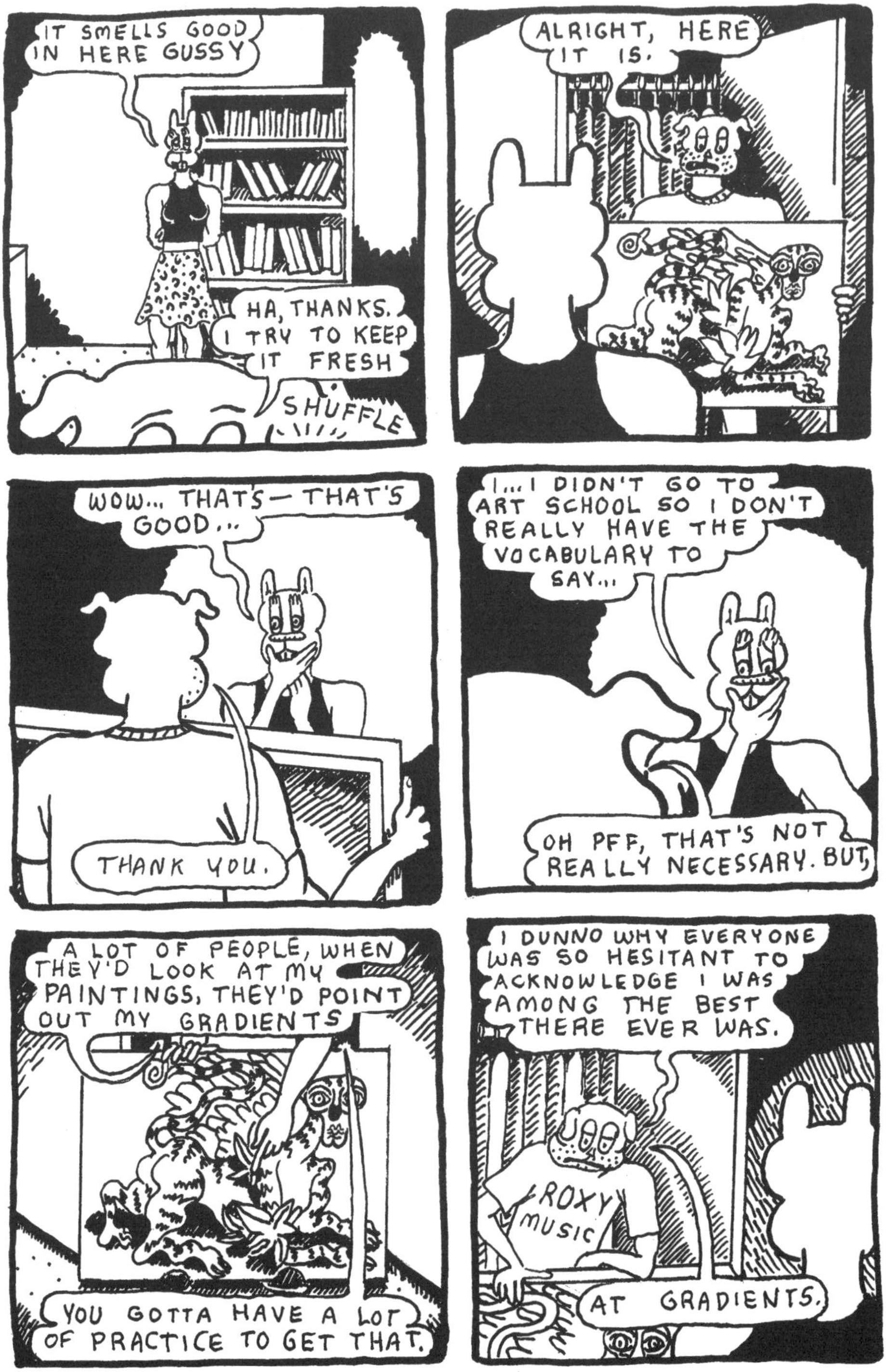
IT SMELLS GOOD IN HERE GUSSY
HA, THANKS. I TRY TO KEEP IT FRESH
SHUFFLE
ALRIGHT, HERE IT IS.
WOW... THAT'S— THAT'S GOOD...
THANK YOU.
I...I DIDN'T GO TO ART SCHOOL SO I DON'T REALLY HAVE THE VOCABULARY TO SAY...
OH PFF, THAT'S NOT REALLY NECESSARY. BUT,
A LOT OF PEOPLE, WHEN THEY'D LOOK AT MY PAINTINGS, THEY'D POINT OUT MY GRADIENTS
YOU GOTTA HAVE A LOT OF PRACTICE TO GET THAT.
I DUNNO WHY EVERYONE WAS SO HESITANT TO ACKNOWLEDGE I WAS AMONG THE BEST THERE EVER WAS.
ROXY MUSIC
AT GRADIENTS.

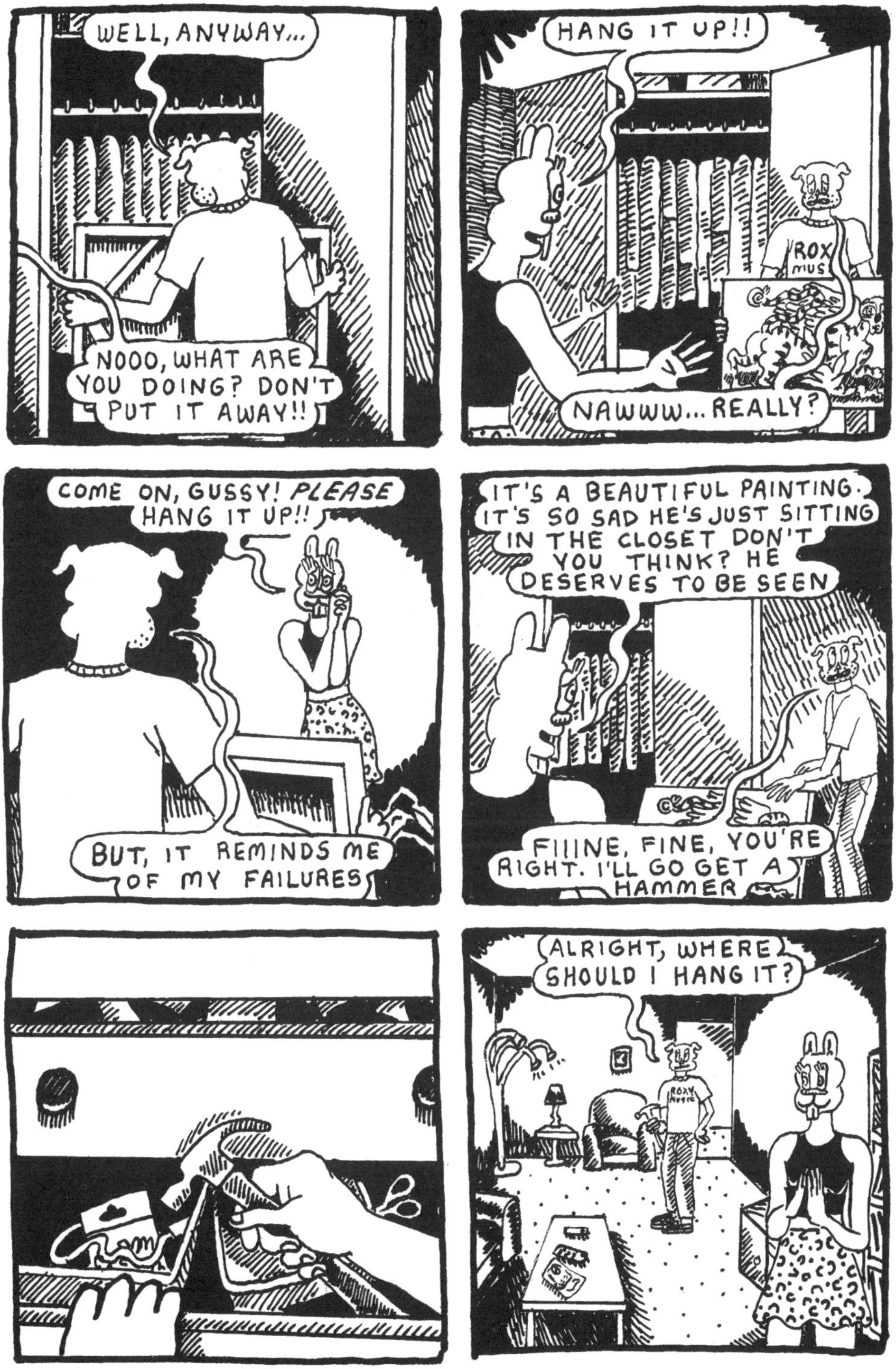

WELL, ANYWAY...
NOOO, WHAT ARE YOU DOING? DON'T PUT IT AWAY!!
HANG IT UP!!
ROX MUS
NAWWW... REALLY?
COME ON, GUSSY! *PLEASE* HANG IT UP!!
BUT, IT REMINDS ME OF MY FAILURES
IT'S A BEAUTIFUL PAINTING. IT'S SO SAD HE'S JUST SITTING IN THE CLOSET DON'T YOU THINK? HE DESERVES TO BE SEEN
FIIINE, FINE, YOU'RE RIGHT. I'LL GO GET A HAMMER
ALRIGHT, WHERE SHOULD I HANG IT?
ROXY MUSIC

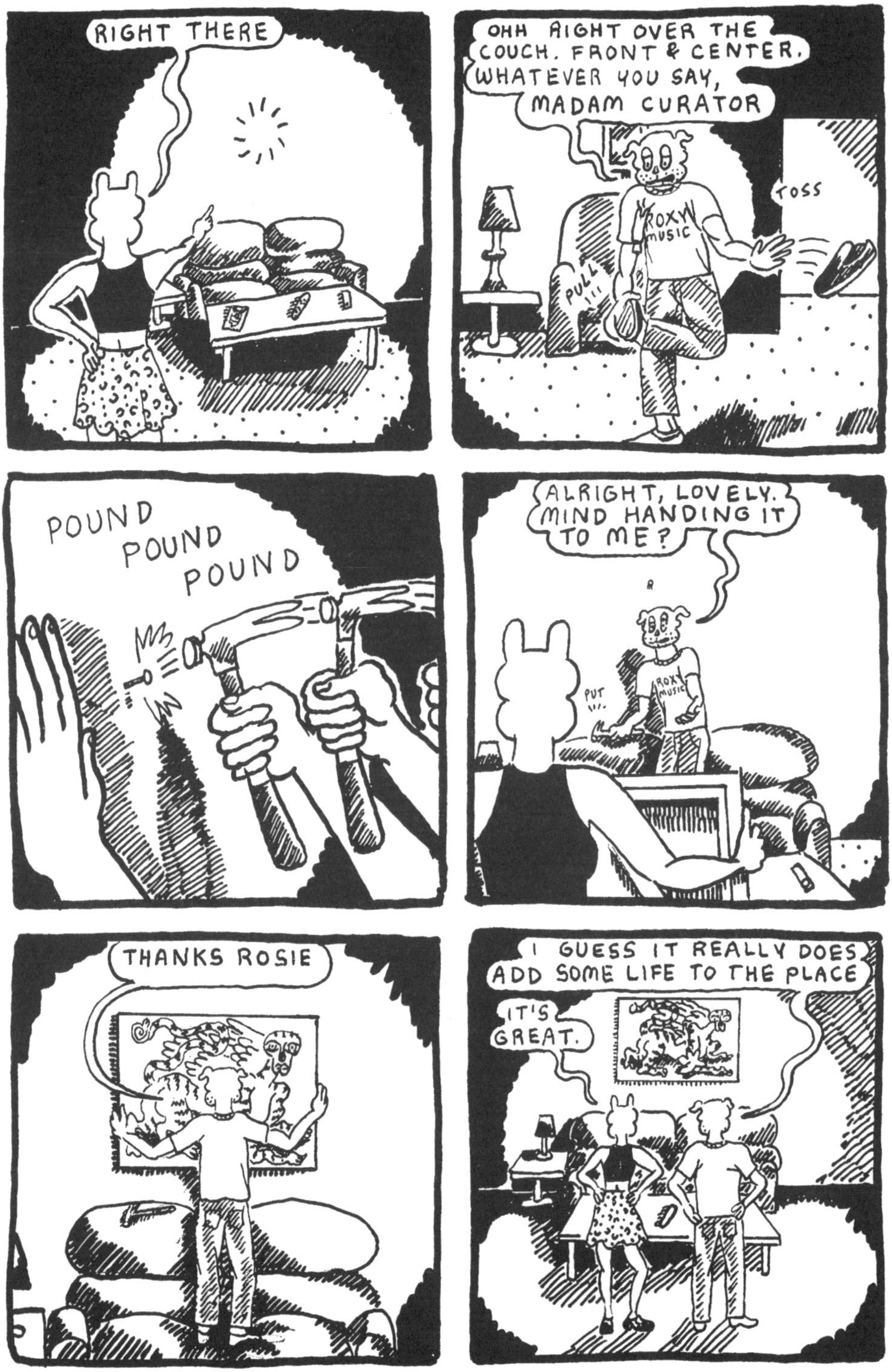
RIGHT THERE
OHH RIGHT OVER THE COUCH. FRONT & CENTER.
WHATEVER YOU SAY, MADAM CURATOR
TOSS
PULL
POUND
POUND
POUND
ALRIGHT, LOVELY. MIND HANDING IT TO ME?
PUT
THANKS ROSIE
I GUESS IT REALLY DOES ADD SOME LIFE TO THE PLACE
IT'S GREAT.

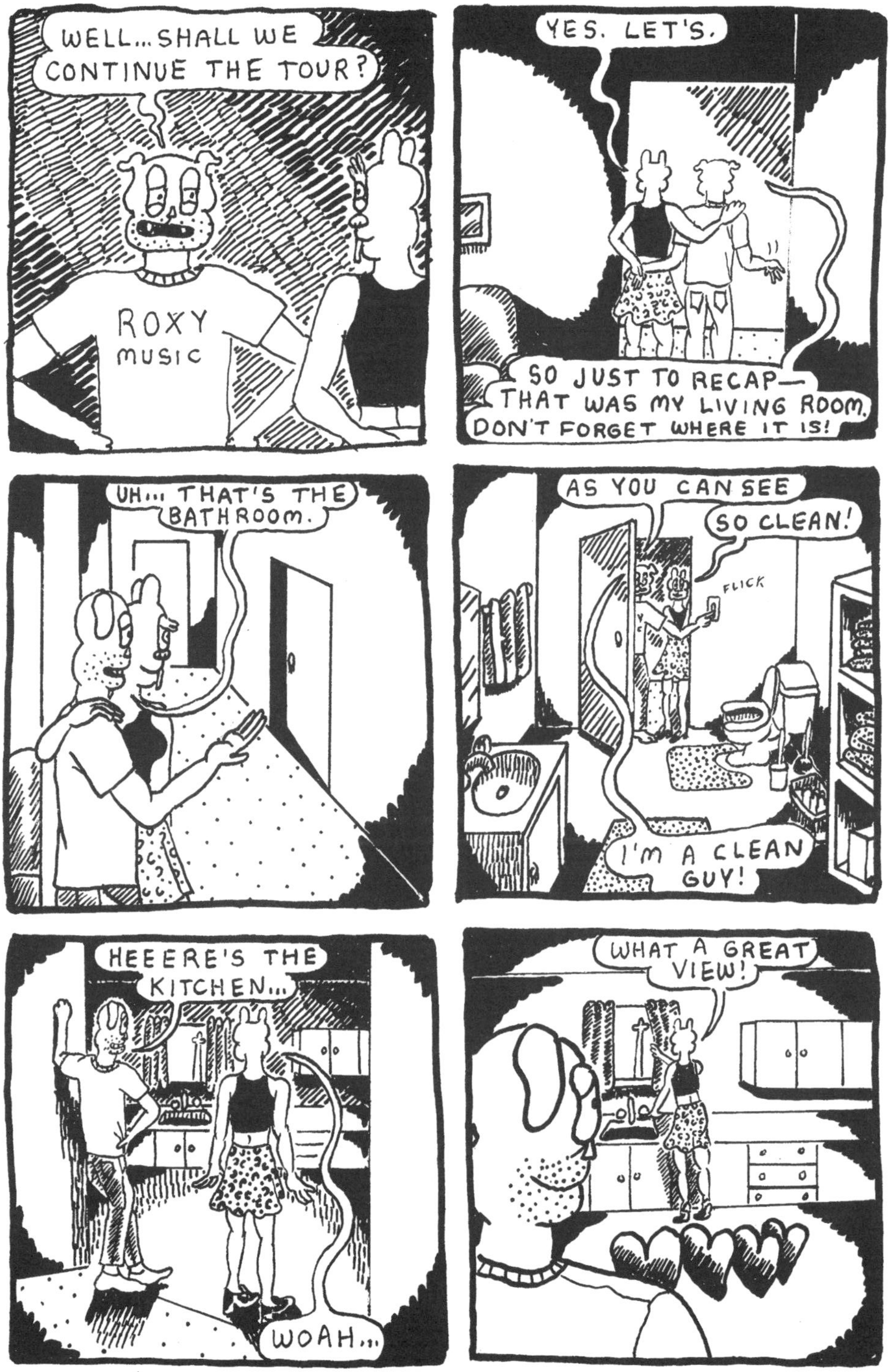
WELL... SHALL WE CONTINUE THE TOUR?
ROXY MUSIC
YES. LET'S.
SO JUST TO RECAP— THAT WAS MY LIVING ROOM. DON'T FORGET WHERE IT IS!
UH... THAT'S THE BATHROOM.
AS YOU CAN SEE
SO CLEAN!
FLICK
I'M A CLEAN GUY!
HEEERE'S THE KITCHEN...
WOAH...
WHAT A GREAT VIEW!

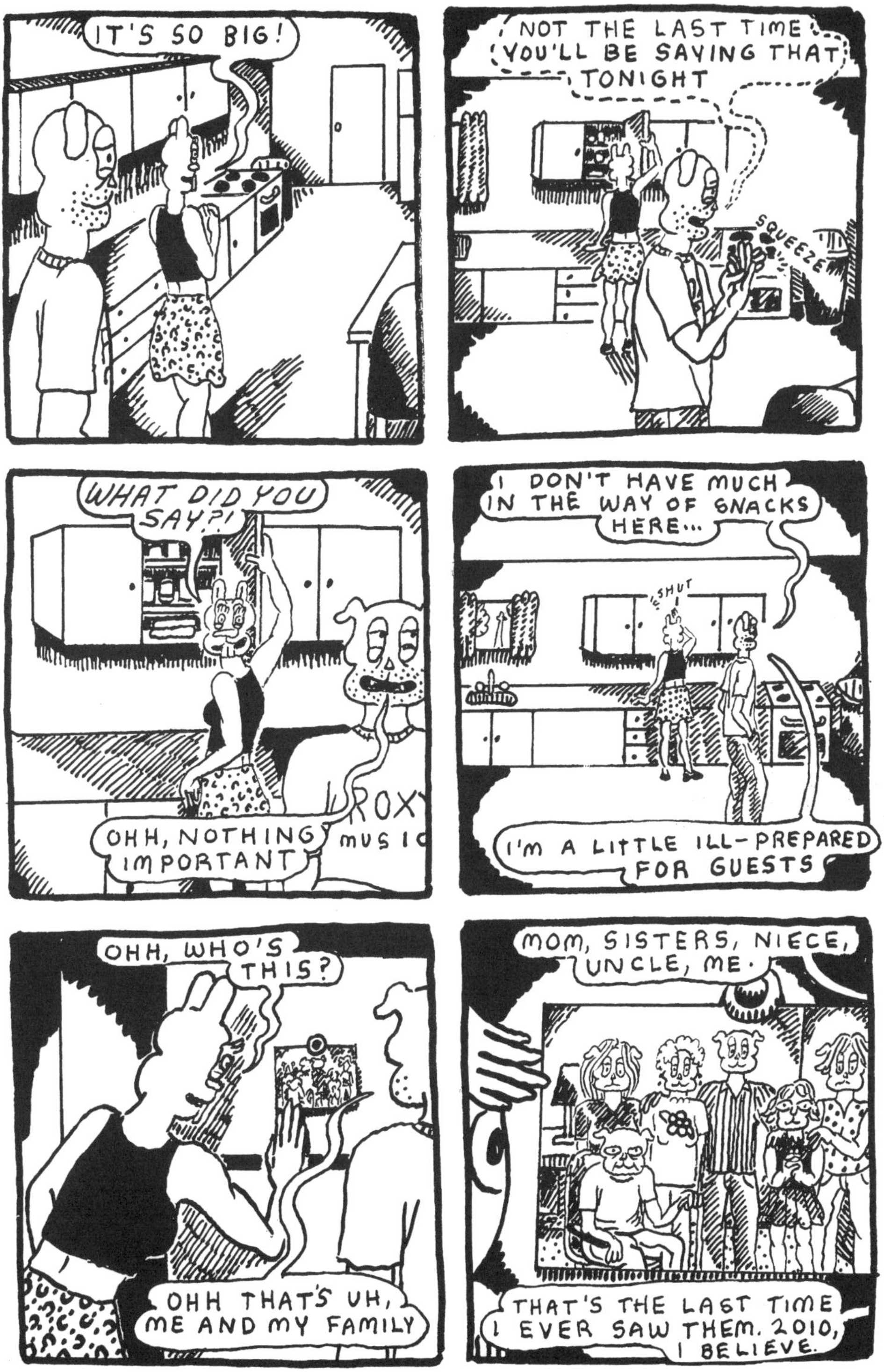
IT'S SO BIG!
NOT THE LAST TIME YOU'LL BE SAYING THAT TONIGHT
SQUEEZE
WHAT DID YOU SAY?!
OHH, NOTHING IMPORTANT
ROXY MUSIC
I DON'T HAVE MUCH IN THE WAY OF SNACKS HERE...
SHUT
I'M A LITTLE ILL-PREPARED FOR GUESTS
OHH, WHO'S THIS?
OHH THAT'S UH, ME AND MY FAMILY
MOM, SISTERS, NIECE, UNCLE, ME.
THAT'S THE LAST TIME I EVER SAW THEM. 2010, I BELIEVE.

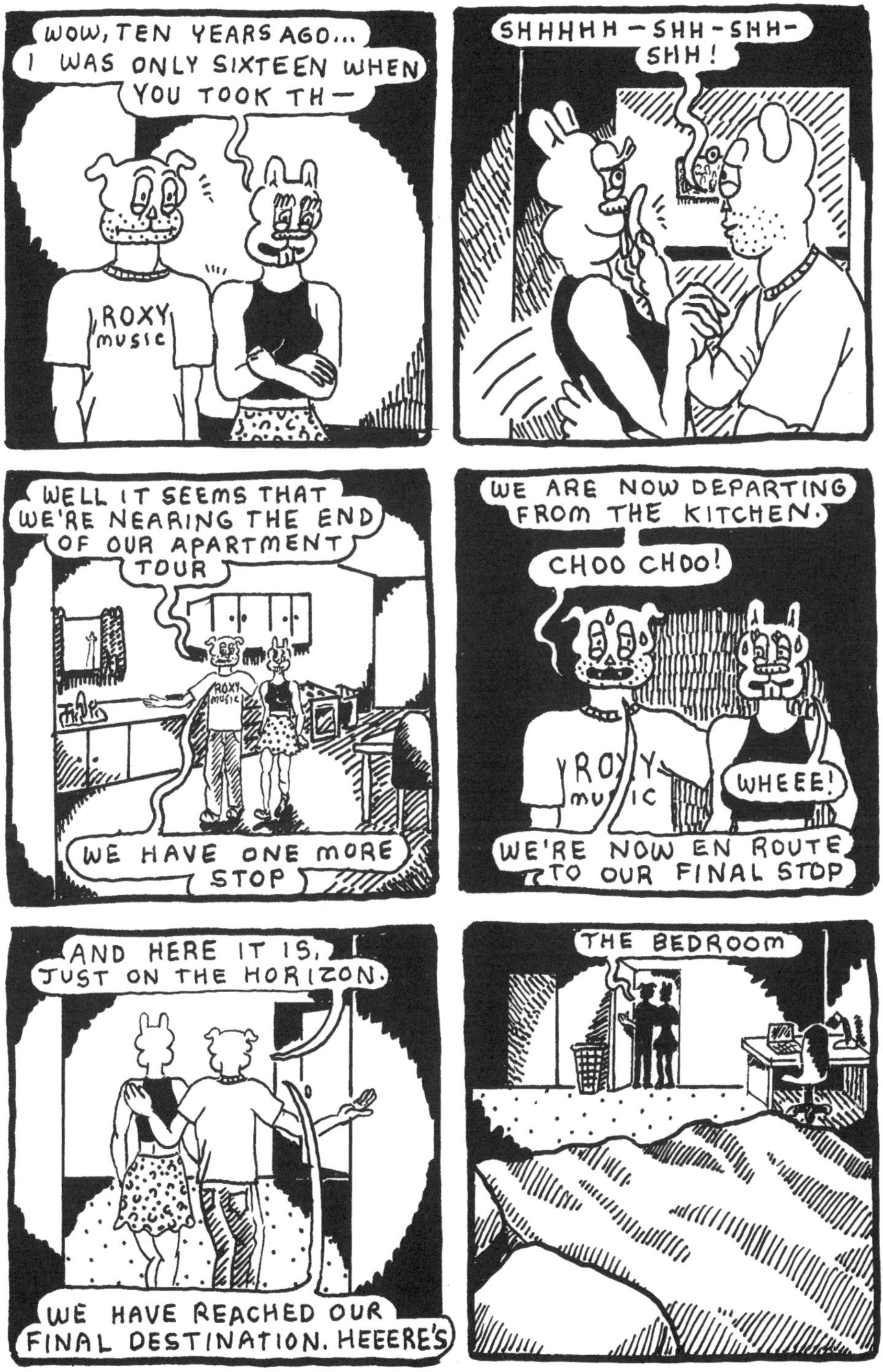
WOW, TEN YEARS AGO... I WAS ONLY SIXTEEN WHEN YOU TOOK TH—
ROXY MUSIC
SHHHHH—SHH—SHH—SHH!
WELL IT SEEMS THAT WE'RE NEARING THE END OF OUR APARTMENT TOUR
ROXY MUSIC
WE HAVE ONE MORE STOP
WE ARE NOW DEPARTING FROM THE KITCHEN.
CHOO CHOO!
ROXY MUSIC
WHEEE!
WE'RE NOW EN ROUTE TO OUR FINAL STOP
AND HERE IT IS, JUST ON THE HORIZON.
WE HAVE REACHED OUR FINAL DESTINATION. HEEERE'S
THE BEDROOM

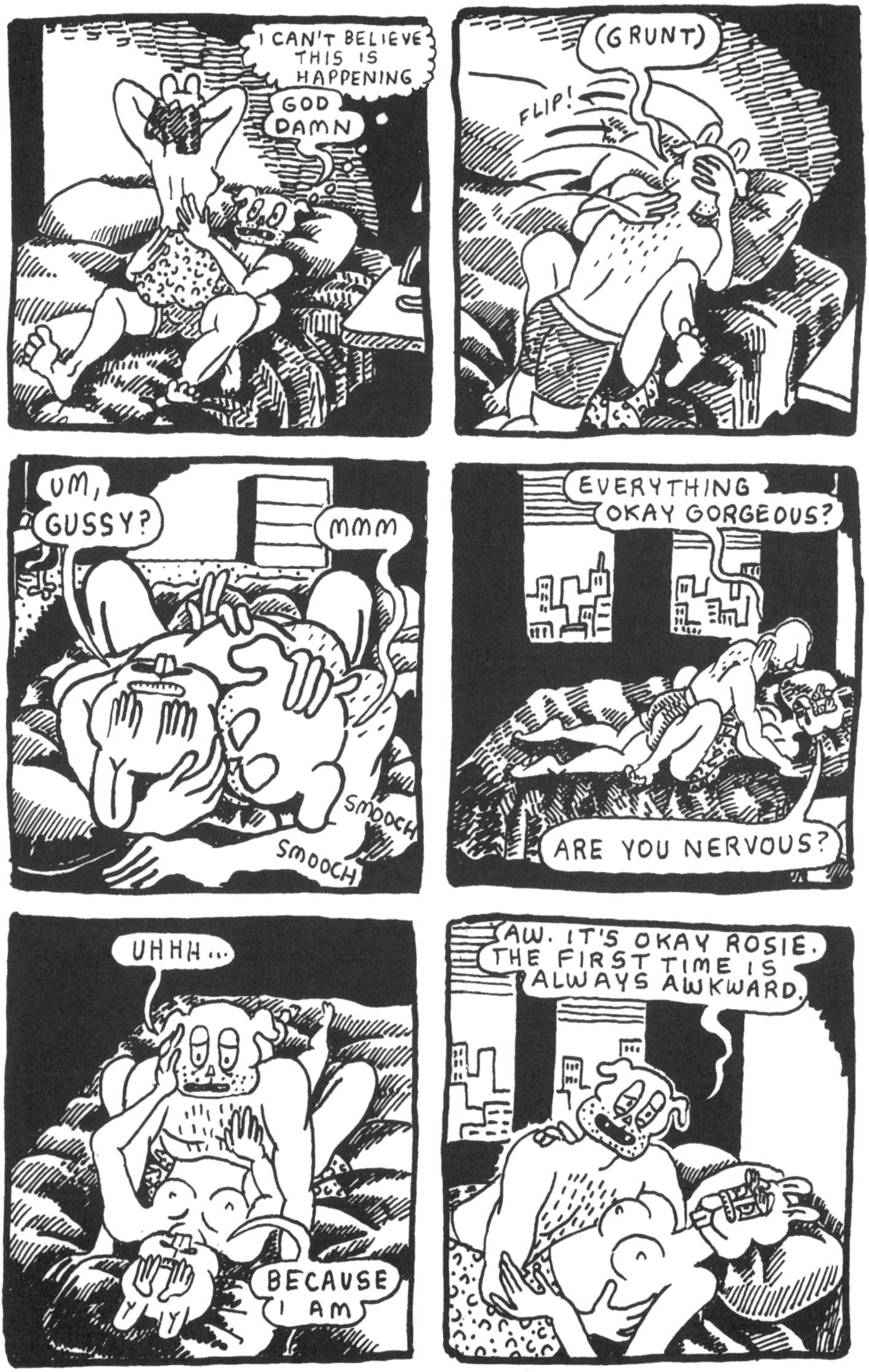
I CAN'T BELIEVE THIS IS HAPPENING
GOD DAMN
(GRUNT)
FLIP!
UM, GUSSY?
MMM
SMOOCH
SMOOCH
EVERYTHING OKAY GORGEOUS?
ARE YOU NERVOUS?
UHHH...
BECAUSE I AM
AW. IT'S OKAY ROSIE. THE FIRST TIME IS ALWAYS AWKWARD.

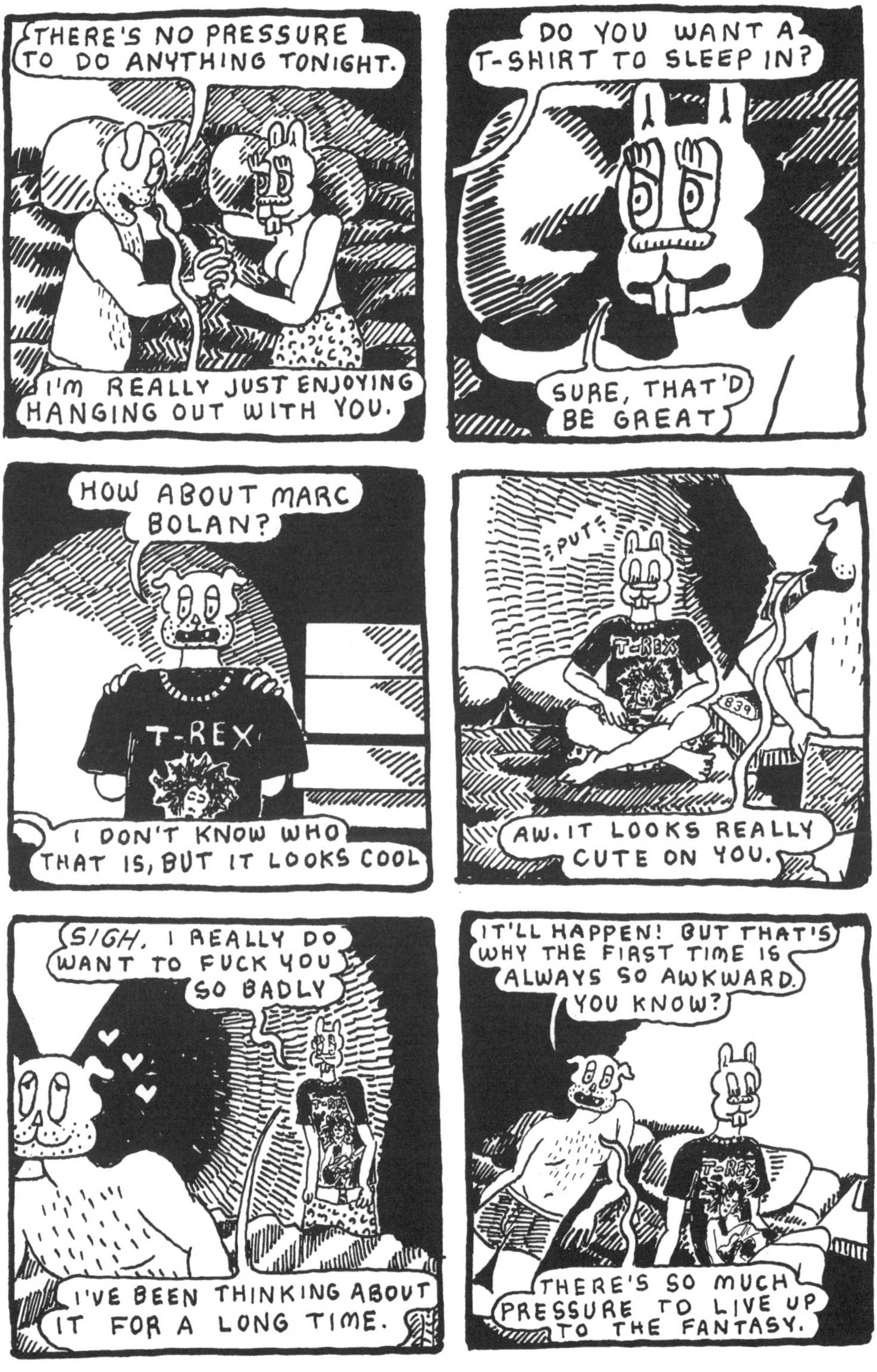
THERE'S NO PRESSURE TO DO ANYTHING TONIGHT.
I'M REALLY JUST ENJOYING HANGING OUT WITH YOU.
DO YOU WANT A T-SHIRT TO SLEEP IN?
SURE, THAT'D BE GREAT
HOW ABOUT MARC BOLAN?
T-REX
I DON'T KNOW WHO THAT IS, BUT IT LOOKS COOL
PUT
T-REX
AW. IT LOOKS REALLY CUTE ON YOU.
SIGH. I REALLY DO WANT TO FUCK YOU SO BADLY
I'VE BEEN THINKING ABOUT IT FOR A LONG TIME.
IT'LL HAPPEN! BUT THAT'S WHY THE FIRST TIME IS ALWAYS SO AWKWARD. YOU KNOW?
THERE'S SO MUCH PRESSURE TO LIVE UP TO THE FANTASY.

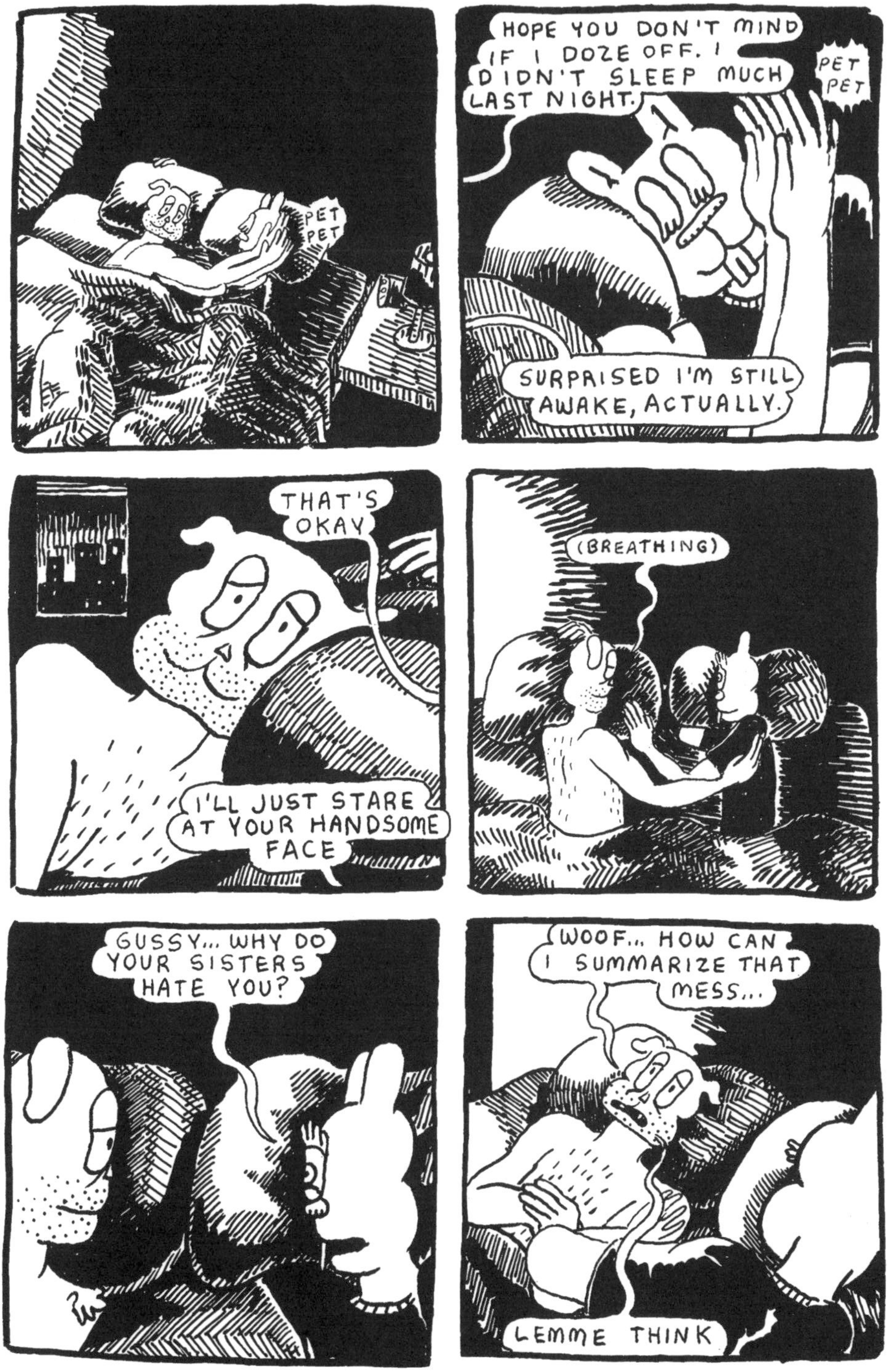
PET PET
HOPE YOU DON'T MIND IF I DOZE OFF. I DIDN'T SLEEP MUCH LAST NIGHT.
PET PET
SURPRISED I'M STILL AWAKE, ACTUALLY.
THAT'S OKAY
I'LL JUST STARE AT YOUR HANDSOME FACE
(BREATHING)
GUSSY... WHY DO YOUR SISTERS HATE YOU?
WOOF... HOW CAN I SUMMARIZE THAT MESS...
LEMME THINK

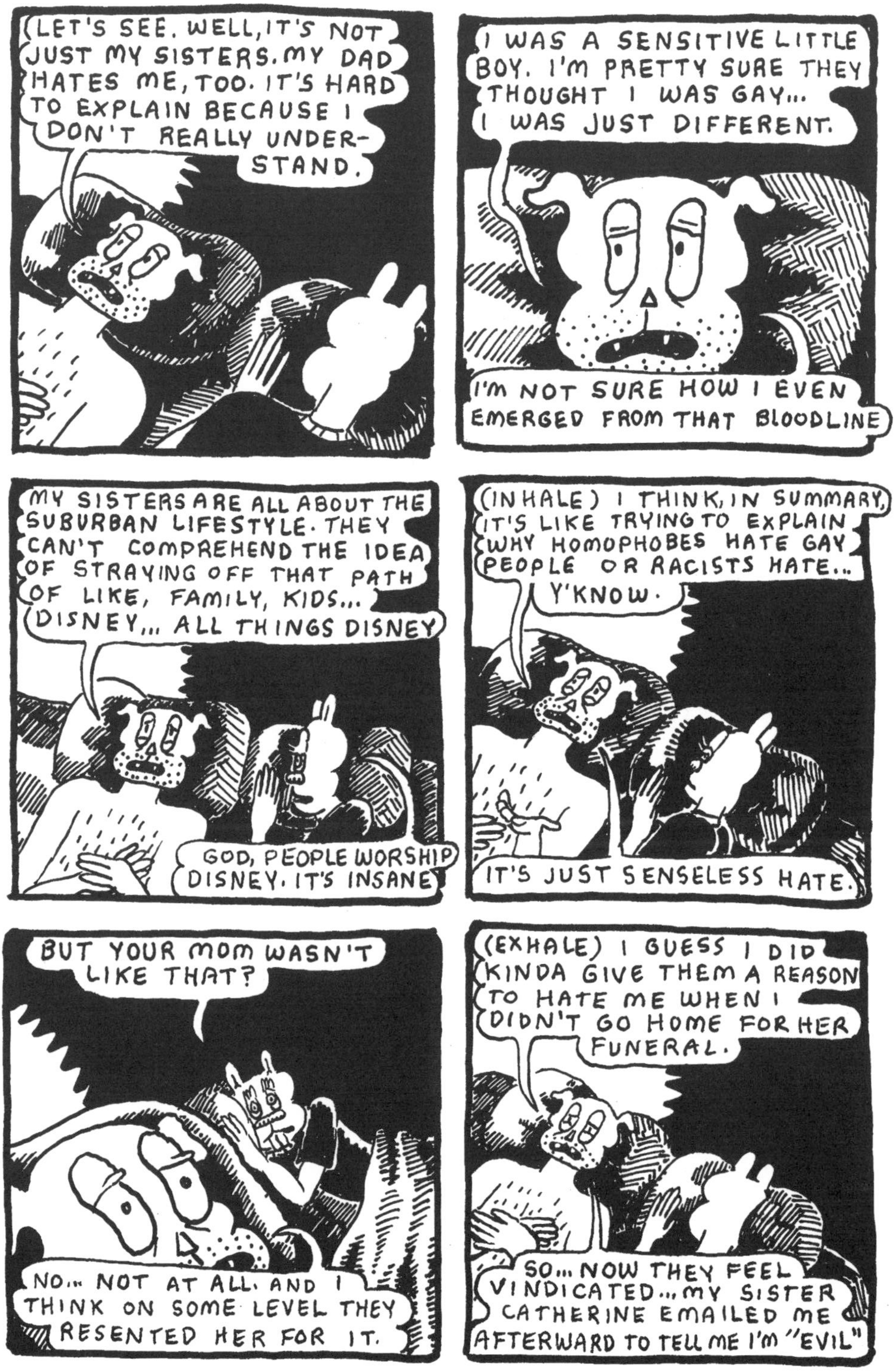
LET'S SEE. WELL, IT'S NOT JUST MY SISTERS. MY DAD HATES ME, TOO. IT'S HARD TO EXPLAIN BECAUSE I DON'T REALLY UNDERSTAND.
I WAS A SENSITIVE LITTLE BOY. I'M PRETTY SURE THEY THOUGHT I WAS GAY... I WAS JUST DIFFERENT.
I'M NOT SURE HOW I EVEN EMERGED FROM THAT BLOODLINE
MY SISTERS ARE ALL ABOUT THE SUBURBAN LIFESTYLE. THEY CAN'T COMPREHEND THE IDEA OF STRAYING OFF THAT PATH OF LIKE, FAMILY, KIDS... DISNEY... ALL THINGS DISNEY
GOD, PEOPLE WORSHIP DISNEY. IT'S INSANE
(INHALE) I THINK, IN SUMMARY, IT'S LIKE TRYING TO EXPLAIN WHY HOMOPHOBES HATE GAY PEOPLE OR RACISTS HATE... Y'KNOW.
IT'S JUST SENSELESS HATE.
BUT YOUR MOM WASN'T LIKE THAT?
NO... NOT AT ALL. AND I THINK ON SOME LEVEL THEY RESENTED HER FOR IT.
(EXHALE) I GUESS I DID KINDA GIVE THEM A REASON TO HATE ME WHEN I DIDN'T GO HOME FOR HER FUNERAL.
SO... NOW THEY FEEL VINDICATED... MY SISTER CATHERINE EMAILED ME AFTERWARD TO TELL ME I'M "EVIL"

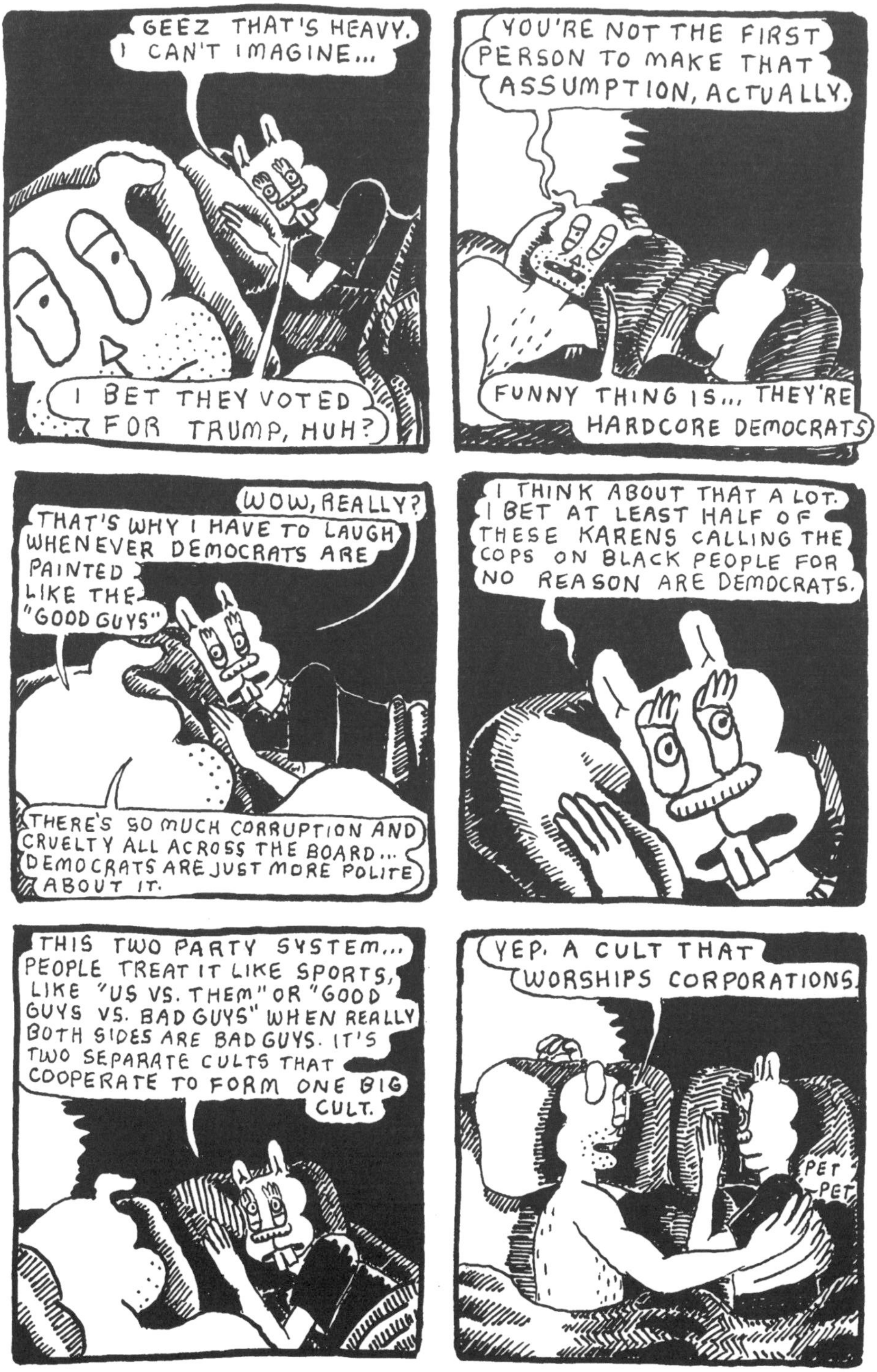
GEEZ THAT'S HEAVY. I CAN'T IMAGINE...
I BET THEY VOTED FOR TRUMP, HUH?
YOU'RE NOT THE FIRST PERSON TO MAKE THAT ASSUMPTION, ACTUALLY.
FUNNY THING IS... THEY'RE HARDCORE DEMOCRATS
WOW, REALLY?
THAT'S WHY I HAVE TO LAUGH WHENEVER DEMOCRATS ARE PAINTED LIKE THE "GOOD GUYS"
THERE'S SO MUCH CORRUPTION AND CRUELTY ALL ACROSS THE BOARD... DEMOCRATS ARE JUST MORE POLITE ABOUT IT.
I THINK ABOUT THAT A LOT. I BET AT LEAST HALF OF THESE KARENS CALLING THE COPS ON BLACK PEOPLE FOR NO REASON ARE DEMOCRATS.
THIS TWO PARTY SYSTEM... PEOPLE TREAT IT LIKE SPORTS, LIKE "US VS. THEM" OR "GOOD GUYS VS. BAD GUYS" WHEN REALLY BOTH SIDES ARE BAD GUYS. IT'S TWO SEPARATE CULTS THAT COOPERATE TO FORM ONE BIG CULT.
YEP. A CULT THAT WORSHIPS CORPORATIONS.
PET PET

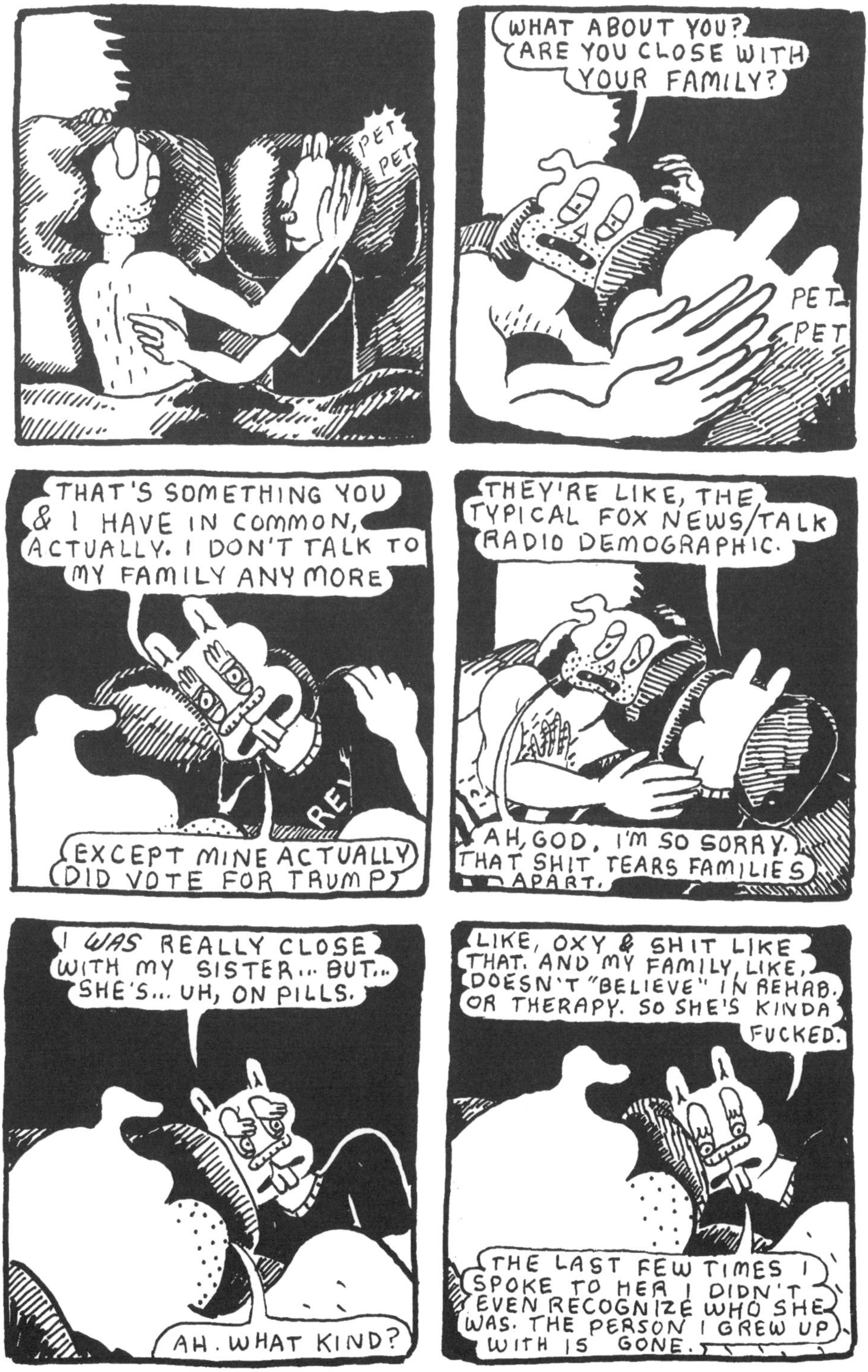
PET PET
WHAT ABOUT YOU? ARE YOU CLOSE WITH YOUR FAMILY?
PET PET
THAT'S SOMETHING YOU & I HAVE IN COMMON, ACTUALLY. I DON'T TALK TO MY FAMILY ANY MORE
EXCEPT MINE ACTUALLY DID VOTE FOR TRUMP
THEY'RE LIKE, THE TYPICAL FOX NEWS/TALK RADIO DEMOGRAPHIC.
AH, GOD, I'M SO SORRY. THAT SHIT TEARS FAMILIES APART.
I *WAS* REALLY CLOSE WITH MY SISTER... BUT... SHE'S... UH, ON PILLS.
AH. WHAT KIND?
LIKE, OXY & SHIT LIKE THAT. AND MY FAMILY, LIKE, DOESN'T "BELIEVE" IN REHAB. OR THERAPY. SO SHE'S KINDA FUCKED.
THE LAST FEW TIMES I SPOKE TO HER I DIDN'T EVEN RECOGNIZE WHO SHE WAS. THE PERSON I GREW UP WITH IS GONE.

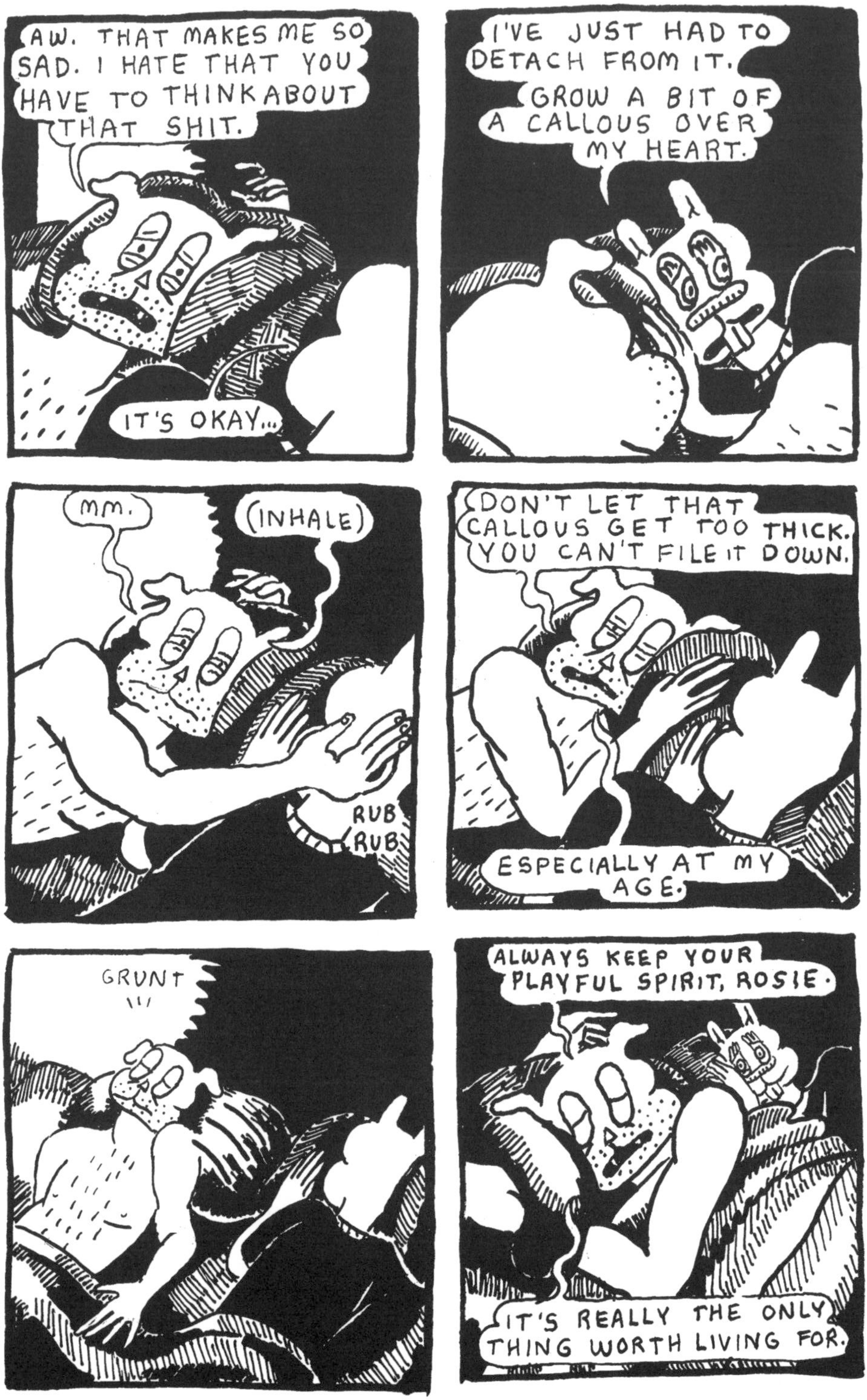
AW. THAT MAKES ME SO SAD. I HATE THAT YOU HAVE TO THINK ABOUT THAT SHIT.
IT'S OKAY...
I'VE JUST HAD TO DETACH FROM IT.
GROW A BIT OF A CALLOUS OVER MY HEART.
MM.
(INHALE)
RUB RUB
DON'T LET THAT CALLOUS GET TOO THICK. YOU CAN'T FILE IT DOWN.
ESPECIALLY AT MY AGE.
GRUNT
ALWAYS KEEP YOUR PLAYFUL SPIRIT, ROSIE.
IT'S REALLY THE ONLY THING WORTH LIVING FOR.

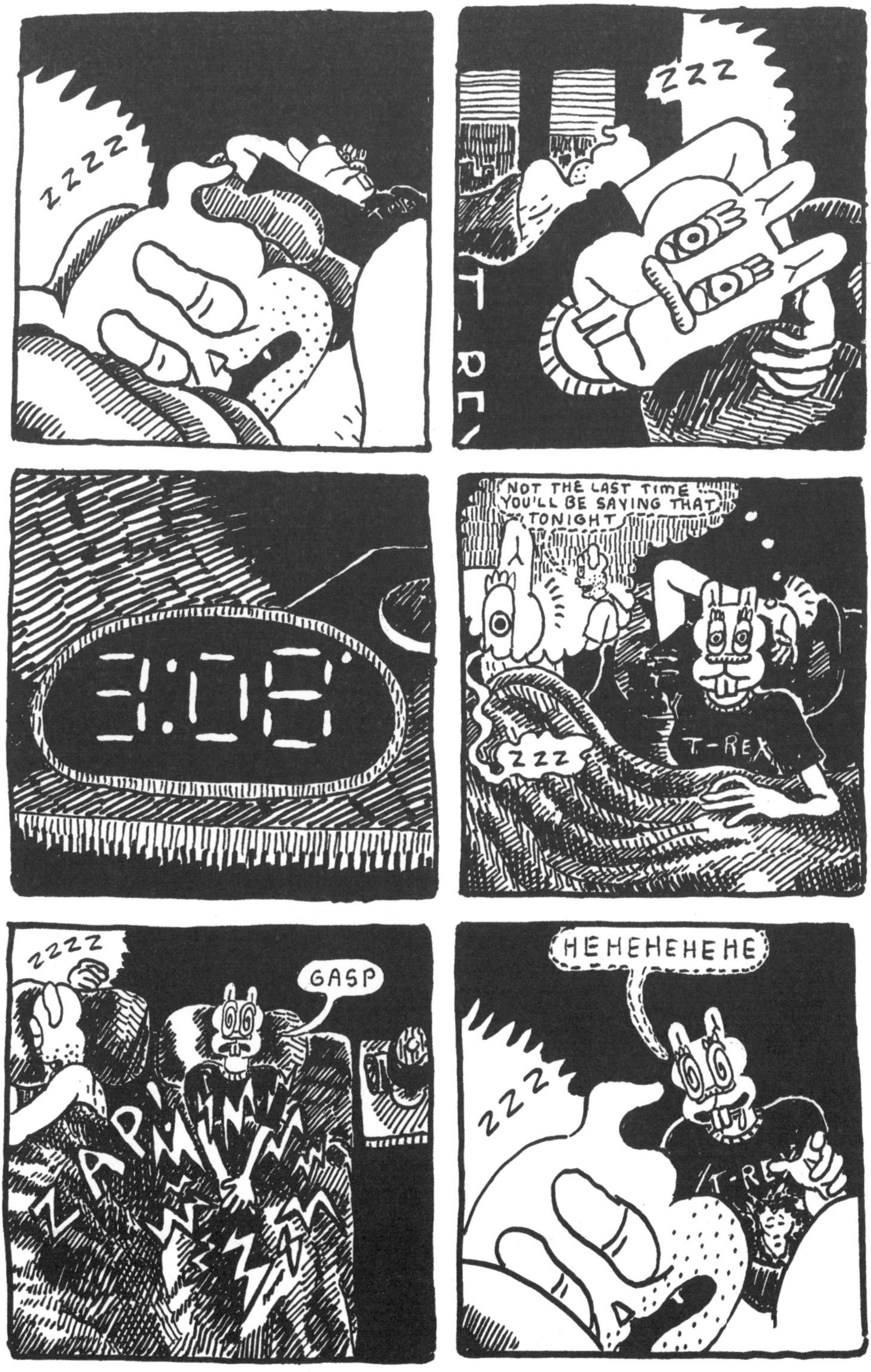
ZZZZ
ZZZ
T-REX
3:08
NOT THE LAST TIME YOU'LL BE SAYING THAT TONIGHT
ZZZ
T-REX
ZZZZ
GASP
ZAP
HEHEHEHEHEHE
ZZZ
T-REX

ZZZZ
SMOOCH
STROKE
STROKE
STROKE
STROKE
THROB
THROB
THROB
HOLY FUCCCK...
THROB
THROB
THROB.
YOU WANNA SEE IT?

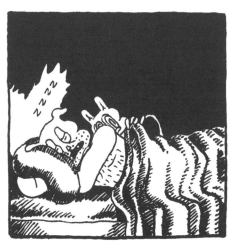

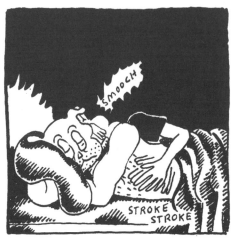

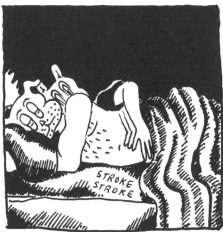

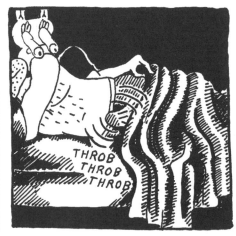

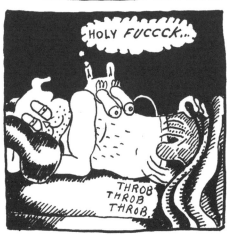

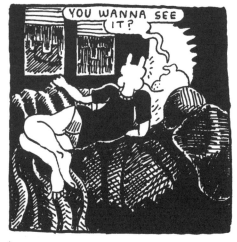

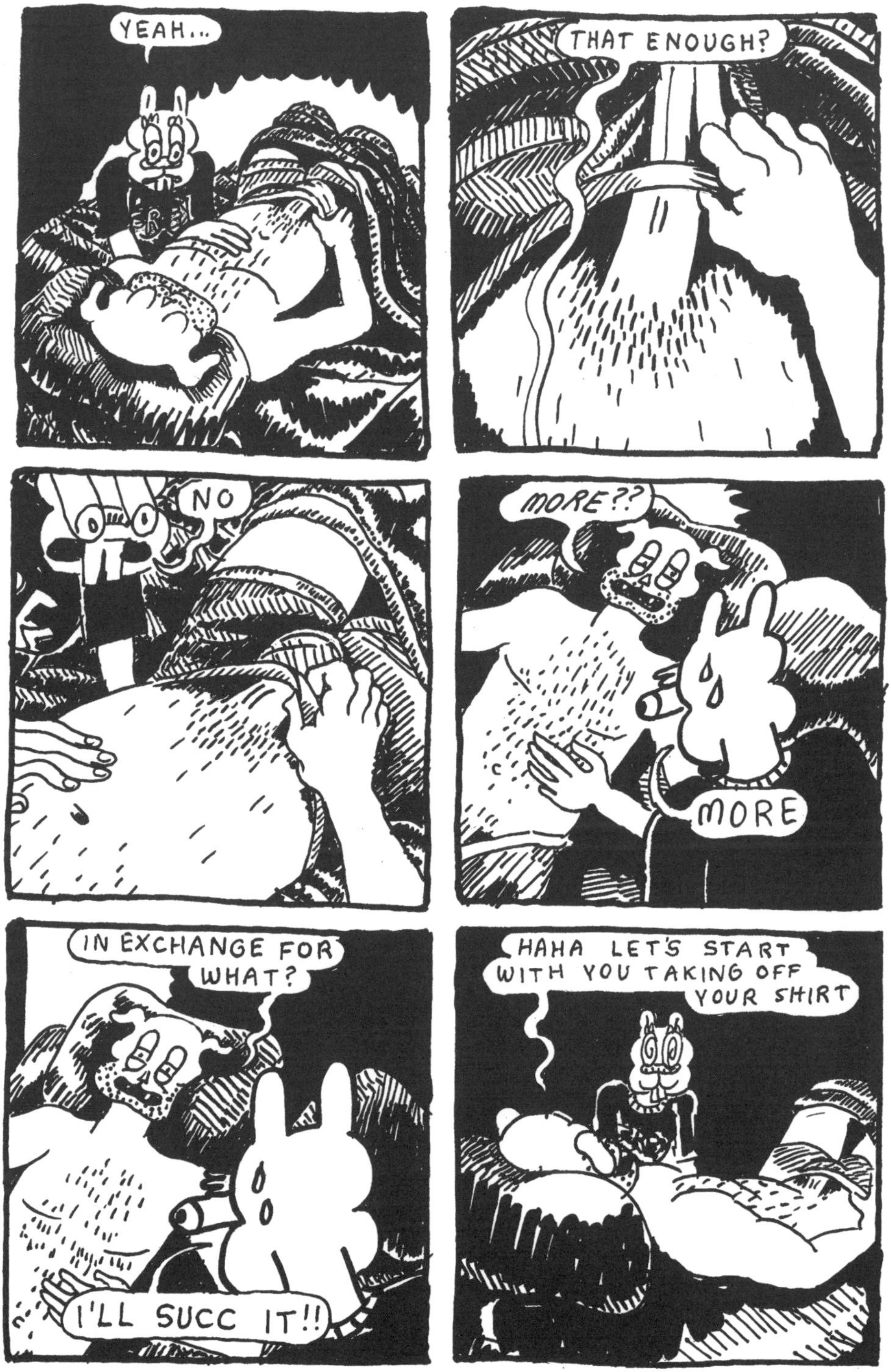
YEAH...
THAT ENOUGH?
NO
MORE??
MORE
IN EXCHANGE FOR WHAT?
I'LL SUCC IT!!
HAHA LET'S START WITH YOU TAKING OFF YOUR SHIRT

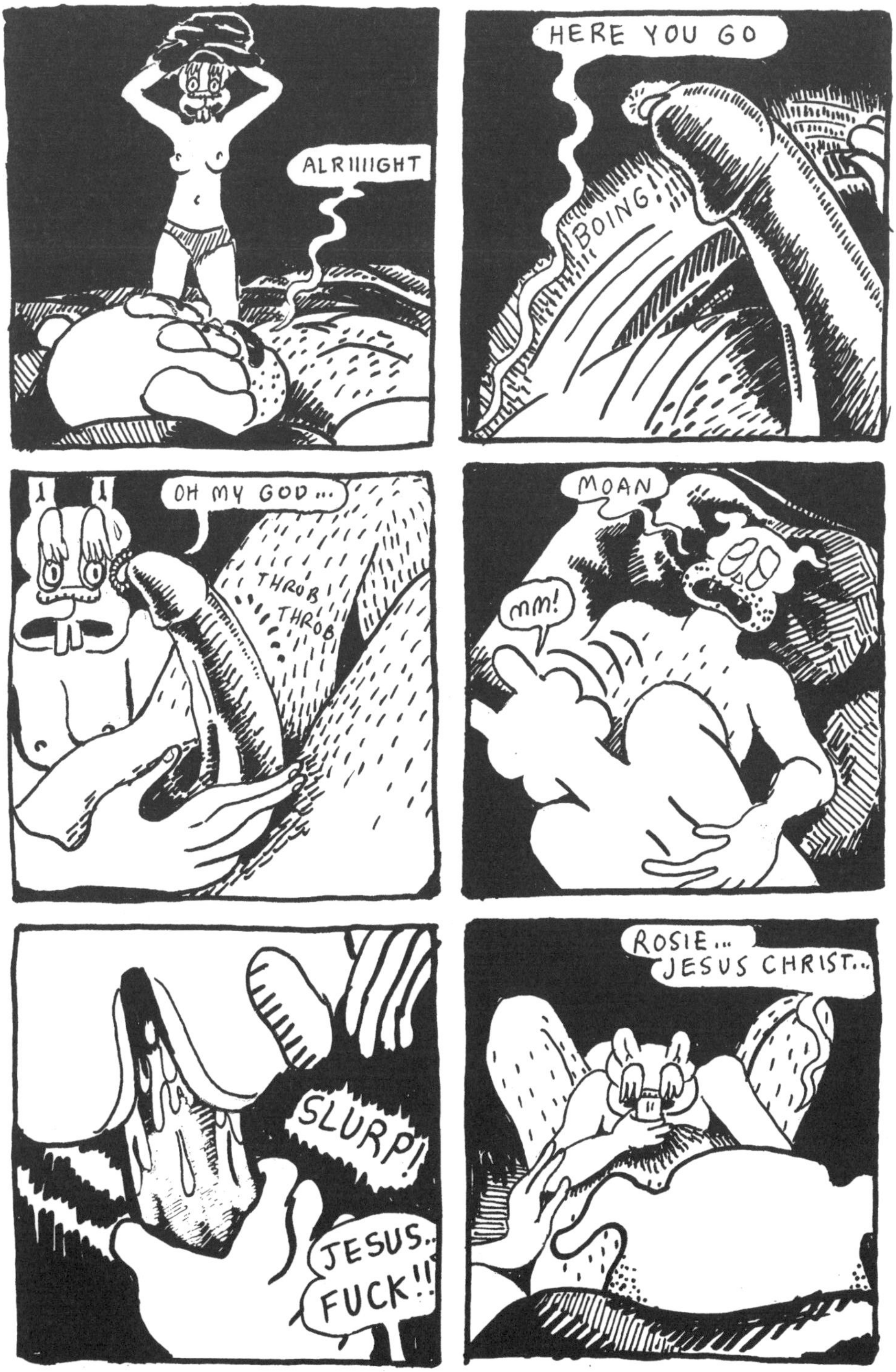
ALRIIIIGHT
HERE YOU GO
BOING!
OH MY GOD...
THROB
THROB
MOAN
mm!
SLURP!
JESUS..
FUCK!!
ROSIE...
JESUS CHRIST...

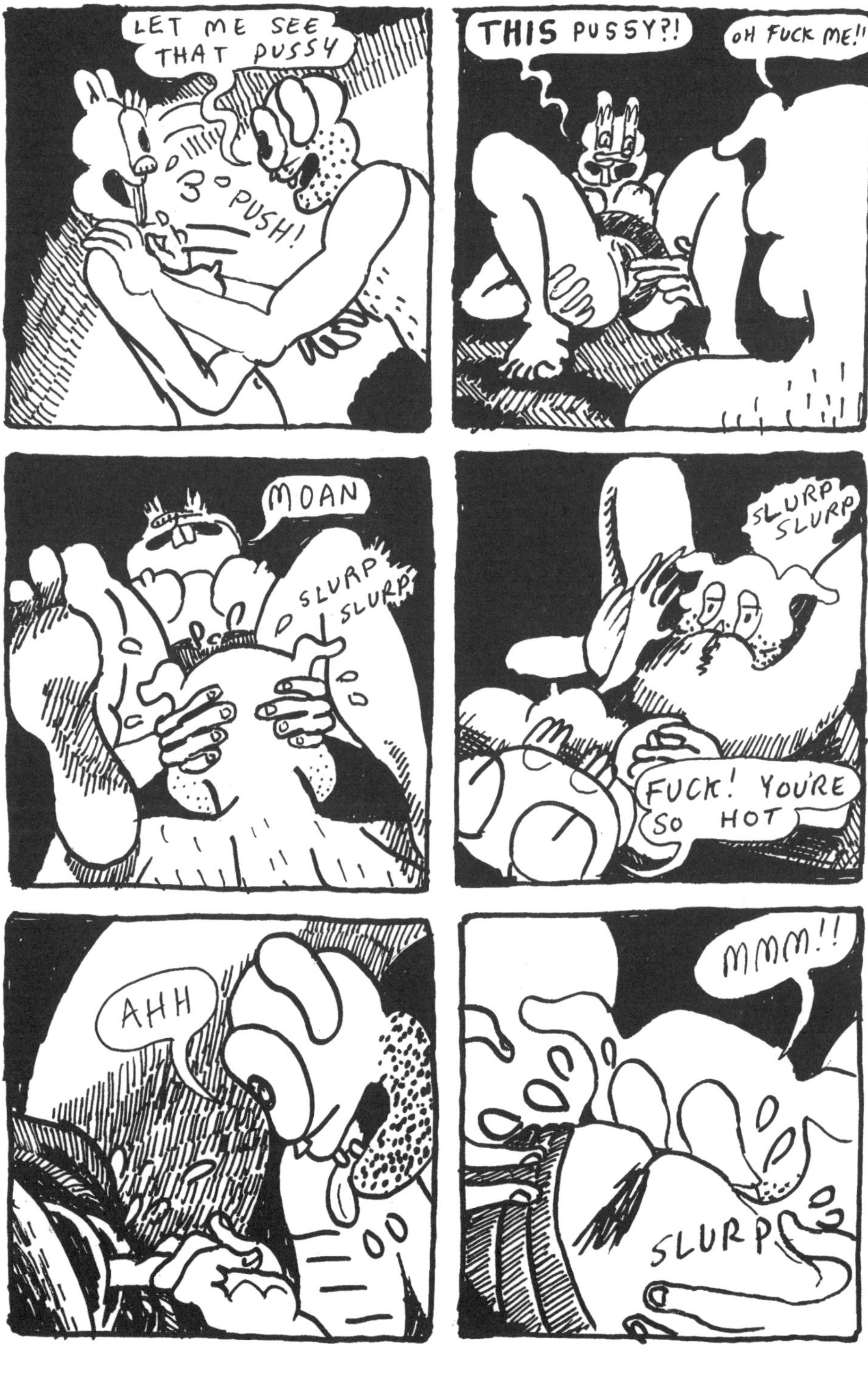
LET ME SEE THAT PUSSY
PUSH!
THIS PUSSY?!
OH FUCK ME!!
MOAN
SLURP SLURP
SLURP SLURP
FUCK! YOU'RE SO HOT
AHH
MMM!!
SLURP

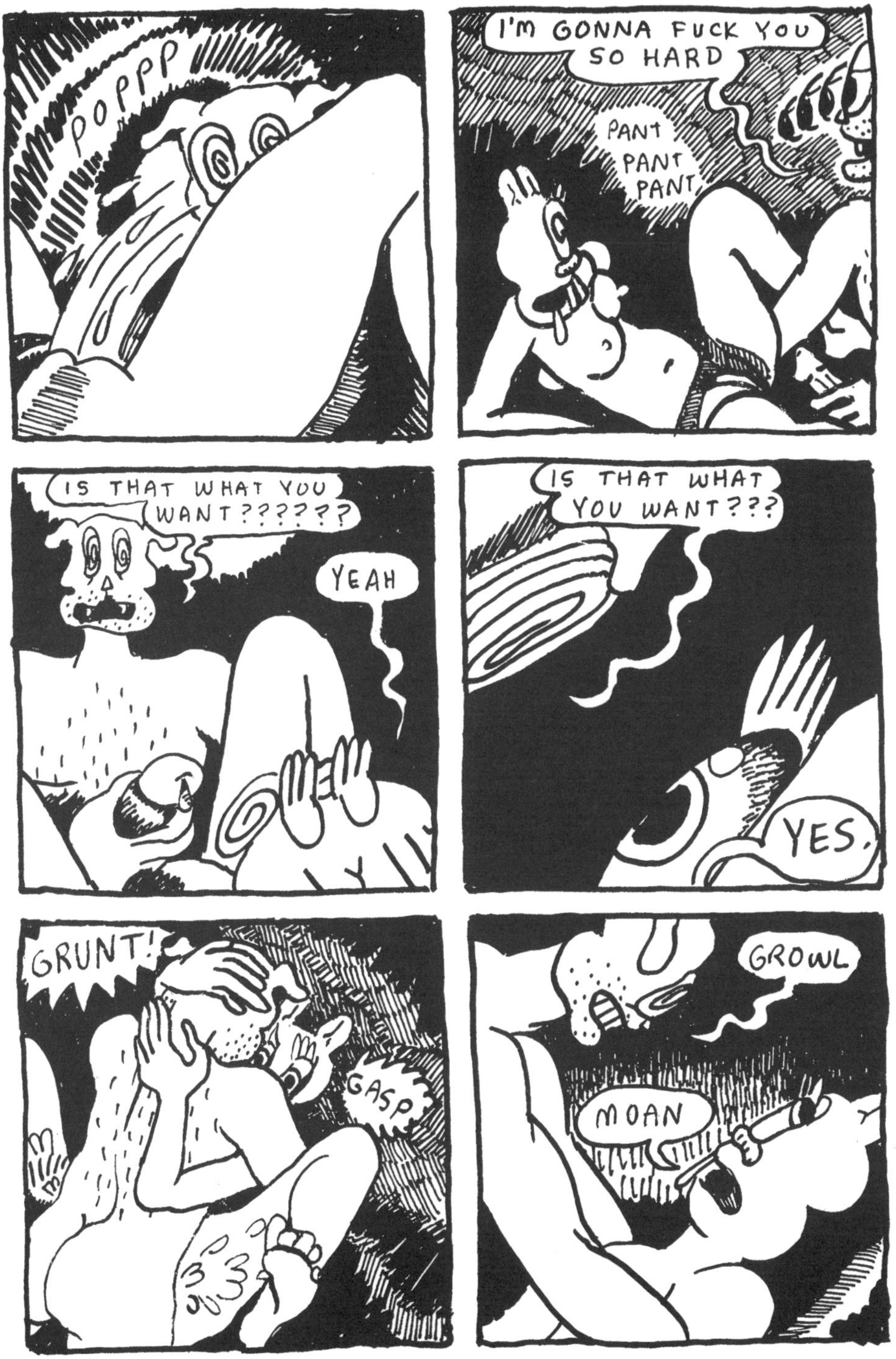
POPPP
I'M GONNA FUCK YOU SO HARD
PANT PANT PANT
IS THAT WHAT YOU WANT??????
YEAH
IS THAT WHAT YOU WANT???
YES.
GRUNT!
GASP
GROWL
MOAN

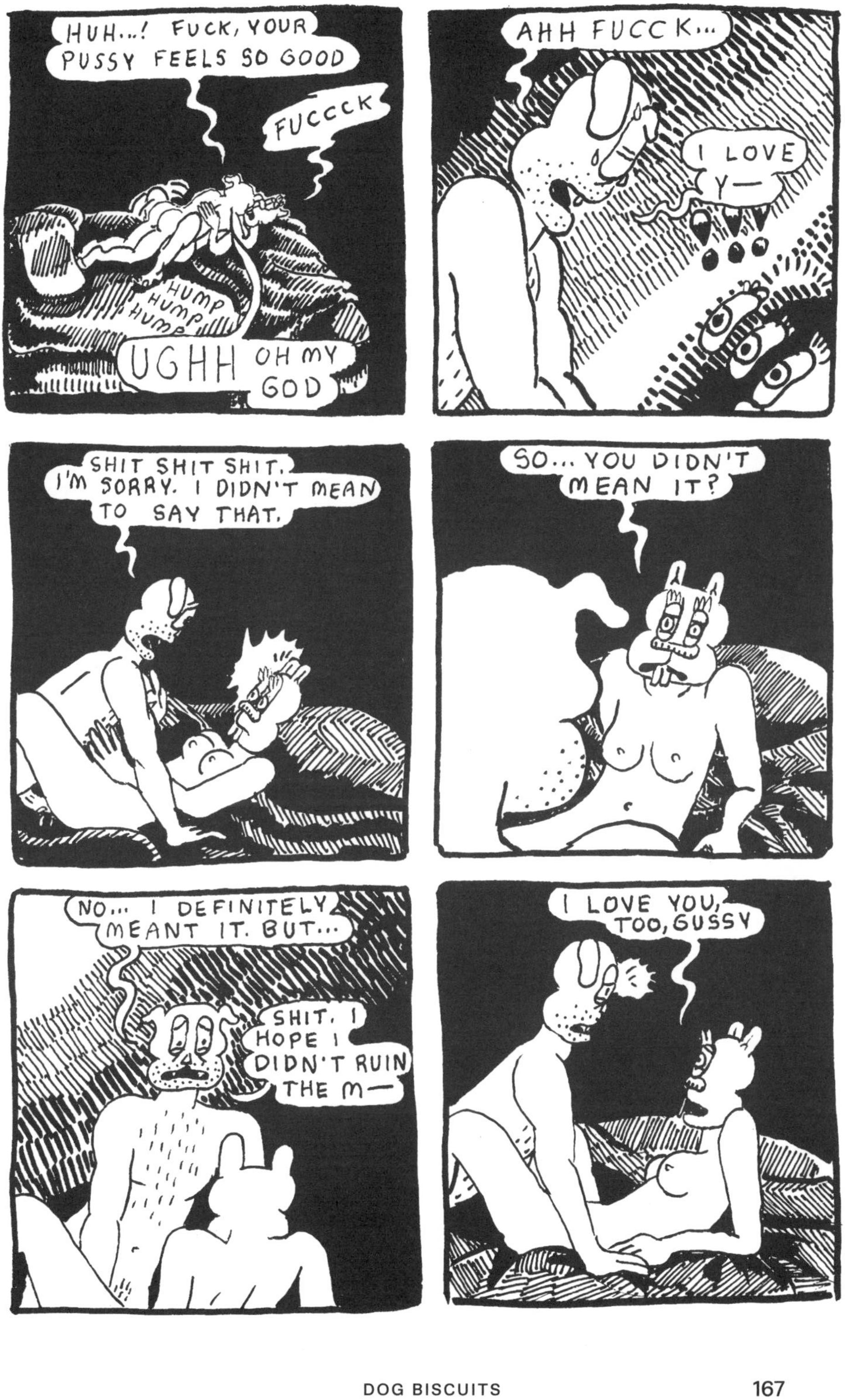
HUH...! FUCK, YOUR PUSSY FEELS SO GOOD
FUCCCK
HUMP HUMP HUMP
UGHH OH MY GOD
AHH FUCCK...
I LOVE Y—
SHIT SHIT SHIT. I'M SORRY. I DIDN'T MEAN TO SAY THAT.
SO... YOU DIDN'T MEAN IT?
NO... I DEFINITELY MEANT IT. BUT...
SHIT. I HOPE I DIDN'T RUIN THE M—
I LOVE YOU, TOO, GUSSY

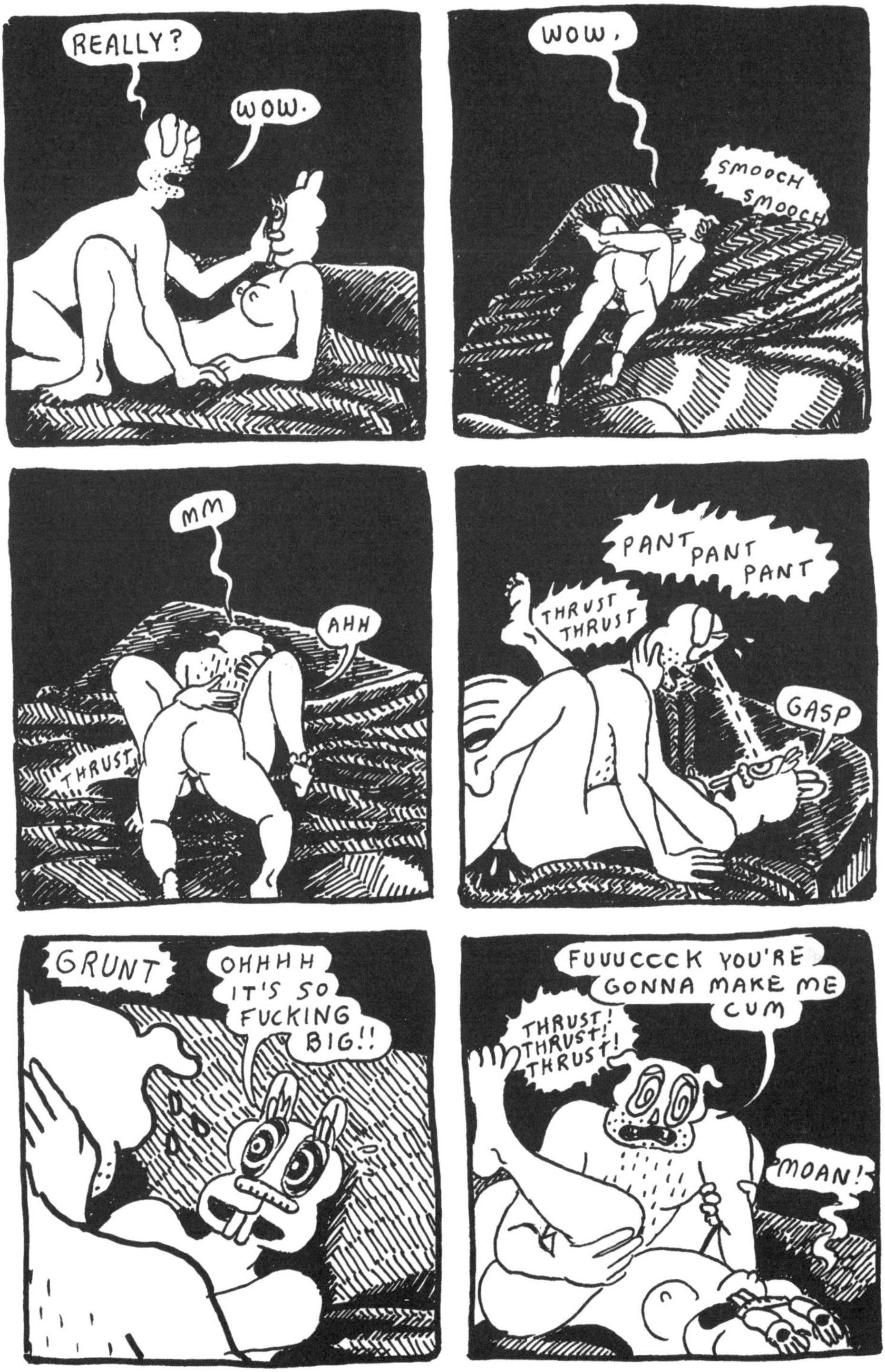
REALLY?
WOW.
WOW.
SMOOCH SMOOCH
MM
AHH
THRUST
PANT PANT PANT
THRUST THRUST
GASP
GRUNT
OHHHH IT'S SO FUCKING BIG!!
FUUUCCCK YOU'RE GONNA MAKE ME CUM
THRUST! THRUST! THRUST!
MOAN!

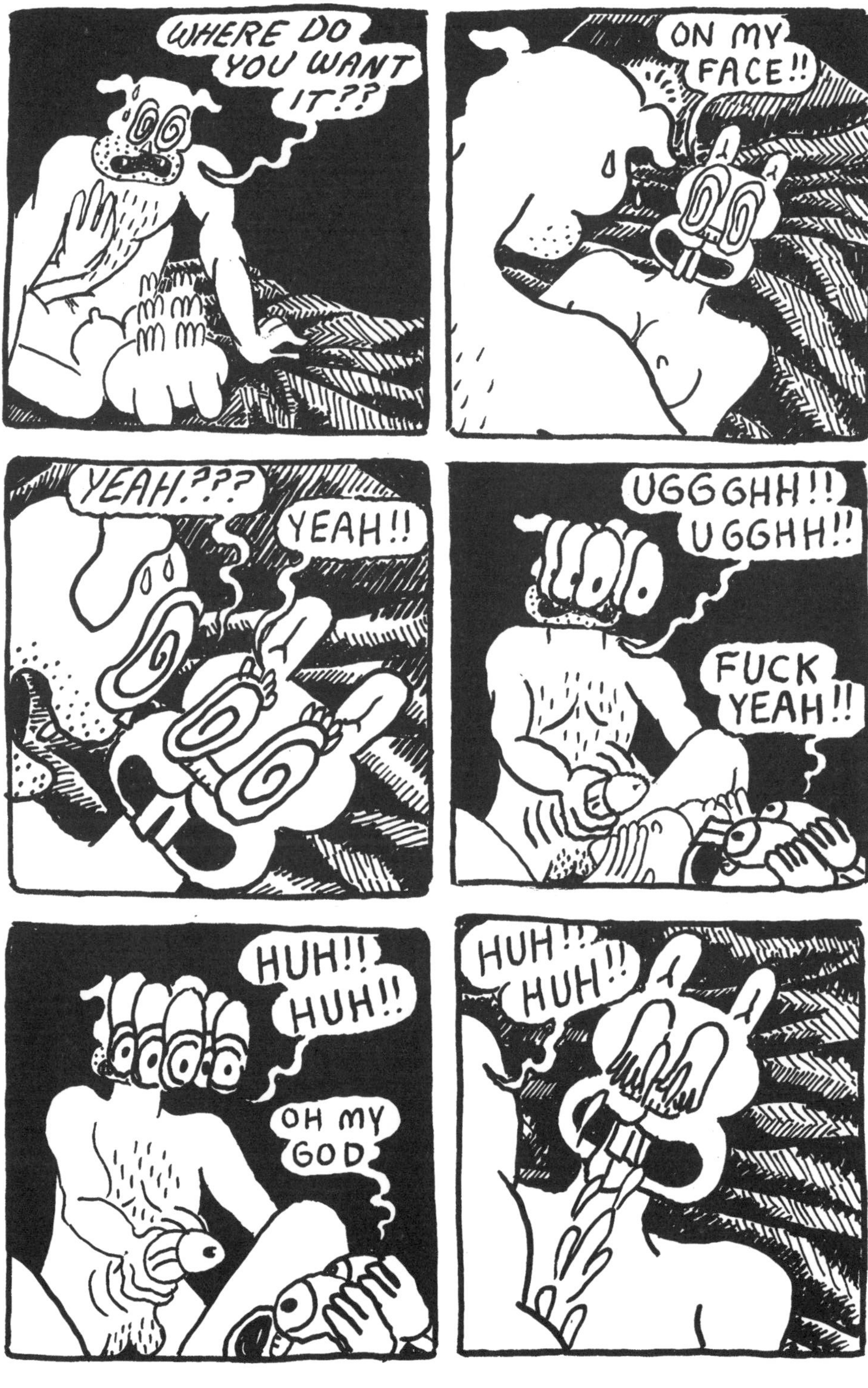
WHERE DO YOU WANT IT??
ON MY FACE!!
YEAH???
YEAH!!
UGGGHH!! UGGHH!!
FUCK YEAH!!
HUH!! HUH!!
OH MY GOD
HUH!! HUH!!

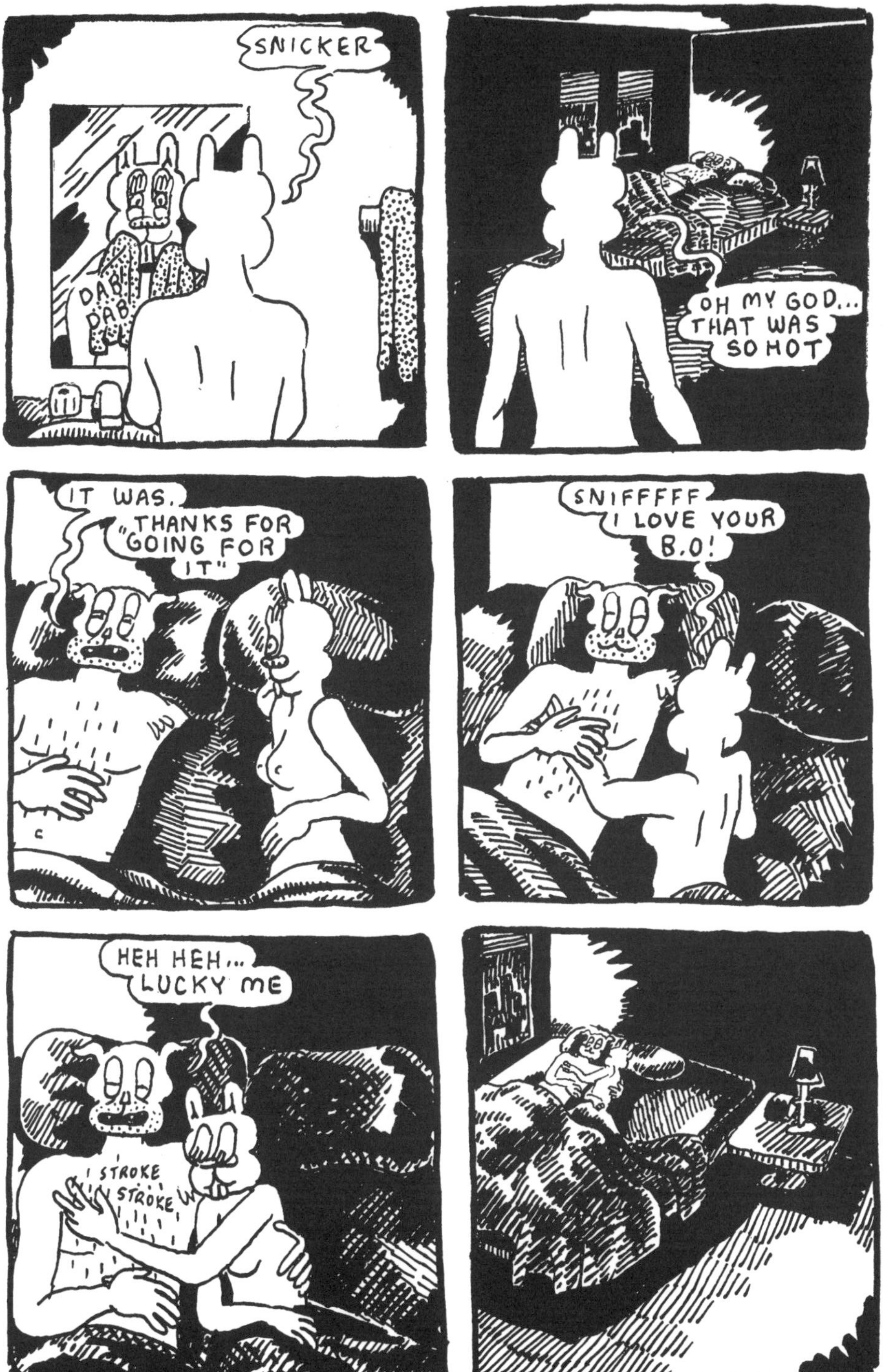

SNICKER
DAB DAB
OH MY GOD... THAT WAS SO HOT
IT WAS.
THANKS FOR "GOING FOR IT"
SNIFFFFF
I LOVE YOUR B.O!
HEH HEH... LUCKY ME
STROKE STROKE

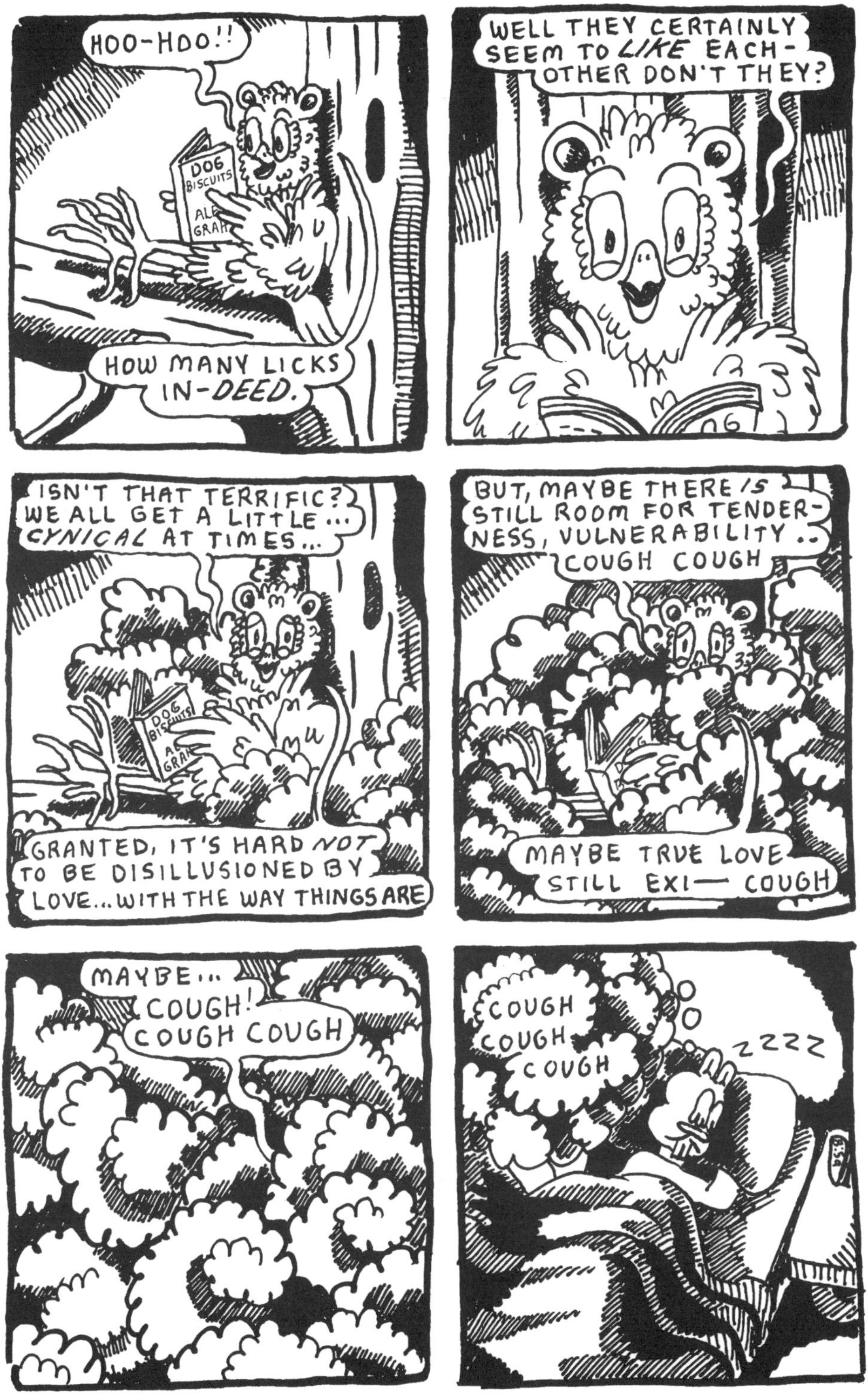
HOO-HOO!!
DOG BISCUITS AL GRAH
HOW MANY LICKS IN-DEED.
WELL THEY CERTAINLY SEEM TO LIKE EACH-OTHER DON'T THEY?
ISN'T THAT TERRIFIC? WE ALL GET A LITTLE... CYNICAL AT TIMES...
DOG BISCUITS A GRAH
GRANTED, IT'S HARD NOT TO BE DISILLUSIONED BY LOVE...WITH THE WAY THINGS ARE
BUT, MAYBE THERE IS STILL ROOM FOR TENDERNESS, VULNERABILITY..
COUGH COUGH
MAYBE TRUE LOVE STILL EXI— COUGH
MAYBE...
COUGH! COUGH COUGH
COUGH COUGH COUGH
ZZZZ

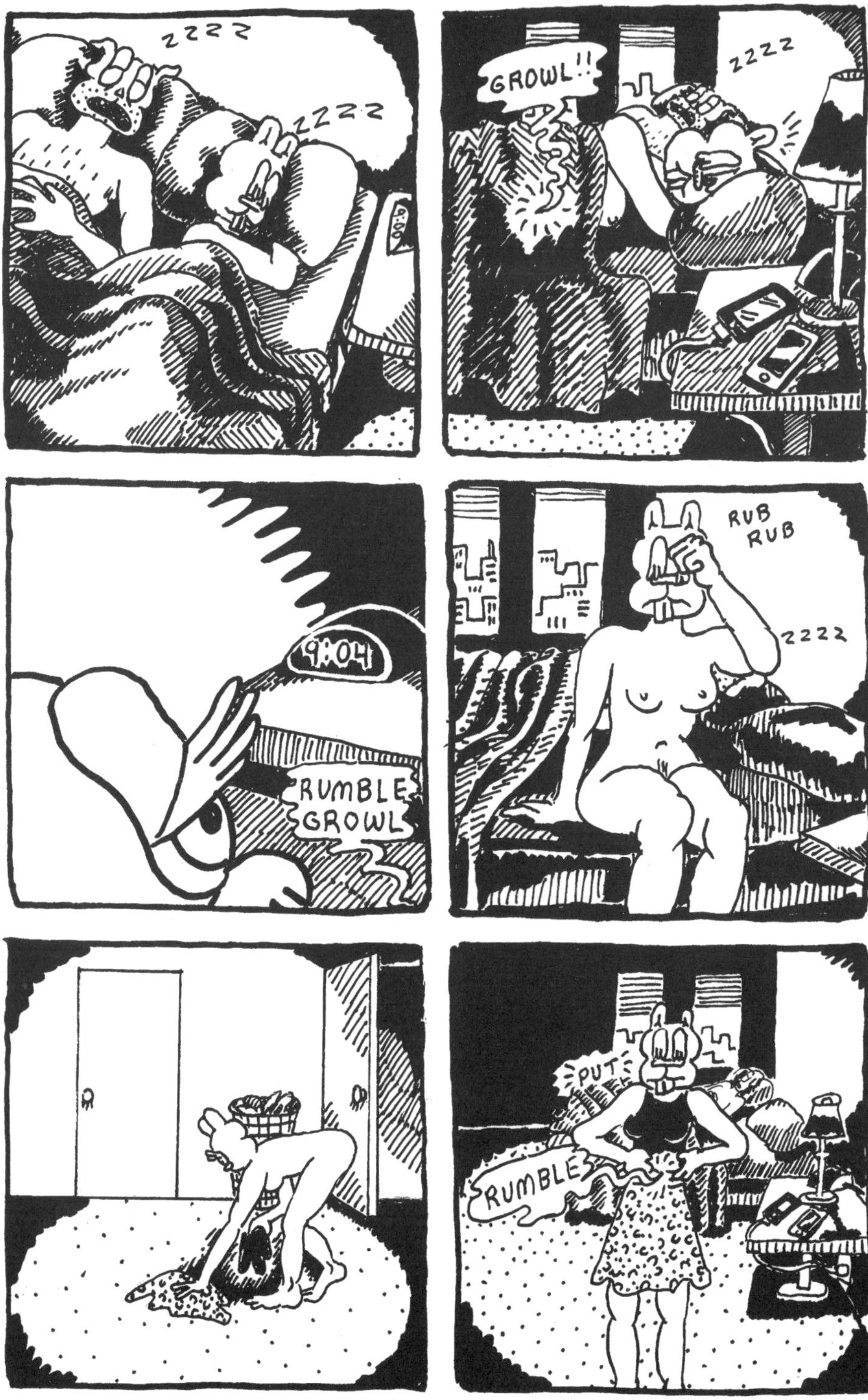
ZZZZ
ZZZZ
GROWL!!
ZZZZ
9:04
RUMBLE
GROWL
RUB
RUB
ZZZZ
PUT
RUMBLE

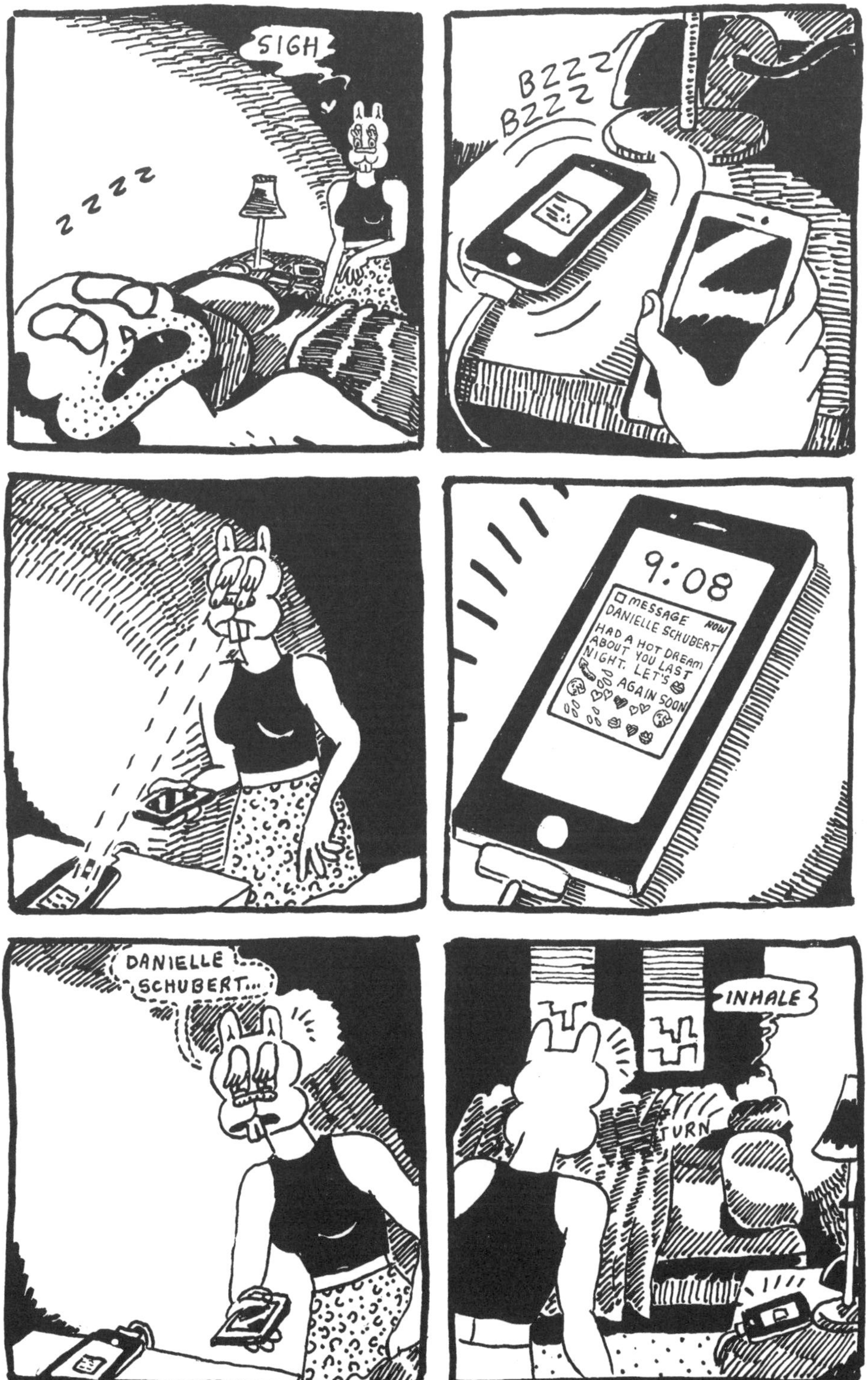
SIGH
ZZZZ
BZZZ
BZZZ
9:08
MESSAGE NOW
DANIELLE SCHUBERT
HAD A HOT DREAM ABOUT YOU LAST NIGHT. LET'S AGAIN SOON
DANIELLE SCHUBERT...
INHALE
TURN

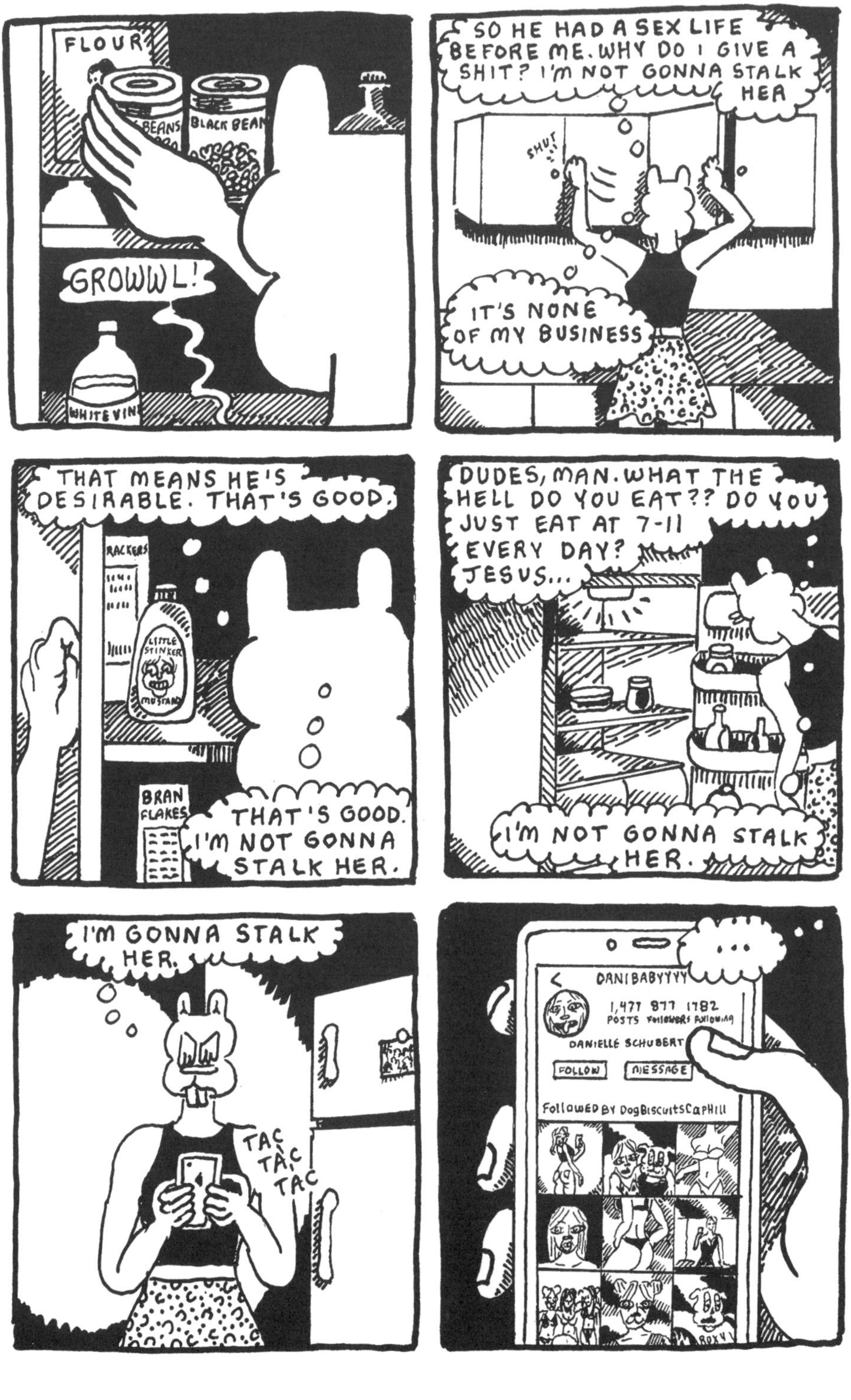
FLOUR
BEANS
BLACK BEAN
GROWWL!
WHITE VIN
SO HE HAD A SEX LIFE BEFORE ME. WHY DO I GIVE A SHIT? I'M NOT GONNA STALK HER
SHUT
IT'S NONE OF MY BUSINESS
THAT MEANS HE'S DESIRABLE. THAT'S GOOD.
RACKERS
LITTLE STINKER MUSTARD
BRAN FLAKES
THAT'S GOOD. I'M NOT GONNA STALK HER.
DUDES, MAN. WHAT THE HELL DO YOU EAT?? DO YOU JUST EAT AT 7-11 EVERY DAY? JESUS...
I'M NOT GONNA STALK HER.
I'M GONNA STALK HER.
TAC TAC TAC
...
DANIBABYYYY
1,477 877 1782
POSTS Followers Following
DANIELLE SCHUBERT
FOLLOW
MESSAGE
Followed by DogBiscuitsCapHill
ROXY

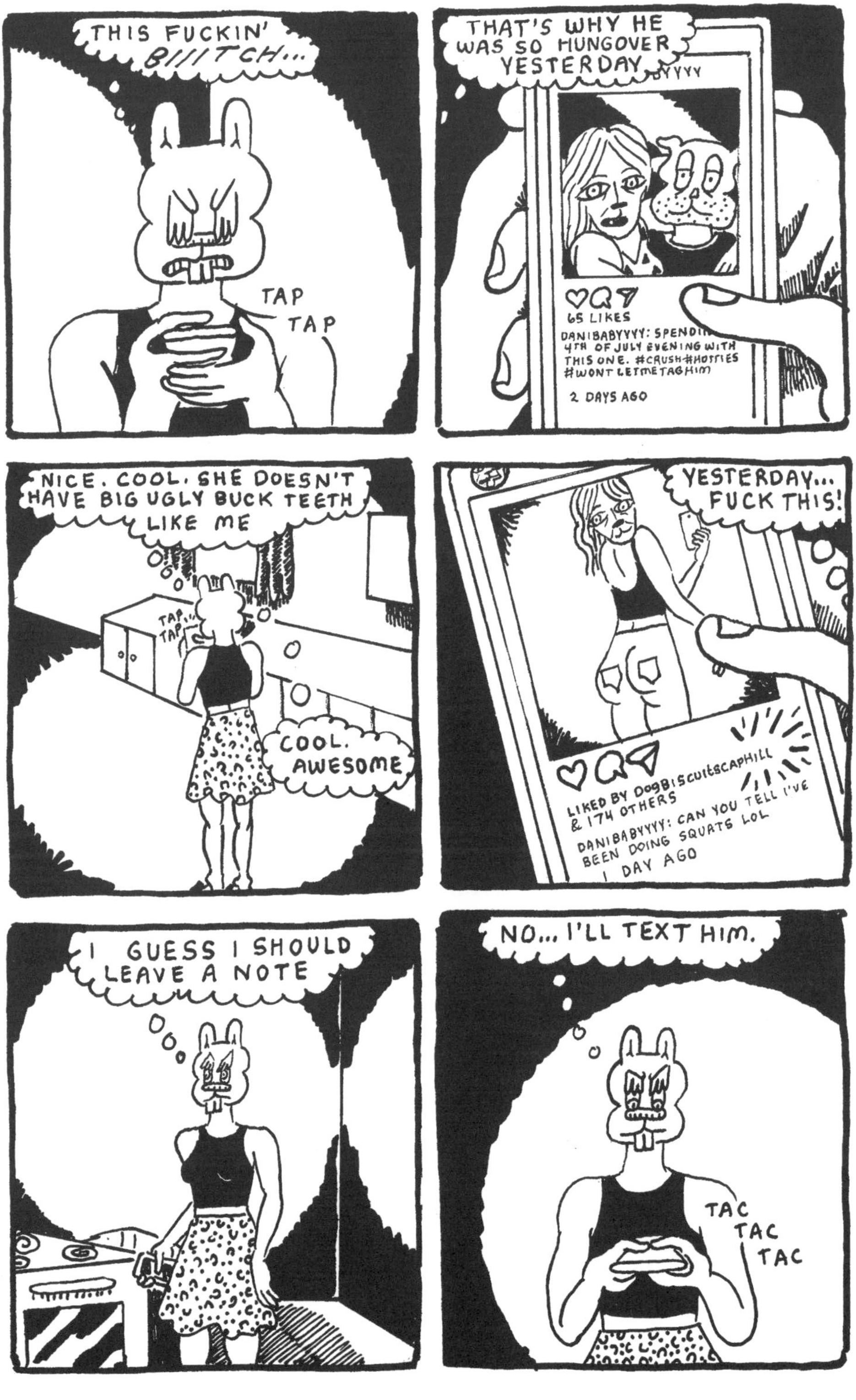
THIS FUCKIN' BIIITCH...
TAP TAP
THAT'S WHY HE WAS SO HUNGOVER YESTERDAY
65 LIKES
DANIBABYYYY: SPENDIN
4TH OF JULY EVENING WITH THIS ONE. #CRUSH #HOTTIES #WONTLETMETAGHIM
2 DAYS AGO
NICE. COOL. SHE DOESN'T HAVE BIG UGLY BUCK TEETH LIKE ME
TAP TAP
COOL. AWESOME
YESTERDAY... FUCK THIS!
LIKED BY DOGBISCUITSCAPHILL & 174 OTHERS
DANIBABYYYY: CAN YOU TELL I'VE BEEN DOING SQUATS LOL
1 DAY AGO
I GUESS I SHOULD LEAVE A NOTE
NO... I'LL TEXT HIM.
TAC TAC TAC

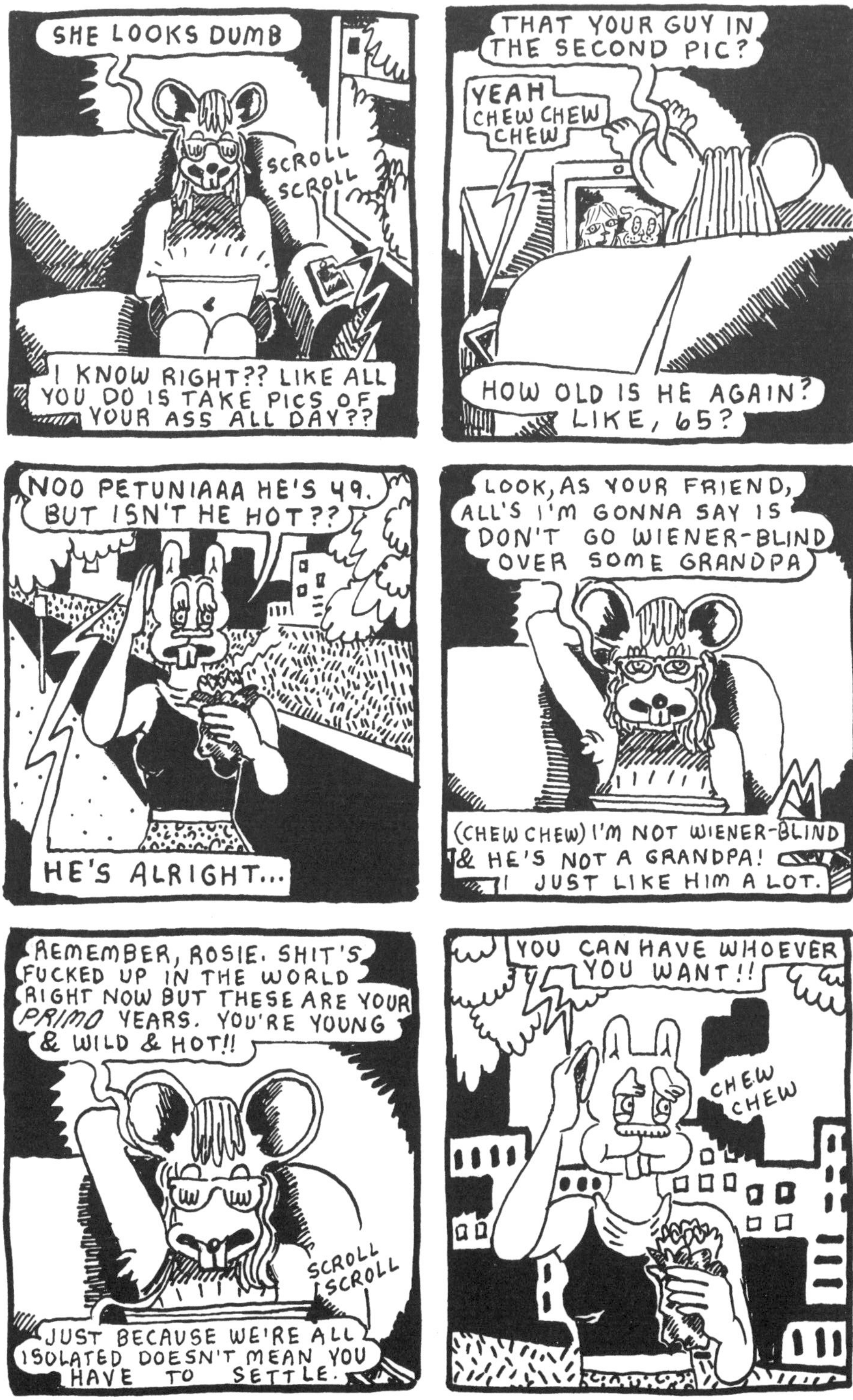
SHE LOOKS DUMB
SCROLL SCROLL
I KNOW RIGHT?? LIKE ALL YOU DO IS TAKE PICS OF YOUR ASS ALL DAY??
THAT YOUR GUY IN THE SECOND PIC?
YEAH CHEW CHEW CHEW
HOW OLD IS HE AGAIN? LIKE, 65?
NOO PETUNIAAA HE'S 49. BUT ISN'T HE HOT??
HE'S ALRIGHT...
LOOK, AS YOUR FRIEND, ALL'S I'M GONNA SAY IS DON'T GO WIENER-BLIND OVER SOME GRANDPA
(CHEW CHEW) I'M NOT WIENER-BLIND & HE'S NOT A GRANDPA! I JUST LIKE HIM A LOT.
REMEMBER, ROSIE. SHIT'S FUCKED UP IN THE WORLD RIGHT NOW BUT THESE ARE YOUR PRIMO YEARS. YOU'RE YOUNG & WILD & HOT!!
SCROLL SCROLL
JUST BECAUSE WE'RE ALL ISOLATED DOESN'T MEAN YOU HAVE TO SETTLE.
YOU CAN HAVE WHOEVER YOU WANT!!
CHEW CHEW

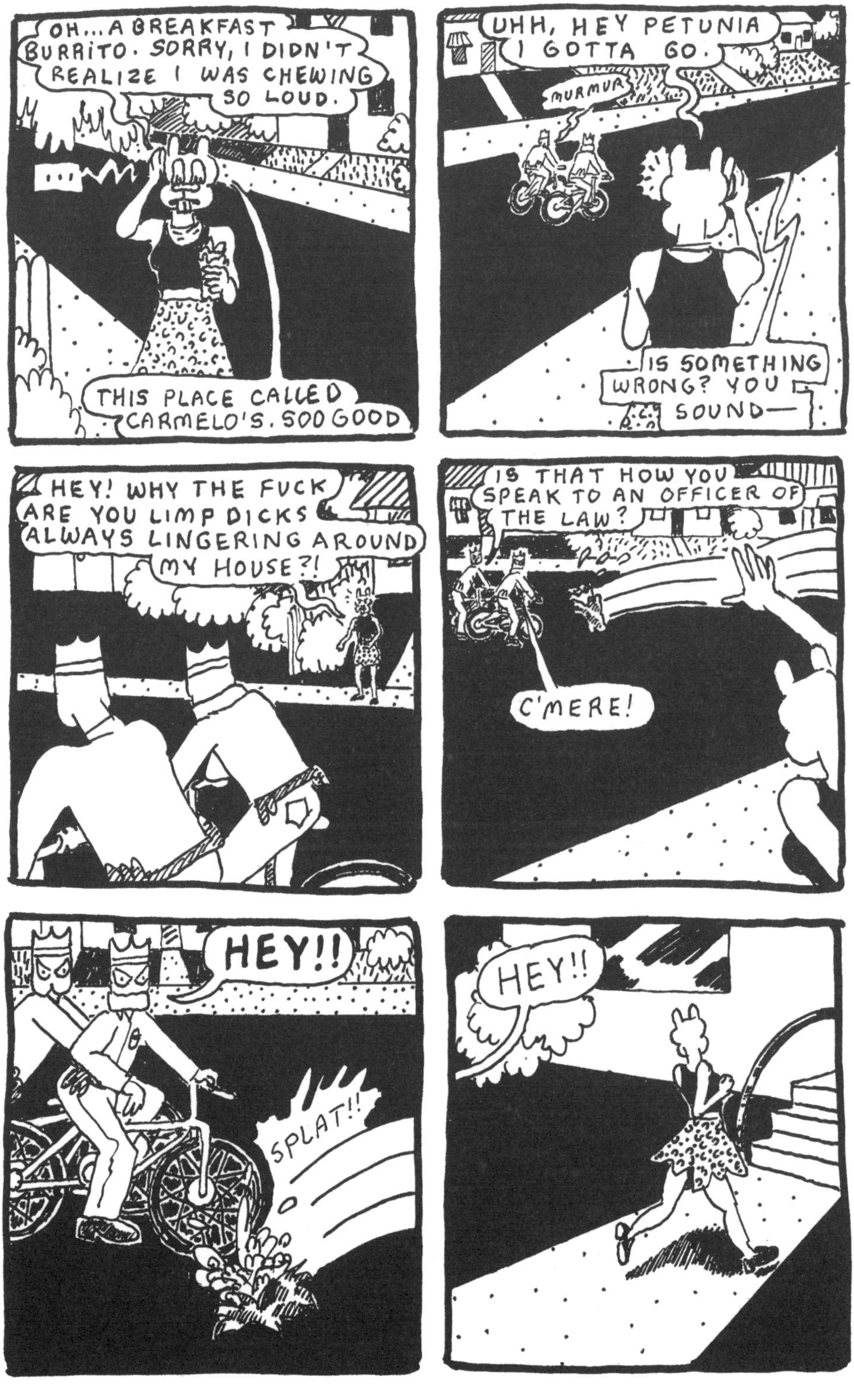

OH... A BREAKFAST BURRITO. SORRY, I DIDN'T REALIZE I WAS CHEWING SO LOUD.
...
THIS PLACE CALLED CARMELO'S. SOO GOOD
UHH, HEY PETUNIA I GOTTA GO.
MURMUR
IS SOMETHING WRONG? YOU SOUND—
HEY! WHY THE FUCK ARE YOU LIMP DICKS ALWAYS LINGERING AROUND MY HOUSE?!
IS THAT HOW YOU SPEAK TO AN OFFICER OF THE LAW?
C'MERE!
HEY!!
SPLAT!!
HEY!!

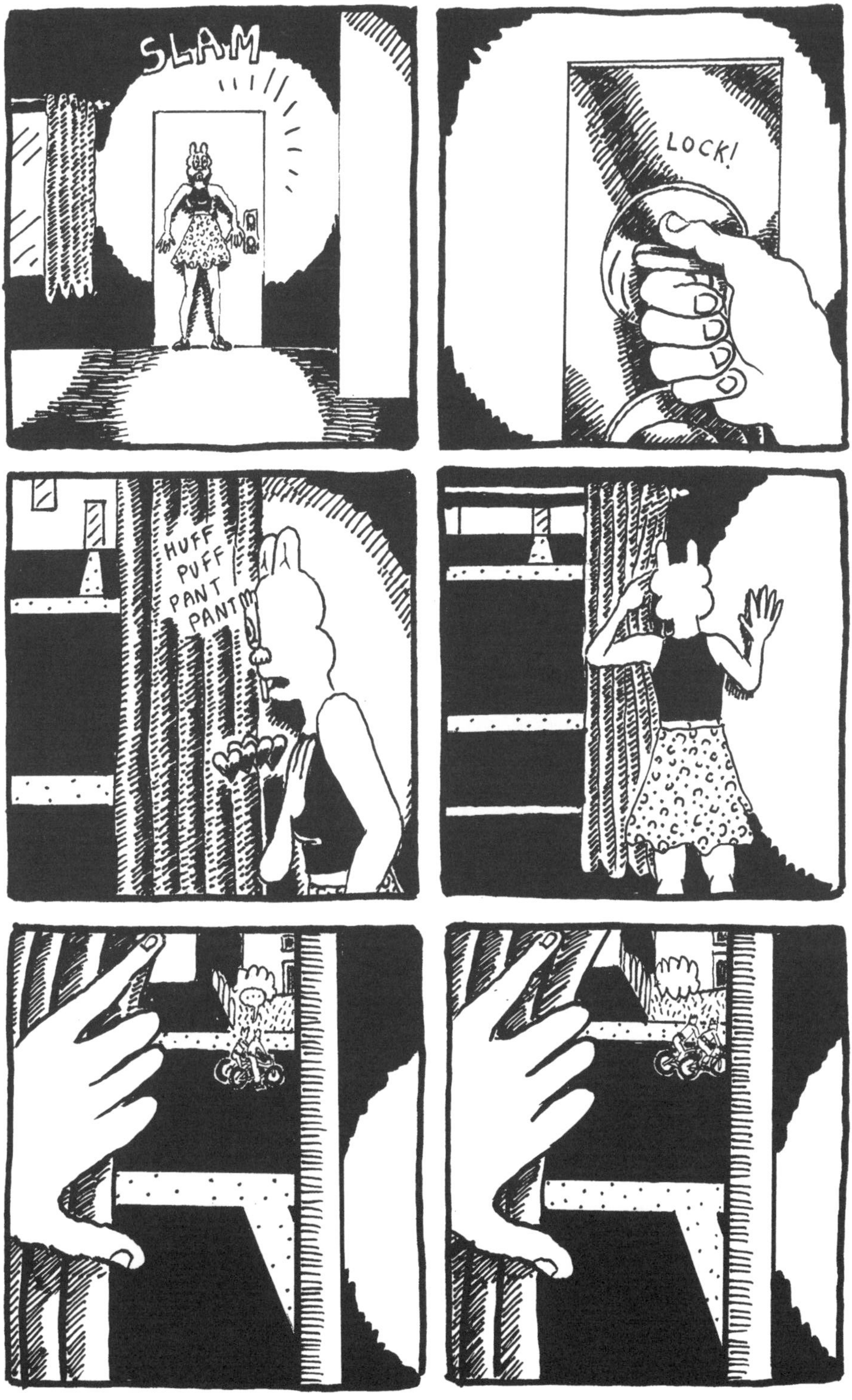
SLAM
LOCK!
HUFF
PUFF
PANT
PANT

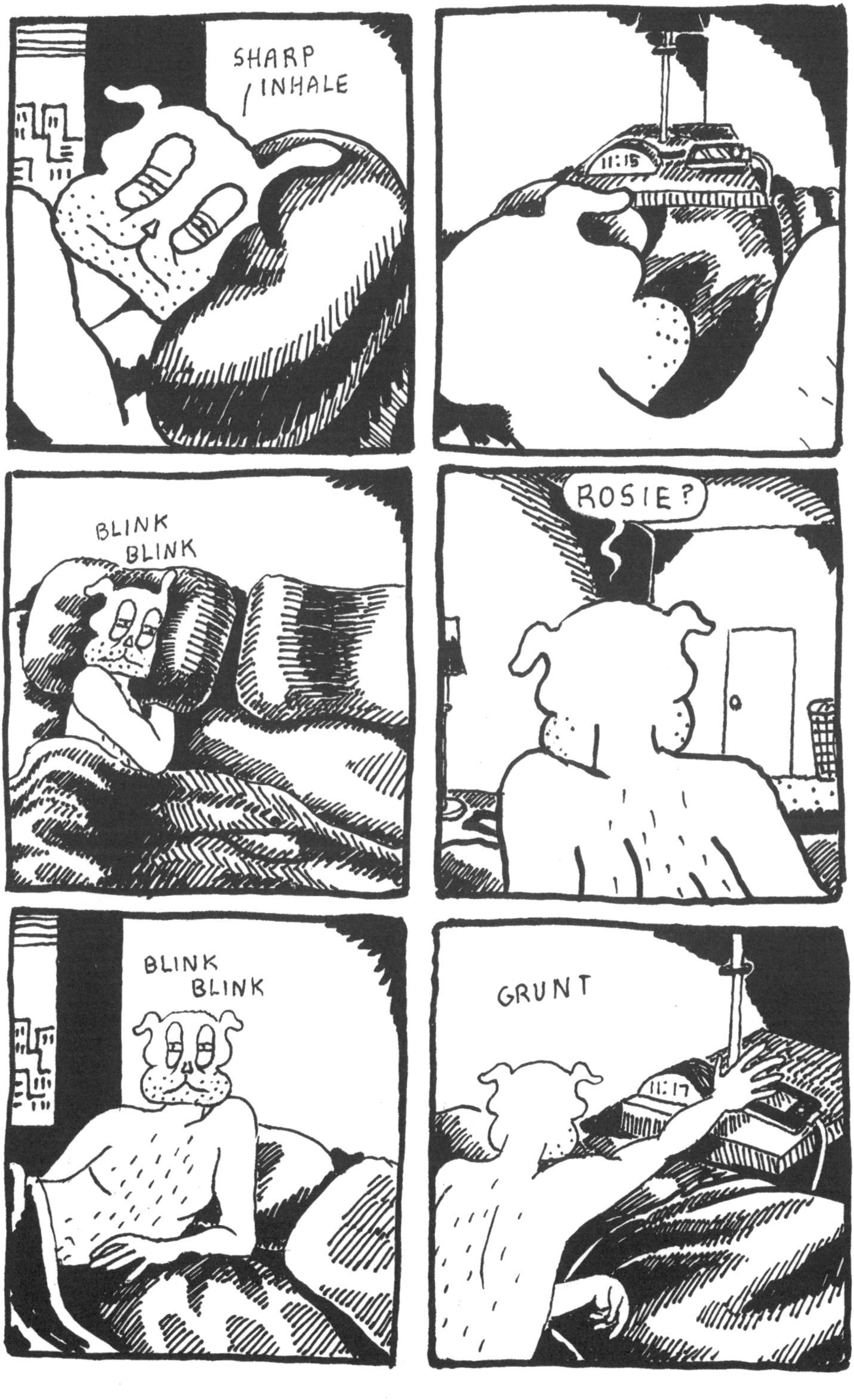
SHARP INHALE
11:15
BLINK BLINK
ROSIE?
BLINK BLINK
GRUNT
11:17

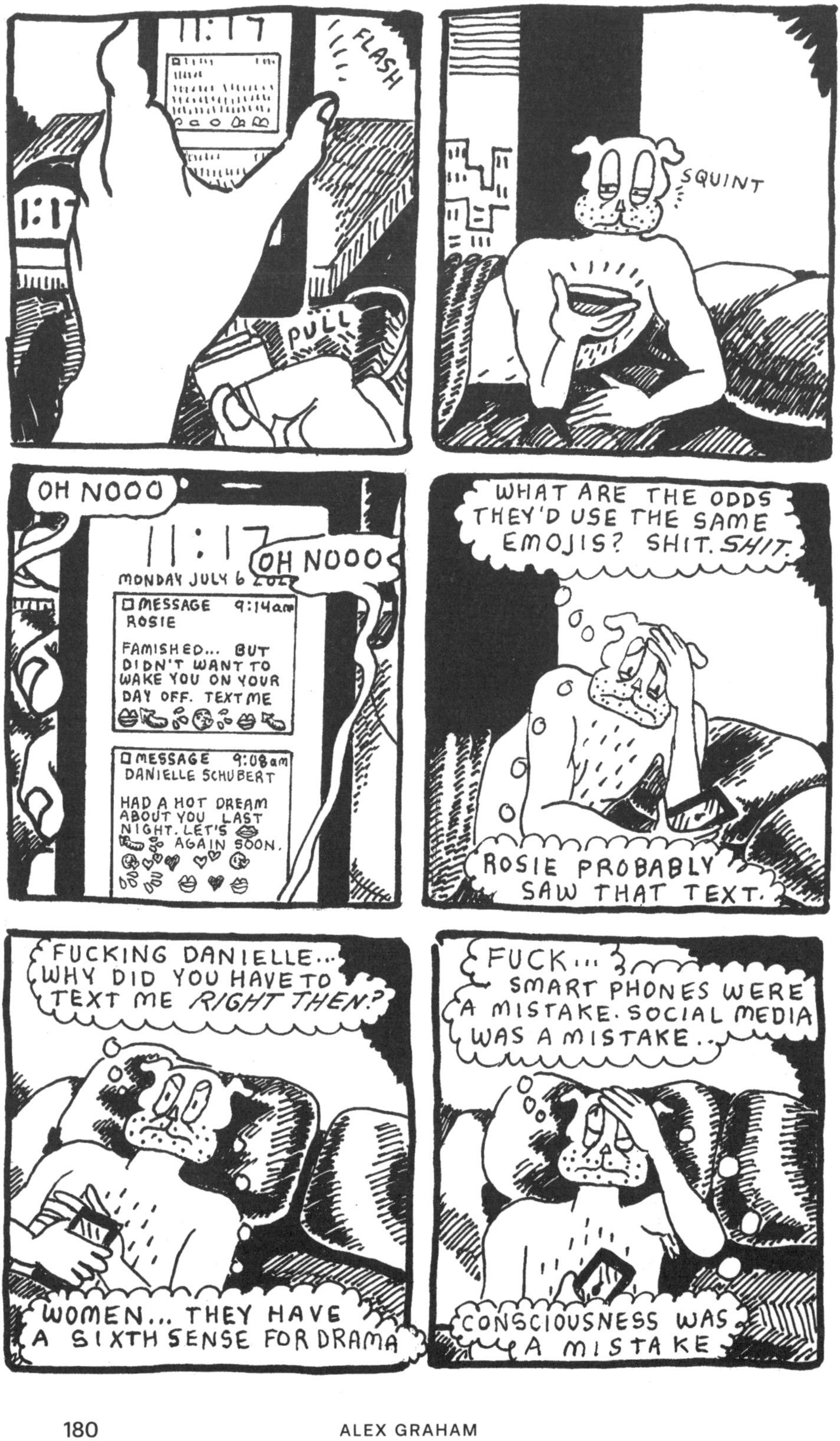
11:17
FLASH
1:17
PULL
SQUINT
OH NOOO
11:17
OH NOOO
MONDAY JULY 6
MESSAGE 9:14am
ROSIE
FAMISHED... BUT DIDN'T WANT TO WAKE YOU ON YOUR DAY OFF. TEXT ME
MESSAGE 9:08am
DANIELLE SCHUBERT
HAD A HOT DREAM ABOUT YOU LAST NIGHT. LET'S AGAIN SOON.
WHAT ARE THE ODDS THEY'D USE THE SAME EMOJIS? SHIT. SHIT.
ROSIE PROBABLY SAW THAT TEXT.
FUCKING DANIELLE... WHY DID YOU HAVE TO TEXT ME RIGHT THEN?
WOMEN... THEY HAVE A SIXTH SENSE FOR DRAMA
FUCK...
SMART PHONES WERE A MISTAKE. SOCIAL MEDIA WAS A MISTAKE..
CONSCIOUSNESS WAS A MISTAKE

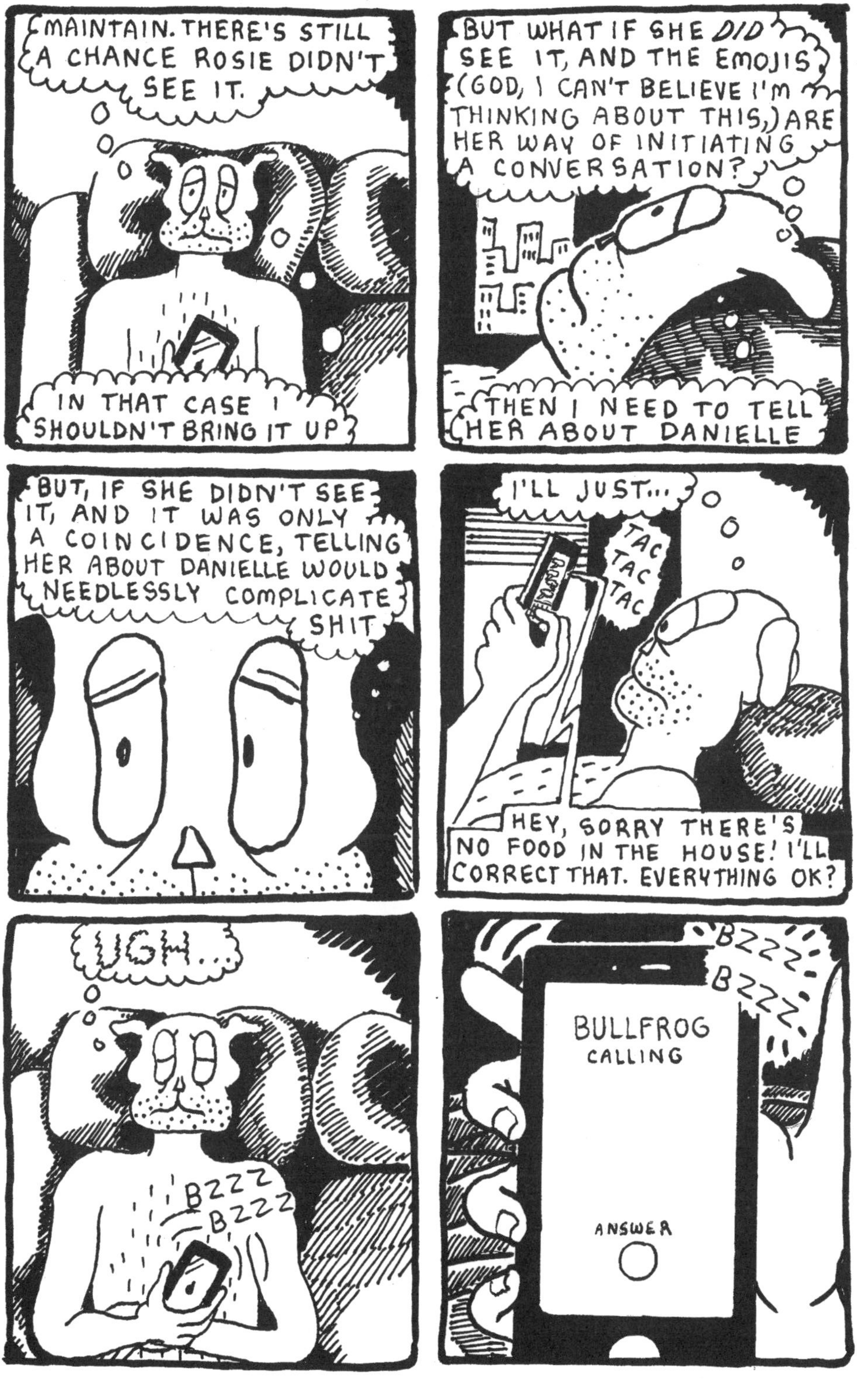
MAINTAIN. THERE'S STILL A CHANCE ROSIE DIDN'T SEE IT.
IN THAT CASE I SHOULDN'T BRING IT UP
BUT WHAT IF SHE DID SEE IT, AND THE EMOJIS (GOD, I CAN'T BELIEVE I'M THINKING ABOUT THIS,) ARE HER WAY OF INITIATING A CONVERSATION?
THEN I NEED TO TELL HER ABOUT DANIELLE
BUT, IF SHE DIDN'T SEE IT, AND IT WAS ONLY A COINCIDENCE, TELLING HER ABOUT DANIELLE WOULD NEEDLESSLY COMPLICATE SHIT
I'LL JUST...
TAC TAC TAC TAC
HEY, SORRY THERE'S NO FOOD IN THE HOUSE! I'LL CORRECT THAT. EVERYTHING OK?
UGH...
BZZZ BZZZ
BZZZ BZZZ
BULLFROG CALLING
ANSWER

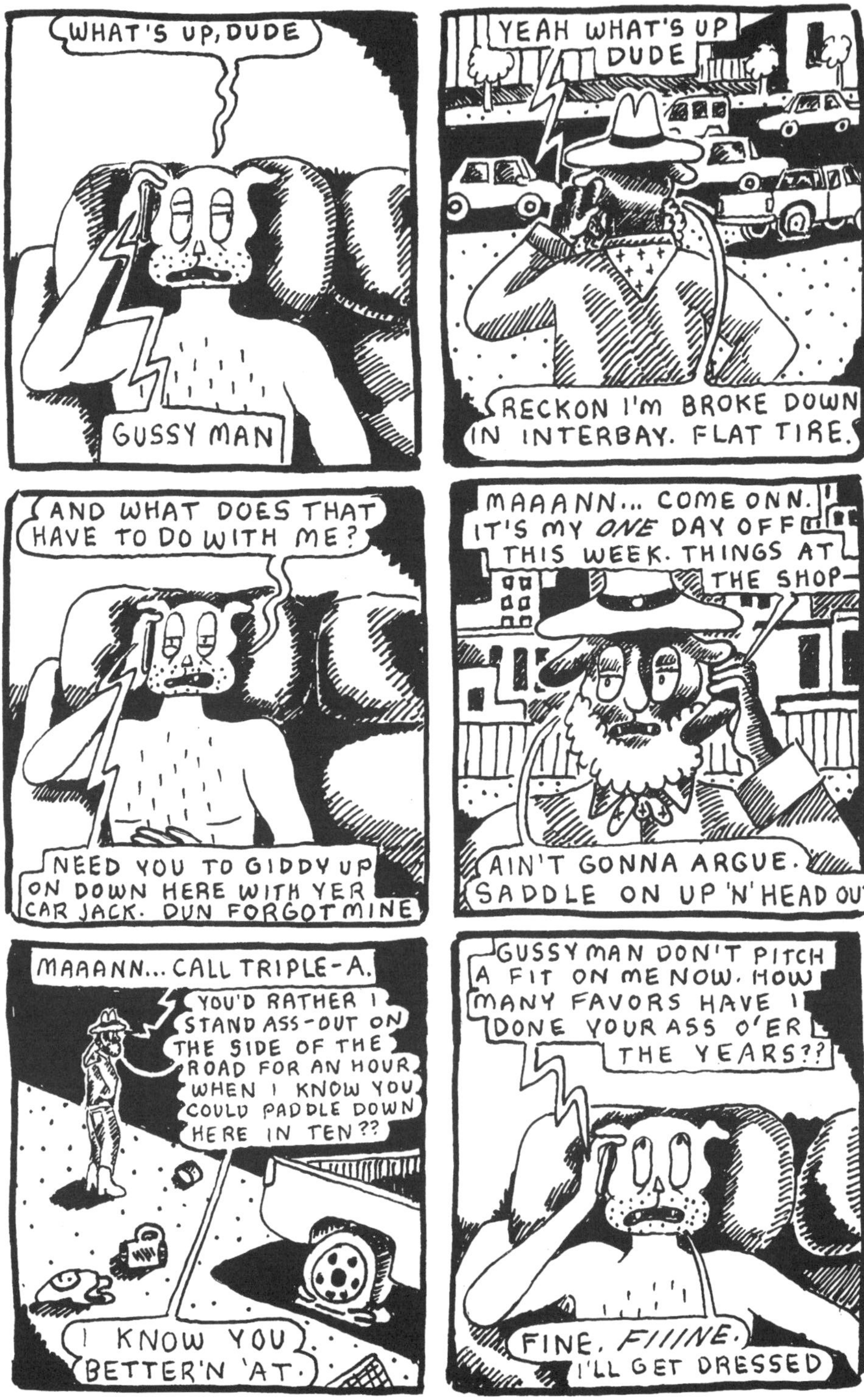
WHAT'S UP, DUDE
GUSSY MAN
YEAH WHAT'S UP DUDE
RECKON I'M BROKE DOWN IN INTERBAY. FLAT TIRE.
AND WHAT DOES THAT HAVE TO DO WITH ME?
NEED YOU TO GIDDY UP ON DOWN HERE WITH YER CAR JACK. DUN FORGOT MINE
MAAANN... COME ONN. IT'S MY *ONE* DAY OFF THIS WEEK. THINGS AT THE SHOP—
AIN'T GONNA ARGUE. SADDLE ON UP 'N' HEAD OUT
MAAANN... CALL TRIPLE-A.
YOU'D RATHER I STAND ASS-OUT ON THE SIDE OF THE ROAD FOR AN HOUR WHEN I KNOW YOU COULD PADDLE DOWN HERE IN TEN??
I KNOW YOU BETTER'N 'AT.
GUSSY MAN DON'T PITCH A FIT ON ME NOW. HOW MANY FAVORS HAVE I DONE YOUR ASS O'ER THE YEARS??
FINE. *FIIINE.* I'LL GET DRESSED

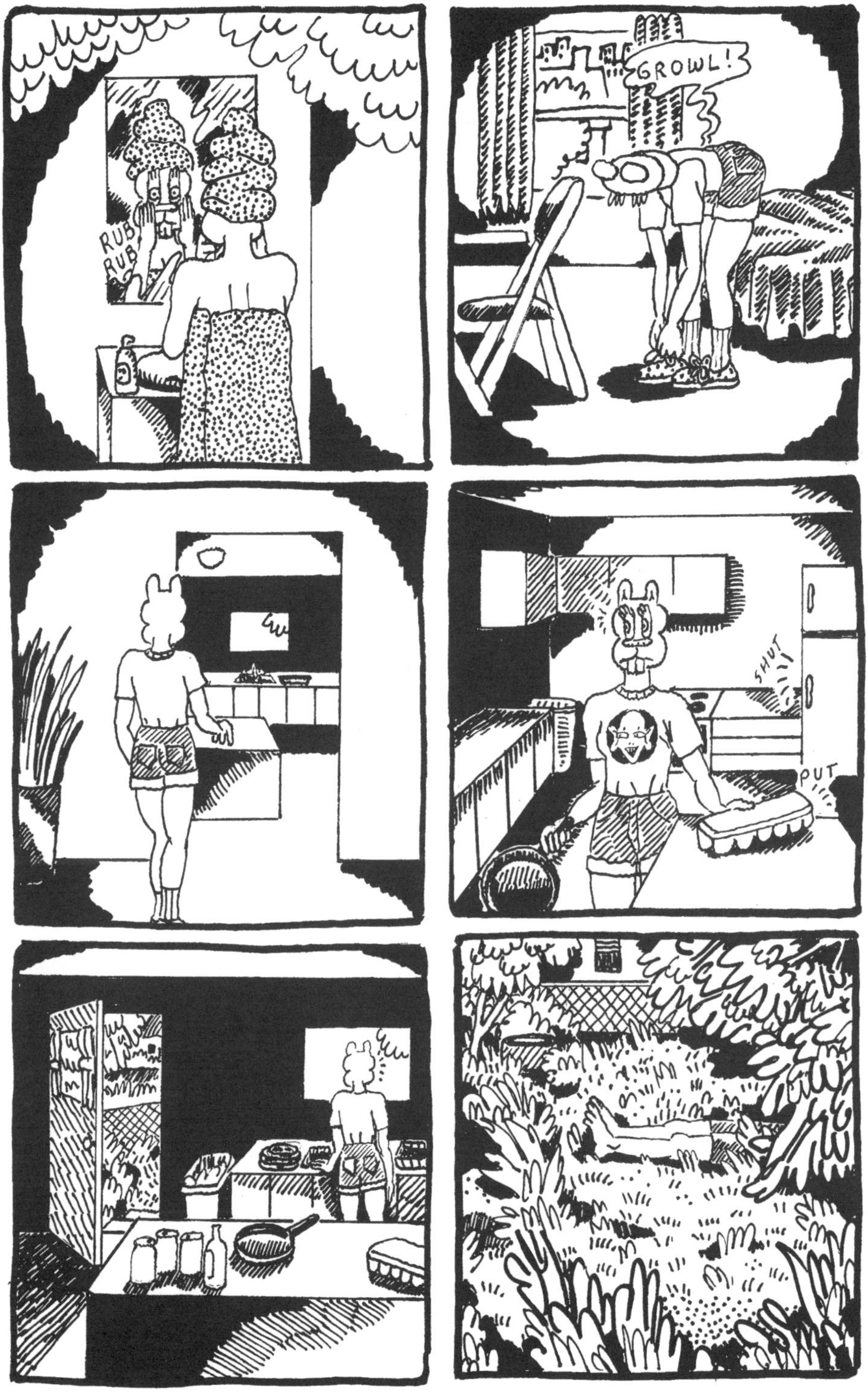
RUB
RUB
GROWL!
SHUT
PUT

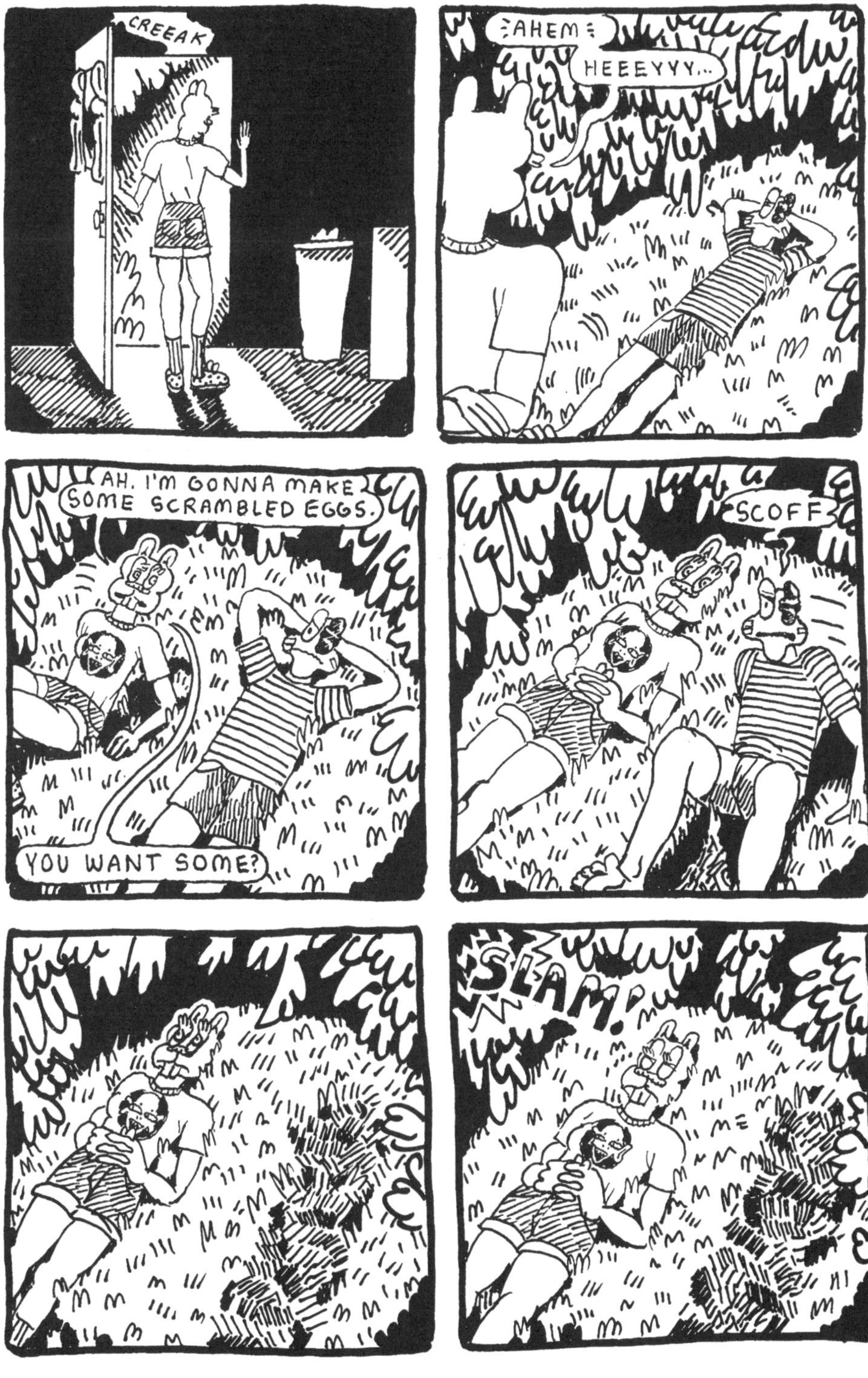
CREEAK
AHEM
HEEEYYY...
AH. I'M GONNA MAKE SOME SCRAMBLED EGGS.
YOU WANT SOME?
SCOFF
SLAM!

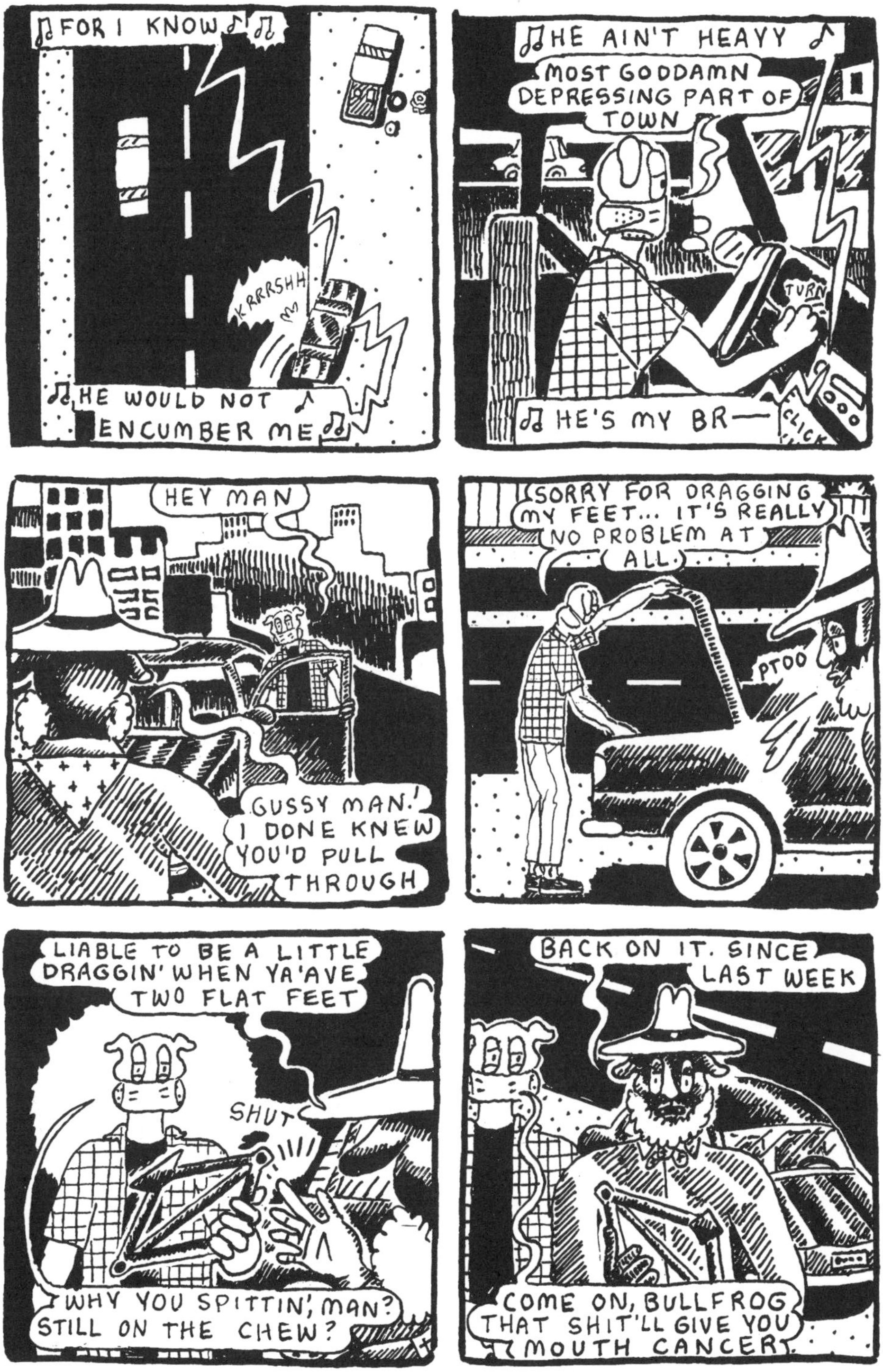

♫ FOR I KNOW ♪ ♫
KRRRSHH
♫ HE WOULD NOT ♪
ENCUMBER ME ♫
♫ HE AIN'T HEAVY ♪
MOST GODDAMN DEPRESSING PART OF TOWN
TURN
♫ HE'S MY BR—
CLICK
HEY MAN
GUSSY MAN! I DONE KNEW YOU'D PULL THROUGH
SORRY FOR DRAGGING MY FEET... IT'S REALLY NO PROBLEM AT ALL
PTOO
LIABLE TO BE A LITTLE DRAGGIN' WHEN YA'AVE TWO FLAT FEET
SHUT
WHY YOU SPITTIN', MAN? STILL ON THE CHEW?
BACK ON IT. SINCE LAST WEEK
COME ON, BULLFROG THAT SHIT'LL GIVE YOU MOUTH CANCER

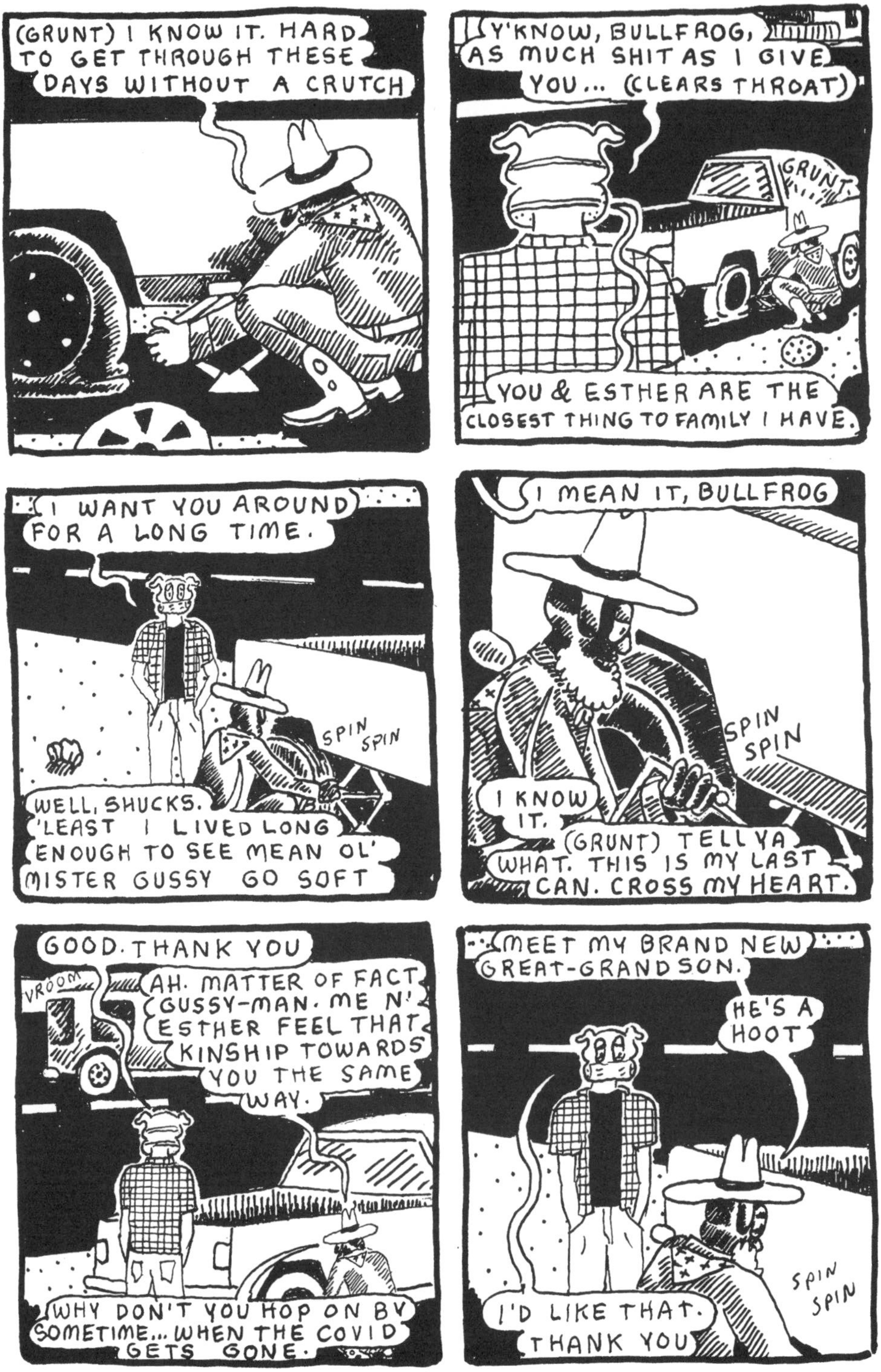
(GRUNT) I KNOW IT. HARD TO GET THROUGH THESE DAYS WITHOUT A CRUTCH
Y'KNOW, BULLFROG, AS MUCH SHIT AS I GIVE YOU... (CLEARS THROAT)
GRUNT
YOU & ESTHER ARE THE CLOSEST THING TO FAMILY I HAVE.
I WANT YOU AROUND FOR A LONG TIME.
SPIN SPIN
WELL, SHUCKS. 'LEAST I LIVED LONG ENOUGH TO SEE MEAN OL' MISTER GUSSY GO SOFT
I MEAN IT, BULLFROG
SPIN SPIN
I KNOW IT.
(GRUNT) TELL YA WHAT. THIS IS MY LAST CAN. CROSS MY HEART.
GOOD. THANK YOU
VROOM
AH. MATTER OF FACT GUSSY-MAN. ME N' ESTHER FEEL THAT KINSHIP TOWARDS YOU THE SAME WAY.
WHY DON'T YOU HOP ON BY SOMETIME... WHEN THE COVID GETS GONE.
MEET MY BRAND NEW GREAT-GRANDSON.
HE'S A HOOT
I'D LIKE THAT. THANK YOU
SPIN SPIN

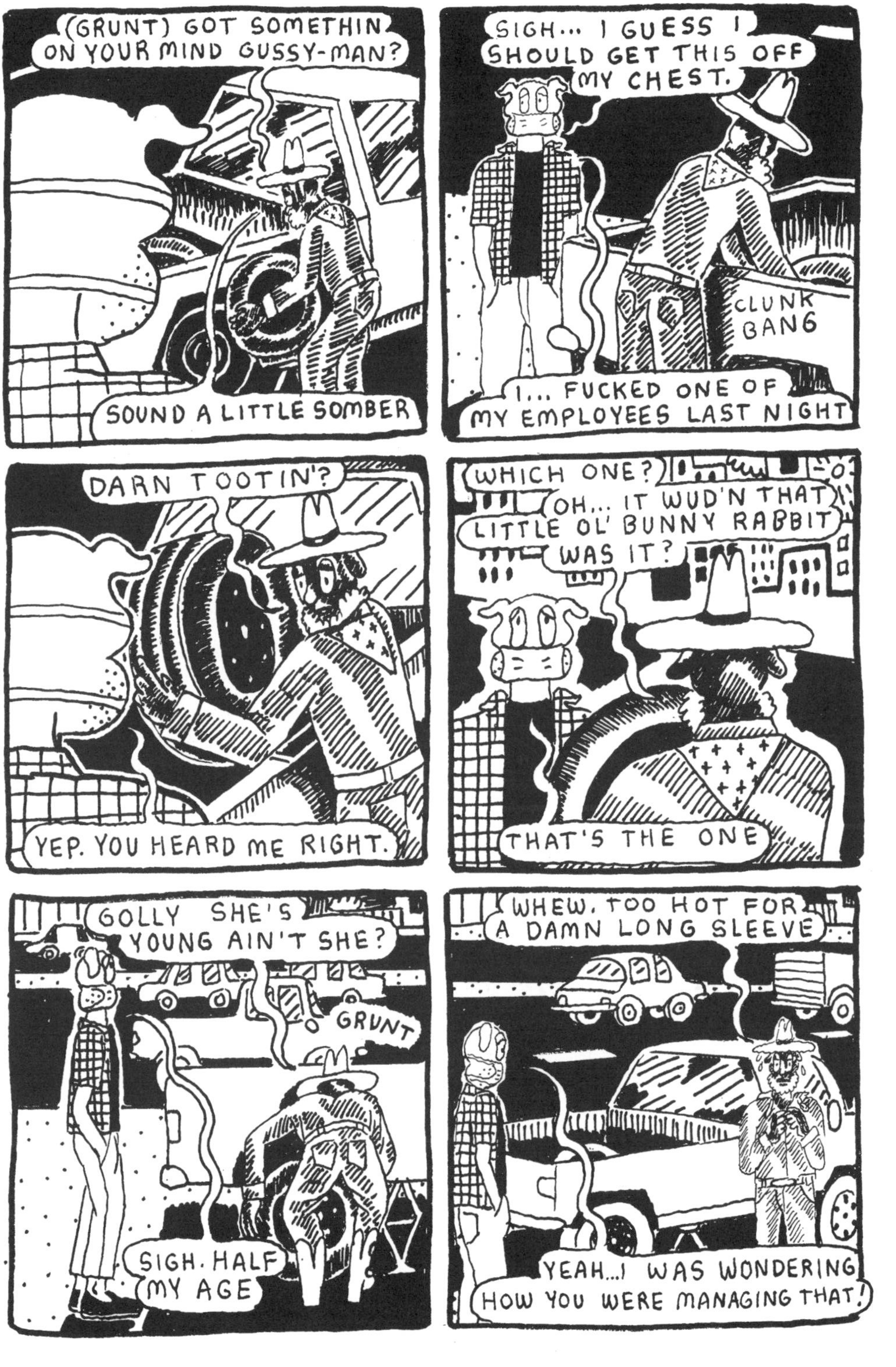
(GRUNT) GOT SOMETHIN ON YOUR MIND GUSSY-MAN?
SOUND A LITTLE SOMBER
SIGH... I GUESS I SHOULD GET THIS OFF MY CHEST.
CLUNK BANG
I... FUCKED ONE OF MY EMPLOYEES LAST NIGHT
DARN TOOTIN'?
YEP. YOU HEARD ME RIGHT.
WHICH ONE?
OH... IT WUD'N THAT LITTLE OL' BUNNY RABBIT WAS IT?
THAT'S THE ONE
GOLLY SHE'S YOUNG AIN'T SHE?
GRUNT
SIGH. HALF MY AGE
WHEW. TOO HOT FOR A DAMN LONG SLEEVE
YEAH...I WAS WONDERING HOW YOU WERE MANAGING THAT!

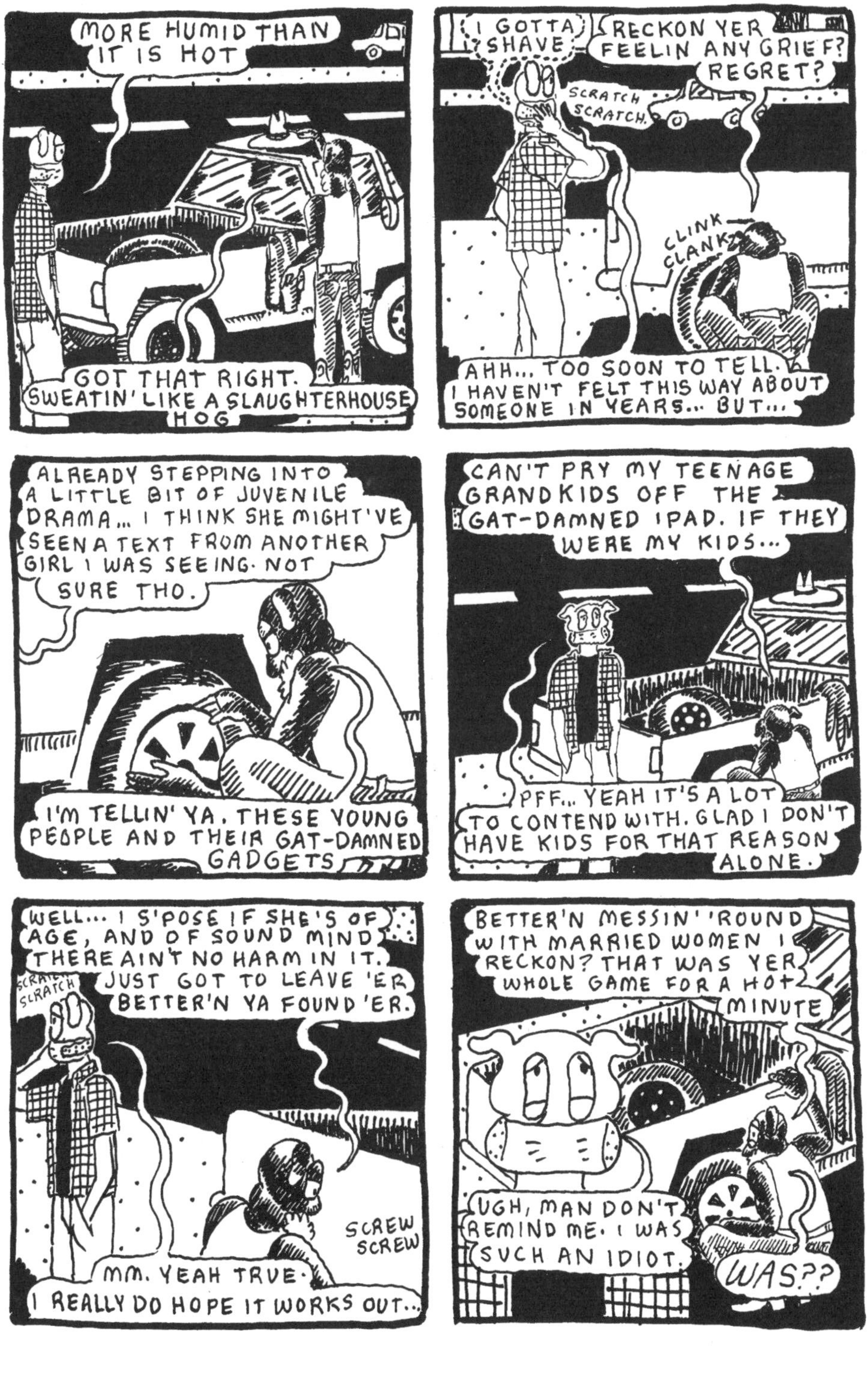
MORE HUMID THAN IT IS HOT
GOT THAT RIGHT. SWEATIN' LIKE A SLAUGHTERHOUSE HOG
I GOTTA SHAVE
RECKON YER FEELIN ANY GRIEF? REGRET?
SCRATCH SCRATCH.
CLINK CLANK
AHH... TOO SOON TO TELL. I HAVEN'T FELT THIS WAY ABOUT SOMEONE IN YEARS... BUT...
ALREADY STEPPING INTO A LITTLE BIT OF JUVENILE DRAMA... I THINK SHE MIGHT'VE SEEN A TEXT FROM ANOTHER GIRL I WAS SEEING. NOT SURE THO.
I'M TELLIN' YA. THESE YOUNG PEOPLE AND THEIR GAT-DAMNED GADGETS
CAN'T PRY MY TEENAGE GRANDKIDS OFF THE GAT-DAMNED IPAD. IF THEY WERE MY KIDS...
PFF... YEAH IT'S A LOT TO CONTEND WITH. GLAD I DON'T HAVE KIDS FOR THAT REASON ALONE.
WELL... I S'POSE IF SHE'S OF AGE, AND OF SOUND MIND THERE AIN'T NO HARM IN IT. JUST GOT TO LEAVE 'ER BETTER'N YA FOUND 'ER.
SCRATCH SCRATCH
SCREW SCREW
MM. YEAH TRUE. I REALLY DO HOPE IT WORKS OUT...
BETTER'N MESSIN' 'ROUND WITH MARRIED WOMEN I RECKON? THAT WAS YER WHOLE GAME FOR A HOT MINUTE
UGH, MAN DON'T REMIND ME. I WAS SUCH AN IDIOT.
WAS??

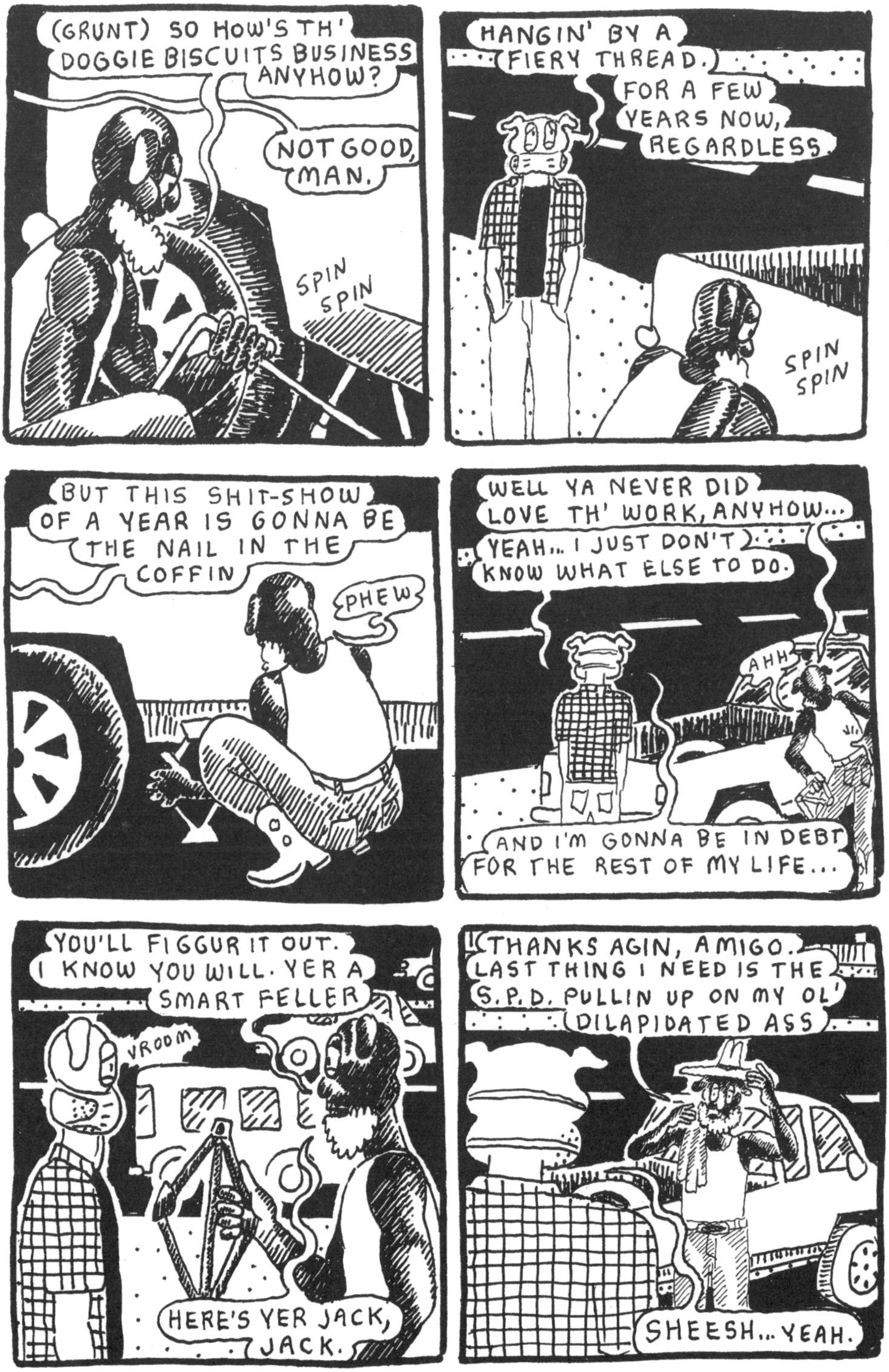
(GRUNT) SO HOW'S TH' DOGGIE BISCUITS BUSINESS ANYHOW?
NOT GOOD, MAN.
SPIN SPIN
HANGIN' BY A FIERY THREAD.
FOR A FEW YEARS NOW, REGARDLESS.
SPIN SPIN
BUT THIS SHIT-SHOW OF A YEAR IS GONNA BE THE NAIL IN THE COFFIN
PHEW
WELL YA NEVER DID LOVE TH' WORK, ANYHOW...
YEAH... I JUST DON'T KNOW WHAT ELSE TO DO.
AHH
AND I'M GONNA BE IN DEBT FOR THE REST OF MY LIFE...
YOU'LL FIGGUR IT OUT. I KNOW YOU WILL. YER A SMART FELLER
VROOM
HERE'S YER JACK, JACK.
THANKS AGIN, AMIGO. LAST THING I NEED IS THE S.P.D. PULLIN UP ON MY OL' DILAPIDATED ASS
SHEESH... YEAH.

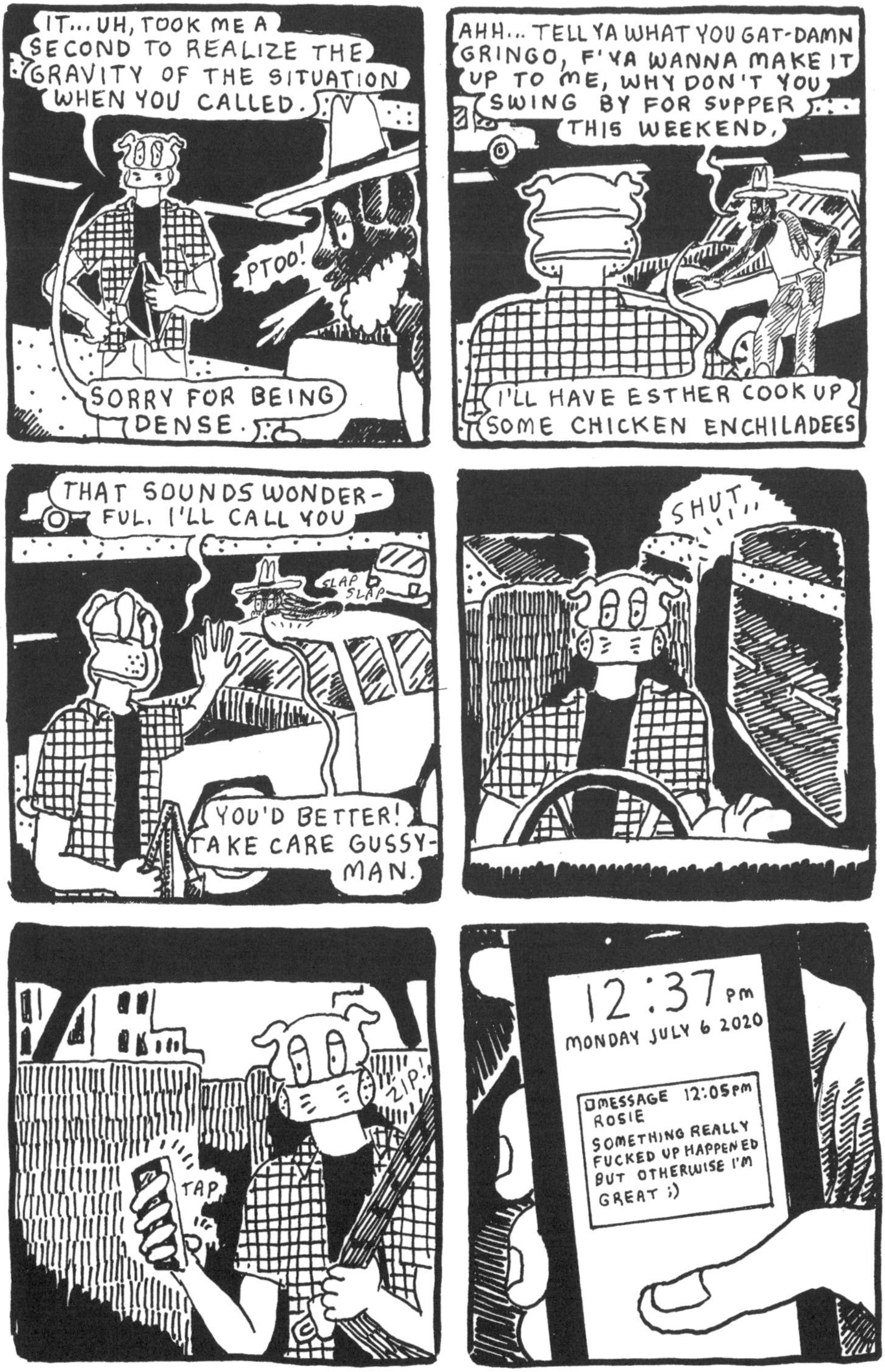
IT... UH, TOOK ME A SECOND TO REALIZE THE GRAVITY OF THE SITUATION WHEN YOU CALLED.
PTOO!
SORRY FOR BEING DENSE.
AHH... TELL YA WHAT YOU GAT-DAMN GRINGO, F'YA WANNA MAKE IT UP TO ME, WHY DON'T YOU SWING BY FOR SUPPER THIS WEEKEND,
I'LL HAVE ESTHER COOK UP SOME CHICKEN ENCHILADEES
THAT SOUNDS WONDER-FUL. I'LL CALL YOU
SLAP SLAP
YOU'D BETTER! TAKE CARE GUSSY-MAN.
SHUT,
ZIP!
TAP
12:37 pm
MONDAY JULY 6 2020
MESSAGE 12:05pm
ROSIE
SOMETHING REALLY FUCKED UP HAPPENED BUT OTHERWISE I'M GREAT ;)

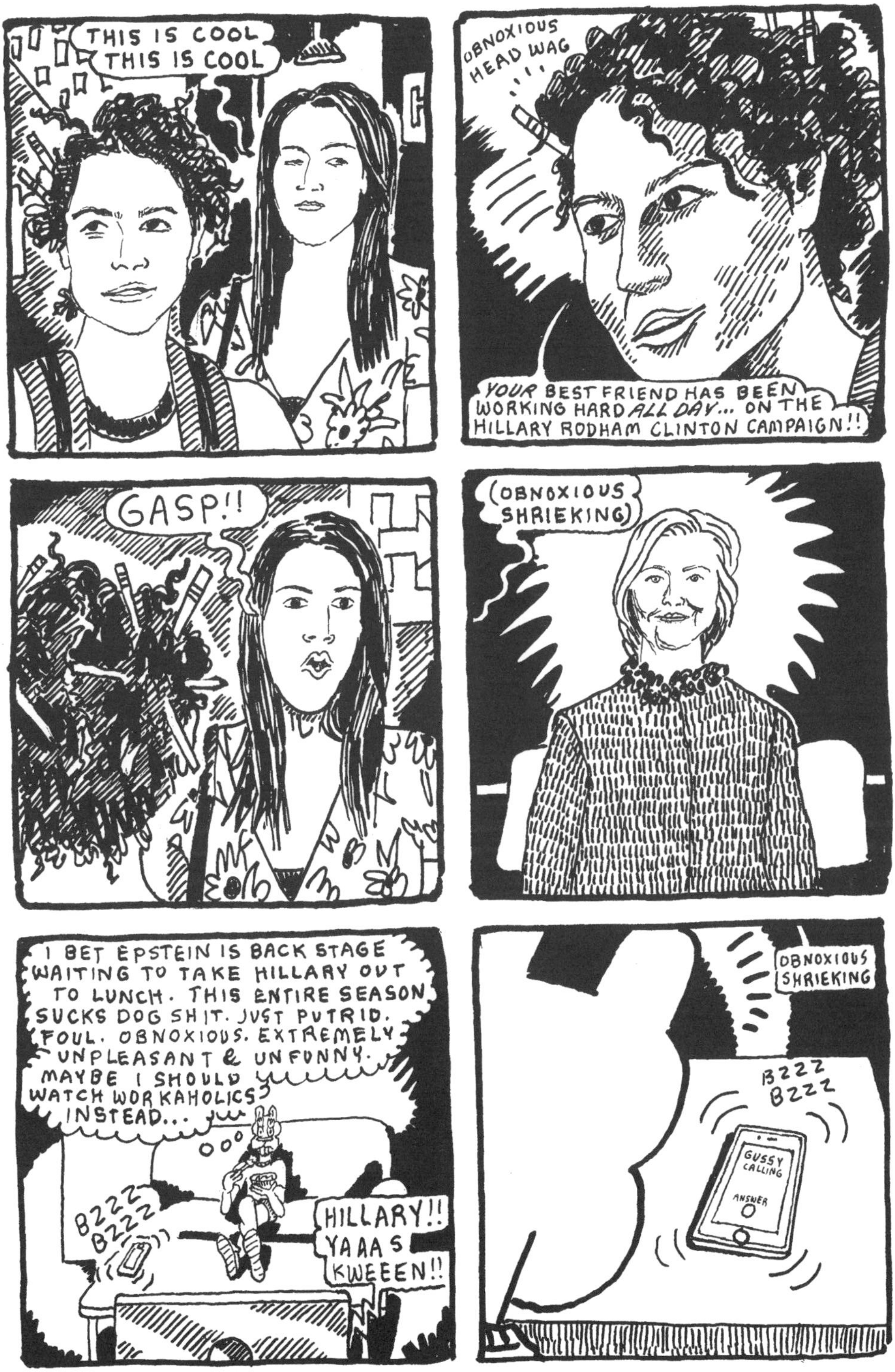
THIS IS COOL THIS IS COOL
OBNOXIOUS HEAD WAG
YOUR BEST FRIEND HAS BEEN WORKING HARD ALL DAY... ON THE HILLARY RODHAM CLINTON CAMPAIGN!!
GASP!!
(OBNOXIOUS SHRIEKING)
I BET EPSTEIN IS BACK STAGE WAITING TO TAKE HILLARY OUT TO LUNCH. THIS ENTIRE SEASON SUCKS DOG SHIT. JUST PUTRID. FOUL. OBNOXIOUS. EXTREMELY UNPLEASANT & UNFUNNY. MAYBE I SHOULD WATCH WORKAHOLICS INSTEAD...
BZZZ BZZZ
HILLARY!! YAAAS KWEEEN!!
OBNOXIOUS SHRIEKING
BZZZ BZZZ
GUSSY CALLING
ANSWER

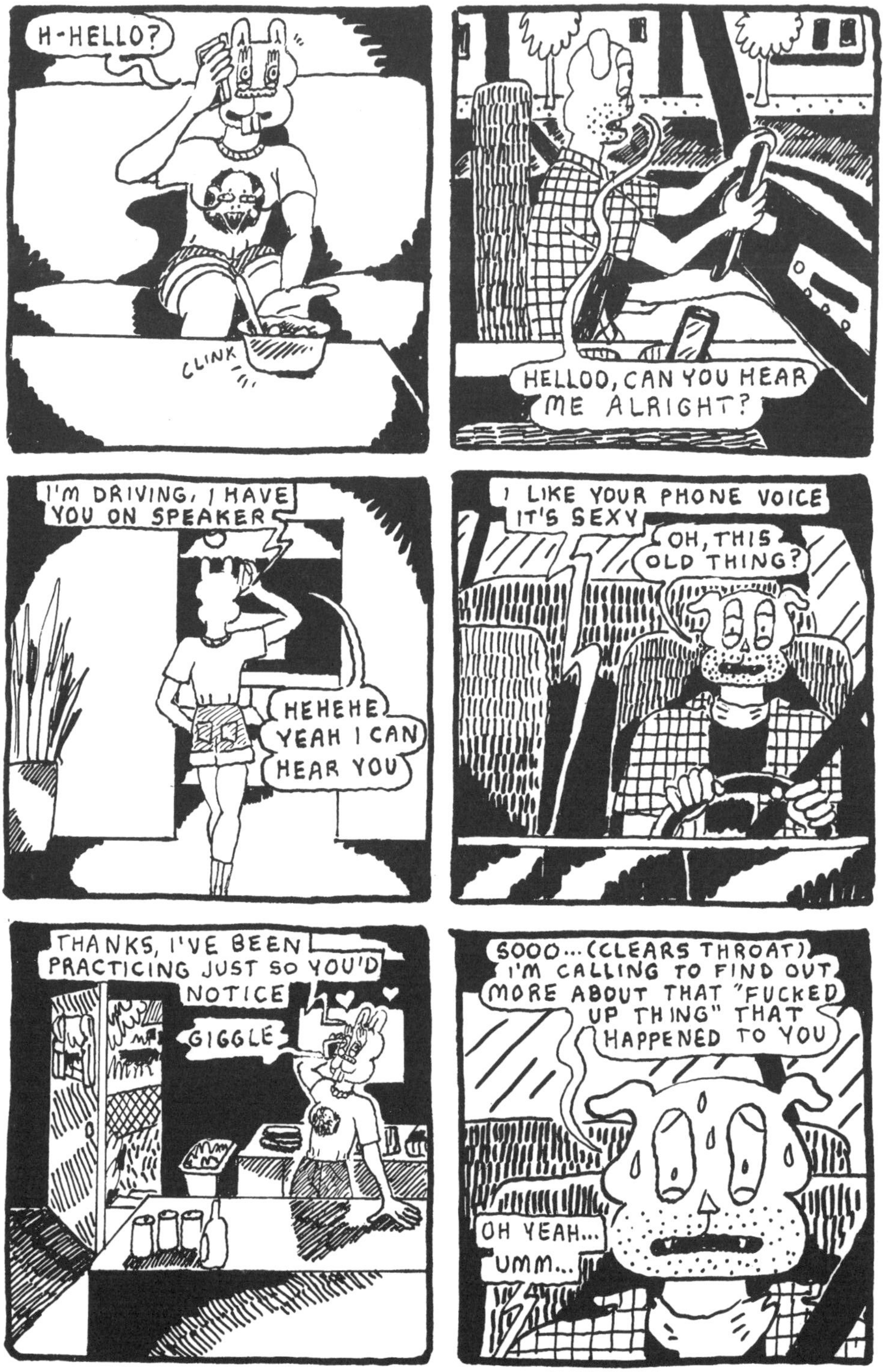
H-HELLO?
CLINK
HELLOO, CAN YOU HEAR ME ALRIGHT?
I'M DRIVING, I HAVE YOU ON SPEAKER
HEHEHE YEAH I CAN HEAR YOU
I LIKE YOUR PHONE VOICE IT'S SEXY
OH, THIS OLD THING?
THANKS, I'VE BEEN PRACTICING JUST SO YOU'D NOTICE
GIGGLE
SOOO... (CLEARS THROAT) I'M CALLING TO FIND OUT MORE ABOUT THAT "FUCKED UP THING" THAT HAPPENED TO YOU
OH YEAH...
UMM...

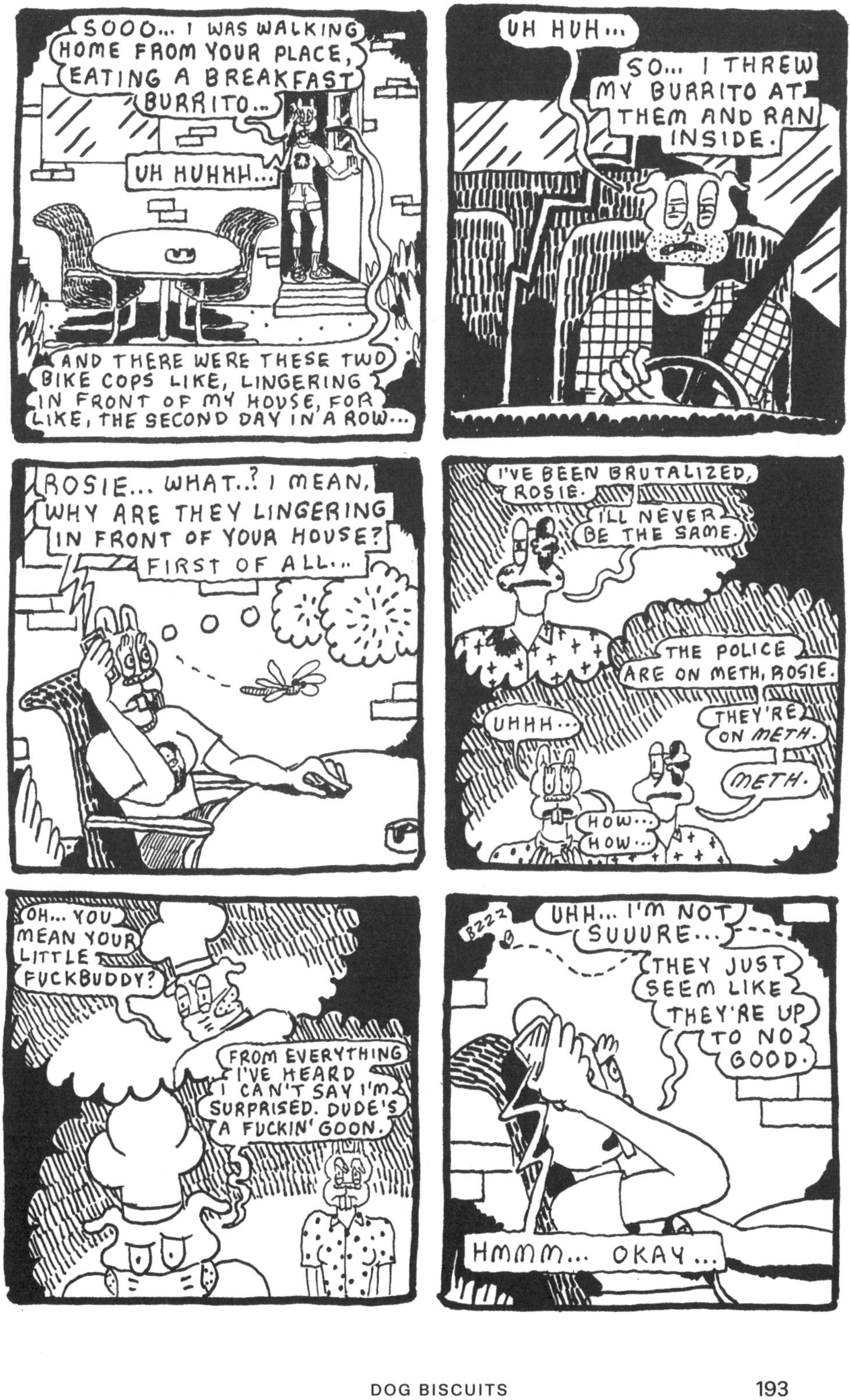
SOOO... I WAS WALKING HOME FROM YOUR PLACE, EATING A BREAKFAST BURRITO...
UH HUHHH...
AND THERE WERE THESE TWO BIKE COPS LIKE, LINGERING IN FRONT OF MY HOUSE, FOR LIKE, THE SECOND DAY IN A ROW...
UH HUH...
SO... I THREW MY BURRITO AT THEM AND RAN INSIDE.
ROSIE... WHAT..? I MEAN, WHY ARE THEY LINGERING IN FRONT OF YOUR HOUSE?
FIRST OF ALL...
I'VE BEEN BRUTALIZED, ROSIE.
I'LL NEVER BE THE SAME.
THE POLICE ARE ON METH, ROSIE.
UHHH...
THEY'RE ON METH.
METH.
HOW...
HOW...
OH... YOU MEAN YOUR LITTLE FUCKBUDDY?
FROM EVERYTHING I'VE HEARD I CAN'T SAY I'M SURPRISED. DUDE'S A FUCKIN' GOON.
BZZZ
UHH... I'M NOT SUUURE...
THEY JUST SEEM LIKE THEY'RE UP TO NO GOOD.
HMMM... OKAY...

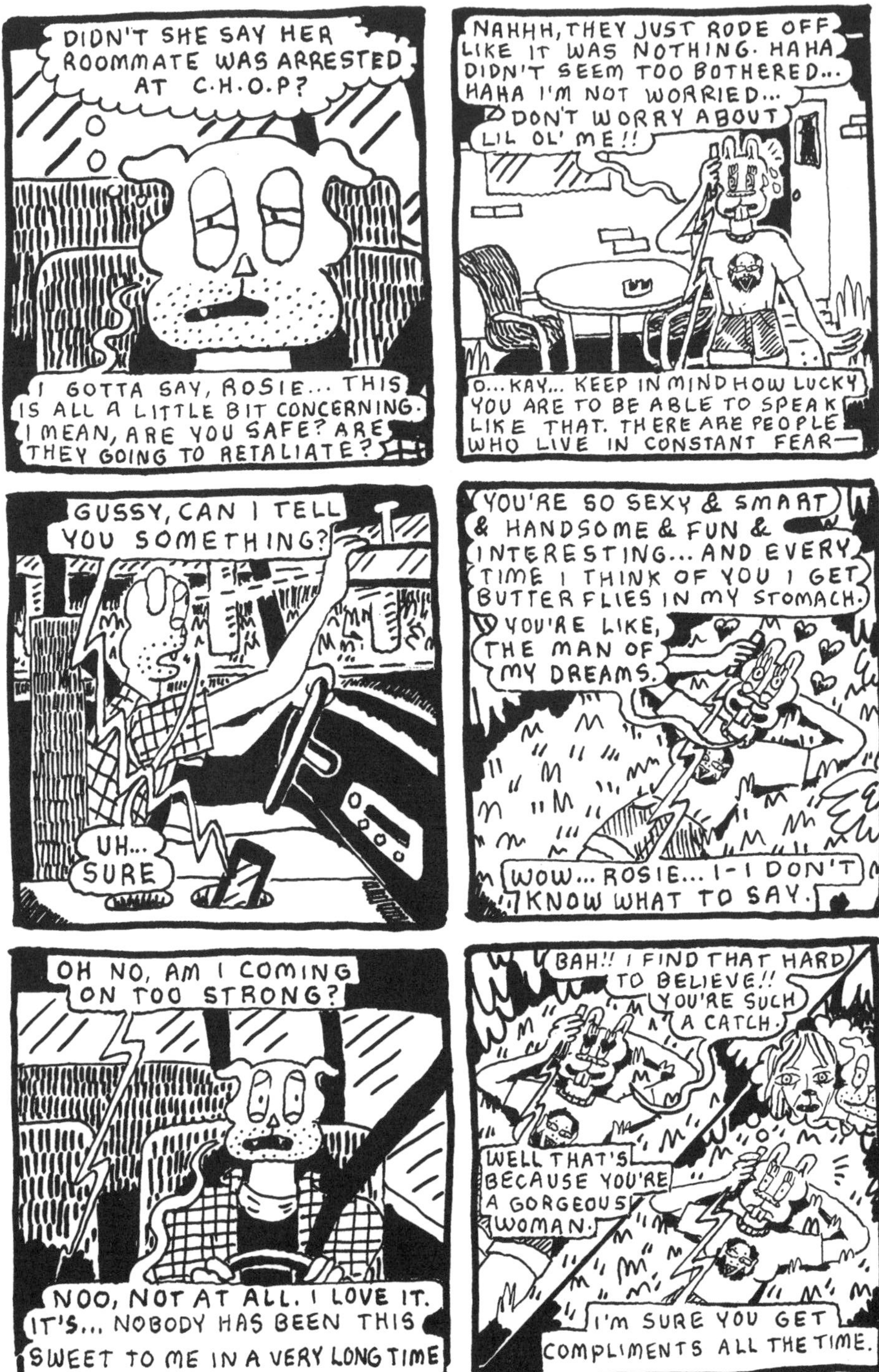
DIDN'T SHE SAY HER ROOMMATE WAS ARRESTED AT C.H.O.P?
I GOTTA SAY, ROSIE... THIS IS ALL A LITTLE BIT CONCERNING. I MEAN, ARE YOU SAFE? ARE THEY GOING TO RETALIATE?
NAHHH, THEY JUST RODE OFF LIKE IT WAS NOTHING. HAHA DIDN'T SEEM TOO BOTHERED... HAHA I'M NOT WORRIED...
DON'T WORRY ABOUT LIL OL' ME!!
O...KAY... KEEP IN MIND HOW LUCKY YOU ARE TO BE ABLE TO SPEAK LIKE THAT. THERE ARE PEOPLE WHO LIVE IN CONSTANT FEAR—
GUSSY, CAN I TELL YOU SOMETHING?
UH... SURE
YOU'RE SO SEXY & SMART & HANDSOME & FUN & INTERESTING... AND EVERY TIME I THINK OF YOU I GET BUTTERFLIES IN MY STOMACH.
YOU'RE LIKE, THE MAN OF MY DREAMS.
WOW... ROSIE... I-I DON'T KNOW WHAT TO SAY.
OH NO, AM I COMING ON TOO STRONG?
NOO, NOT AT ALL. I LOVE IT. IT'S... NOBODY HAS BEEN THIS SWEET TO ME IN A VERY LONG TIME
BAH!! I FIND THAT HARD TO BELIEVE!! YOU'RE SUCH A CATCH.
WELL THAT'S BECAUSE YOU'RE A GORGEOUS WOMAN.
I'M SURE YOU GET COMPLIMENTS ALL THE TIME.

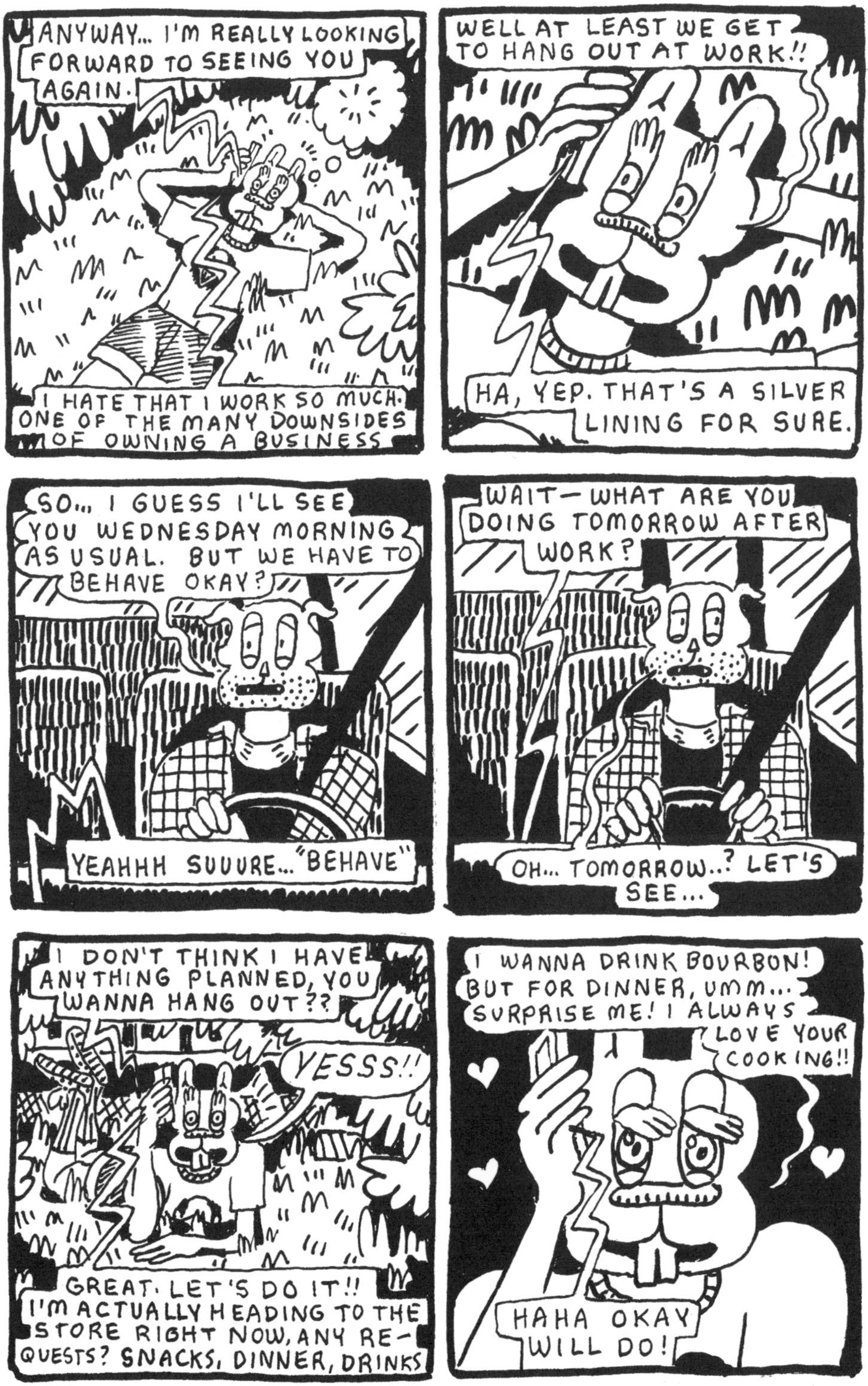
ANYWAY... I'M REALLY LOOKING FORWARD TO SEEING YOU AGAIN.
I HATE THAT I WORK SO MUCH. ONE OF THE MANY DOWNSIDES OF OWNING A BUSINESS
WELL AT LEAST WE GET TO HANG OUT AT WORK!!
HA, YEP. THAT'S A SILVER LINING FOR SURE.
SO... I GUESS I'LL SEE YOU WEDNESDAY MORNING AS USUAL. BUT WE HAVE TO BEHAVE OKAY?
YEAHHH SUUURE... "BEHAVE"
WAIT— WHAT ARE YOU DOING TOMORROW AFTER WORK?
OH... TOMORROW...? LET'S SEE...
I DON'T THINK I HAVE ANYTHING PLANNED, YOU WANNA HANG OUT??
YESSS!!
GREAT. LET'S DO IT!! I'M ACTUALLY HEADING TO THE STORE RIGHT NOW, ANY REQUESTS? SNACKS, DINNER, DRINKS
I WANNA DRINK BOURBON! BUT FOR DINNER, UMM... SURPRISE ME! I ALWAYS LOVE YOUR COOKING!!
HAHA OKAY WILL DO!

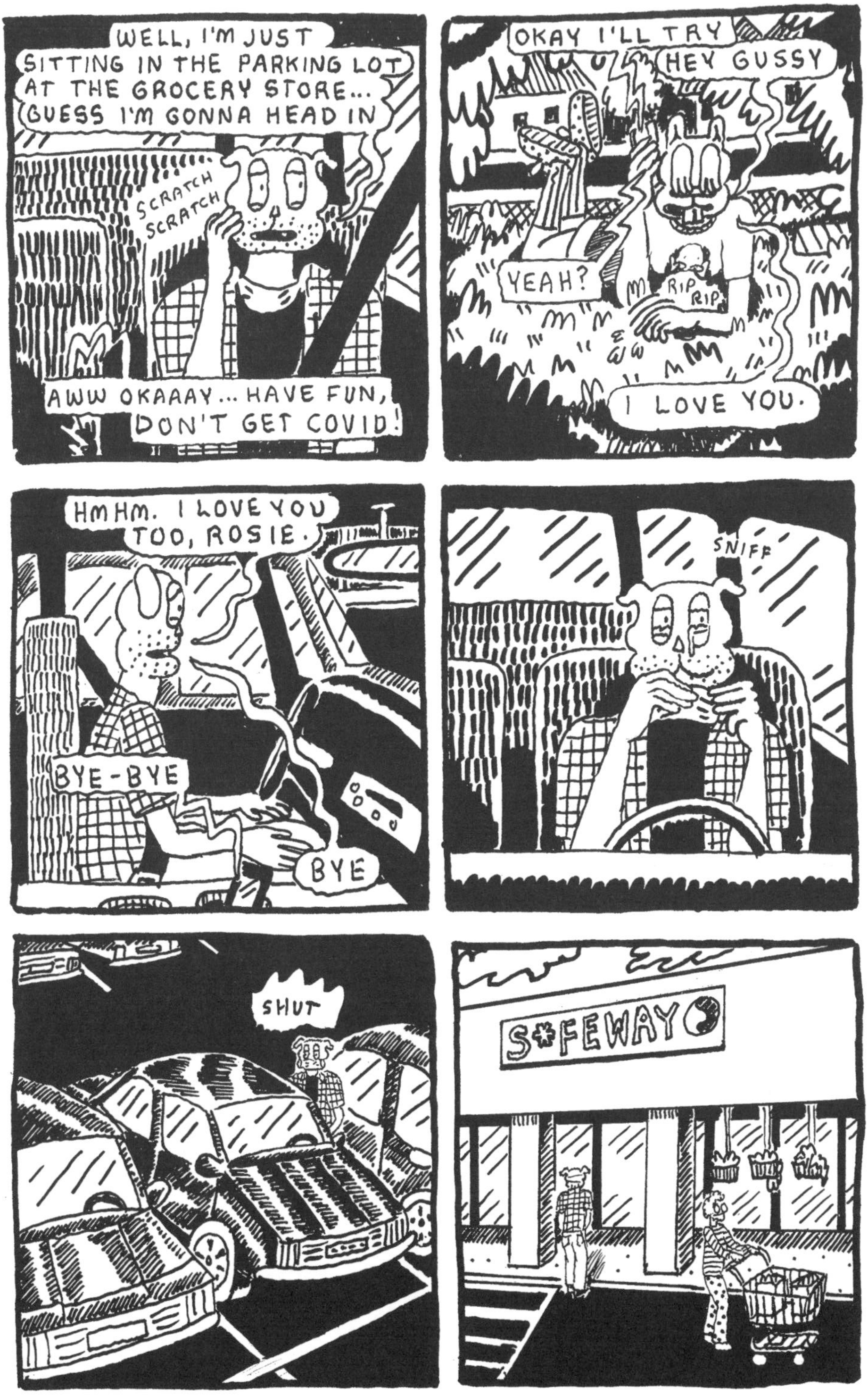
WELL, I'M JUST SITTING IN THE PARKING LOT AT THE GROCERY STORE... GUESS I'M GONNA HEAD IN
SCRATCH SCRATCH
AWW OKAAAY... HAVE FUN, DON'T GET COVID!
OKAY I'LL TRY
HEY GUSSY
YEAH?
RIP RIP
I LOVE YOU.
HMHM. I LOVE YOU TOO, ROSIE.
BYE-BYE
BYE
SNIFF
SHUT
S*FEWAY

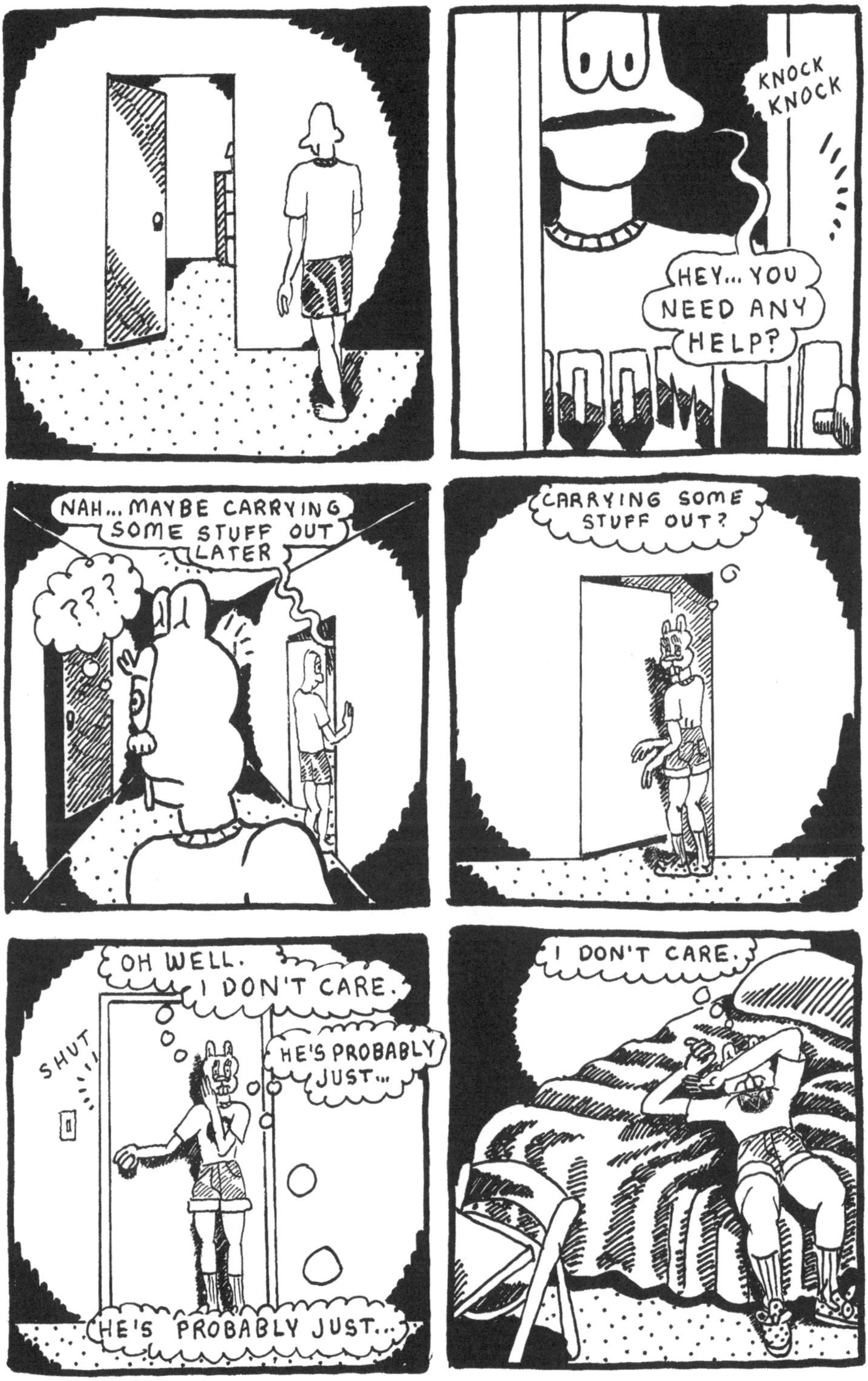
KNOCK KNOCK
HEY... YOU NEED ANY HELP?
NAH... MAYBE CARRYING SOME STUFF OUT LATER
???
CARRYING SOME STUFF OUT?
OH WELL.
I DON'T CARE.
SHUT
HE'S PROBABLY JUST...
HE'S PROBABLY JUST...
I DON'T CARE.

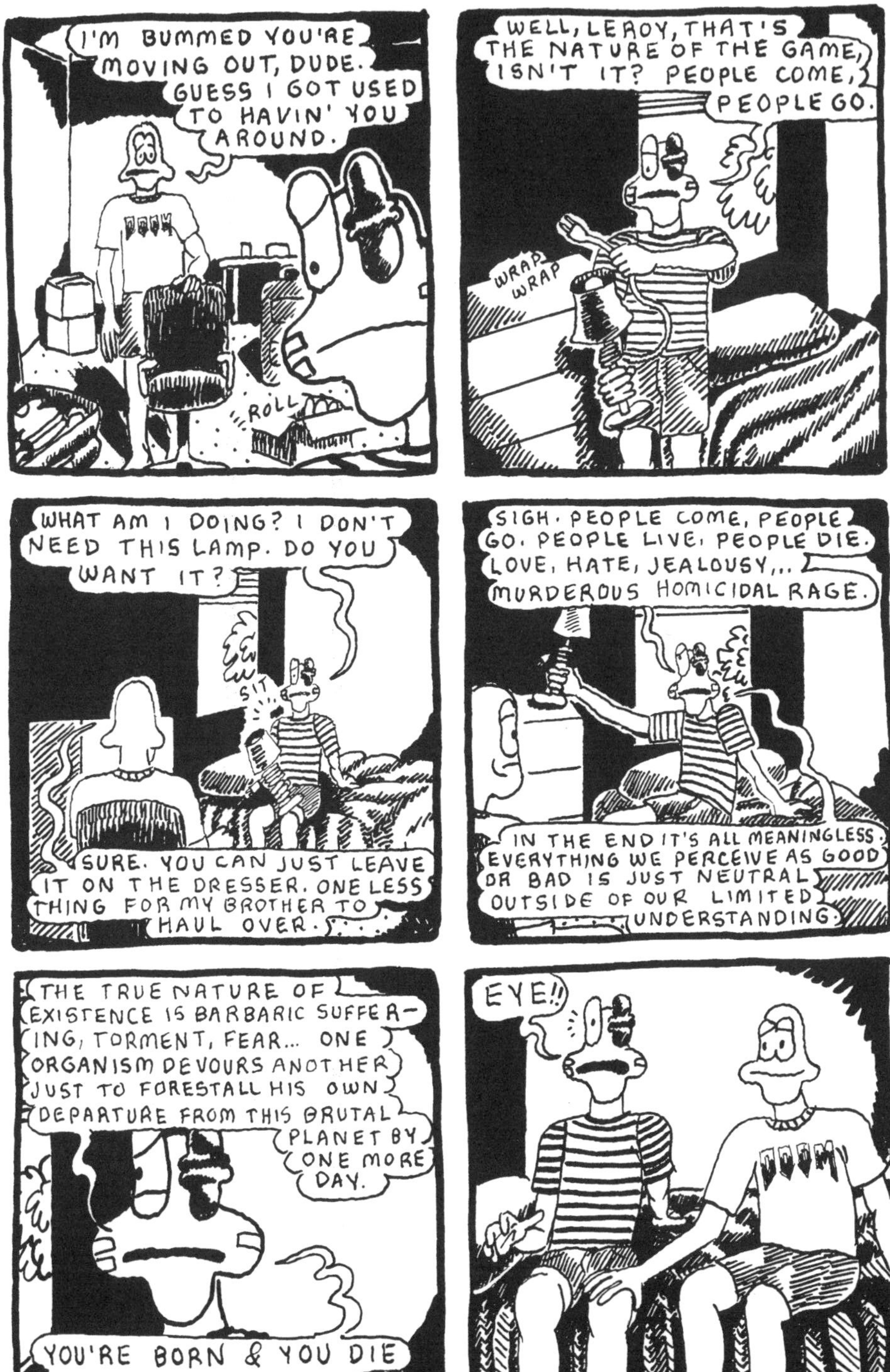
I'M BUMMED YOU'RE MOVING OUT, DUDE.
GUESS I GOT USED TO HAVIN' YOU AROUND.
ROLL
WELL, LEROY, THAT'S THE NATURE OF THE GAME, ISN'T IT? PEOPLE COME,
PEOPLE GO.
WRAP WRAP
WHAT AM I DOING? I DON'T NEED THIS LAMP. DO YOU WANT IT?
SIT
SURE. YOU CAN JUST LEAVE IT ON THE DRESSER. ONE LESS THING FOR MY BROTHER TO HAUL OVER.
SIGH. PEOPLE COME, PEOPLE GO. PEOPLE LIVE, PEOPLE DIE. LOVE, HATE, JEALOUSY,.. MURDEROUS HOMICIDAL RAGE.
IN THE END IT'S ALL MEANINGLESS. EVERYTHING WE PERCEIVE AS GOOD OR BAD IS JUST NEUTRAL OUTSIDE OF OUR LIMITED UNDERSTANDING.
THE TRUE NATURE OF EXISTENCE IS BARBARIC SUFFERING, TORMENT, FEAR... ONE ORGANISM DEVOURS ANOTHER JUST TO FORESTALL HIS OWN DEPARTURE FROM THIS BRUTAL PLANET BY ONE MORE DAY.
YOU'RE BORN & YOU DIE IN THE BLINK OF AN
EYE!!

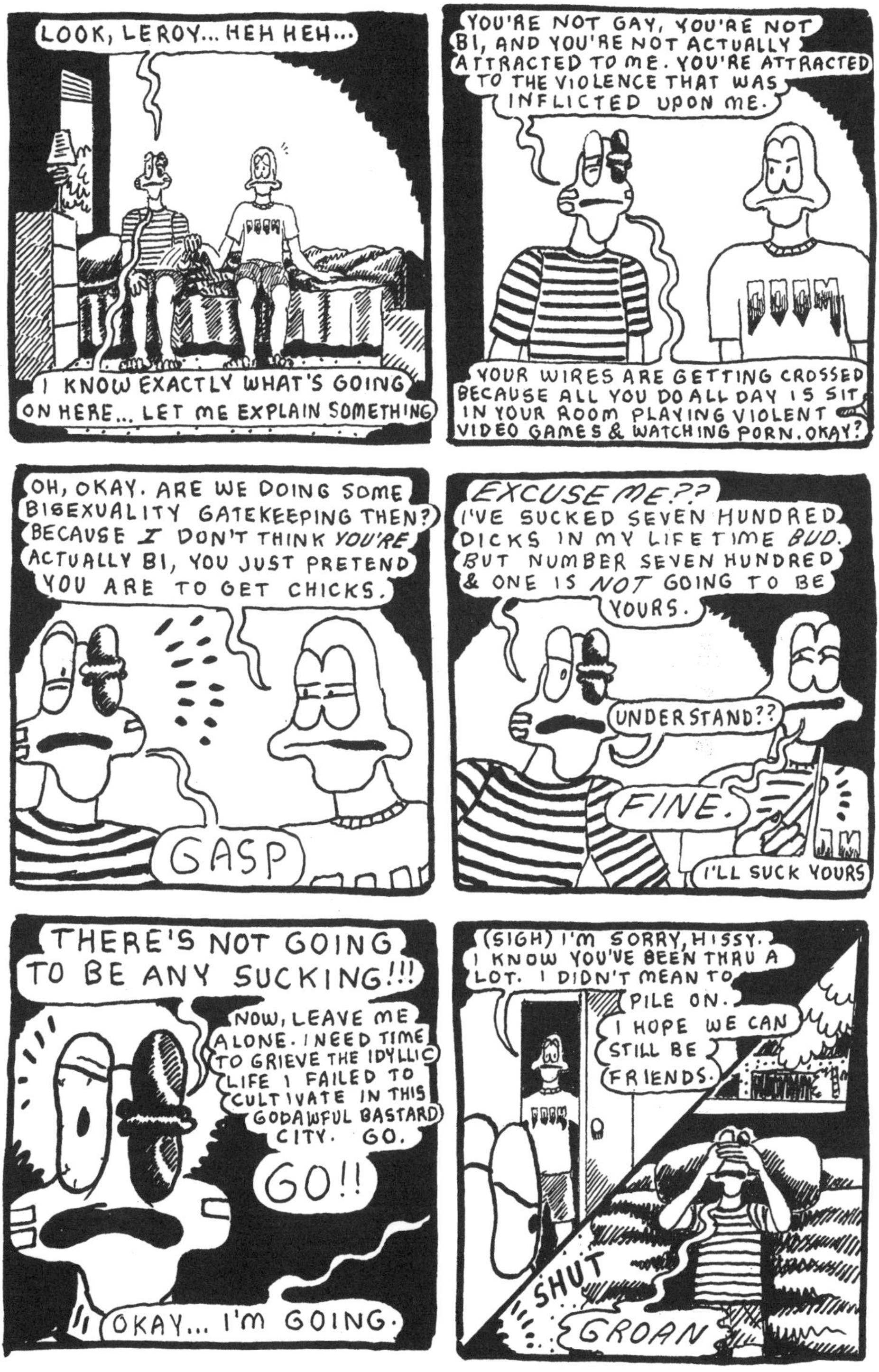
LOOK, LEROY... HEH HEH...
I KNOW EXACTLY WHAT'S GOING ON HERE... LET ME EXPLAIN SOMETHING
YOU'RE NOT GAY, YOU'RE NOT BI, AND YOU'RE NOT ACTUALLY ATTRACTED TO ME. YOU'RE ATTRACTED TO THE VIOLENCE THAT WAS INFLICTED UPON ME.
YOUR WIRES ARE GETTING CROSSED BECAUSE ALL YOU DO ALL DAY IS SIT IN YOUR ROOM PLAYING VIOLENT VIDEO GAMES & WATCHING PORN. OKAY?
OH, OKAY. ARE WE DOING SOME BISEXUALITY GATEKEEPING THEN? BECAUSE I DON'T THINK YOU'RE ACTUALLY BI, YOU JUST PRETEND YOU ARE TO GET CHICKS.
GASP
EXCUSE ME???
I'VE SUCKED SEVEN HUNDRED DICKS IN MY LIFETIME BUD. BUT NUMBER SEVEN HUNDRED & ONE IS NOT GOING TO BE YOURS.
UNDERSTAND??
FINE.
I'LL SUCK YOURS
THERE'S NOT GOING TO BE ANY SUCKING!!!
NOW, LEAVE ME ALONE. I NEED TIME TO GRIEVE THE IDYLLIC LIFE I FAILED TO CULTIVATE IN THIS GODAWFUL BASTARD CITY. GO.
GO!!
OKAY... I'M GOING.
(SIGH) I'M SORRY, HISSY. I KNOW YOU'VE BEEN THRU A LOT. I DIDN'T MEAN TO PILE ON.
I HOPE WE CAN STILL BE FRIENDS.
SHUT
GROAN

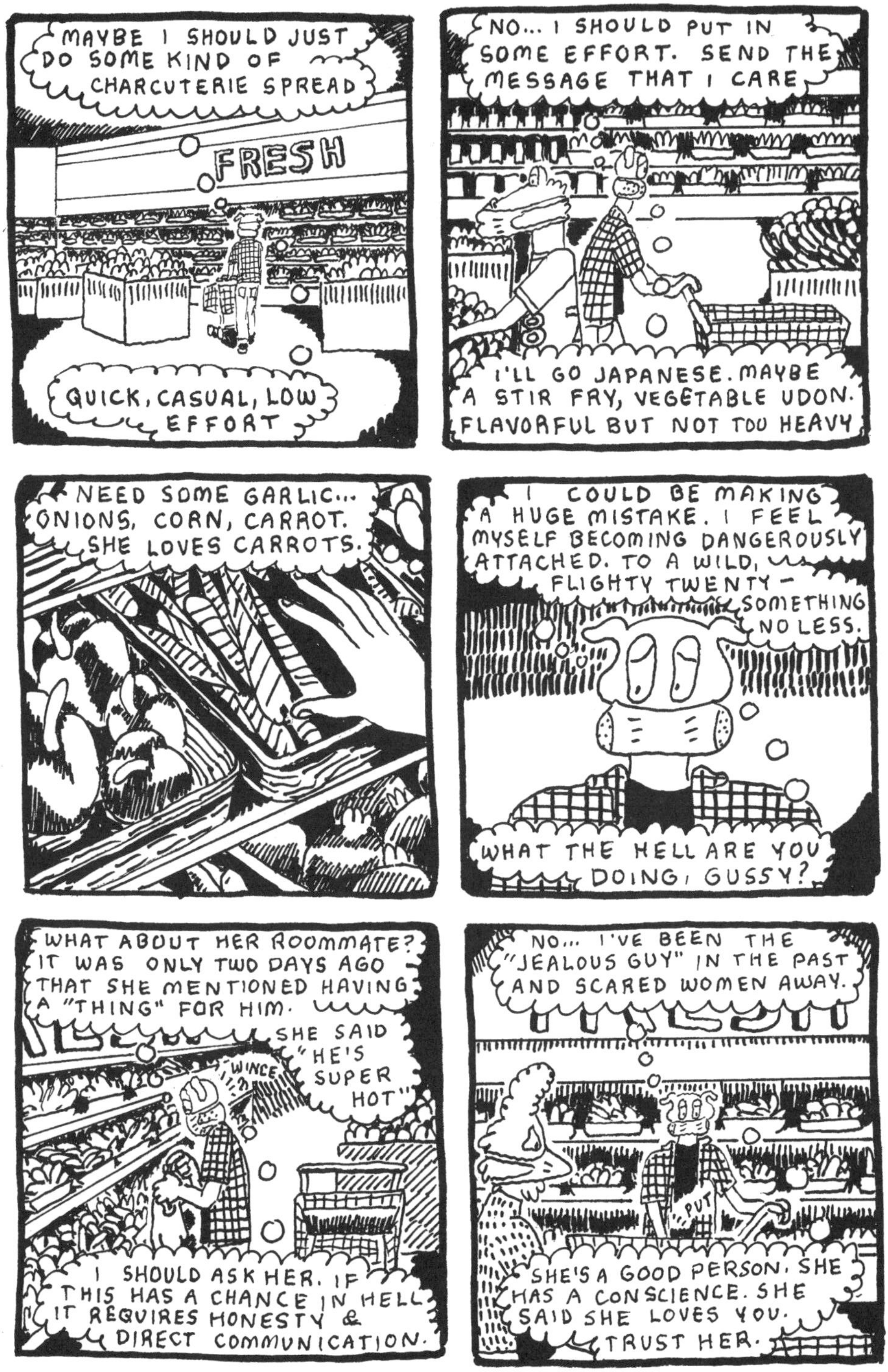

MAYBE I SHOULD JUST DO SOME KIND OF CHARCUTERIE SPREAD
FRESH
QUICK, CASUAL, LOW EFFORT
NO... I SHOULD PUT IN SOME EFFORT. SEND THE MESSAGE THAT I CARE
I'LL GO JAPANESE. MAYBE A STIR FRY, VEGETABLE UDON. FLAVORFUL BUT NOT TOO HEAVY
NEED SOME GARLIC... ONIONS, CORN, CARROT. SHE LOVES CARROTS.
I COULD BE MAKING A HUGE MISTAKE. I FEEL MYSELF BECOMING DANGEROUSLY ATTACHED. TO A WILD, FLIGHTY TWENTY-SOMETHING NO LESS.
WHAT THE HELL ARE YOU DOING, GUSSY?
WHAT ABOUT HER ROOMMATE? IT WAS ONLY TWO DAYS AGO THAT SHE MENTIONED HAVING A "THING" FOR HIM.
SHE SAID "HE'S SUPER HOT"
WINCE
I SHOULD ASK HER. IF THIS HAS A CHANCE IN HELL IT REQUIRES HONESTY & DIRECT COMMUNICATION.
NO... I'VE BEEN THE "JEALOUS GUY" IN THE PAST AND SCARED WOMEN AWAY.
PUT
SHE'S A GOOD PERSON. SHE HAS A CONSCIENCE. SHE SAID SHE LOVES YOU. TRUST HER.

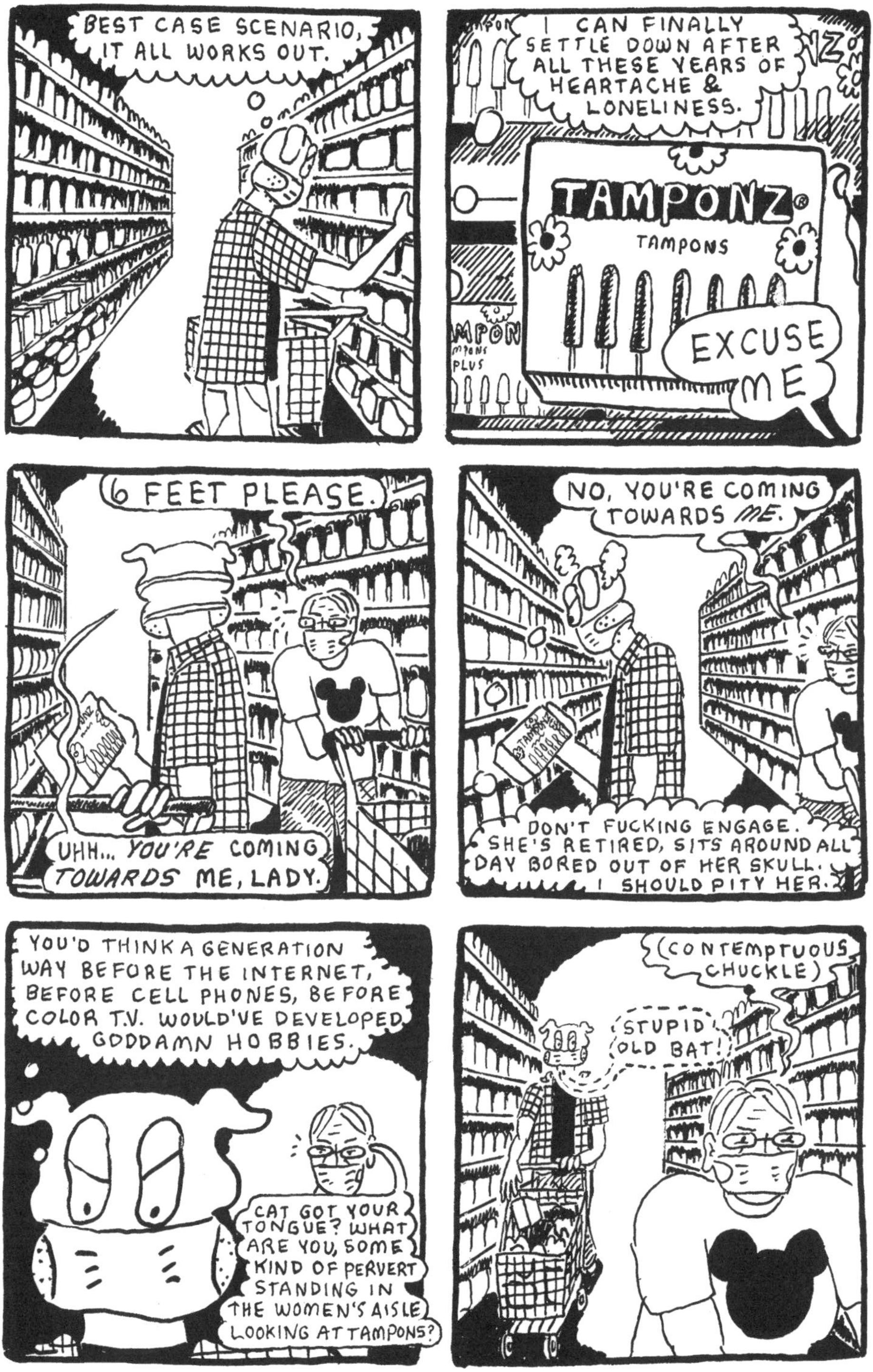
BEST CASE SCENARIO, IT ALL WORKS OUT.
I CAN FINALLY SETTLE DOWN AFTER ALL THESE YEARS OF HEARTACHE & LONELINESS.
TAMPONZ®
TAMPONS
EXCUSE ME
6 FEET PLEASE.
UHH... YOU'RE COMING TOWARDS ME, LADY.
NO, YOU'RE COMING TOWARDS ME.
DON'T FUCKING ENGAGE. SHE'S RETIRED, SITS AROUND ALL DAY BORED OUT OF HER SKULL. I SHOULD PITY HER.
YOU'D THINK A GENERATION WAY BEFORE THE INTERNET, BEFORE CELL PHONES, BEFORE COLOR T.V. WOULD'VE DEVELOPED GODDAMN HOBBIES.
CAT GOT YOUR TONGUE? WHAT ARE YOU, SOME KIND OF PERVERT STANDING IN THE WOMEN'S AISLE LOOKING AT TAMPONS?
(CONTEMPTUOUS CHUCKLE)
STUPID OLD BAT!

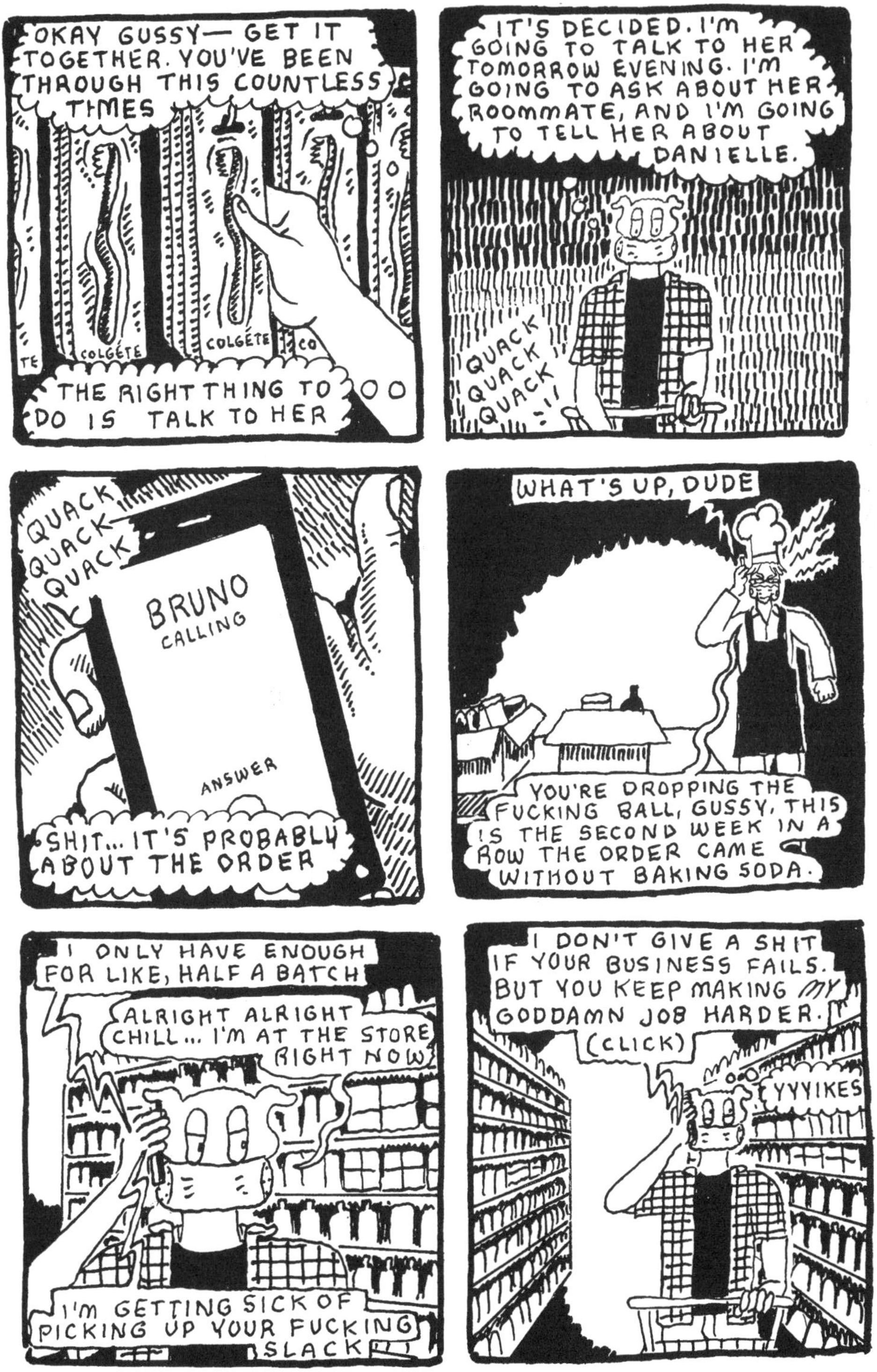
OKAY GUSSY— GET IT TOGETHER. YOU'VE BEEN THROUGH THIS COUNTLESS TIMES
TE
COLGÉTE
COLGÉTE
CO
THE RIGHT THING TO DO IS TALK TO HER
IT'S DECIDED. I'M GOING TO TALK TO HER TOMORROW EVENING. I'M GOING TO ASK ABOUT HER ROOMMATE, AND I'M GOING TO TELL HER ABOUT DANIELLE.
QUACK QUACK QUACK
QUACK QUACK QUACK
BRUNO CALLING
ANSWER
SHIT... IT'S PROBABLY ABOUT THE ORDER
WHAT'S UP, DUDE
YOU'RE DROPPING THE FUCKING BALL, GUSSY. THIS IS THE SECOND WEEK IN A ROW THE ORDER CAME WITHOUT BAKING SODA.
I ONLY HAVE ENOUGH FOR LIKE, HALF A BATCH
ALRIGHT ALRIGHT CHILL... I'M AT THE STORE RIGHT NOW
I'M GETTING SICK OF PICKING UP YOUR FUCKING SLACK
I DON'T GIVE A SHIT IF YOUR BUSINESS FAILS. BUT YOU KEEP MAKING MY GODDAMN JOB HARDER. (CLICK)
YYYIKES

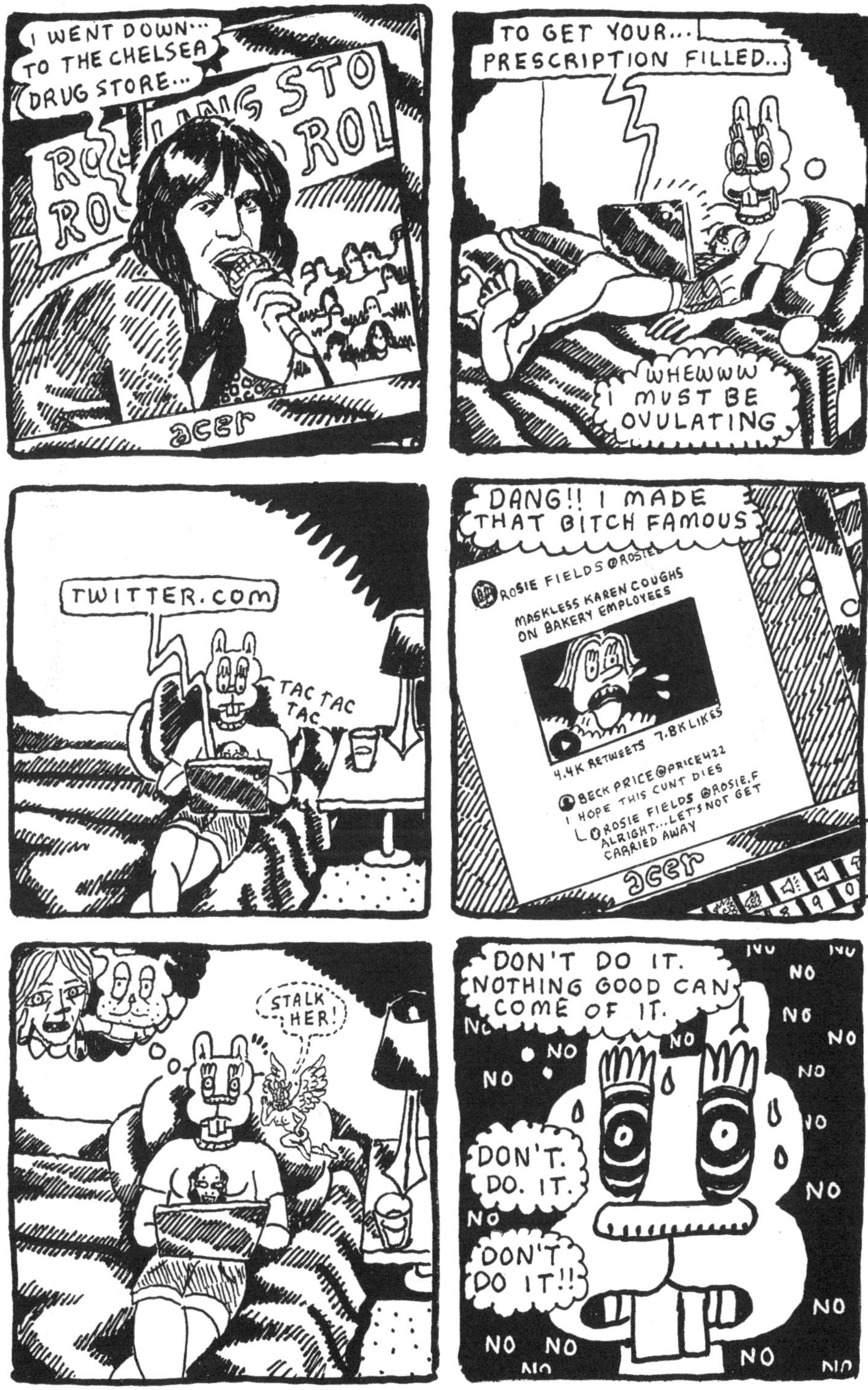

I WENT DOWN... TO THE CHELSEA DRUG STORE...
acer
TO GET YOUR... PRESCRIPTION FILLED...
WHEWWW I MUST BE OVULATING
TWITTER.COM
TAC TAC TAC
DANG!! I MADE THAT BITCH FAMOUS
ROSIE FIELDS @ROSIE
ROSIE FIELDS
MASKLESS KAREN COUGHS ON BAKERY EMPLOYEES
4.4K RETWEETS 7.8K LIKES
BECK PRICE @PRICE422
I HOPE THIS CUNT DIES
ROSIE FIELDS @ROSIE.F
ALRIGHT...LET'S NOT GET CARRIED AWAY
acer
STALK HER!
DON'T DO IT. NOTHING GOOD CAN COME OF IT.
DON'T. DO. IT.
DON'T DO IT!!
NO NO NO NO NO NO NO NO NO NO NO NO NO NO NO

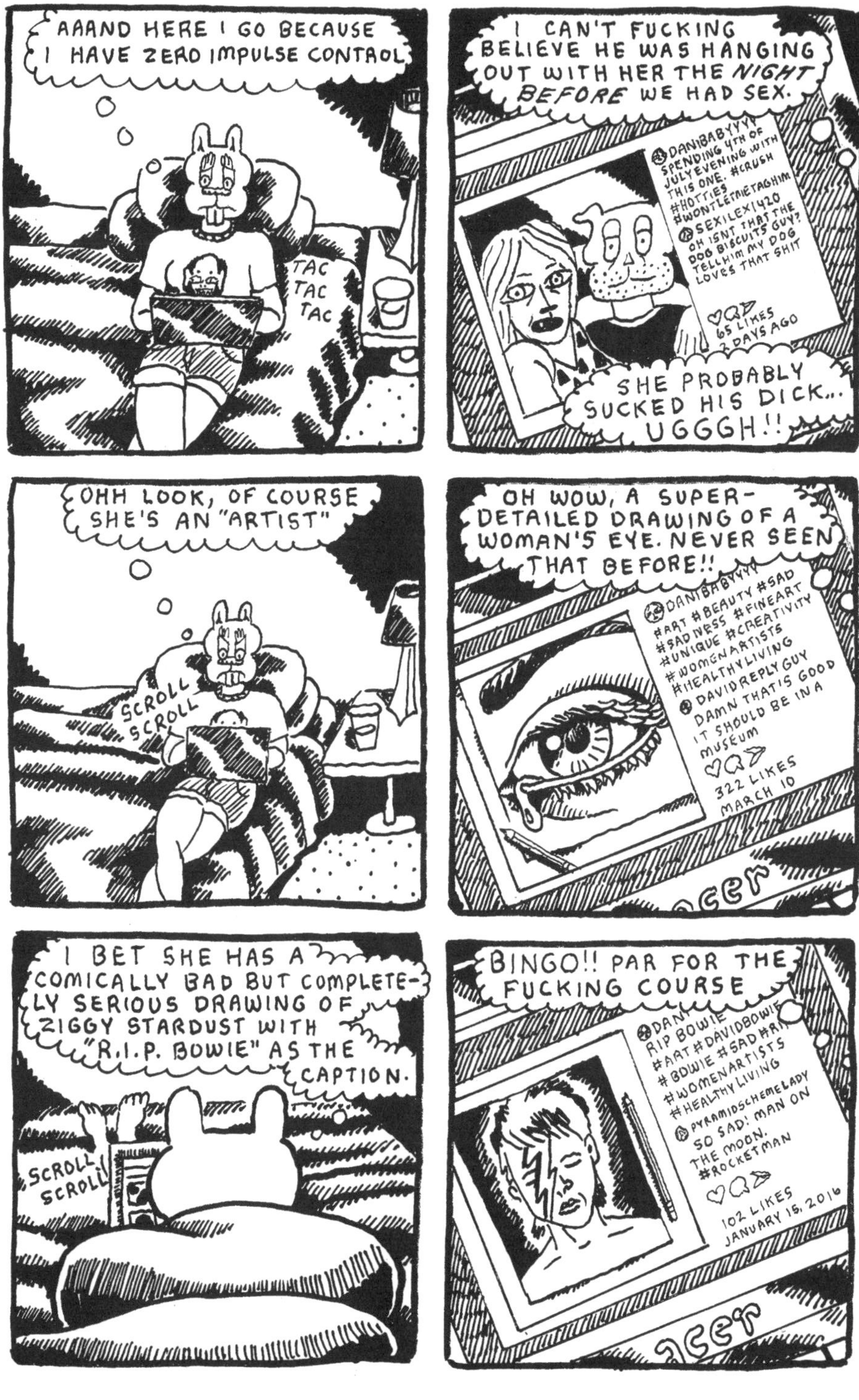
AAAND HERE I GO BECAUSE I HAVE ZERO IMPULSE CONTROL
TAC TAC TAC
I CAN'T FUCKING BELIEVE HE WAS HANGING OUT WITH HER THE NIGHT BEFORE WE HAD SEX.
DANIBABYYYY SPENDING 4TH OF JULY EVENING WITH THIS ONE. #CRUSH #HOTTIES #WONTLETMETAGHIM
SEXILEXI420 OH ISNT THAT THE DOG BISCUITS GUY? TELLHIM MY DOG LOVES THAT SHIT
65 LIKES
2 DAYS AGO
SHE PROBABLY SUCKED HIS DICK... UGGGH!!
OHH LOOK, OF COURSE SHE'S AN "ARTIST"
SCROLL SCROLL
OH WOW, A SUPER-DETAILED DRAWING OF A WOMAN'S EYE. NEVER SEEN THAT BEFORE!!
DANIBABYYYY #ART #BEAUTY #SAD #SADNESS #FINEART #UNIQUE #CREATIVITY #WOMENARTISTS #HEALTHYLIVING
DAVIDREPLYGUY DAMN THAT IS GOOD IT SHOULD BE IN A MUSEUM
322 LIKES
MARCH 10
I BET SHE HAS A COMICALLY BAD BUT COMPLETELY SERIOUS DRAWING OF ZIGGY STARDUST WITH "R.I.P. BOWIE" AS THE CAPTION.
SCROLL SCROLL
BINGO!! PAR FOR THE FUCKING COURSE
RIP BOWIE #ART #DAVIDBOWIE #BOWIE #SAD #WOMENARTISTS #HEALTHYLIVING
PYRAMIDSCHEMELADY SO SAD! MAN ON THE MOON. #ROCKETMAN
102 LIKES
JANUARY 15, 2016

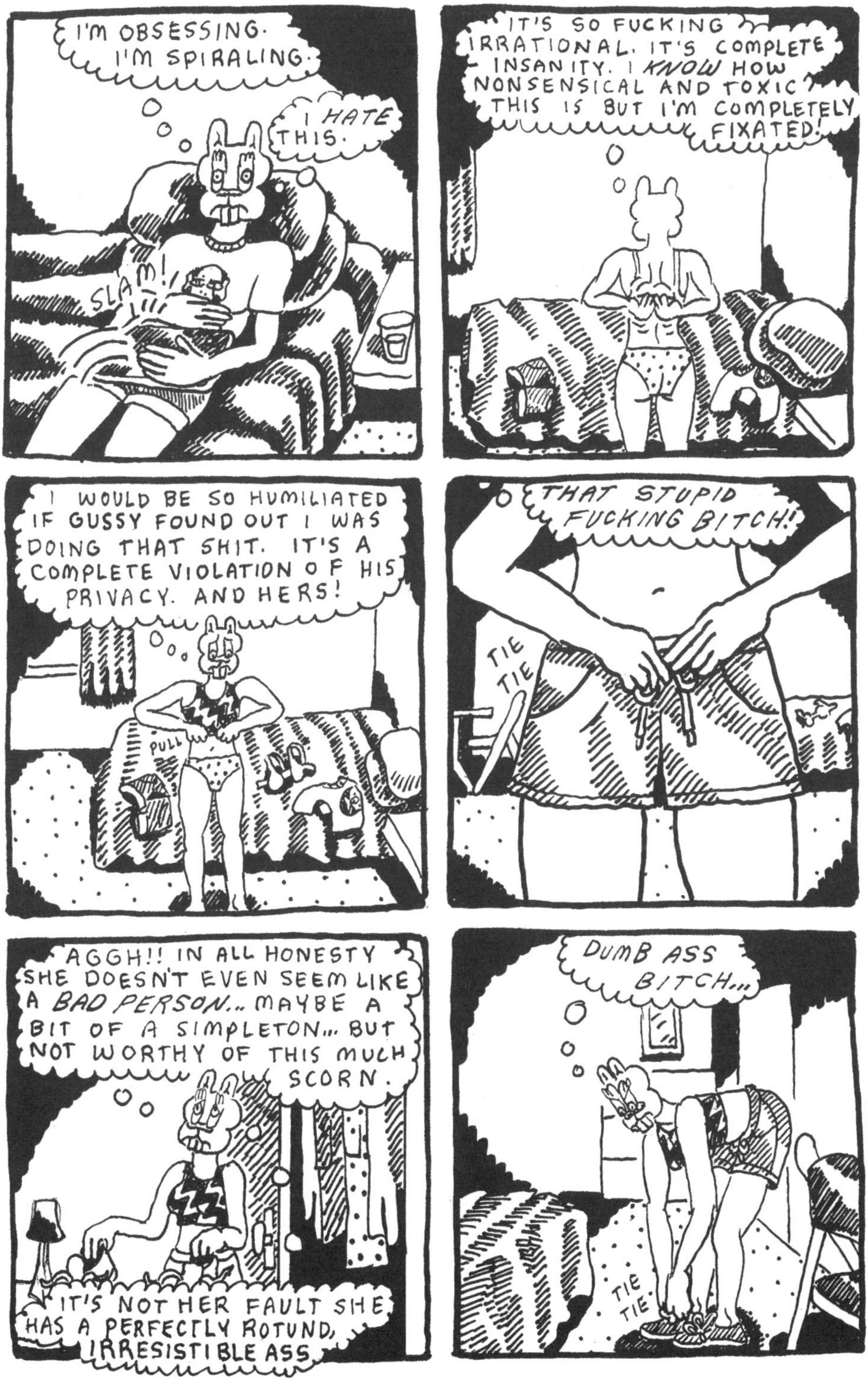

I'M OBSESSING. I'M SPIRALING.
I HATE THIS.
SLAM!
IT'S SO FUCKING IRRATIONAL. IT'S COMPLETE INSANITY. I KNOW HOW NONSENSICAL AND TOXIC THIS IS BUT I'M COMPLETELY FIXATED!
I WOULD BE SO HUMILIATED IF GUSSY FOUND OUT I WAS DOING THAT SHIT. IT'S A COMPLETE VIOLATION OF HIS PRIVACY. AND HERS!
PULL
THAT STUPID FUCKING BITCH!
TIE TIE
AGGH!! IN ALL HONESTY SHE DOESN'T EVEN SEEM LIKE A BAD PERSON... MAYBE A BIT OF A SIMPLETON... BUT NOT WORTHY OF THIS MUCH SCORN.
IT'S NOT HER FAULT SHE HAS A PERFECTLY ROTUND, IRRESISTIBLE ASS
DUMB ASS BITCH...
TIE TIE

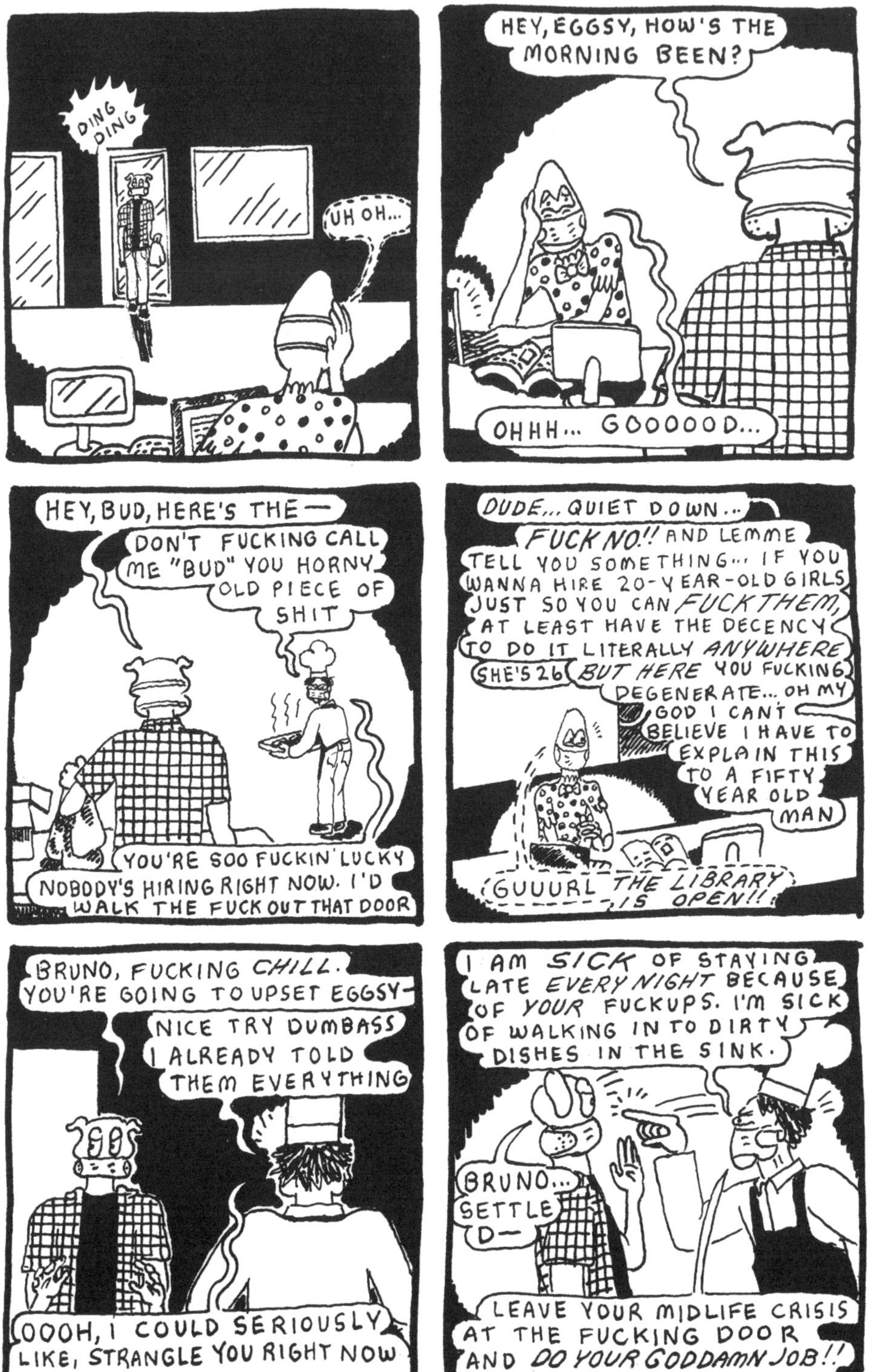
DING DING
UH OH...
HEY, EGGSY, HOW'S THE MORNING BEEN?
OHHH... GOOOOOD...
HEY, BUD, HERE'S THE—
DON'T FUCKING CALL ME "BUD" YOU HORNY OLD PIECE OF SHIT
YOU'RE SOO FUCKIN' LUCKY NOBODY'S HIRING RIGHT NOW. I'D WALK THE FUCK OUT THAT DOOR
DUDE... QUIET DOWN...
FUCK NO!! AND LEMME TELL YOU SOMETHING... IF YOU WANNA HIRE 20-YEAR-OLD GIRLS JUST SO YOU CAN FUCK THEM, AT LEAST HAVE THE DECENCY TO DO IT LITERALLY ANYWHERE
SHE'S 26
BUT HERE YOU FUCKING DEGENERATE... OH MY GOD I CAN'T BELIEVE I HAVE TO EXPLAIN THIS TO A FIFTY YEAR OLD MAN
GUUURL THE LIBRARY IS OPEN!!
BRUNO, FUCKING CHILL. YOU'RE GOING TO UPSET EGGSY—
NICE TRY DUMBASS I ALREADY TOLD THEM EVERYTHING
OOOH, I COULD SERIOUSLY LIKE, STRANGLE YOU RIGHT NOW
I AM SICK OF STAYING LATE EVERY NIGHT BECAUSE OF YOUR FUCKUPS. I'M SICK OF WALKING INTO DIRTY DISHES IN THE SINK.
BRUNO... SETTLE D—
LEAVE YOUR MIDLIFE CRISIS AT THE FUCKING DOOR AND DO YOUR GODDAMN JOB!!

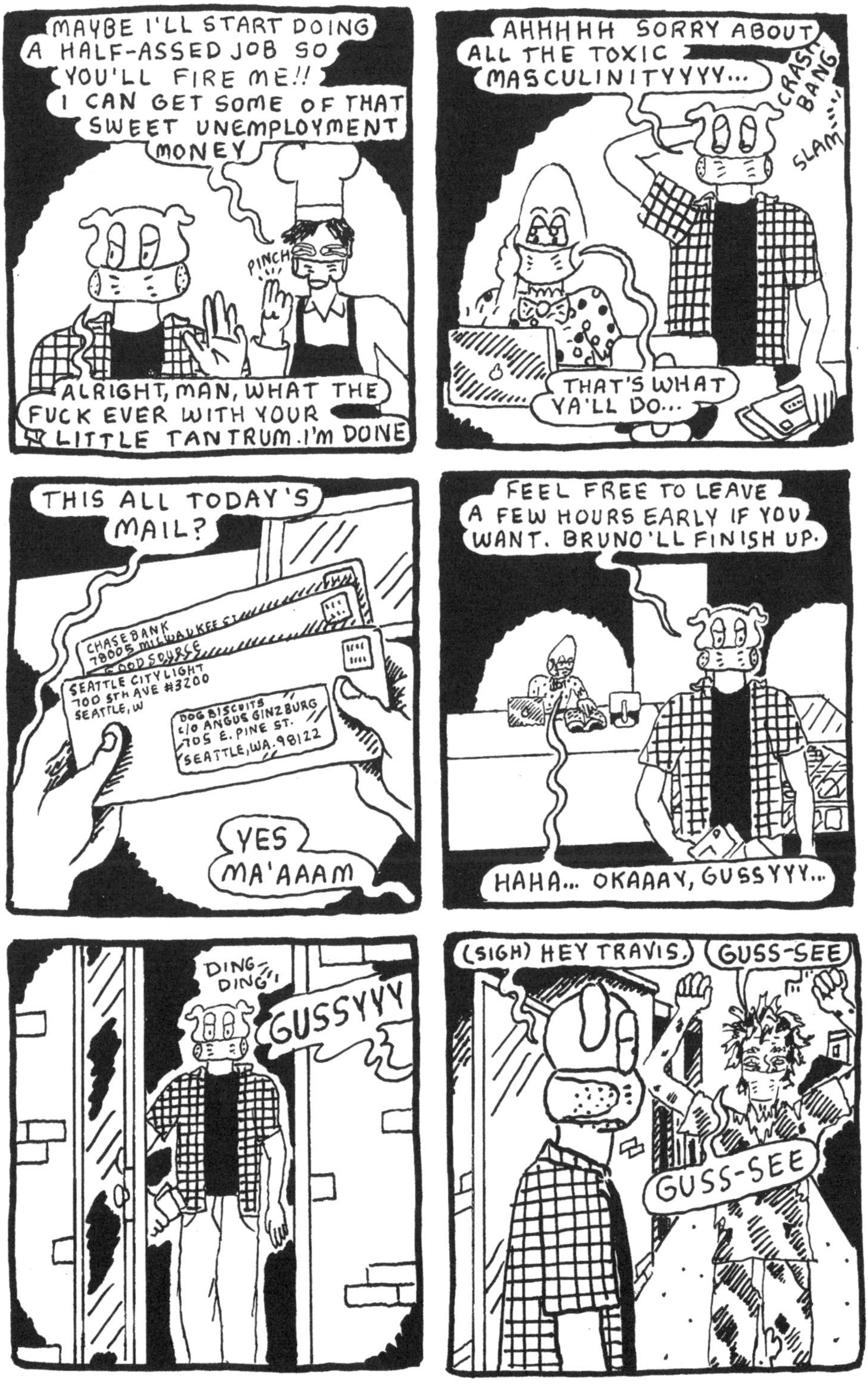
MAYBE I'LL START DOING A HALF-ASSED JOB SO YOU'LL FIRE ME!! I CAN GET SOME OF THAT SWEET UNEMPLOYMENT MONEY
PINCH
ALRIGHT, MAN, WHAT THE FUCK EVER WITH YOUR LITTLE TANTRUM. I'M DONE
AHHHHH SORRY ABOUT ALL THE TOXIC MASCULINITYYYY...
CRASH BANG
SLAM
THAT'S WHAT YA'LL DO...
THIS ALL TODAY'S MAIL?
CHASE BANK
FOOD SOURCE
SEATTLE CITY LIGHT
700 5TH AVE #3200
SEATTLE, W
DOG BISCUITS
c/o ANGUS GINZBURG
705 E. PINE ST.
SEATTLE, WA. 98122
YES MA'AAAM
FEEL FREE TO LEAVE A FEW HOURS EARLY IF YOU WANT. BRUNO'LL FINISH UP.
HAHA... OKAAAY, GUSSYYY...
DING DING
GUSSYYY
(SIGH) HEY TRAVIS.
GUSS-SEE
GUSS-SEE

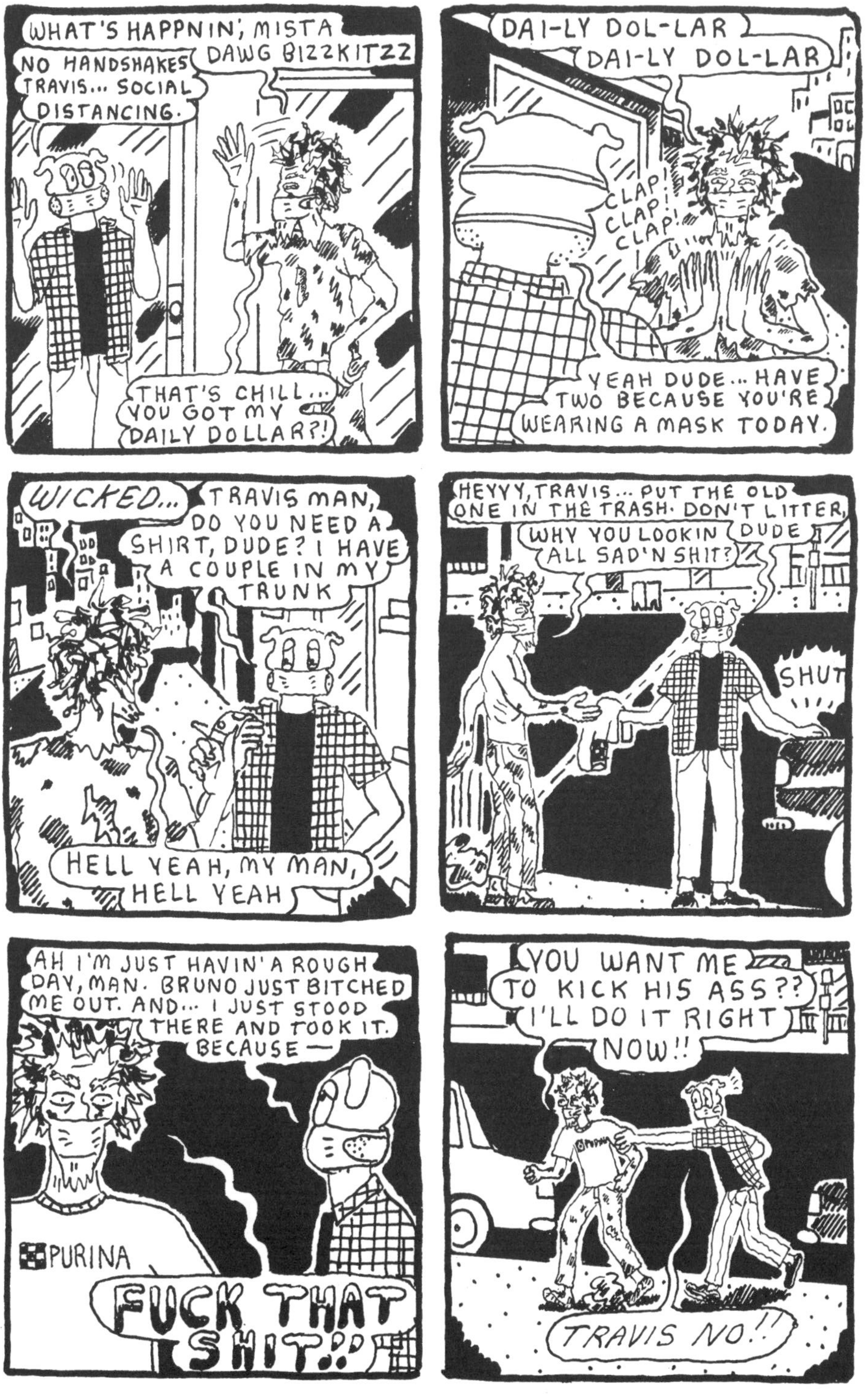

WHAT'S HAPPNIN', MISTA DAWG BIZZKITZZ
NO HANDSHAKES TRAVIS... SOCIAL DISTANCING.
THAT'S CHILL... YOU GOT MY DAILY DOLLAR?!
DAI-LY DOL-LAR
DAI-LY DOL-LAR
CLAP! CLAP! CLAP!
YEAH DUDE... HAVE TWO BECAUSE YOU'RE WEARING A MASK TODAY.
WICKED...
TRAVIS MAN, DO YOU NEED A SHIRT, DUDE? I HAVE A COUPLE IN MY TRUNK
HELL YEAH, MY MAN, HELL YEAH
HEYYY, TRAVIS... PUT THE OLD ONE IN THE TRASH. DON'T LITTER, DUDE
WHY YOU LOOKIN ALL SAD'N SHIT?
SHUT
AH I'M JUST HAVIN' A ROUGH DAY, MAN. BRUNO JUST BITCHED ME OUT. AND... I JUST STOOD THERE AND TOOK IT. BECAUSE —
PURINA
FUCK THAT SHIT!!
YOU WANT ME TO KICK HIS ASS?? I'LL DO IT RIGHT NOW!!
PURINA
TRAVIS NO!!

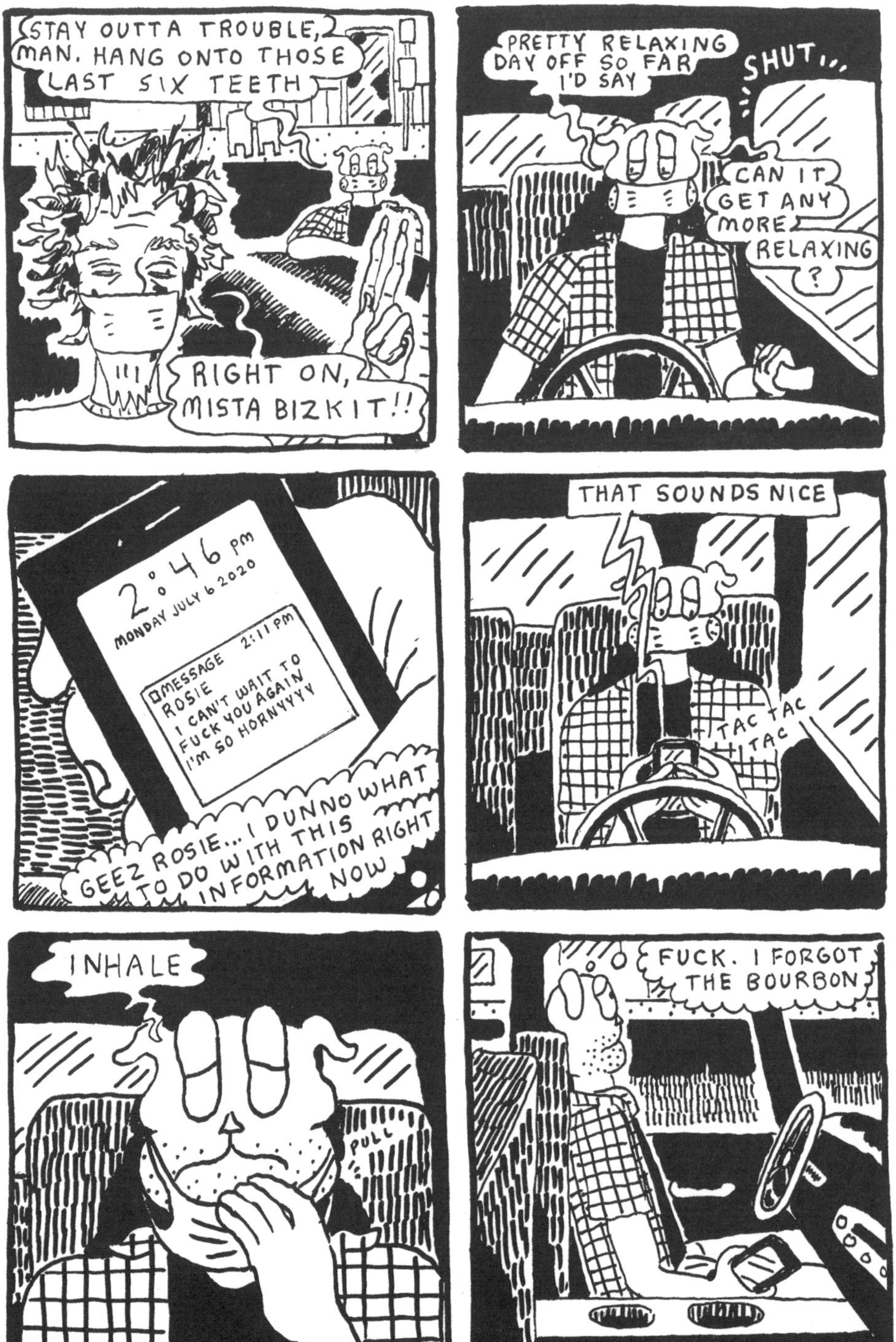
STAY OUTTA TROUBLE, MAN. HANG ONTO THOSE LAST SIX TEETH
RIGHT ON, MISTA BIZKIT!!
PRETTY RELAXING DAY OFF SO FAR I'D SAY
SHUT
CAN IT GET ANY MORE RELAXING ?
2:46 pm
MONDAY JULY 6 2020
MESSAGE 2:11 PM
ROSIE
I CAN'T WAIT TO FUCK YOU AGAIN I'M SO HORNYYYY
GEEZ ROSIE... I DUNNO WHAT TO DO WITH THIS INFORMATION RIGHT NOW
THAT SOUNDS NICE
TAC TAC TAC
INHALE
PULL
FUCK. I FORGOT THE BOURBON

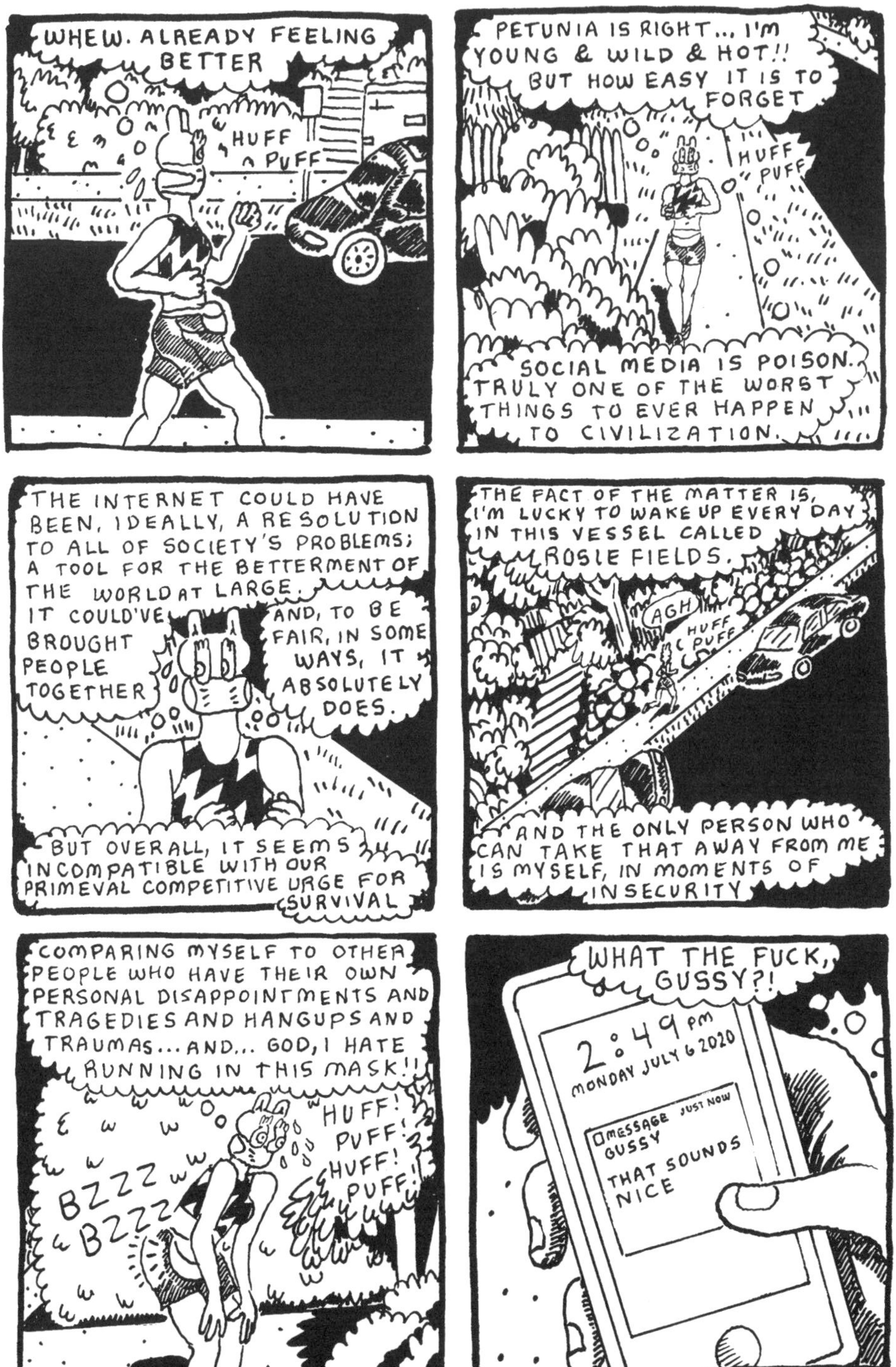
WHEW. ALREADY FEELING BETTER
HUFF PUFF
PETUNIA IS RIGHT... I'M YOUNG & WILD & HOT!! BUT HOW EASY IT IS TO FORGET
HUFF PUFF
SOCIAL MEDIA IS POISON. TRULY ONE OF THE WORST THINGS TO EVER HAPPEN TO CIVILIZATION.
THE INTERNET COULD HAVE BEEN, IDEALLY, A RESOLUTION TO ALL OF SOCIETY'S PROBLEMS; A TOOL FOR THE BETTERMENT OF THE WORLD AT LARGE.
IT COULD'VE BROUGHT PEOPLE TOGETHER
AND, TO BE FAIR, IN SOME WAYS, IT ABSOLUTELY DOES.
BUT OVERALL, IT SEEMS INCOMPATIBLE WITH OUR PRIMEVAL COMPETITIVE URGE FOR SURVIVAL
THE FACT OF THE MATTER IS, I'M LUCKY TO WAKE UP EVERY DAY IN THIS VESSEL CALLED ROSIE FIELDS.
AGH
HUFF PUFF
AND THE ONLY PERSON WHO CAN TAKE THAT AWAY FROM ME IS MYSELF, IN MOMENTS OF INSECURITY
COMPARING MYSELF TO OTHER PEOPLE WHO HAVE THEIR OWN PERSONAL DISAPPOINTMENTS AND TRAGEDIES AND HANGUPS AND TRAUMAS... AND... GOD, I HATE RUNNING IN THIS MASK!!
HUFF! PUFF! HUFF! PUFF!
BZZZ BZZZ
WHAT THE FUCK, GUSSY?!
2:49 pm
MONDAY JULY 6 2020
MESSAGE JUST NOW
GUSSY
THAT SOUNDS NICE

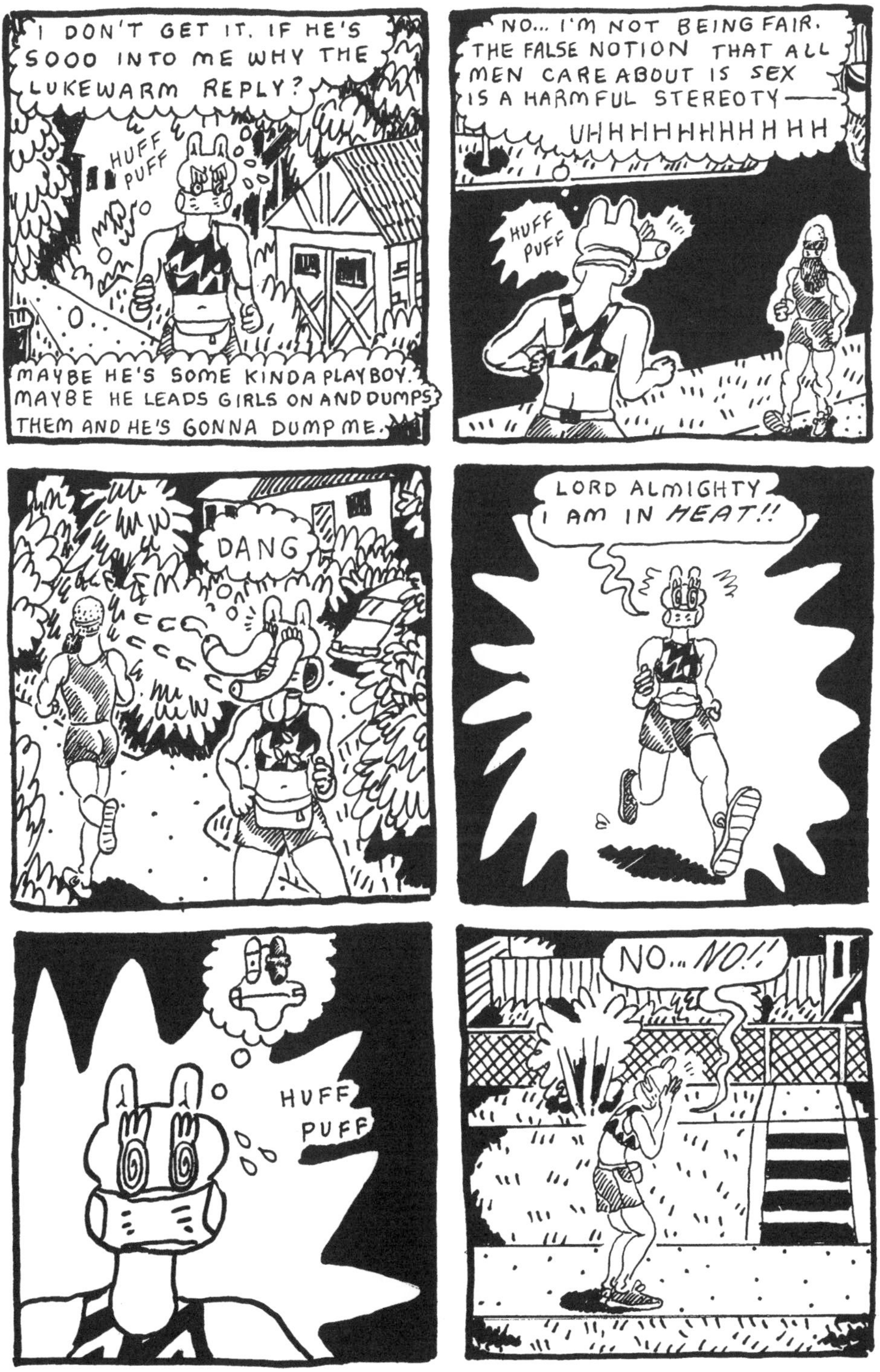
I DON'T GET IT. IF HE'S SOOO INTO ME WHY THE LUKEWARM REPLY?
HUFF PUFF
MAYBE HE'S SOME KINDA PLAYBOY. MAYBE HE LEADS GIRLS ON AND DUMPS THEM AND HE'S GONNA DUMP ME.
NO... I'M NOT BEING FAIR. THE FALSE NOTION THAT ALL MEN CARE ABOUT IS SEX IS A HARMFUL STEREOTY——
UHHHHHHHHHHHH
HUFF PUFF
DANG
LORD ALMIGHTY I AM IN HEAT!!
HUFF PUFF
NO... NO!!

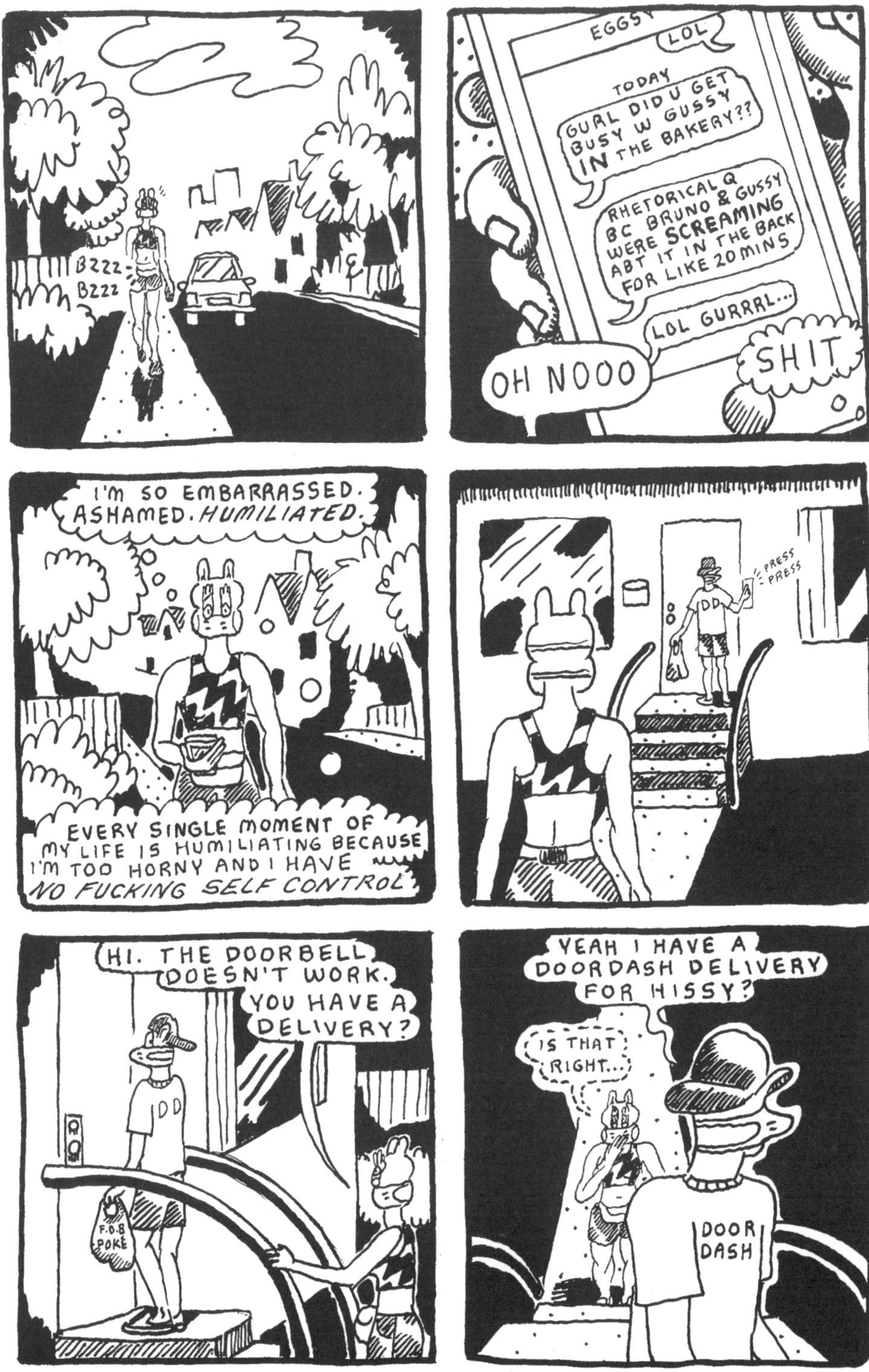
BZZZ
BZZZ
EGGS
LOL
TODAY
GURL DID U GET BUSY W GUSSY IN THE BAKERY??
RHETORICAL Q BC BRUNO & GUSSY WERE SCREAMING ABT IT IN THE BACK FOR LIKE 20 MINS
LOL GURRRL...
OH NOOO
SHIT
I'M SO EMBARRASSED. ASHAMED. HUMILIATED.
EVERY SINGLE MOMENT OF MY LIFE IS HUMILIATING BECAUSE I'M TOO HORNY AND I HAVE NO FUCKING SELF CONTROL
PRESS PRESS
DD
HI. THE DOORBELL DOESN'T WORK.
YOU HAVE A DELIVERY?
DD
F.O.B POKE
YEAH I HAVE A DOORDASH DELIVERY FOR HISSY?
IS THAT RIGHT...
DOOR DASH

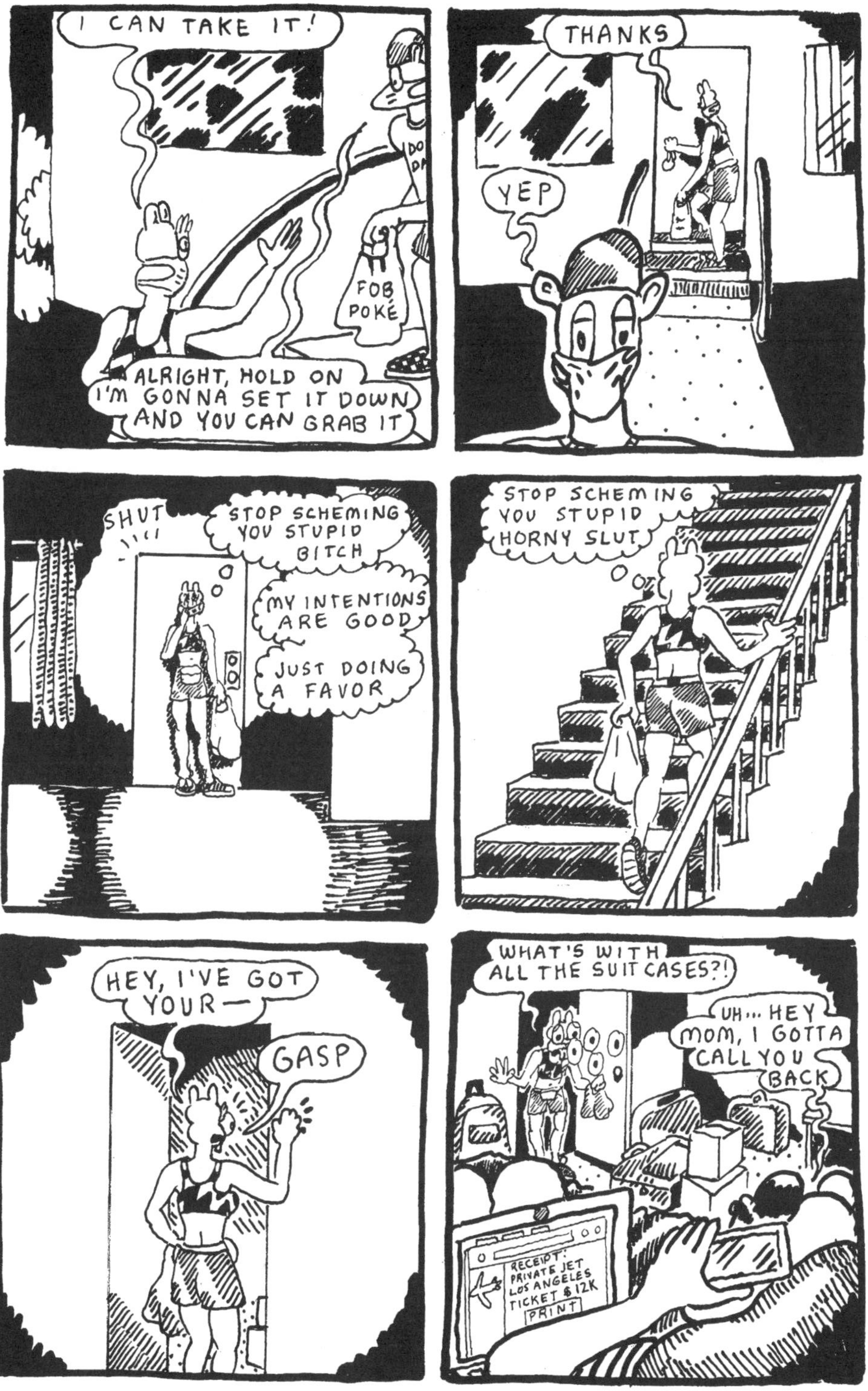
I CAN TAKE IT!
FOB POKÉ
ALRIGHT, HOLD ON I'M GONNA SET IT DOWN AND YOU CAN GRAB IT
THANKS
YEP
SHUT
STOP SCHEMING YOU STUPID BITCH
MY INTENTIONS ARE GOOD
JUST DOING A FAVOR
STOP SCHEMING YOU STUPID HORNY SLUT
HEY, I'VE GOT YOUR—
GASP
WHAT'S WITH ALL THE SUITCASES?!
UH... HEY MOM, I GOTTA CALL YOU BACK
RECEIPT: PRIVATE JET LOS ANGELES TICKET $12K
PRINT

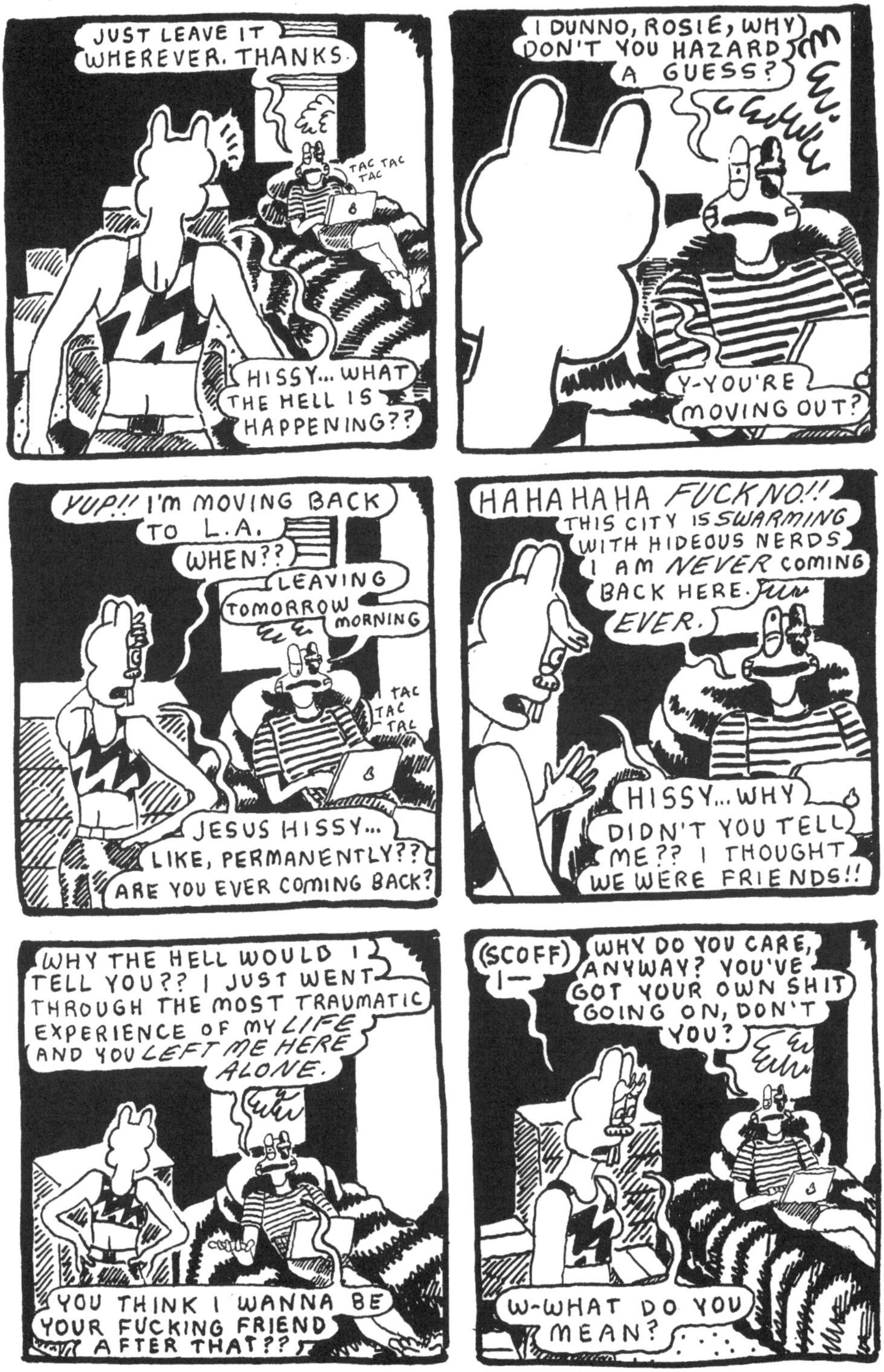
JUST LEAVE IT WHEREVER. THANKS.
TAC TAC TAC
HISSY... WHAT THE HELL IS HAPPENING??
I DUNNO, ROSIE, WHY DON'T YOU HAZARD A GUESS?
Y-YOU'RE MOVING OUT?
YUP!! I'M MOVING BACK TO L.A.
WHEN??
LEAVING TOMORROW MORNING
TAC TAC TAC
JESUS HISSY... LIKE, PERMANENTLY?? ARE YOU EVER COMING BACK?
HAHAHAHA FUCK NO!! THIS CITY IS SWARMING WITH HIDEOUS NERDS. I AM NEVER COMING BACK HERE. EVER.
HISSY... WHY DIDN'T YOU TELL ME?? I THOUGHT WE WERE FRIENDS!!
WHY THE HELL WOULD I TELL YOU?? I JUST WENT THROUGH THE MOST TRAUMATIC EXPERIENCE OF MY LIFE AND YOU LEFT ME HERE ALONE.
YOU THINK I WANNA BE YOUR FUCKING FRIEND AFTER THAT??
(SCOFF) I—
WHY DO YOU CARE, ANYWAY? YOU'VE GOT YOUR OWN SHIT GOING ON, DON'T YOU?
W-WHAT DO YOU MEAN?

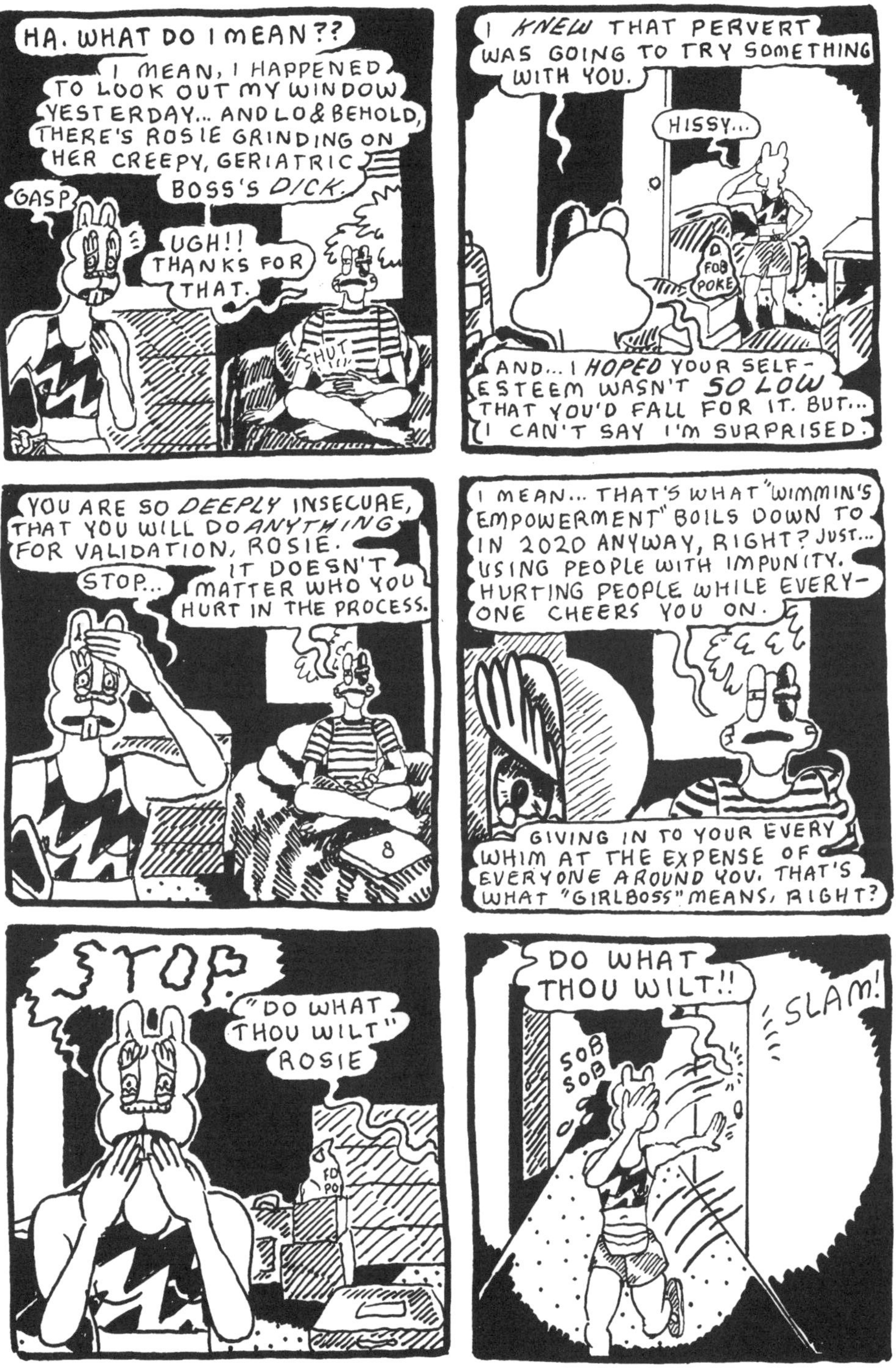
HA. WHAT DO I MEAN??
I MEAN, I HAPPENED TO LOOK OUT MY WINDOW YESTERDAY... AND LO & BEHOLD, THERE'S ROSIE GRINDING ON HER CREEPY, GERIATRIC BOSS'S *DICK*.
GASP
UGH!! THANKS FOR THAT.
SHUT
I *KNEW* THAT PERVERT WAS GOING TO TRY SOMETHING WITH YOU.
HISSY...
FOB POKE
AND... I *HOPED* YOUR SELF-ESTEEM WASN'T *SO LOW* THAT YOU'D FALL FOR IT. BUT... I CAN'T SAY I'M SURPRISED.
YOU ARE SO *DEEPLY* INSECURE, THAT YOU WILL DO *ANYTHING* FOR VALIDATION, ROSIE.
STOP...
IT DOESN'T MATTER WHO YOU HURT IN THE PROCESS.
I MEAN... THAT'S WHAT "WIMMIN'S EMPOWERMENT" BOILS DOWN TO IN 2020 ANYWAY, RIGHT? JUST... USING PEOPLE WITH IMPUNITY. HURTING PEOPLE WHILE EVERYONE CHEERS YOU ON.
GIVING IN TO YOUR EVERY WHIM AT THE EXPENSE OF EVERYONE AROUND YOU. THAT'S WHAT "GIRLBOSS" MEANS, RIGHT?
STOP
"DO WHAT THOU WILT" ROSIE
DO WHAT THOU WILT!!
SLAM!
SOB SOB

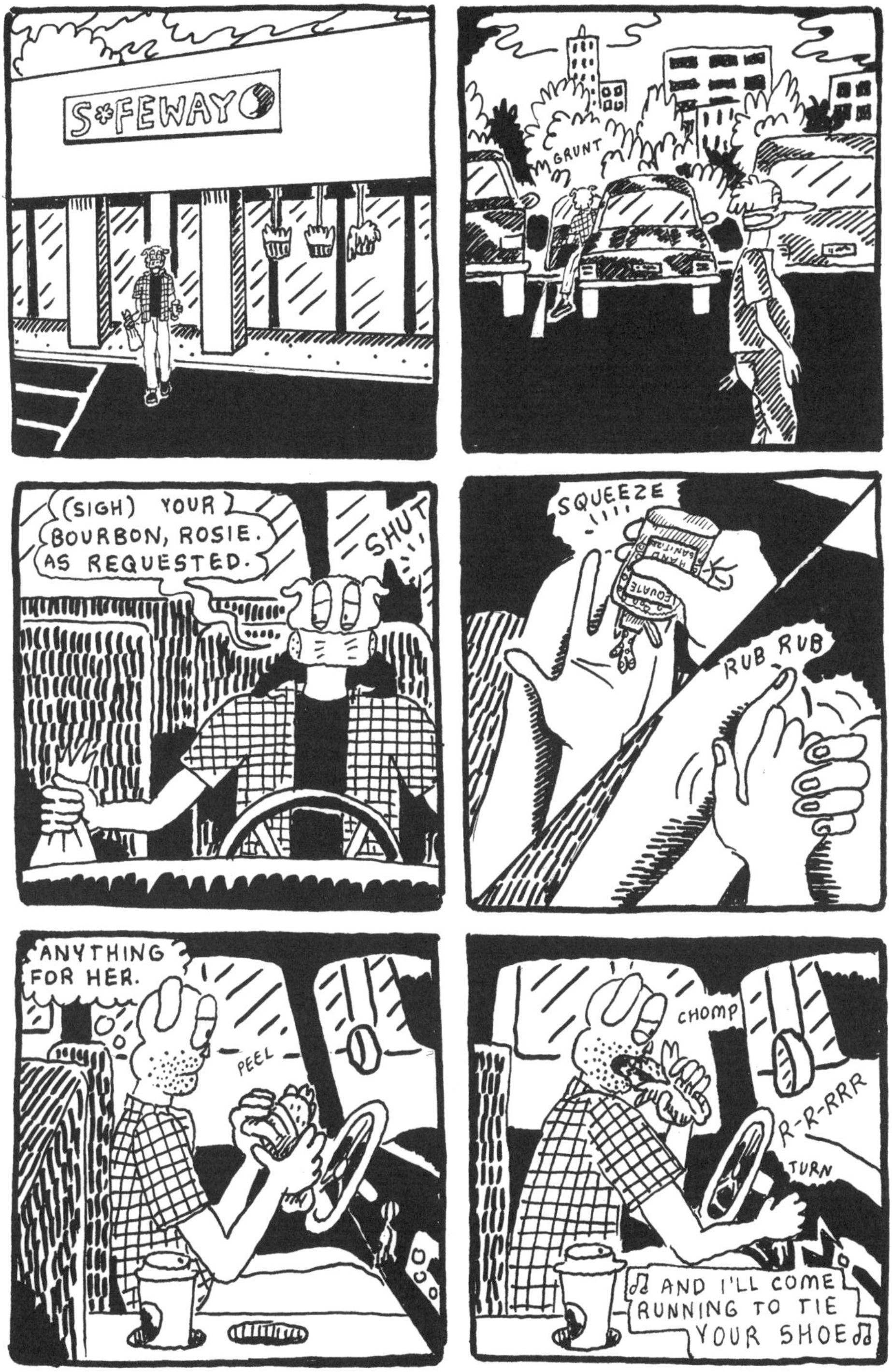
S*FEWAY
GRUNT
(SIGH) YOUR BOURBON, ROSIE. AS REQUESTED.
SHUT
SQUEEZE
RUB RUB
ANYTHING FOR HER.
PEEL
CHOMP
R-R-RRR
TURN
♫ AND I'LL COME RUNNING TO TIE YOUR SHOE ♫

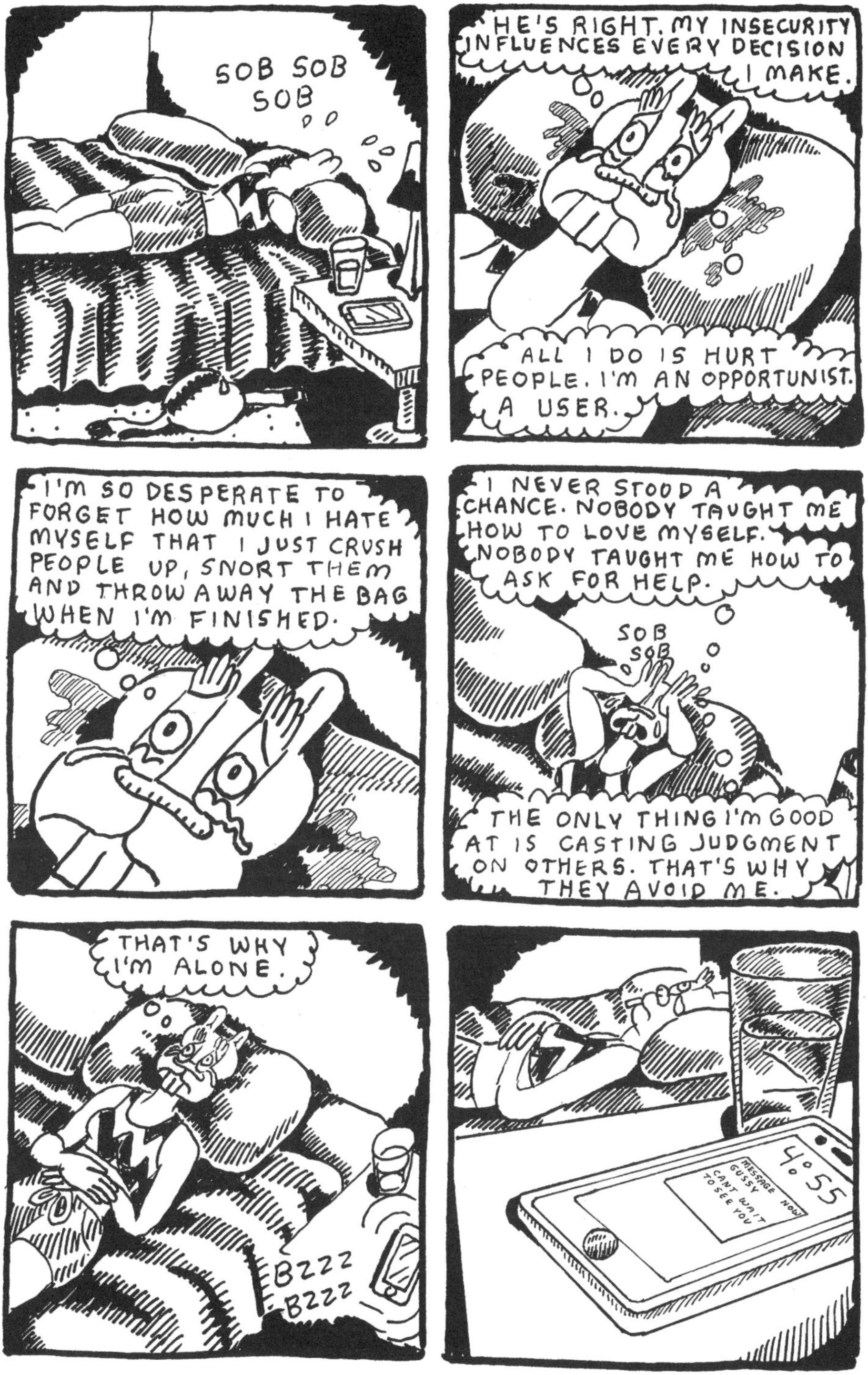
SOB SOB SOB
HE'S RIGHT. MY INSECURITY INFLUENCES EVERY DECISION I MAKE.
ALL I DO IS HURT PEOPLE. I'M AN OPPORTUNIST. A USER.
I'M SO DESPERATE TO FORGET HOW MUCH I HATE MYSELF THAT I JUST CRUSH PEOPLE UP, SNORT THEM AND THROW AWAY THE BAG WHEN I'M FINISHED.
I NEVER STOOD A CHANCE. NOBODY TAUGHT ME HOW TO LOVE MYSELF. NOBODY TAUGHT ME HOW TO ASK FOR HELP.
SOB SOB
THE ONLY THING I'M GOOD AT IS CASTING JUDGMENT ON OTHERS. THAT'S WHY THEY AVOID ME.
THAT'S WHY I'M ALONE.
BZZZ BZZZ
4:55
MESSAGE NOW
GUSSY
CANT WAIT TO SEE YOU

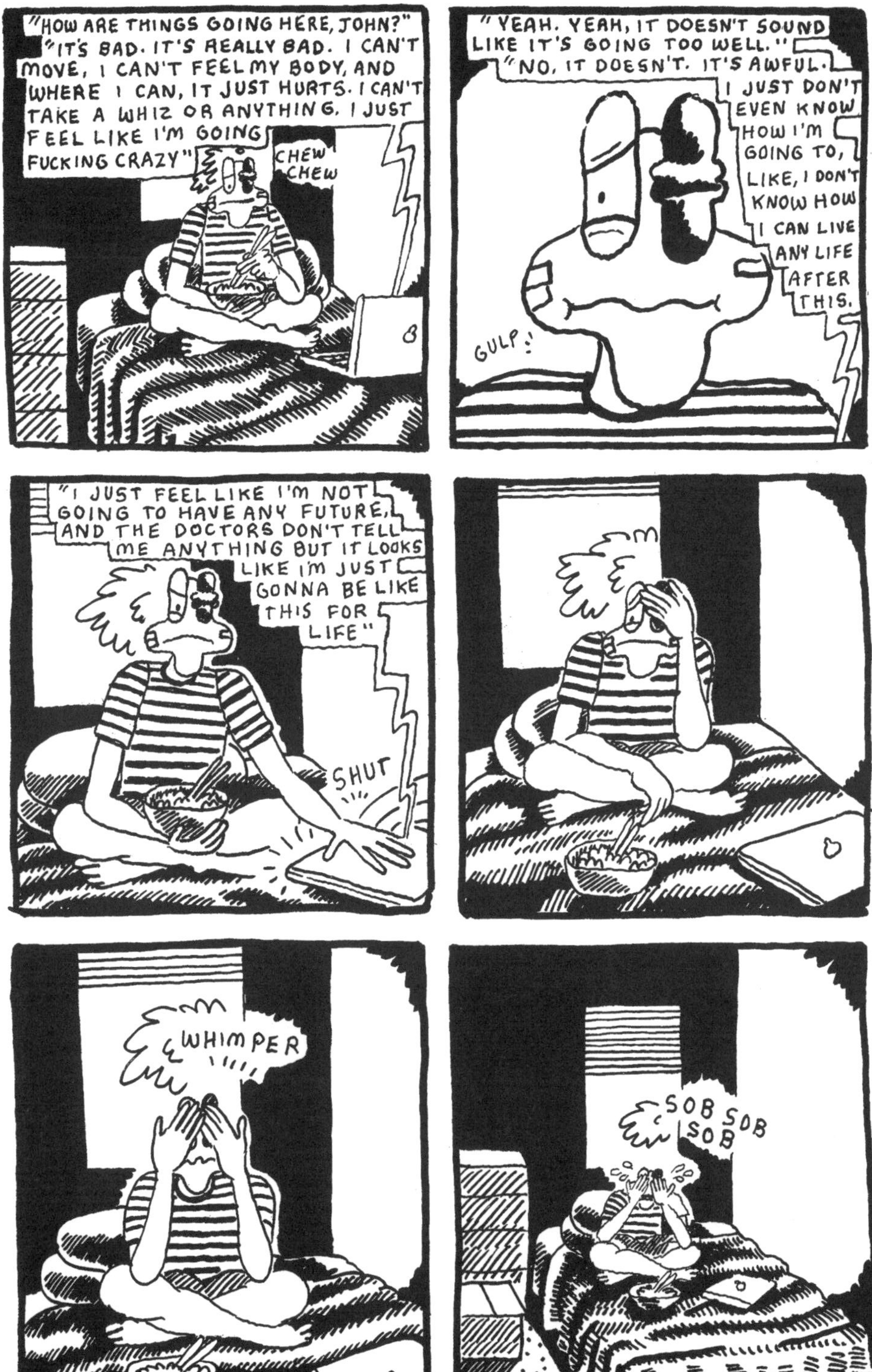
"HOW ARE THINGS GOING HERE, JOHN?"
"IT'S BAD. IT'S REALLY BAD. I CAN'T MOVE, I CAN'T FEEL MY BODY, AND WHERE I CAN, IT JUST HURTS. I CAN'T TAKE A WHIZ OR ANYTHING. I JUST FEEL LIKE I'M GOING FUCKING CRAZY"
CHEW CHEW
"YEAH. YEAH, IT DOESN'T SOUND LIKE IT'S GOING TOO WELL."
"NO, IT DOESN'T. IT'S AWFUL. I JUST DON'T EVEN KNOW HOW I'M GOING TO, LIKE, I DON'T KNOW HOW I CAN LIVE ANY LIFE AFTER THIS.
GULP
"I JUST FEEL LIKE I'M NOT GOING TO HAVE ANY FUTURE, AND THE DOCTORS DON'T TELL ME ANYTHING BUT IT LOOKS LIKE I'M JUST GONNA BE LIKE THIS FOR LIFE"
SHUT
WHIMPER
SOB SOB SOB

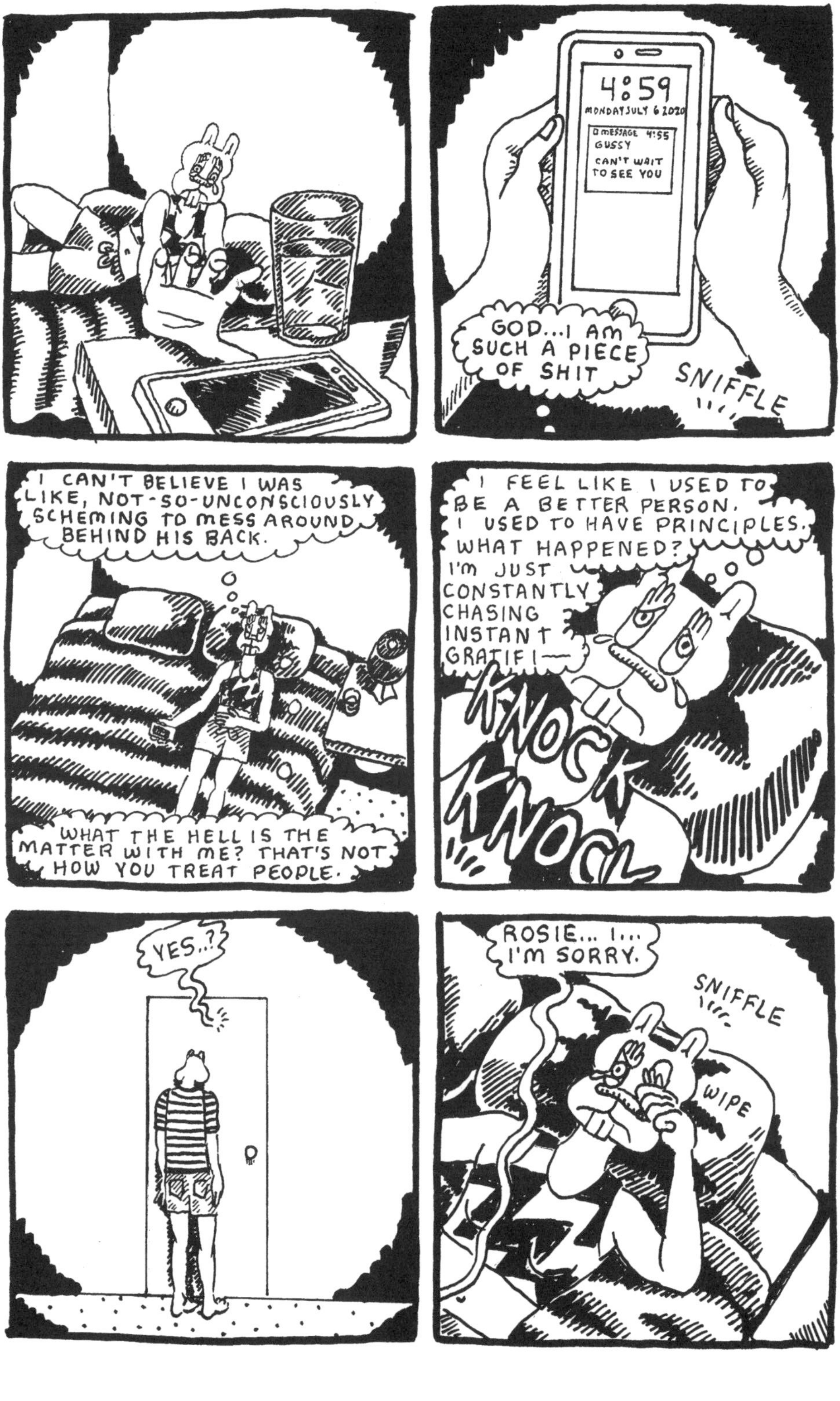
4:59
MONDAY JULY 6 2020
MESSAGE 4:55
GUSSY
CAN'T WAIT TO SEE YOU
GOD...I AM SUCH A PIECE OF SHIT
SNIFFLE
I CAN'T BELIEVE I WAS LIKE, NOT-SO-UNCONSCIOUSLY SCHEMING TO MESS AROUND BEHIND HIS BACK.
WHAT THE HELL IS THE MATTER WITH ME? THAT'S NOT HOW YOU TREAT PEOPLE.
I FEEL LIKE I USED TO BE A BETTER PERSON. I USED TO HAVE PRINCIPLES. WHAT HAPPENED?
I'M JUST CONSTANTLY CHASING INSTANT GRATIFI—
KNOCK KNOCK
YES..?
ROSIE... I... I'M SORRY.
SNIFFLE
WIPE

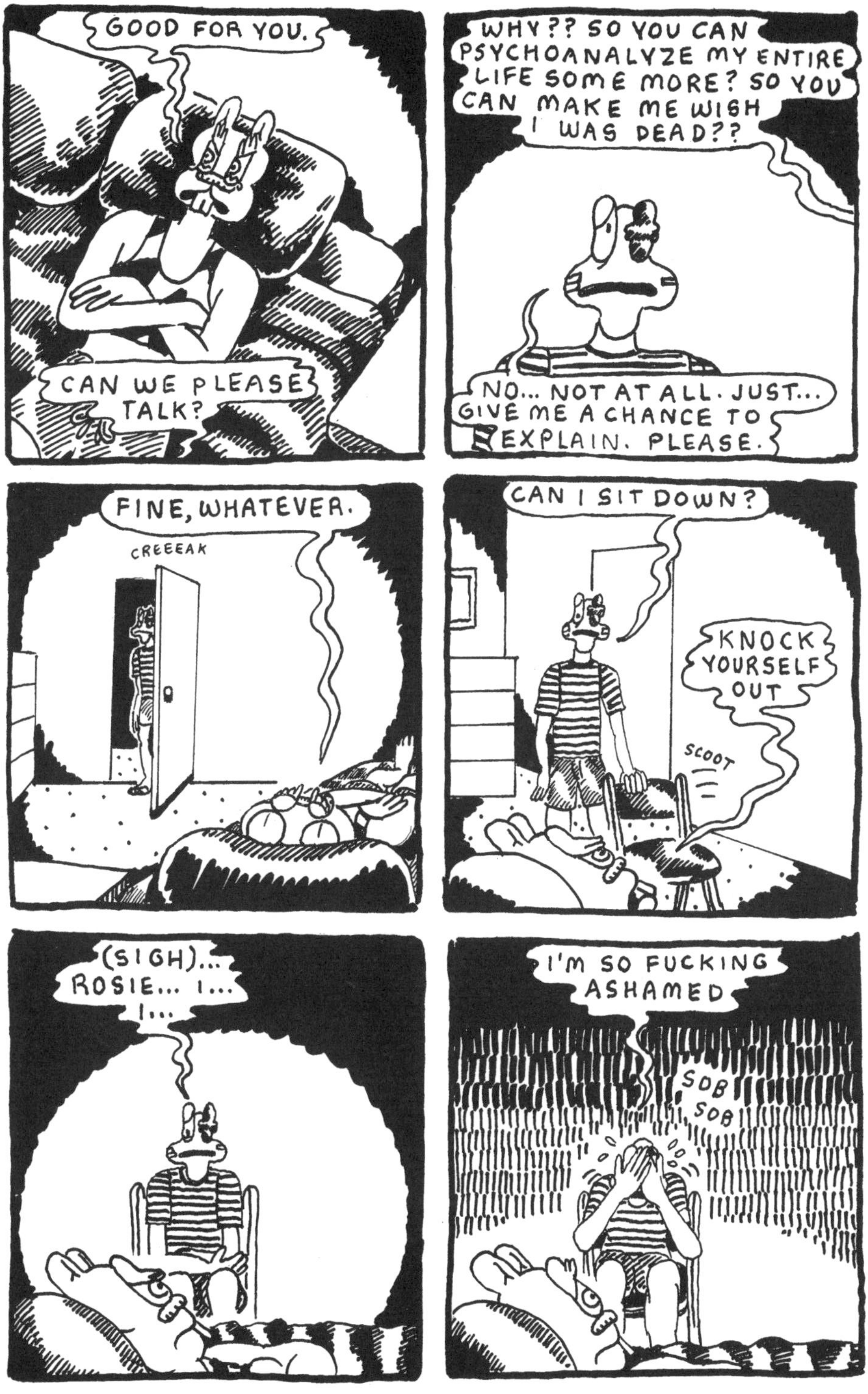
GOOD FOR YOU.
CAN WE PLEASE TALK?
WHY?? SO YOU CAN PSYCHOANALYZE MY ENTIRE LIFE SOME MORE? SO YOU CAN MAKE ME WISH I WAS DEAD??
NO... NOT AT ALL. JUST... GIVE ME A CHANCE TO EXPLAIN. PLEASE.
FINE, WHATEVER.
CREEEAK
CAN I SIT DOWN?
KNOCK YOURSELF OUT
SCOOT
(SIGH)... ROSIE... I... I...
I'M SO FUCKING ASHAMED
SOB SOB

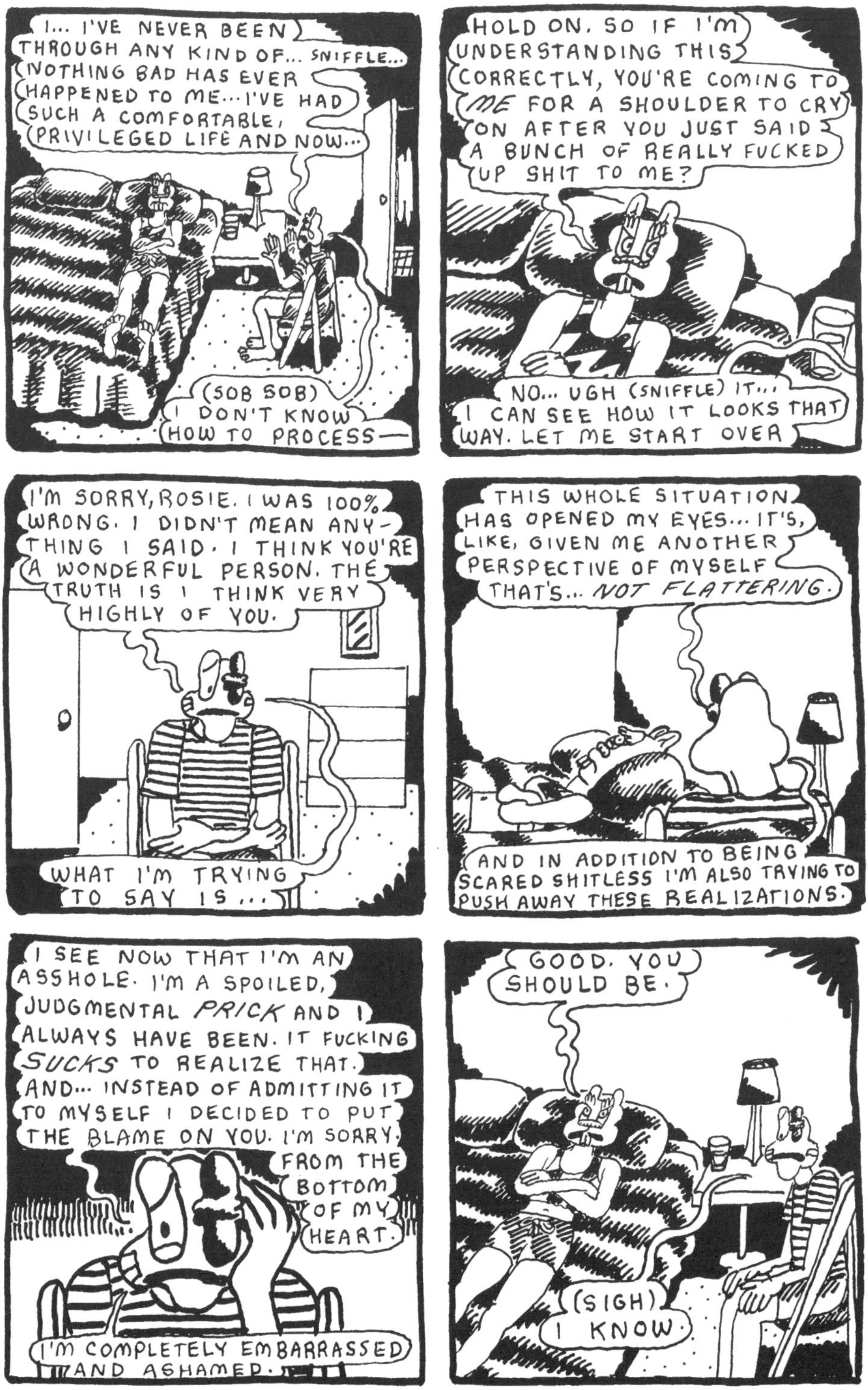
I... I'VE NEVER BEEN THROUGH ANY KIND OF... SNIFFLE... NOTHING BAD HAS EVER HAPPENED TO ME... I'VE HAD SUCH A COMFORTABLE, PRIVILEGED LIFE AND NOW...
(SOB SOB) I DON'T KNOW HOW TO PROCESS—
HOLD ON. SO IF I'M UNDERSTANDING THIS CORRECTLY, YOU'RE COMING TO ME FOR A SHOULDER TO CRY ON AFTER YOU JUST SAID A BUNCH OF REALLY FUCKED UP SHIT TO ME?
NO... UGH (SNIFFLE) IT... I CAN SEE HOW IT LOOKS THAT WAY. LET ME START OVER
I'M SORRY, ROSIE. I WAS 100% WRONG. I DIDN'T MEAN ANYTHING I SAID. I THINK YOU'RE A WONDERFUL PERSON. THE TRUTH IS I THINK VERY HIGHLY OF YOU.
WHAT I'M TRYING TO SAY IS...
THIS WHOLE SITUATION HAS OPENED MY EYES... IT'S, LIKE, GIVEN ME ANOTHER PERSPECTIVE OF MYSELF THAT'S... NOT FLATTERING.
AND IN ADDITION TO BEING SCARED SHITLESS I'M ALSO TRYING TO PUSH AWAY THESE REALIZATIONS.
I SEE NOW THAT I'M AN ASSHOLE. I'M A SPOILED, JUDGMENTAL PRICK AND I ALWAYS HAVE BEEN. IT FUCKING SUCKS TO REALIZE THAT. AND... INSTEAD OF ADMITTING IT TO MYSELF I DECIDED TO PUT THE BLAME ON YOU. I'M SORRY.
FROM THE BOTTOM OF MY HEART.
I'M COMPLETELY EMBARRASSED AND ASHAMED.
GOOD. YOU SHOULD BE.
(SIGH) I KNOW.

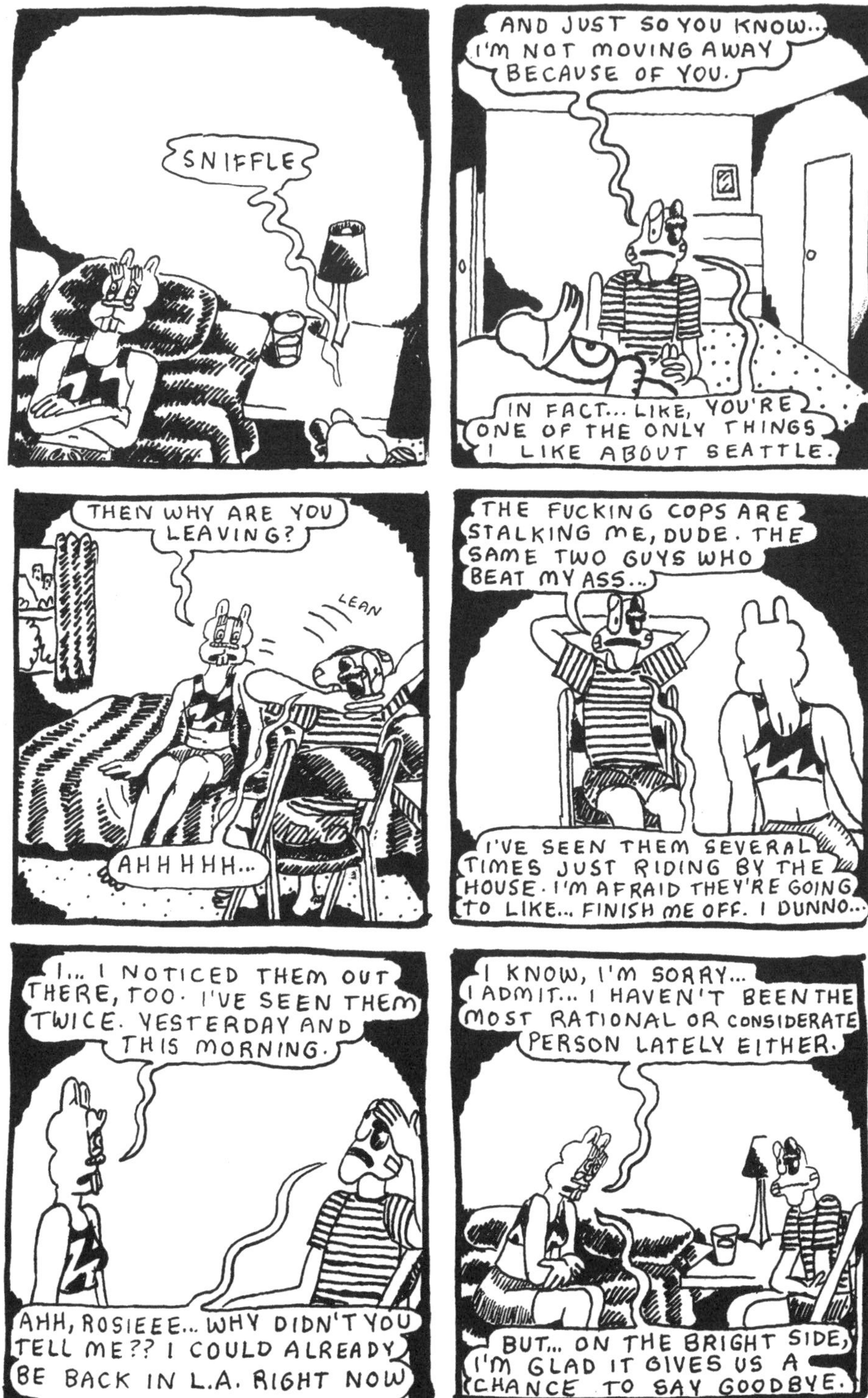
SNIFFLE
AND JUST SO YOU KNOW... I'M NOT MOVING AWAY BECAUSE OF YOU.
IN FACT... LIKE, YOU'RE ONE OF THE ONLY THINGS I LIKE ABOUT SEATTLE.
THEN WHY ARE YOU LEAVING?
LEAN
AHHHHH...
THE FUCKING COPS ARE STALKING ME, DUDE. THE SAME TWO GUYS WHO BEAT MY ASS...
I'VE SEEN THEM SEVERAL TIMES JUST RIDING BY THE HOUSE. I'M AFRAID THEY'RE GOING TO LIKE... FINISH ME OFF. I DUNNO...
I... I NOTICED THEM OUT THERE, TOO. I'VE SEEN THEM TWICE. YESTERDAY AND THIS MORNING.
AHH, ROSIEEE... WHY DIDN'T YOU TELL ME?? I COULD ALREADY BE BACK IN L.A. RIGHT NOW
I KNOW, I'M SORRY... I ADMIT... I HAVEN'T BEEN THE MOST RATIONAL OR CONSIDERATE PERSON LATELY EITHER.
BUT... ON THE BRIGHT SIDE, I'M GLAD IT GIVES US A CHANCE TO SAY GOODBYE.

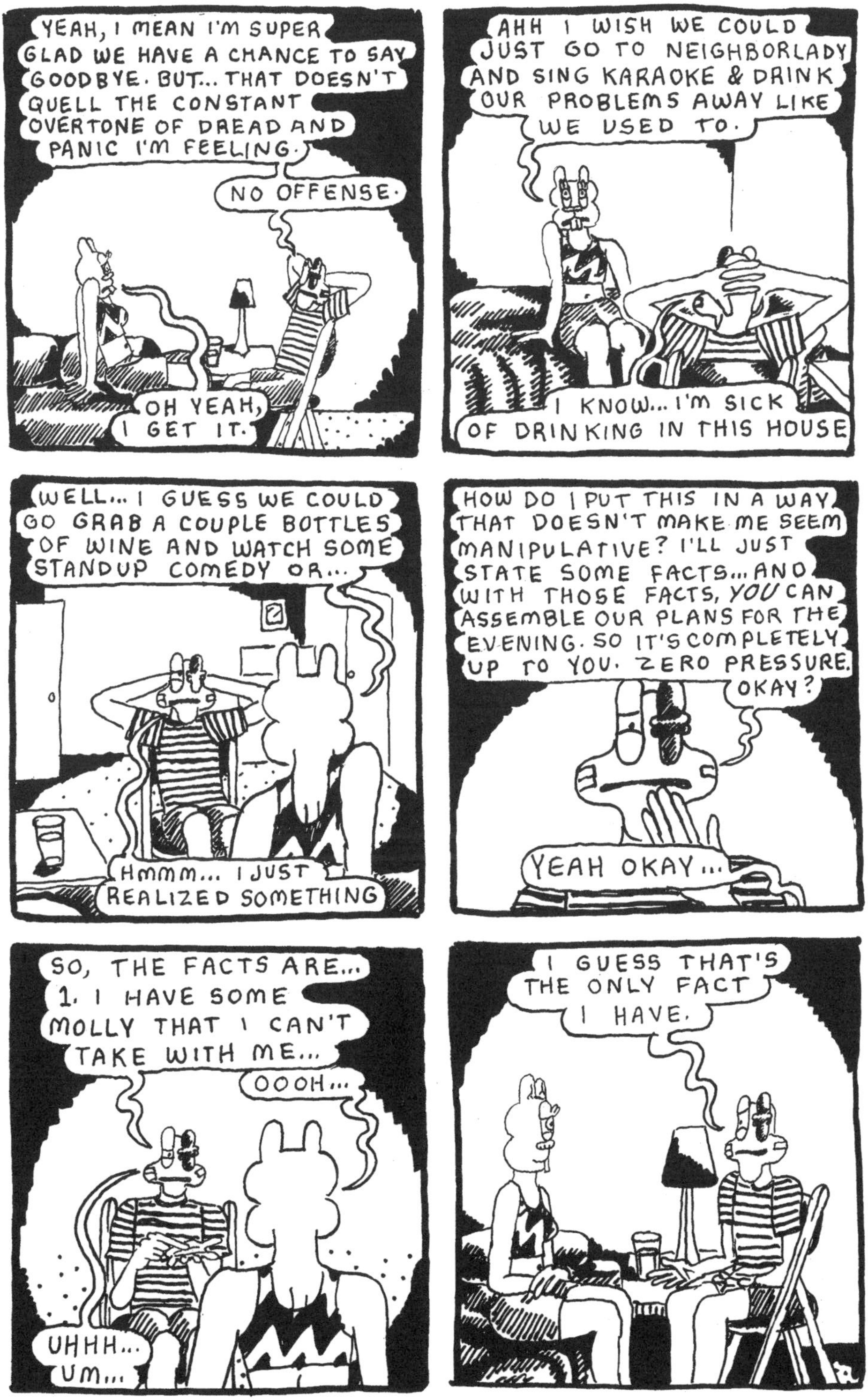
YEAH, I MEAN I'M SUPER GLAD WE HAVE A CHANCE TO SAY GOODBYE. BUT... THAT DOESN'T QUELL THE CONSTANT OVERTONE OF DREAD AND PANIC I'M FEELING.
NO OFFENSE.
OH YEAH, I GET IT.
AHH I WISH WE COULD JUST GO TO NEIGHBORLADY AND SING KARAOKE & DRINK OUR PROBLEMS AWAY LIKE WE USED TO.
I KNOW... I'M SICK OF DRINKING IN THIS HOUSE
WELL... I GUESS WE COULD GO GRAB A COUPLE BOTTLES OF WINE AND WATCH SOME STANDUP COMEDY OR...
HMMM... I JUST REALIZED SOMETHING
HOW DO I PUT THIS IN A WAY THAT DOESN'T MAKE ME SEEM MANIPULATIVE? I'LL JUST STATE SOME FACTS... AND WITH THOSE FACTS, YOU CAN ASSEMBLE OUR PLANS FOR THE EVENING. SO IT'S COMPLETELY UP TO YOU. ZERO PRESSURE.
OKAY?
YEAH OKAY...
SO, THE FACTS ARE... 1. I HAVE SOME MOLLY THAT I CAN'T TAKE WITH ME...
OOOH...
UHHH... UM...
I GUESS THAT'S THE ONLY FACT I HAVE.

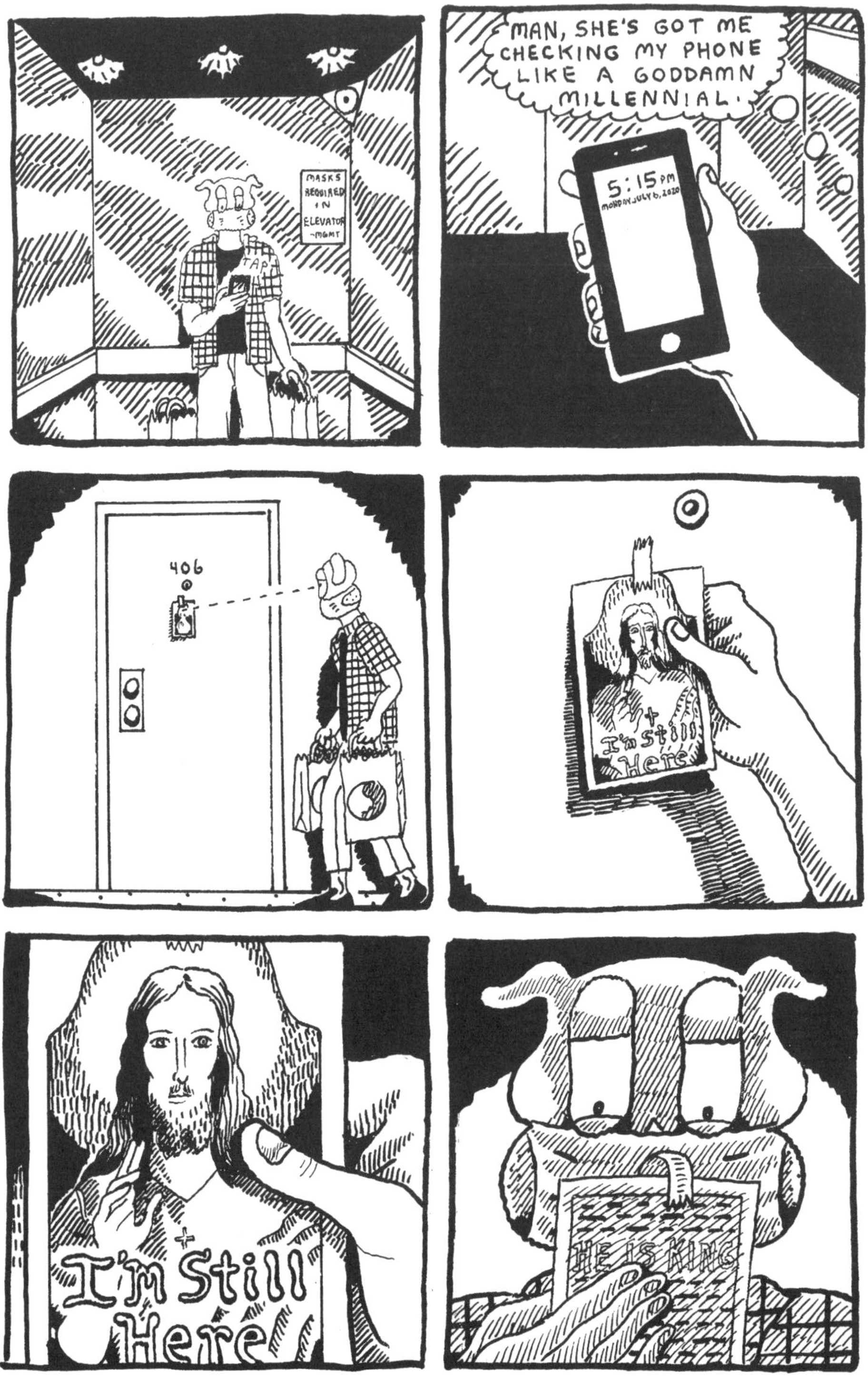
MASKS REQUIRED IN ELEVATOR ~MGMT
TAP
MAN, SHE'S GOT ME CHECKING MY PHONE LIKE A GODDAMN MILLENNIAL.
5:15PM
MONDAY, JULY 6, 2020
406
I'm Still Here
I'm Still Here
HE IS KING

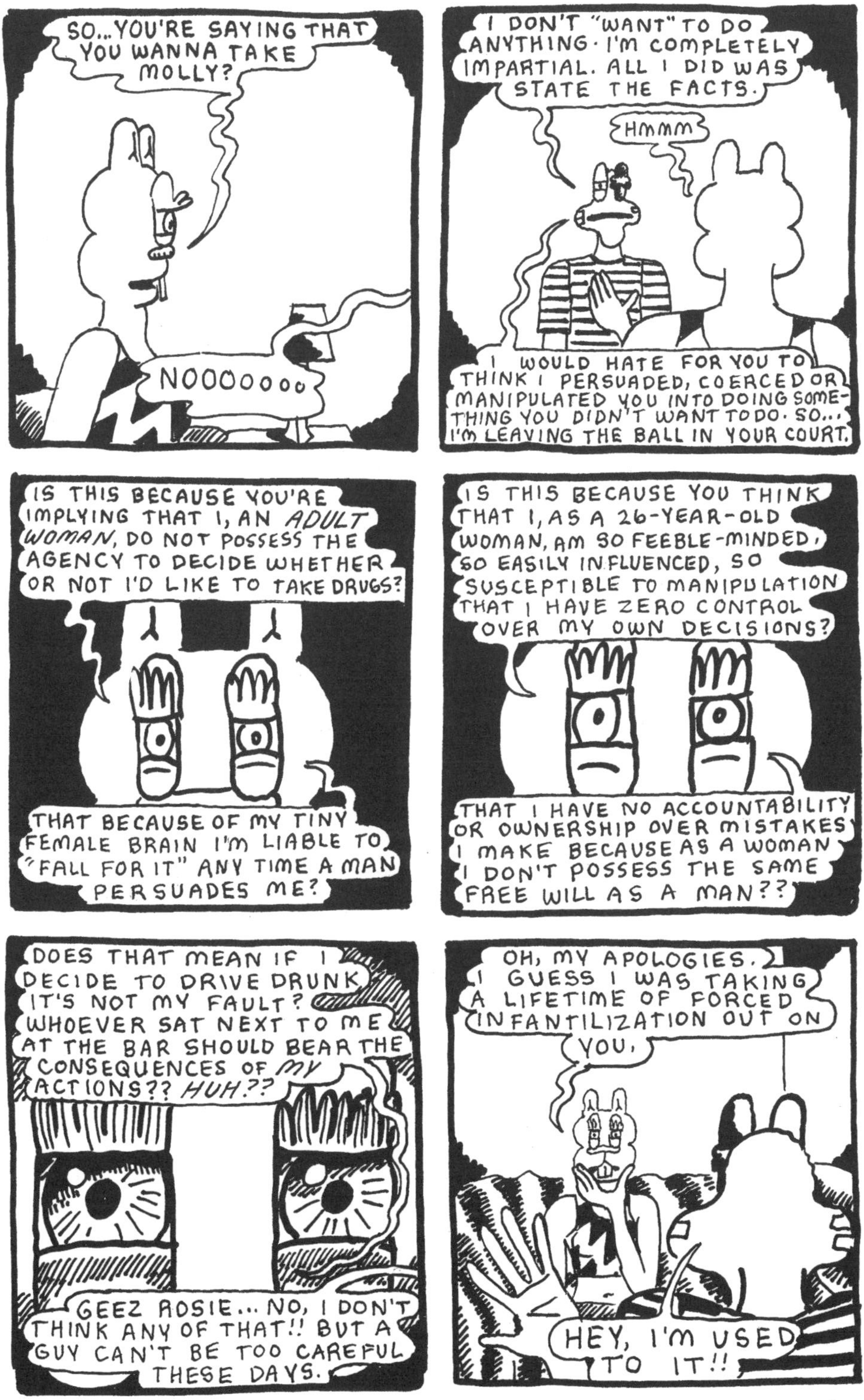
SO...YOU'RE SAYING THAT YOU WANNA TAKE MOLLY?
NOOOoooo
I DON'T "WANT" TO DO ANYTHING. I'M COMPLETELY IMPARTIAL. ALL I DID WAS STATE THE FACTS.
HMMM
I WOULD HATE FOR YOU TO THINK I PERSUADED, COERCED OR MANIPULATED YOU INTO DOING SOMETHING YOU DIDN'T WANT TO DO. SO... I'M LEAVING THE BALL IN YOUR COURT.
IS THIS BECAUSE YOU'RE IMPLYING THAT I, AN ADULT WOMAN, DO NOT POSSESS THE AGENCY TO DECIDE WHETHER OR NOT I'D LIKE TO TAKE DRUGS?
THAT BECAUSE OF MY TINY FEMALE BRAIN I'M LIABLE TO "FALL FOR IT" ANY TIME A MAN PERSUADES ME?
IS THIS BECAUSE YOU THINK THAT I, AS A 26-YEAR-OLD WOMAN, AM SO FEEBLE-MINDED, SO EASILY INFLUENCED, SO SUSCEPTIBLE TO MANIPULATION THAT I HAVE ZERO CONTROL OVER MY OWN DECISIONS?
THAT I HAVE NO ACCOUNTABILITY OR OWNERSHIP OVER MISTAKES I MAKE BECAUSE AS A WOMAN I DON'T POSSESS THE SAME FREE WILL AS A MAN??
DOES THAT MEAN IF I DECIDE TO DRIVE DRUNK IT'S NOT MY FAULT? WHOEVER SAT NEXT TO ME AT THE BAR SHOULD BEAR THE CONSEQUENCES OF MY ACTIONS?? HUH??
GEEZ ROSIE... NO, I DON'T THINK ANY OF THAT!! BUT A GUY CAN'T BE TOO CAREFUL THESE DAYS.
OH, MY APOLOGIES. I GUESS I WAS TAKING A LIFETIME OF FORCED INFANTILIZATION OUT ON YOU.
HEY, I'M USED TO IT!!

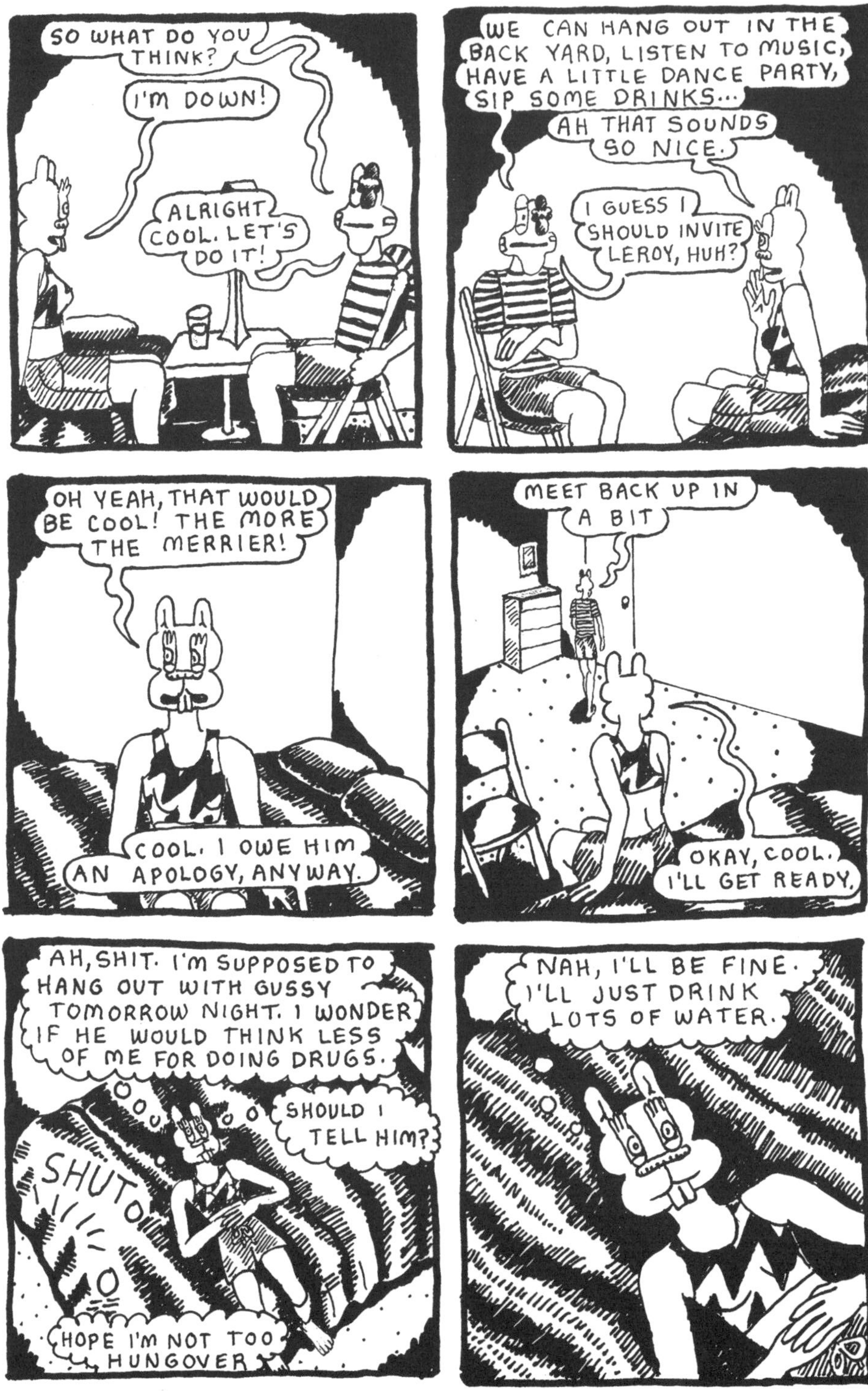
SO WHAT DO YOU THINK?
I'M DOWN!
ALRIGHT COOL. LET'S DO IT!
WE CAN HANG OUT IN THE BACK YARD, LISTEN TO MUSIC, HAVE A LITTLE DANCE PARTY, SIP SOME DRINKS...
AH THAT SOUNDS SO NICE.
I GUESS I SHOULD INVITE LEROY, HUH?
OH YEAH, THAT WOULD BE COOL! THE MORE THE MERRIER!
COOL. I OWE HIM AN APOLOGY, ANYWAY.
MEET BACK UP IN A BIT
OKAY, COOL. I'LL GET READY.
AH, SHIT. I'M SUPPOSED TO HANG OUT WITH GUSSY TOMORROW NIGHT. I WONDER IF HE WOULD THINK LESS OF ME FOR DOING DRUGS.
SHOULD I TELL HIM?
SHUT
HOPE I'M NOT TOO HUNGOVER
NAH, I'LL BE FINE. I'LL JUST DRINK LOTS OF WATER.

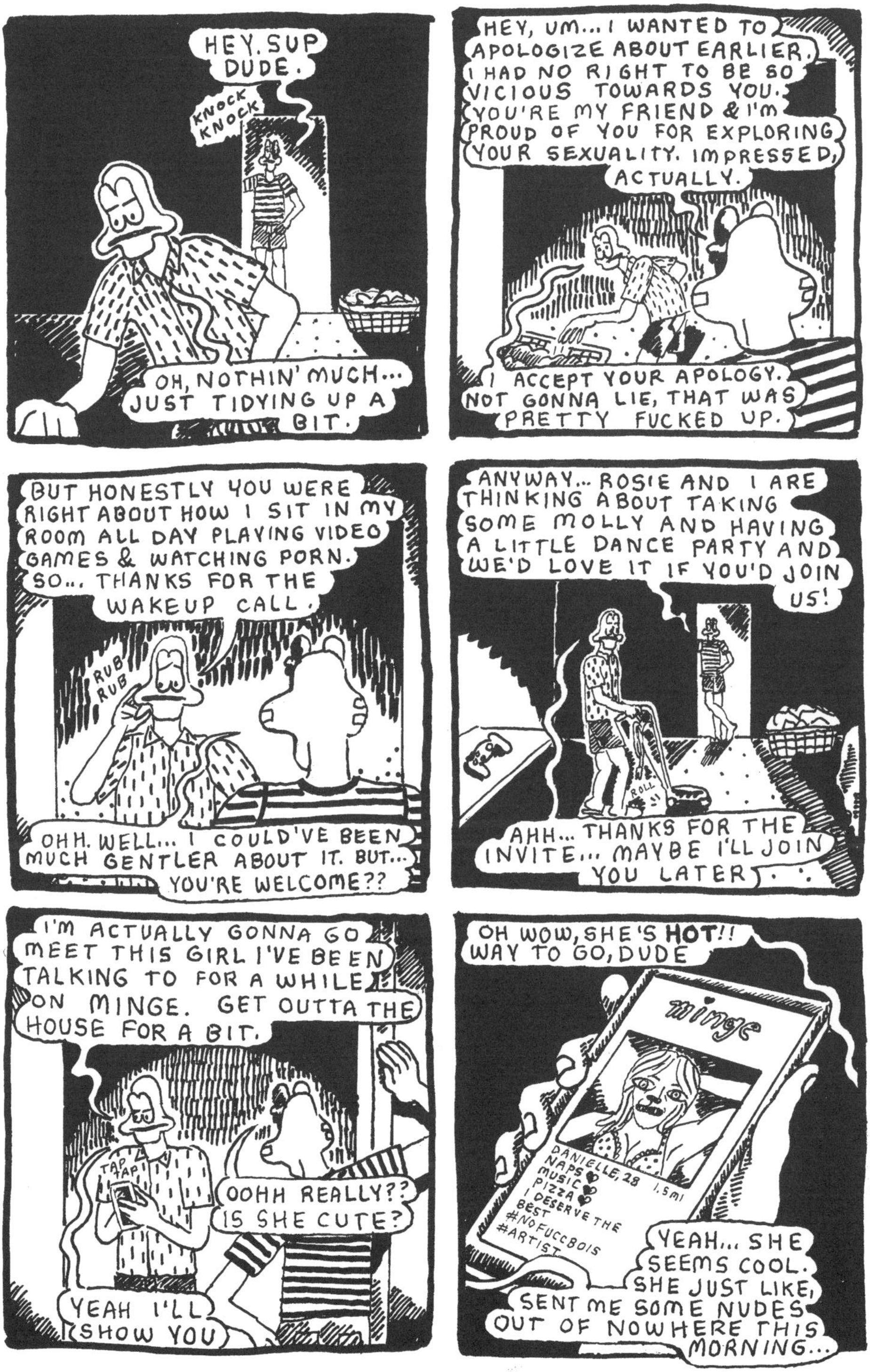
HEY. SUP DUDE.
KNOCK KNOCK
OH, NOTHIN' MUCH... JUST TIDYING UP A BIT.
HEY, UM... I WANTED TO APOLOGIZE ABOUT EARLIER. I HAD NO RIGHT TO BE SO VICIOUS TOWARDS YOU. YOU'RE MY FRIEND & I'M PROUD OF YOU FOR EXPLORING YOUR SEXUALITY. IMPRESSED, ACTUALLY.
I ACCEPT YOUR APOLOGY. NOT GONNA LIE, THAT WAS PRETTY FUCKED UP.
BUT HONESTLY YOU WERE RIGHT ABOUT HOW I SIT IN MY ROOM ALL DAY PLAYING VIDEO GAMES & WATCHING PORN. SO... THANKS FOR THE WAKEUP CALL.
RUB RUB
OHH. WELL... I COULD'VE BEEN MUCH GENTLER ABOUT IT. BUT... YOU'RE WELCOME??
ANYWAY... ROSIE AND I ARE THINKING ABOUT TAKING SOME MOLLY AND HAVING A LITTLE DANCE PARTY AND WE'D LOVE IT IF YOU'D JOIN US!
ROLL
AHH... THANKS FOR THE INVITE... MAYBE I'LL JOIN YOU LATER
I'M ACTUALLY GONNA GO MEET THIS GIRL I'VE BEEN TALKING TO FOR A WHILE ON MINGE. GET OUTTA THE HOUSE FOR A BIT.
TAP TAP
OOHH REALLY?? IS SHE CUTE?
YEAH I'LL SHOW YOU
OH WOW, SHE'S HOT!! WAY TO GO, DUDE
minge
DANIELLE, 28 1.5MI
NAPS
MUSIC
PIZZA
I DESERVE THE BEST
#NOFUCCBOIS
#ARTIST
YEAH... SHE SEEMS COOL. SHE JUST LIKE, SENT ME SOME NUDES OUT OF NOWHERE THIS MORNING...

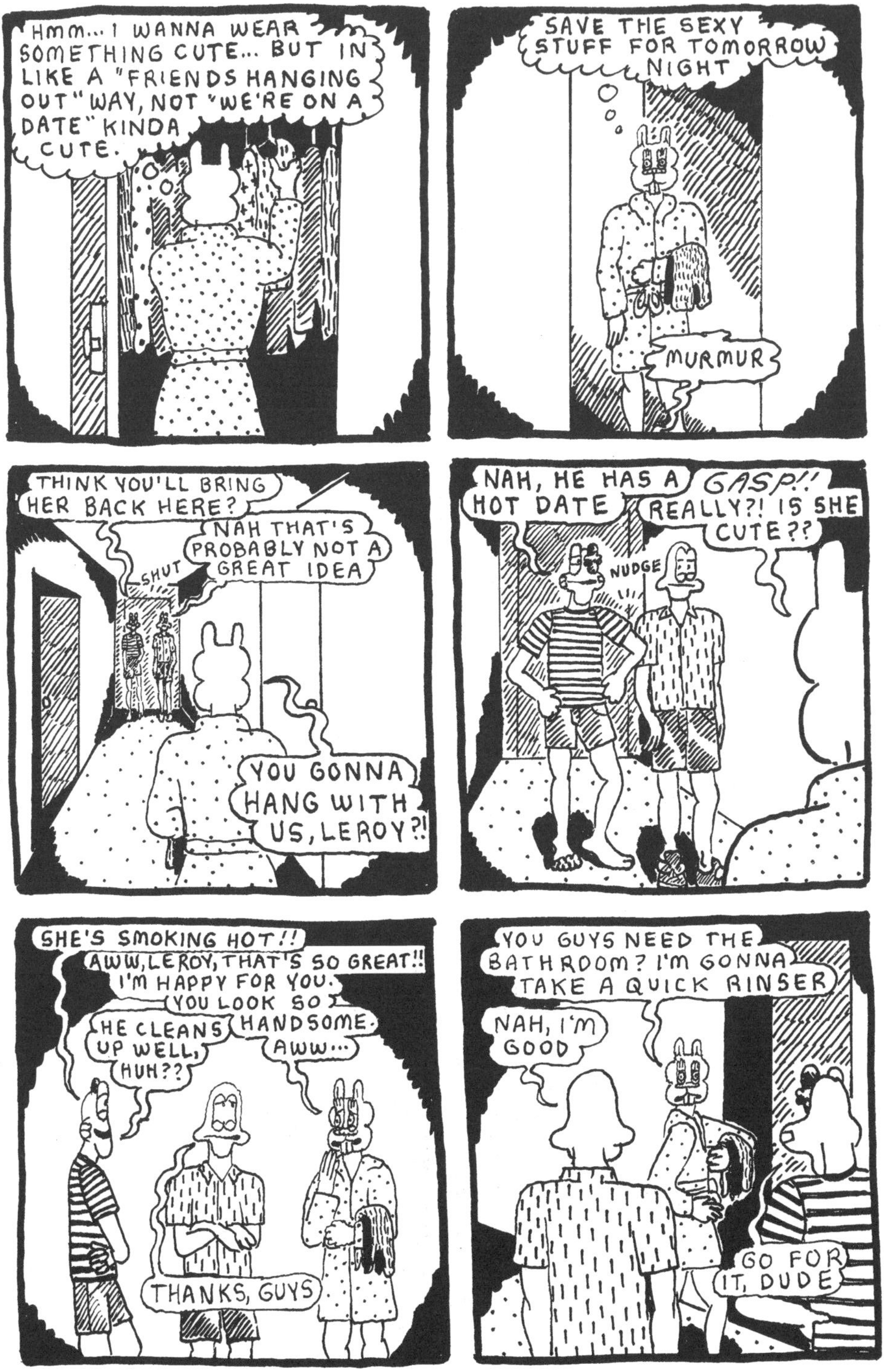
HMM... I WANNA WEAR SOMETHING CUTE... BUT IN LIKE A "FRIENDS HANGING OUT" WAY, NOT "WE'RE ON A DATE" KINDA CUTE.
SAVE THE SEXY STUFF FOR TOMORROW NIGHT
MURMUR
THINK YOU'LL BRING HER BACK HERE?
SHUT
NAH THAT'S PROBABLY NOT A GREAT IDEA
YOU GONNA HANG WITH US, LEROY?!
NAH, HE HAS A HOT DATE
NUDGE
GASP!!
REALLY?! IS SHE CUTE??
SHE'S SMOKING HOT!!
AWW, LEROY, THAT'S SO GREAT!! I'M HAPPY FOR YOU.
YOU LOOK SO HANDSOME.
HE CLEANS UP WELL, HUH??
AWW...
THANKS, GUYS
YOU GUYS NEED THE BATHROOM? I'M GONNA TAKE A QUICK RINSER
NAH, I'M GOOD
GO FOR IT, DUDE

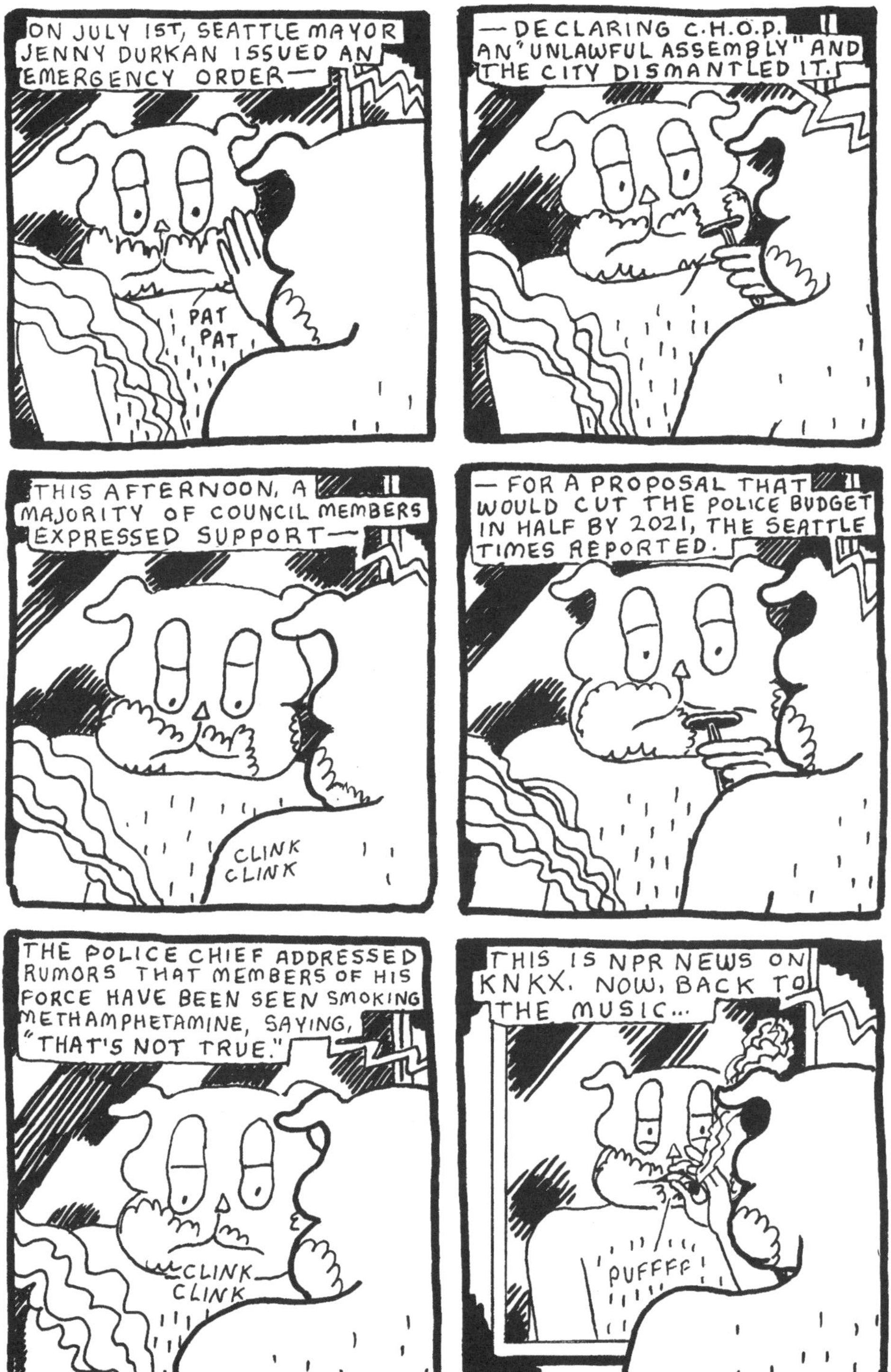
ON JULY 1ST, SEATTLE MAYOR JENNY DURKAN ISSUED AN EMERGENCY ORDER—
PAT PAT
—DECLARING C.H.O.P. AN "UNLAWFUL ASSEMBLY" AND THE CITY DISMANTLED IT.
THIS AFTERNOON, A MAJORITY OF COUNCIL MEMBERS EXPRESSED SUPPORT—
CLINK CLINK
—FOR A PROPOSAL THAT WOULD CUT THE POLICE BUDGET IN HALF BY 2021, THE SEATTLE TIMES REPORTED.
THE POLICE CHIEF ADDRESSED RUMORS THAT MEMBERS OF HIS FORCE HAVE BEEN SEEN SMOKING METHAMPHETAMINE, SAYING, "THAT'S NOT TRUE."
CLINK CLINK
THIS IS NPR NEWS ON KNKX. NOW, BACK TO THE MUSIC...
PUFFFF

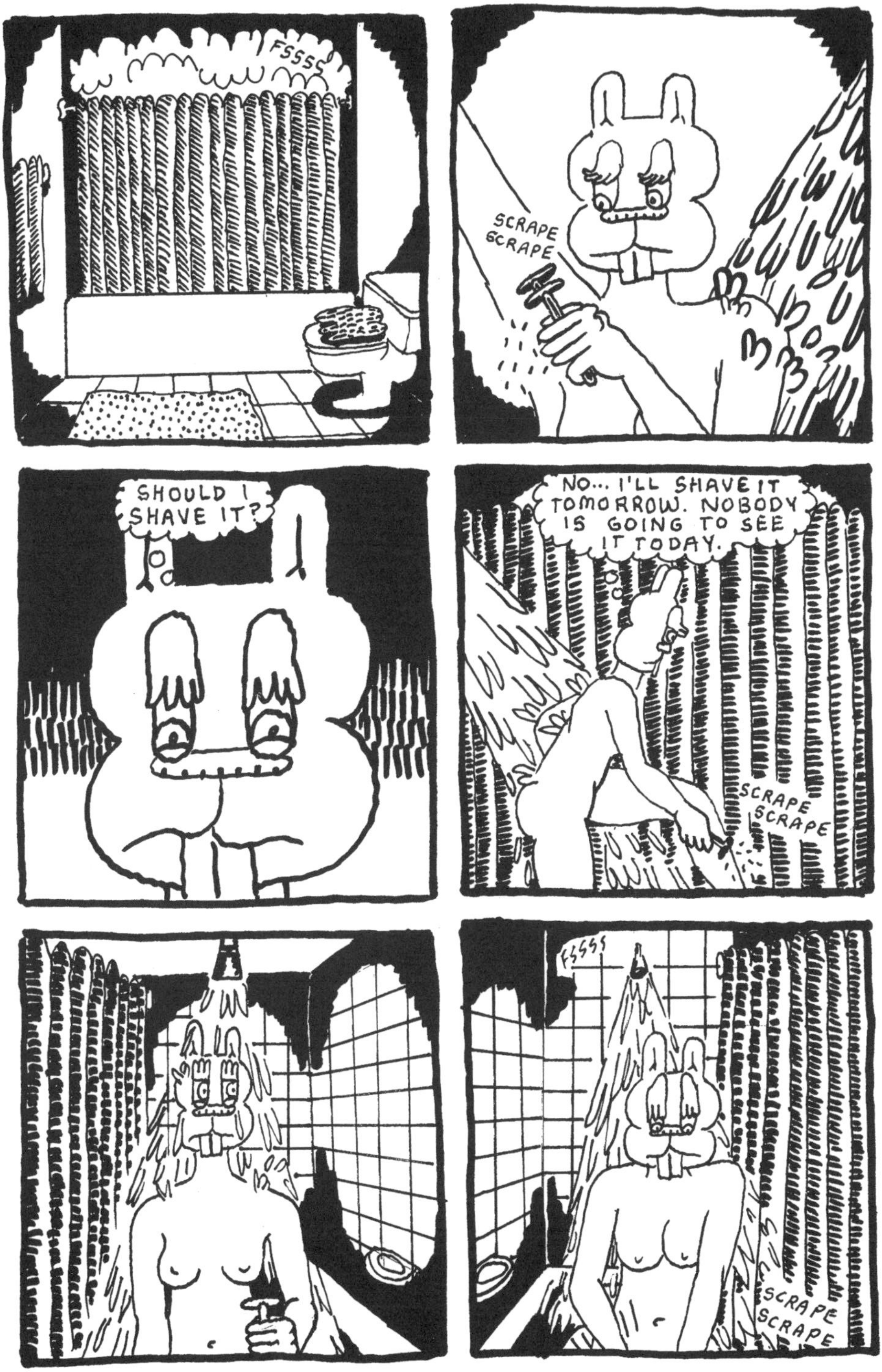
FSSSS
SCRAPE
SCRAPE
SHOULD I SHAVE IT?
NO... I'LL SHAVE IT TOMORROW. NOBODY IS GOING TO SEE IT TODAY.
SCRAPE
SCRAPE
FSSSS
SCRAPE
SCRAPE

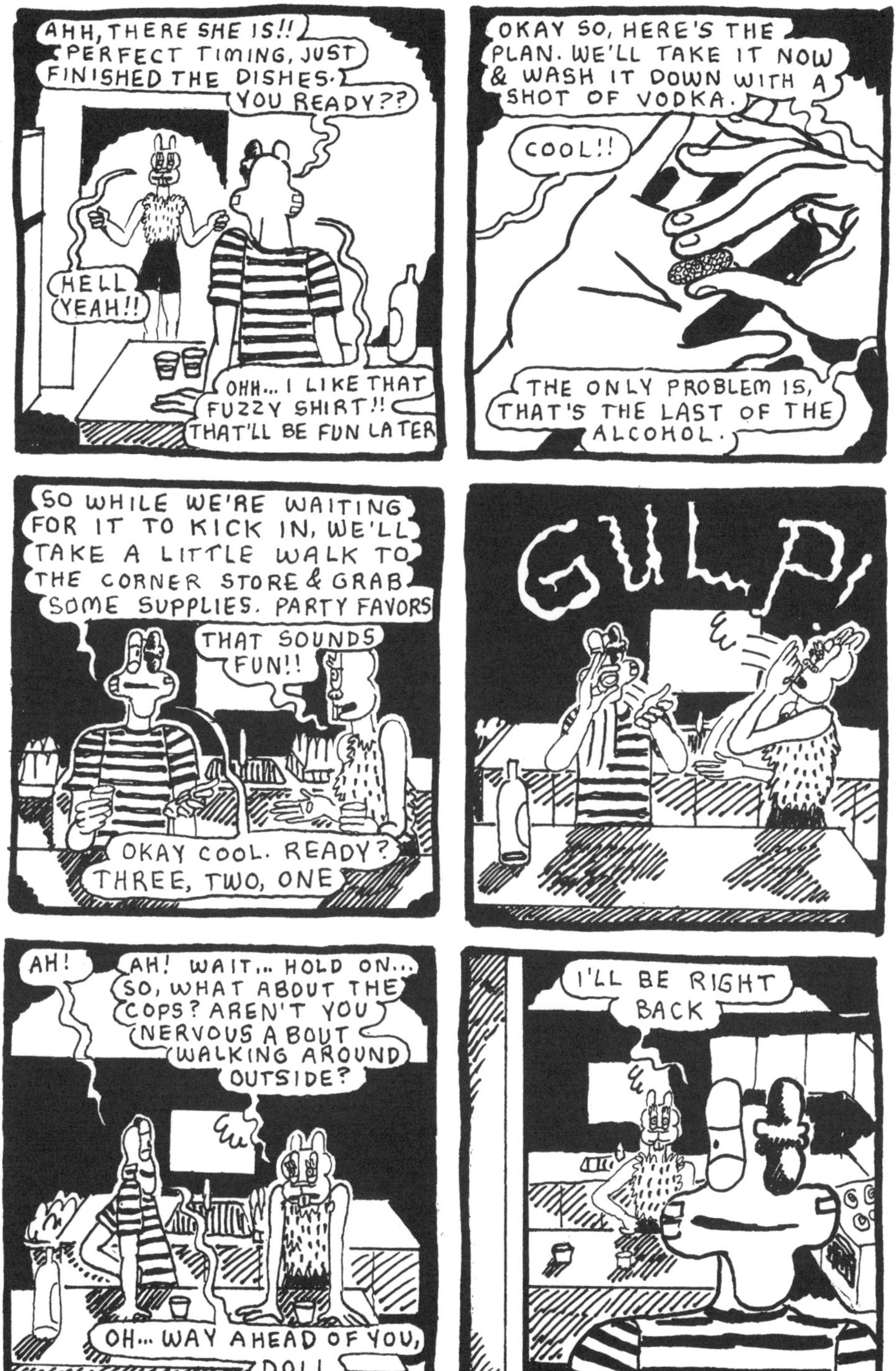
AHH, THERE SHE IS!! PERFECT TIMING, JUST FINISHED THE DISHES.
YOU READY??
HELL YEAH!!
OHH... I LIKE THAT FUZZY SHIRT!! THAT'LL BE FUN LATER
OKAY SO, HERE'S THE PLAN. WE'LL TAKE IT NOW & WASH IT DOWN WITH A SHOT OF VODKA.
COOL!!
THE ONLY PROBLEM IS, THAT'S THE LAST OF THE ALCOHOL.
SO WHILE WE'RE WAITING FOR IT TO KICK IN, WE'LL TAKE A LITTLE WALK TO THE CORNER STORE & GRAB SOME SUPPLIES. PARTY FAVORS
THAT SOUNDS FUN!!
OKAY COOL. READY? THREE, TWO, ONE
GULP,
AH!
AH! WAIT... HOLD ON... SO, WHAT ABOUT THE COPS? AREN'T YOU NERVOUS ABOUT WALKING AROUND OUTSIDE?
OH... WAY AHEAD OF YOU, DOLL
I'LL BE RIGHT BACK

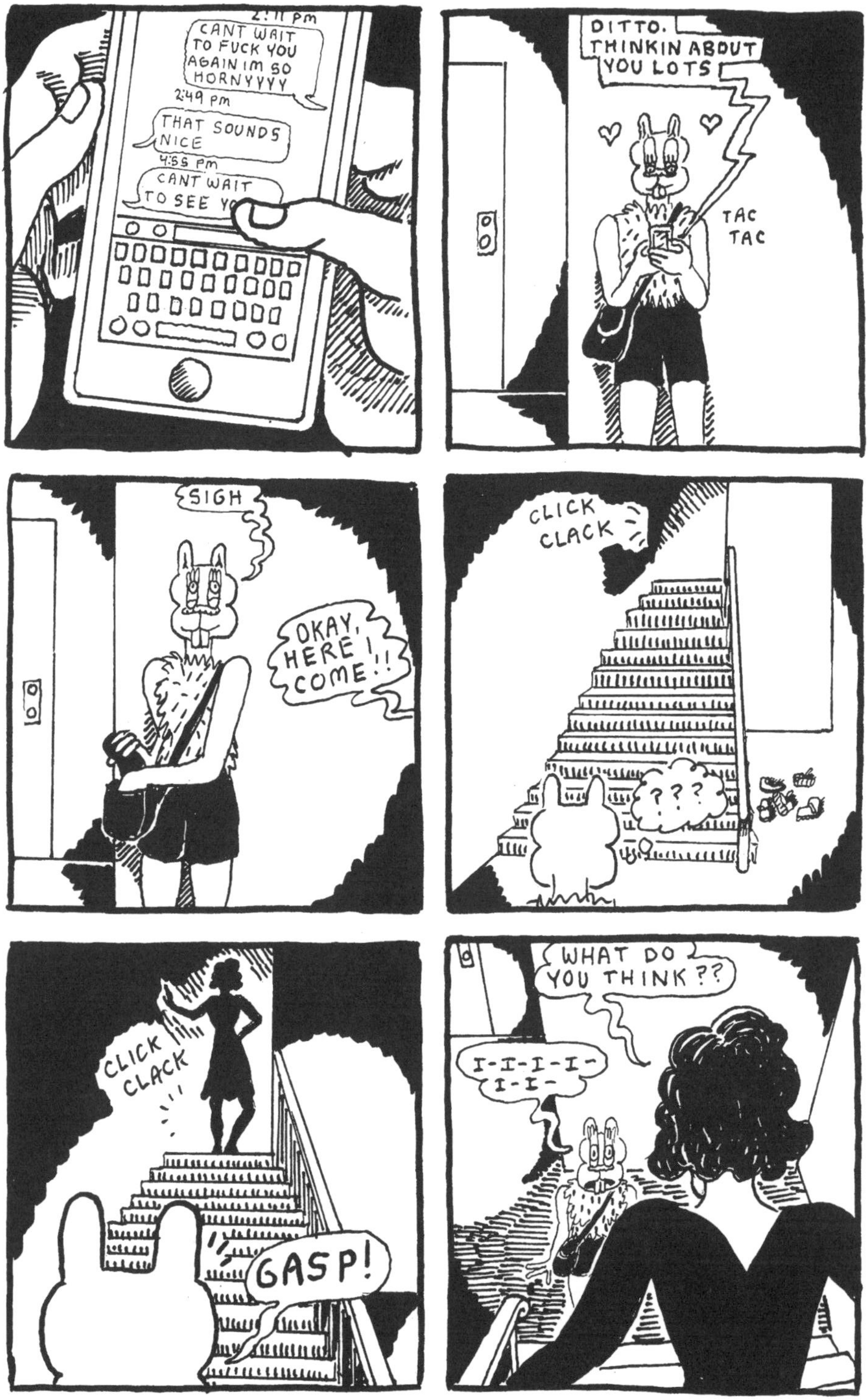
2:11 pm
CANT WAIT TO FUCK YOU AGAIN IM SO HORNYYYY
2:49 pm
THAT SOUNDS NICE
4:55 pm
CANT WAIT TO SEE YO
DITTO. THINKIN ABOUT YOU LOTS
TAC TAC
SIGH
OKAY, HERE I COME!!
CLICK CLACK
???
CLICK CLACK
GASP!
WHAT DO YOU THINK??
I-I-I-I-I-I-

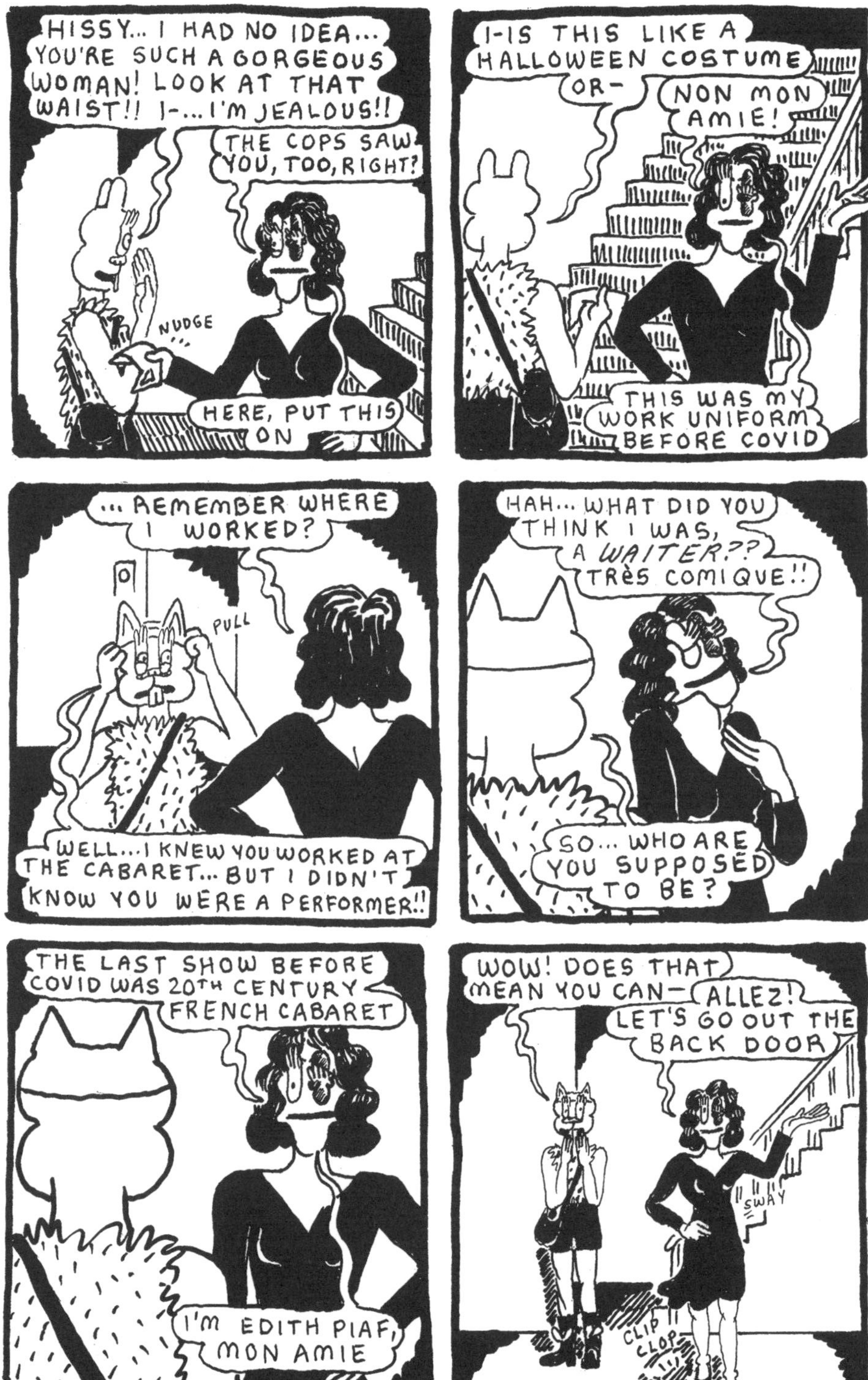
HISSY... I HAD NO IDEA... YOU'RE SUCH A GORGEOUS WOMAN! LOOK AT THAT WAIST!! I-... I'M JEALOUS!!
THE COPS SAW YOU, TOO, RIGHT?
NUDGE
HERE, PUT THIS ON
I-IS THIS LIKE A HALLOWEEN COSTUME OR-
NON MON AMIE!
THIS WAS MY WORK UNIFORM BEFORE COVID
... REMEMBER WHERE I WORKED?
PULL
WELL... I KNEW YOU WORKED AT THE CABARET... BUT I DIDN'T KNOW YOU WERE A PERFORMER!!
HAH... WHAT DID YOU THINK I WAS, A *WAITER*?? TRèS COMIQUE!!
SO... WHO ARE YOU SUPPOSED TO BE?
THE LAST SHOW BEFORE COVID WAS 20TH CENTURY FRENCH CABARET
I'M EDITH PIAF, MON AMIE
WOW! DOES THAT MEAN YOU CAN-
ALLEZ! LET'S GO OUT THE BACK DOOR
SWAY
CLIP CLOP

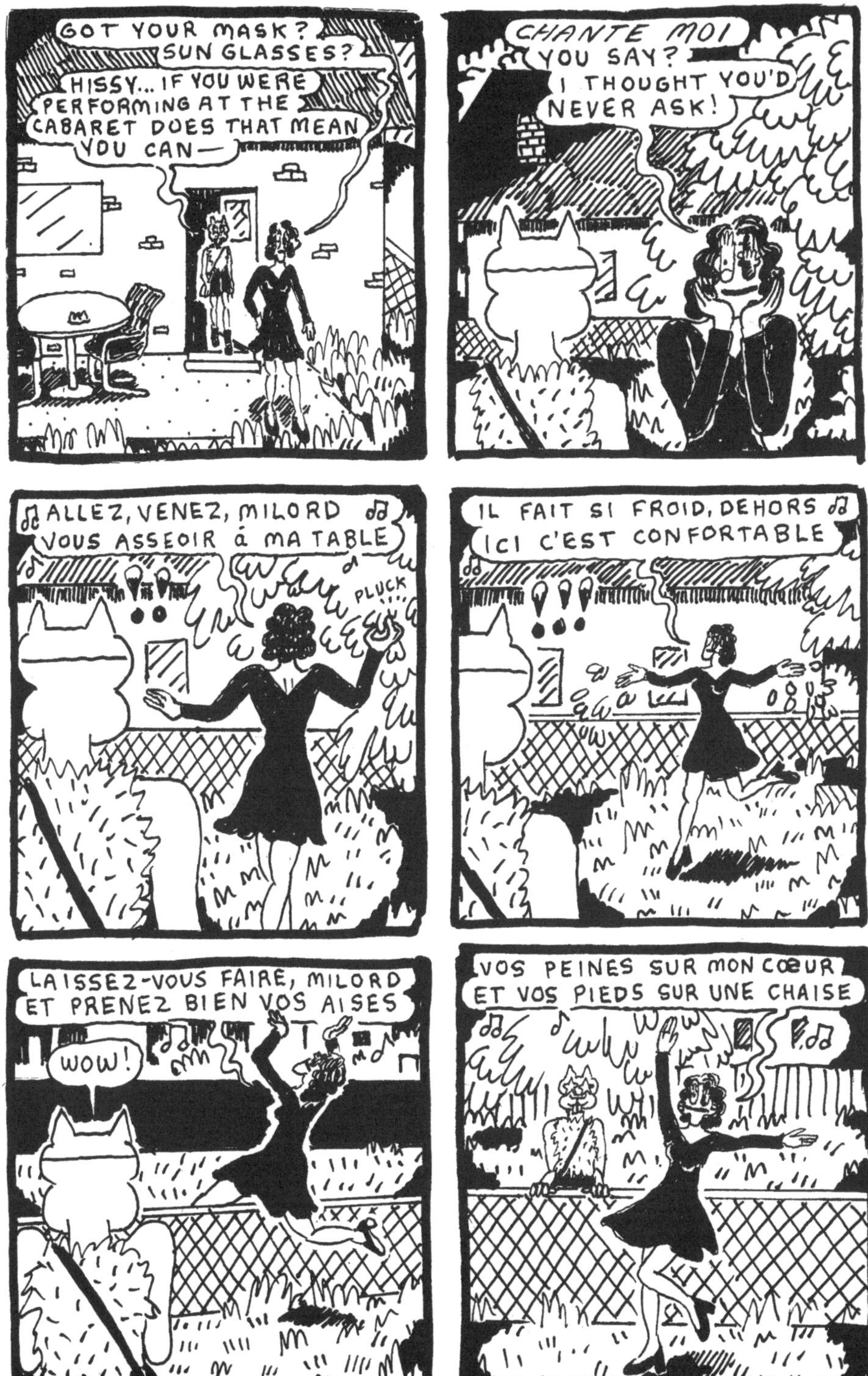
GOT YOUR MASK? SUN GLASSES?
HISSY... IF YOU WERE PERFORMING AT THE CABARET DOES THAT MEAN YOU CAN—
CHANTE MOI YOU SAY? I THOUGHT YOU'D NEVER ASK!
ALLEZ, VENEZ, MILORD VOUS ASSEOIR á MA TABLE
PLUCK
IL FAIT SI FROID, DEHORS ICI C'EST CONFORTABLE
LAISSEZ-VOUS FAIRE, MILORD ET PRENEZ BIEN VOS AISES
WOW!
VOS PEINES SUR MON CŒUR ET VOS PIEDS SUR UNE CHAISE

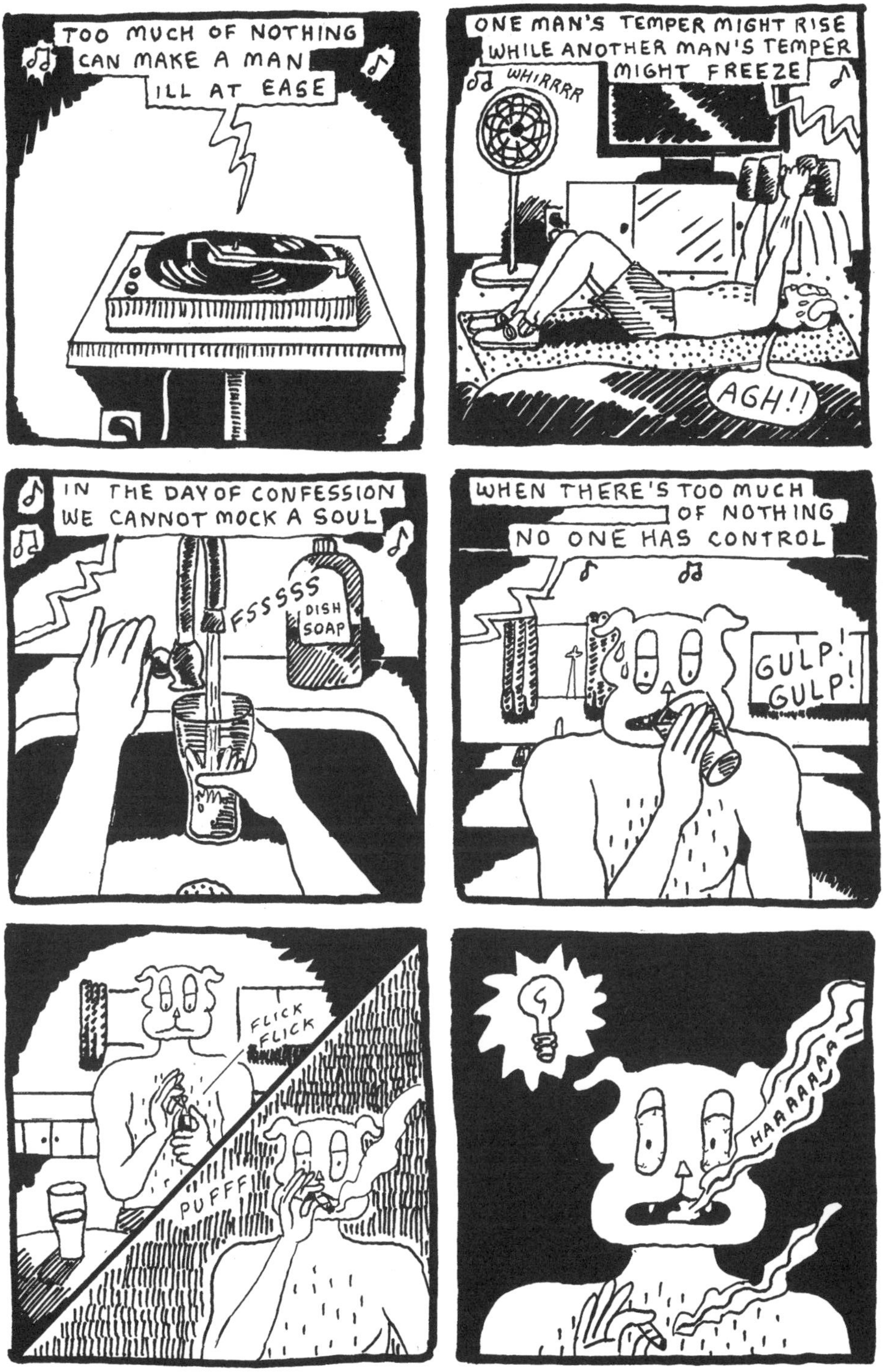
TOO MUCH OF NOTHING CAN MAKE A MAN ILL AT EASE
ONE MAN'S TEMPER MIGHT RISE WHILE ANOTHER MAN'S TEMPER MIGHT FREEZE
WHIRRRR
AGH!!
IN THE DAY OF CONFESSION WE CANNOT MOCK A SOUL
FSSSSS
DISH SOAP
WHEN THERE'S TOO MUCH OF NOTHING NO ONE HAS CONTROL
GULP! GULP!
FLICK FLICK
PUFFF
HAAAAAAA

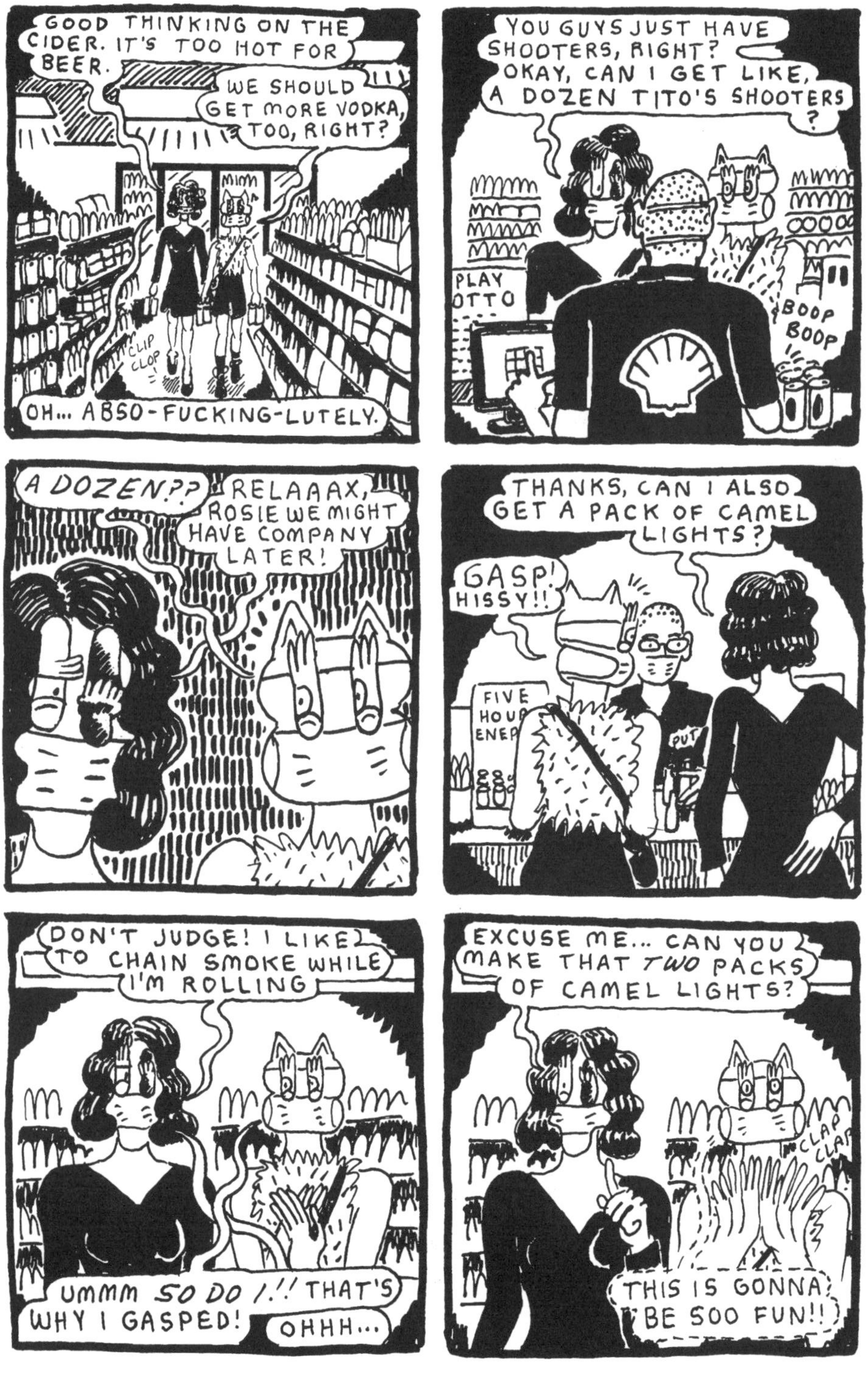
GOOD THINKING ON THE CIDER. IT'S TOO HOT FOR BEER.
WE SHOULD GET MORE VODKA, TOO, RIGHT?
CLIP CLOP
OH... ABSO-FUCKING-LUTELY.
YOU GUYS JUST HAVE SHOOTERS, RIGHT?
OKAY, CAN I GET LIKE, A DOZEN TITO'S SHOOTERS?
PLAY
OTTO
BOOP BOOP
A DOZEN??
RELAAAX, ROSIE WE MIGHT HAVE COMPANY LATER!
THANKS, CAN I ALSO GET A PACK OF CAMEL LIGHTS?
GASP! HISSY!!
FIVE HOU ENE
PUT
DON'T JUDGE! I LIKE TO CHAIN SMOKE WHILE I'M ROLLING
UMMM SO DO I.!! THAT'S WHY I GASPED!
OHHH...
EXCUSE ME... CAN YOU MAKE THAT TWO PACKS OF CAMEL LIGHTS?
CLAP CLAP
THIS IS GONNA BE SOO FUN!!

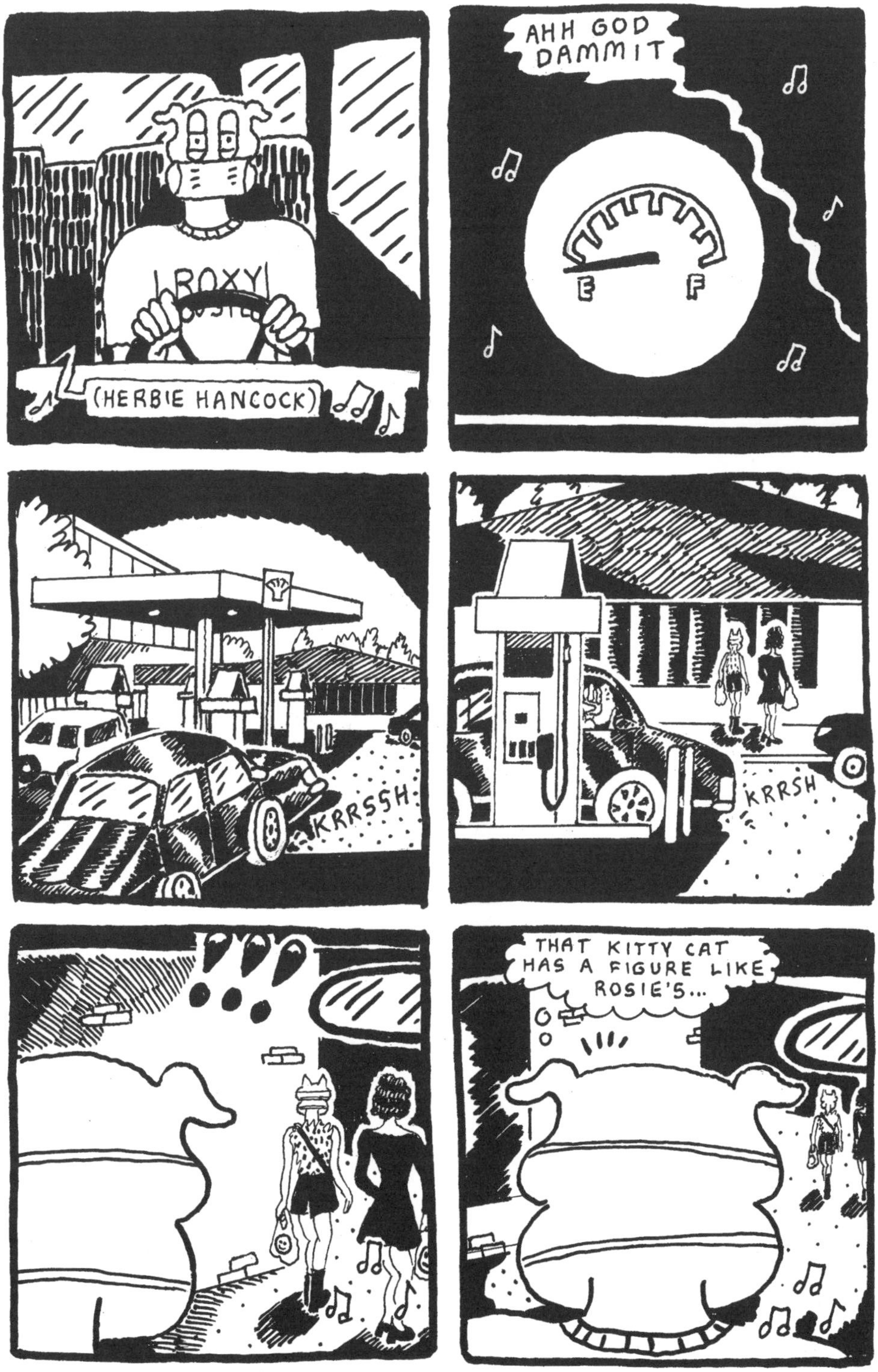
ROXY
(HERBIE HANCOCK)
AHH GOD DAMMIT
E
F
KRRSSH
KRRSH
THAT KITTY CAT HAS A FIGURE LIKE ROSIE'S...

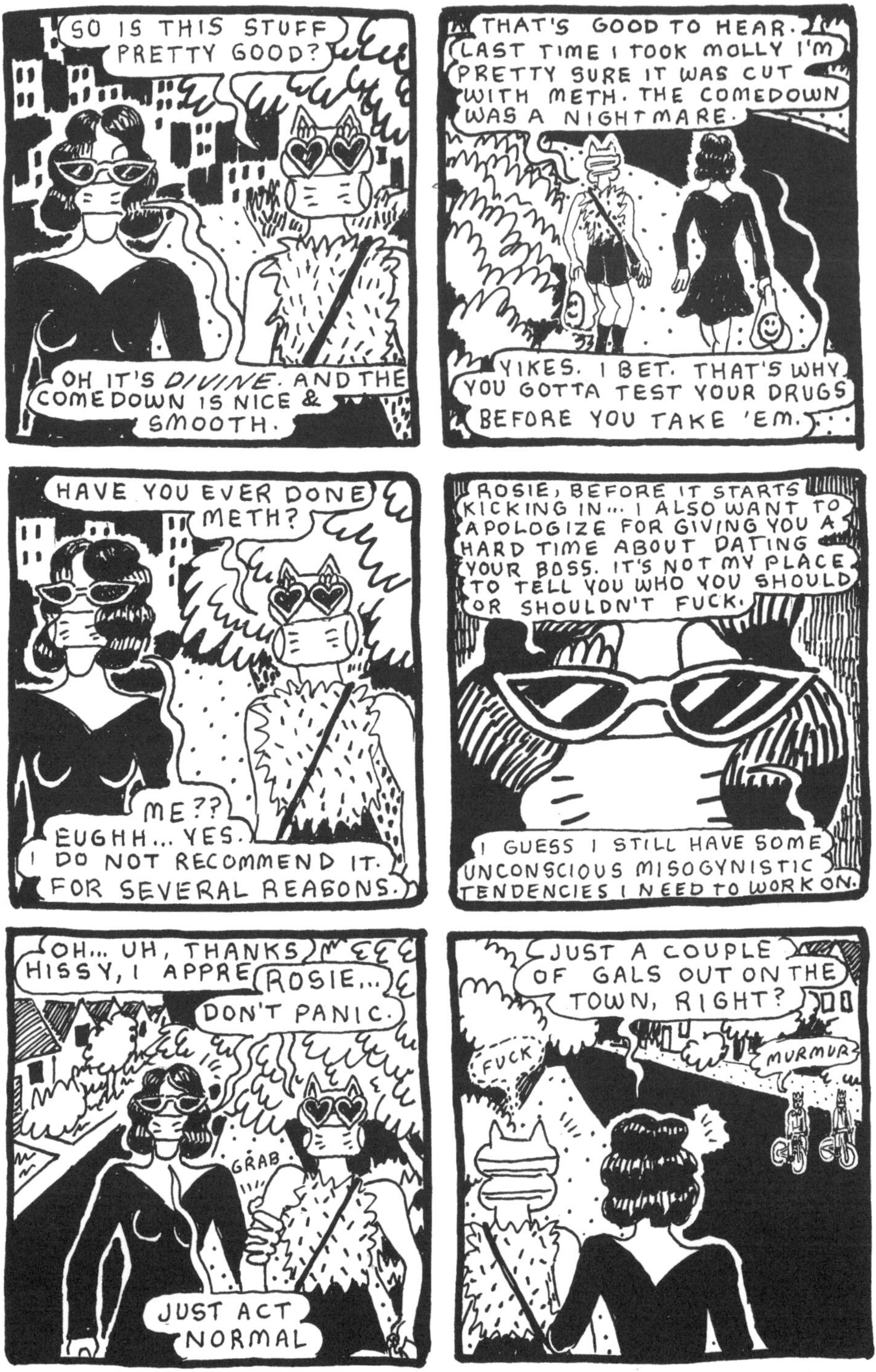
SO IS THIS STUFF PRETTY GOOD?
OH IT'S *DIVINE*. AND THE COMEDOWN IS NICE & SMOOTH.
THAT'S GOOD TO HEAR. LAST TIME I TOOK MOLLY I'M PRETTY SURE IT WAS CUT WITH METH. THE COMEDOWN WAS A NIGHTMARE.
YIKES. I BET. THAT'S WHY YOU GOTTA TEST YOUR DRUGS BEFORE YOU TAKE 'EM.
HAVE YOU EVER DONE METH?
ME??
EUGHH... YES. I DO NOT RECOMMEND IT. FOR SEVERAL REASONS.
ROSIE, BEFORE IT STARTS KICKING IN... I ALSO WANT TO APOLOGIZE FOR GIVING YOU A HARD TIME ABOUT DATING YOUR BOSS. IT'S NOT MY PLACE TO TELL YOU WHO YOU SHOULD OR SHOULDN'T FUCK.
I GUESS I STILL HAVE SOME UNCONSCIOUS MISOGYNISTIC TENDENCIES I NEED TO WORK ON.
OH... UH, THANKS HISSY, I APPRE
ROSIE... DON'T PANIC.
GRAB
JUST ACT NORMAL
JUST A COUPLE OF GALS OUT ON THE TOWN, RIGHT?
FUCK
MURMUR

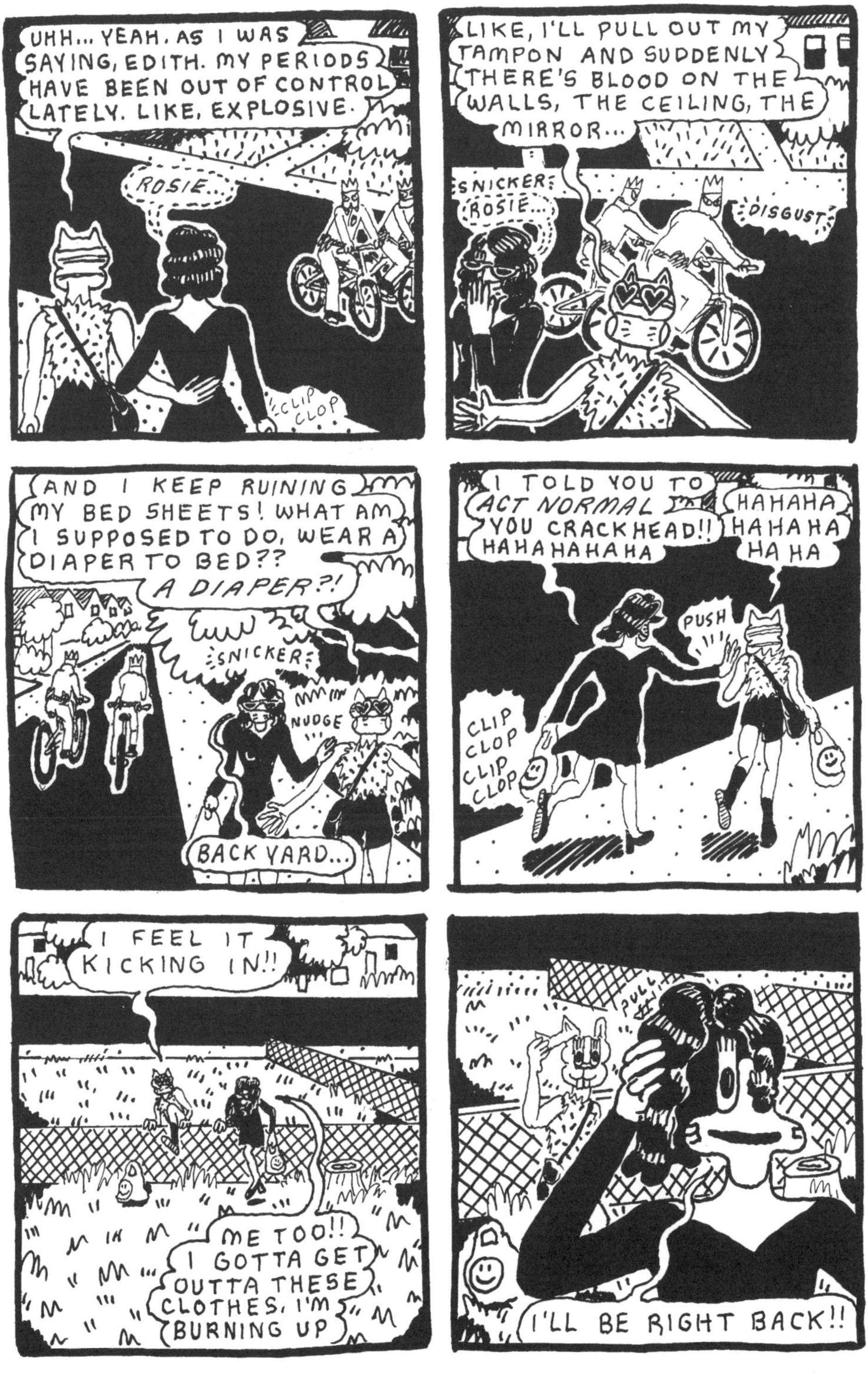
UHH... YEAH. AS I WAS SAYING, EDITH. MY PERIODS HAVE BEEN OUT OF CONTROL LATELY. LIKE, EXPLOSIVE.
ROSIE...
CLIP CLOP
LIKE, I'LL PULL OUT MY TAMPON AND SUDDENLY THERE'S BLOOD ON THE WALLS, THE CEILING, THE MIRROR...
SNICKER
ROSIE...
DISGUST
AND I KEEP RUINING MY BED SHEETS! WHAT AM I SUPPOSED TO DO, WEAR A DIAPER TO BED??
A DIAPER?!
EWW
SNICKER
NUDGE
BACK YARD...
I TOLD YOU TO ACT NORMAL YOU CRACKHEAD!! HAHAHAHAHA
HAHAHA HAHAHA HA HA
PUSH
CLIP CLOP CLIP CLOP
I FEEL IT KICKING IN!!
ME TOO!! I GOTTA GET OUTTA THESE CLOTHES, I'M BURNING UP
PULL
I'LL BE RIGHT BACK!!

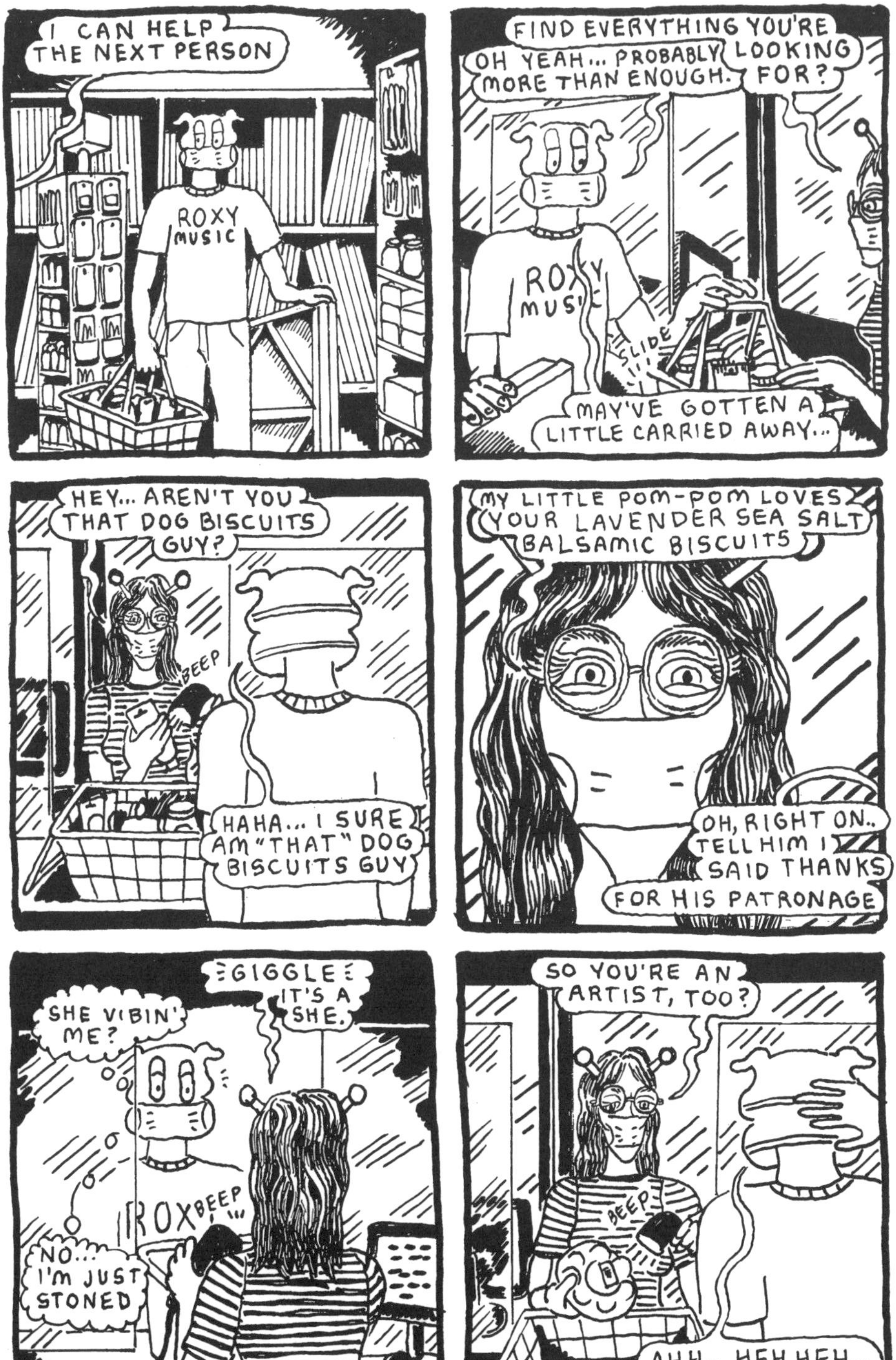
I CAN HELP THE NEXT PERSON
ROXY MUSIC
FIND EVERYTHING YOU'RE LOOKING FOR?
OH YEAH... PROBABLY MORE THAN ENOUGH.
ROXY MUSIC
SLIDE
MAY'VE GOTTEN A LITTLE CARRIED AWAY...
HEY... AREN'T YOU THAT DOG BISCUITS GUY?
BEEP
HAHA... I SURE AM "THAT" DOG BISCUITS GUY
MY LITTLE POM-POM LOVES YOUR LAVENDER SEA SALT BALSAMIC BISCUITS
OH, RIGHT ON.. TELL HIM I SAID THANKS
FOR HIS PATRONAGE
SHE VIBIN' ME?
GIGGLE
IT'S A SHE.
ROX
BEEP
NO... I'M JUST STONED
SO YOU'RE AN ARTIST, TOO?
BEEP
AHH... HEH HEH..

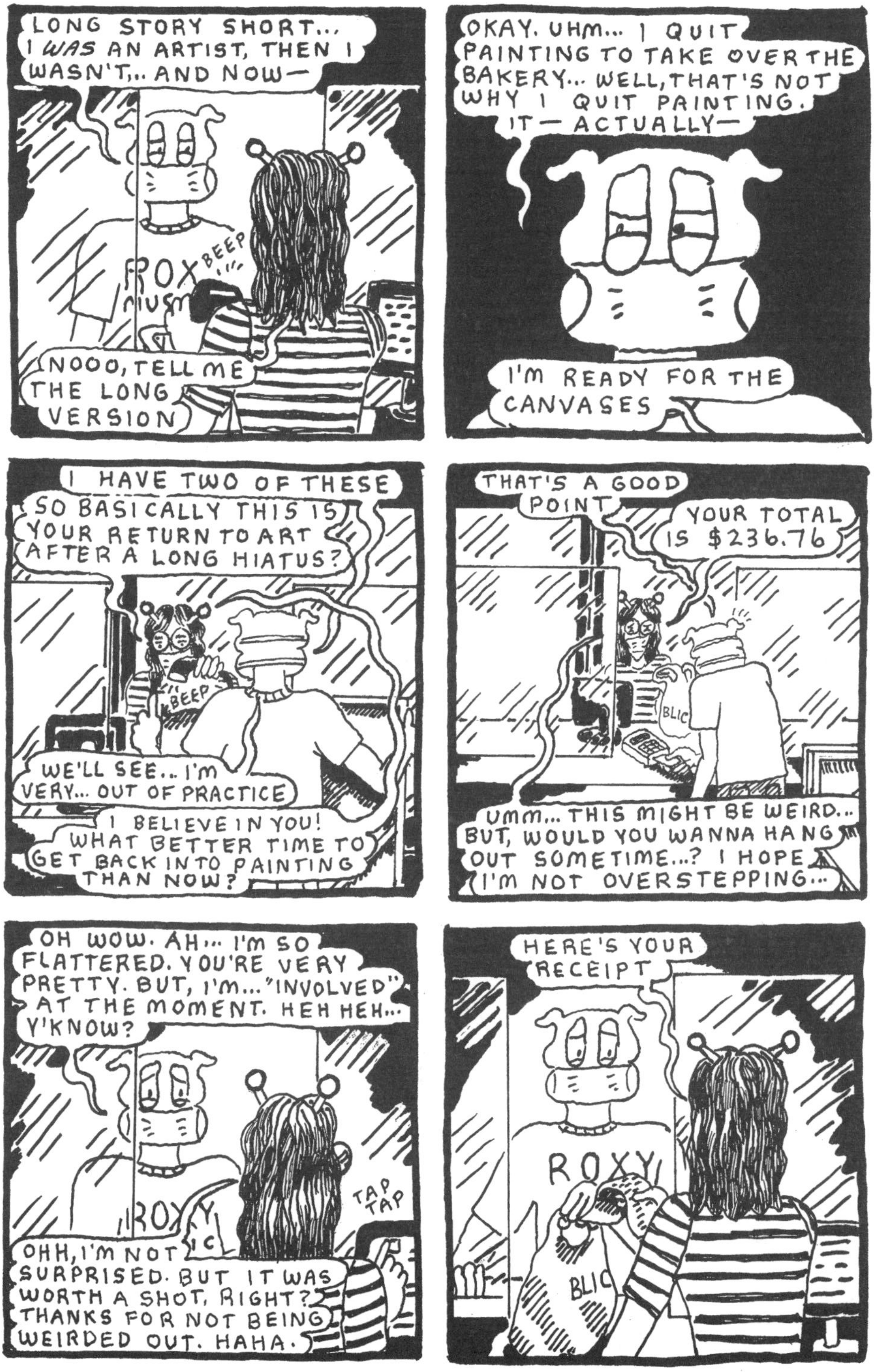
LONG STORY SHORT... I WAS AN ARTIST, THEN I WASN'T... AND NOW—
BEEP
NOOO, TELL ME THE LONG VERSION
OKAY. UHM... I QUIT PAINTING TO TAKE OVER THE BAKERY... WELL, THAT'S NOT WHY I QUIT PAINTING. IT— ACTUALLY—
I'M READY FOR THE CANVASES
I HAVE TWO OF THESE
SO BASICALLY THIS IS YOUR RETURN TO ART AFTER A LONG HIATUS?
BEEP
WE'LL SEE... I'M VERY... OUT OF PRACTICE
I BELIEVE IN YOU! WHAT BETTER TIME TO GET BACK INTO PAINTING THAN NOW?
THAT'S A GOOD POINT
YOUR TOTAL IS $236.76
UMM... THIS MIGHT BE WEIRD... BUT, WOULD YOU WANNA HANG OUT SOMETIME...? I HOPE I'M NOT OVERSTEPPING...
OH WOW. AH... I'M SO FLATTERED. YOU'RE VERY PRETTY. BUT, I'M... "INVOLVED" AT THE MOMENT. HEH HEH... Y'KNOW?
TAP TAP
OHH, I'M NOT SURPRISED. BUT IT WAS WORTH A SHOT, RIGHT? THANKS FOR NOT BEING WEIRDED OUT. HAHA.
HERE'S YOUR RECEIPT
ROXY

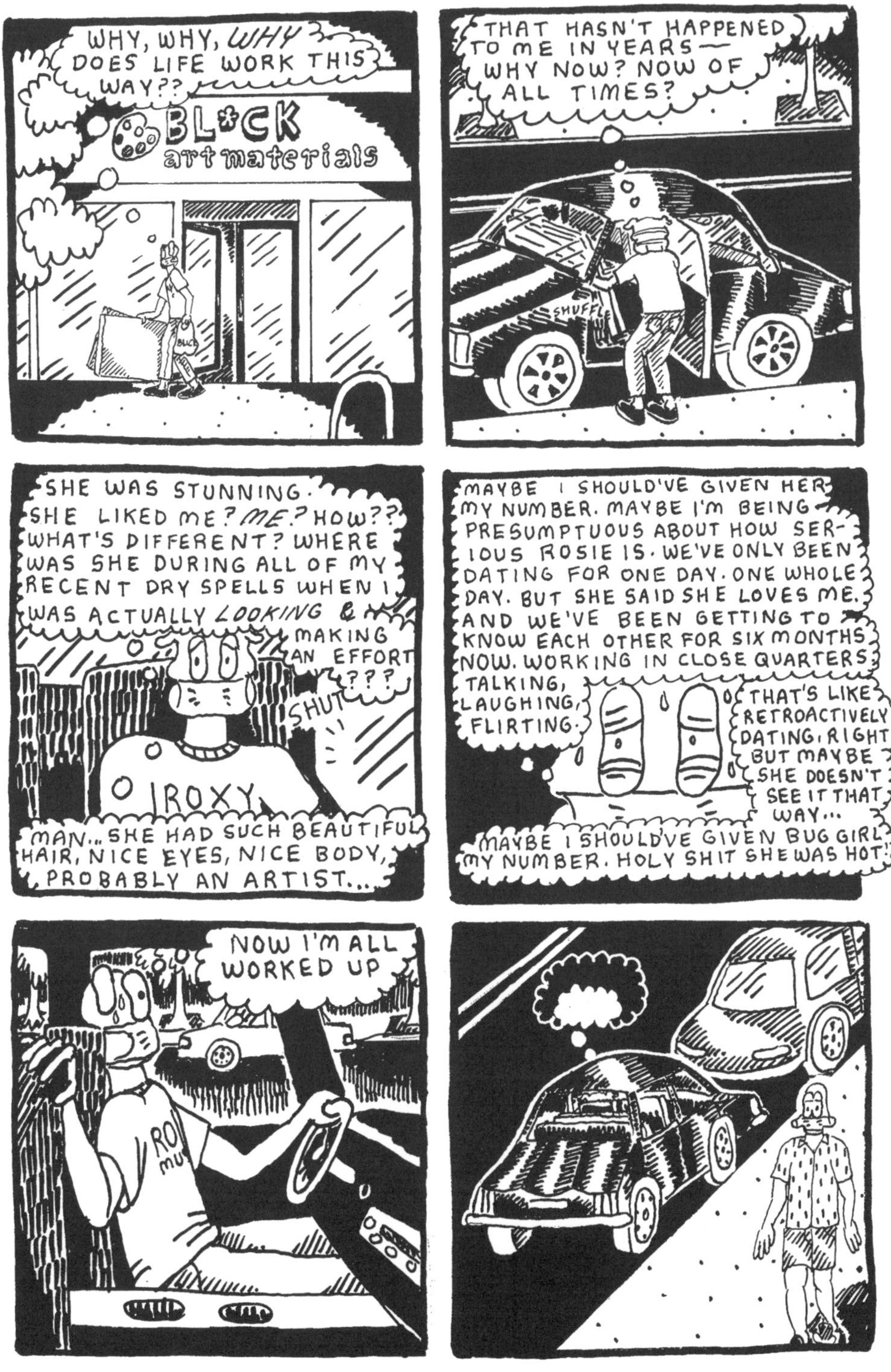

WHY, WHY, WHY DOES LIFE WORK THIS WAY??
BL*CK art materials
THAT HASN'T HAPPENED TO ME IN YEARS— WHY NOW? NOW OF ALL TIMES?
SHUFFLE
SHE WAS STUNNING. SHE LIKED ME? ME? HOW?? WHAT'S DIFFERENT? WHERE WAS SHE DURING ALL OF MY RECENT DRY SPELLS WHEN I WAS ACTUALLY LOOKING & MAKING AN EFFORT???
SHUT
ROXY
MAN... SHE HAD SUCH BEAUTIFUL HAIR, NICE EYES, NICE BODY, PROBABLY AN ARTIST...
MAYBE I SHOULD'VE GIVEN HER MY NUMBER. MAYBE I'M BEING PRESUMPTUOUS ABOUT HOW SERIOUS ROSIE IS. WE'VE ONLY BEEN DATING FOR ONE DAY. ONE WHOLE DAY. BUT SHE SAID SHE LOVES ME. AND WE'VE BEEN GETTING TO KNOW EACH OTHER FOR SIX MONTHS NOW. WORKING IN CLOSE QUARTERS. TALKING, LAUGHING, FLIRTING.
THAT'S LIKE RETROACTIVELY DATING, RIGHT? BUT MAYBE SHE DOESN'T SEE IT THAT WAY...
MAYBE I SHOULD'VE GIVEN BUG GIRL MY NUMBER. HOLY SHIT SHE WAS HOT!
NOW I'M ALL WORKED UP

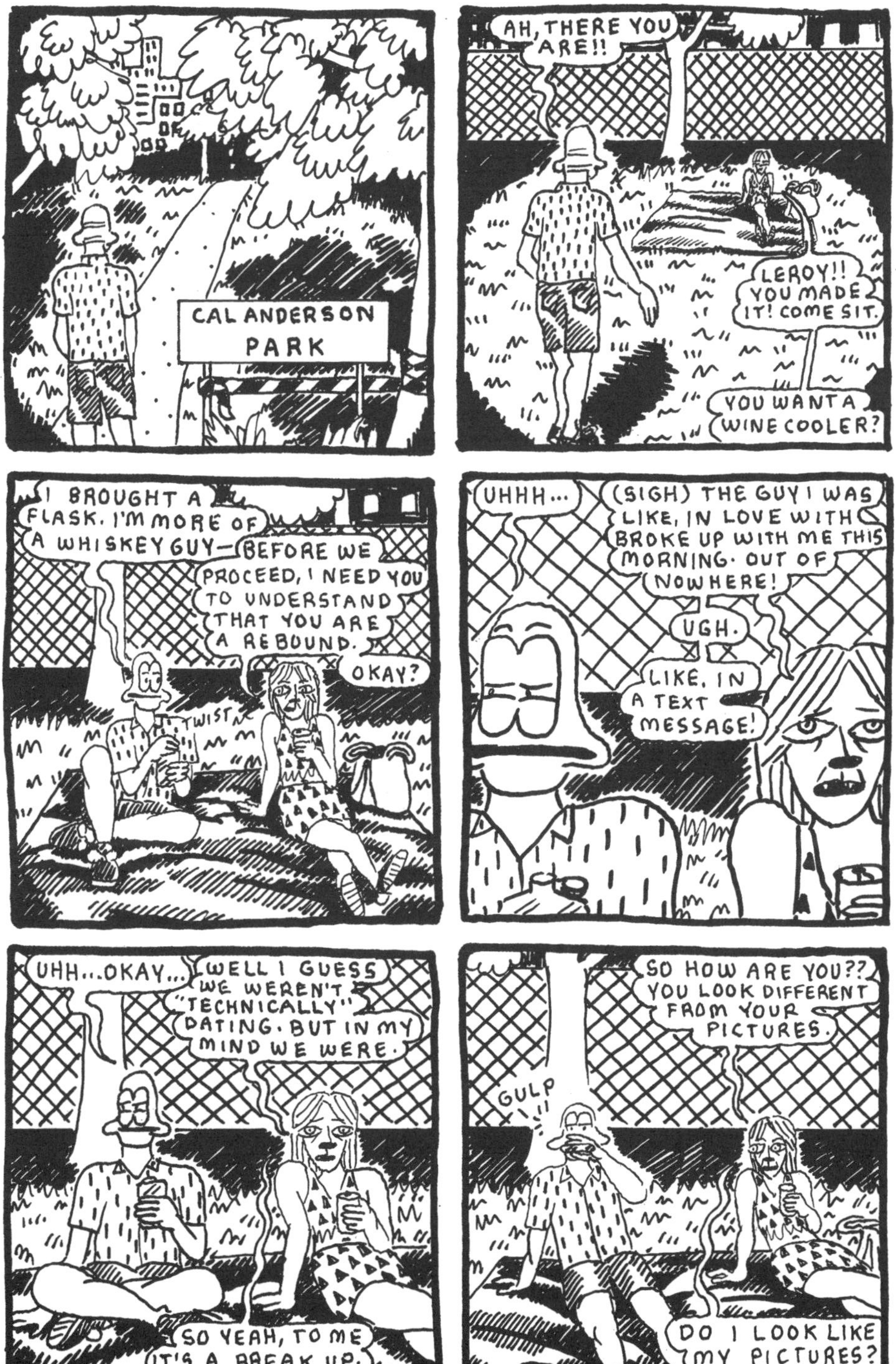
CAL ANDERSON PARK
AH, THERE YOU ARE!!
LEROY!! YOU MADE IT! COME SIT.
YOU WANT A WINE COOLER?
I BROUGHT A FLASK. I'M MORE OF A WHISKEY GUY—
BEFORE WE PROCEED, I NEED YOU TO UNDERSTAND THAT YOU ARE A REBOUND.
OKAY?
TWIST
UHHH...
(SIGH) THE GUY I WAS LIKE, IN LOVE WITH BROKE UP WITH ME THIS MORNING. OUT OF NOWHERE!
UGH.
LIKE, IN A TEXT MESSAGE!
UHH...OKAY...
WELL I GUESS WE WEREN'T "TECHNICALLY" DATING. BUT IN MY MIND WE WERE.
SO YEAH, TO ME IT'S A BREAK UP.
SO HOW ARE YOU?? YOU LOOK DIFFERENT FROM YOUR PICTURES.
GULP
DO I LOOK LIKE MY PICTURES?

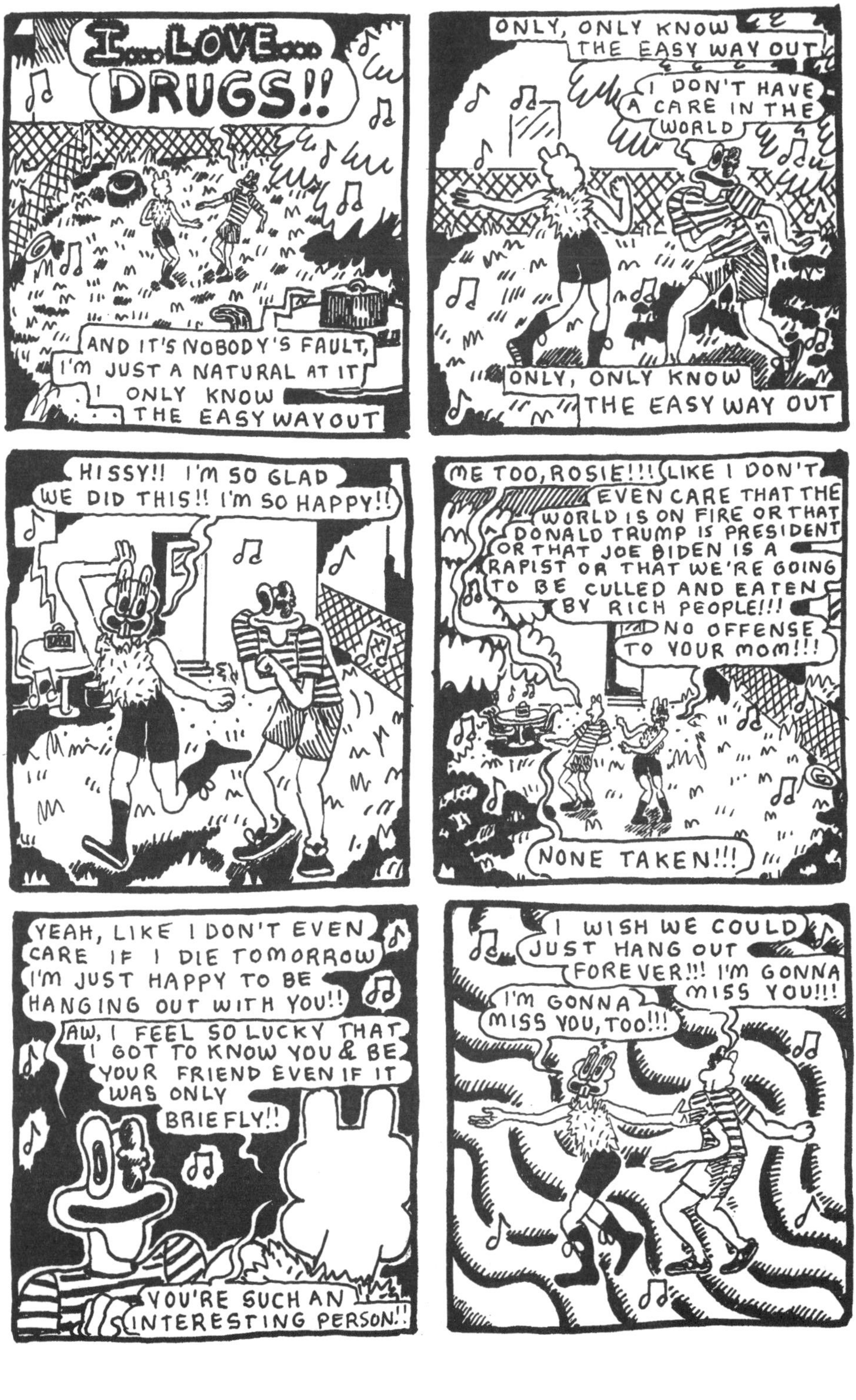
I...LOVE...DRUGS!!
AND IT'S NOBODY'S FAULT, I'M JUST A NATURAL AT IT
I ONLY KNOW THE EASY WAY OUT
ONLY, ONLY KNOW THE EASY WAY OUT
I DON'T HAVE A CARE IN THE WORLD
ONLY, ONLY KNOW THE EASY WAY OUT
HISSY!! I'M SO GLAD WE DID THIS!! I'M SO HAPPY!!
ME TOO, ROSIE!!!
LIKE I DON'T EVEN CARE THAT THE WORLD IS ON FIRE OR THAT DONALD TRUMP IS PRESIDENT OR THAT JOE BIDEN IS A RAPIST OR THAT WE'RE GOING TO BE CULLED AND EATEN BY RICH PEOPLE!!!
NO OFFENSE TO YOUR MOM!!!
NONE TAKEN!!!
YEAH, LIKE I DON'T EVEN CARE IF I DIE TOMORROW I'M JUST HAPPY TO BE HANGING OUT WITH YOU!!
AW, I FEEL SO LUCKY THAT I GOT TO KNOW YOU & BE YOUR FRIEND EVEN IF IT WAS ONLY BRIEFLY!!
YOU'RE SUCH AN INTERESTING PERSON!!
I WISH WE COULD JUST HANG OUT FOREVER!!! I'M GONNA MISS YOU!!!
I'M GONNA MISS YOU, TOO!!!

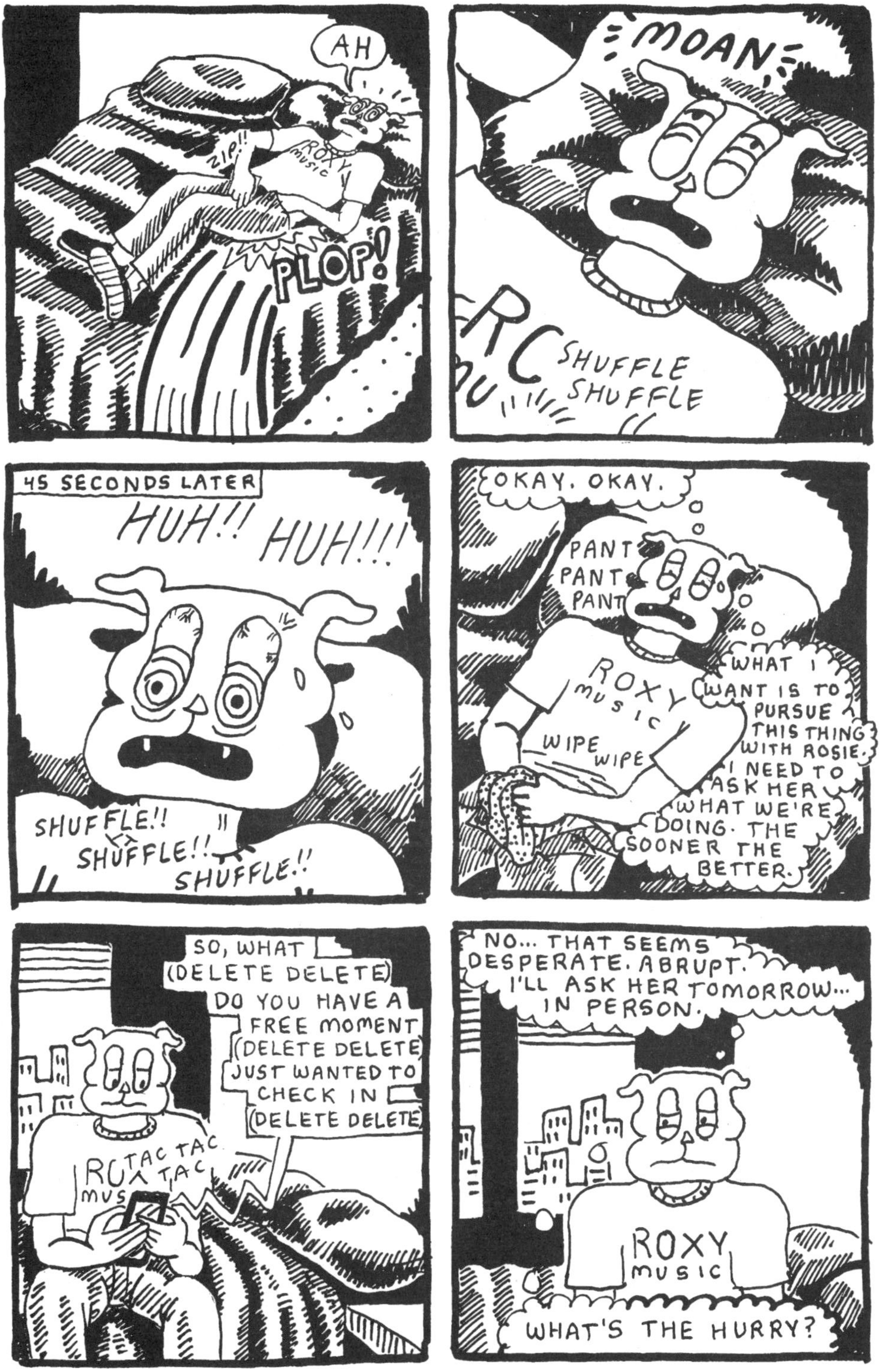
AH
ZIP!!
ROXY MUSIC
PLOP!
MOAN
SHUFFLE
SHUFFLE
45 SECONDS LATER
HUH!! HUH!!!
SHUFFLE!!
SHUFFLE!!
SHUFFLE!!
OKAY. OKAY.
PANT
PANT
PANT
ROXY MUSIC
WIPE WIPE
WHAT I WANT IS TO PURSUE THIS THING WITH ROSIE. I NEED TO ASK HER WHAT WE'RE DOING. THE SOONER THE BETTER.
SO, WHAT (DELETE DELETE) DO YOU HAVE A FREE MOMENT (DELETE DELETE) JUST WANTED TO CHECK IN (DELETE DELETE)
TAC TAC TAC
NO... THAT SEEMS DESPERATE. ABRUPT. I'LL ASK HER TOMORROW... IN PERSON.
ROXY MUSIC
WHAT'S THE HURRY?

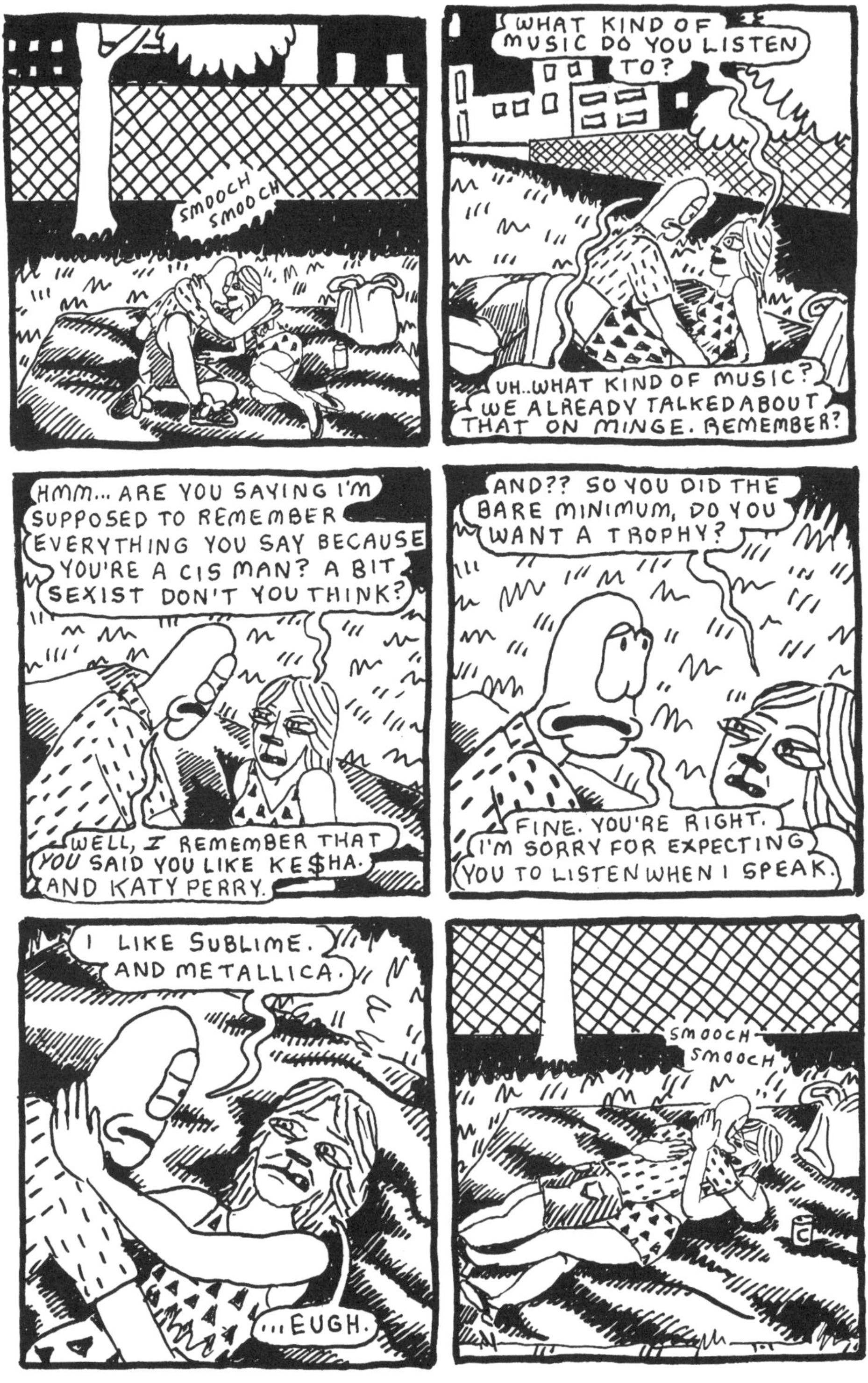
SMOOCH SMOOCH
WHAT KIND OF MUSIC DO YOU LISTEN TO?
UH..WHAT KIND OF MUSIC? WE ALREADY TALKED ABOUT THAT ON MINGE. REMEMBER?
HMM... ARE YOU SAYING I'M SUPPOSED TO REMEMBER EVERYTHING YOU SAY BECAUSE YOU'RE A CIS MAN? A BIT SEXIST DON'T YOU THINK?
WELL, I REMEMBER THAT YOU SAID YOU LIKE KE$HA. AND KATY PERRY.
AND?? SO YOU DID THE BARE MINIMUM, DO YOU WANT A TROPHY?
FINE. YOU'RE RIGHT. I'M SORRY FOR EXPECTING YOU TO LISTEN WHEN I SPEAK.
I LIKE SUBLIME. AND METALLICA.
...EUGH.
SMOOCH SMOOCH

I THINK IT'S SO FUCKING COOL THAT YOU DO DRAG. I'VE NEVER HEARD OF A BISEXUAL GUY THAT WAS A DRAG QUEEN BEFORE!

YEAH I GET THAT A LOT. SOMETIMES WITH A JUDGMENTAL, ACCUSATORY TONE... FROM THE SAME PPL WHO CALL THEMSELVES "SEX POSITIVE"

Y'KNOW, I THINK ITS SO FUCKING WEIRD HOW OUR GENERATION PRETENDS TO BE SO SEXUALLY LIBERATED & FORWARD THINKING, YET WHENEVER SOMEONE DOES OR SAYS SOMETHING OUTSIDE OF THE STRICT LANGUAGE PARAMETERS WE'VE CONSTRUCTED, ITS SEEN AS A THING TO BE JUDGED AT MINIMUM, OR EVEN A REASON TO DENOUNCE SOMEONE ENTIRELY.

MM HMM!

PUEFFF..

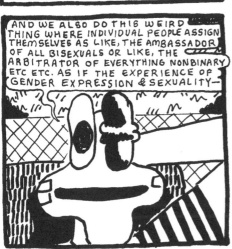

AND WE ALSO DO THIS WEIRD THING WHERE INDIVIDUAL PEOPLE ASSIGN THEMSELVES AS LIKE, THE AMBASSADOR OF ALL BISEXUALS OR LIKE, THE ARBITRATOR OF EVERYTHING NONBINARY ETC ETC. AS IF THE EXPERIENCE OF GENDER EXPRESSION & SEXUALITY—

— BELONG ONLY TO PEOPLE WHO (HAVE THE PRIVILEGE TO) LEARN THE STRINGENT LANGUAGE THRESHOLDS, RATHER THAN BEING SOMETHING THAT EVERY HUMAN BEING ON EARTH GRAPPLES WITH IN DIFFERENT, UNIQUE WAYS AND ALLOWING FOR VARIATION BEYOND THE CONFINES OF ONE'S INDIVIDUAL SENSE OF REALITY.

SOUNDS LIKE A TYPE OF FASCISM TO ME!!

IT IS!! IT'S A TYPE OF FASCISM THAT WE ENFORCE ON EACH OTHER— ESPECIALLY WHEN IT COMES TO POLICING ART & SELF EXPRESSION.

THE MOST ABSURD THING ABOUT IT IS, THESE TYPES OF FASCISTIC, PURITANICAL SOCIAL CONTRACTS ARE THE SAME THINGS WE DESPISE ABOUT WHITE ANGLO SAXON PROTESTANTS & BABY BOOMERS

WOW — YOU'RE RIGHT!! IT'S COME FULL CIRCLE HASN'T IT?

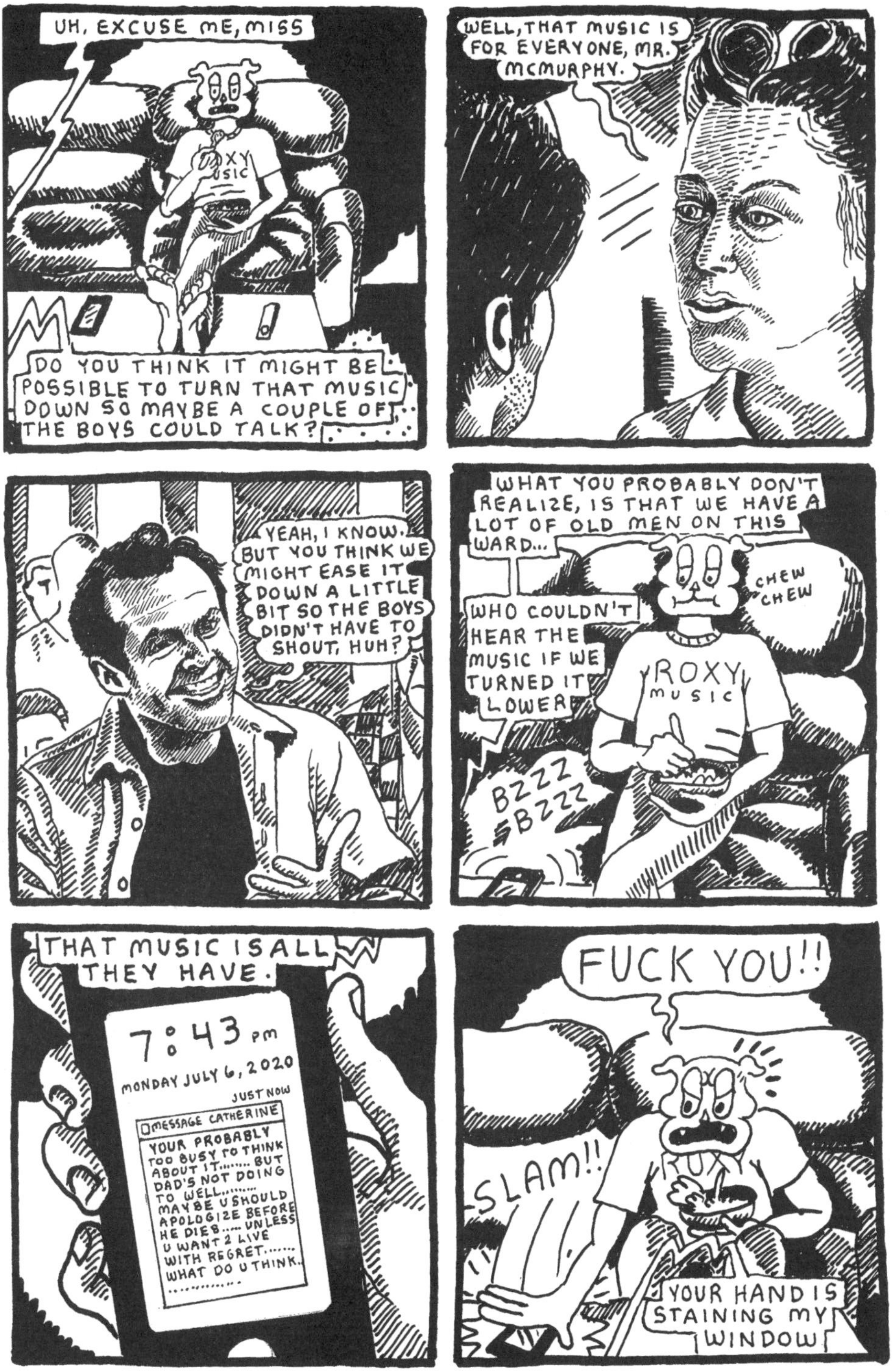
UH, EXCUSE ME, MISS
OXY USIC
DO YOU THINK IT MIGHT BE POSSIBLE TO TURN THAT MUSIC DOWN SO MAYBE A COUPLE OF THE BOYS COULD TALK?
WELL, THAT MUSIC IS FOR EVERYONE, MR. MCMURPHY.
YEAH, I KNOW. BUT YOU THINK WE MIGHT EASE IT DOWN A LITTLE BIT SO THE BOYS DIDN'T HAVE TO SHOUT, HUH?
WHAT YOU PROBABLY DON'T REALIZE, IS THAT WE HAVE A LOT OF OLD MEN ON THIS WARD...
WHO COULDN'T HEAR THE MUSIC IF WE TURNED IT LOWER
CHEW CHEW
ROXY MUSIC
BZZZ BZZZ
THAT MUSIC IS ALL THEY HAVE.
7:43 pm
MONDAY JULY 6, 2020
JUST NOW
MESSAGE CATHERINE
YOUR PROBABLY TOO BUSY TO THINK ABOUT IT....... BUT DAD'S NOT DOING TO WELL......... MAYBE U SHOULD APOLOGIZE BEFORE HE DIES..... UNLESS U WANT 2 LIVE WITH REGRET....... WHAT DO U THINK. ....
FUCK YOU!!
SLAM!!
YOUR HAND IS STAINING MY WINDOW

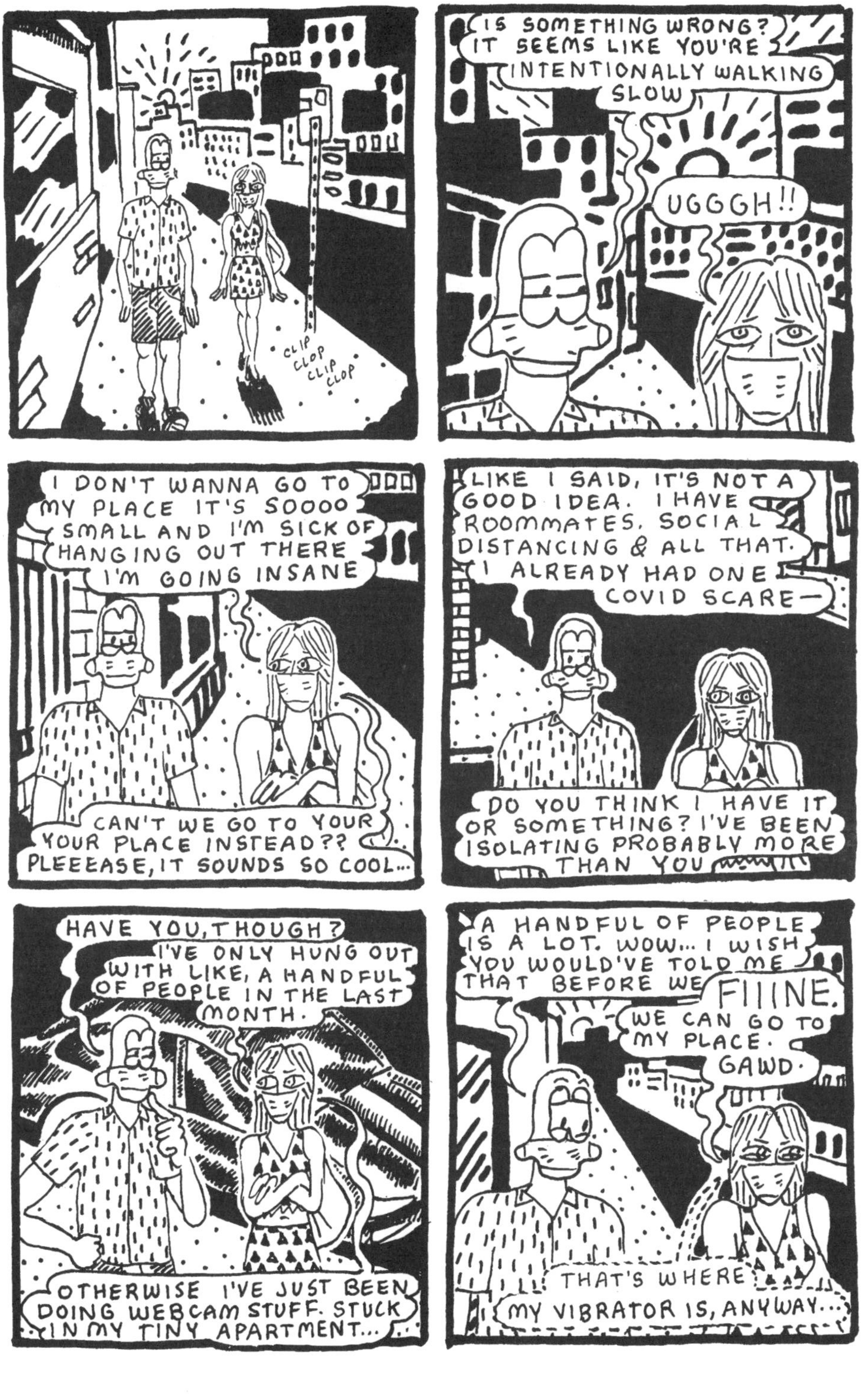
CLIP CLOP CLIP CLOP
IS SOMETHING WRONG? IT SEEMS LIKE YOU'RE
INTENTIONALLY WALKING SLOW
UGGGH!!
I DON'T WANNA GO TO MY PLACE IT'S SOOOO SMALL AND I'M SICK OF HANGING OUT THERE I'M GOING INSANE
CAN'T WE GO TO YOUR YOUR PLACE INSTEAD?? PLEEEASE, IT SOUNDS SO COOL...
LIKE I SAID, IT'S NOT A GOOD IDEA. I HAVE ROOMMATES, SOCIAL DISTANCING & ALL THAT.
I ALREADY HAD ONE COVID SCARE—
DO YOU THINK I HAVE IT OR SOMETHING? I'VE BEEN ISOLATING PROBABLY MORE THAN YOU
HAVE YOU, THOUGH?
I'VE ONLY HUNG OUT WITH LIKE, A HANDFUL OF PEOPLE IN THE LAST MONTH.
OTHERWISE I'VE JUST BEEN DOING WEBCAM STUFF. STUCK IN MY TINY APARTMENT...
A HANDFUL OF PEOPLE IS A LOT. WOW... I WISH YOU WOULD'VE TOLD ME THAT BEFORE WE
FIIINE.
WE CAN GO TO MY PLACE. GAWD.
THAT'S WHERE
MY VIBRATOR IS, ANYWAY...

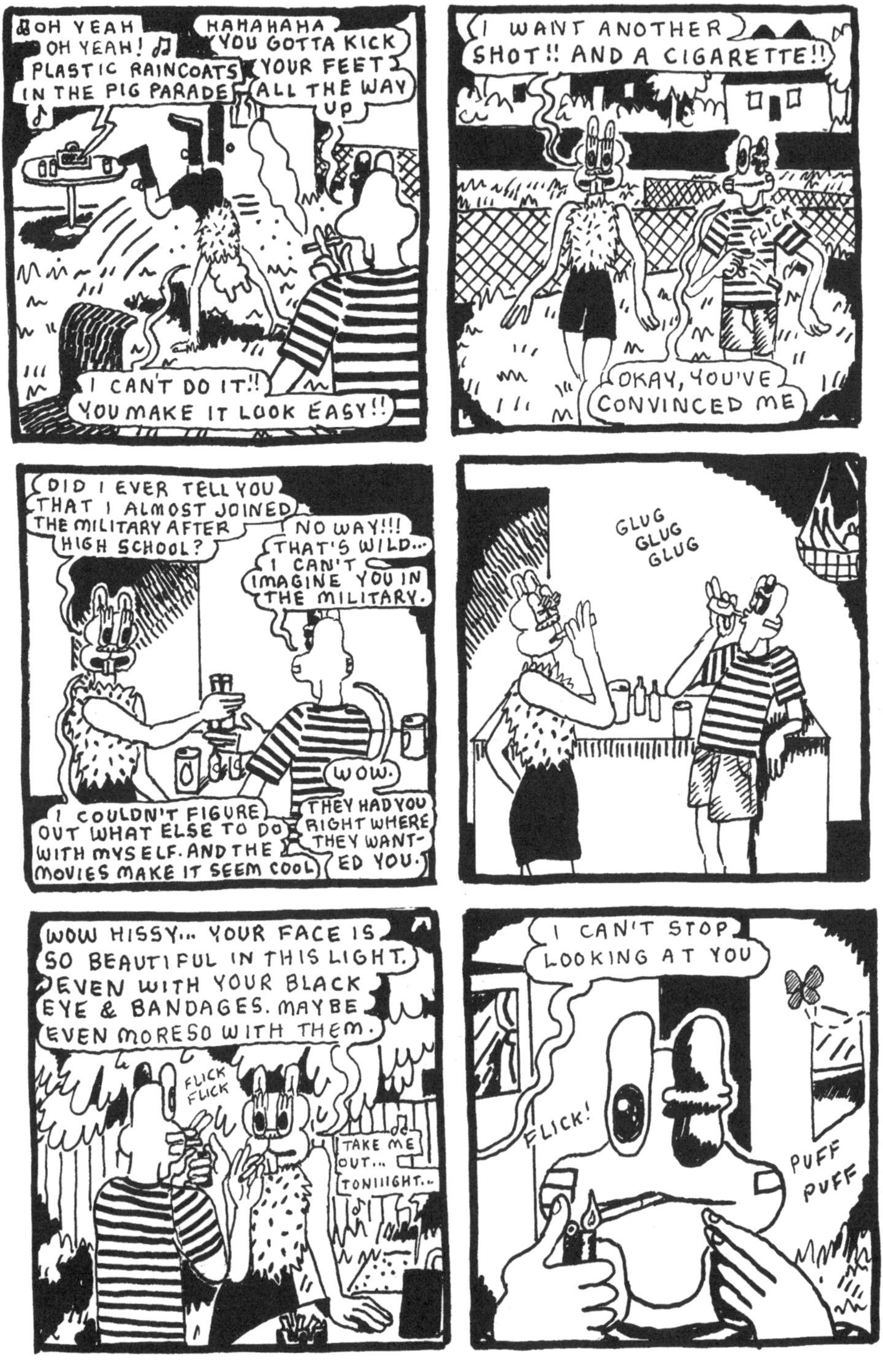
♫ OH YEAH OH YEAH! ♫ PLASTIC RAINCOATS IN THE PIG PARADE ♪
HAHAHAHA YOU GOTTA KICK YOUR FEET ALL THE WAY UP
I CAN'T DO IT!! YOU MAKE IT LOOK EASY!!
I WANT ANOTHER SHOT!! AND A CIGARETTE!!
FLICK
OKAY, YOU'VE CONVINCED ME
DID I EVER TELL YOU THAT I ALMOST JOINED THE MILITARY AFTER HIGH SCHOOL?
NO WAY!!! THAT'S WILD... I CAN'T IMAGINE YOU IN THE MILITARY.
WOW.
I COULDN'T FIGURE OUT WHAT ELSE TO DO WITH MYSELF. AND THE MOVIES MAKE IT SEEM COOL
THEY HAD YOU RIGHT WHERE THEY WANTED YOU.
GLUG GLUG GLUG
WOW HISSY... YOUR FACE IS SO BEAUTIFUL IN THIS LIGHT. EVEN WITH YOUR BLACK EYE & BANDAGES. MAYBE EVEN MORESO WITH THEM.
FLICK FLICK
♫ TAKE ME OUT... TONIIIGHT...
I CAN'T STOP LOOKING AT YOU
FLICK!
PUFF PUFF

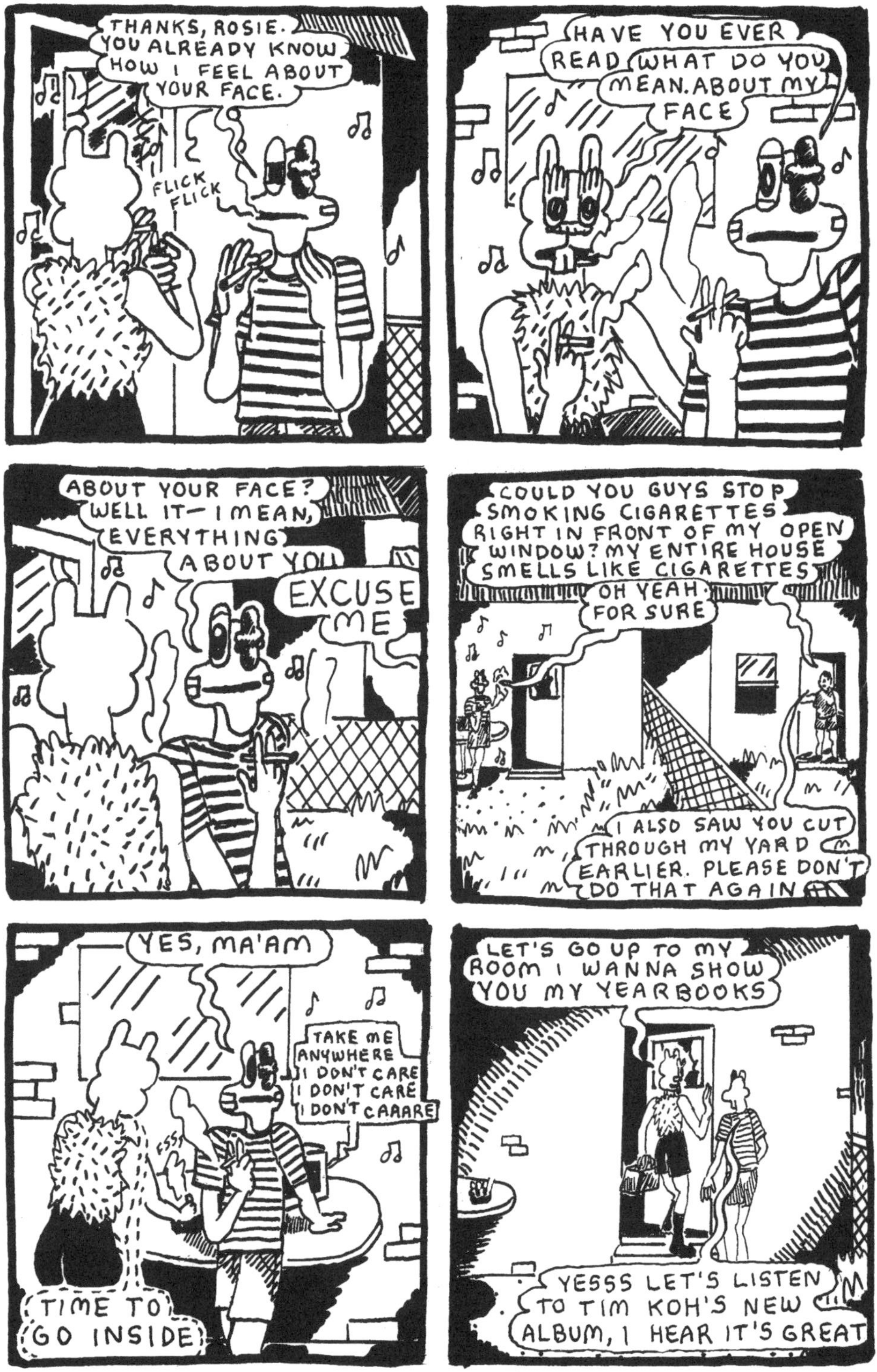

THANKS, ROSIE. YOU ALREADY KNOW HOW I FEEL ABOUT YOUR FACE.
FLICK FLICK
HAVE YOU EVER READ
WHAT DO YOU MEAN. ABOUT MY FACE
ABOUT YOUR FACE? WELL IT— I MEAN, EVERYTHING
ABOUT YOU
EXCUSE ME
COULD YOU GUYS STOP SMOKING CIGARETTES RIGHT IN FRONT OF MY OPEN WINDOW? MY ENTIRE HOUSE SMELLS LIKE CIGARETTES
OH YEAH FOR SURE
I ALSO SAW YOU CUT THROUGH MY YARD EARLIER. PLEASE DON'T DO THAT AGAIN
YES, MA'AM
TAKE ME ANYWHERE I DON'T CARE I DON'T CARE I DON'T CAAARE
TIME TO GO INSIDE
LET'S GO UP TO MY ROOM I WANNA SHOW YOU MY YEARBOOKS
YESSS LET'S LISTEN TO TIM KOH'S NEW ALBUM, I HEAR IT'S GREAT

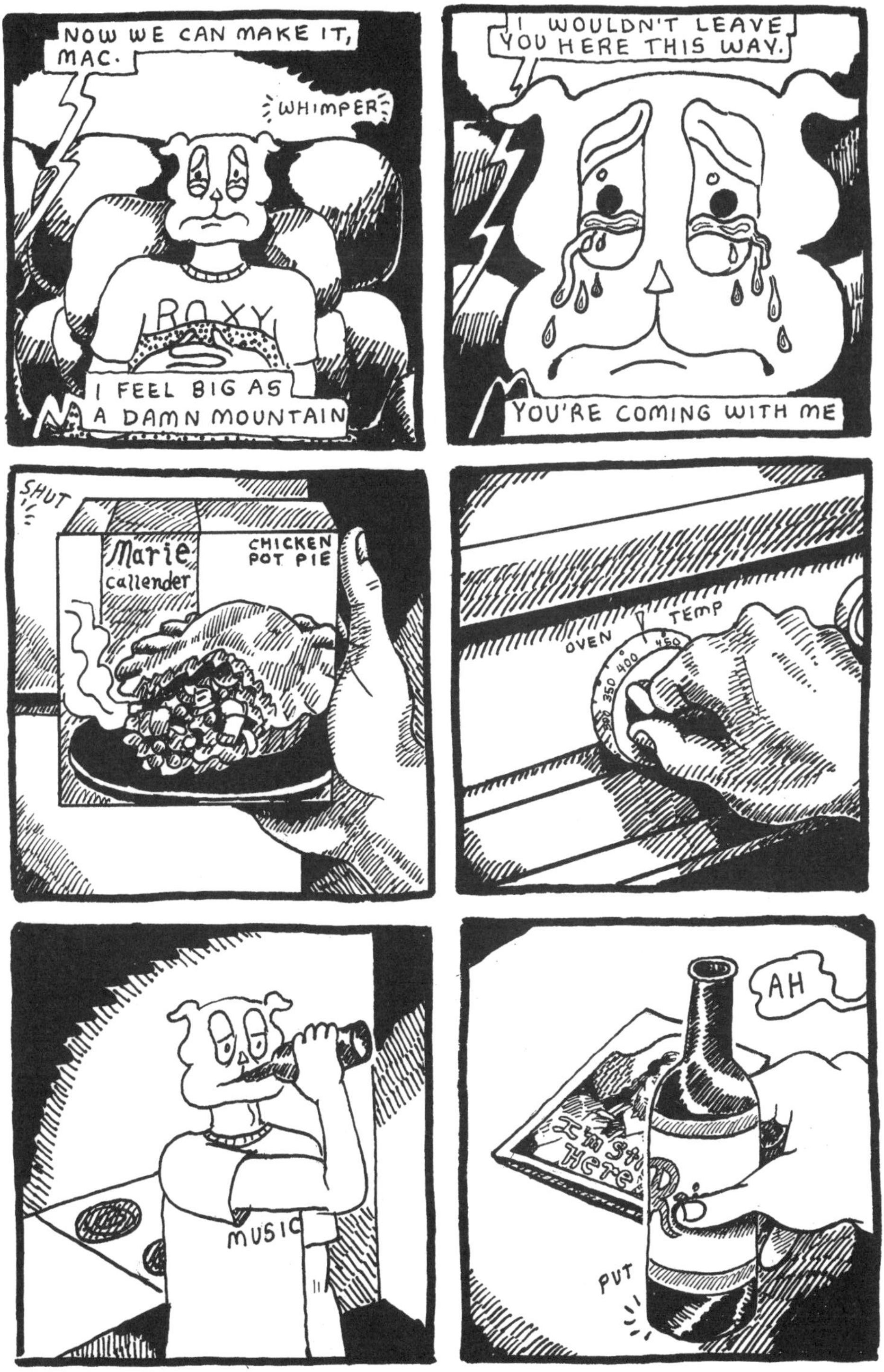
NOW WE CAN MAKE IT, MAC.
WHIMPER
ROXY
I FEEL BIG AS A DAMN MOUNTAIN
I WOULDN'T LEAVE YOU HERE THIS WAY.
YOU'RE COMING WITH ME
SHUT
Marie callender
CHICKEN POT PIE
OVEN TEMP
350 400 450
MUSIC
AH
PUT

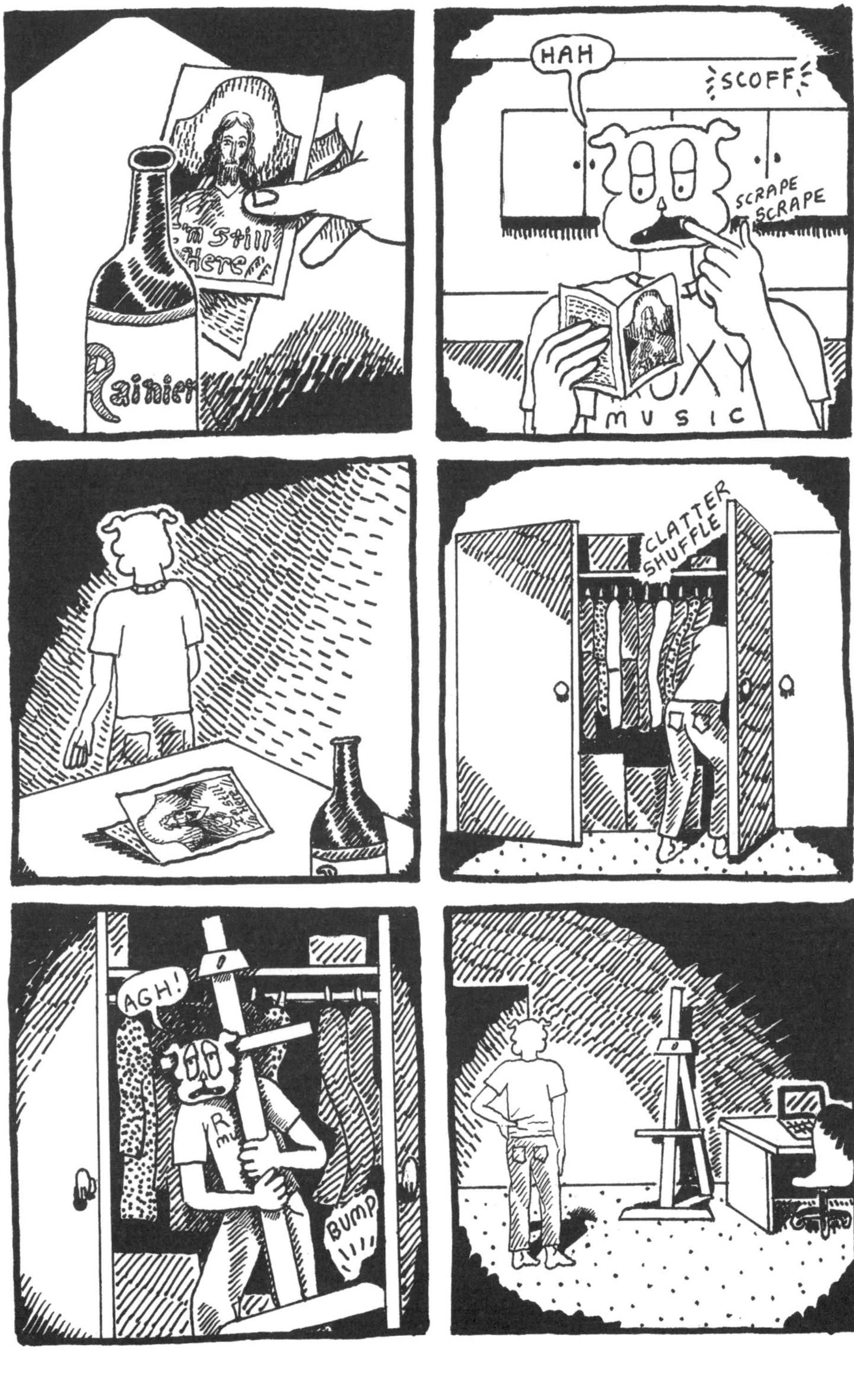

'm Still
Here
Rainier
HAH
SCOFF
SCRAPE
SCRAPE
MUSIC
CLATTER
SHUFFLE
AGH!
BUMP

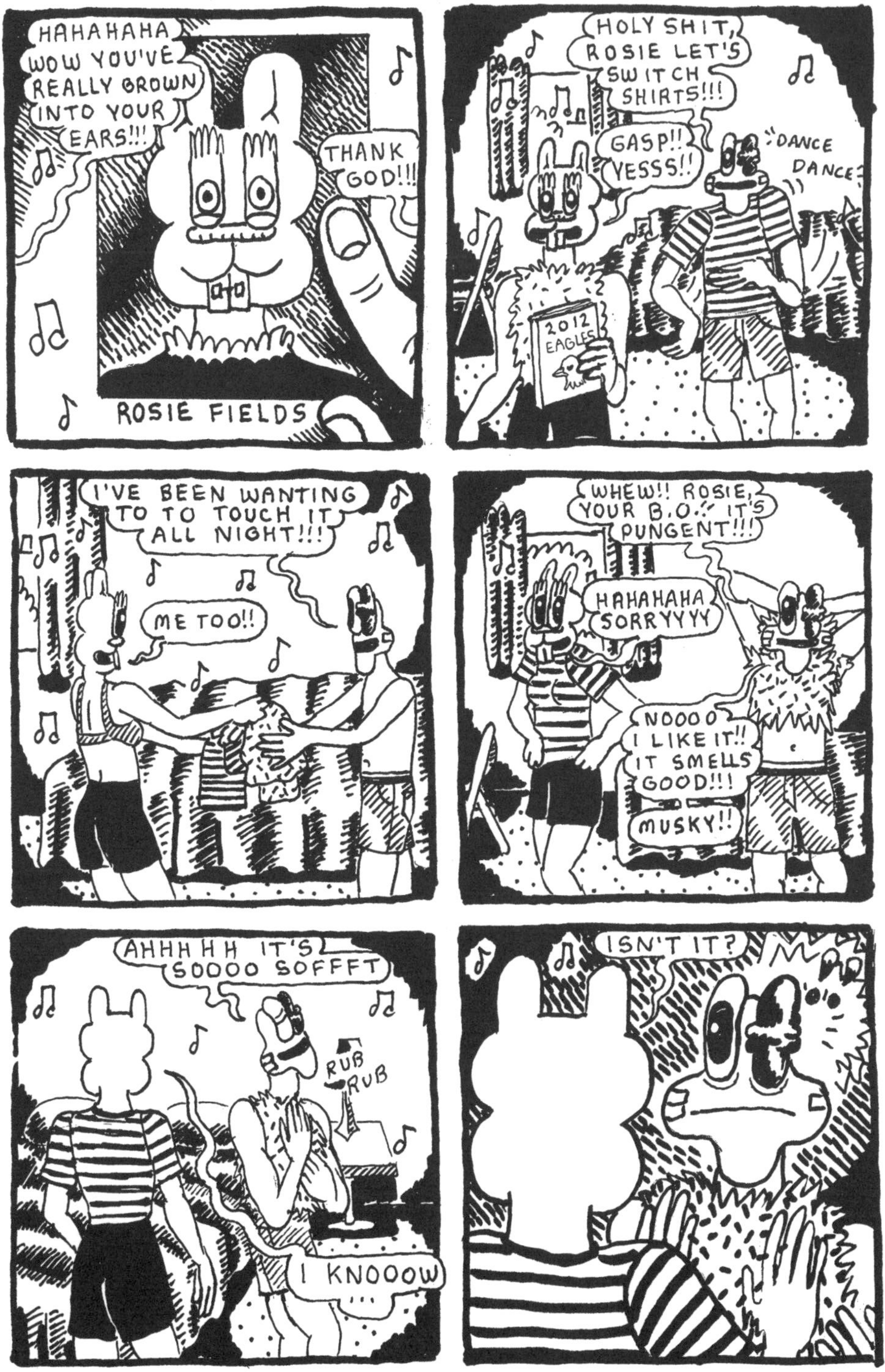
HAHAHAHA WOW YOU'VE REALLY GROWN INTO YOUR EARS!!!
THANK GOD!!!
ROSIE FIELDS
HOLY SHIT, ROSIE LET'S SWITCH SHIRTS!!!
GASP!! YESSS!!
DANCE DANCE
2012 EAGLES
I'VE BEEN WANTING TO TO TOUCH IT ALL NIGHT!!!
ME TOO!!
WHEW!! ROSIE, YOUR B.O. IT'S PUNGENT!!!
HAHAHAHA SORRYYYY
NOOOO I LIKE IT!! IT SMELLS GOOD!!!
MUSKY!!
AHHHHH IT'S SOOOO SOFFFT
RUB RUB
I KNOOOW ...
ISN'T IT?

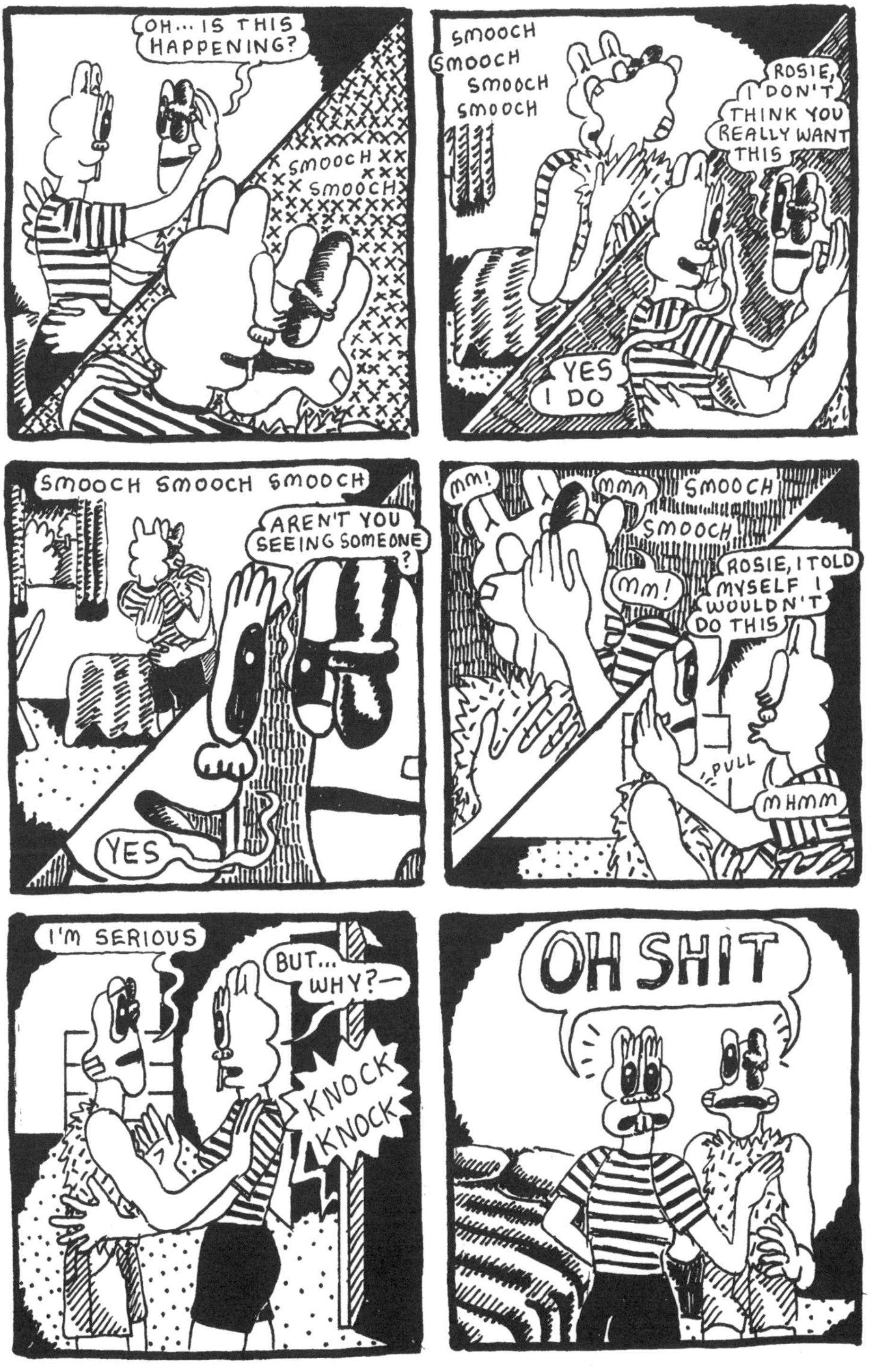
OH... IS THIS HAPPENING?
SMOOCH
SMOOCH
SMOOCH
SMOOCH
SMOOCH
SMOOCH
ROSIE, I DON'T THINK YOU REALLY WANT THIS
YES I DO
SMOOCH SMOOCH SMOOCH
AREN'T YOU SEEING SOMEONE?
YES
MM!
MMM
SMOOCH
SMOOCH
MM!
ROSIE, I TOLD MYSELF I WOULDN'T DO THIS
PULL
MHMM
I'M SERIOUS
BUT... WHY?—
KNOCK KNOCK
OH SHIT

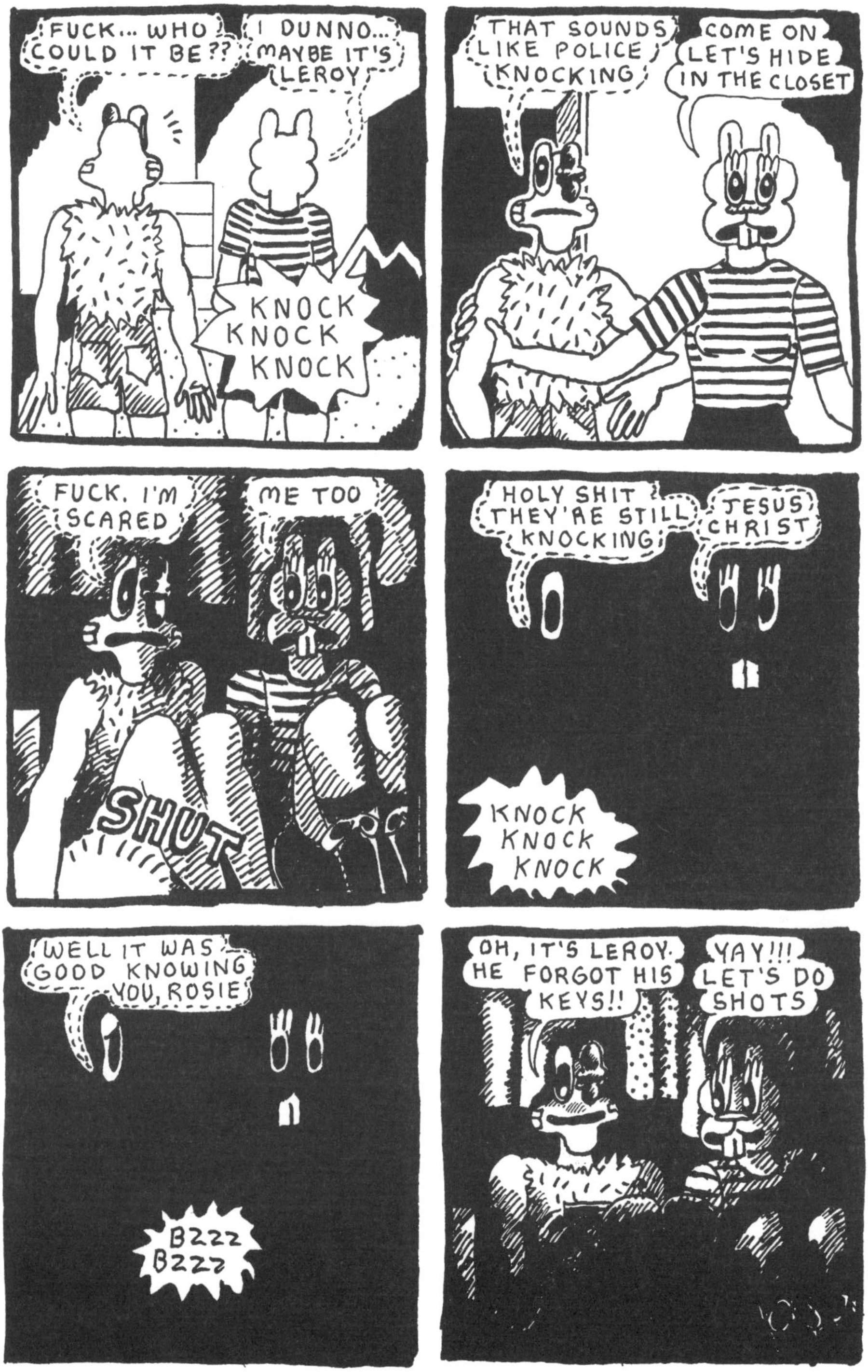
FUCK... WHO COULD IT BE??
I DUNNO... MAYBE IT'S LEROY
KNOCK KNOCK KNOCK
THAT SOUNDS LIKE POLICE KNOCKING
COME ON LET'S HIDE IN THE CLOSET
FUCK. I'M SCARED
ME TOO
SHUT
HOLY SHIT THEY'RE STILL KNOCKING
JESUS CHRIST
KNOCK KNOCK KNOCK
WELL IT WAS GOOD KNOWING YOU, ROSIE
BZZZ BZZZ
OH, IT'S LEROY. HE FORGOT HIS KEYS!!
YAY!!! LET'S DO SHOTS

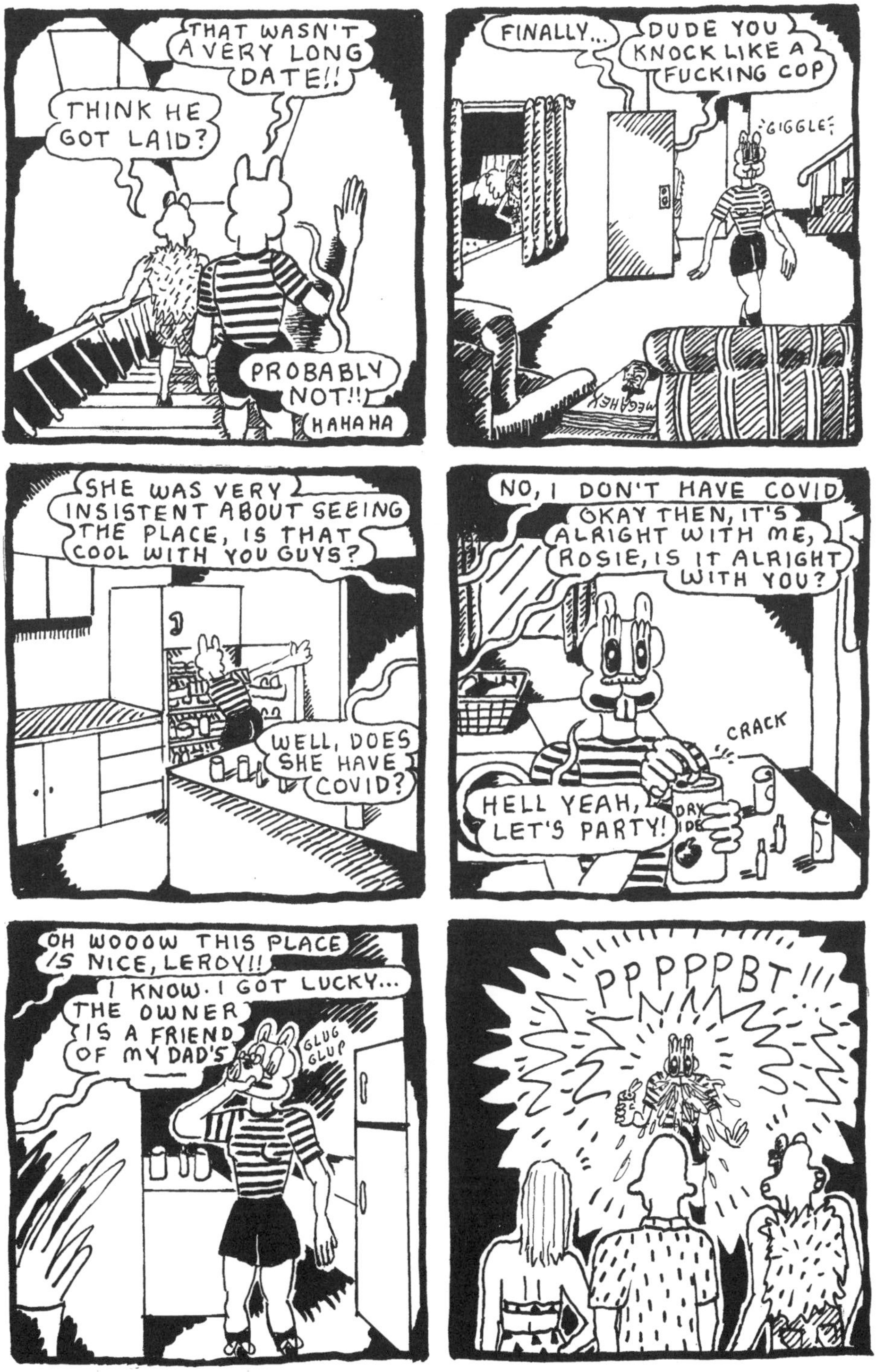

THAT WASN'T A VERY LONG DATE!!
THINK HE GOT LAID?
PROBABLY NOT!!
HAHAHA
FINALLY...
DUDE YOU KNOCK LIKE A FUCKING COP
GIGGLE
MEGAHEX
SHE WAS VERY INSISTENT ABOUT SEEING THE PLACE, IS THAT COOL WITH YOU GUYS?
WELL, DOES SHE HAVE COVID?
NO, I DON'T HAVE COVID
OKAY THEN, IT'S ALRIGHT WITH ME, ROSIE, IS IT ALRIGHT WITH YOU?
CRACK
HELL YEAH, LET'S PARTY!
OH WOOOW THIS PLACE IS NICE, LEROY!!
I KNOW. I GOT LUCKY... THE OWNER IS A FRIEND OF MY DAD'S
GLUG GLUP
PPPPPBT!!!

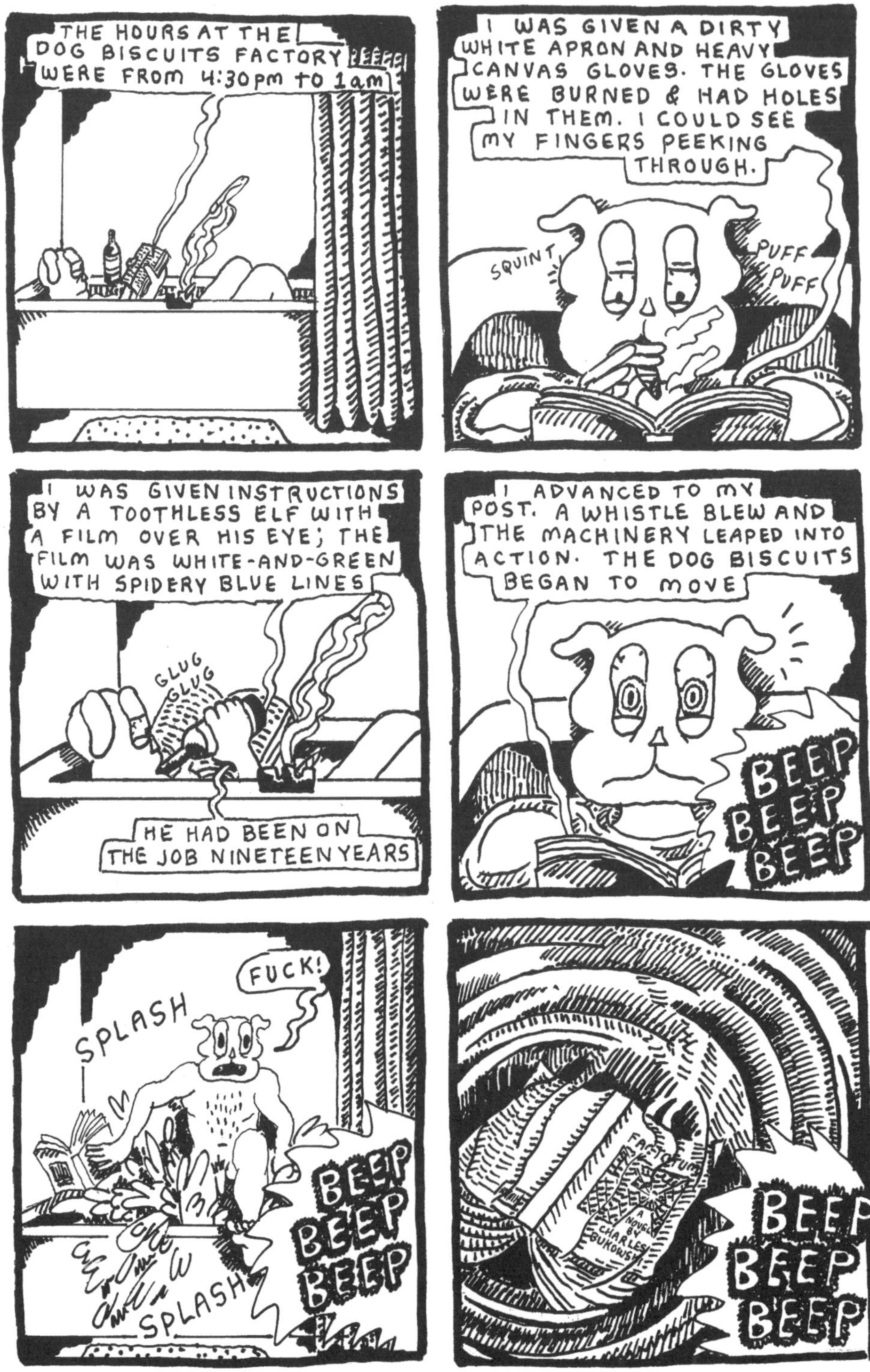
THE HOURS AT THE DOG BISCUITS FACTORY WERE FROM 4:30pm TO 1am
I WAS GIVEN A DIRTY WHITE APRON AND HEAVY CANVAS GLOVES. THE GLOVES WERE BURNED & HAD HOLES IN THEM. I COULD SEE MY FINGERS PEEKING THROUGH.
SQUINT
PUFF PUFF
I WAS GIVEN INSTRUCTIONS BY A TOOTHLESS ELF WITH A FILM OVER HIS EYE; THE FILM WAS WHITE-AND-GREEN WITH SPIDERY BLUE LINES
GLUG GLUG
HE HAD BEEN ON THE JOB NINETEEN YEARS
I ADVANCED TO MY POST. A WHISTLE BLEW AND THE MACHINERY LEAPED INTO ACTION. THE DOG BISCUITS BEGAN TO MOVE
BEEP BEEP BEEP
FUCK!
SPLASH
SPLASH
BEEP BEEP BEEP
BEEP BEEP BEEP

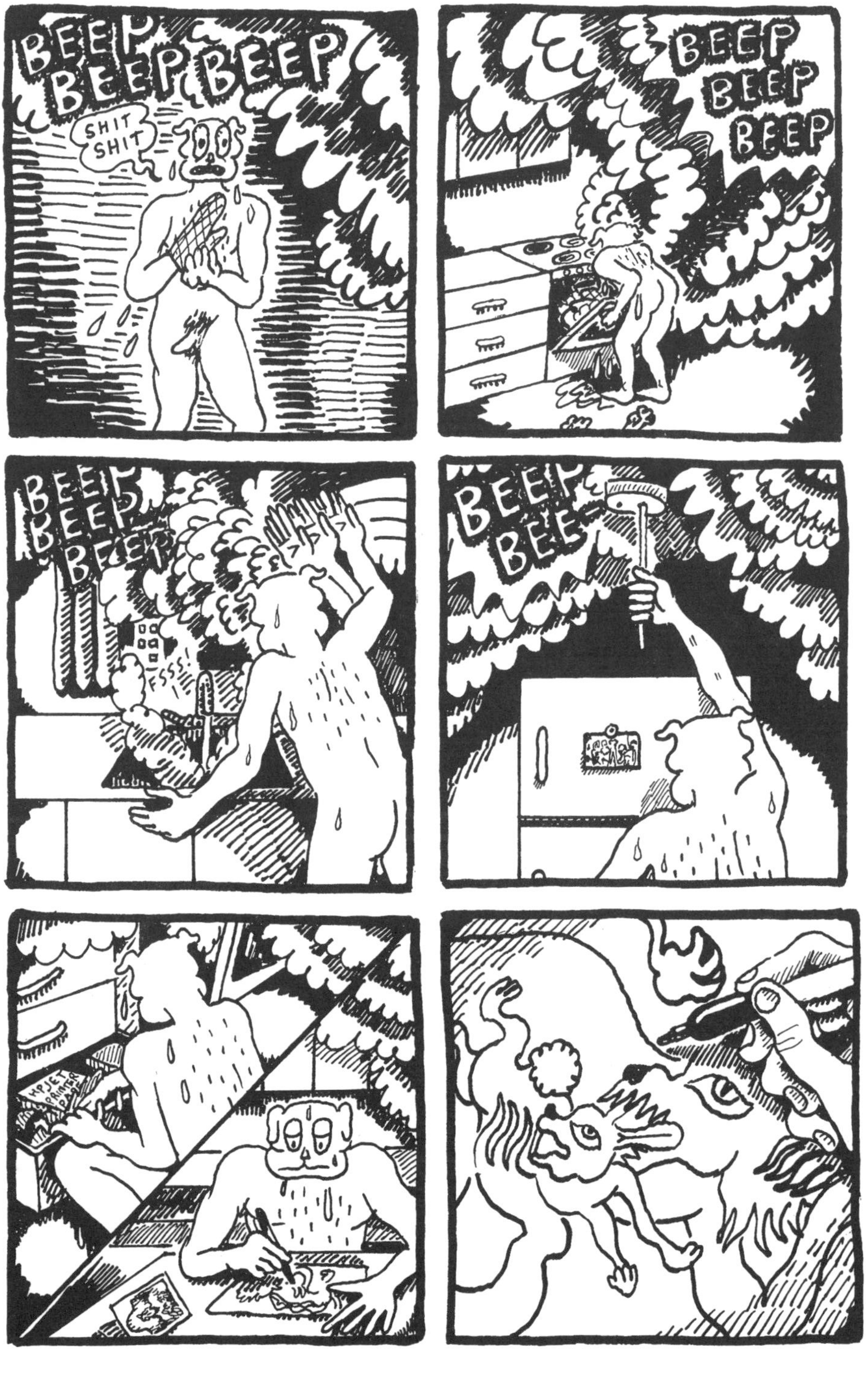
BEEP BEEP BEEP
SHIT SHIT
BEEP BEEP BEEP
BEEP BEEP BEEP
FSSS!
BEEP BEE-
HP JET PRINTER PAPER

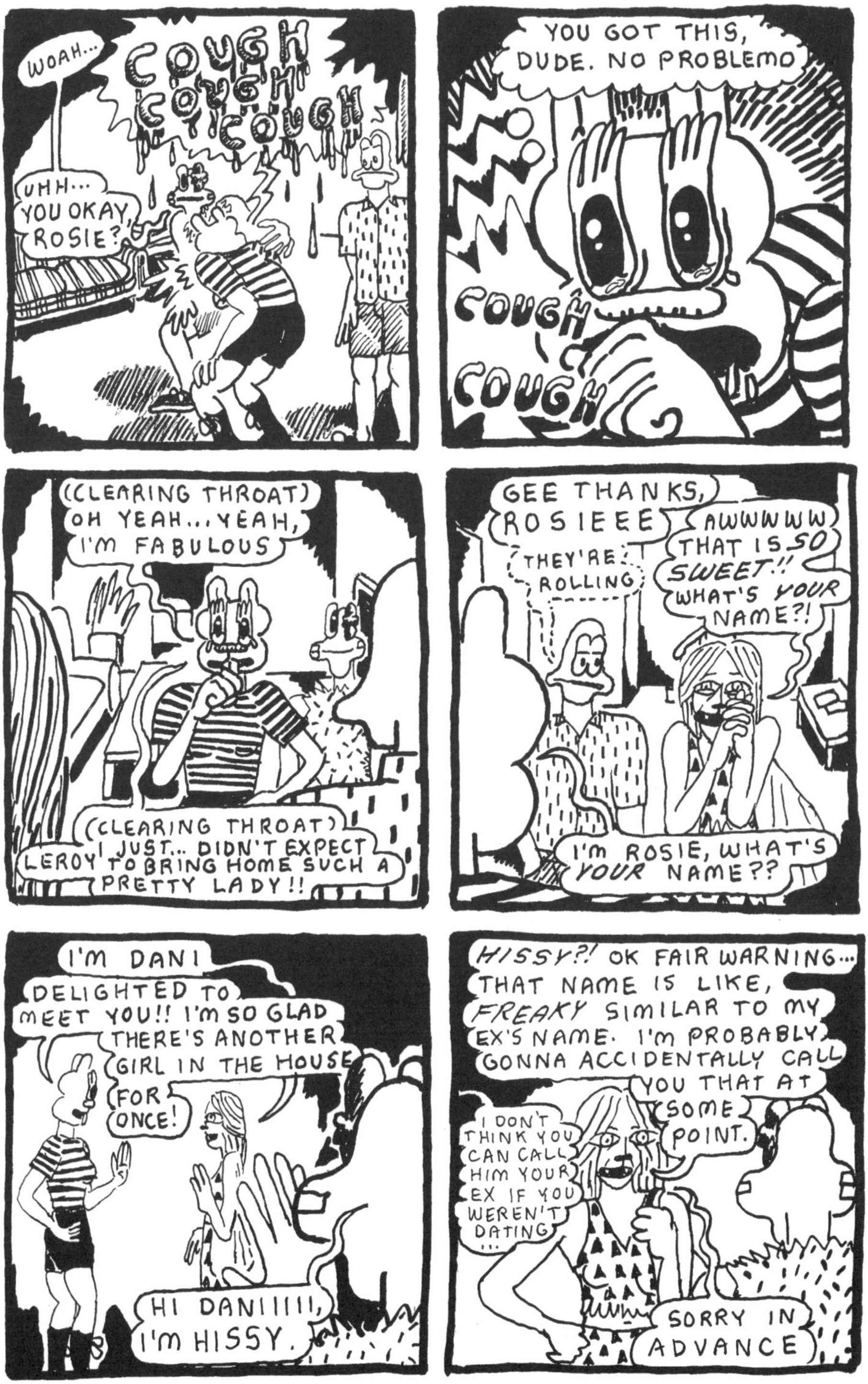
WOAH...
COUGH COUGH COUGH
UHH... YOU OKAY, ROSIE?
YOU GOT THIS, DUDE. NO PROBLEMO
COUGH
COUGH
(CLEARING THROAT) OH YEAH... YEAH, I'M FABULOUS
(CLEARING THROAT) I JUST... DIDN'T EXPECT LEROY TO BRING HOME SUCH A PRETTY LADY!!
GEE THANKS, ROSIEEE
THEY'RE ROLLING
AWWWWW THAT IS SO SWEET!! WHAT'S YOUR NAME?!
I'M ROSIE, WHAT'S YOUR NAME??
I'M DANI
DELIGHTED TO MEET YOU!! I'M SO GLAD THERE'S ANOTHER GIRL IN THE HOUSE FOR ONCE!
HI DANI!!!!, I'M HISSY.
HISSY?! OK FAIR WARNING... THAT NAME IS LIKE, FREAKY SIMILAR TO MY EX'S NAME. I'M PROBABLY GONNA ACCIDENTALLY CALL YOU THAT AT SOME POINT.
I DON'T THINK YOU CAN CALL HIM YOUR EX IF YOU WEREN'T DATING...
SORRY IN ADVANCE

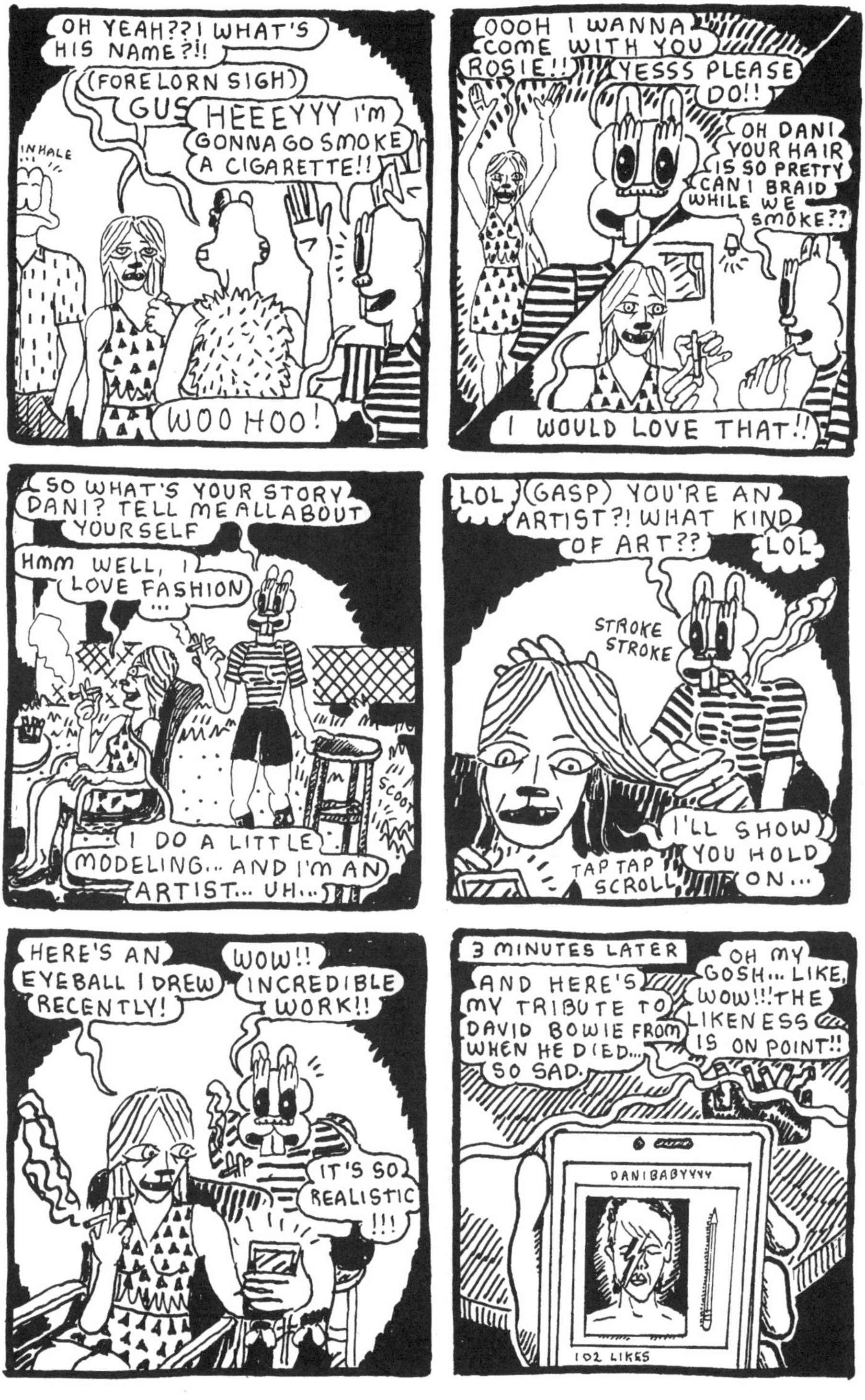
OH YEAH??! WHAT'S HIS NAME?!!
(FORELORN SIGH) GUS
HEEEYYY I'M GONNA GO SMOKE A CIGARETTE!!
INHALE
WOO HOO!
OOOH I WANNA COME WITH YOU ROSIE!!
YESSS PLEASE DO!!
OH DANI YOUR HAIR IS SO PRETTY CAN I BRAID WHILE WE SMOKE??
I WOULD LOVE THAT!!
SO WHAT'S YOUR STORY DANI? TELL ME ALL ABOUT YOURSELF
HMM WELL, I LOVE FASHION...
I DO A LITTLE MODELING... AND I'M AN ARTIST... UH...
SCOOT
LOL
(GASP) YOU'RE AN ARTIST?! WHAT KIND OF ART??
LOL
STROKE STROKE
TAP TAP SCROLL
I'LL SHOW YOU HOLD ON...
HERE'S AN EYEBALL I DREW RECENTLY!
WOW!! INCREDIBLE WORK!!
IT'S SO REALISTIC!!!
3 MINUTES LATER
AND HERE'S MY TRIBUTE TO DAVID BOWIE FROM WHEN HE DIED... SO SAD.
OH MY GOSH... LIKE, WOW!!! THE LIKENESS IS ON POINT!!
DANIBABYYYY
102 LIKES

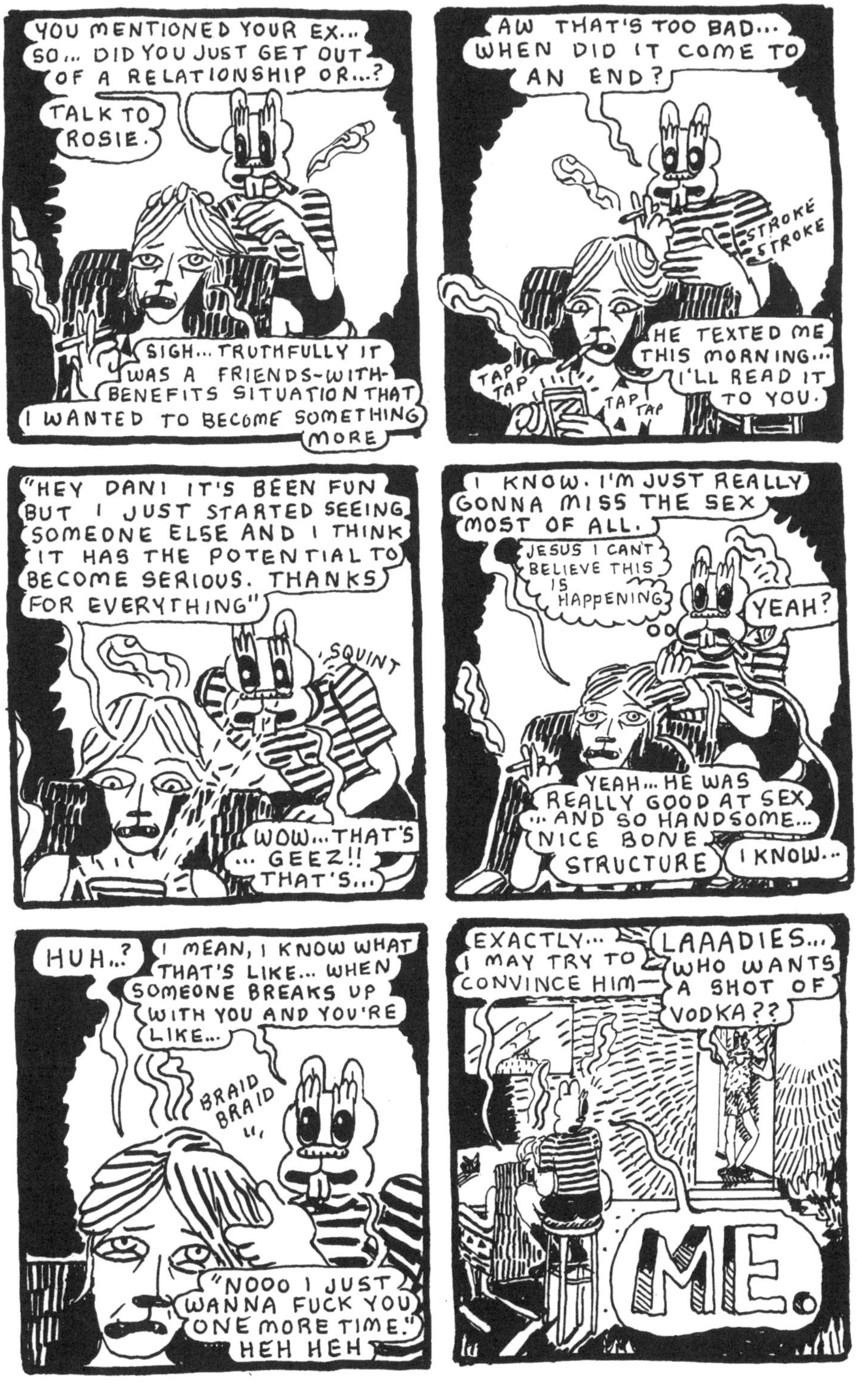
YOU MENTIONED YOUR EX... SO... DID YOU JUST GET OUT OF A RELATIONSHIP OR...?
TALK TO ROSIE.
SIGH... TRUTHFULLY IT WAS A FRIENDS-WITH-BENEFITS SITUATION THAT I WANTED TO BECOME SOMETHING MORE
AW THAT'S TOO BAD... WHEN DID IT COME TO AN END?
STROKE STROKE
TAP TAP
TAP TAP
HE TEXTED ME THIS MORNING... I'LL READ IT TO YOU.
"HEY DANI IT'S BEEN FUN BUT I JUST STARTED SEEING SOMEONE ELSE AND I THINK IT HAS THE POTENTIAL TO BECOME SERIOUS. THANKS FOR EVERYTHING"
SQUINT
WOW... THAT'S ... GEEZ!! THAT'S...
I KNOW. I'M JUST REALLY GONNA MISS THE SEX MOST OF ALL.
JESUS I CAN'T BELIEVE THIS IS HAPPENING
YEAH?
YEAH... HE WAS REALLY GOOD AT SEX ... AND SO HANDSOME... NICE BONE STRUCTURE
I KNOW...
HUH..?
I MEAN, I KNOW WHAT THAT'S LIKE... WHEN SOMEONE BREAKS UP WITH YOU AND YOU'RE LIKE...
BRAID BRAID
"NOOO I JUST WANNA FUCK YOU ONE MORE TIME." HEH HEH
EXACTLY... I MAY TRY TO CONVINCE HIM—
LAAADIES... WHO WANTS A SHOT OF VODKA??
ME.

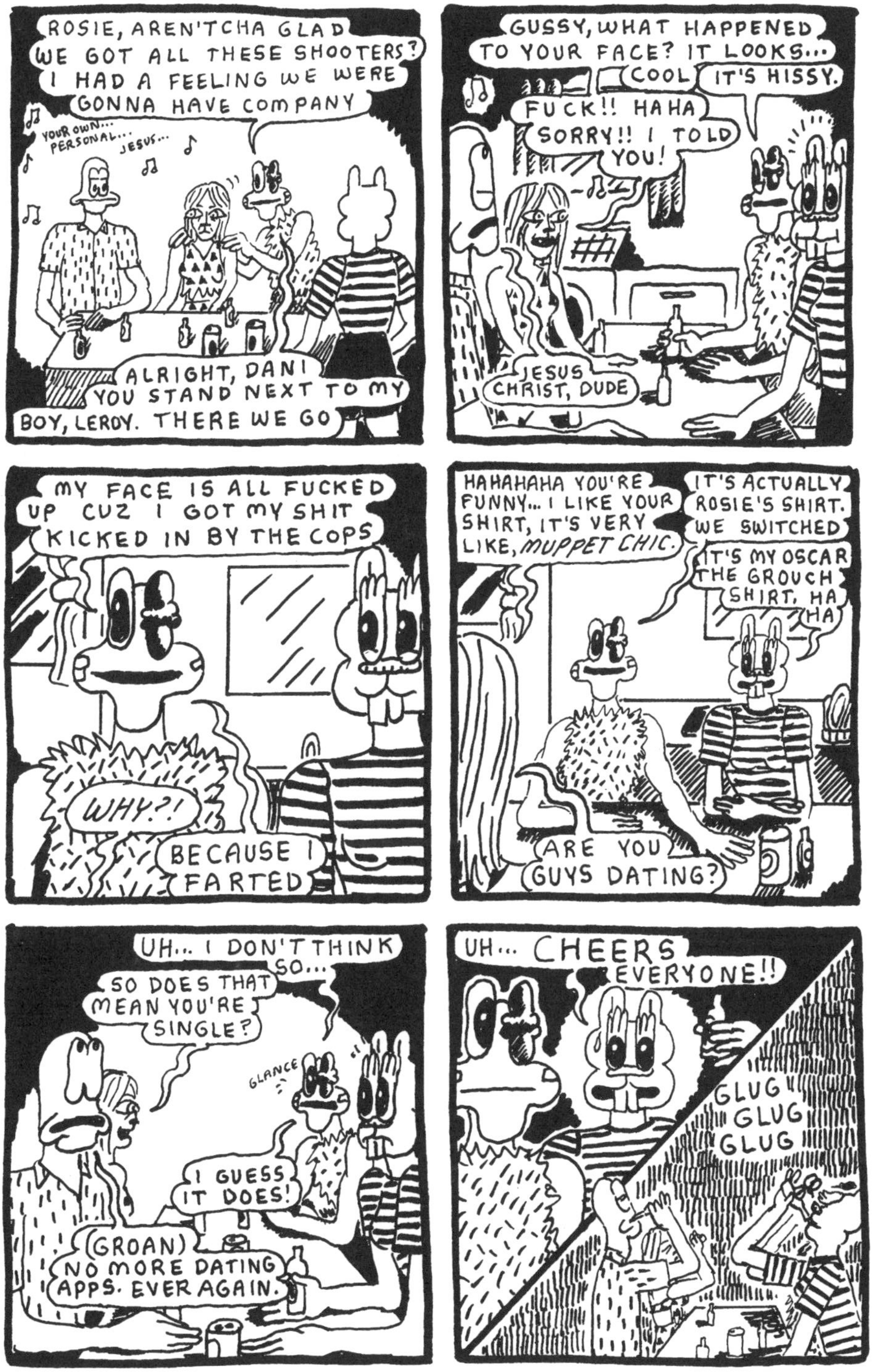

ROSIE, AREN'TCHA GLAD WE GOT ALL THESE SHOOTERS? I HAD A FEELING WE WERE GONNA HAVE COMPANY
YOUR OWN... PERSONAL... JESUS...
ALRIGHT, DANI YOU STAND NEXT TO MY BOY, LEROY. THERE WE GO
GUSSY, WHAT HAPPENED TO YOUR FACE? IT LOOKS...
COOL
IT'S HISSY.
FUCK!! HAHA SORRY!! I TOLD YOU!
JESUS CHRIST, DUDE
MY FACE IS ALL FUCKED UP CUZ I GOT MY SHIT KICKED IN BY THE COPS
WHY?!
BECAUSE I FARTED
HAHAHAHA YOU'RE FUNNY... I LIKE YOUR SHIRT, IT'S VERY LIKE, *MUPPET CHIC.*
IT'S ACTUALLY ROSIE'S SHIRT. WE SWITCHED
IT'S MY OSCAR THE GROUCH SHIRT, HA HA
ARE YOU GUYS DATING?
UH... I DON'T THINK SO...
SO DOES THAT MEAN YOU'RE SINGLE?
GLANCE
I GUESS IT DOES!
(GROAN) NO MORE DATING APPS. EVER AGAIN.
UH... CHEERS EVERYONE!!
GLUG GLUG GLUG

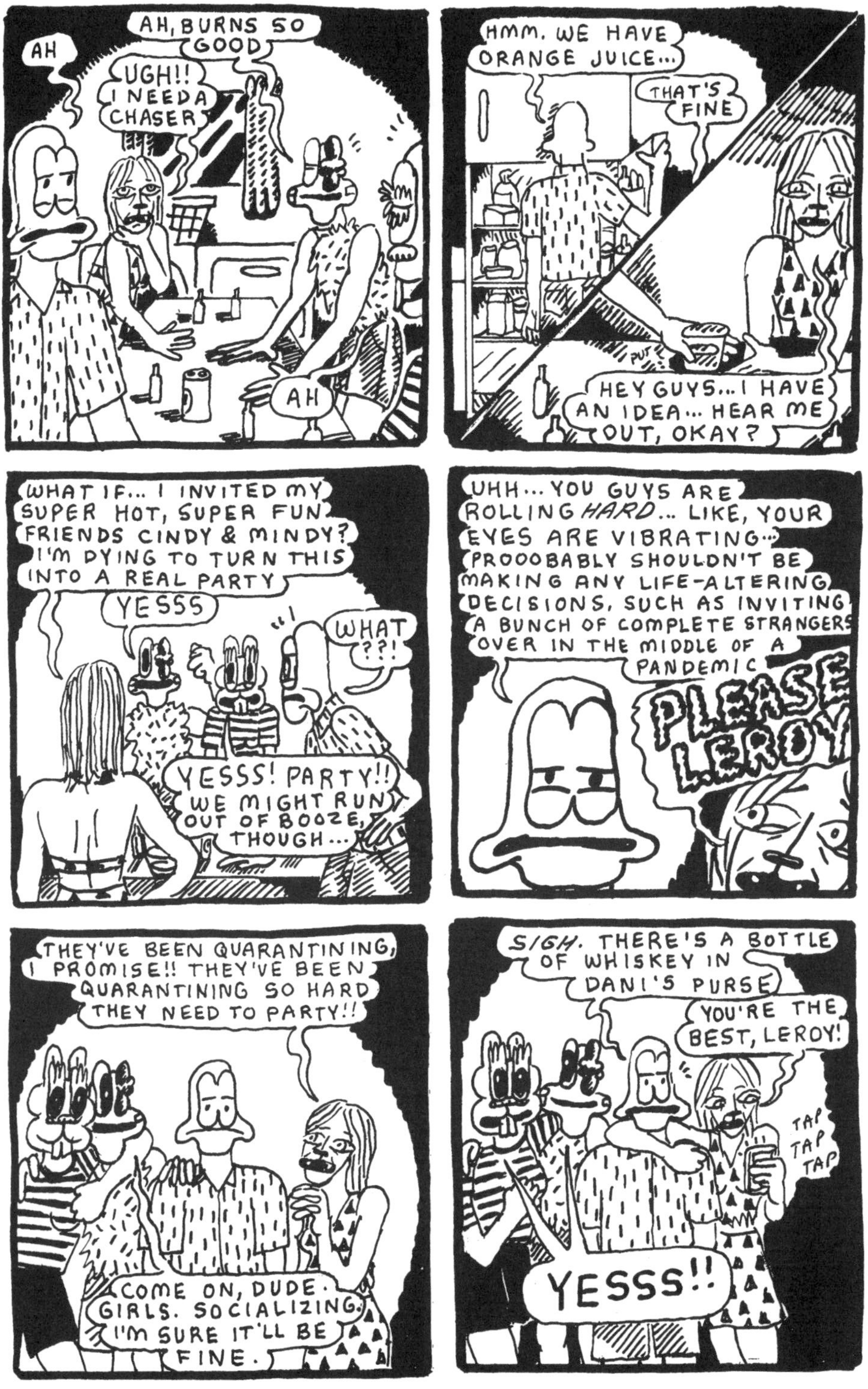
AH
AH, BURNS SO GOOD
UGH!! I NEEDA CHASER
AH
HMM. WE HAVE ORANGE JUICE...
THAT'S FINE
PUT
HEY GUYS... I HAVE AN IDEA... HEAR ME OUT, OKAY?
WHAT IF... I INVITED MY SUPER HOT, SUPER FUN FRIENDS CINDY & MINDY? I'M DYING TO TURN THIS INTO A REAL PARTY
YESSS
WHAT ??!
YESSS! PARTY!! WE MIGHT RUN OUT OF BOOZE, THOUGH...
UHH... YOU GUYS ARE ROLLING HARD... LIKE, YOUR EYES ARE VIBRATING... PROOOBABLY SHOULDN'T BE MAKING ANY LIFE-ALTERING DECISIONS, SUCH AS INVITING A BUNCH OF COMPLETE STRANGERS OVER IN THE MIDDLE OF A PANDEMIC
PLEASE LEROY
THEY'VE BEEN QUARANTINING, I PROMISE!! THEY'VE BEEN QUARANTINING SO HARD THEY NEED TO PARTY!!
COME ON, DUDE. GIRLS. SOCIALIZING. I'M SURE IT'LL BE FINE.
SIGH. THERE'S A BOTTLE OF WHISKEY IN DANI'S PURSE
YOU'RE THE BEST, LEROY!
TAP TAP TAP
YESSS!!

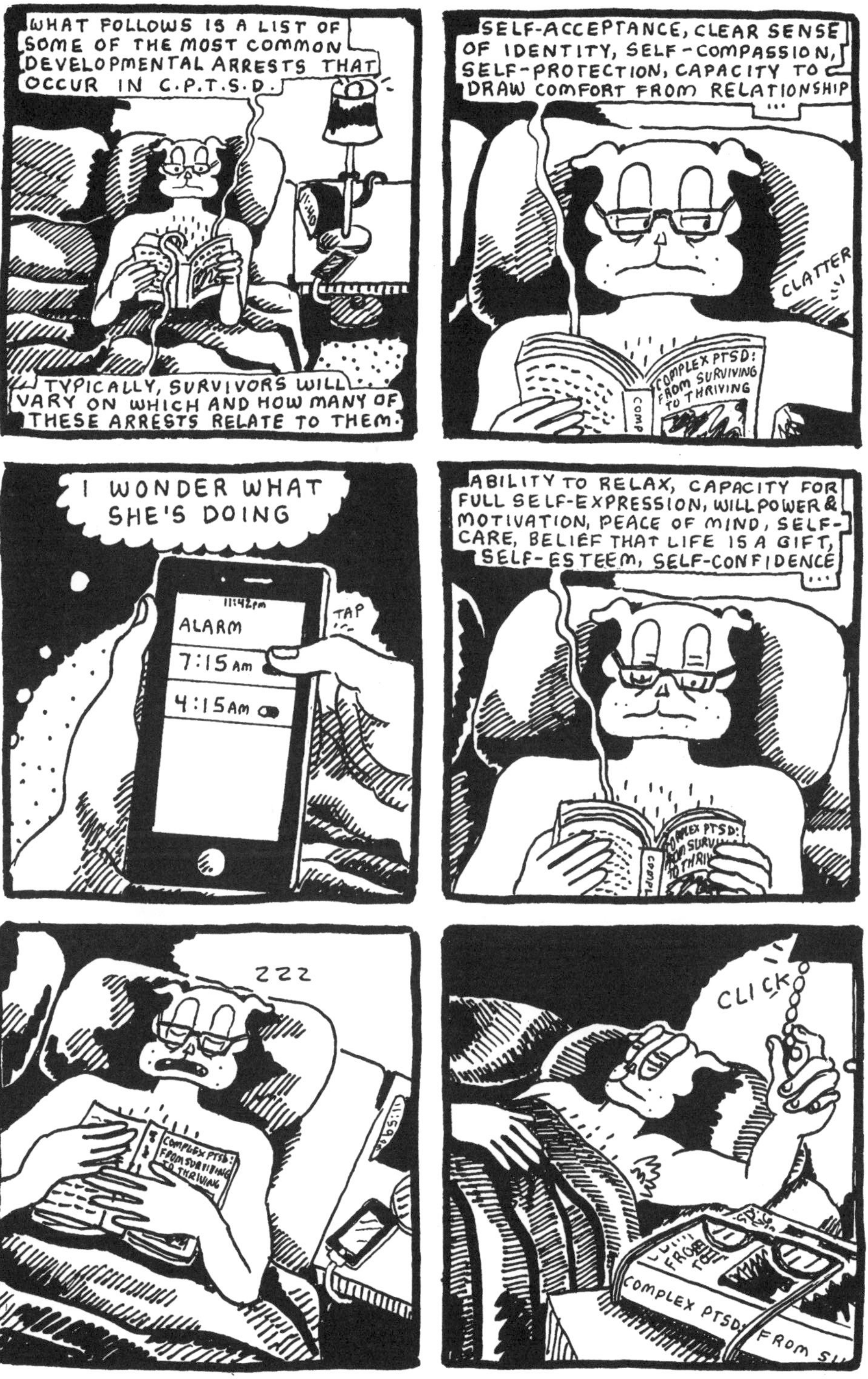
WHAT FOLLOWS IS A LIST OF SOME OF THE MOST COMMON DEVELOPMENTAL ARRESTS THAT OCCUR IN C.P.T.S.D.
TYPICALLY, SURVIVORS WILL VARY ON WHICH AND HOW MANY OF THESE ARRESTS RELATE TO THEM.
SELF-ACCEPTANCE, CLEAR SENSE OF IDENTITY, SELF-COMPASSION, SELF-PROTECTION, CAPACITY TO DRAW COMFORT FROM RELATIONSHIP ...
CLATTER
COMPLEX PTSD: FROM SURVIVING TO THRIVING
I WONDER WHAT SHE'S DOING
11:42pm
ALARM
7:15 AM
4:15 AM
TAP
ABILITY TO RELAX, CAPACITY FOR FULL SELF-EXPRESSION, WILLPOWER & MOTIVATION, PEACE OF MIND, SELF-CARE, BELIEF THAT LIFE IS A GIFT, SELF-ESTEEM, SELF-CONFIDENCE ...
COMPLEX PTSD: FROM SURVIVING TO THRIVING
ZZZ
COMPLEX PTSD: FROM SURVIVING TO THRIVING
CLICK
COMPLEX PTSD: FROM SU

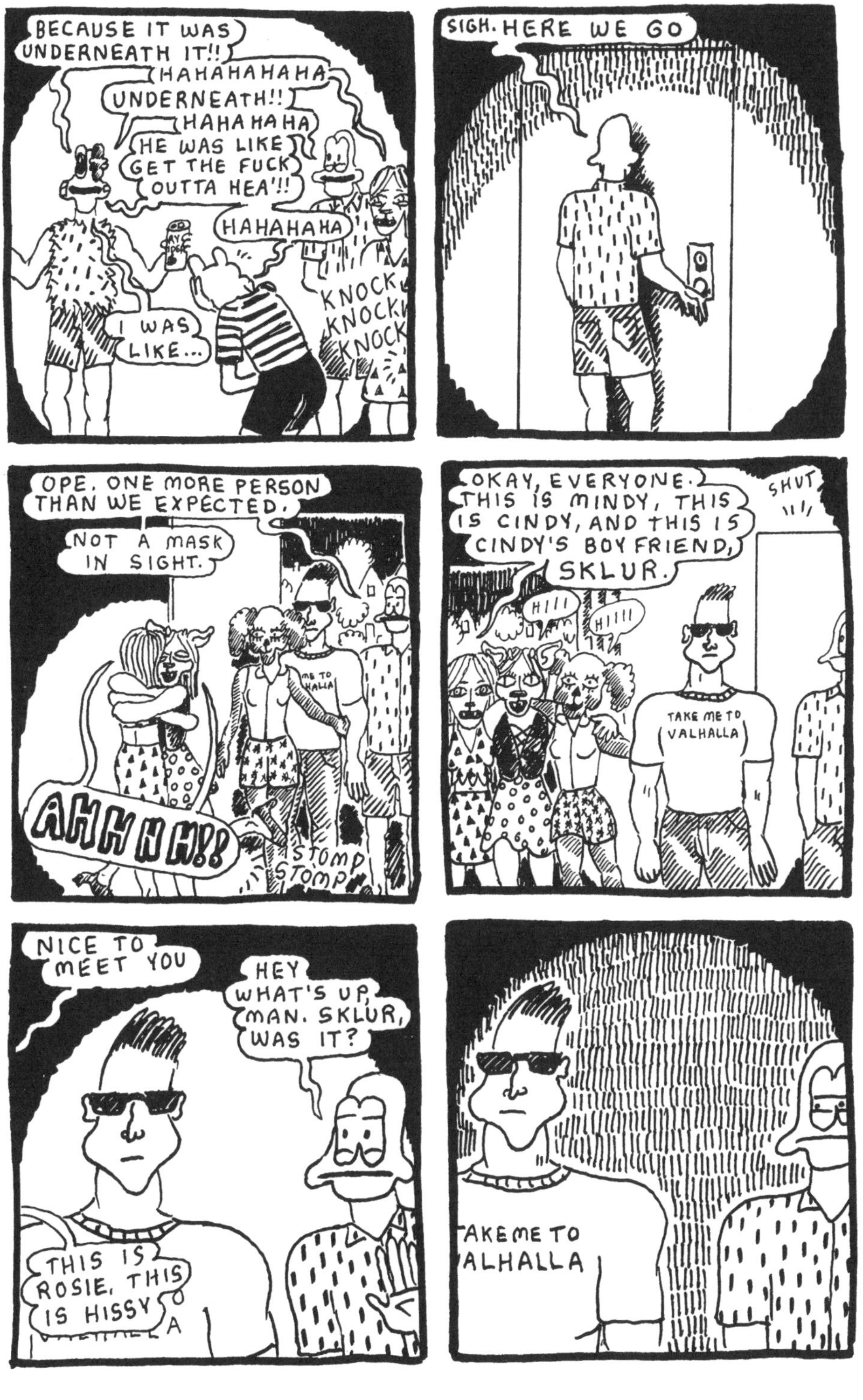
BECAUSE IT WAS UNDERNEATH IT!!
HAHAHAHAHAHA
UNDERNEATH!!
HAHAHAHAHA
HE WAS LIKE GET THE FUCK OUTTA HEA'!!
HAHAHAHA
I WAS LIKE...
KNOCK KNOCK KNOCK
SIGH. HERE WE GO
OPE. ONE MORE PERSON THAN WE EXPECTED.
NOT A MASK IN SIGHT.
AHHHH!!
STOMP STOMP
OKAY, EVERYONE. THIS IS MINDY, THIS IS CINDY, AND THIS IS CINDY'S BOYFRIEND, SKLUR.
SHUT
HI!!
HI!!!
TAKE ME TO VALHALLA
NICE TO MEET YOU
HEY WHAT'S UP, MAN. SKLUR, WAS IT?
THIS IS ROSIE, THIS IS HISSY
AKE ME TO
ALHALLA

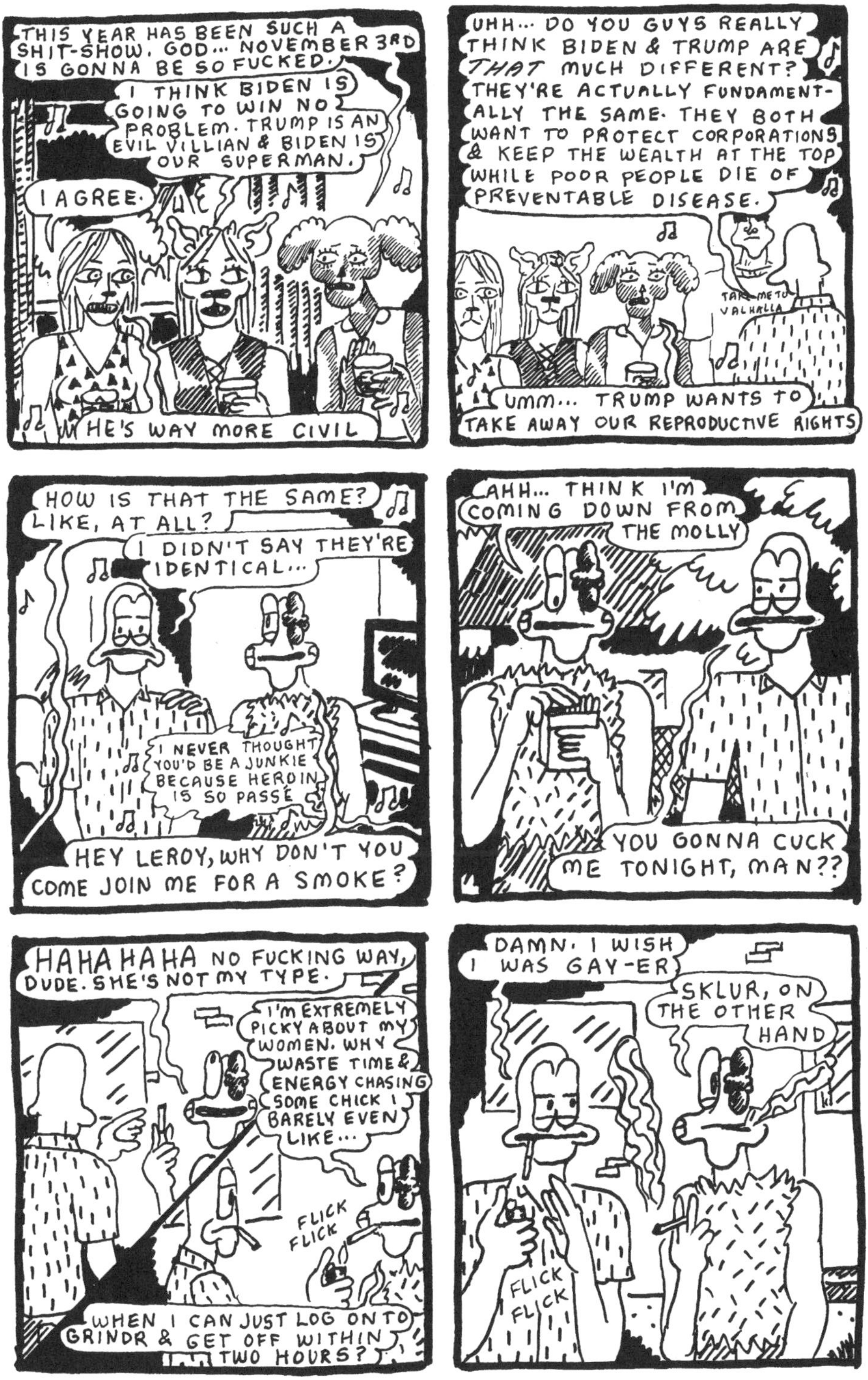
THIS YEAR HAS BEEN SUCH A SHIT-SHOW. GOD... NOVEMBER 3RD IS GONNA BE SO FUCKED.
I THINK BIDEN IS GOING TO WIN NO PROBLEM. TRUMP IS AN EVIL VILLIAN & BIDEN IS OUR SUPERMAN.
I AGREE.
HE'S WAY MORE CIVIL
UHH... DO YOU GUYS REALLY THINK BIDEN & TRUMP ARE THAT MUCH DIFFERENT? THEY'RE ACTUALLY FUNDAMENTALLY THE SAME. THEY BOTH WANT TO PROTECT CORPORATIONS & KEEP THE WEALTH AT THE TOP WHILE POOR PEOPLE DIE OF PREVENTABLE DISEASE.
TAKE ME TO VALHALLA
UMM... TRUMP WANTS TO TAKE AWAY OUR REPRODUCTIVE RIGHTS
HOW IS THAT THE SAME? LIKE, AT ALL?
I DIDN'T SAY THEY'RE IDENTICAL...
I NEVER THOUGHT YOU'D BE A JUNKIE BECAUSE HEROIN IS SO PASSÉ
HEY LEROY, WHY DON'T YOU COME JOIN ME FOR A SMOKE?
AHH... THINK I'M COMING DOWN FROM THE MOLLY
YOU GONNA CUCK ME TONIGHT, MAN??
HAHAHAHA NO FUCKING WAY, DUDE. SHE'S NOT MY TYPE.
I'M EXTREMELY PICKY ABOUT MY WOMEN. WHY WASTE TIME & ENERGY CHASING SOME CHICK I BARELY EVEN LIKE...
FLICK FLICK
WHEN I CAN JUST LOG ONTO GRINDR & GET OFF WITHIN TWO HOURS?
DAMN. I WISH I WAS GAY-ER
SKLUR, ON THE OTHER HAND
FLICK FLICK

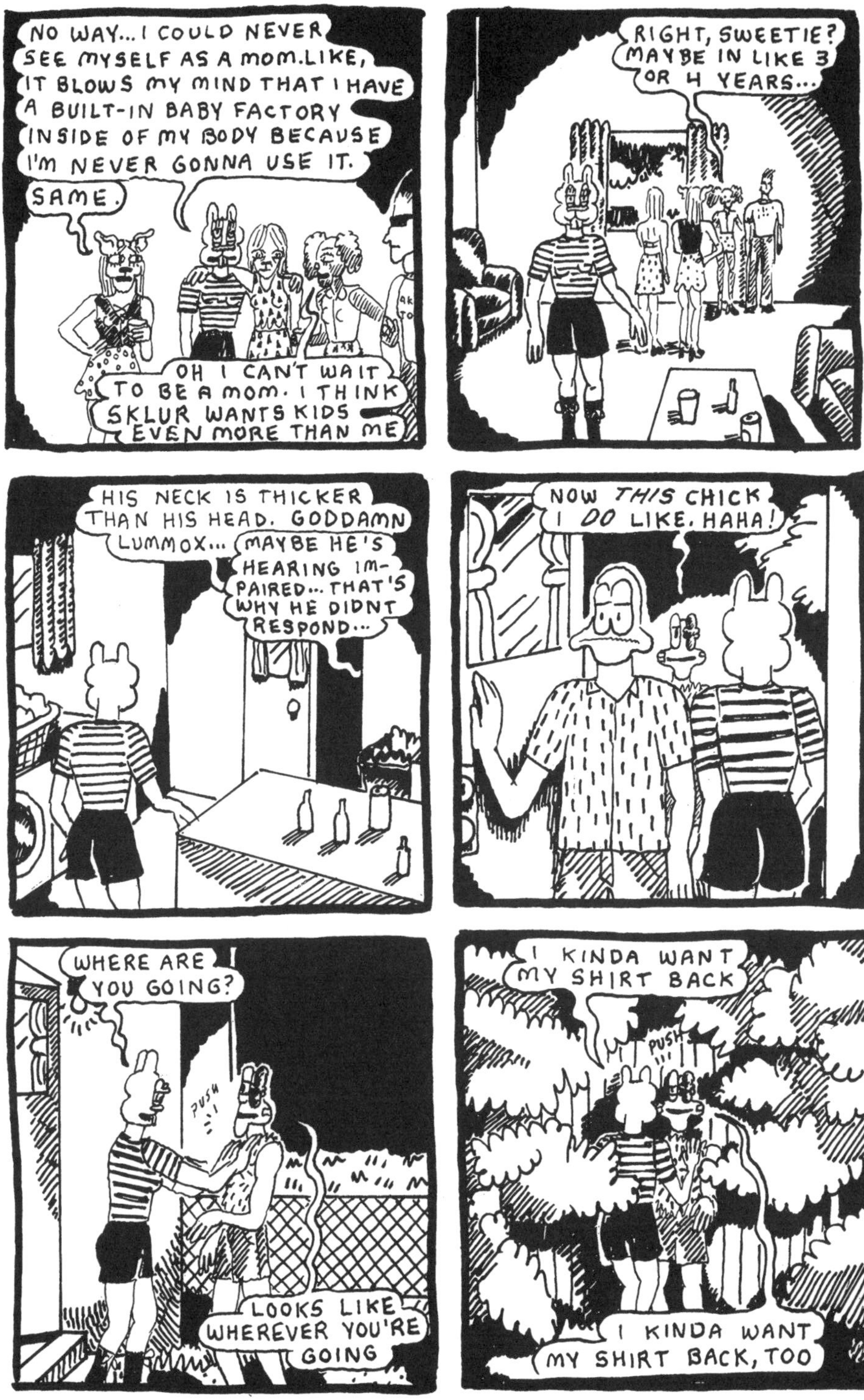
NO WAY... I COULD NEVER SEE MYSELF AS A MOM. LIKE, IT BLOWS MY MIND THAT I HAVE A BUILT-IN BABY FACTORY INSIDE OF MY BODY BECAUSE I'M NEVER GONNA USE IT.
SAME.
OH I CAN'T WAIT TO BE A MOM. I THINK SKLUR WANTS KIDS EVEN MORE THAN ME
RIGHT, SWEETIE? MAYBE IN LIKE 3 OR 4 YEARS...
HIS NECK IS THICKER THAN HIS HEAD. GODDAMN LUMMOX...
MAYBE HE'S HEARING IM-PAIRED... THAT'S WHY HE DIDNT RESPOND...
NOW THIS CHICK I DO LIKE. HAHA!
WHERE ARE YOU GOING?
PUSH
LOOKS LIKE WHEREVER YOU'RE GOING
I KINDA WANT MY SHIRT BACK
PUSH
I KINDA WANT MY SHIRT BACK, TOO

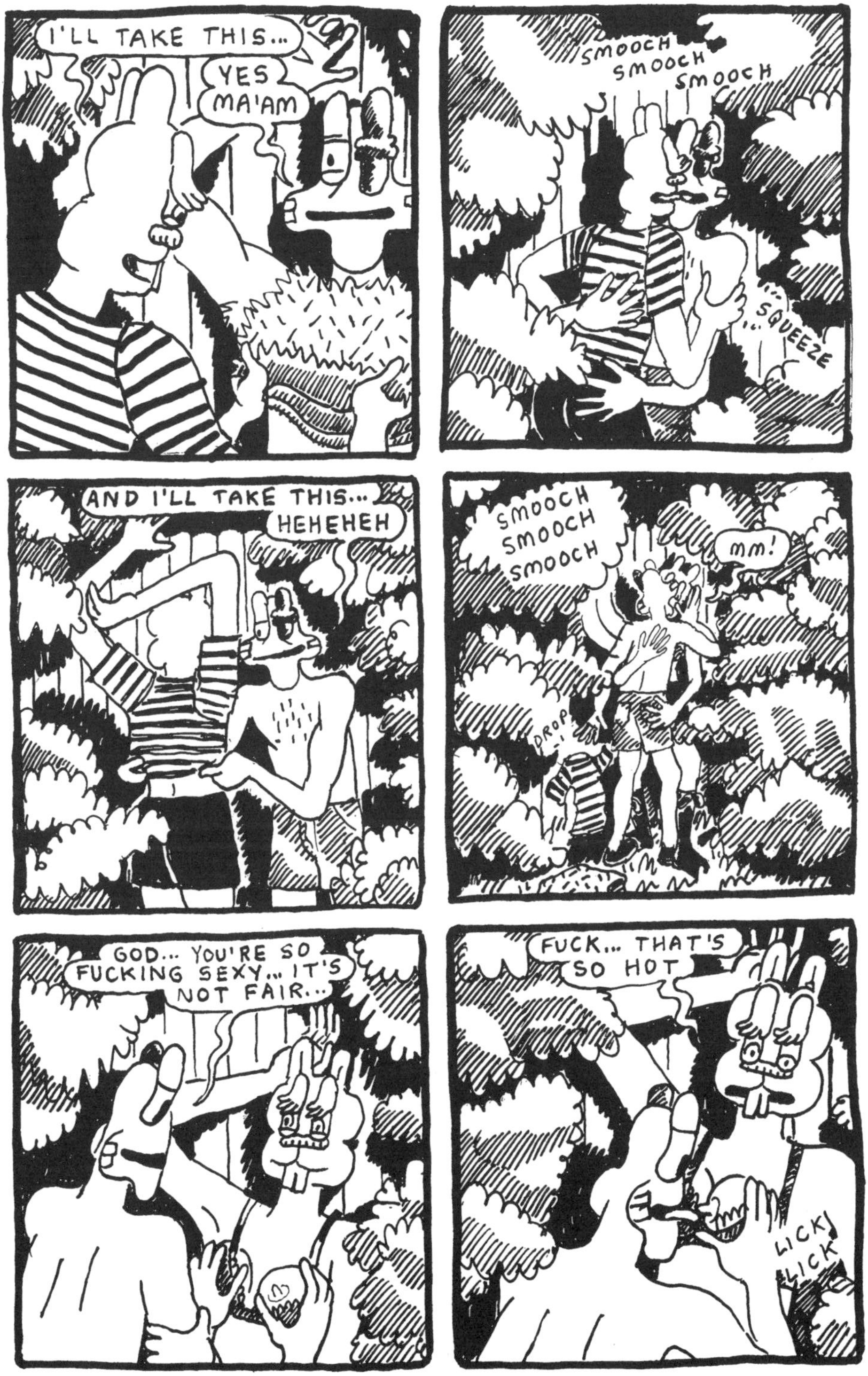
I'LL TAKE THIS...
YES MA'AM
SMOOCH SMOOCH SMOOCH
SQUEEZE
AND I'LL TAKE THIS...
HEHEHEH
SMOOCH SMOOCH SMOOCH
mm!
DROP
GOD... YOU'RE SO FUCKING SEXY... IT'S NOT FAIR...
FUCK... THAT'S SO HOT
LICK LICK

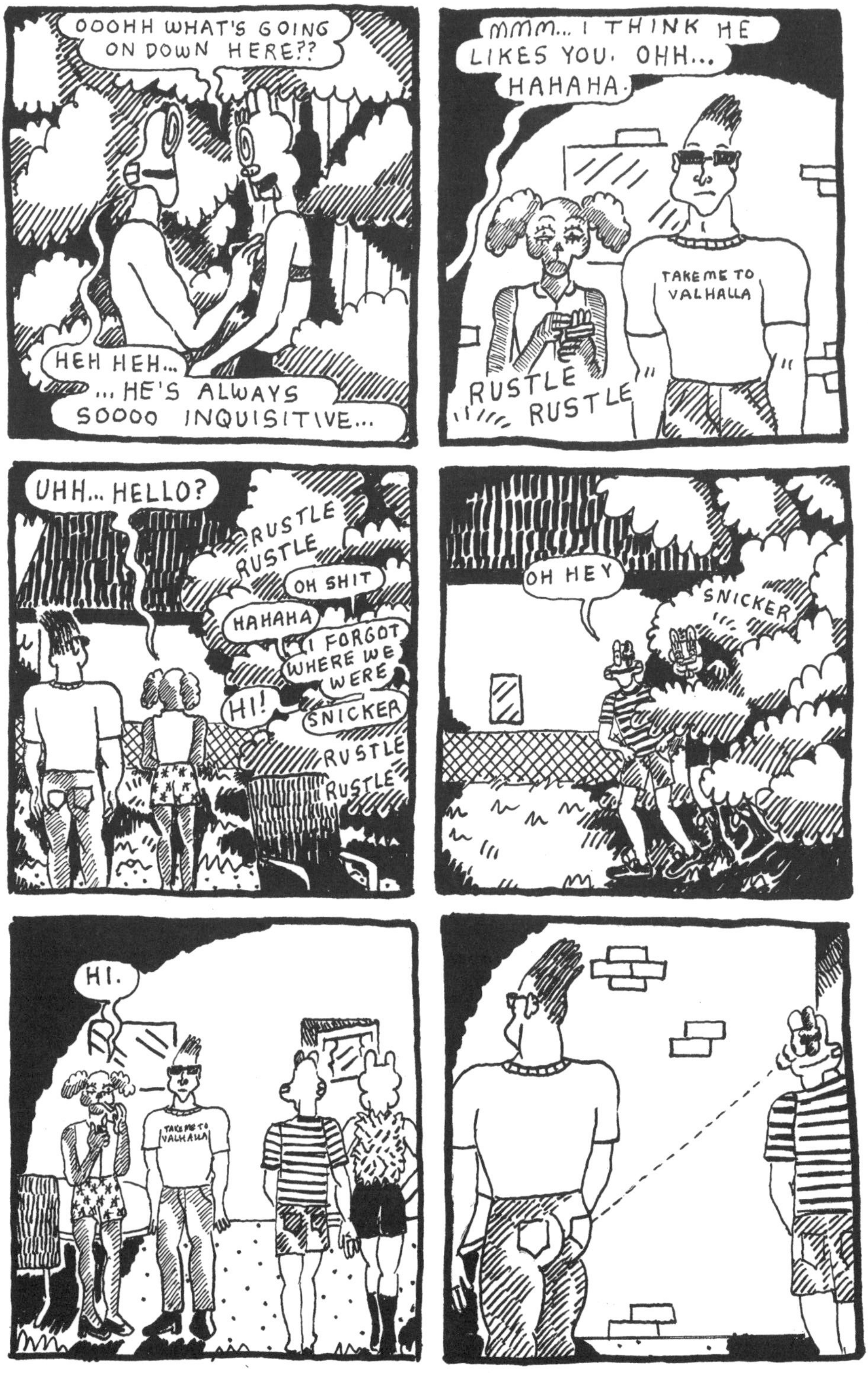
OOOHH WHAT'S GOING ON DOWN HERE??
HEH HEH...
... HE'S ALWAYS SOOOO INQUISITIVE...
MMM... I THINK HE LIKES YOU. OHH... HAHAHA.
TAKE ME TO VALHALLA
RUSTLE RUSTLE
UHH... HELLO?
RUSTLE RUSTLE
OH SHIT
HAHAHA
I FORGOT WHERE WE WERE
HI!
SNICKER
RUSTLE RUSTLE
OH HEY
SNICKER
HI.
TAKE ME TO VALHALLA

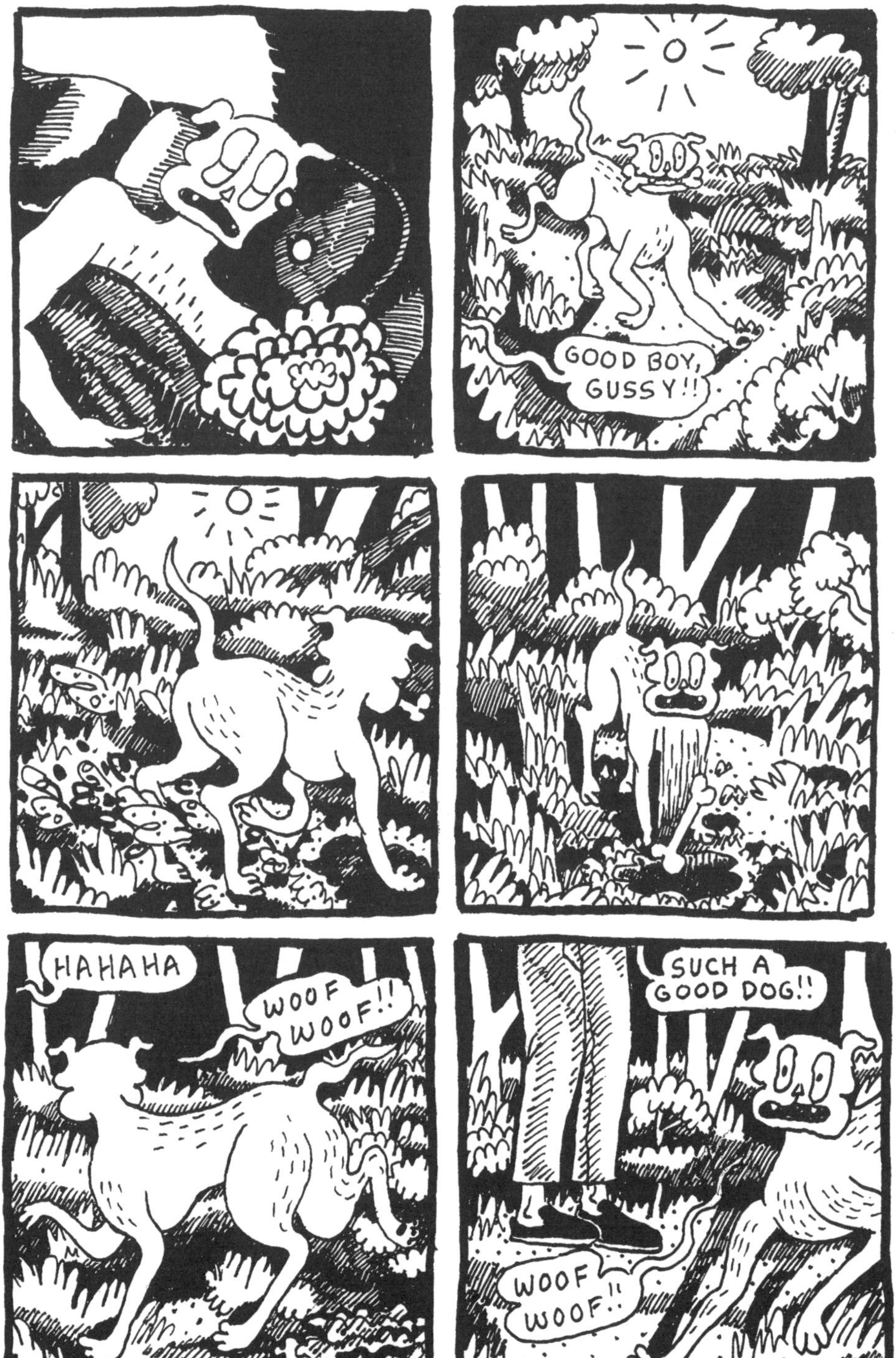
GOOD BOY, GUSSY!!
HAHAHA
WOOF WOOF!!
SUCH A GOOD DOG!!
WOOF WOOF!!

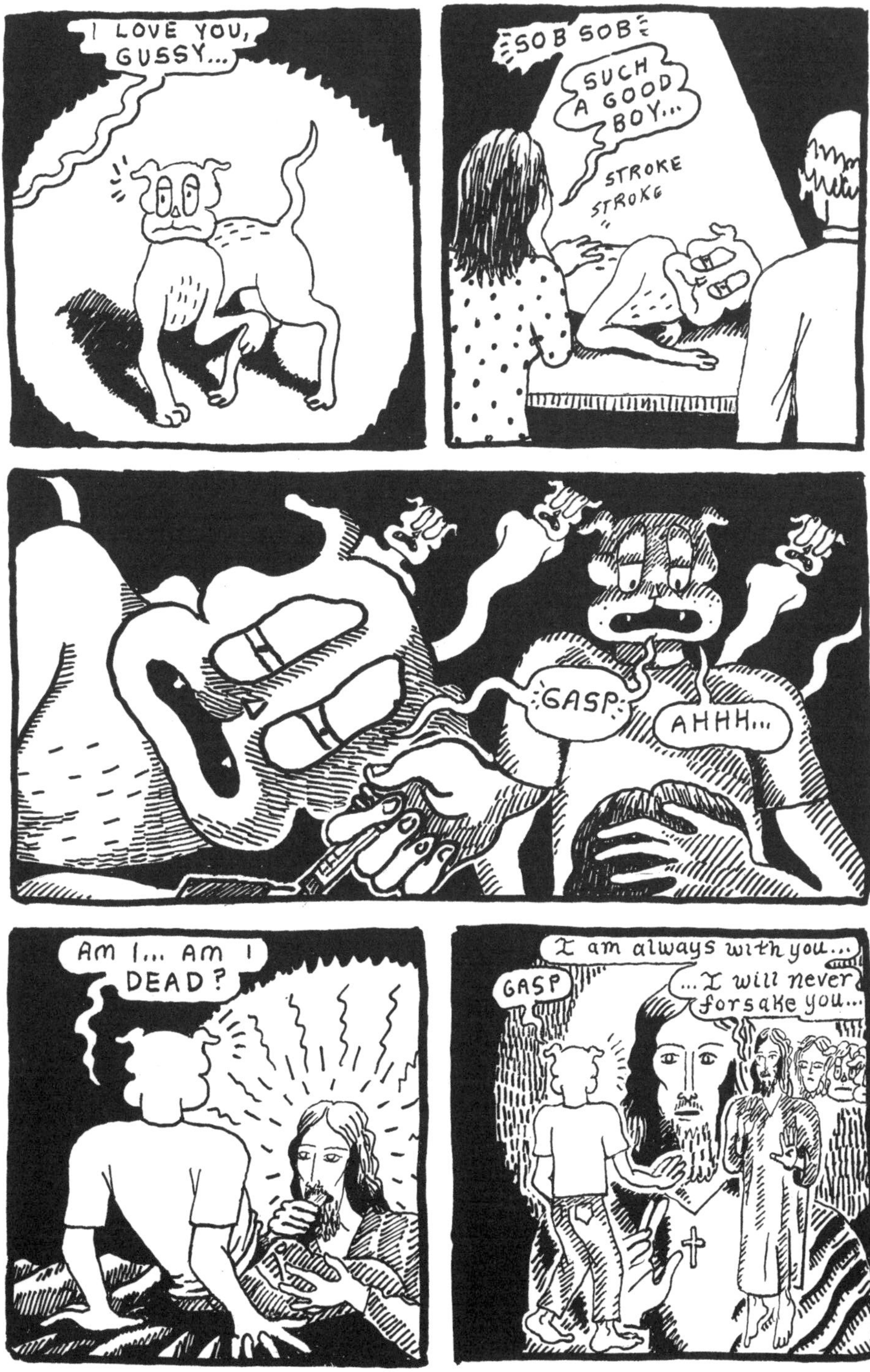
I LOVE YOU, GUSSY...
SOB SOB
SUCH A GOOD BOY...
STROKE STROKE
GASP
AHHH...
Am I... Am I DEAD?
I am always with you...
GASP
...I will never forsake you...

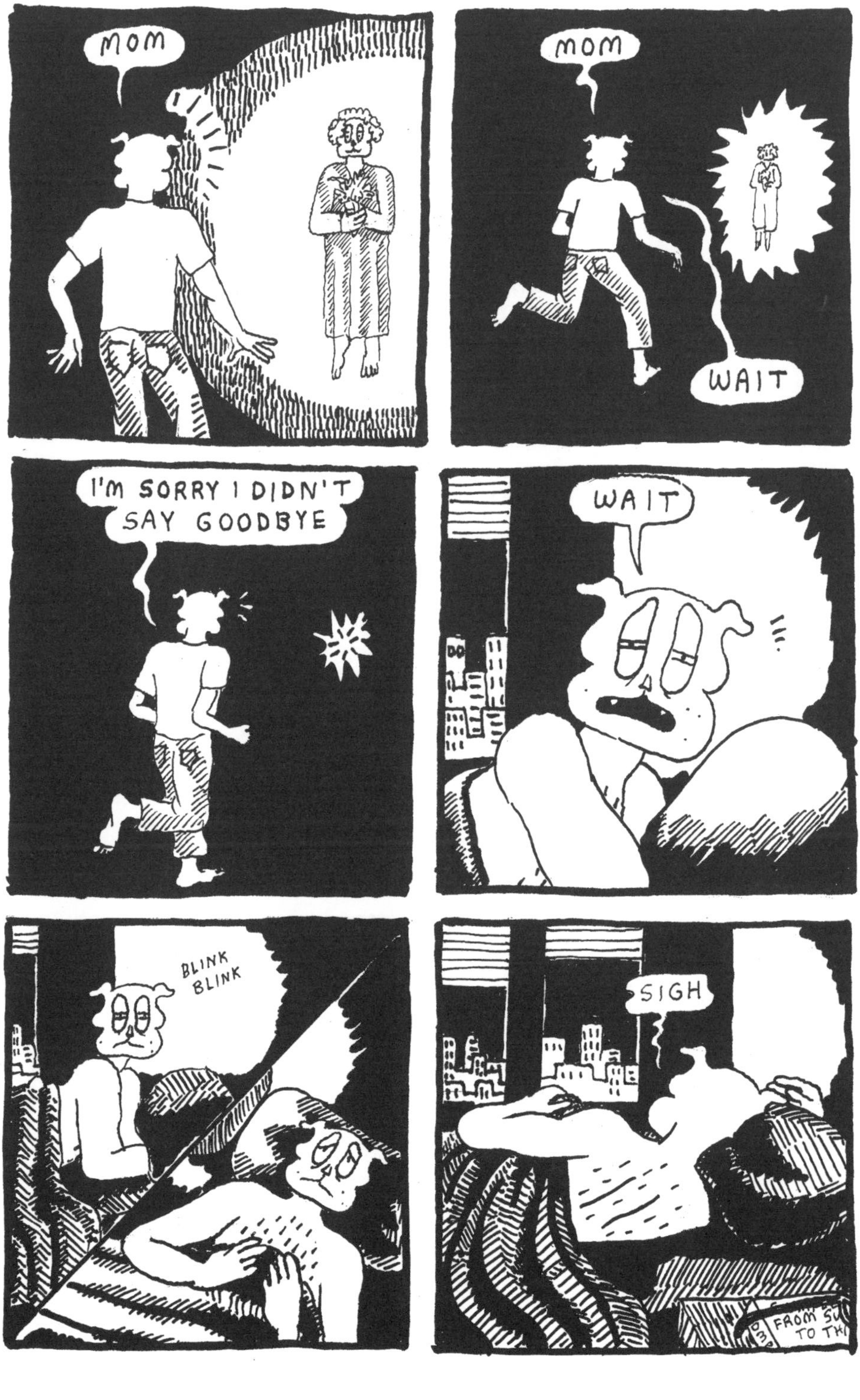
MOM
MOM
WAIT
I'M SORRY I DIDN'T SAY GOODBYE
WAIT
BLINK BLINK
SIGH

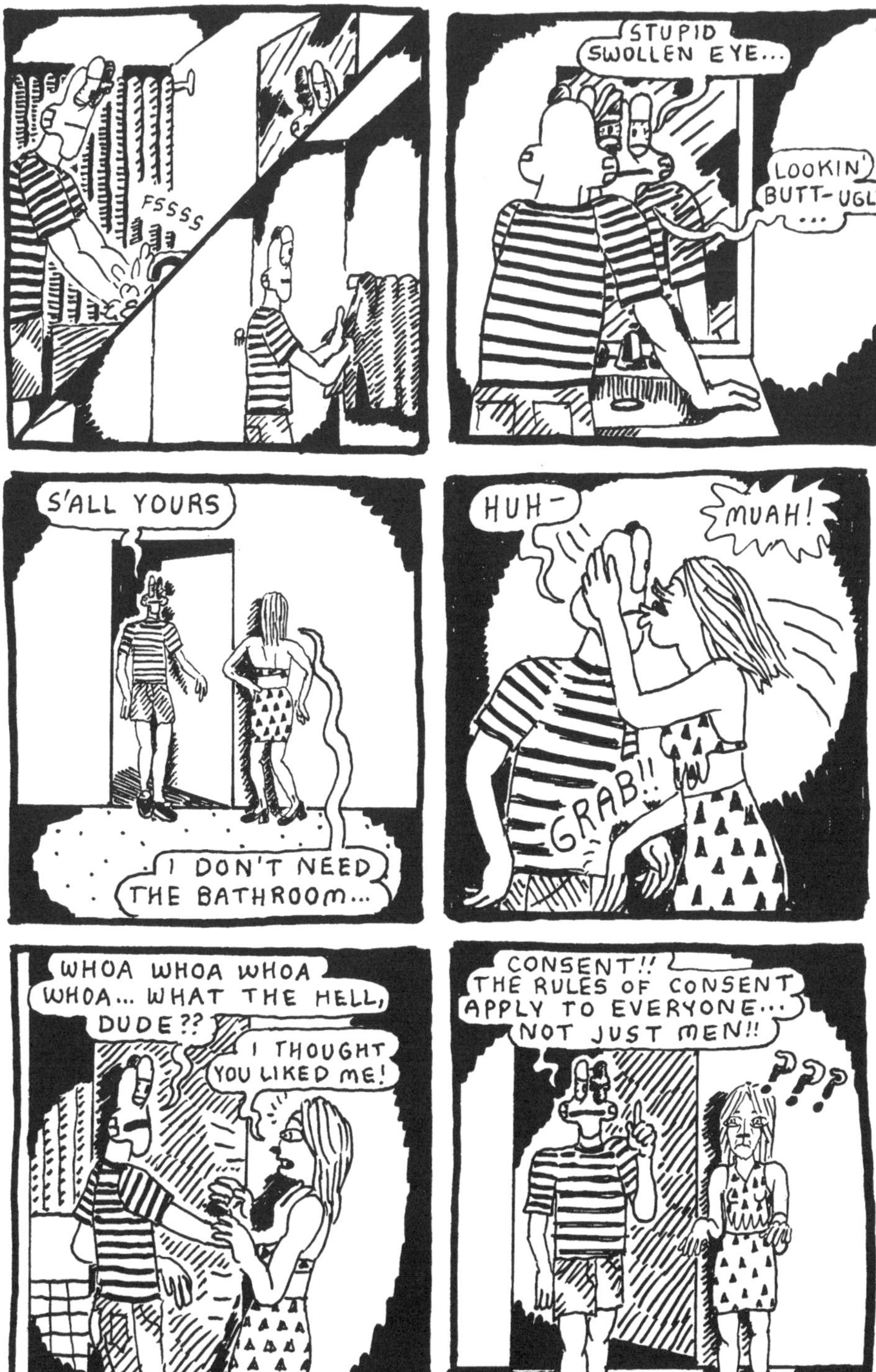
FSSSS
STUPID SWOLLEN EYE...
LOOKIN' BUTT-UGLY ...
S'ALL YOURS
I DON'T NEED THE BATHROOM...
HUH-
MUAH!
GRAB!!
WHOA WHOA WHOA WHOA... WHAT THE HELL, DUDE??
I THOUGHT YOU LIKED ME!
CONSENT!! THE RULES OF CONSENT APPLY TO EVERYONE... NOT JUST MEN!!
???

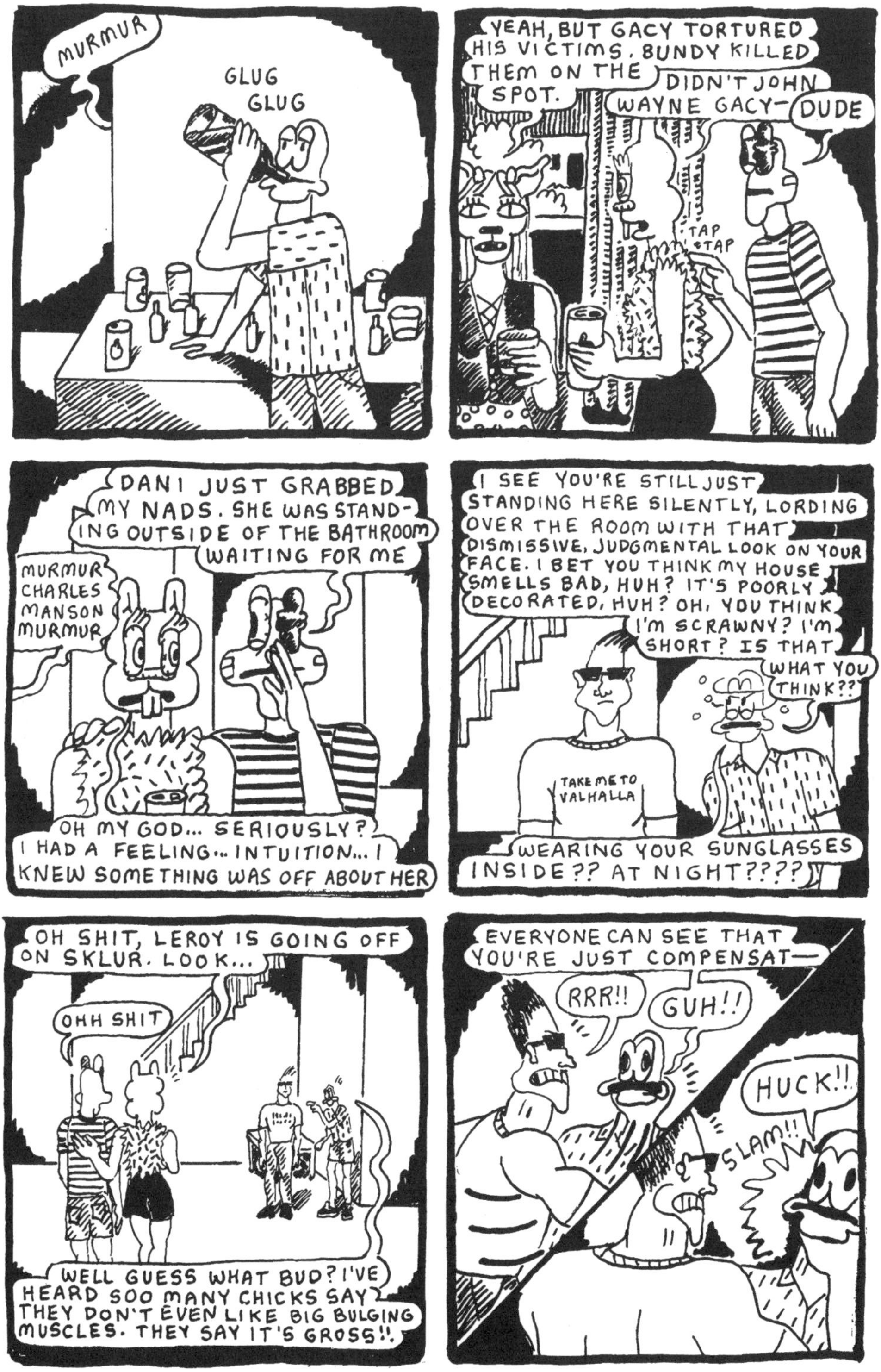
MURMUR
GLUG
GLUG
YEAH, BUT GACY TORTURED HIS VICTIMS. BUNDY KILLED THEM ON THE SPOT.
DIDN'T JOHN WAYNE GACY—
DUDE
TAP
TAP
DANI JUST GRABBED MY NADS. SHE WAS STANDING OUTSIDE OF THE BATHROOM WAITING FOR ME
MURMUR CHARLES MANSON MURMUR
OH MY GOD... SERIOUSLY? I HAD A FEELING... INTUITION... I KNEW SOMETHING WAS OFF ABOUT HER
I SEE YOU'RE STILL JUST STANDING HERE SILENTLY, LORDING OVER THE ROOM WITH THAT DISMISSIVE, JUDGMENTAL LOOK ON YOUR FACE. I BET YOU THINK MY HOUSE SMELLS BAD, HUH? IT'S POORLY DECORATED, HUH? OH, YOU THINK I'M SCRAWNY? I'M SHORT? IS THAT WHAT YOU THINK??
TAKE ME TO VALHALLA
WEARING YOUR SUNGLASSES INSIDE?? AT NIGHT????
OH SHIT, LEROY IS GOING OFF ON SKLUR. LOOK...
OHH SHIT
WELL GUESS WHAT BUD? I'VE HEARD SOO MANY CHICKS SAY THEY DON'T EVEN LIKE BIG BULGING MUSCLES. THEY SAY IT'S GROSS!!
EVERYONE CAN SEE THAT YOU'RE JUST COMPENSAT—
RRR!!
GUH!!
HUCK!!
SLAM!!

UGH!! CHK...

HERE IS MY HAND... GRIPPING THE NECK OF A MAN... WHIPPED BY THE WRATH OF HIS OWN INADEQUACY. THE STING OF IT BETRAYS YOU... IT IS OBVIOUS TO ALL EXCEPT THE COVETOUS ONE... THAT HIS SHARP TONGUE IS A CONSEQUENCE OF SORROW, DISAPPOINT-MENT, DISILLUSIONMENT IN THE MATER-IAL WORLD; AND THE HUBRISTIC VIOLENCE HE INFLICTS UPON HIS NEIGHBOR SPRINGS FORTH FROM A PLACE OF DEEP, INSURMOUNTABLE SADNESS.

TO EXIST IN THIS WORLD IS TO YEARN, TO SEEK, TO BECOME DISILLU-SIONED. WHAT WE ARE LOOKING FOR DOES NOT EXIST... THE FANTASIES WE CONSTRUCT AS CHILDREN ARE MIND GAMES; SURVIVAL MECHANISMS; THEY INSPIRE US TO ENDURE REALITY, TO PROLIFERATE THE HUMAN RACE.

CHOKE
SPUTTER

BUT AS LIFE PROCEEDS... AS WE MOVE THROUGH THE TEDIUM OF EACH DAY... OF EACH MONTH... OF EACH PASSING YEAR... THESE ILLUSIONS DISSOLVE UNTIL WE ARE LEFT ONLY WITH AN ACHING, STINGING VOID; THE AGONY OF WHICH CAUSES ONE TO BRUTALLY, VIOLENTLY COVET WHAT OTHERS HAVE UNTIL ONE'S OWN SOUL IS IRREPARABLY DESTROYED; DAY BY DAY, IT IS BITTEN & RIPPED AWAY BY THE HOWLING WINDS OF REGRET.

I DO PITY YOU.

GASP!!!

SLIDE

YOU GOOD, LEROY?

OH MY GOSH...

WHEEZE COUGH COUGH COUGH

WHEEZE COUGH COUGH

CLEARING THROAT MUCH RESPECT BROTHAH

PAT PAT

ALEX GRAHAM

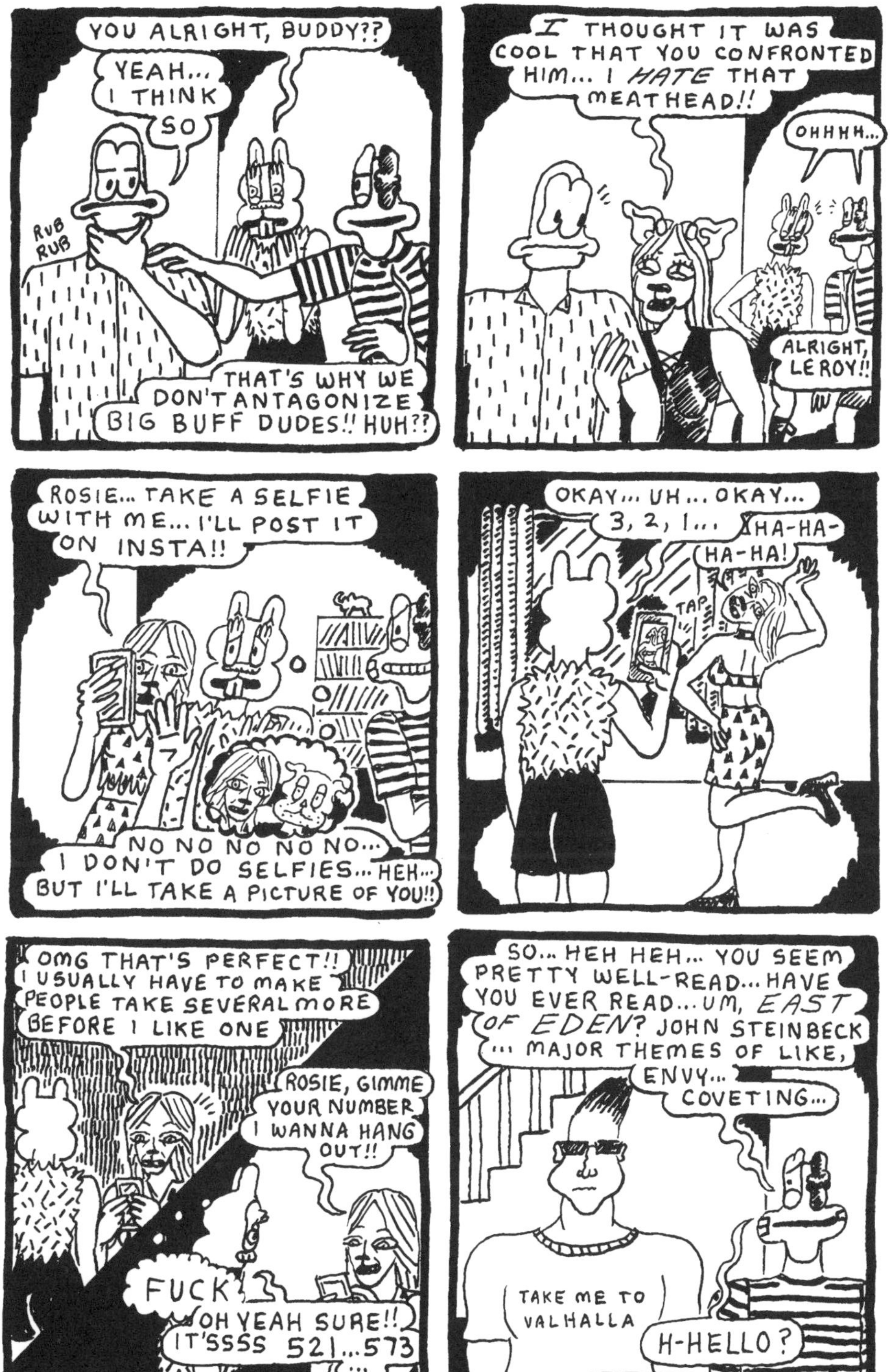
YOU ALRIGHT, BUDDY??
YEAH... I THINK SO
RUB RUB
THAT'S WHY WE DON'T ANTAGONIZE BIG BUFF DUDES!! HUH??
I THOUGHT IT WAS COOL THAT YOU CONFRONTED HIM... I HATE THAT MEATHEAD!!
OHHHH...
ALRIGHT, LEROY!!
ROSIE... TAKE A SELFIE WITH ME... I'LL POST IT ON INSTA!!
NO NO NO NO NO... I DON'T DO SELFIES... HEH... BUT I'LL TAKE A PICTURE OF YOU!!
OKAY... UH... OKAY... 3, 2, 1...
HA-HA-HA-HA!
TAP
OMG THAT'S PERFECT!! I USUALLY HAVE TO MAKE PEOPLE TAKE SEVERAL MORE BEFORE I LIKE ONE
ROSIE, GIMME YOUR NUMBER I WANNA HANG OUT!!
FUCK
OH YEAH SURE!! IT'SSSS 521...573 ...
SO... HEH HEH... YOU SEEM PRETTY WELL-READ... HAVE YOU EVER READ... UM, EAST OF EDEN? JOHN STEINBECK ... MAJOR THEMES OF LIKE, ENVY...
COVETING...
TAKE ME TO VALHALLA
H-HELLO?

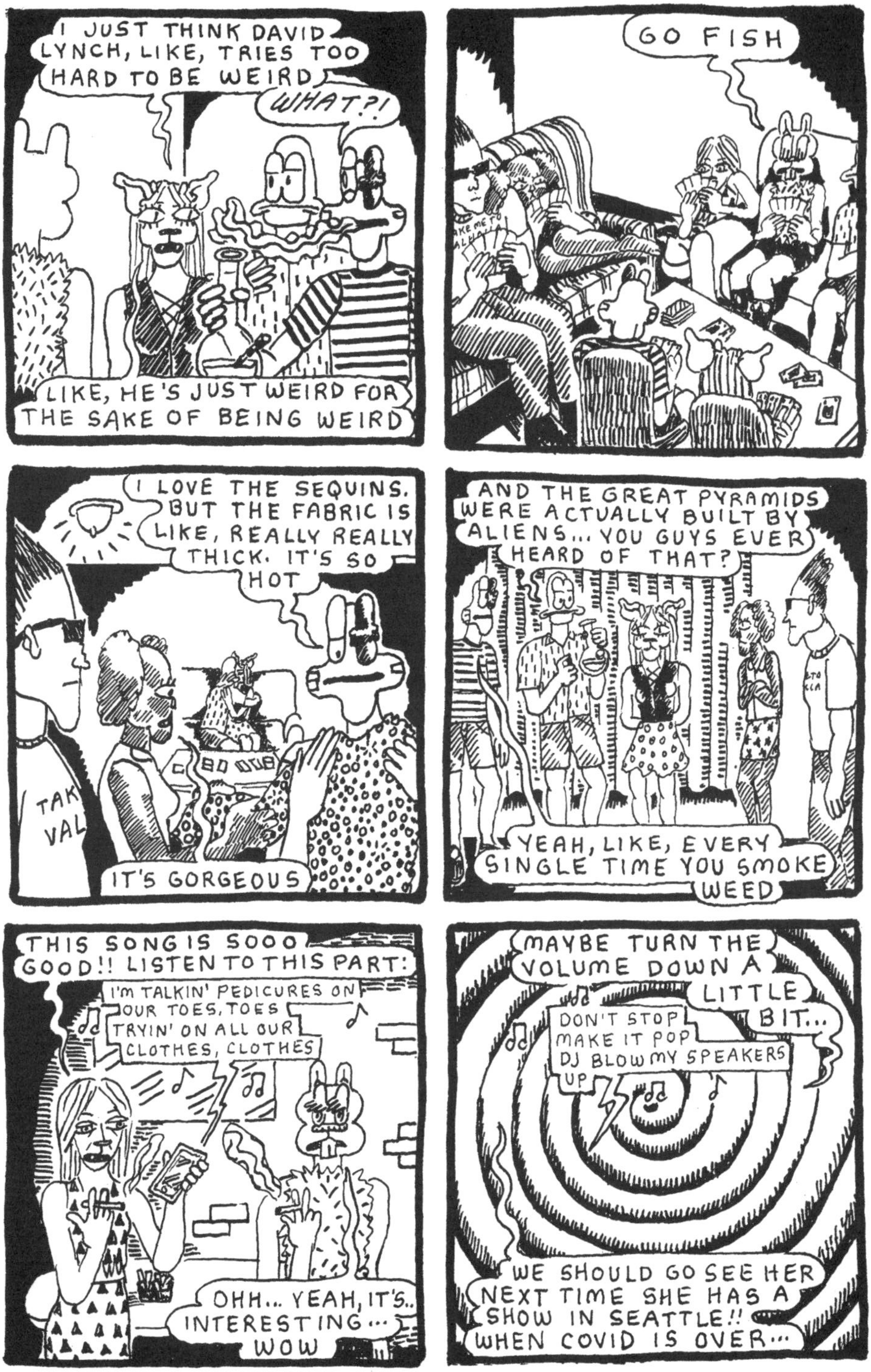
I JUST THINK DAVID LYNCH, LIKE, TRIES TOO HARD TO BE WEIRD
WHAT?!
LIKE, HE'S JUST WEIRD FOR THE SAKE OF BEING WEIRD
GO FISH
I LOVE THE SEQUINS. BUT THE FABRIC IS LIKE, REALLY REALLY THICK. IT'S SO HOT
IT'S GORGEOUS
AND THE GREAT PYRAMIDS WERE ACTUALLY BUILT BY ALIENS... YOU GUYS EVER HEARD OF THAT?
YEAH, LIKE, EVERY SINGLE TIME YOU SMOKE WEED
THIS SONG IS SOOO GOOD!! LISTEN TO THIS PART:
I'M TALKIN' PEDICURES ON OUR TOES, TOES TRYIN' ON ALL OUR CLOTHES, CLOTHES
OHH... YEAH, IT'S.. INTERESTING... WOW
MAYBE TURN THE VOLUME DOWN A LITTLE BIT...
DON'T STOP MAKE IT POP DJ BLOW MY SPEAKERS UP
WE SHOULD GO SEE HER NEXT TIME SHE HAS A SHOW IN SEATTLE!! WHEN COVID IS OVER...

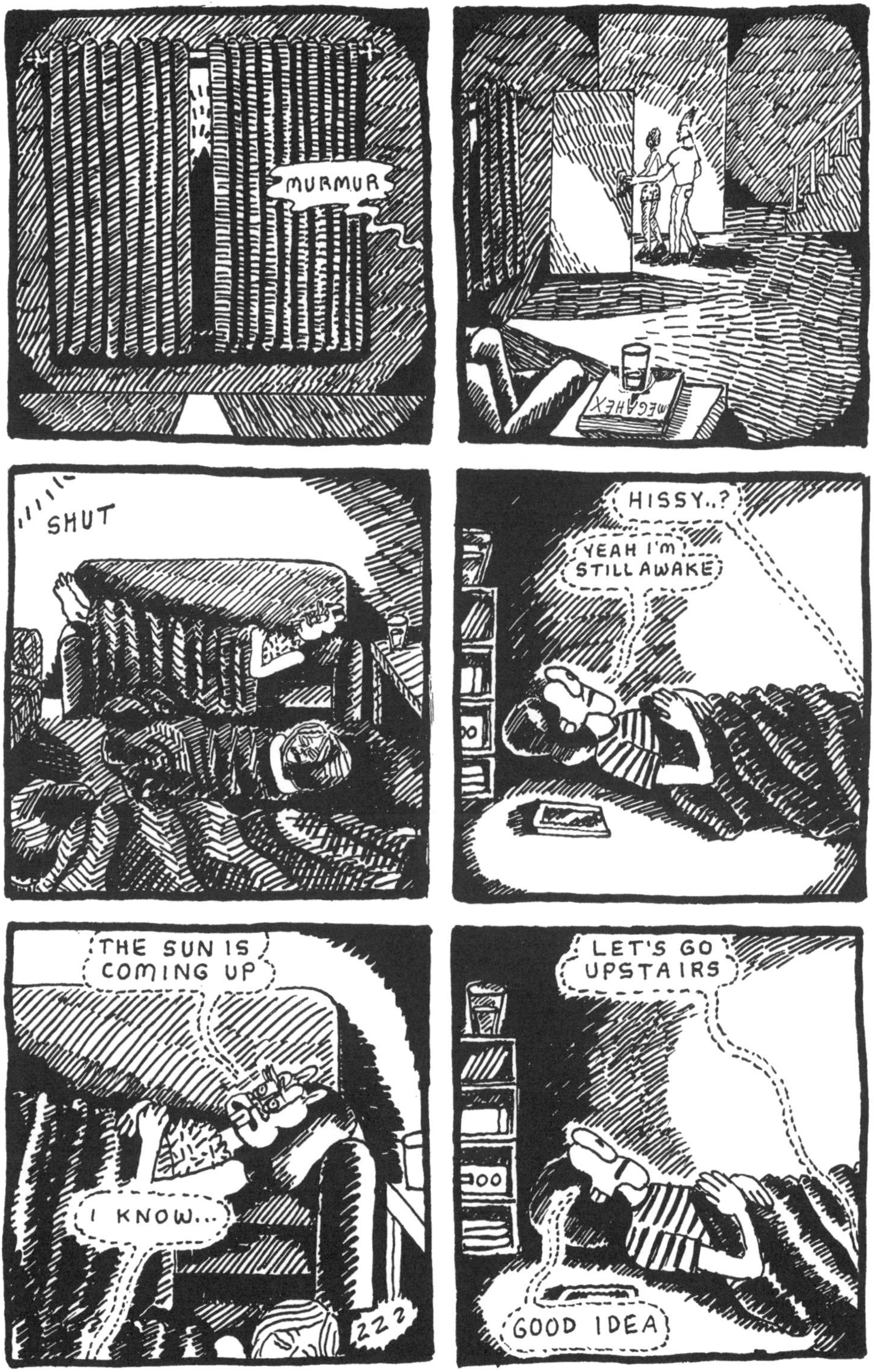
MURMUR
MEGAHEX
SHUT
HISSY..?
YEAH I'M STILL AWAKE
THE SUN IS COMING UP
I KNOW...
ZZZ
LET'S GO UPSTAIRS
GOOD IDEA

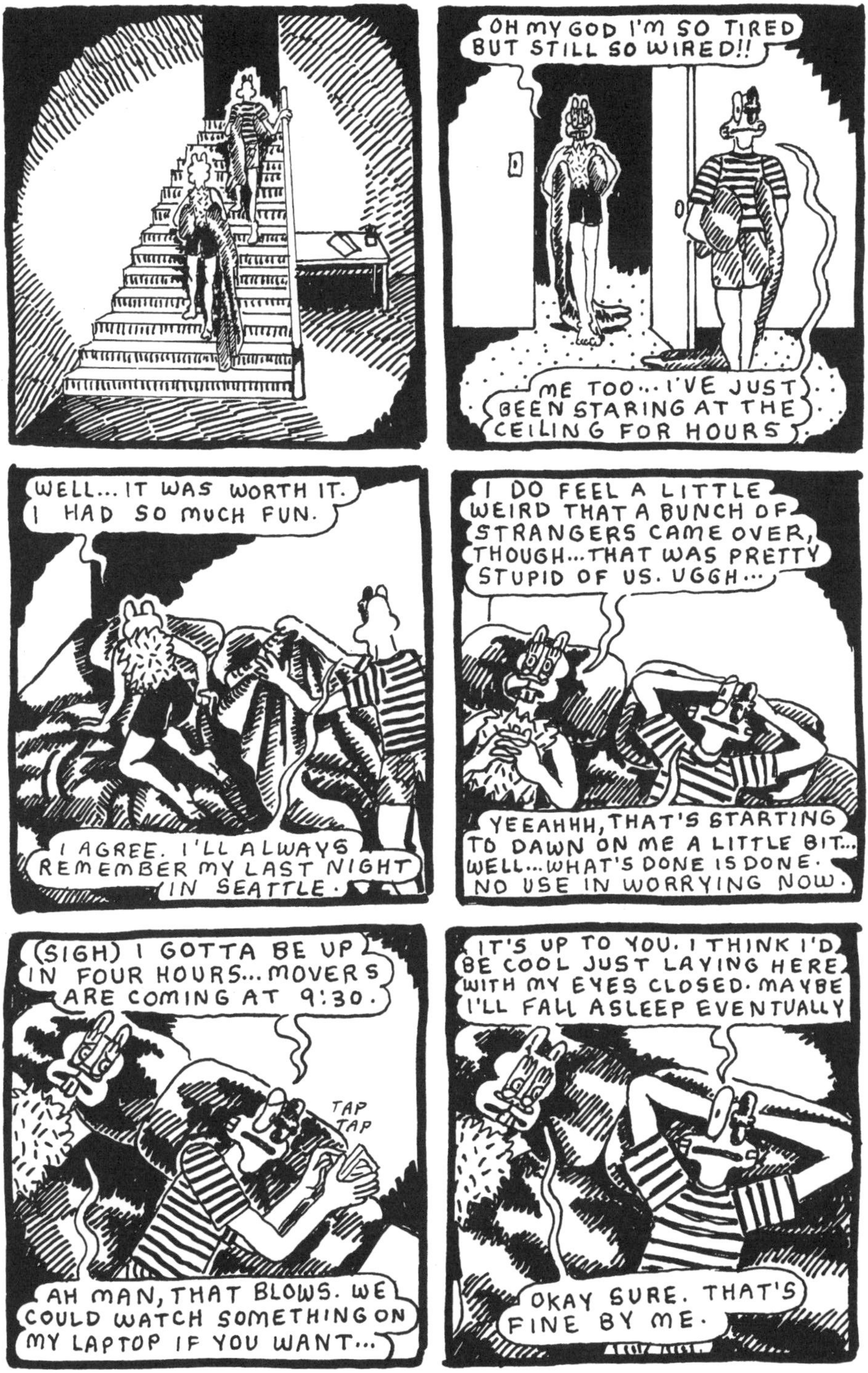
OH MY GOD I'M SO TIRED BUT STILL SO WIRED!!
ME TOO... I'VE JUST BEEN STARING AT THE CEILING FOR HOURS
WELL... IT WAS WORTH IT. I HAD SO MUCH FUN.
I AGREE. I'LL ALWAYS REMEMBER MY LAST NIGHT IN SEATTLE.
I DO FEEL A LITTLE WEIRD THAT A BUNCH OF STRANGERS CAME OVER, THOUGH... THAT WAS PRETTY STUPID OF US. UGGH...
YEEAHHH, THAT'S STARTING TO DAWN ON ME A LITTLE BIT... WELL... WHAT'S DONE IS DONE. NO USE IN WORRYING NOW.
(SIGH) I GOTTA BE UP IN FOUR HOURS... MOVERS ARE COMING AT 9:30.
TAP TAP
AH MAN, THAT BLOWS. WE COULD WATCH SOMETHING ON MY LAPTOP IF YOU WANT...
IT'S UP TO YOU. I THINK I'D BE COOL JUST LAYING HERE WITH MY EYES CLOSED. MAYBE I'LL FALL ASLEEP EVENTUALLY
OKAY SURE. THAT'S FINE BY ME.

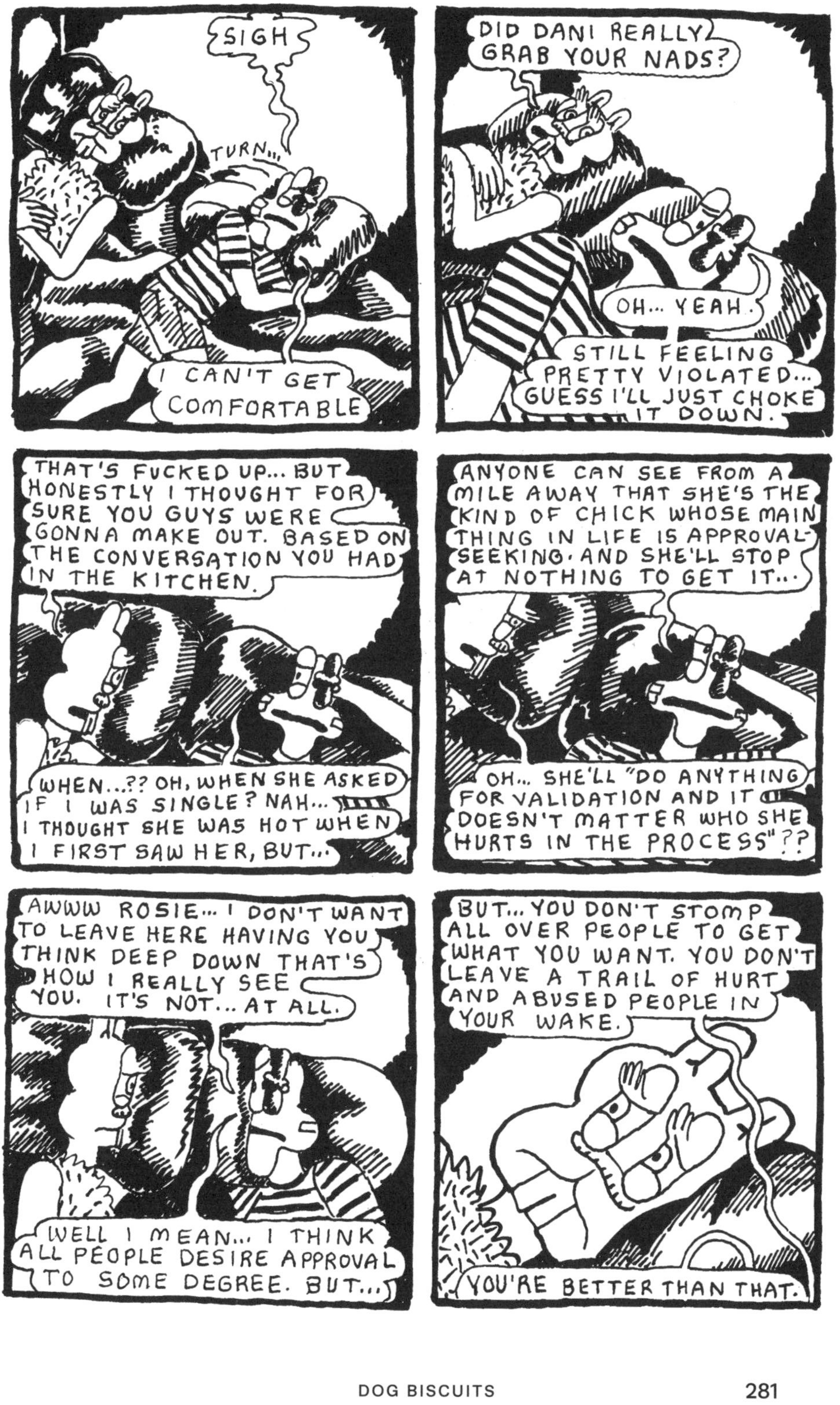
SIGH
TURN...
I CAN'T GET COMFORTABLE
DID DANI REALLY GRAB YOUR NADS?
OH... YEAH.
STILL FEELING PRETTY VIOLATED... GUESS I'LL JUST CHOKE IT DOWN.
THAT'S FUCKED UP... BUT HONESTLY I THOUGHT FOR SURE YOU GUYS WERE GONNA MAKE OUT. BASED ON THE CONVERSATION YOU HAD IN THE KITCHEN.
WHEN...?? OH, WHEN SHE ASKED IF I WAS SINGLE? NAH... I THOUGHT SHE WAS HOT WHEN I FIRST SAW HER, BUT...
ANYONE CAN SEE FROM A MILE AWAY THAT SHE'S THE KIND OF CHICK WHOSE MAIN THING IN LIFE IS APPROVAL-SEEKING. AND SHE'LL STOP AT NOTHING TO GET IT...
OH... SHE'LL "DO ANYTHING FOR VALIDATION AND IT DOESN'T MATTER WHO SHE HURTS IN THE PROCESS"??
AWWW ROSIE... I DON'T WANT TO LEAVE HERE HAVING YOU THINK DEEP DOWN THAT'S HOW I REALLY SEE YOU. IT'S NOT... AT ALL.
WELL I MEAN... I THINK ALL PEOPLE DESIRE APPROVAL TO SOME DEGREE. BUT...
BUT... YOU DON'T STOMP ALL OVER PEOPLE TO GET WHAT YOU WANT. YOU DON'T LEAVE A TRAIL OF HURT AND ABUSED PEOPLE IN YOUR WAKE.
YOU'RE BETTER THAN THAT.

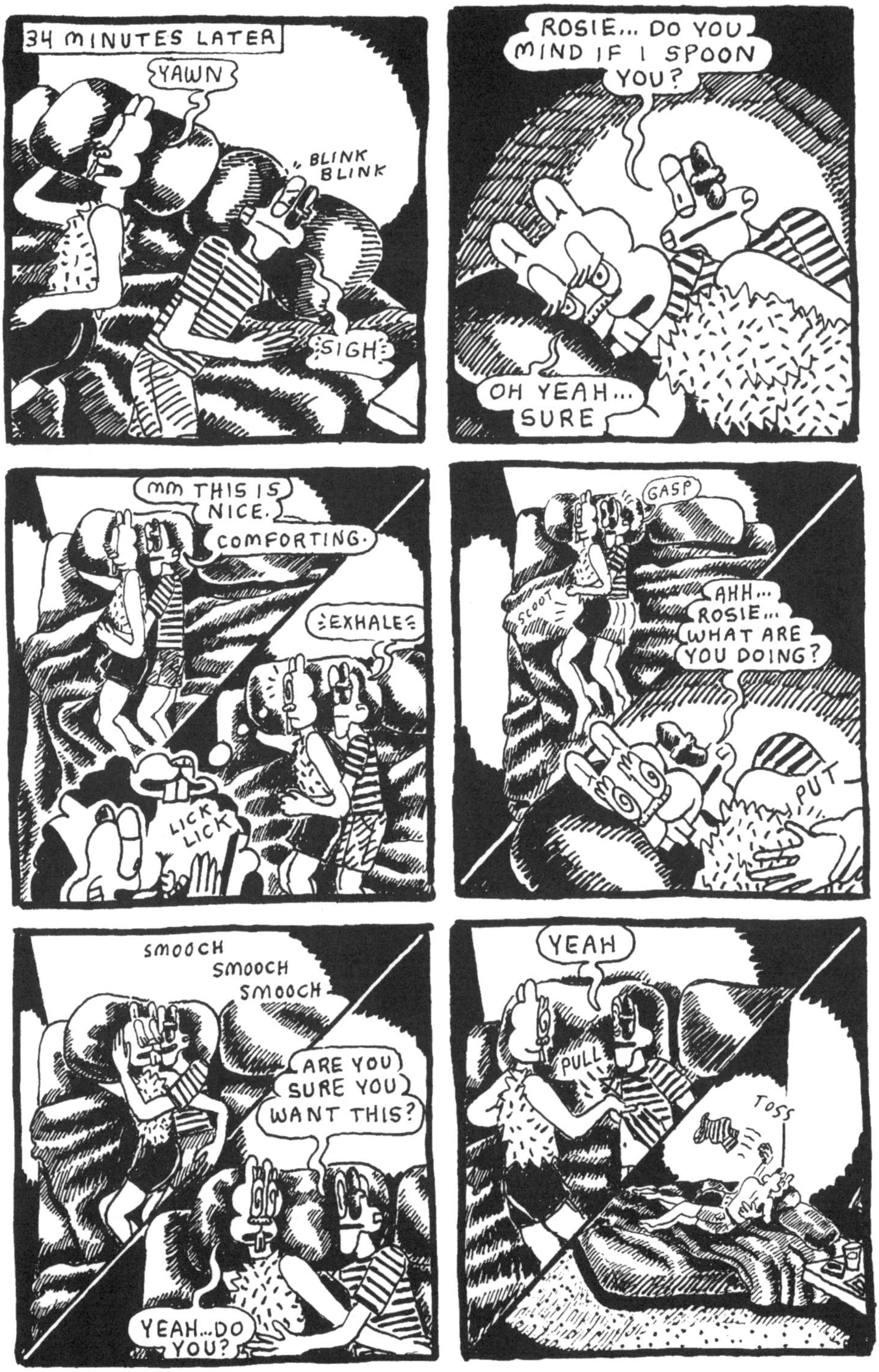
34 MINUTES LATER
YAWN
BLINK BLINK
SIGH
ROSIE... DO YOU MIND IF I SPOON YOU?
OH YEAH... SURE
MM THIS IS NICE.
COMFORTING.
EXHALE
LICK LICK
GASP
SCOOT
AHH... ROSIE... WHAT ARE YOU DOING?
PUT
SMOOCH SMOOCH SMOOCH
ARE YOU SURE YOU WANT THIS?
YEAH...DO YOU?
YEAH
PULL
TOSS

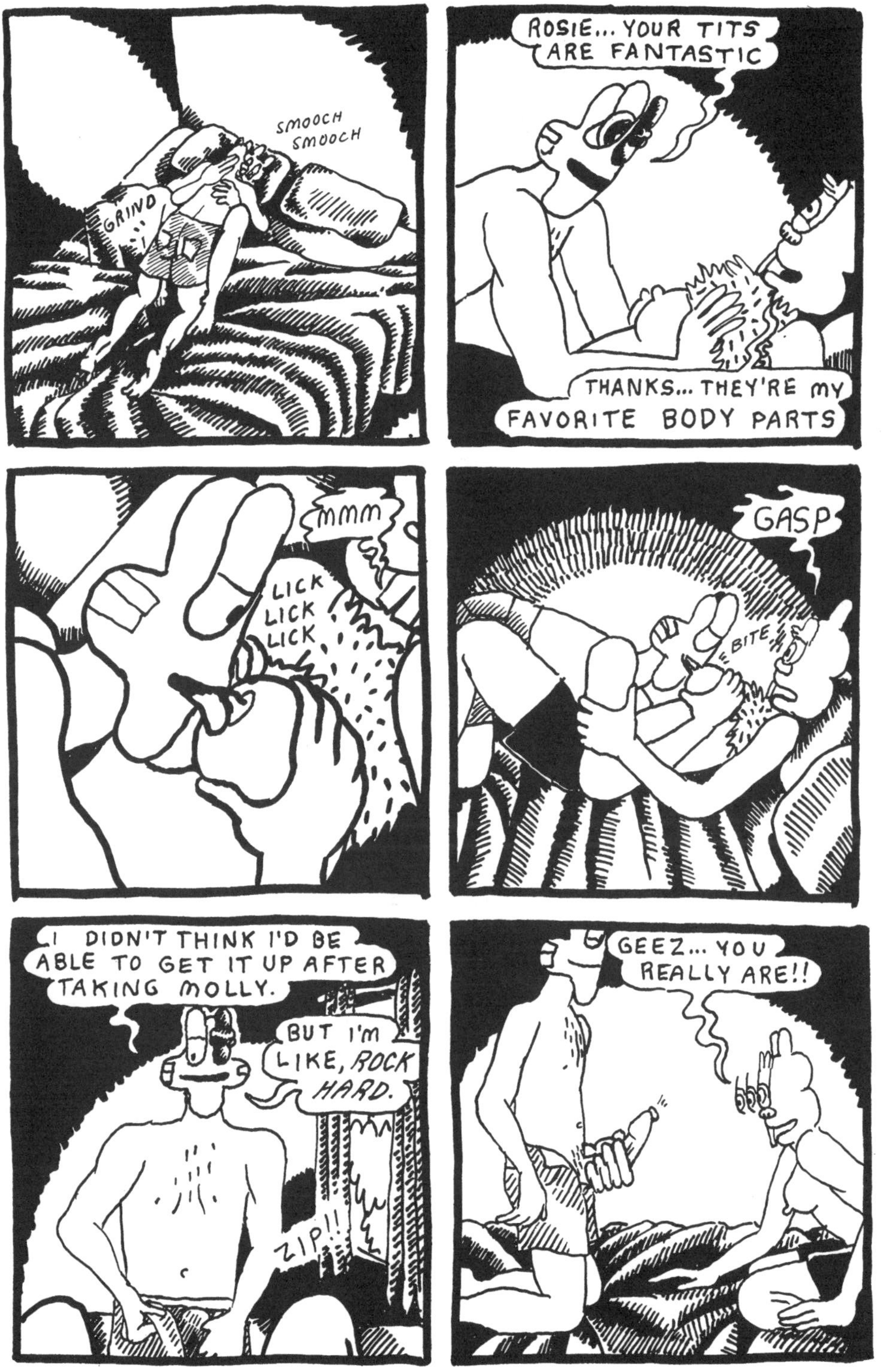
SMOOCH SMOOCH
GRIND
ROSIE... YOUR TITS ARE FANTASTIC
THANKS... THEY'RE MY FAVORITE BODY PARTS
MMM
LICK LICK LICK
GASP
BITE
I DIDN'T THINK I'D BE ABLE TO GET IT UP AFTER TAKING MOLLY.
BUT I'M LIKE, ROCK HARD.
ZIP!!
GEEZ... YOU REALLY ARE!!

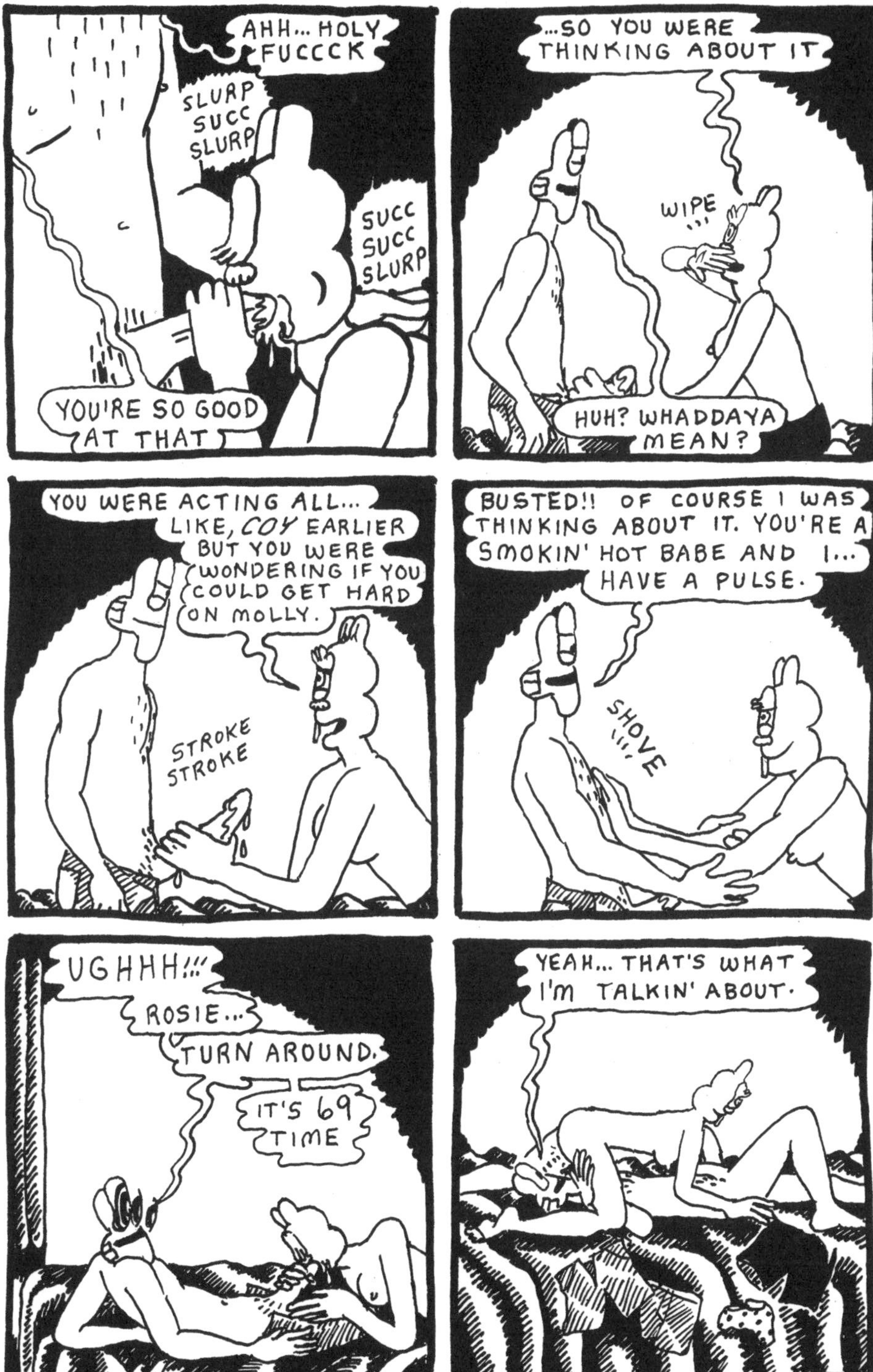
AHH... HOLY FUCCCK
SLURP SUCC SLURP
SUCC SUCC SLURP
YOU'RE SO GOOD AT THAT
...SO YOU WERE THINKING ABOUT IT
WIPE
HUH? WHADDAYA MEAN?
YOU WERE ACTING ALL... LIKE, COY EARLIER BUT YOU WERE WONDERING IF YOU COULD GET HARD ON MOLLY.
STROKE STROKE
BUSTED!! OF COURSE I WAS THINKING ABOUT IT. YOU'RE A SMOKIN' HOT BABE AND I... HAVE A PULSE.
SHOVE
UGHHH!!!
ROSIE...
TURN AROUND.
IT'S 69 TIME
YEAH... THAT'S WHAT I'M TALKIN' ABOUT.

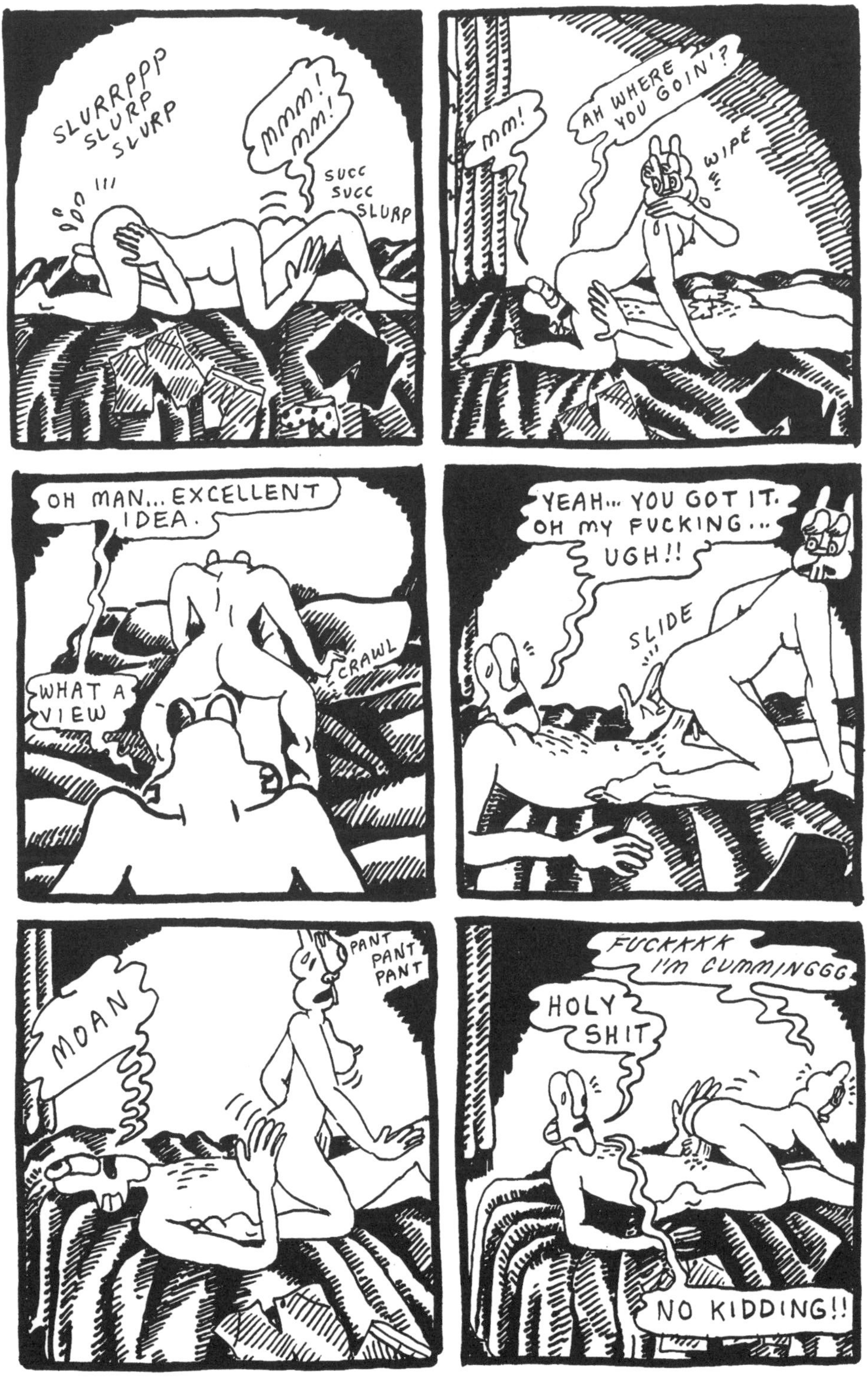
SLURRPPP
SLURP
SLURP
MMMM! MM!
SUCC
SUCC
SLURP
MM!
AH WHERE YOU GOIN'?
WIPE
OH MAN... EXCELLENT IDEA.
WHAT A VIEW
CRAWL
YEAH... YOU GOT IT. OH MY FUCKING... UGH!!
SLIDE
MOAN
PANT
PANT
PANT
FUCKKKK I'M CUMMINGGG
HOLY SHIT
NO KIDDING!!

TURN AROUND REAL QUICK
PANT PANT PANT
POP
FUCK!!!
SLURP SLURP
WOW YOUR PUSSY IS THROBBING... I CAN SEE IT!!
PANT PANT PANT PANT
I'M STILL CUMMING
FUCK... THAT'S WILD!!
...I WANNA FEEL IT THROBBING AROUND MY COCK...
HOW DOES THAT SOUND?
WOULD YOU LIKE THAT?
PANT PANT PANT PANT PANT
THROB THROB
YES
HEH HEH.. IF MY DICK GETS ANY HARDER IT'S GOING TO EXPLODE
UGHHHH PLEASE FUCK ME
YEAH?? LIKE... RIGHT NOW??
YES!!
STROKE STROKE

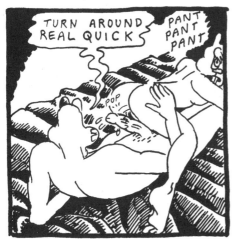

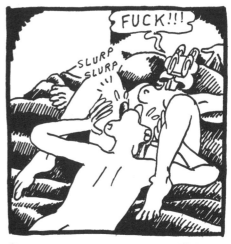

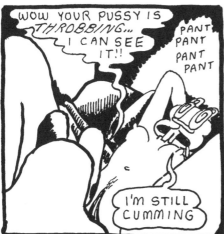

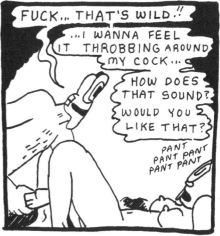

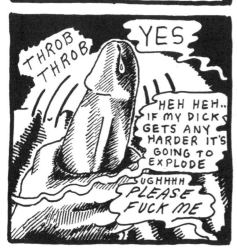

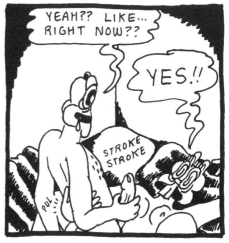

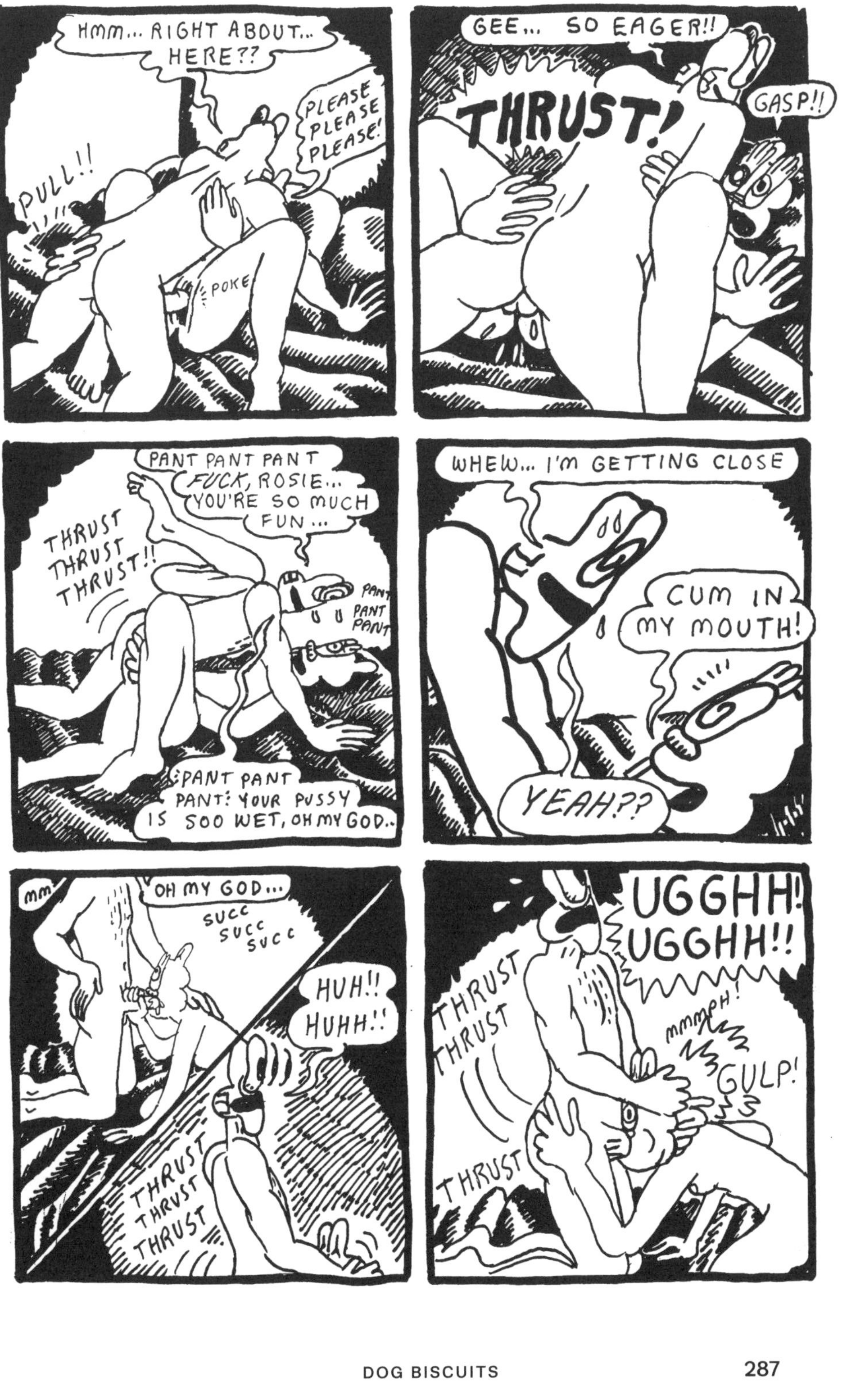
HMM... RIGHT ABOUT... HERE??
PLEASE PLEASE PLEASE!
PULL!!
POKE
GEE... SO EAGER!!
THRUST!
GASP!!
PANT PANT PANT FUCK, ROSIE... YOU'RE SO MUCH FUN...
THRUST THRUST THRUST!!
PANT PANT PANT
PANT PANT PANT! YOUR PUSSY IS SOO WET, OH MY GOD..
WHEW... I'M GETTING CLOSE
CUM IN MY MOUTH!
YEAH??
mm
OH MY GOD...
SUCC SUCC SUCC
HUH!! HUHH!!
THRUST THRUST THRUST
UGGHH! UGGHH!!
THRUST THRUST
MMMPH!
GULP!
THRUST

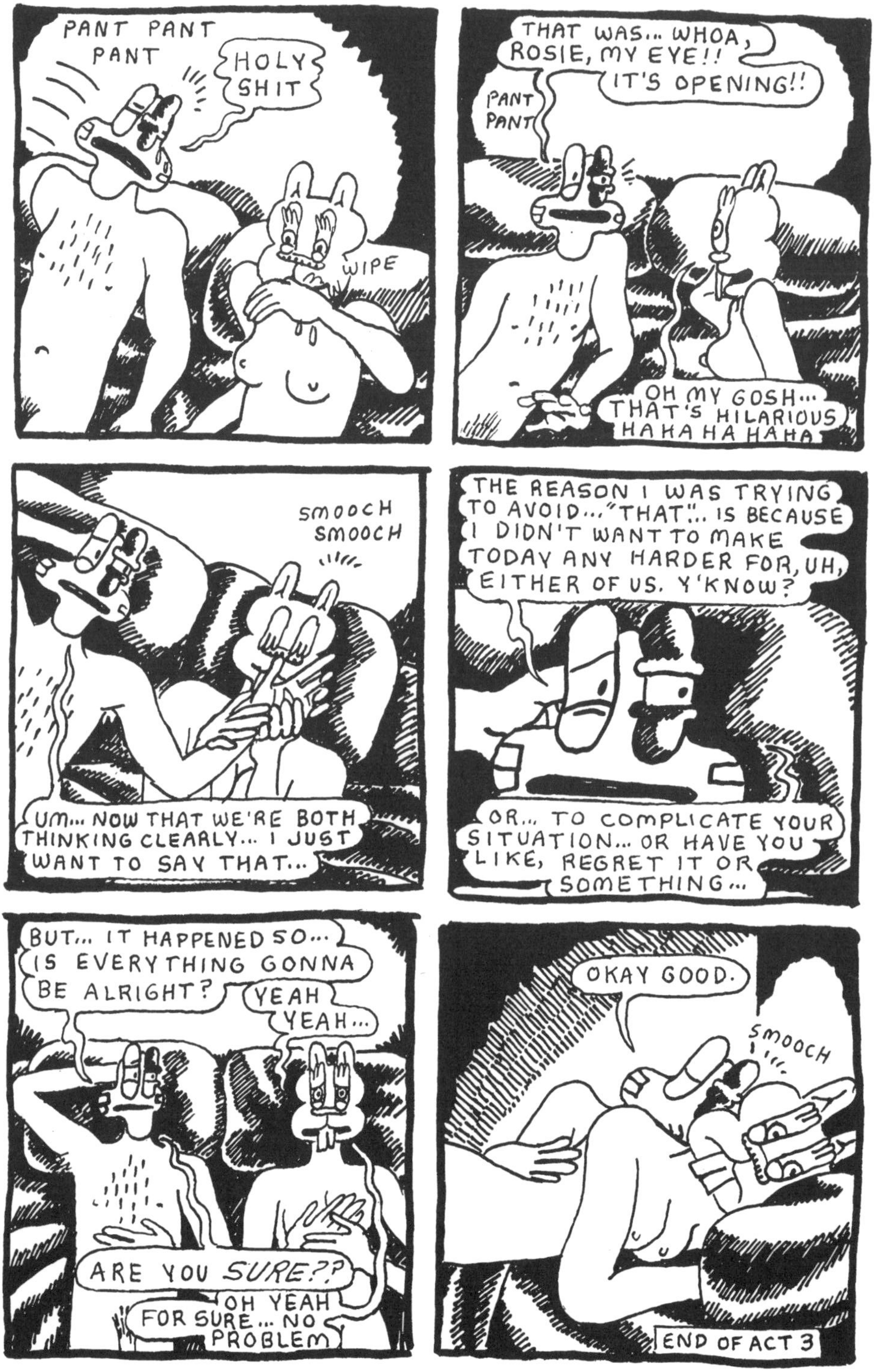
PANT PANT
PANT
HOLY SHIT
WIPE
THAT WAS... WHOA, ROSIE, MY EYE!!
IT'S OPENING!!
PANT PANT
OH MY GOSH... THAT'S HILARIOUS HAHA HA HAHA
SMOOCH SMOOCH
UM... NOW THAT WE'RE BOTH THINKING CLEARLY... I JUST WANT TO SAY THAT...
THE REASON I WAS TRYING TO AVOID..."THAT"... IS BECAUSE I DIDN'T WANT TO MAKE TODAY ANY HARDER FOR, UH, EITHER OF US. Y'KNOW?
OR... TO COMPLICATE YOUR SITUATION... OR HAVE YOU LIKE, REGRET IT OR SOMETHING...
BUT... IT HAPPENED SO... IS EVERYTHING GONNA BE ALRIGHT?
YEAH YEAH...
ARE YOU SURE??
OH YEAH FOR SURE... NO PROBLEM
OKAY GOOD.
SMOOCH
END OF ACT 3

“Down Bad”

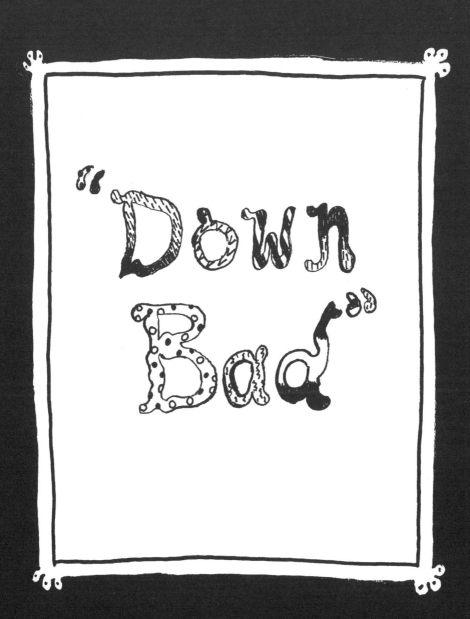

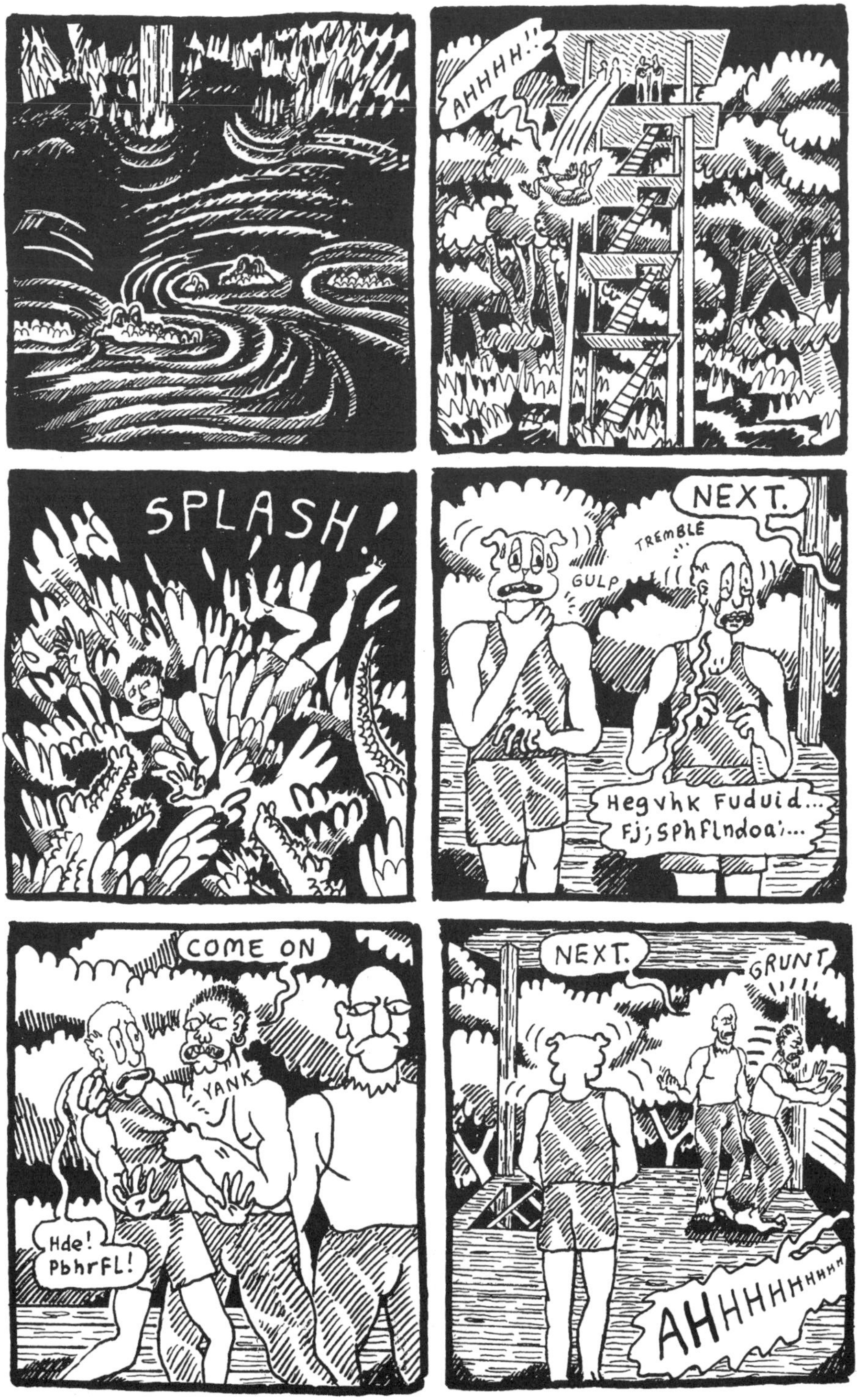
AHHHH!!
SPLASH!
NEXT.
TREMBLE
GULP
Hegvhk Fuduid...
Fj; Sphflndoa;...
COME ON
YANK
Hde!
PbhrFL!
NEXT.
GRUNT
AHHHHHHHHH

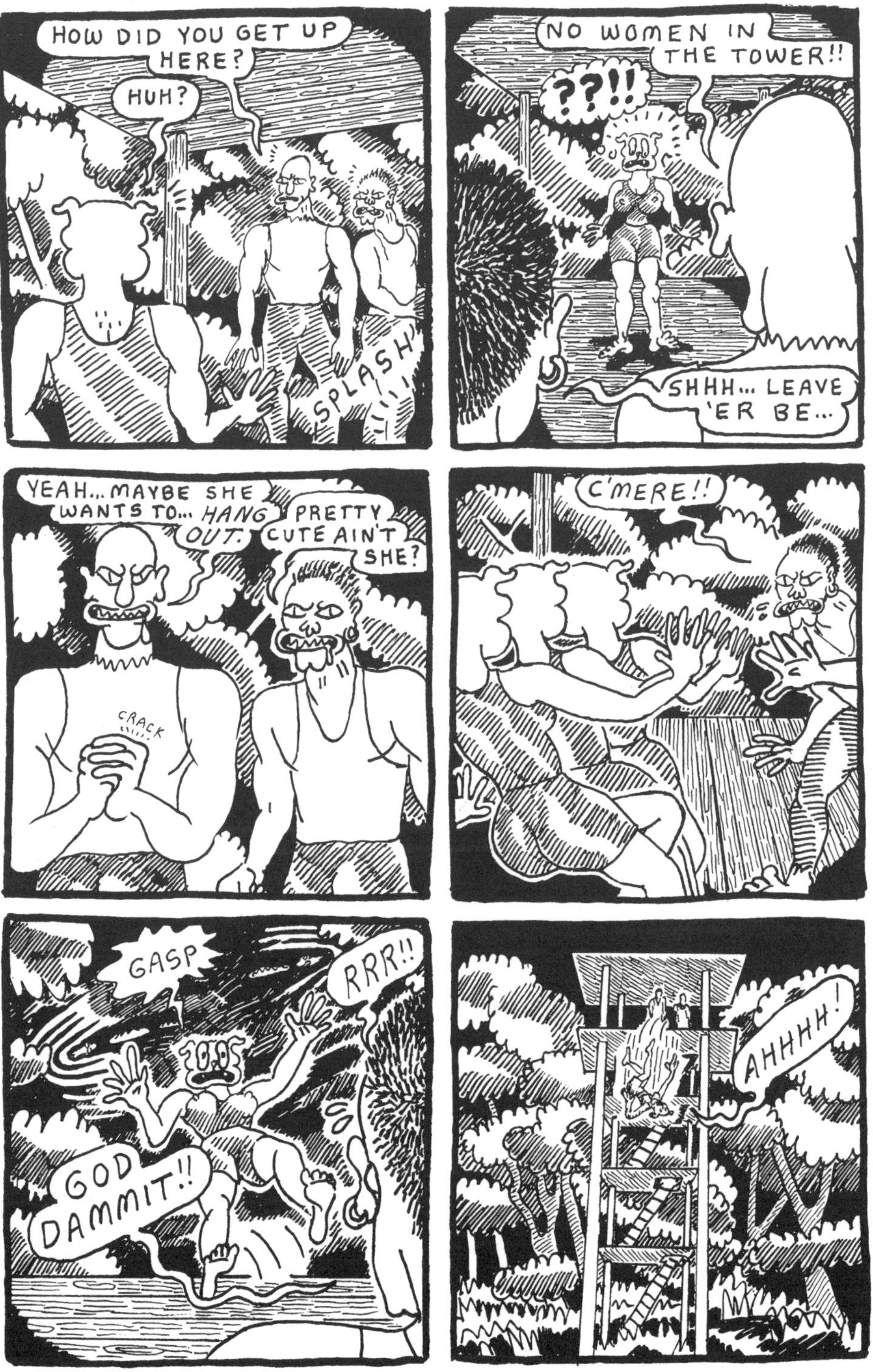
HOW DID YOU GET UP HERE?
HUH?
SPLASH
NO WOMEN IN THE TOWER!!
??!!
SHHH... LEAVE 'ER BE...
YEAH... MAYBE SHE WANTS TO... HANG OUT.
PRETTY CUTE AIN'T SHE?
CRACK
C'MERE!!
GASP
RRR!!
GOD DAMMIT!!
AHHHH!

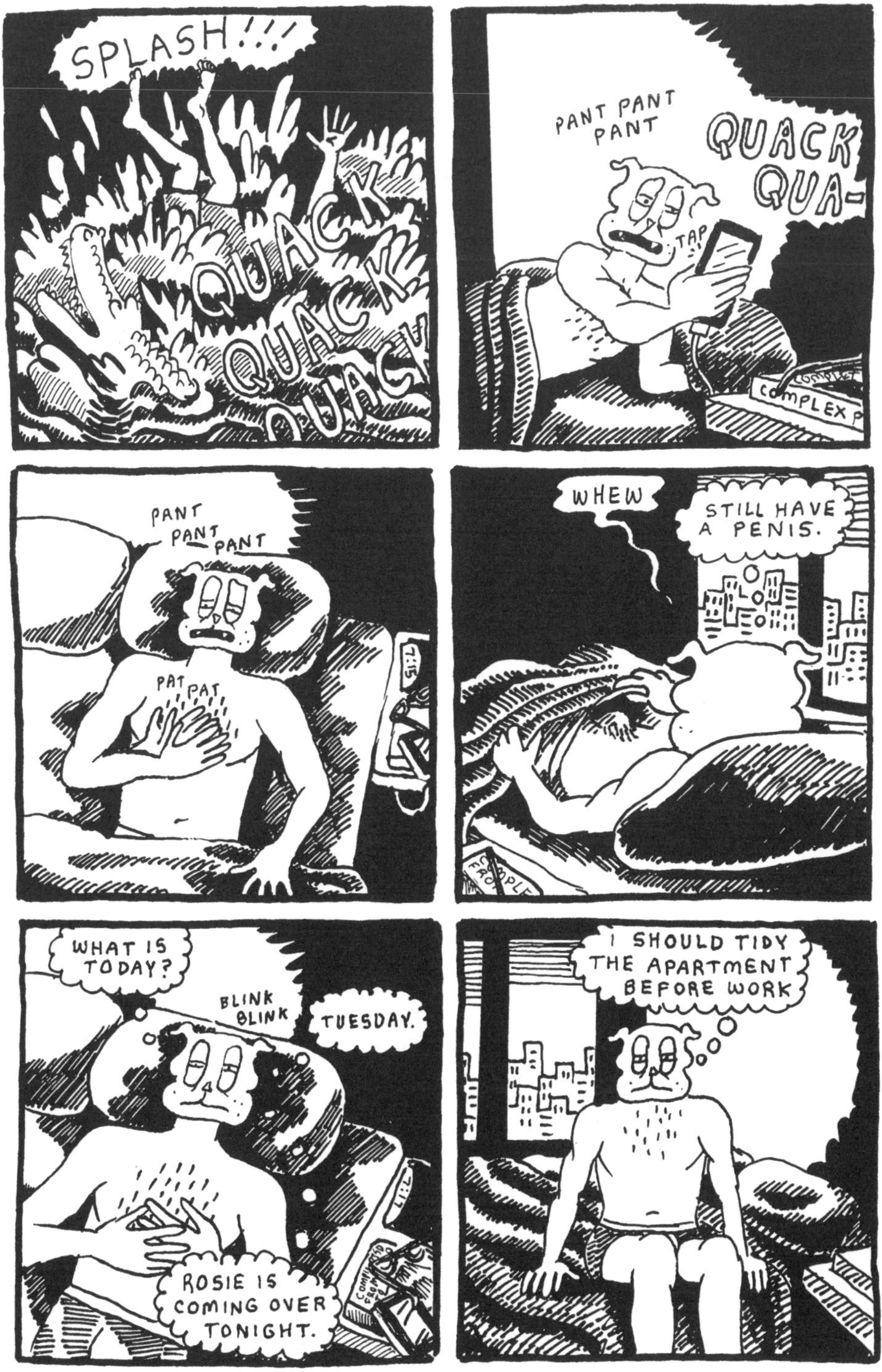
SPLASH!!!
QUACK
QUACK
PANT PANT PANT
QUACK QUA-
TAP
PANT PANT PANT
PAT PAT
7:15
WHEW
STILL HAVE A PENIS.
WHAT IS TODAY?
BLINK BLINK
TUESDAY.
ROSIE IS COMING OVER TONIGHT.
I SHOULD TIDY THE APARTMENT BEFORE WORK

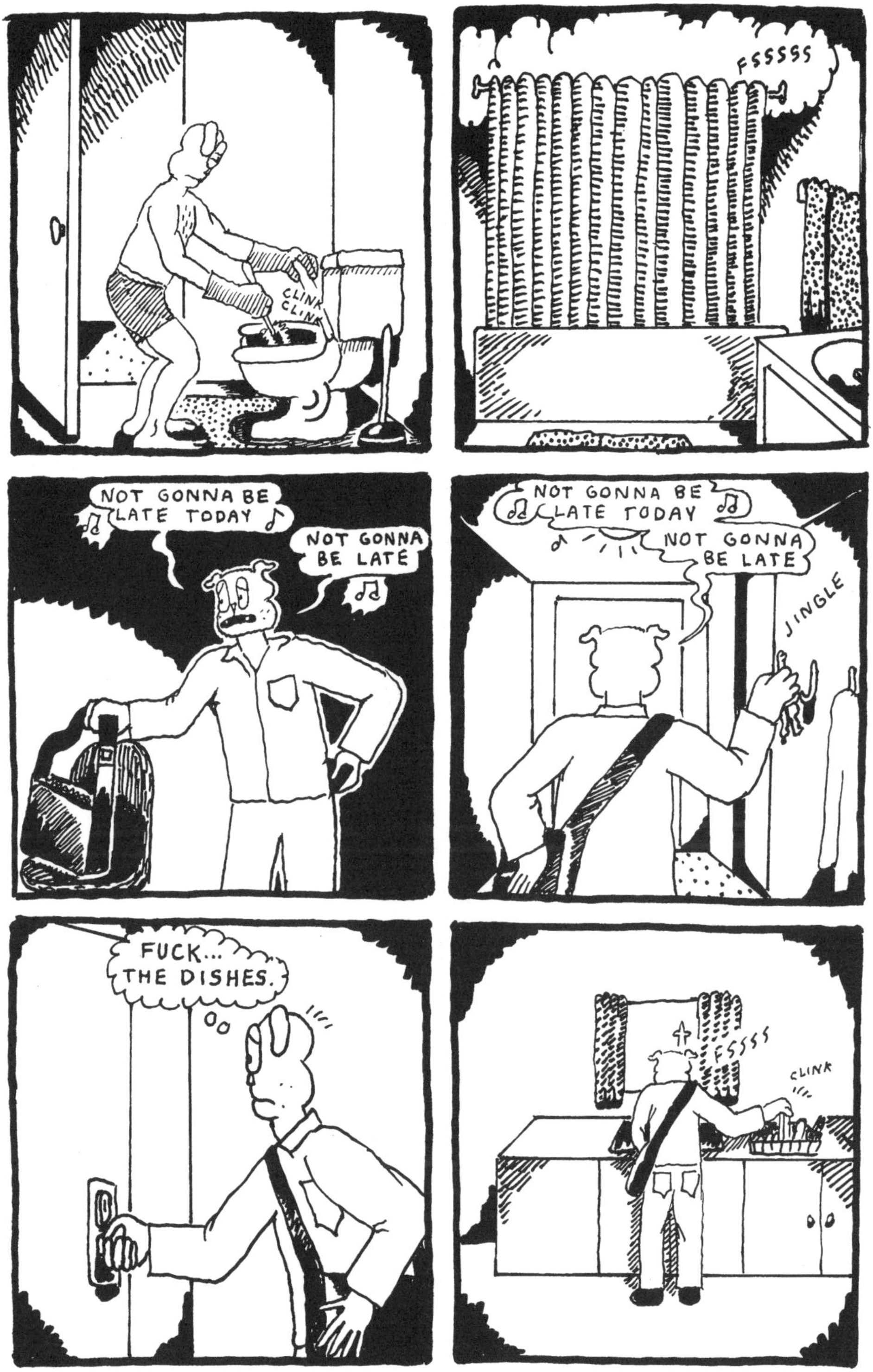
CLINK
CLINK
FSSSSS
NOT GONNA BE LATE TODAY
NOT GONNA BE LATE
NOT GONNA BE LATE TODAY
NOT GONNA BE LATE
JINGLE
FUCK... THE DISHES.
FSSSS
CLINK

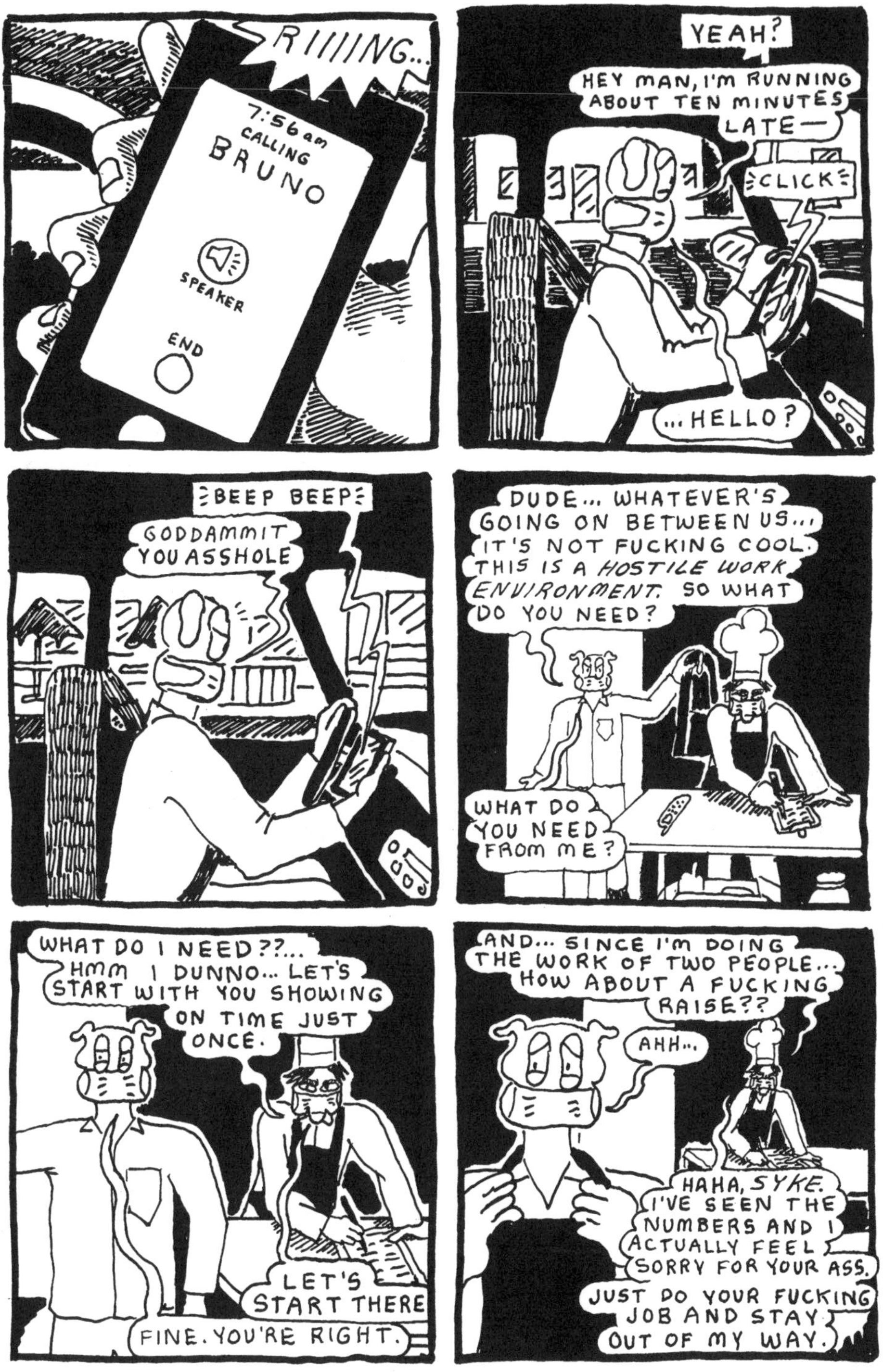
RIIIING...
7:56 am
CALLING
BRUNO
SPEAKER
END
YEAH?
HEY MAN, I'M RUNNING ABOUT TEN MINUTES LATE—
CLICK
...HELLO?
BEEP BEEP
GODDAMMIT YOU ASSHOLE
DUDE... WHATEVER'S GOING ON BETWEEN US... IT'S NOT FUCKING COOL. THIS IS A *HOSTILE WORK ENVIRONMENT.* SO WHAT DO YOU NEED?
WHAT DO YOU NEED FROM ME?
WHAT DO I NEED??... HMM I DUNNO... LET'S START WITH YOU SHOWING ON TIME JUST ONCE.
LET'S START THERE
FINE. YOU'RE RIGHT.
AND... SINCE I'M DOING THE WORK OF TWO PEOPLE... HOW ABOUT A FUCKING RAISE??
AHH...
HAHA, *SYKE.* I'VE SEEN THE NUMBERS AND I ACTUALLY FEEL SORRY FOR YOUR ASS.
JUST DO YOUR FUCKING JOB AND STAY OUT OF MY WAY.

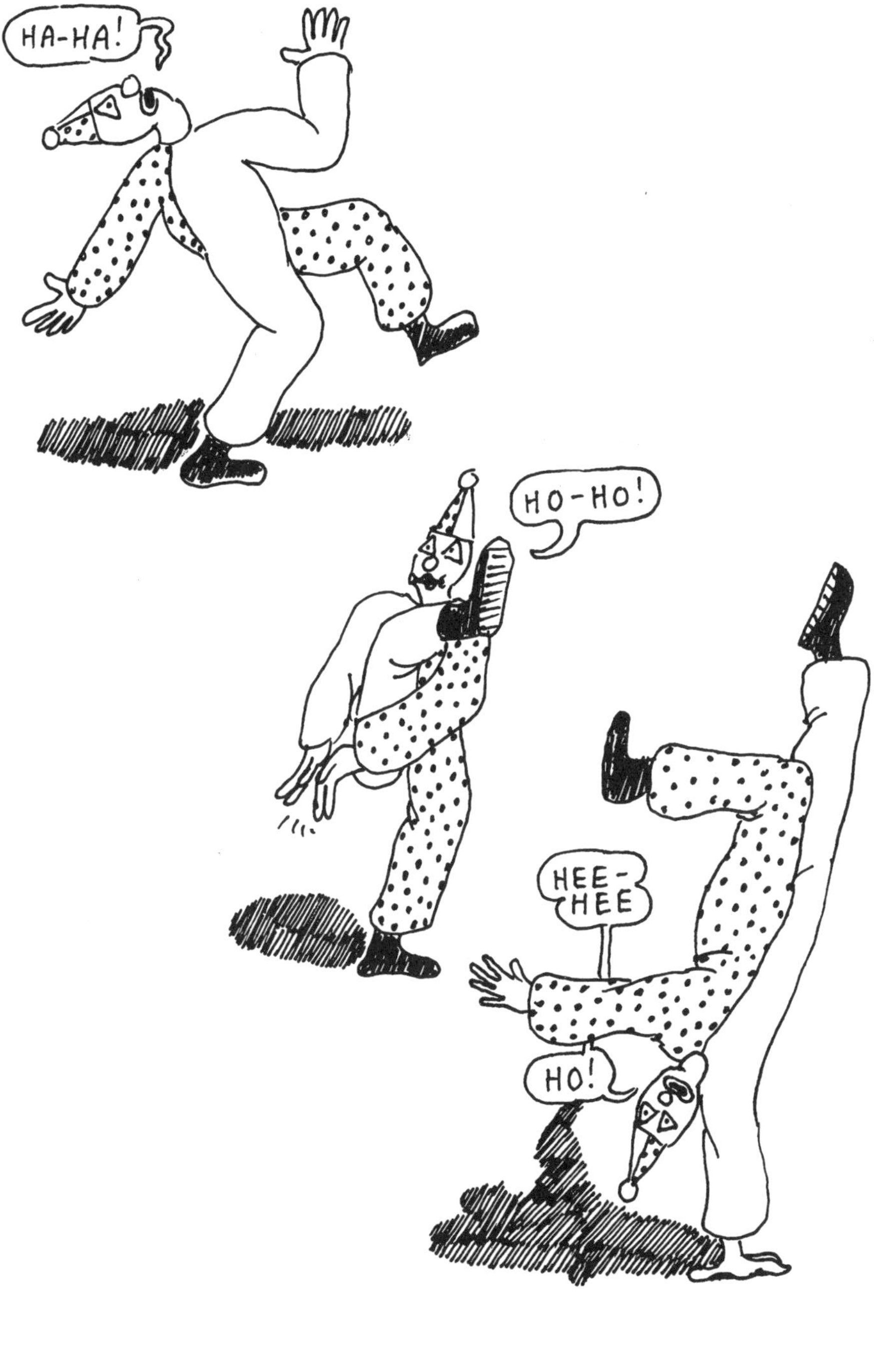
HA-HA!
HO-HO!
HEE-HEE
HO!

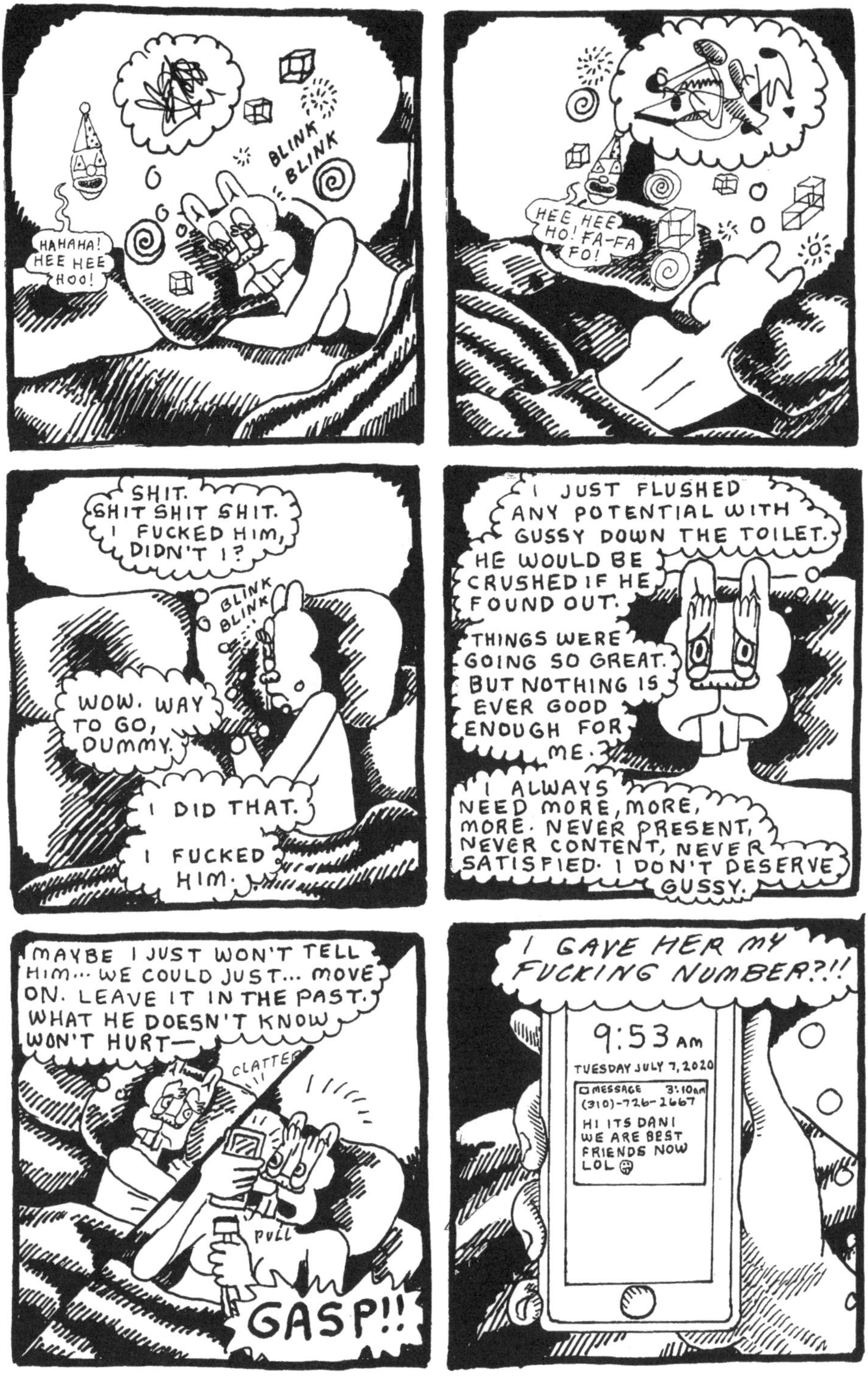
HAHAHA! HEE HEE HOO!
BLINK BLINK
HEE HEE HO! FA-FA FO!
SHIT. SHIT SHIT SHIT. I FUCKED HIM, DIDN'T I?
BLINK BLINK
WOW. WAY TO GO, DUMMY.
I DID THAT.
I FUCKED HIM.
I JUST FLUSHED ANY POTENTIAL WITH GUSSY DOWN THE TOILET.
HE WOULD BE CRUSHED IF HE FOUND OUT.
THINGS WERE GOING SO GREAT. BUT NOTHING IS EVER GOOD ENOUGH FOR ME.
I ALWAYS NEED MORE, MORE, MORE. NEVER PRESENT, NEVER CONTENT, NEVER SATISFIED. I DON'T DESERVE GUSSY.
MAYBE I JUST WON'T TELL HIM... WE COULD JUST... MOVE ON. LEAVE IT IN THE PAST. WHAT HE DOESN'T KNOW WON'T HURT—
CLATTER
PULL
GASP!!
I GAVE HER MY FUCKING NUMBER?!!
9:53 AM
TUESDAY JULY 7, 2020
MESSAGE 3:10am
(310)-726-2667
HI ITS DANI WE ARE BEST FRIENDS NOW LOL

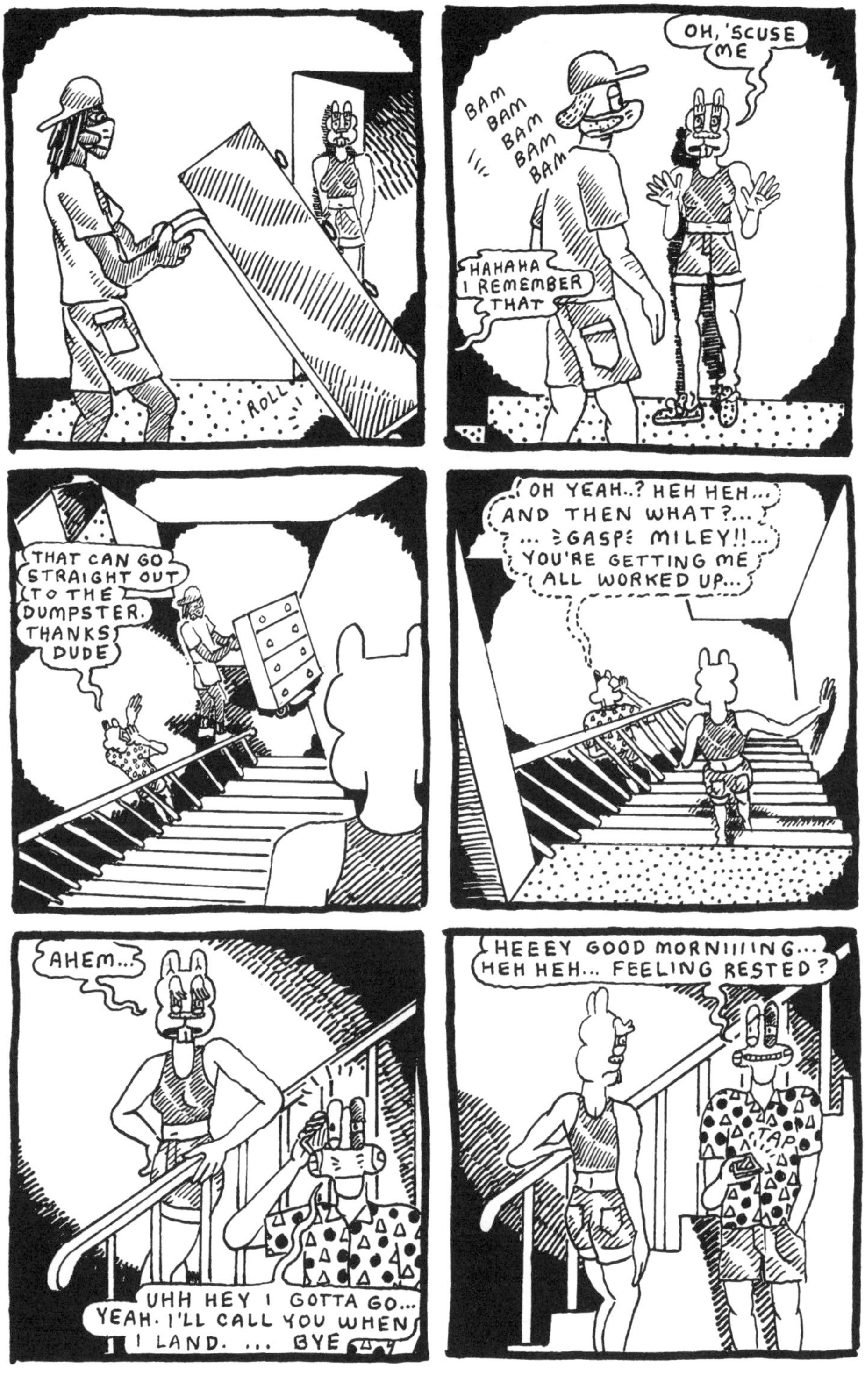
ROLL
BAM BAM BAM BAM BAM
OH, 'SCUSE ME
HAHAHA I REMEMBER THAT
THAT CAN GO STRAIGHT OUT TO THE DUMPSTER. THANKS DUDE
OH YEAH..? HEH HEH... AND THEN WHAT?... ... GASP MILEY!!... YOU'RE GETTING ME ALL WORKED UP...
AHEM...
UHH HEY I GOTTA GO... YEAH. I'LL CALL YOU WHEN I LAND. ... BYE
HEEEY GOOD MORNIIIING... HEH HEH... FEELING RESTED?
TAP

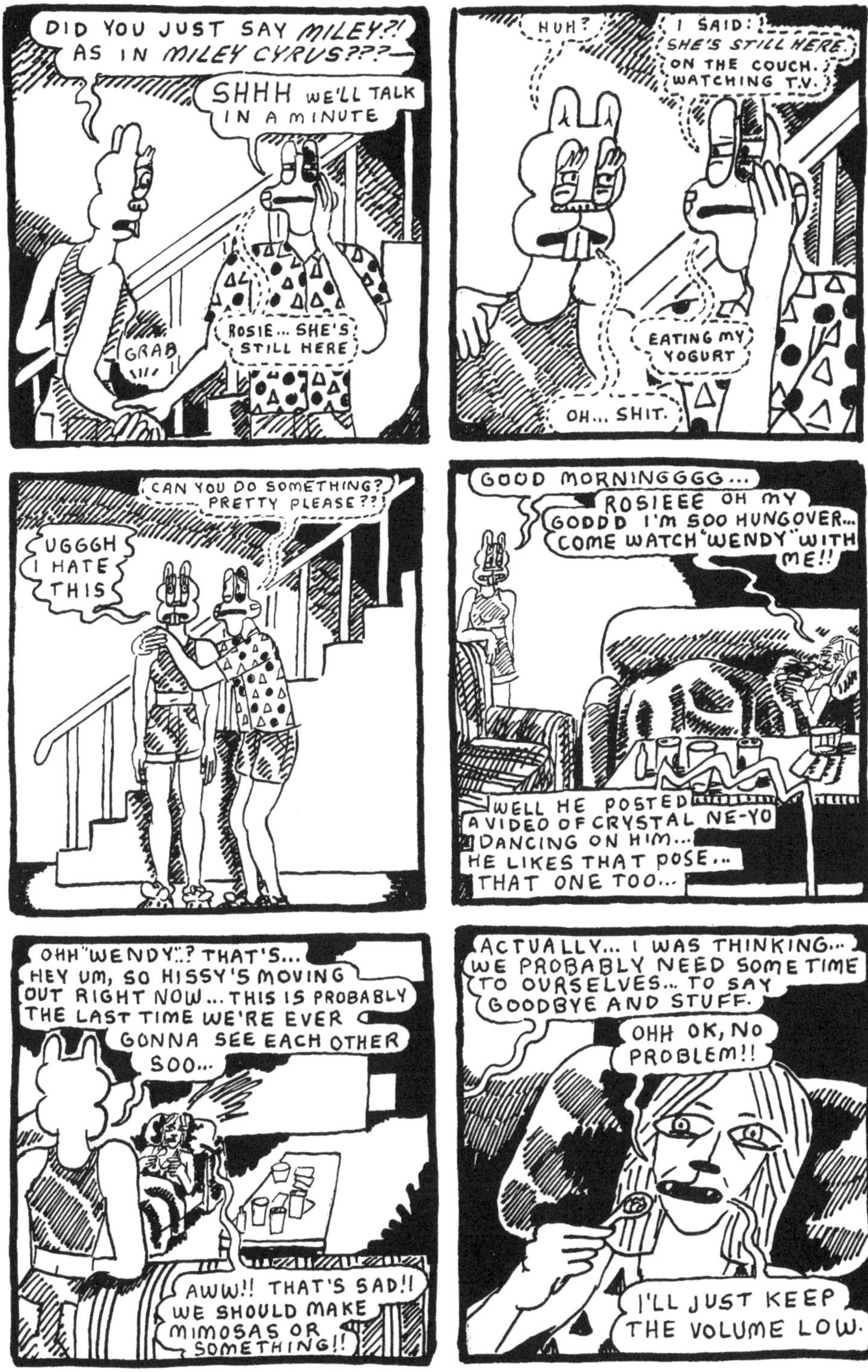
DID YOU JUST SAY MILEY?! AS IN MILEY CYRUS???
SHHH WE'LL TALK IN A MINUTE
ROSIE... SHE'S STILL HERE
GRAB
HUH?
I SAID: SHE'S STILL HERE. ON THE COUCH. WATCHING T.V.
EATING MY YOGURT
OH... SHIT.
CAN YOU DO SOMETHING? PRETTY PLEASE??
UGGGH I HATE THIS
GOOD MORNINGGGG...
ROSIEEE OH MY GODDD I'M SOO HUNGOVER... COME WATCH "WENDY" WITH ME!!
WELL HE POSTED A VIDEO OF CRYSTAL NE-YO DANCING ON HIM... HE LIKES THAT POSE... THAT ONE TOO...
OHH "WENDY"..? THAT'S... HEY UM, SO HISSY'S MOVING OUT RIGHT NOW... THIS IS PROBABLY THE LAST TIME WE'RE EVER GONNA SEE EACH OTHER SOO...
AWW!! THAT'S SAD!! WE SHOULD MAKE MIMOSAS OR SOMETHING!!
ACTUALLY... I WAS THINKING... WE PROBABLY NEED SOME TIME TO OURSELVES... TO SAY GOODBYE AND STUFF.
OHH OK, NO PROBLEM!!
I'LL JUST KEEP THE VOLUME LOW.

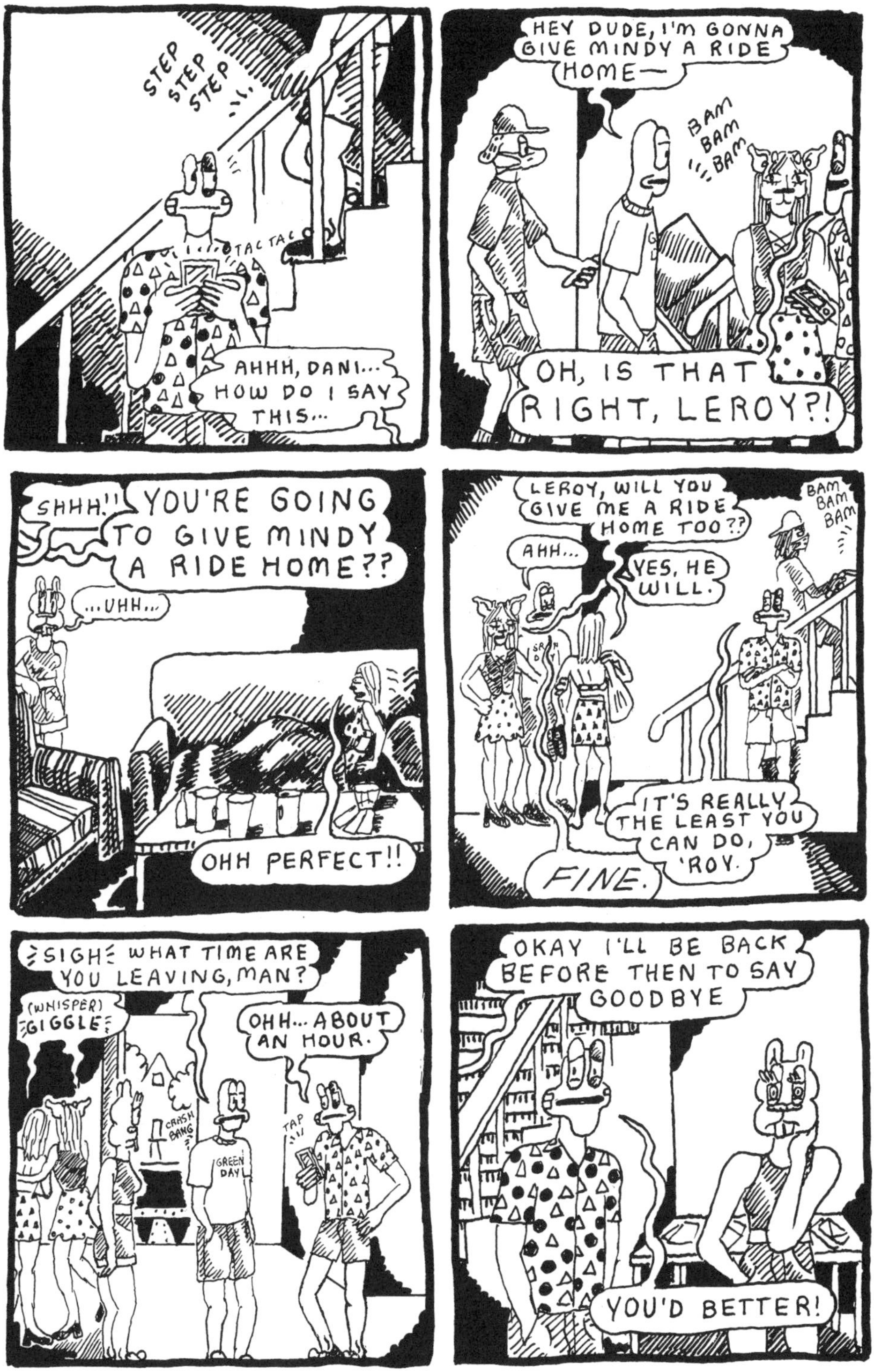
STEP
STEP
STEP
TAC TAC
AHHH, DANI... HOW DO I SAY THIS...
HEY DUDE, I'M GONNA GIVE MINDY A RIDE HOME—
BAM BAM BAM
OH, IS THAT RIGHT, LEROY?!
SHHH!!
YOU'RE GOING TO GIVE MINDY A RIDE HOME??
...UHH...
OHH PERFECT!!
LEROY, WILL YOU GIVE ME A RIDE HOME TOO??
BAM BAM BAM
AHH...
YES, HE WILL.
IT'S REALLY THE LEAST YOU CAN DO, 'ROY.
FINE.
SIGH WHAT TIME ARE YOU LEAVING, MAN?
(WHISPER) GIGGLE
OHH... ABOUT AN HOUR.
CRASH BANG
TAP
GREEN DAY
OKAY I'LL BE BACK BEFORE THEN TO SAY GOODBYE
YOU'D BETTER!

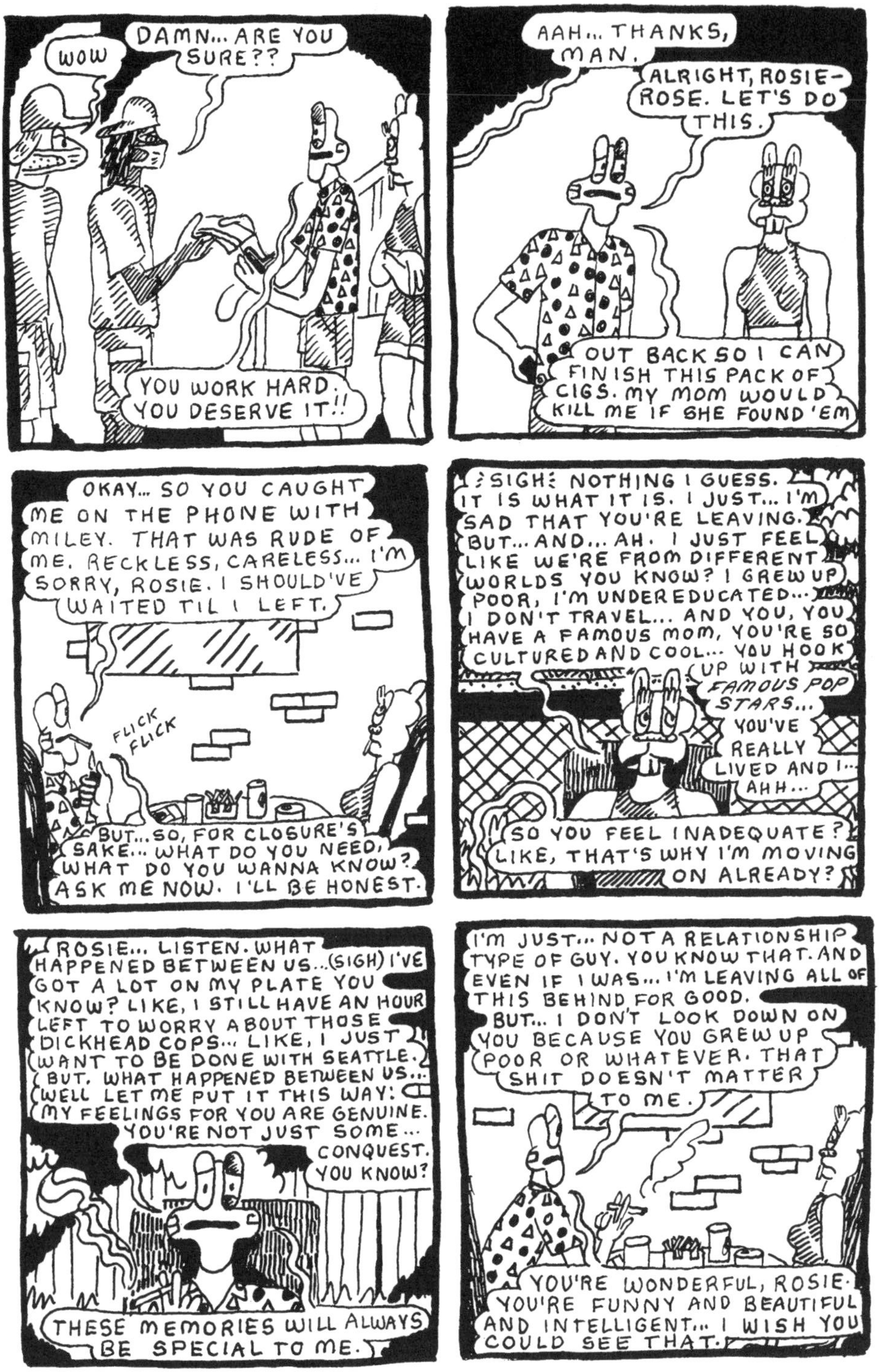
WOW
DAMN... ARE YOU SURE??
YOU WORK HARD. YOU DESERVE IT!!
AAH... THANKS, MAN.
ALRIGHT, ROSIE-ROSE. LET'S DO THIS.
OUT BACK SO I CAN FINISH THIS PACK OF CIGS. MY MOM WOULD KILL ME IF SHE FOUND 'EM
OKAY... SO YOU CAUGHT ME ON THE PHONE WITH MILEY. THAT WAS RUDE OF ME. RECKLESS, CARELESS... I'M SORRY, ROSIE. I SHOULD'VE WAITED TIL I LEFT.
FLICK FLICK
BUT... SO, FOR CLOSURE'S SAKE... WHAT DO YOU NEED, WHAT DO YOU WANNA KNOW? ASK ME NOW. I'LL BE HONEST.
:SIGH: NOTHING I GUESS. IT IS WHAT IT IS. I JUST... I'M SAD THAT YOU'RE LEAVING. BUT... AND... AH. I JUST FEEL LIKE WE'RE FROM DIFFERENT WORLDS YOU KNOW? I GREW UP POOR, I'M UNDEREDUCATED... I DON'T TRAVEL... AND YOU, YOU HAVE A FAMOUS MOM, YOU'RE SO CULTURED AND COOL... YOU HOOK UP WITH FAMOUS POP STARS... YOU'VE REALLY LIVED AND I... AHH...
SO YOU FEEL INADEQUATE? LIKE, THAT'S WHY I'M MOVING ON ALREADY?
ROSIE... LISTEN. WHAT HAPPENED BETWEEN US... (SIGH) I'VE GOT A LOT ON MY PLATE YOU KNOW? LIKE, I STILL HAVE AN HOUR LEFT TO WORRY ABOUT THOSE DICKHEAD COPS... LIKE, I JUST WANT TO BE DONE WITH SEATTLE. BUT, WHAT HAPPENED BETWEEN US... WELL LET ME PUT IT THIS WAY: MY FEELINGS FOR YOU ARE GENUINE. YOU'RE NOT JUST SOME... CONQUEST. YOU KNOW?
THESE MEMORIES WILL ALWAYS BE SPECIAL TO ME.
I'M JUST... NOT A RELATIONSHIP TYPE OF GUY. YOU KNOW THAT. AND EVEN IF I WAS... I'M LEAVING ALL OF THIS BEHIND FOR GOOD. BUT... I DON'T LOOK DOWN ON YOU BECAUSE YOU GREW UP POOR OR WHATEVER. THAT SHIT DOESN'T MATTER TO ME.
YOU'RE WONDERFUL, ROSIE. YOU'RE FUNNY AND BEAUTIFUL AND INTELLIGENT... I WISH YOU COULD SEE THAT.

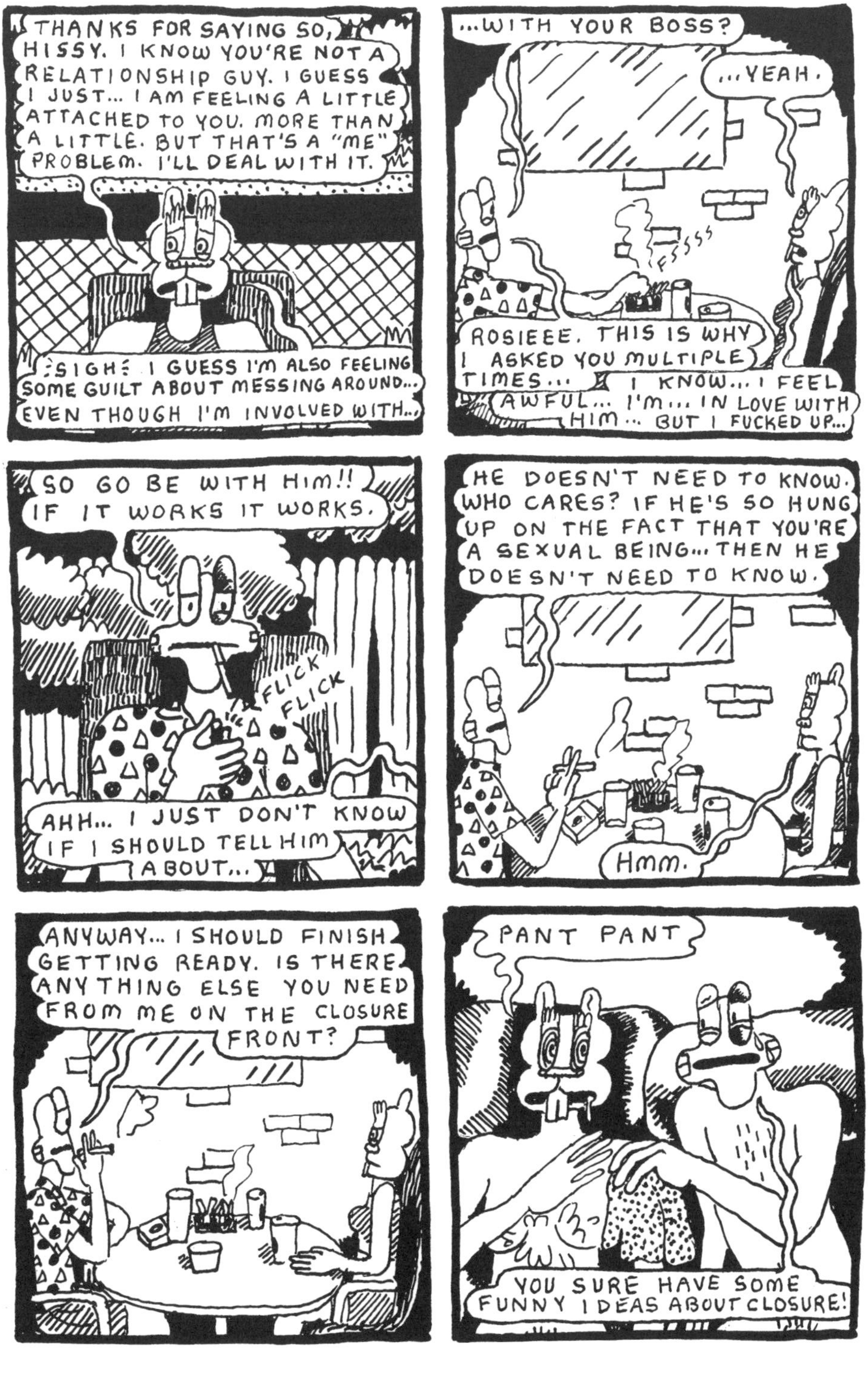
THANKS FOR SAYING SO, HISSY. I KNOW YOU'RE NOT A RELATIONSHIP GUY. I GUESS I JUST... I AM FEELING A LITTLE ATTACHED TO YOU. MORE THAN A LITTLE. BUT THAT'S A "ME" PROBLEM. I'LL DEAL WITH IT.
:SIGH: I GUESS I'M ALSO FEELING SOME GUILT ABOUT MESSING AROUND... EVEN THOUGH I'M INVOLVED WITH...
...WITH YOUR BOSS?
...YEAH.
FSSSS
ROSIEEE. THIS IS WHY I ASKED YOU MULTIPLE TIMES...
I KNOW... I FEEL AWFUL... I'M... IN LOVE WITH HIM... BUT I FUCKED UP...
SO GO BE WITH HIM!! IF IT WORKS IT WORKS.
FLICK FLICK
AHH... I JUST DON'T KNOW IF I SHOULD TELL HIM ABOUT...
HE DOESN'T NEED TO KNOW. WHO CARES? IF HE'S SO HUNG UP ON THE FACT THAT YOU'RE A SEXUAL BEING... THEN HE DOESN'T NEED TO KNOW.
HMM.
ANYWAY... I SHOULD FINISH GETTING READY. IS THERE ANYTHING ELSE YOU NEED FROM ME ON THE CLOSURE FRONT?
PANT PANT
YOU SURE HAVE SOME FUNNY IDEAS ABOUT CLOSURE!

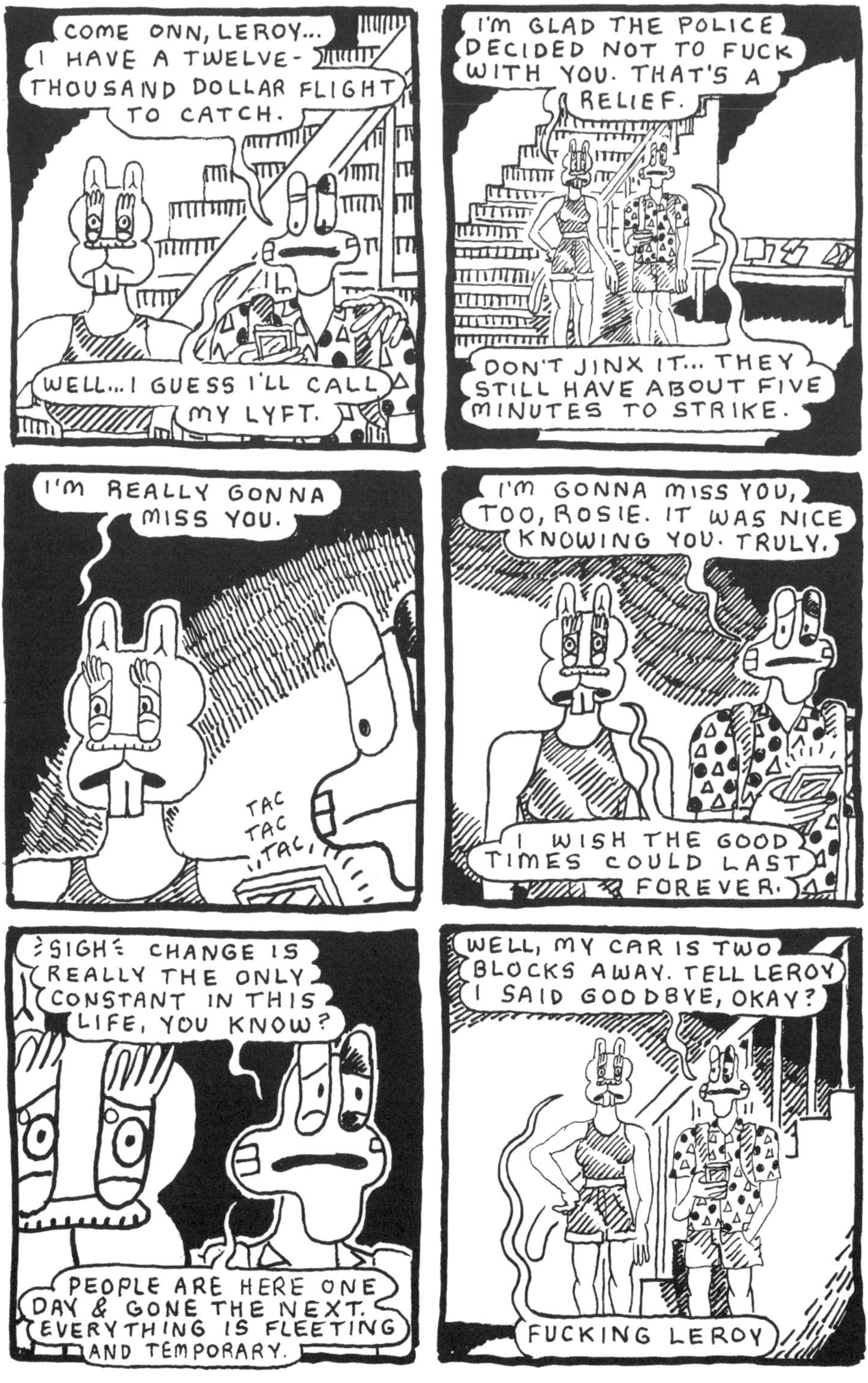
COME ONN, LEROY... I HAVE A TWELVE-THOUSAND DOLLAR FLIGHT TO CATCH.
WELL... I GUESS I'LL CALL MY LYFT.
I'M GLAD THE POLICE DECIDED NOT TO FUCK WITH YOU. THAT'S A RELIEF.
DON'T JINX IT... THEY STILL HAVE ABOUT FIVE MINUTES TO STRIKE.
I'M REALLY GONNA MISS YOU.
TAC TAC TAC
I'M GONNA MISS YOU, TOO, ROSIE. IT WAS NICE KNOWING YOU. TRULY.
I WISH THE GOOD TIMES COULD LAST FOREVER.
SIGH CHANGE IS REALLY THE ONLY CONSTANT IN THIS LIFE, YOU KNOW?
PEOPLE ARE HERE ONE DAY & GONE THE NEXT. EVERYTHING IS FLEETING AND TEMPORARY.
WELL, MY CAR IS TWO BLOCKS AWAY. TELL LEROY I SAID GOODBYE, OKAY?
FUCKING LEROY

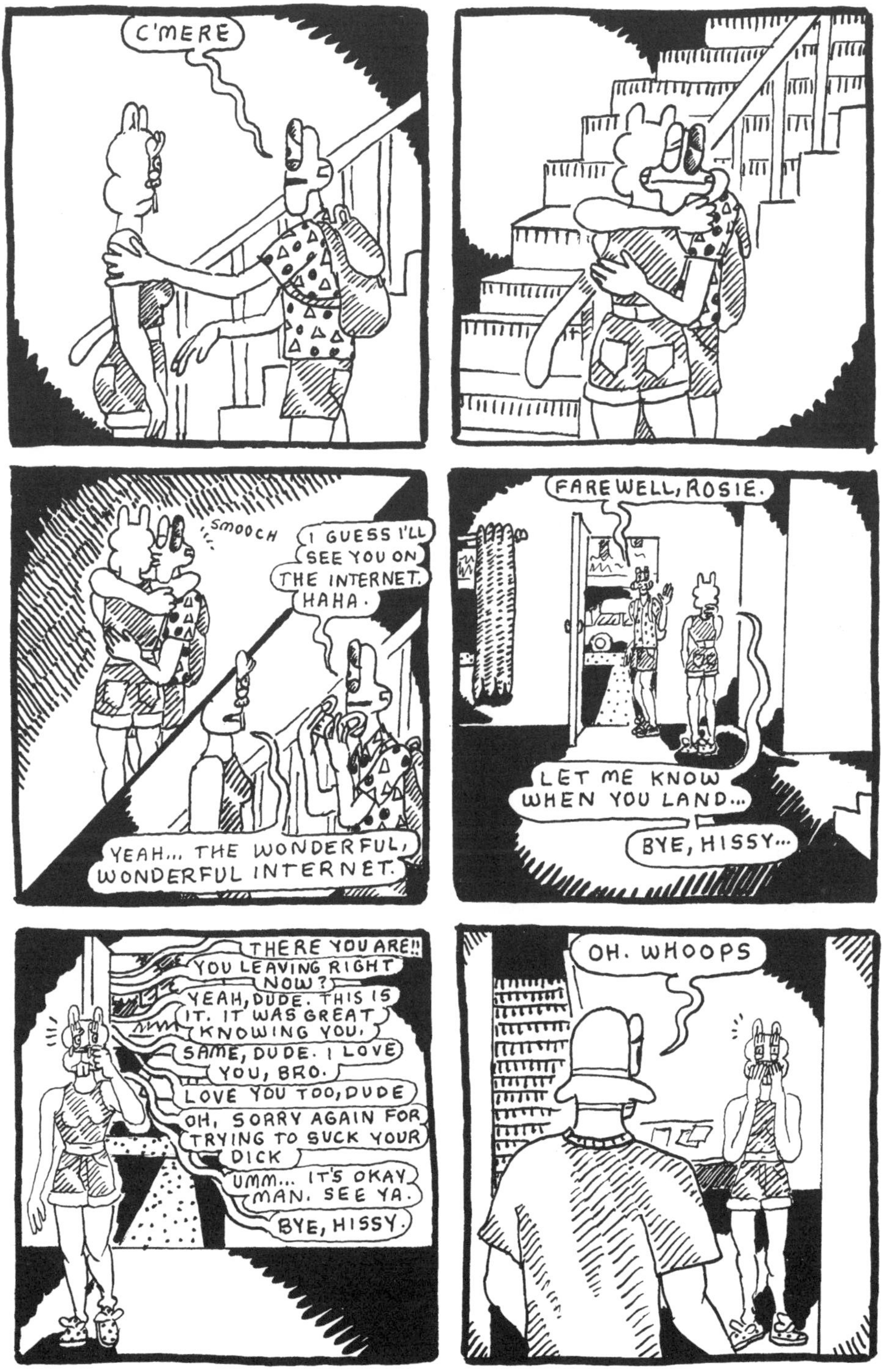
C'MERE
SMOOCH
I GUESS I'LL SEE YOU ON THE INTERNET. HAHA.
YEAH... THE WONDERFUL, WONDERFUL INTERNET.
FAREWELL, ROSIE.
LET ME KNOW WHEN YOU LAND...
BYE, HISSY...
THERE YOU ARE!!
YOU LEAVING RIGHT NOW?
YEAH, DUDE. THIS IS IT. IT WAS GREAT KNOWING YOU.
SAME, DUDE. I LOVE YOU, BRO.
LOVE YOU TOO, DUDE
OH, SORRY AGAIN FOR TRYING TO SUCK YOUR DICK
UMM... IT'S OKAY MAN. SEE YA.
BYE, HISSY.
OH. WHOOPS

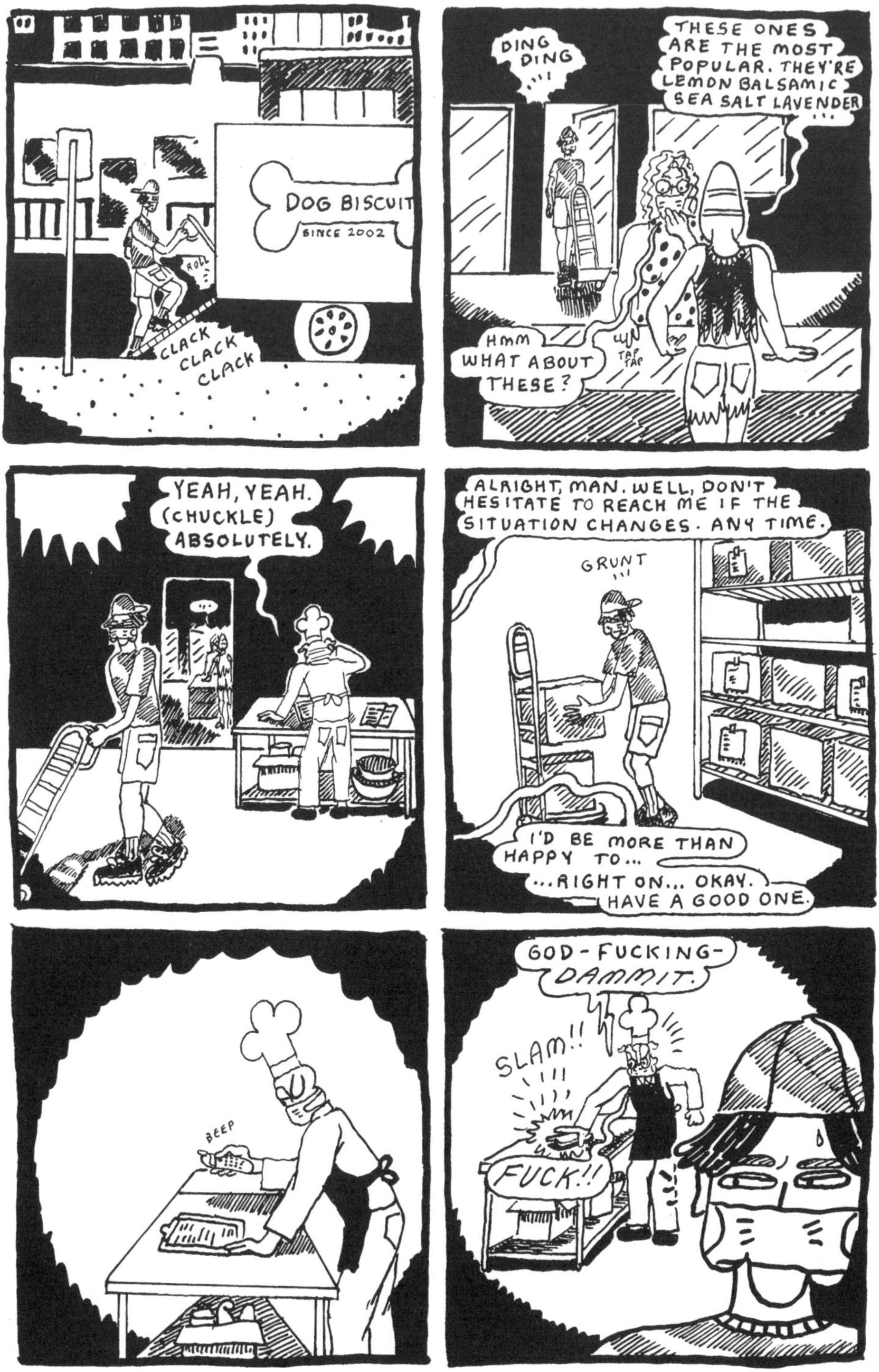
DOG BISCUIT
SINCE 2002
ROLL
CLACK
CLACK
CLACK
DING
DING
THESE ONES ARE THE MOST POPULAR. THEY'RE LEMON BALSAMIC SEA SALT LAVENDER ...
HMM WHAT ABOUT THESE?
TAP TAP
YEAH, YEAH. (CHUCKLE) ABSOLUTELY.
ALRIGHT, MAN. WELL, DON'T HESITATE TO REACH ME IF THE SITUATION CHANGES. ANY TIME.
GRUNT
I'D BE MORE THAN HAPPY TO...
...RIGHT ON... OKAY. HAVE A GOOD ONE.
BEEP
GOD-FUCKING-DAMMIT.
SLAM!!
FUCK!!

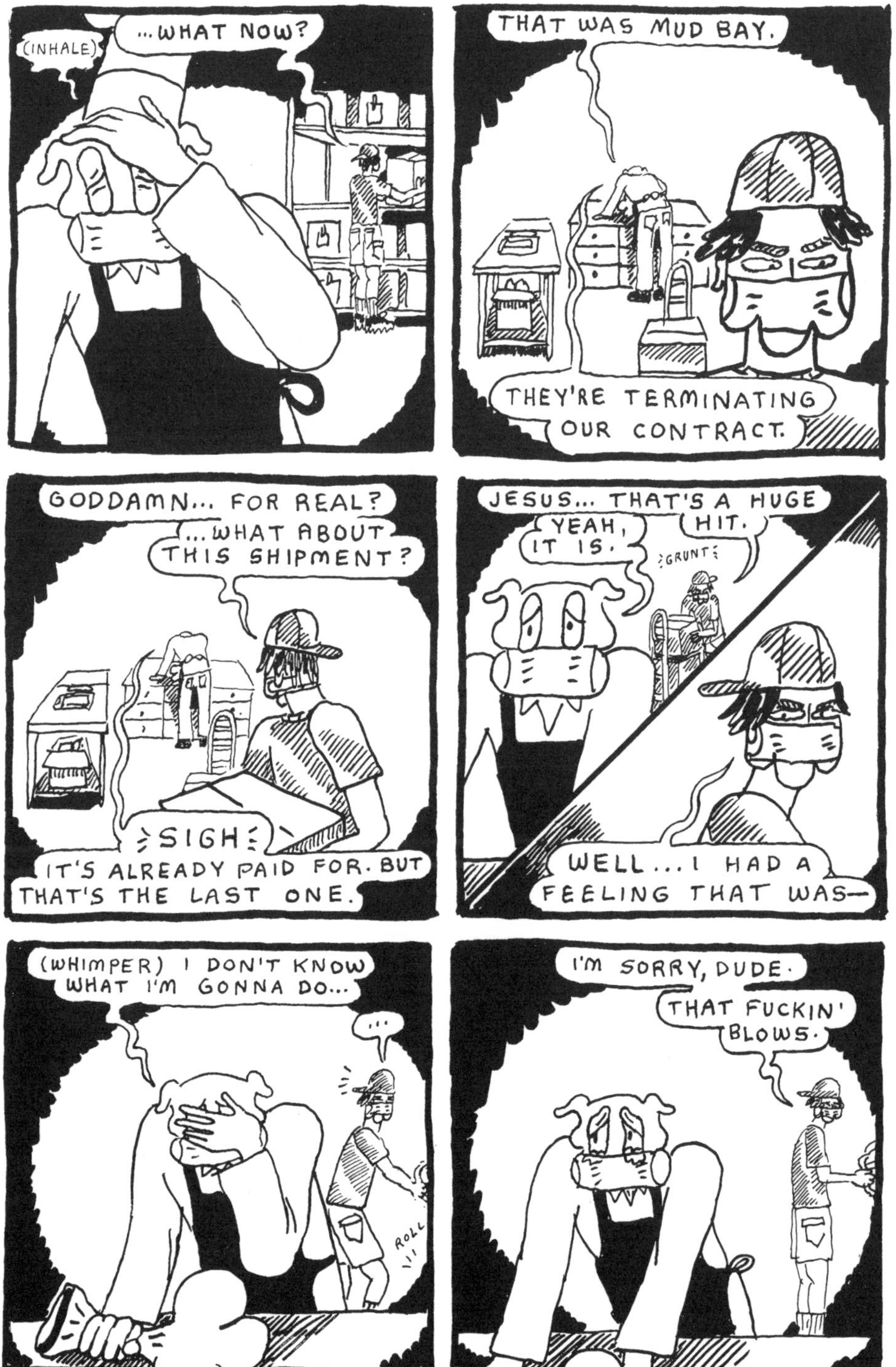
(INHALE)
...WHAT NOW?
THAT WAS MUD BAY.
THEY'RE TERMINATING OUR CONTRACT.
GODDAMN... FOR REAL?
...WHAT ABOUT THIS SHIPMENT?
SIGH
IT'S ALREADY PAID FOR. BUT THAT'S THE LAST ONE.
JESUS... THAT'S A HUGE HIT.
YEAH, IT IS.
GRUNT
WELL... I HAD A FEELING THAT WAS—
(WHIMPER) I DON'T KNOW WHAT I'M GONNA DO...
...
ROLL
I'M SORRY, DUDE.
THAT FUCKIN' BLOWS.

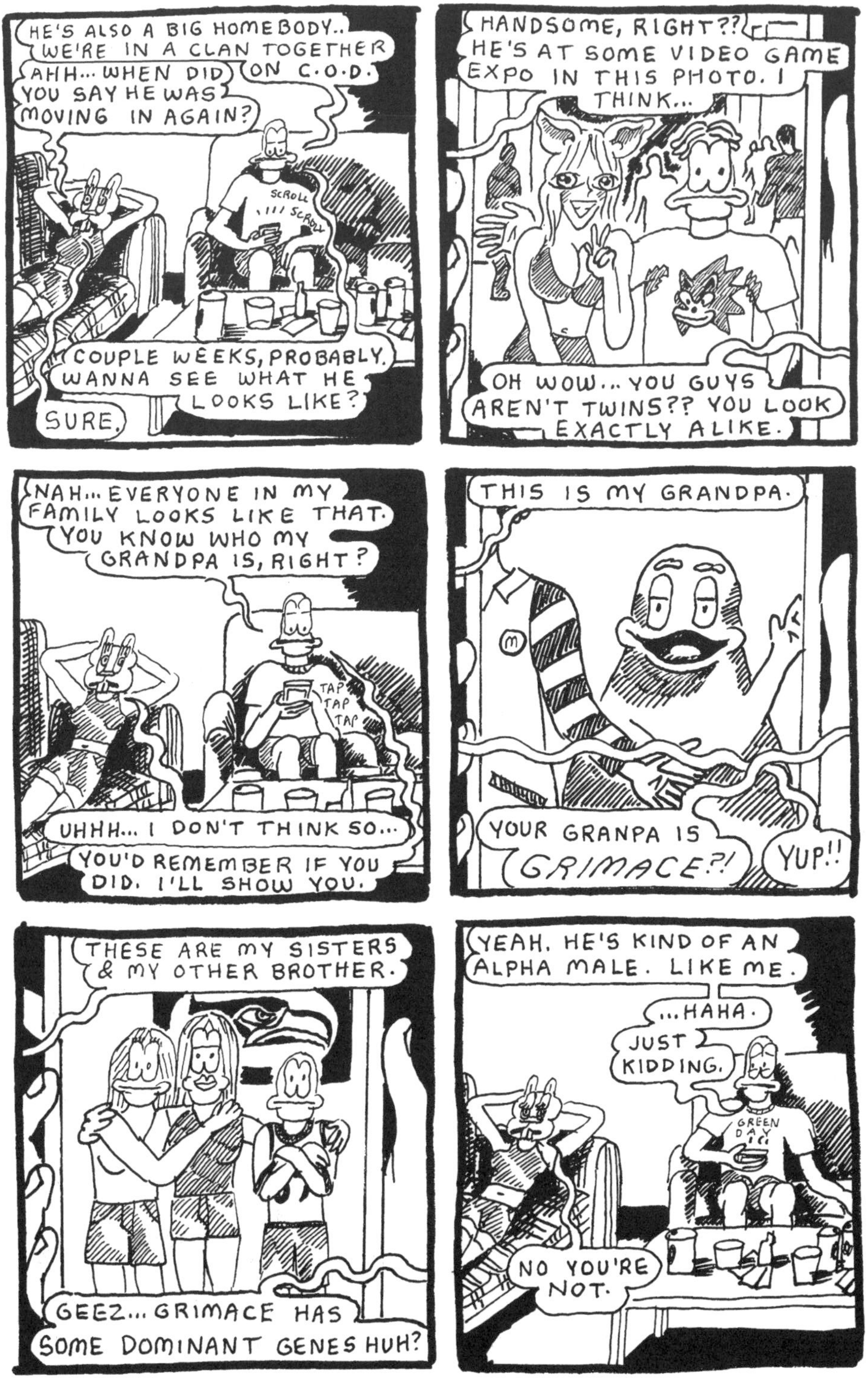
HE'S ALSO A BIG HOMEBODY.. WE'RE IN A CLAN TOGETHER ON C.O.D.
AHH... WHEN DID YOU SAY HE WAS MOVING IN AGAIN?
SCROLL SCROLL
COUPLE WEEKS, PROBABLY. WANNA SEE WHAT HE LOOKS LIKE?
SURE.
HANDSOME, RIGHT?? HE'S AT SOME VIDEO GAME EXPO IN THIS PHOTO. I THINK...
OH WOW... YOU GUYS AREN'T TWINS?? YOU LOOK EXACTLY ALIKE.
NAH... EVERYONE IN MY FAMILY LOOKS LIKE THAT.
YOU KNOW WHO MY GRANDPA IS, RIGHT?
TAP TAP TAP
UHHH... I DON'T THINK SO...
YOU'D REMEMBER IF YOU DID. I'LL SHOW YOU.
THIS IS MY GRANDPA.
YOUR GRANPA IS GRIMACE?!
YUP!!
THESE ARE MY SISTERS & MY OTHER BROTHER.
GEEZ... GRIMACE HAS SOME DOMINANT GENES HUH?
YEAH. HE'S KIND OF AN ALPHA MALE. LIKE ME.
...HAHA. JUST KIDDING.
GREEN DAY
NO YOU'RE NOT.

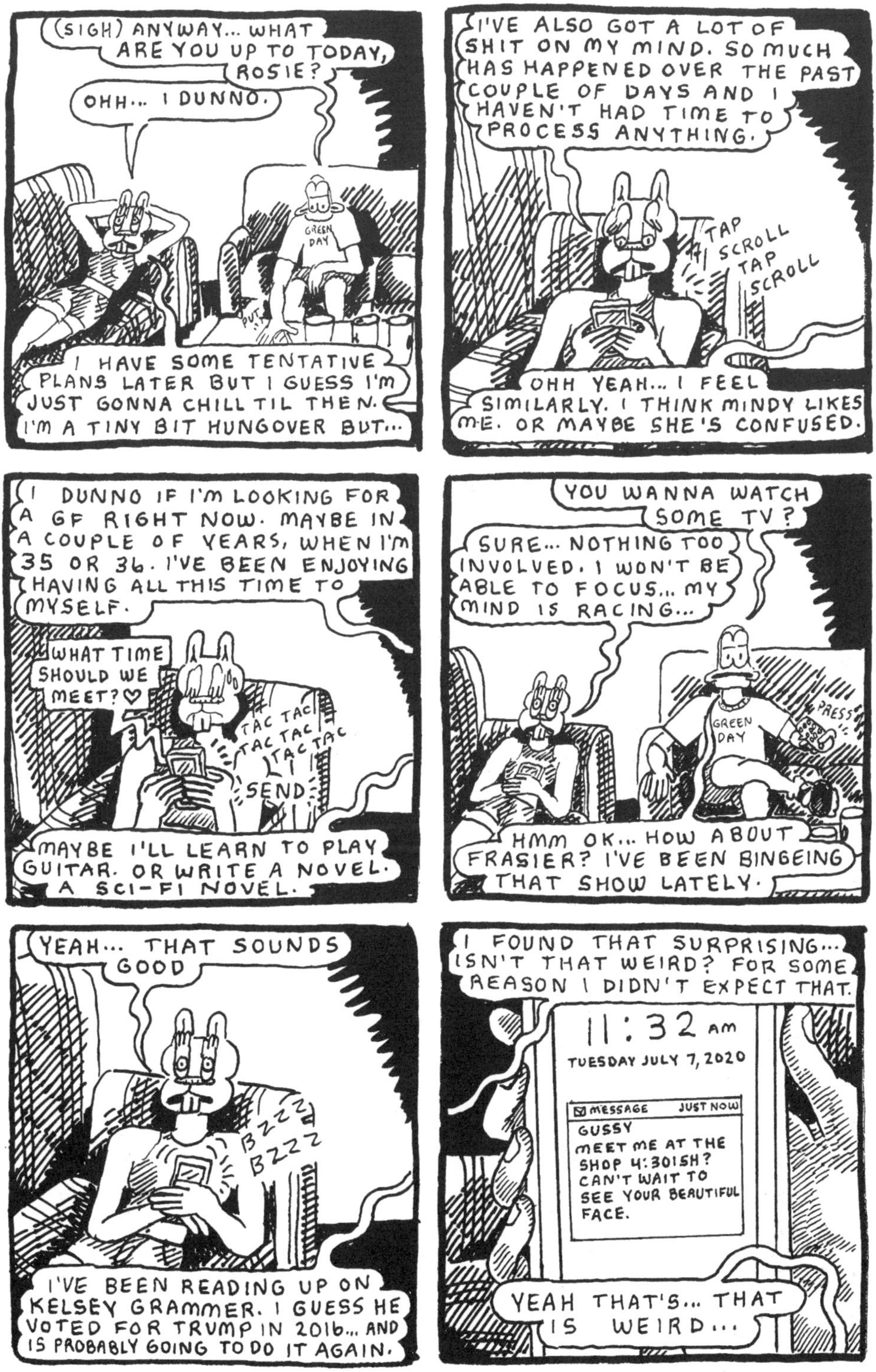
(SIGH) ANYWAY... WHAT ARE YOU UP TO TODAY, ROSIE?
OHH... I DUNNO.
PUT
I HAVE SOME TENTATIVE PLANS LATER BUT I GUESS I'M JUST GONNA CHILL TIL THEN. I'M A TINY BIT HUNGOVER BUT...
GREEN DAY
I'VE ALSO GOT A LOT OF SHIT ON MY MIND. SO MUCH HAS HAPPENED OVER THE PAST COUPLE OF DAYS AND I HAVEN'T HAD TIME TO PROCESS ANYTHING.
TAP SCROLL TAP SCROLL
OHH YEAH... I FEEL SIMILARLY. I THINK MINDY LIKES ME. OR MAYBE SHE'S CONFUSED.
I DUNNO IF I'M LOOKING FOR A GF RIGHT NOW. MAYBE IN A COUPLE OF YEARS, WHEN I'M 35 OR 36. I'VE BEEN ENJOYING HAVING ALL THIS TIME TO MYSELF.
WHAT TIME SHOULD WE MEET? ♡
TAC TAC TAC TAC TAC TAC
SEND
MAYBE I'LL LEARN TO PLAY GUITAR. OR WRITE A NOVEL. A SCI-FI NOVEL.
YOU WANNA WATCH SOME TV?
SURE... NOTHING TOO INVOLVED. I WON'T BE ABLE TO FOCUS... MY MIND IS RACING...
GREEN DAY
PRESS
HMM OK... HOW ABOUT FRASIER? I'VE BEEN BINGEING THAT SHOW LATELY.
YEAH... THAT SOUNDS GOOD
BZZZ BZZZ
I'VE BEEN READING UP ON KELSEY GRAMMER. I GUESS HE VOTED FOR TRUMP IN 2016... AND IS PROBABLY GOING TO DO IT AGAIN.
I FOUND THAT SURPRISING... ISN'T THAT WEIRD? FOR SOME REASON I DIDN'T EXPECT THAT.
11:32 AM
TUESDAY JULY 7, 2020
MESSAGE JUST NOW
GUSSY
MEET ME AT THE SHOP 4:30ISH? CAN'T WAIT TO SEE YOUR BEAUTIFUL FACE.
YEAH THAT'S... THAT IS WEIRD...

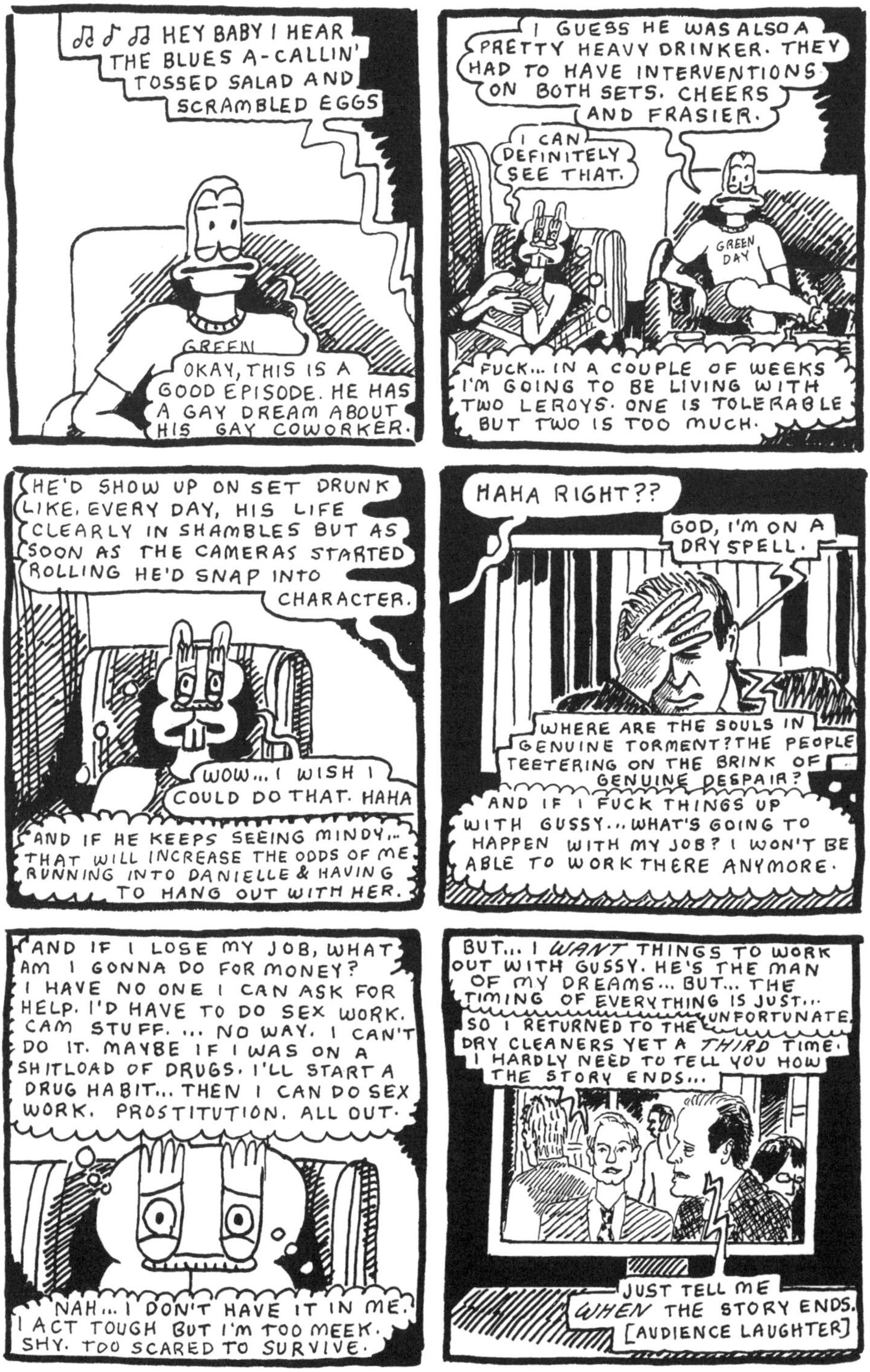

♫♪♫ HEY BABY I HEAR THE BLUES A-CALLIN' TOSSED SALAD AND SCRAMBLED EGGS
GREEN
OKAY, THIS IS A GOOD EPISODE. HE HAS A GAY DREAM ABOUT HIS GAY COWORKER.
I GUESS HE WAS ALSO A PRETTY HEAVY DRINKER. THEY HAD TO HAVE INTERVENTIONS ON BOTH SETS. CHEERS AND FRASIER.
I CAN DEFINITELY SEE THAT.
GREEN DAY
FUCK... IN A COUPLE OF WEEKS I'M GOING TO BE LIVING WITH TWO LEROYS. ONE IS TOLERABLE BUT TWO IS TOO MUCH.
HE'D SHOW UP ON SET DRUNK LIKE, EVERY DAY, HIS LIFE CLEARLY IN SHAMBLES BUT AS SOON AS THE CAMERAS STARTED ROLLING HE'D SNAP INTO CHARACTER.
WOW... I WISH I COULD DO THAT. HAHA
AND IF HE KEEPS SEEING MINDY... THAT WILL INCREASE THE ODDS OF ME RUNNING INTO DANIELLE & HAVING TO HANG OUT WITH HER.
HAHA RIGHT??
GOD, I'M ON A DRY SPELL.
WHERE ARE THE SOULS IN GENUINE TORMENT? THE PEOPLE TEETERING ON THE BRINK OF GENUINE DESPAIR?
AND IF I FUCK THINGS UP WITH GUSSY... WHAT'S GOING TO HAPPEN WITH MY JOB? I WON'T BE ABLE TO WORK THERE ANYMORE.
AND IF I LOSE MY JOB, WHAT AM I GONNA DO FOR MONEY? I HAVE NO ONE I CAN ASK FOR HELP. I'D HAVE TO DO SEX WORK. CAM STUFF. ... NO WAY. I CAN'T DO IT. MAYBE IF I WAS ON A SHITLOAD OF DRUGS. I'LL START A DRUG HABIT... THEN I CAN DO SEX WORK. PROSTITUTION. ALL OUT.
NAH... I DON'T HAVE IT IN ME. I ACT TOUGH BUT I'M TOO MEEK. SHY. TOO SCARED TO SURVIVE.
BUT... I *WANT* THINGS TO WORK OUT WITH GUSSY. HE'S THE MAN OF MY DREAMS... BUT... THE TIMING OF EVERYTHING IS JUST... UNFORTUNATE.
SO I RETURNED TO THE DRY CLEANERS YET A *THIRD* TIME. I HARDLY NEED TO TELL YOU HOW THE STORY ENDS...
JUST TELL ME *WHEN* THE STORY ENDS. [AUDIENCE LAUGHTER]

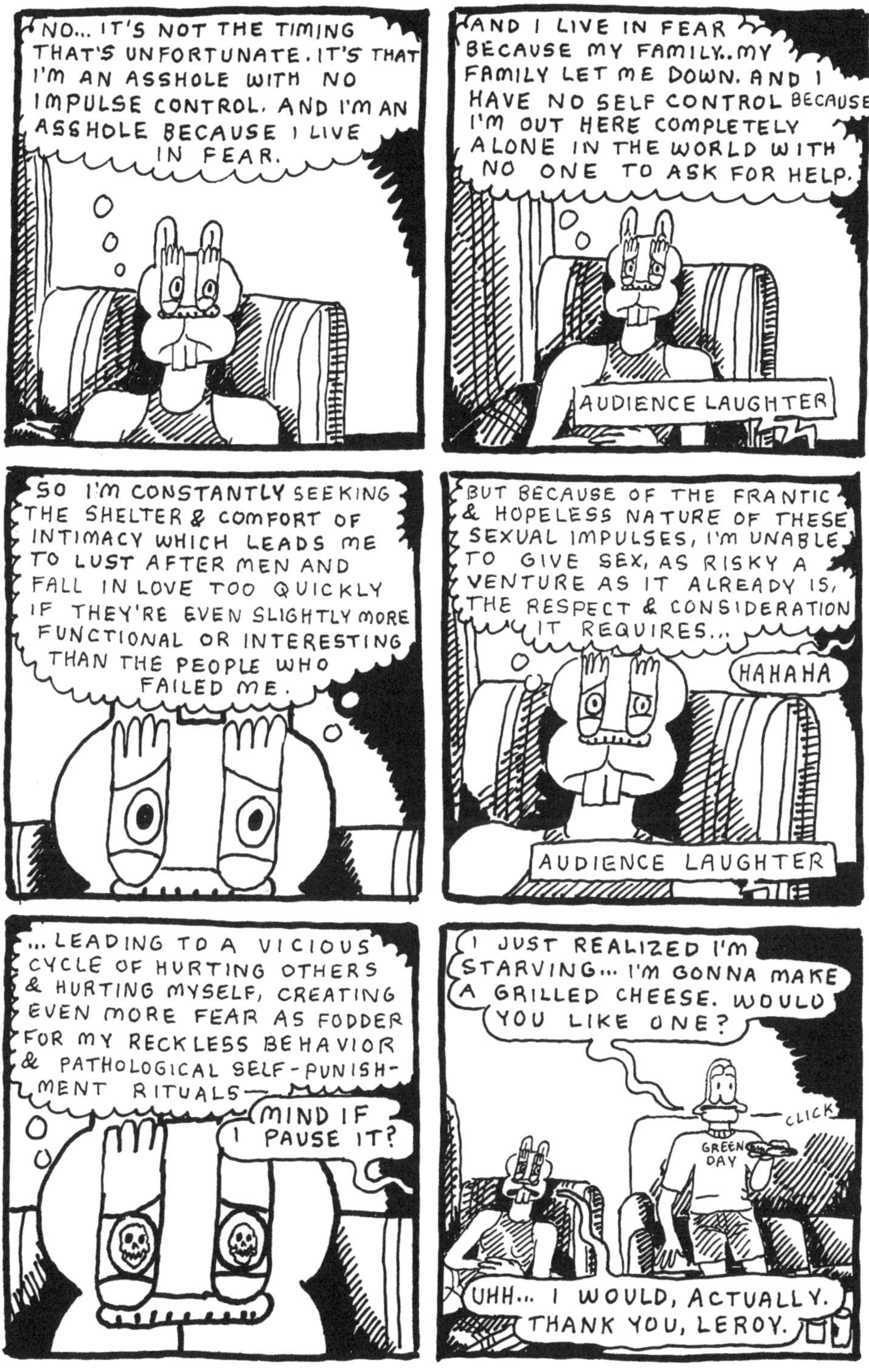
NO... IT'S NOT THE TIMING THAT'S UNFORTUNATE. IT'S THAT I'M AN ASSHOLE WITH NO IMPULSE CONTROL. AND I'M AN ASSHOLE BECAUSE I LIVE IN FEAR.
AND I LIVE IN FEAR BECAUSE MY FAMILY.. MY FAMILY LET ME DOWN. AND I HAVE NO SELF CONTROL BECAUSE I'M OUT HERE COMPLETELY ALONE IN THE WORLD WITH NO ONE TO ASK FOR HELP.
AUDIENCE LAUGHTER
SO I'M CONSTANTLY SEEKING THE SHELTER & COMFORT OF INTIMACY WHICH LEADS ME TO LUST AFTER MEN AND FALL IN LOVE TOO QUICKLY IF THEY'RE EVEN SLIGHTLY MORE FUNCTIONAL OR INTERESTING THAN THE PEOPLE WHO FAILED ME.
BUT BECAUSE OF THE FRANTIC & HOPELESS NATURE OF THESE SEXUAL IMPULSES, I'M UNABLE TO GIVE SEX, AS RISKY A VENTURE AS IT ALREADY IS, THE RESPECT & CONSIDERATION IT REQUIRES...
HAHAHA
AUDIENCE LAUGHTER
...LEADING TO A VICIOUS CYCLE OF HURTING OTHERS & HURTING MYSELF, CREATING EVEN MORE FEAR AS FODDER FOR MY RECKLESS BEHAVIOR & PATHOLOGICAL SELF-PUNISHMENT RITUALS—
MIND IF I PAUSE IT?
I JUST REALIZED I'M STARVING... I'M GONNA MAKE A GRILLED CHEESE. WOULD YOU LIKE ONE?
CLICK
GREEN DAY
UHH... I WOULD, ACTUALLY. THANK YOU, LEROY.

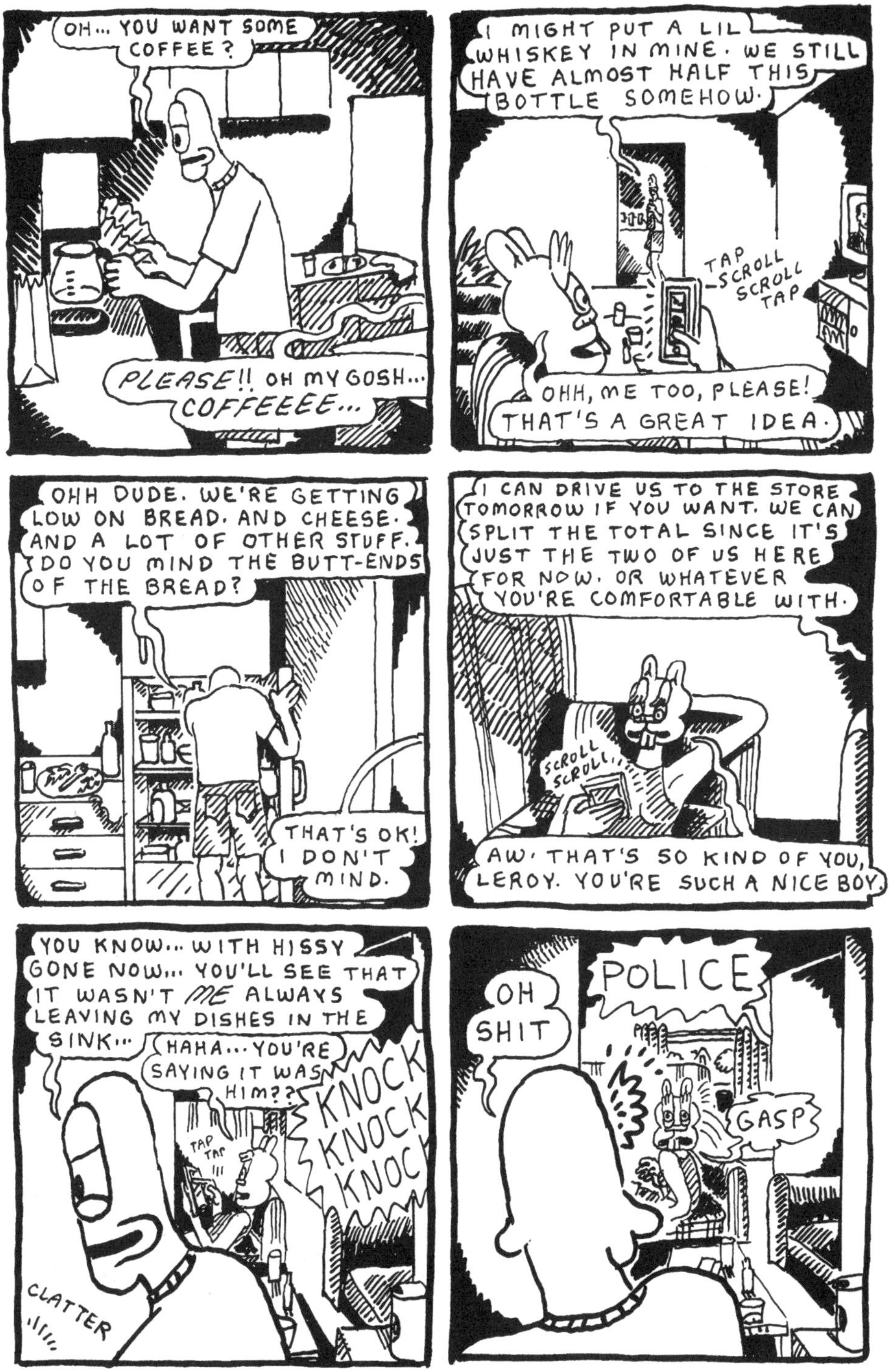
OH... YOU WANT SOME COFFEE?
PLEASE!! OH MY GOSH... COFFEEEE...
I MIGHT PUT A LIL WHISKEY IN MINE. WE STILL HAVE ALMOST HALF THIS BOTTLE SOMEHOW.
TAP SCROLL SCROLL TAP
OHH, ME TOO, PLEASE! THAT'S A GREAT IDEA.
OHH DUDE. WE'RE GETTING LOW ON BREAD. AND CHEESE. AND A LOT OF OTHER STUFF. DO YOU MIND THE BUTT-ENDS OF THE BREAD?
THAT'S OK! I DON'T MIND.
I CAN DRIVE US TO THE STORE TOMORROW IF YOU WANT. WE CAN SPLIT THE TOTAL SINCE IT'S JUST THE TWO OF US HERE FOR NOW. OR WHATEVER YOU'RE COMFORTABLE WITH.
SCROLL SCROLL
AW. THAT'S SO KIND OF YOU, LEROY. YOU'RE SUCH A NICE BOY.
YOU KNOW... WITH HISSY GONE NOW... YOU'LL SEE THAT IT WASN'T ME ALWAYS LEAVING MY DISHES IN THE SINK...
HAHA... YOU'RE SAYING IT WAS HIM??
TAP TAP
KNOCK KNOCK KNOC
CLATTER
OH SHIT
POLICE
GASP

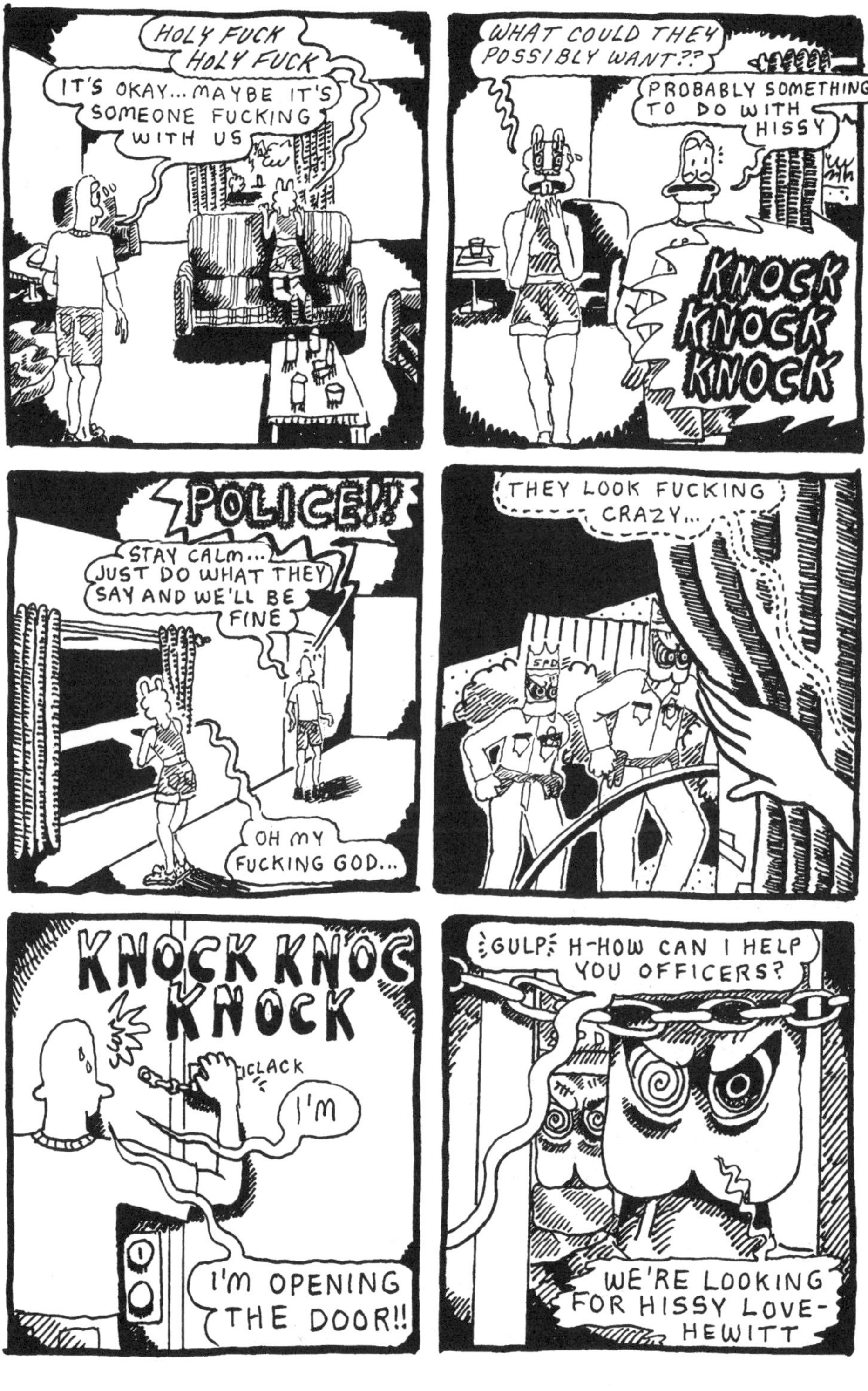
HOLY FUCK HOLY FUCK
IT'S OKAY... MAYBE IT'S SOMEONE FUCKING WITH US
WHAT COULD THEY POSSIBLY WANT??
PROBABLY SOMETHING TO DO WITH HISSY
KNOCK KNOCK KNOCK
POLICE!!
STAY CALM... JUST DO WHAT THEY SAY AND WE'LL BE FINE
OH MY FUCKING GOD...
THEY LOOK FUCKING CRAZY...
SPD
KNOCK KNOC KNOCK
CLACK
I'M
I'M OPENING THE DOOR!!
GULP H-HOW CAN I HELP YOU OFFICERS?
WE'RE LOOKING FOR HISSY LOVE-HEWITT

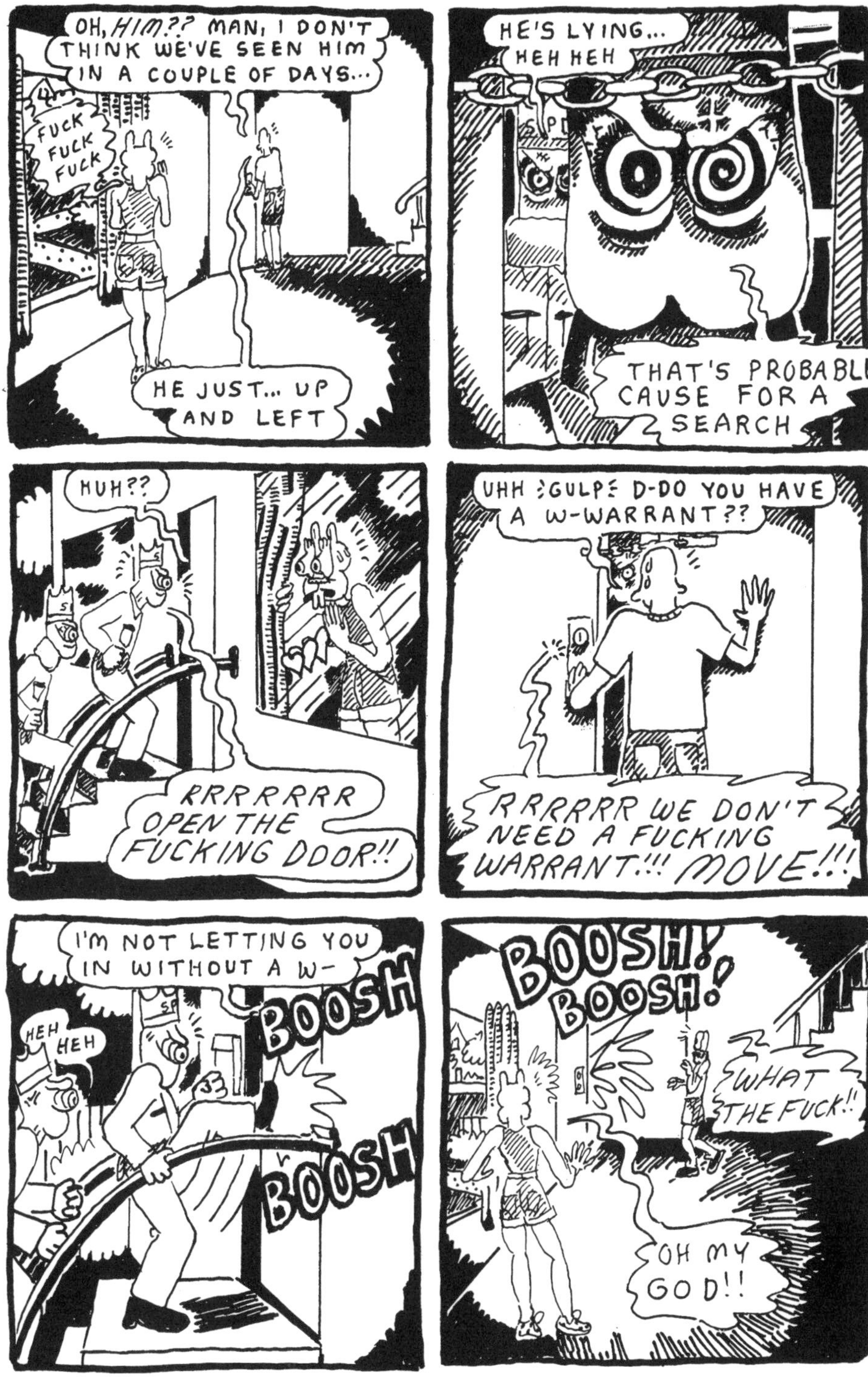
OH, HIM?? MAN, I DON'T THINK WE'VE SEEN HIM IN A COUPLE OF DAYS...
FUCK FUCK FUCK
HE JUST... UP AND LEFT
HE'S LYING... HEH HEH
THAT'S PROBABLE CAUSE FOR A SEARCH
HUH??
RRRRRRR OPEN THE FUCKING DOOR!!
UHH :GULP: D-DO YOU HAVE A W-WARRANT??
RRRRRR WE DON'T NEED A FUCKING WARRANT!!! MOVE!!!
I'M NOT LETTING YOU IN WITHOUT A W-
HEH HEH
BOOSH
BOOSH
BOOSH! BOOSH!
WHAT THE FUCK!!
OH MY GOD!!

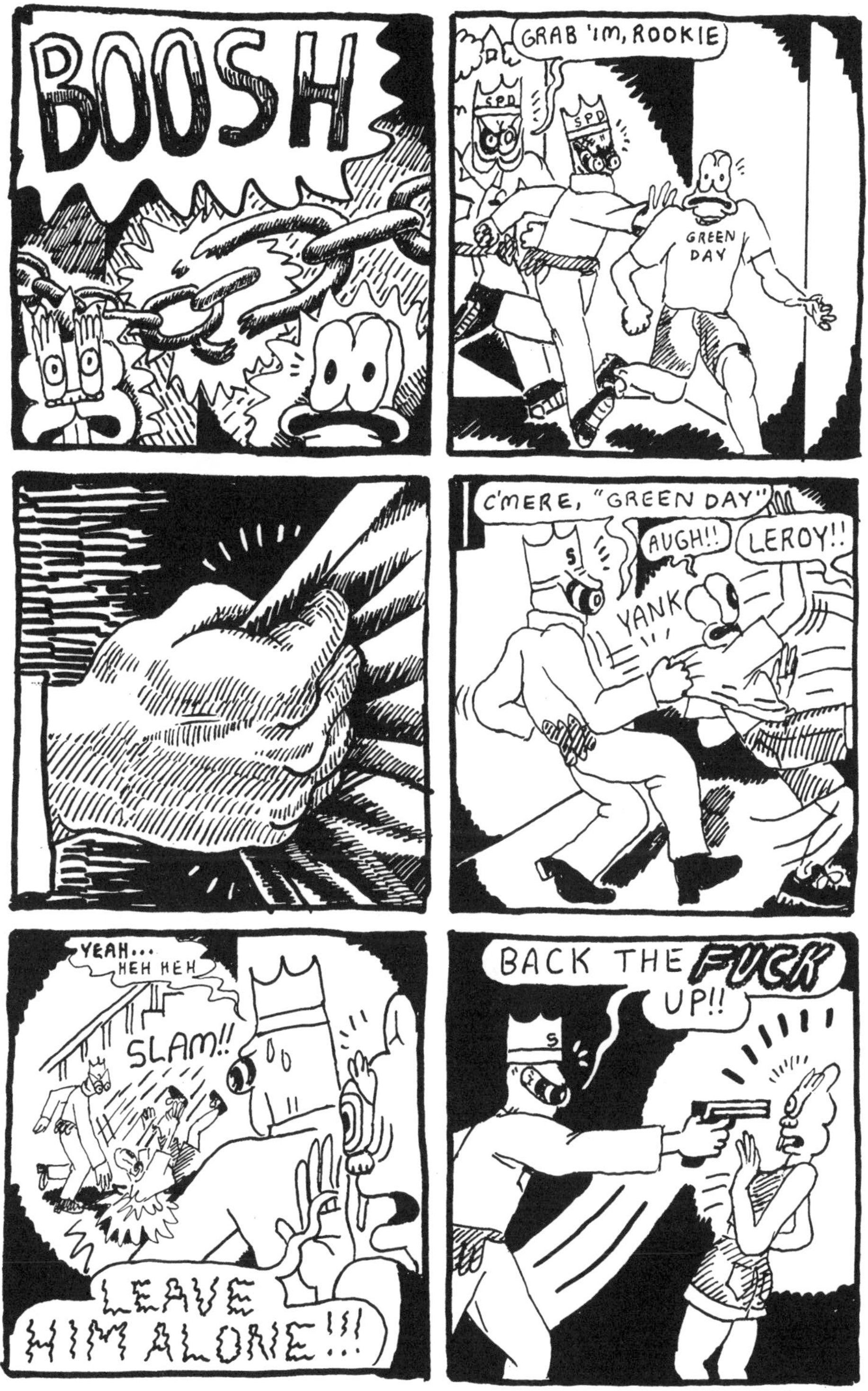
BOOSH
GRAB 'IM, ROOKIE
SPD
SPD
GREEN DAY
C'MERE, "GREEN DAY"
AUGH!!
LEROY!!
YANK
YEAH... HEH HEH
SLAM!!
LEAVE HIM ALONE!!!
BACK THE FUCK UP!!

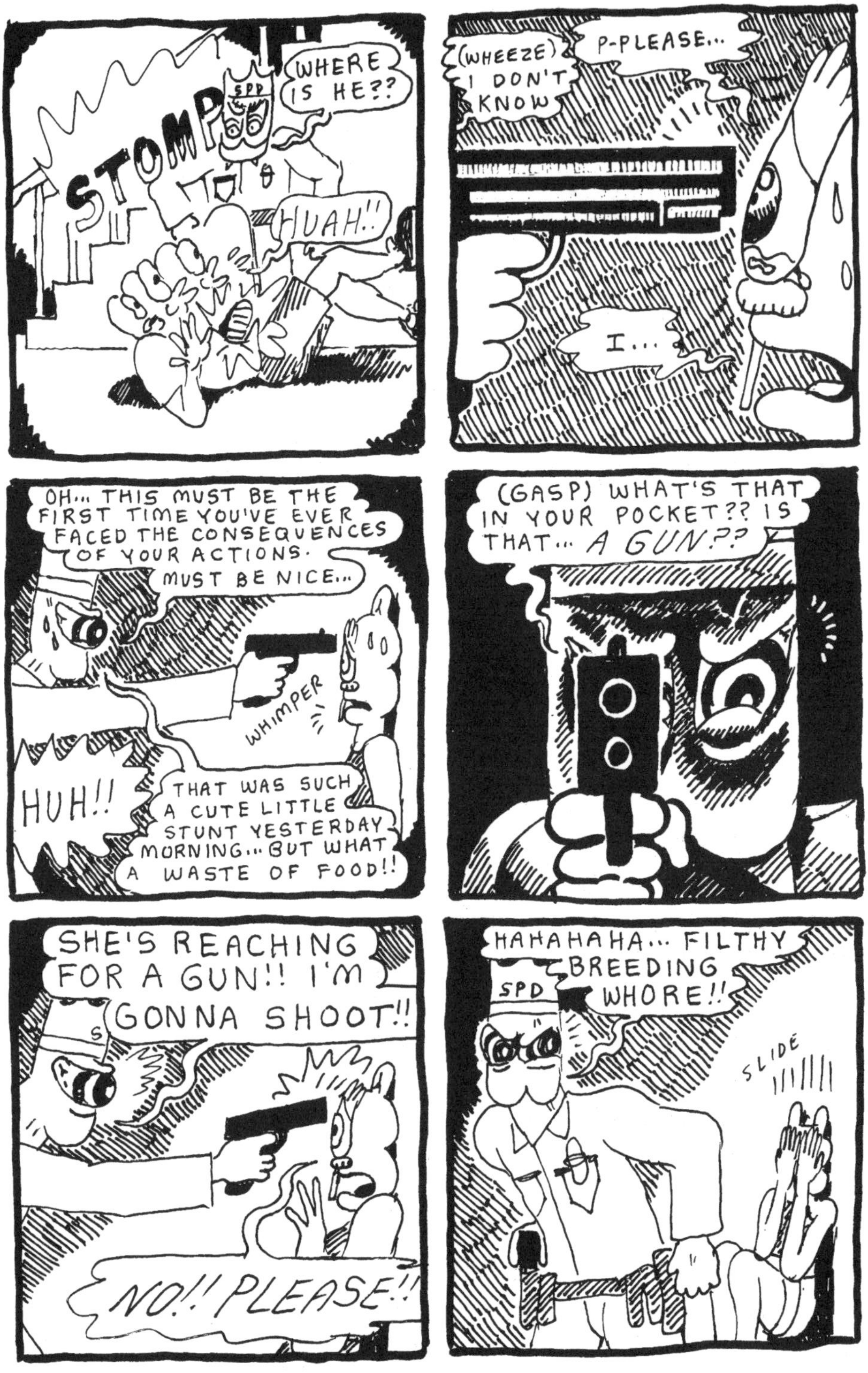
STOMP
WHERE IS HE??
SPD
HUAH!!
(WHEEZE) I DON'T KNOW
P-PLEASE...
I...
OH... THIS MUST BE THE FIRST TIME YOU'VE EVER FACED THE CONSEQUENCES OF YOUR ACTIONS.
MUST BE NICE...
WHIMPER
HUH!!
THAT WAS SUCH A CUTE LITTLE STUNT YESTERDAY MORNING... BUT WHAT A WASTE OF FOOD!!
(GASP) WHAT'S THAT IN YOUR POCKET?? IS THAT... A GUN??
SHE'S REACHING FOR A GUN!! I'M GONNA SHOOT!!
NO!! PLEASE!!
HAHAHAHA... FILTHY BREEDING WHORE!!
SPD
SLIDE

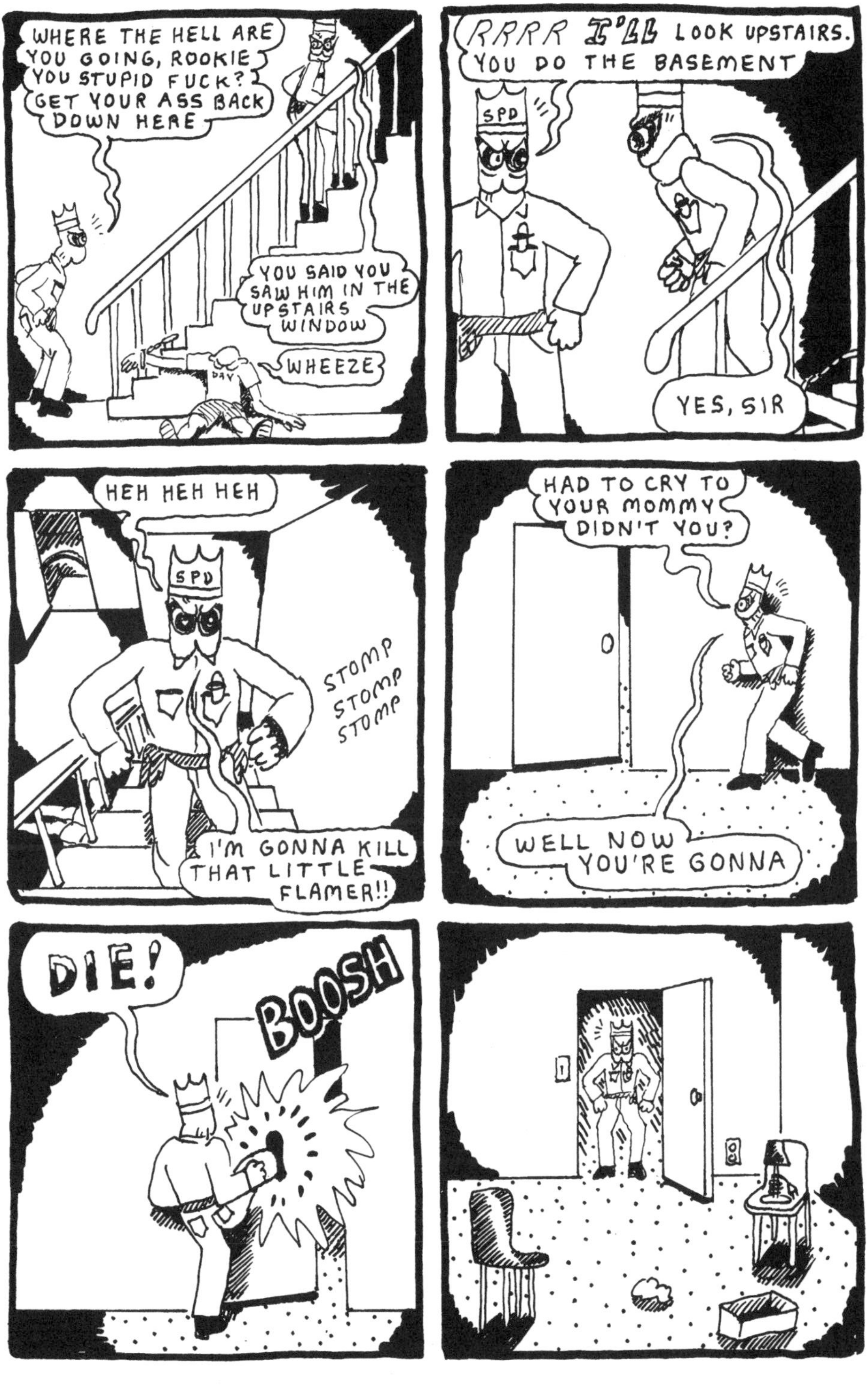
WHERE THE HELL ARE YOU GOING, ROOKIE YOU STUPID FUCK? GET YOUR ASS BACK DOWN HERE
YOU SAID YOU SAW HIM IN THE UPSTAIRS WINDOW
WHEEZE
RRRR I'LL LOOK UPSTAIRS. YOU DO THE BASEMENT
YES, SIR
HEH HEH HEH
STOMP STOMP STOMP
I'M GONNA KILL THAT LITTLE FLAMER!!
HAD TO CRY TO YOUR MOMMY DIDN'T YOU?
WELL NOW YOU'RE GONNA
DIE!
BOOSH

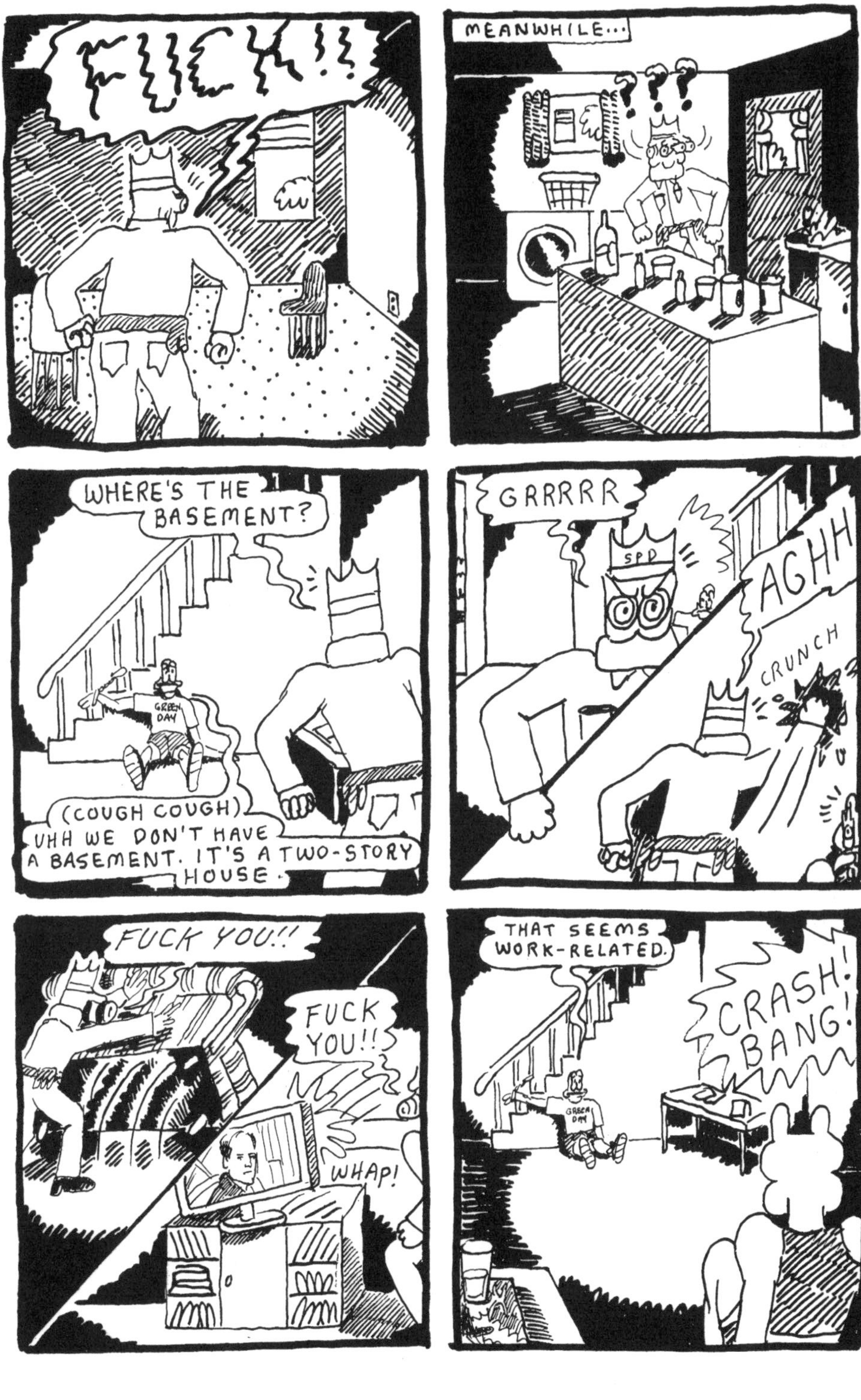
FUCK!!
MEANWHILE...
???
WHERE'S THE BASEMENT?
GREEN DAY
(COUGH COUGH) UHH WE DON'T HAVE A BASEMENT. IT'S A TWO-STORY HOUSE.
GRRRRR
SPD
AGHH
CRUNCH
FUCK YOU!!
FUCK YOU!!
WHAP!
THAT SEEMS WORK-RELATED.
GREEN DAY
CRASH! BANG!

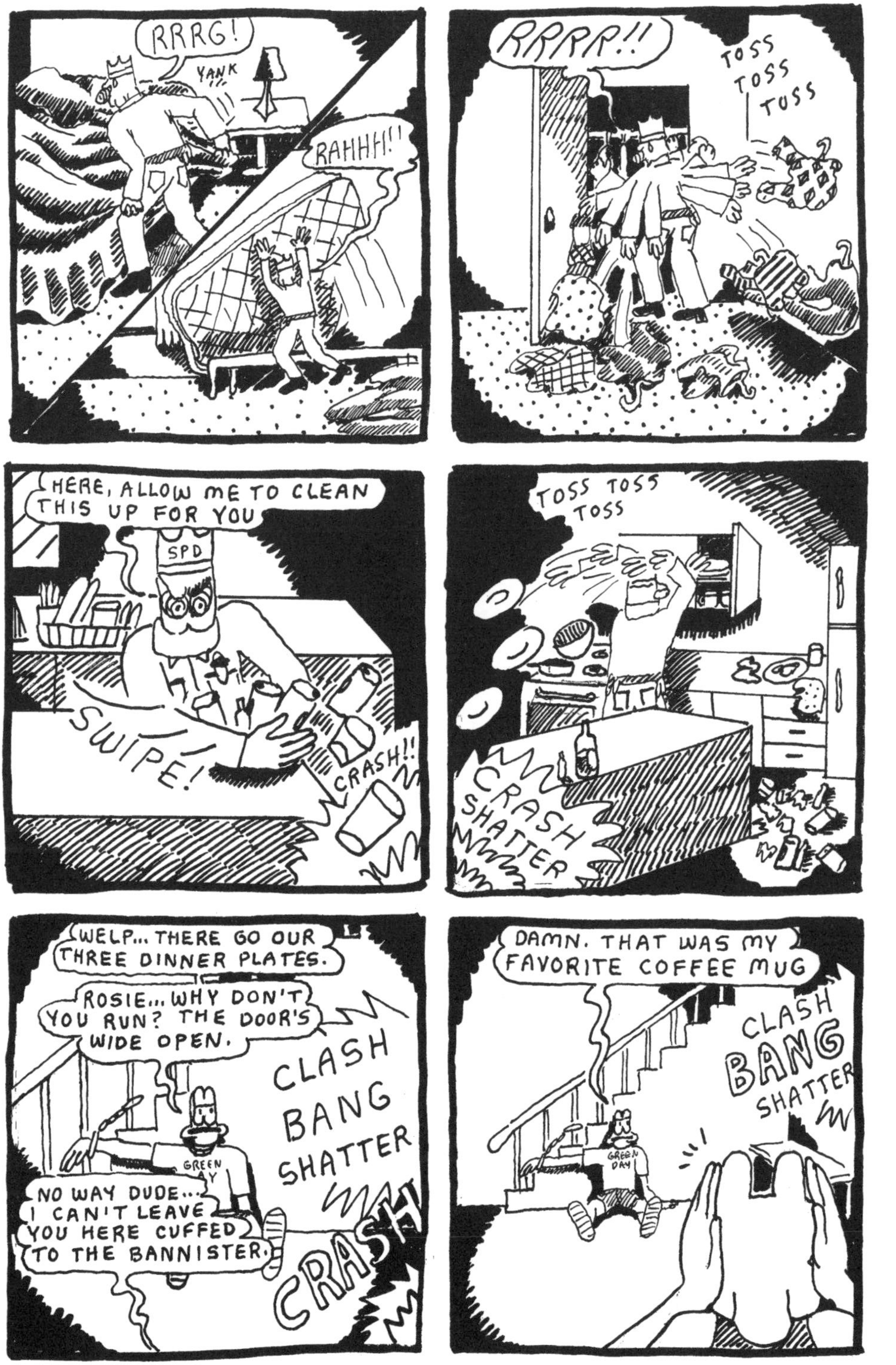
RRRG!
YANK
RAHHH!!
RRRR!!
TOSS
TOSS
TUSS
HERE, ALLOW ME TO CLEAN THIS UP FOR YOU
SPD
SWIPE!
CRASH!!
TOSS TOSS TOSS
CRASH
SHATTER
WELP... THERE GO OUR THREE DINNER PLATES.
ROSIE... WHY DON'T YOU RUN? THE DOOR'S WIDE OPEN.
CLASH
BANG
SHATTER
NO WAY DUDE... I CAN'T LEAVE YOU HERE CUFFED TO THE BANNISTER.
CRASH
DAMN. THAT WAS MY FAVORITE COFFEE MUG
CLASH
BANG
SHATTER
GREEN DAY

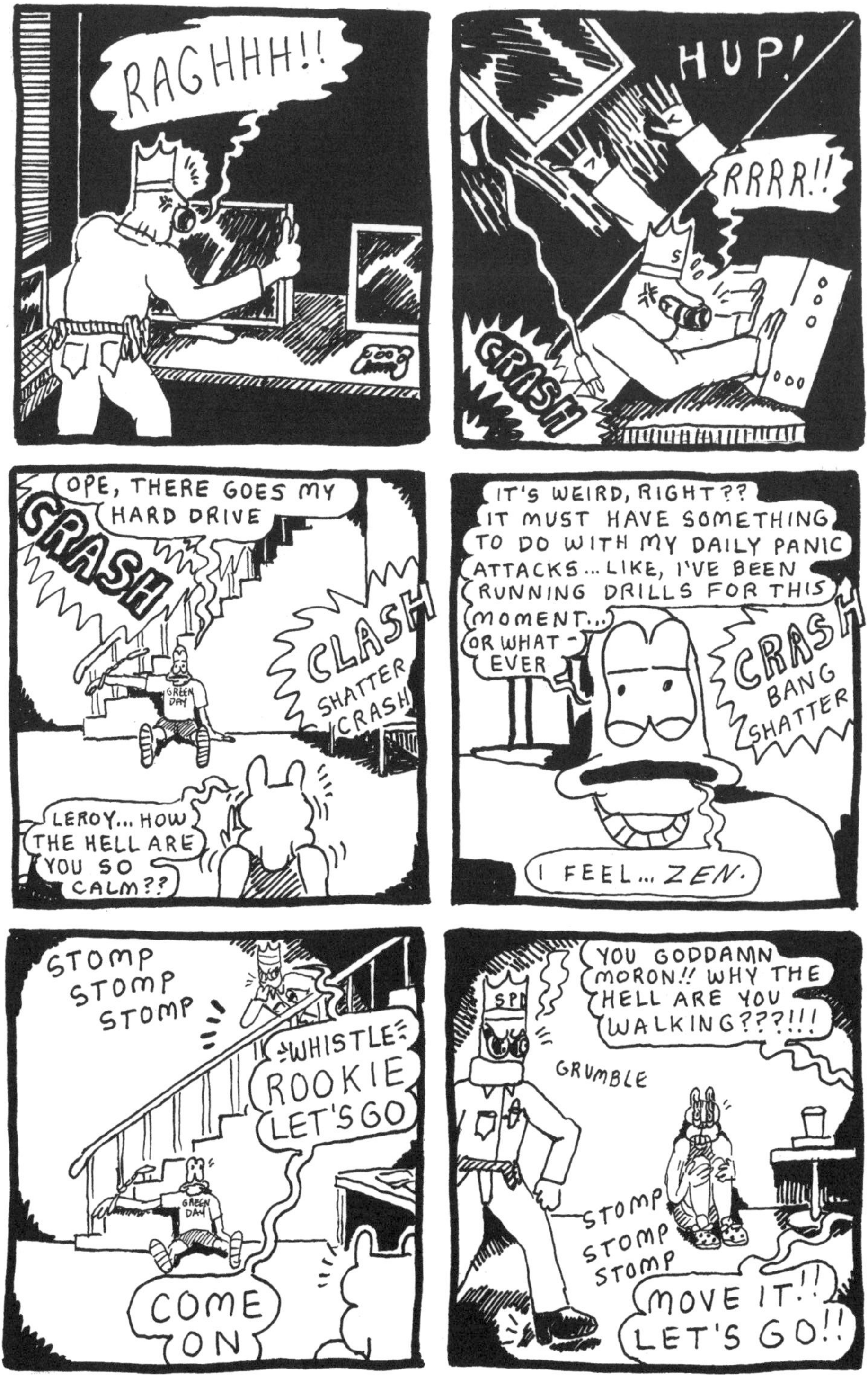
RAGHHH!!
HUP!
RRRR!!
CRASH
CRASH
OPE, THERE GOES MY HARD DRIVE
CLASH
SHATTER
CRASH
GREEN DAY
LEROY... HOW THE HELL ARE YOU SO CALM??
IT'S WEIRD, RIGHT?? IT MUST HAVE SOMETHING TO DO WITH MY DAILY PANIC ATTACKS... LIKE, I'VE BEEN RUNNING DRILLS FOR THIS MOMENT...
OR WHAT-EVER
CRASH
BANG
SHATTER
I FEEL... ZEN.
STOMP
STOMP
STOMP
WHISTLE
ROOKIE LET'S GO
GREEN DAY
COME ON
YOU GODDAMN MORON!! WHY THE HELL ARE YOU WALKING???!!!
SPD
GRUMBLE
STOMP
STOMP
STOMP
MOVE IT!! LET'S GO!!

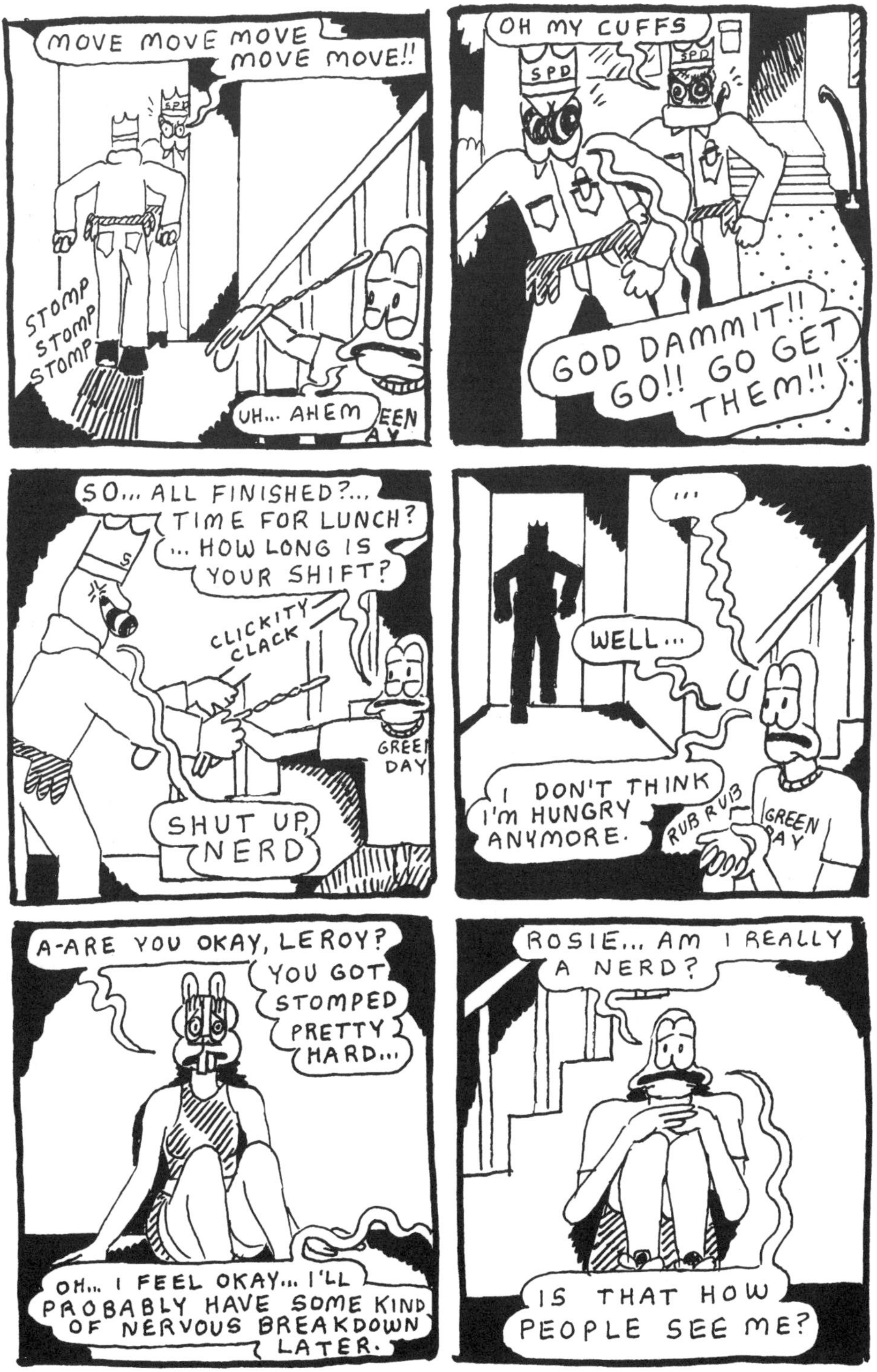
MOVE MOVE MOVE MOVE MOVE MOVE!!
STOMP STOMP STOMP
UH... AHEM
OH MY CUFFS
GOD DAMMIT!! GO!! GO GET THEM!!
SO... ALL FINISHED?... TIME FOR LUNCH? ... HOW LONG IS YOUR SHIFT?
CLICKITY CLACK
SHUT UP, NERD
GREEN DAY
...
WELL...
I DON'T THINK I'M HUNGRY ANYMORE.
RUB RUB
A-ARE YOU OKAY, LEROY? YOU GOT STOMPED PRETTY HARD...
OH... I FEEL OKAY... I'LL PROBABLY HAVE SOME KIND OF NERVOUS BREAKDOWN LATER.
ROSIE... AM I REALLY A NERD?
IS THAT HOW PEOPLE SEE ME?

AND NOW, SEVERAL TIMES A DAY I'M BLASTED WITH THESE INTRUSIVE THOUGHTS... I HAVE THIS VISCERAL, FULL-BODY AWARENESS OF ALL THE SUFFERING THAT'S OCCURRING RIGHT AT THIS MOMENT ALL OVER THE PLANET.

ALL THESE EARTHLY PROCESSES... THE NATURE OF EXISTENCE ON THIS PLANET IS... WHAT'S THE WORD? ALL THIS ISOLATION IS GIVING ME BRAIN DAMAGE...

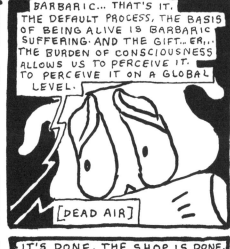

BARBARIC... THAT'S IT. THE DEFAULT PROCESS, THE BASIS OF BEING ALIVE IS BARBARIC SUFFERING. AND THE GIFT... ER,... THE BURDEN OF CONSCIOUSNESS ALLOWS US TO PERCEIVE IT. TO PERCEIVE IT ON A GLOBAL LEVEL.

[DEAD AIR]

YOU'RE LISTENING TO *THIS AMERICAN LIFE*... THIS WEEK WE'RE TALKING ABOUT CARTOONING IN THE AGE OF COVID, AND WE'VE BEEN SPEAKING WITH CARTOONIST ARGYLE GUMGORBA

CLICK

I'M ON A SINKING SHIP.

IT'S DONE. THE SHOP IS DONE. I'M JUST GOING THROUGH THE MOTIONS NOW. THIS IS POINTLESS. WHAT AM I DOING?

BEEP BEEP BEEP

THIS CHAPTER OF MY LIFE IS OVER. WHAT NOW?

WHAT AM I GONNA DO WITH MYSELF? BECOME THE GENERAL MANAGER OF A RITE-AID?

BEEP BEE—

1:00

START   MODE   PRESS

A DRUG STORE CASHIER?

I BET ROSIE WOULD LOVE THAT IDEA. A LIVELY, GORGEOUS YOUNG WOMAN DATING A FIFTY-YEAR-OLD DRUG STORE CASHIER.

PULL

CAUSE & EFFECT. THAT'S THE REALITY OF THE SITUATION OL' GUSSY-BOY. ALL OF THE DECISIONS YOU'VE MADE UP TO THIS POINT HAVE LED YOU HERE. TO THIS MOMENT IN TIME...

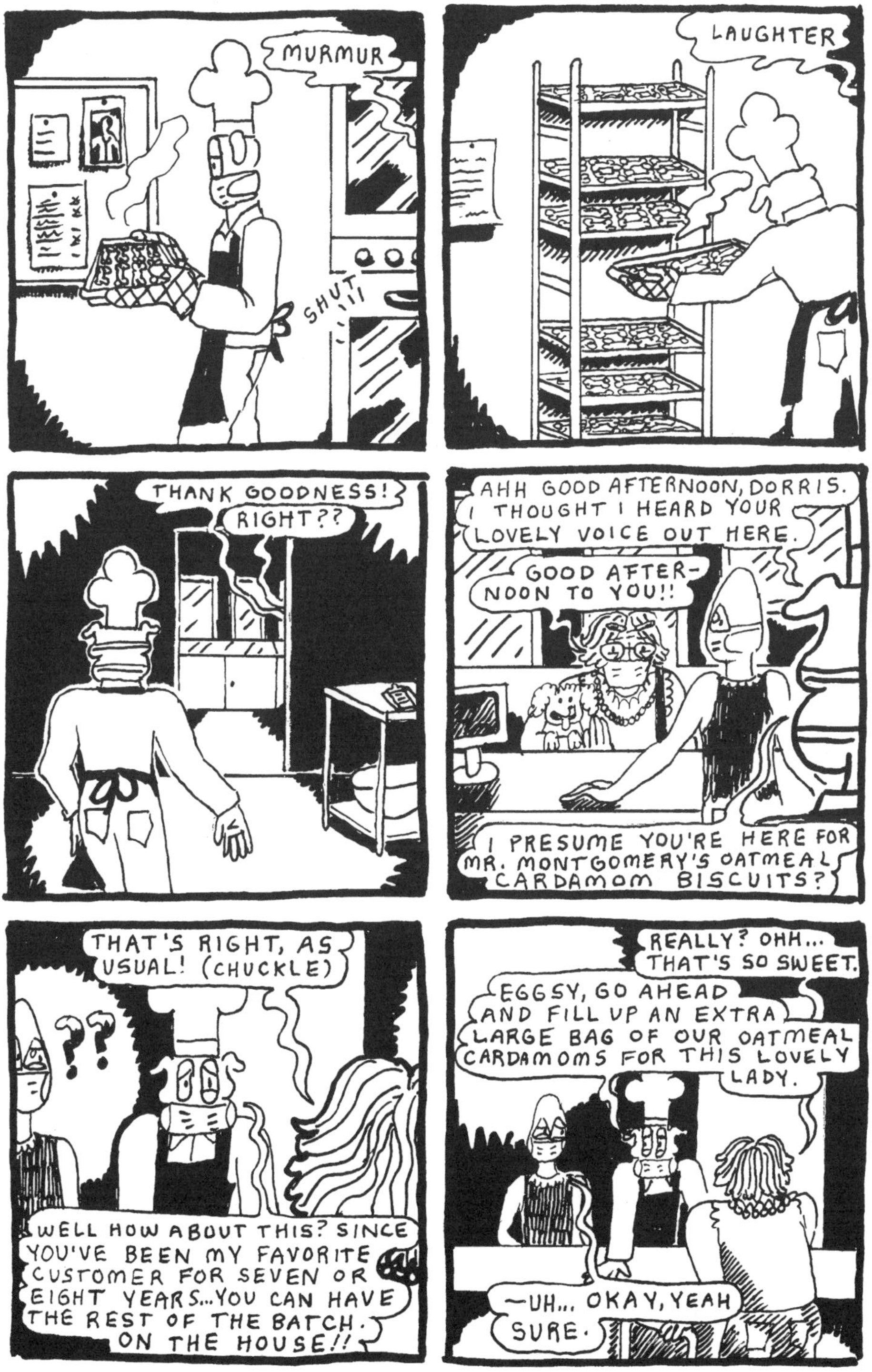
MURMUR
SHUT
LAUGHTER
THANK GOODNESS!
RIGHT??
AHH GOOD AFTERNOON, DORRIS. I THOUGHT I HEARD YOUR LOVELY VOICE OUT HERE.
GOOD AFTER-NOON TO YOU!!
I PRESUME YOU'RE HERE FOR MR. MONTGOMERY'S OATMEAL CARDAMOM BISCUITS?
THAT'S RIGHT, AS USUAL! (CHUCKLE)
??
WELL HOW ABOUT THIS? SINCE YOU'VE BEEN MY FAVORITE CUSTOMER FOR SEVEN OR EIGHT YEARS...YOU CAN HAVE THE REST OF THE BATCH. ON THE HOUSE!!
REALLY? OHH... THAT'S SO SWEET.
EGGSY, GO AHEAD AND FILL UP AN EXTRA LARGE BAG OF OUR OATMEAL CARDAMOMS FOR THIS LOVELY LADY.
~UH... OKAY, YEAH SURE.

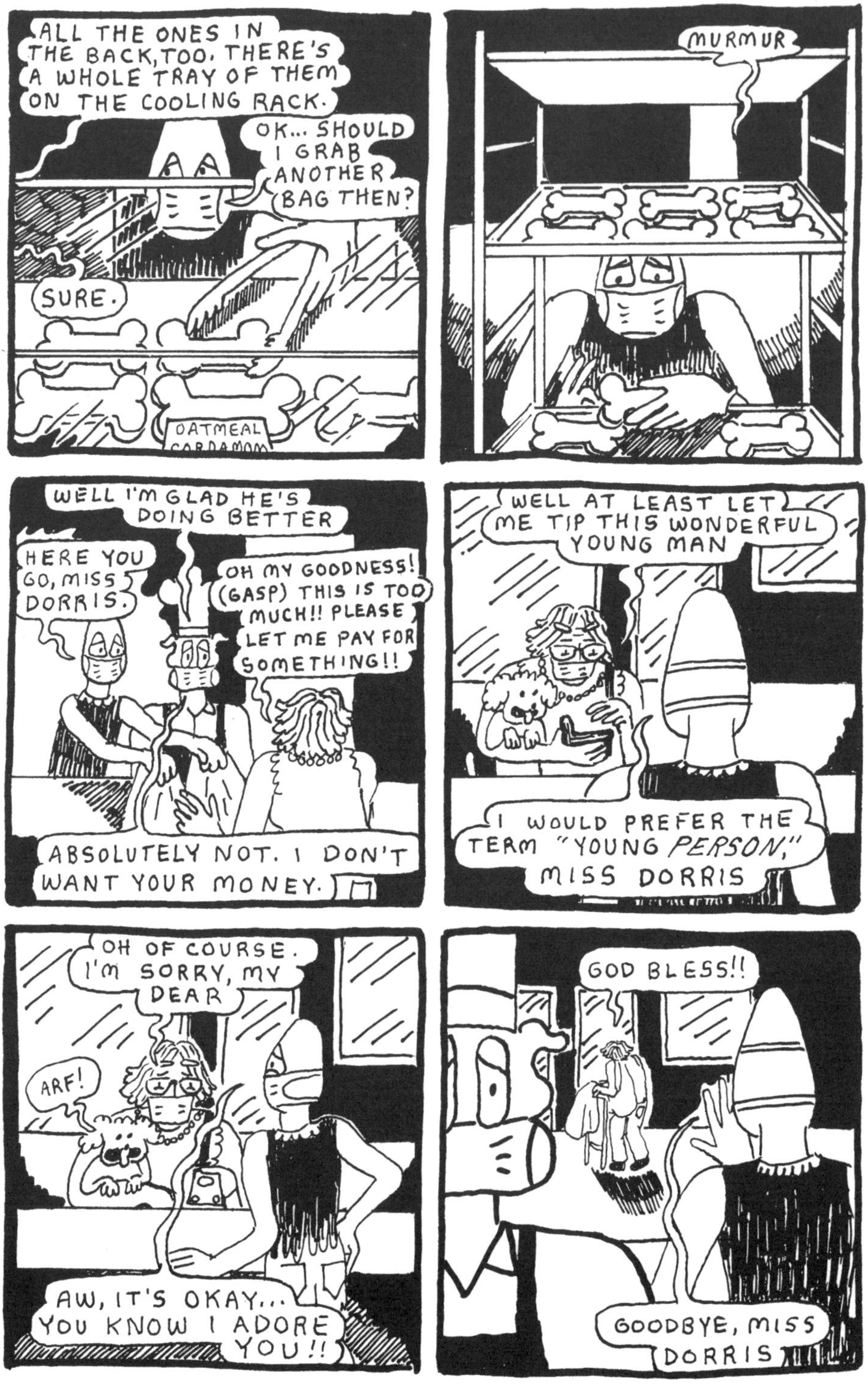
ALL THE ONES IN THE BACK, TOO. THERE'S A WHOLE TRAY OF THEM ON THE COOLING RACK.
OK... SHOULD I GRAB ANOTHER BAG THEN?
SURE.
OATMEAL
MURMUR
WELL I'M GLAD HE'S DOING BETTER
HERE YOU GO, MISS DORRIS.
OH MY GOODNESS! (GASP) THIS IS TOO MUCH!! PLEASE LET ME PAY FOR SOMETHING!!
ABSOLUTELY NOT. I DON'T WANT YOUR MONEY.
WELL AT LEAST LET ME TIP THIS WONDERFUL YOUNG MAN
I WOULD PREFER THE TERM "YOUNG PERSON," MISS DORRIS
OH OF COURSE. I'M SORRY, MY DEAR
ARF!
AW, IT'S OKAY... YOU KNOW I ADORE YOU!!
GOD BLESS!!
GOODBYE, MISS DORRIS

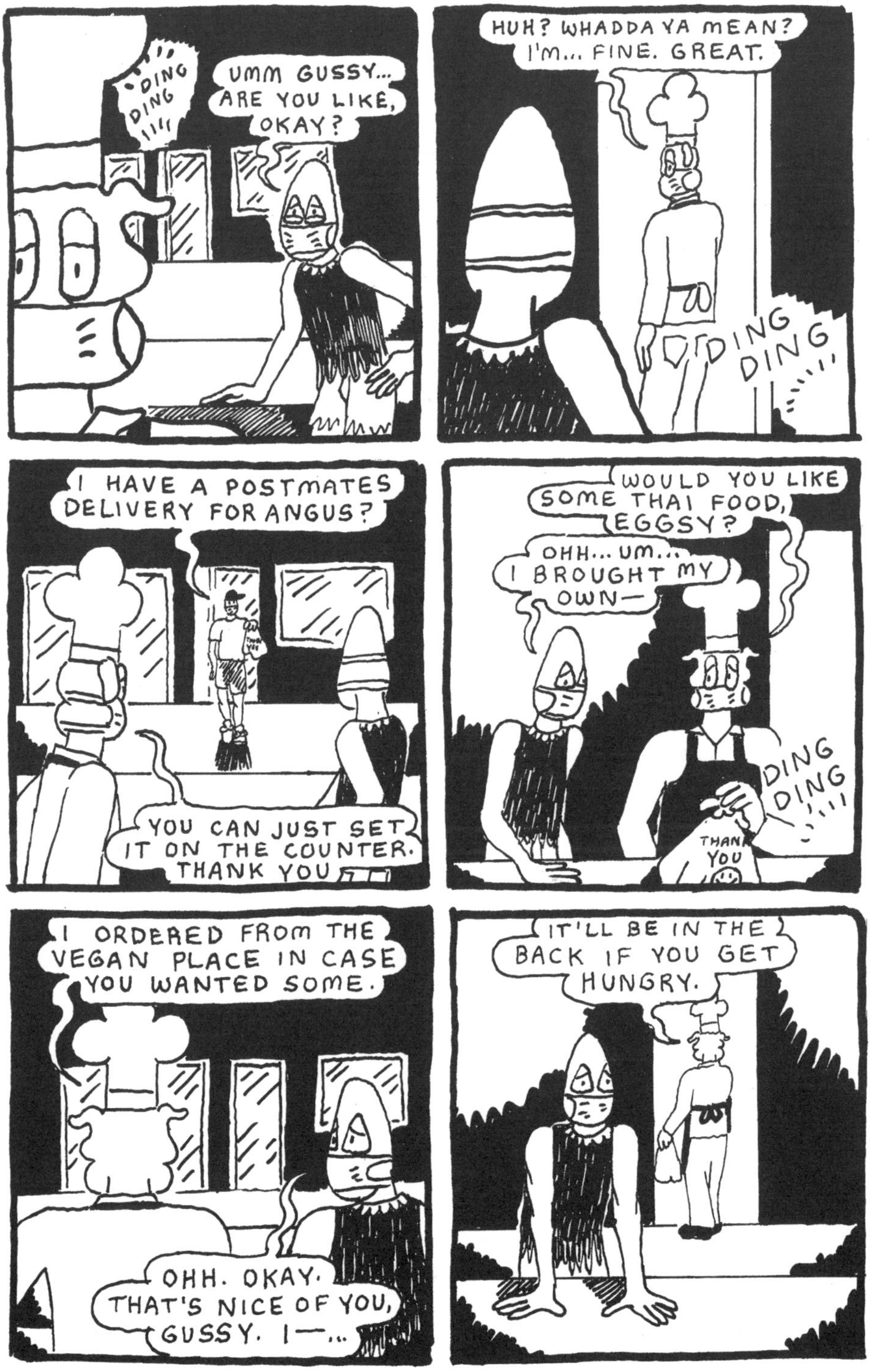
DING DING
UMM GUSSY... ARE YOU LIKE, OKAY?
HUH? WHADDA YA MEAN? I'M... FINE. GREAT.
DING DING
I HAVE A POSTMATES DELIVERY FOR ANGUS?
YOU CAN JUST SET IT ON THE COUNTER. THANK YOU
WOULD YOU LIKE SOME THAI FOOD, EGGSY?
OHH... UM... I BROUGHT MY OWN—
DING DING
THANK YOU
I ORDERED FROM THE VEGAN PLACE IN CASE YOU WANTED SOME.
OHH. OKAY. THAT'S NICE OF YOU, GUSSY. I—...
IT'LL BE IN THE BACK IF YOU GET HUNGRY.

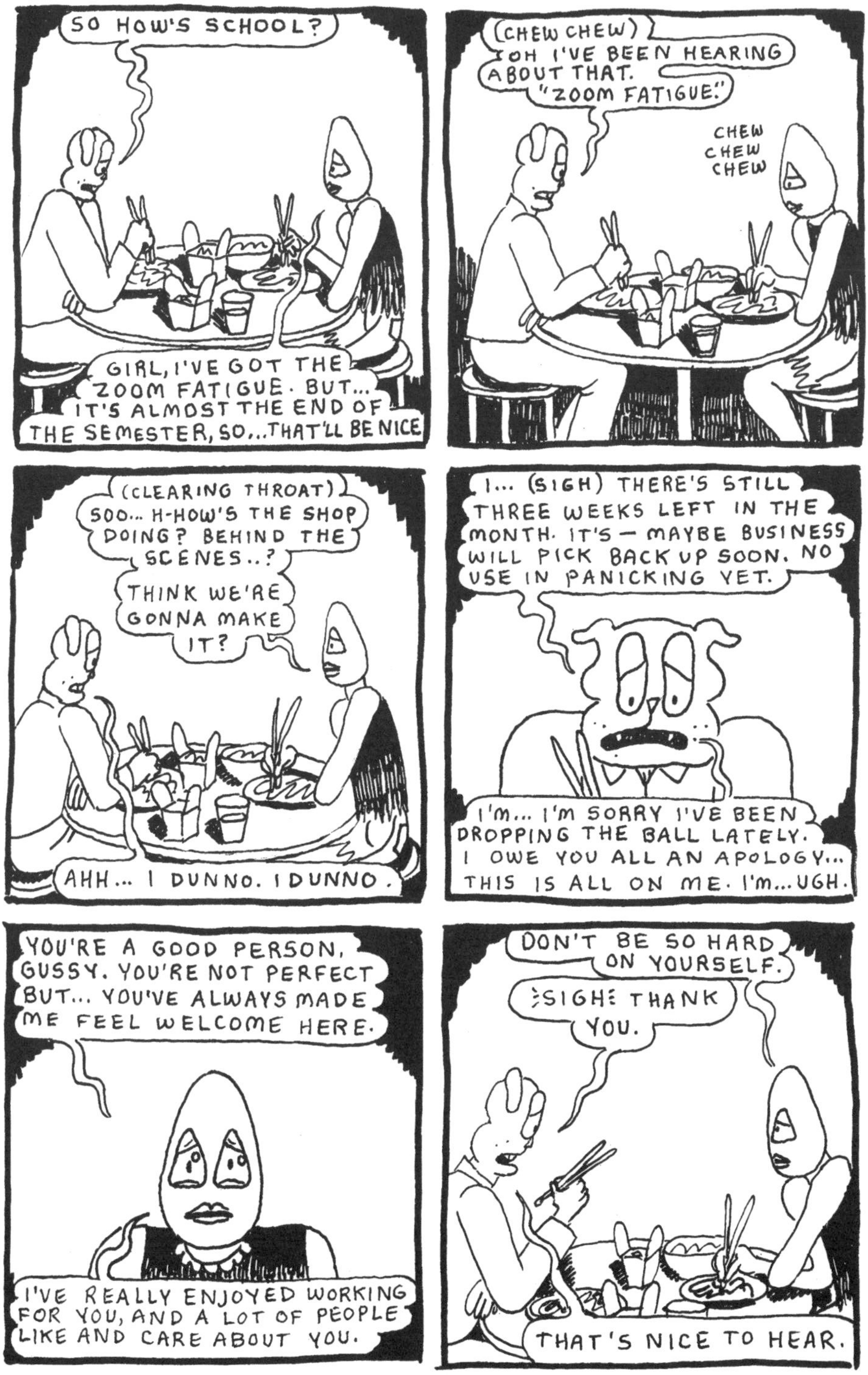
SO HOW'S SCHOOL?
GIRL, I'VE GOT THE ZOOM FATIGUE. BUT... IT'S ALMOST THE END OF THE SEMESTER, SO... THAT'LL BE NICE
(CHEW CHEW) OH I'VE BEEN HEARING ABOUT THAT. "ZOOM FATIGUE."
CHEW CHEW CHEW
(CLEARING THROAT) SOO... H-HOW'S THE SHOP DOING? BEHIND THE SCENES..?
THINK WE'RE GONNA MAKE IT?
AHH... I DUNNO. I DUNNO.
I... (SIGH) THERE'S STILL THREE WEEKS LEFT IN THE MONTH. IT'S — MAYBE BUSINESS WILL PICK BACK UP SOON. NO USE IN PANICKING YET.
I'M... I'M SORRY I'VE BEEN DROPPING THE BALL LATELY. I OWE YOU ALL AN APOLOGY... THIS IS ALL ON ME. I'M... UGH.
YOU'RE A GOOD PERSON, GUSSY. YOU'RE NOT PERFECT BUT... YOU'VE ALWAYS MADE ME FEEL WELCOME HERE.
I'VE REALLY ENJOYED WORKING FOR YOU, AND A LOT OF PEOPLE LIKE AND CARE ABOUT YOU.
DON'T BE SO HARD ON YOURSELF.
:SIGH: THANK YOU.
THAT'S NICE TO HEAR.

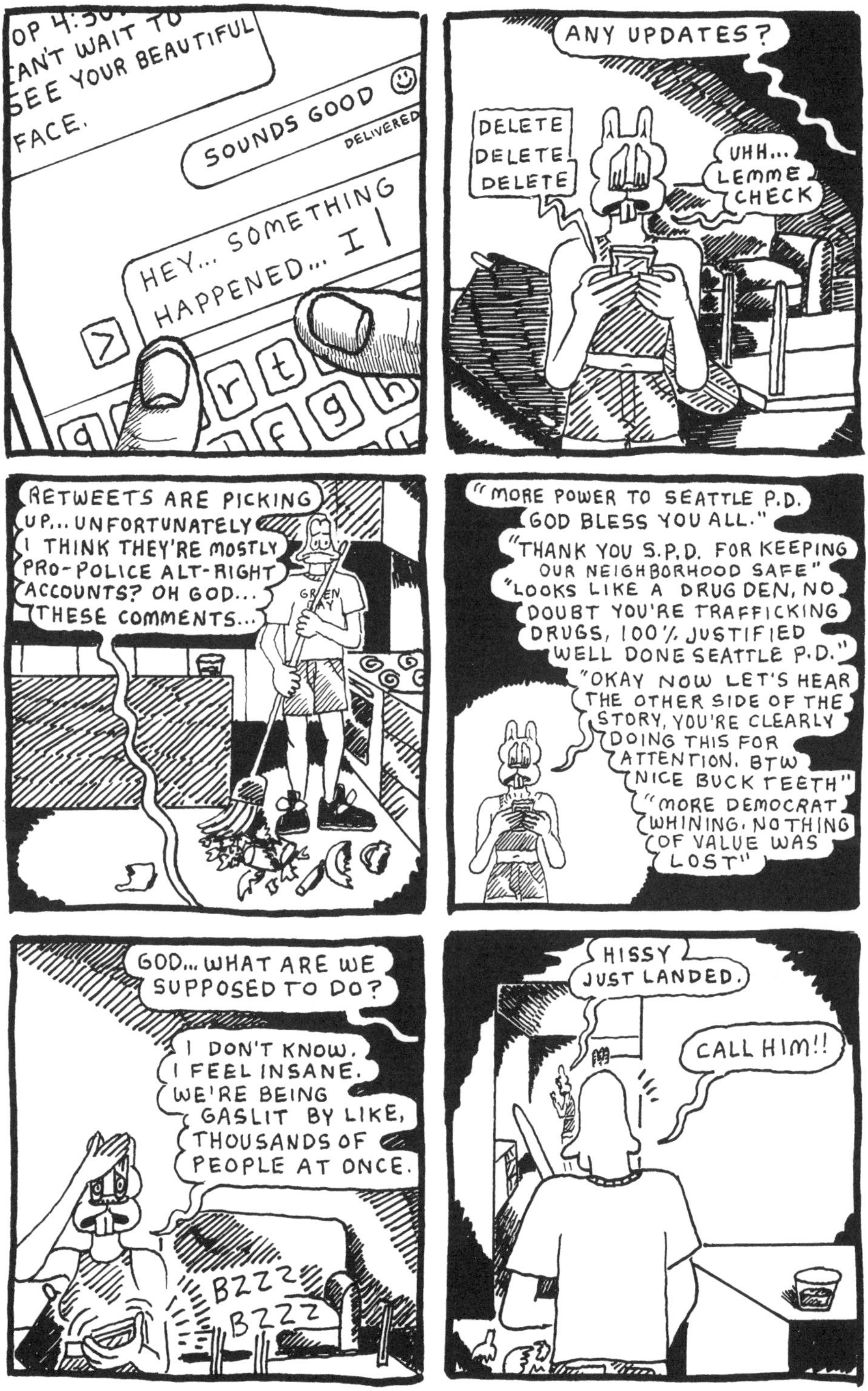
OP 4:30 CAN'T WAIT TO SEE YOUR BEAUTIFUL FACE.
SOUNDS GOOD
DELIVERED
HEY... SOMETHING HAPPENED... I
ANY UPDATES?
DELETE DELETE DELETE
UHH... LEMME CHECK
RETWEETS ARE PICKING UP... UNFORTUNATELY I THINK THEY'RE MOSTLY PRO-POLICE ALT-RIGHT ACCOUNTS? OH GOD... THESE COMMENTS...
GREEN DAY
"MORE POWER TO SEATTLE P.D. GOD BLESS YOU ALL."
"THANK YOU S.P.D. FOR KEEPING OUR NEIGHBORHOOD SAFE"
"LOOKS LIKE A DRUG DEN, NO DOUBT YOU'RE TRAFFICKING DRUGS, 100% JUSTIFIED WELL DONE SEATTLE P.D."
"OKAY NOW LET'S HEAR THE OTHER SIDE OF THE STORY, YOU'RE CLEARLY DOING THIS FOR ATTENTION. BTW NICE BUCK TEETH"
"MORE DEMOCRAT WHINING. NOTHING OF VALUE WAS LOST"
GOD... WHAT ARE WE SUPPOSED TO DO?
I DON'T KNOW. I FEEL INSANE. WE'RE BEING GASLIT BY LIKE, THOUSANDS OF PEOPLE AT ONCE.
BZZZ BZZZ
HISSY JUST LANDED.
CALL HIM!!

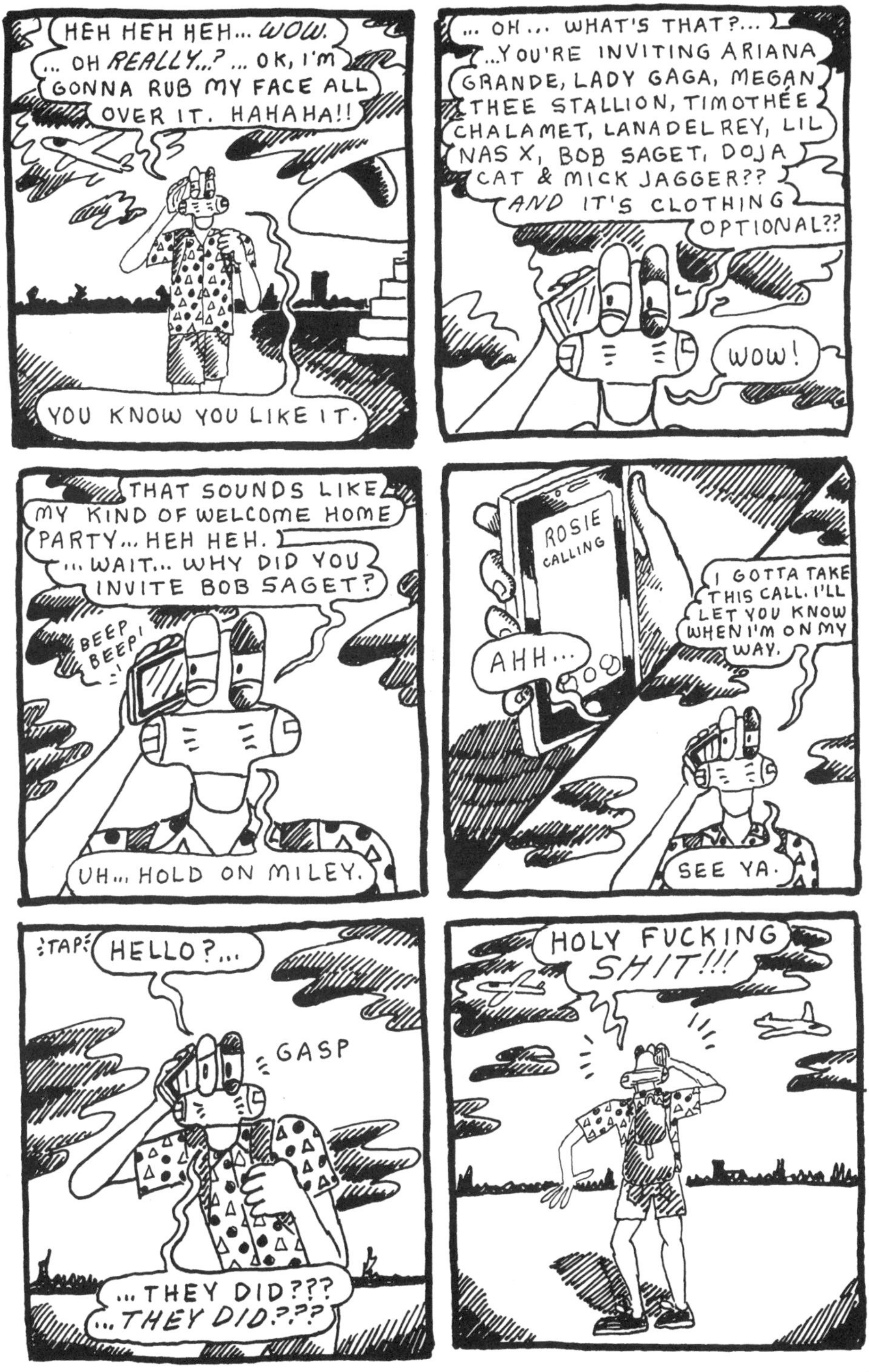
HEH HEH HEH... WOW. ... OH REALLY...? ... OK, I'M GONNA RUB MY FACE ALL OVER IT. HAHAHA!!
YOU KNOW YOU LIKE IT.
... OH ... WHAT'S THAT?... ...YOU'RE INVITING ARIANA GRANDE, LADY GAGA, MEGAN THEE STALLION, TIMOTHÉE CHALAMET, LANADELREY, LIL NAS X, BOB SAGET, DOJA CAT & MICK JAGGER?? AND IT'S CLOTHING OPTIONAL??
WOW!
THAT SOUNDS LIKE MY KIND OF WELCOME HOME PARTY... HEH HEH. ... WAIT... WHY DID YOU INVITE BOB SAGET?
BEEP BEEP!
UH... HOLD ON MILEY.
ROSIE CALLING
AHH...
I GOTTA TAKE THIS CALL. I'LL LET YOU KNOW WHEN I'M ON MY WAY.
SEE YA.
TAP
HELLO?...
GASP
... THEY DID??? ... THEY DID???
HOLY FUCKING SHIT!!!

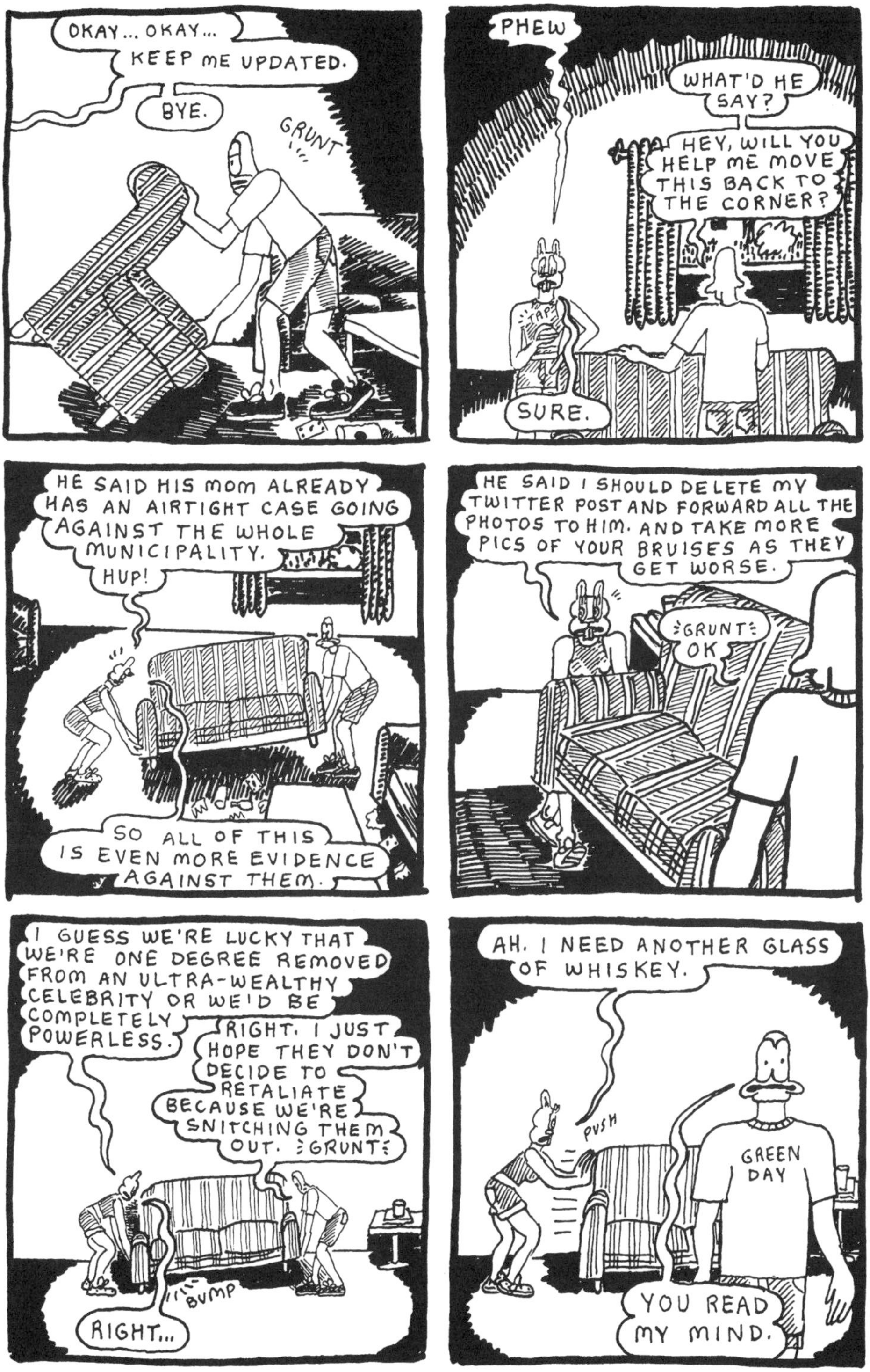
OKAY... OKAY...
KEEP ME UPDATED.
BYE.
GRUNT
PHEW
WHAT'D HE SAY?
HEY, WILL YOU HELP ME MOVE THIS BACK TO THE CORNER?
TAP
SURE.
HE SAID HIS MOM ALREADY HAS AN AIRTIGHT CASE GOING AGAINST THE WHOLE MUNICIPALITY.
HUP!
SO ALL OF THIS IS EVEN MORE EVIDENCE AGAINST THEM.
HE SAID I SHOULD DELETE MY TWITTER POST AND FORWARD ALL THE PHOTOS TO HIM. AND TAKE MORE PICS OF YOUR BRUISES AS THEY GET WORSE.
GRUNT
OK
I GUESS WE'RE LUCKY THAT WE'RE ONE DEGREE REMOVED FROM AN ULTRA-WEALTHY CELEBRITY OR WE'D BE COMPLETELY POWERLESS.
RIGHT. I JUST HOPE THEY DON'T DECIDE TO RETALIATE BECAUSE WE'RE SNITCHING THEM OUT.
GRUNT
BUMP
RIGHT...
AH. I NEED ANOTHER GLASS OF WHISKEY.
PUSH
GREEN DAY
YOU READ MY MIND.

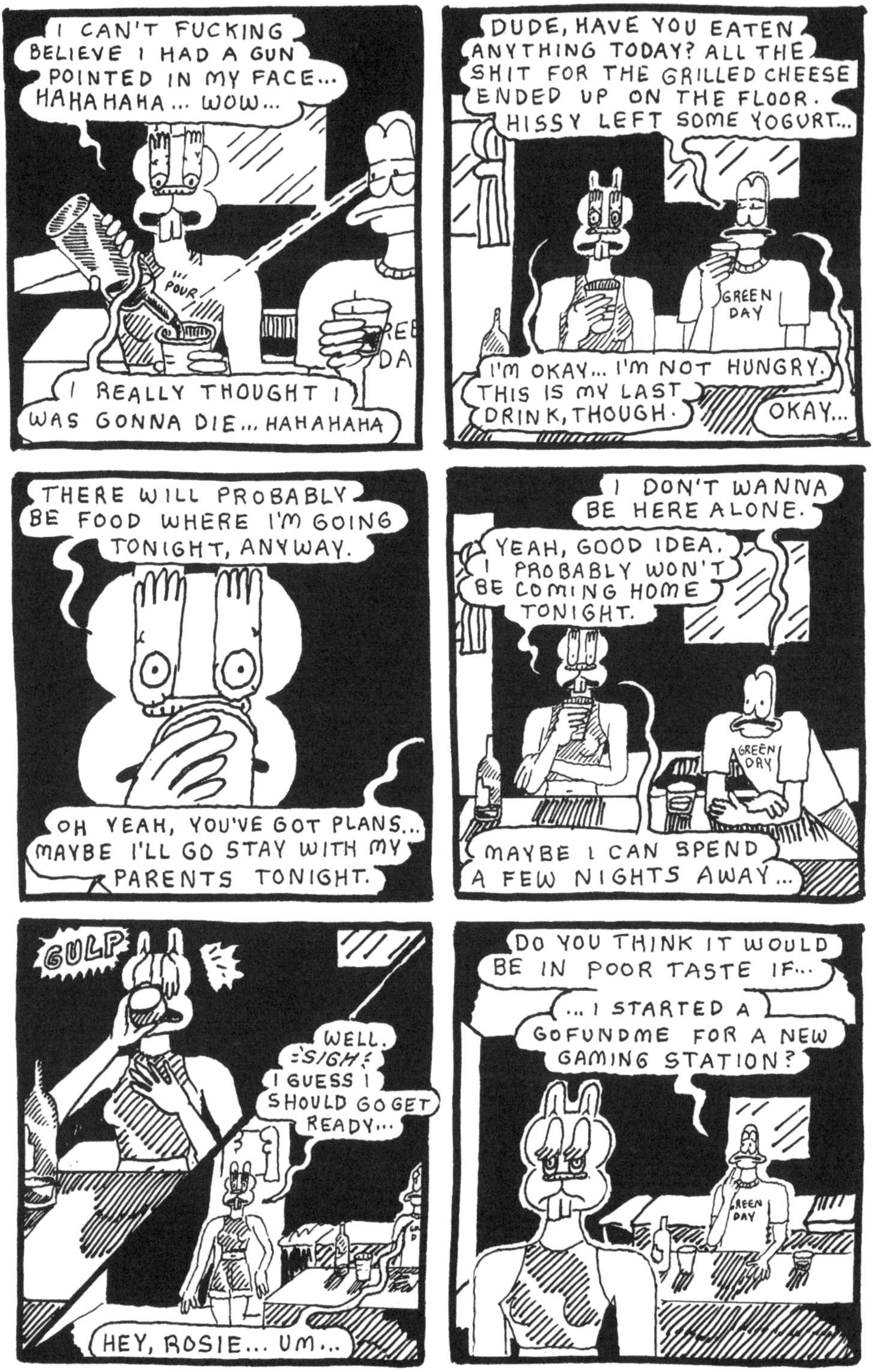
I CAN'T FUCKING BELIEVE I HAD A GUN POINTED IN MY FACE... HAHAHAHA... WOW...
POUR
I REALLY THOUGHT I WAS GONNA DIE... HAHAHAHA
DUDE, HAVE YOU EATEN ANYTHING TODAY? ALL THE SHIT FOR THE GRILLED CHEESE ENDED UP ON THE FLOOR. HISSY LEFT SOME YOGURT...
GREEN DAY
I'M OKAY... I'M NOT HUNGRY. THIS IS MY LAST DRINK, THOUGH.
OKAY...
THERE WILL PROBABLY BE FOOD WHERE I'M GOING TONIGHT, ANYWAY.
OH YEAH, YOU'VE GOT PLANS... MAYBE I'LL GO STAY WITH MY PARENTS TONIGHT.
I DON'T WANNA BE HERE ALONE.
YEAH, GOOD IDEA. I PROBABLY WON'T BE COMING HOME TONIGHT.
GREEN DAY
MAYBE I CAN SPEND A FEW NIGHTS AWAY...
GULP
WELL. SIGH I GUESS I SHOULD GO GET READY...
HEY, ROSIE... UM...
DO YOU THINK IT WOULD BE IN POOR TASTE IF...
... I STARTED A GOFUNDME FOR A NEW GAMING STATION?
GREEN DAY

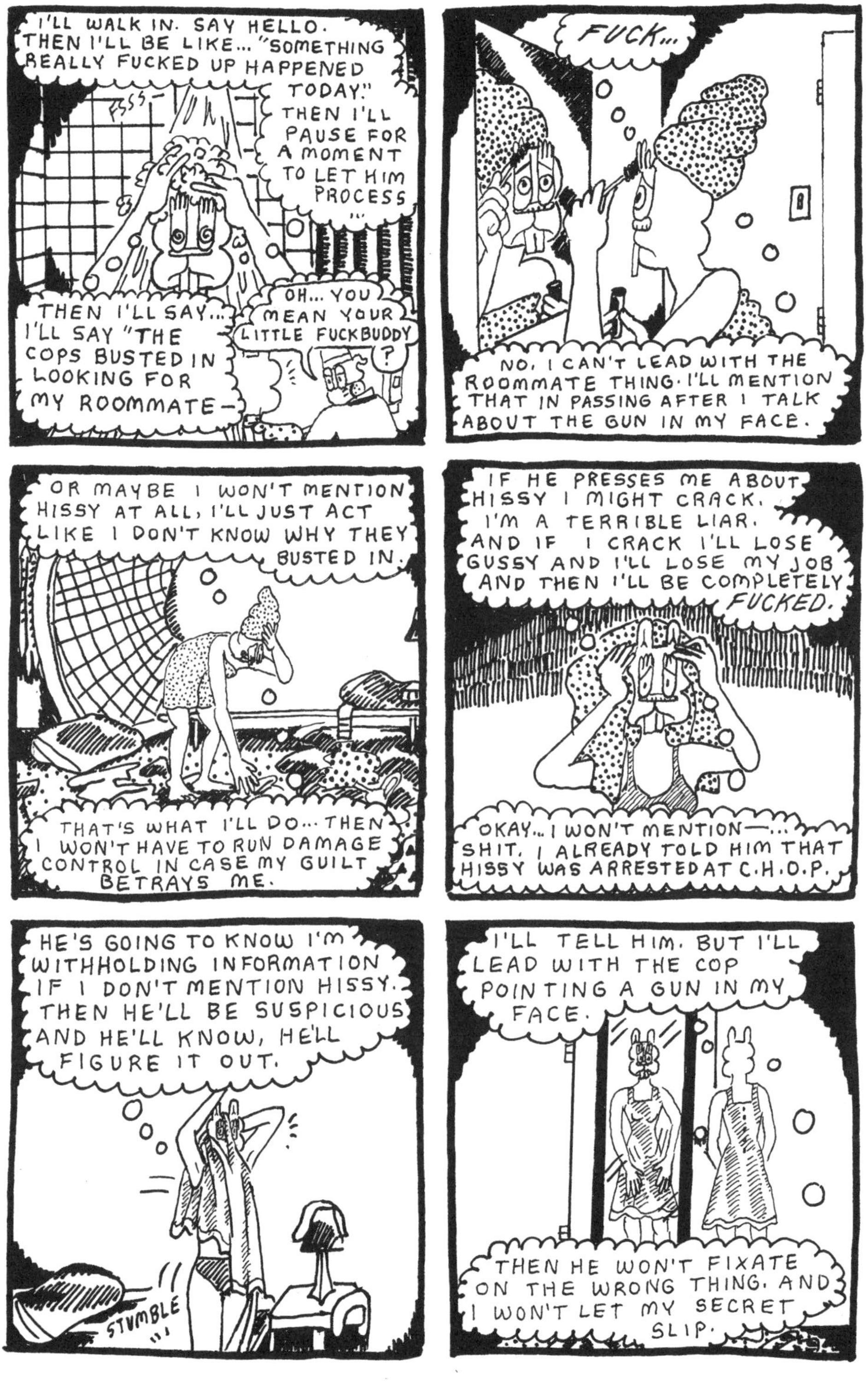
I'LL WALK IN. SAY HELLO. THEN I'LL BE LIKE... "SOMETHING REALLY FUCKED UP HAPPENED TODAY." THEN I'LL PAUSE FOR A MOMENT TO LET HIM PROCESS...
FSSS
THEN I'LL SAY... I'LL SAY "THE COPS BUSTED IN LOOKING FOR MY ROOMMATE—
OH... YOU MEAN YOUR LITTLE FUCKBUDDY?
FUCK...
NO, I CAN'T LEAD WITH THE ROOMMATE THING. I'LL MENTION THAT IN PASSING AFTER I TALK ABOUT THE GUN IN MY FACE.
OR MAYBE I WON'T MENTION HISSY AT ALL, I'LL JUST ACT LIKE I DON'T KNOW WHY THEY BUSTED IN.
THAT'S WHAT I'LL DO... THEN I WON'T HAVE TO RUN DAMAGE CONTROL IN CASE MY GUILT BETRAYS ME.
IF HE PRESSES ME ABOUT HISSY I MIGHT CRACK. I'M A TERRIBLE LIAR. AND IF I CRACK I'LL LOSE GUSSY AND I'LL LOSE MY JOB AND THEN I'LL BE COMPLETELY FUCKED.
OKAY... I WON'T MENTION—... SHIT, I ALREADY TOLD HIM THAT HISSY WAS ARRESTED AT C.H.O.P.
HE'S GOING TO KNOW I'M WITHHOLDING INFORMATION IF I DON'T MENTION HISSY. THEN HE'LL BE SUSPICIOUS AND HE'LL KNOW, HE'LL FIGURE IT OUT.
STUMBLE
I'LL TELL HIM. BUT I'LL LEAD WITH THE COP POINTING A GUN IN MY FACE.
THEN HE WON'T FIXATE ON THE WRONG THING. AND I WON'T LET MY SECRET SLIP.

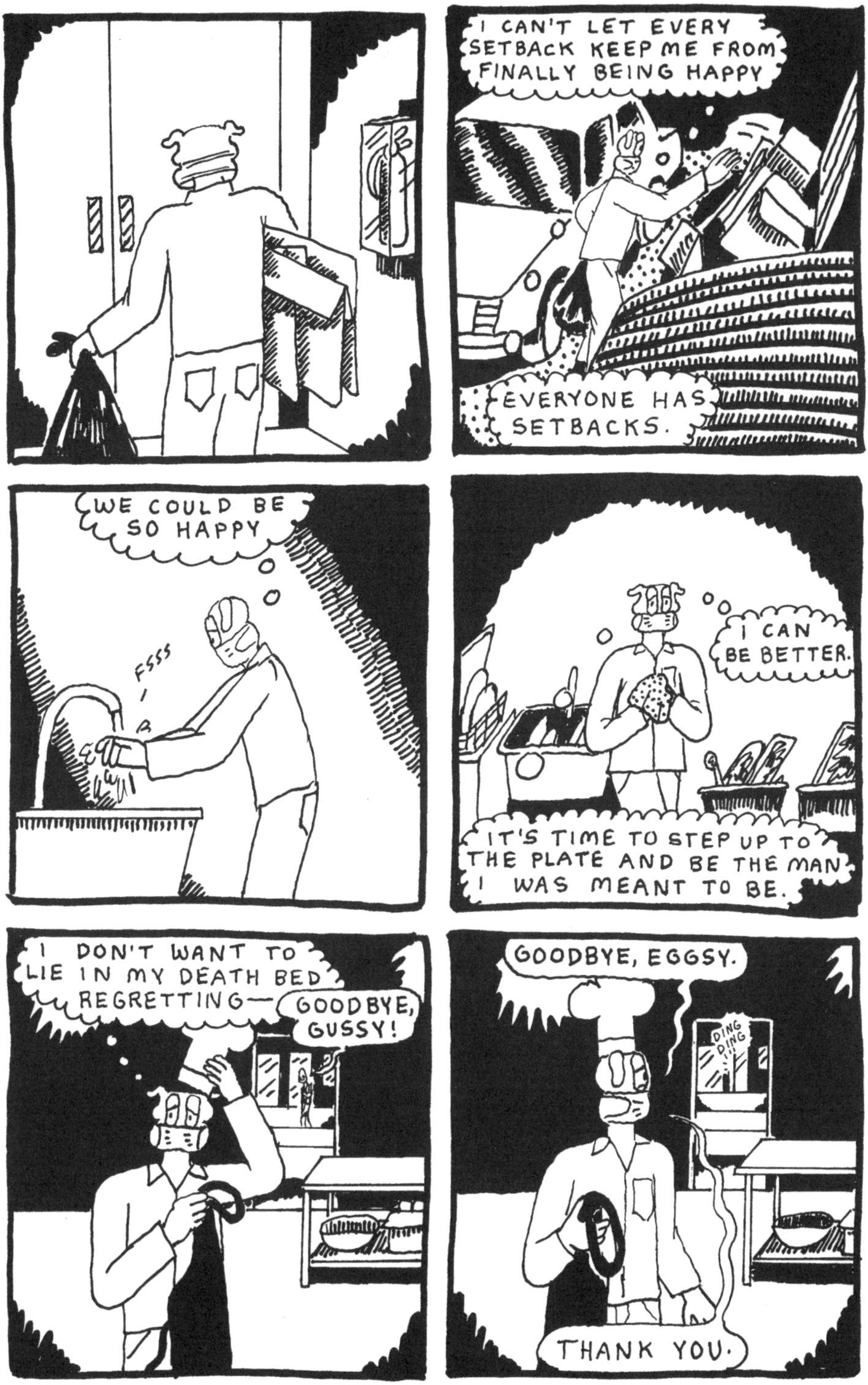
I CAN'T LET EVERY SETBACK KEEP ME FROM FINALLY BEING HAPPY
EVERYONE HAS SETBACKS.
WE COULD BE SO HAPPY
FSSS
I CAN BE BETTER.
IT'S TIME TO STEP UP TO THE PLATE AND BE THE MAN I WAS MEANT TO BE.
I DON'T WANT TO LIE IN MY DEATH BED REGRETTING—
GOODBYE, GUSSY!
GOODBYE, EGGSY.
DING DING
THANK YOU.

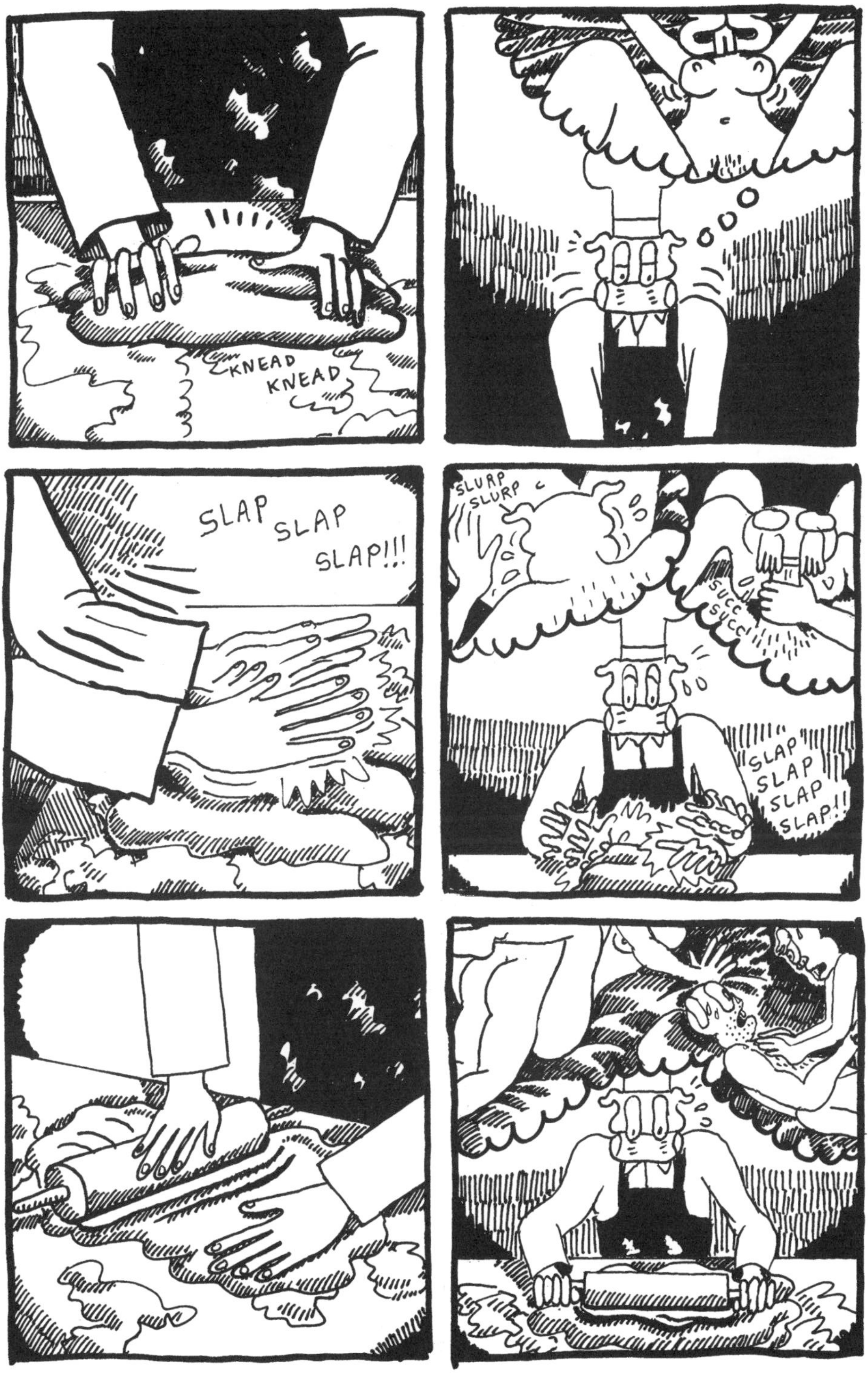
KNEAD KNEAD
SLAP SLAP SLAP!!!
SLURP SLURP
SUCC SUCC
SLAP SLAP SLAP SLAP!!

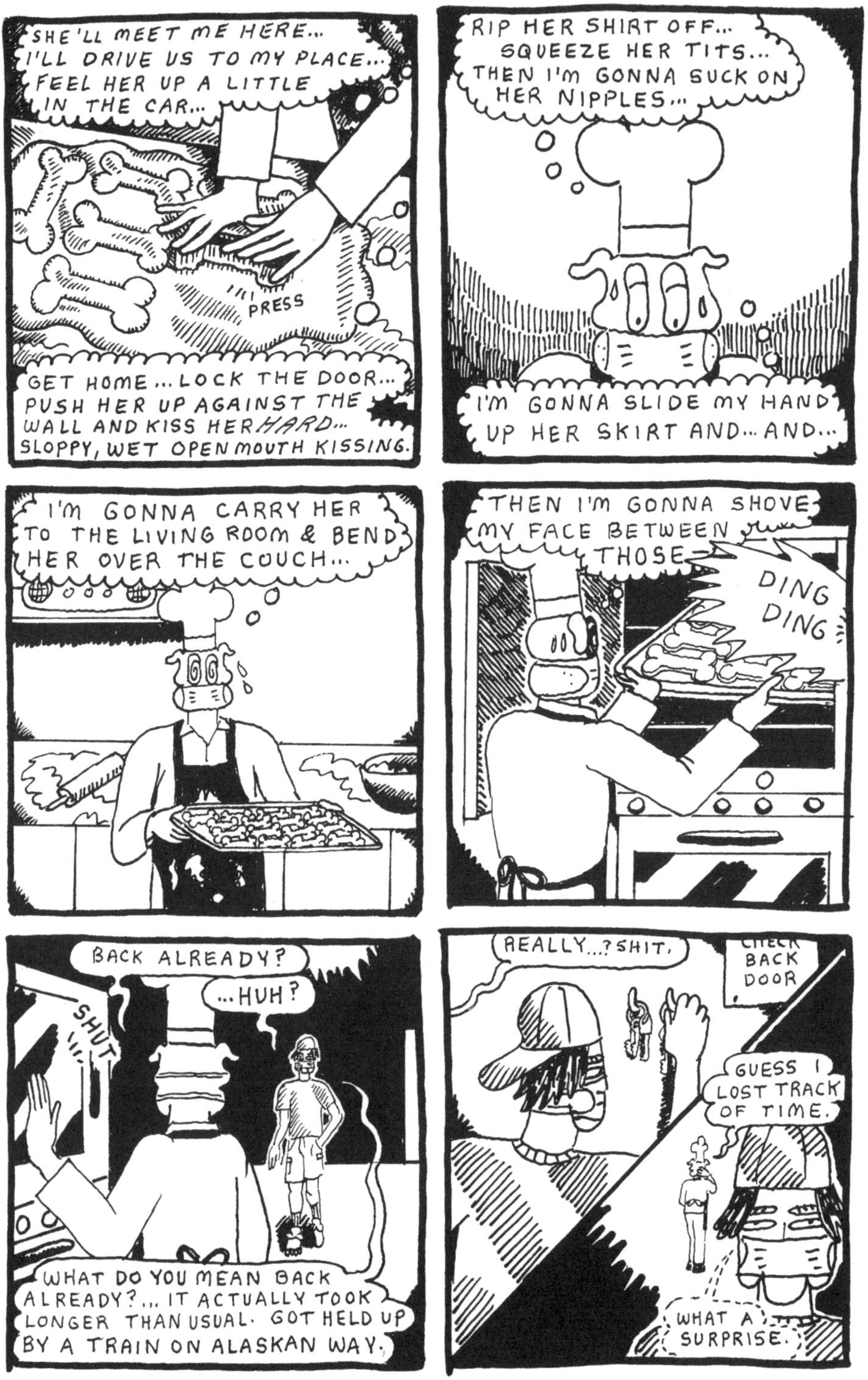
SHE'LL MEET ME HERE... I'LL DRIVE US TO MY PLACE... FEEL HER UP A LITTLE IN THE CAR...
PRESS
GET HOME... LOCK THE DOOR... PUSH HER UP AGAINST THE WALL AND KISS HER HARD... SLOPPY, WET OPEN MOUTH KISSING.
RIP HER SHIRT OFF... SQUEEZE HER TITS... THEN I'M GONNA SUCK ON HER NIPPLES...
I'M GONNA SLIDE MY HAND UP HER SKIRT AND... AND...
I'M GONNA CARRY HER TO THE LIVING ROOM & BEND HER OVER THE COUCH...
THEN I'M GONNA SHOVE MY FACE BETWEEN THOSE
DING DING
BACK ALREADY?
...HUH?
SHUT
WHAT DO YOU MEAN BACK ALREADY?... IT ACTUALLY TOOK LONGER THAN USUAL. GOT HELD UP BY A TRAIN ON ALASKAN WAY.
REALLY...? SHIT.
BACK DOOR
GUESS I LOST TRACK OF TIME.
WHAT A SURPRISE.

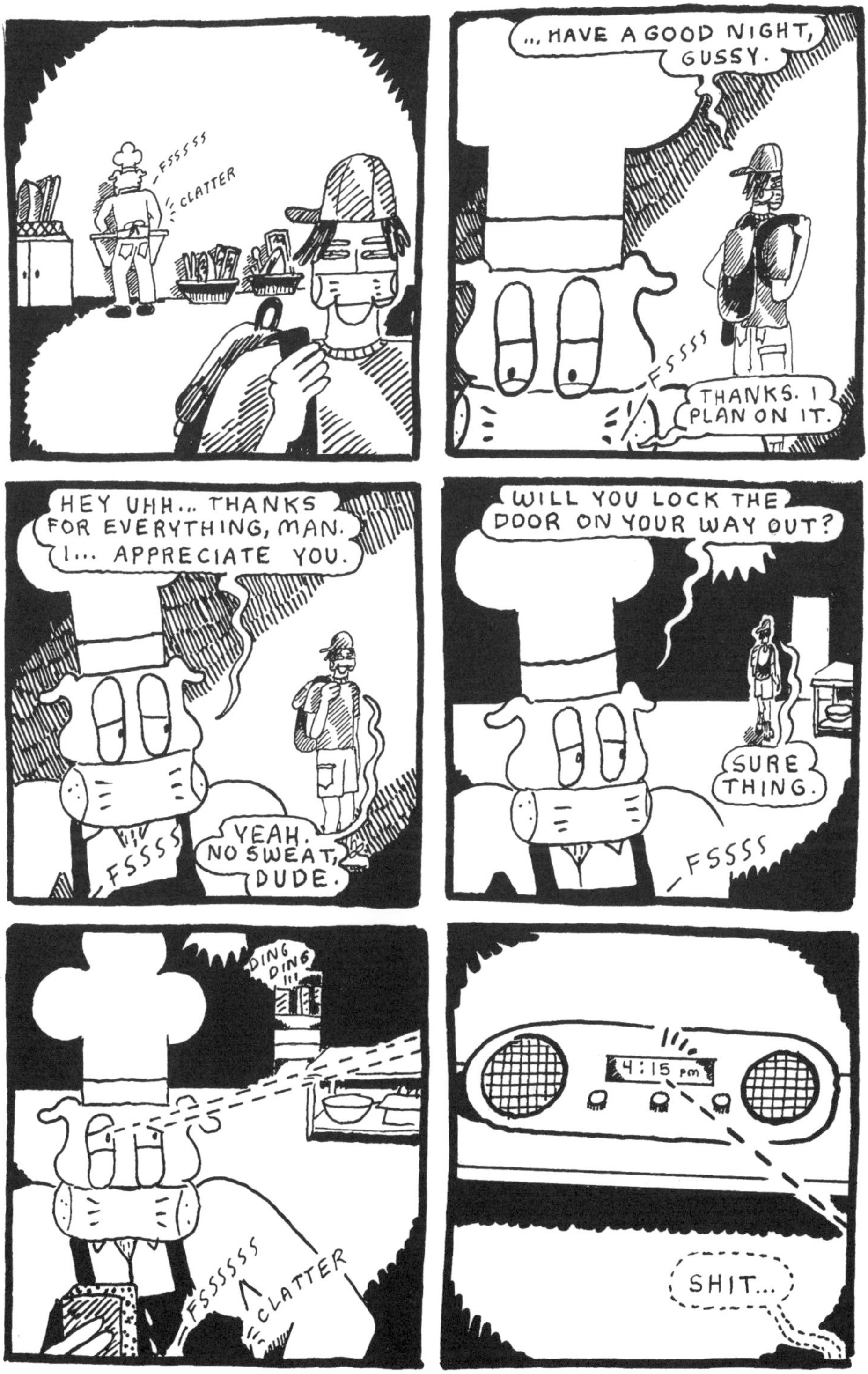
FSSSSS
CLATTER
..., HAVE A GOOD NIGHT, GUSSY.
FSSSS
THANKS. I PLAN ON IT.
HEY UHH... THANKS FOR EVERYTHING, MAN. I... APPRECIATE YOU.
FSSSS
YEAH. NO SWEAT, DUDE.
WILL YOU LOCK THE DOOR ON YOUR WAY OUT?
SURE THING.
FSSSS
DING DING !!!
FSSSSS
CLATTER
4:15 pm
SHIT...

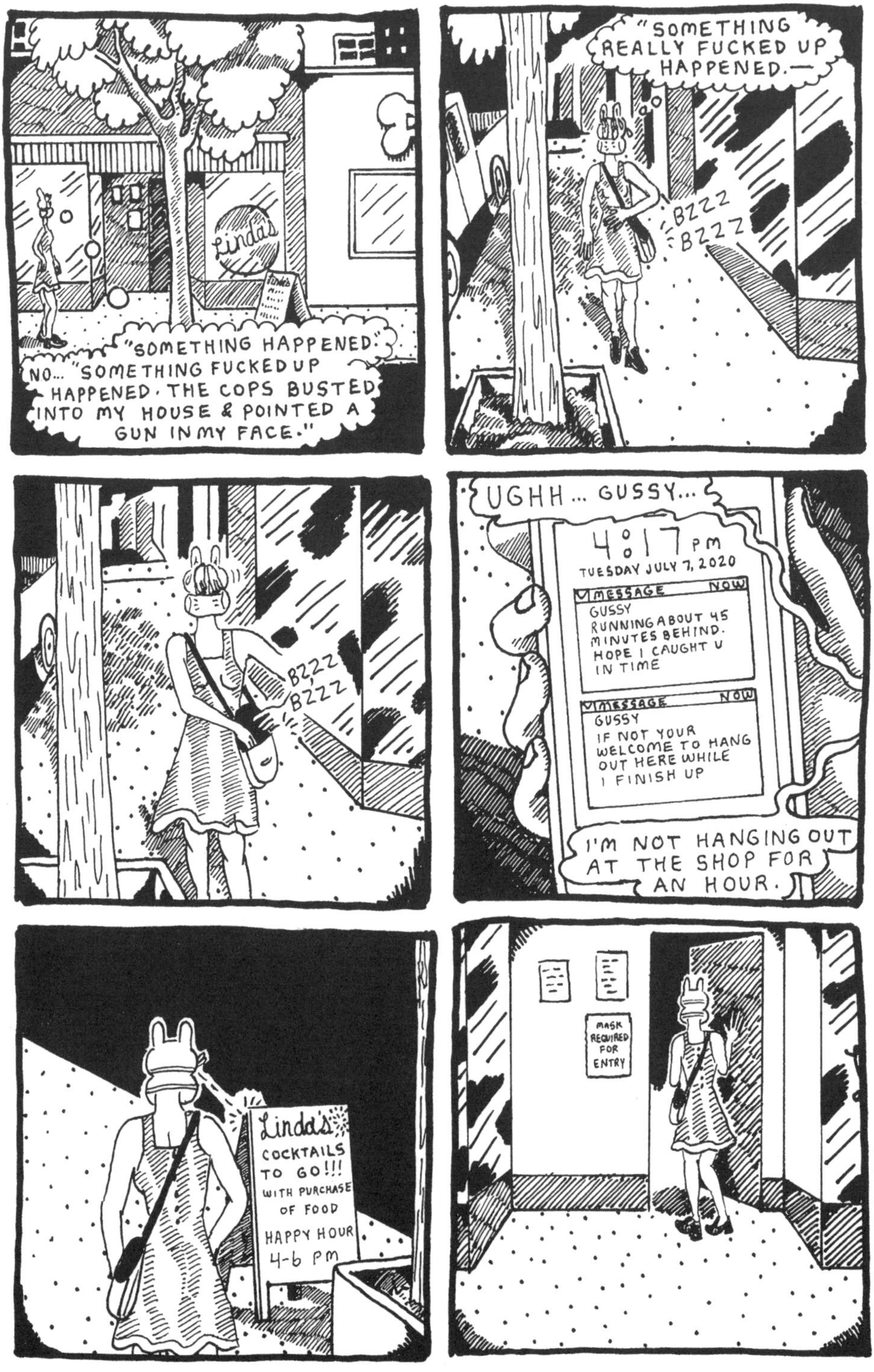
"SOMETHING HAPPENED."
NO... "SOMETHING FUCKED UP HAPPENED. THE COPS BUSTED INTO MY HOUSE & POINTED A GUN IN MY FACE."
Linda's
"SOMETHING REALLY FUCKED UP HAPPENED.—
BZZZ BZZZ
BZZZ BZZZ
UGHH... GUSSY...
4:17 PM
TUESDAY JULY 7, 2020
MESSAGE NOW
GUSSY
RUNNING ABOUT 45 MINUTES BEHIND. HOPE I CAUGHT U IN TIME
MESSAGE NOW
GUSSY
IF NOT YOUR WELCOME TO HANG OUT HERE WHILE I FINISH UP
I'M NOT HANGING OUT AT THE SHOP FOR AN HOUR.
Linda's
COCKTAILS TO GO!!!
WITH PURCHASE OF FOOD
HAPPY HOUR 4-6 PM
MASK REQUIRED FOR ENTRY

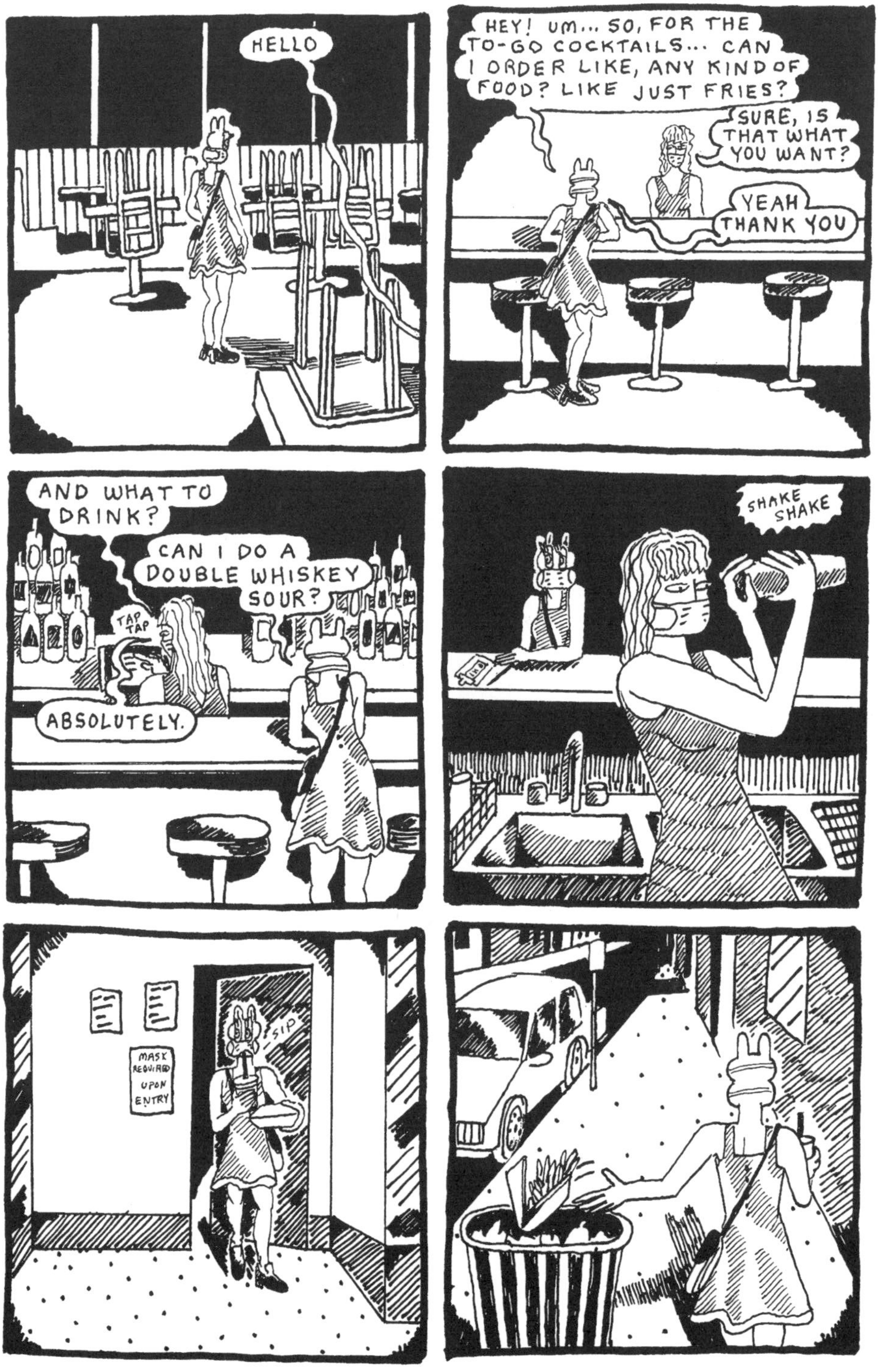
HELLO
HEY! UM... SO, FOR THE TO-GO COCKTAILS... CAN I ORDER LIKE, ANY KIND OF FOOD? LIKE JUST FRIES?
SURE, IS THAT WHAT YOU WANT?
YEAH THANK YOU
AND WHAT TO DRINK?
CAN I DO A DOUBLE WHISKEY SOUR?
TAP TAP
ABSOLUTELY.
SHAKE SHAKE
MASK REQUIRED UPON ENTRY
SIP

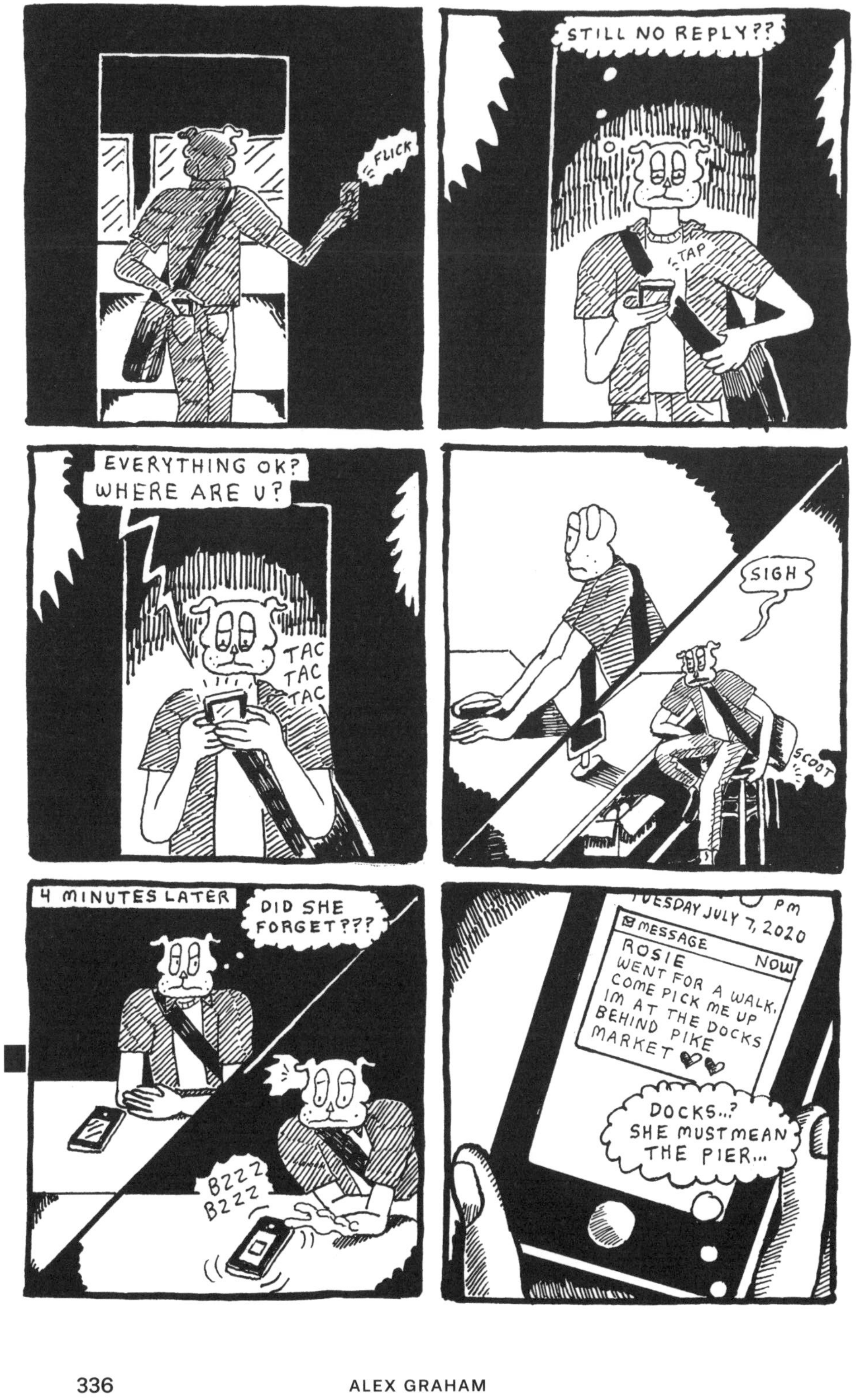
FLICK
STILL NO REPLY??
TAP
EVERYTHING OK? WHERE ARE U?
TAC TAC TAC
SIGH
SCOOT
4 MINUTES LATER
DID SHE FORGET???
BZZZ BZZZ
TUESDAY JULY 7, 2020
PM
MESSAGE
ROSIE
NOW
WENT FOR A WALK, COME PICK ME UP IM AT THE DOCKS BEHIND PIKE MARKET
DOCKS..? SHE MUST MEAN THE PIER...

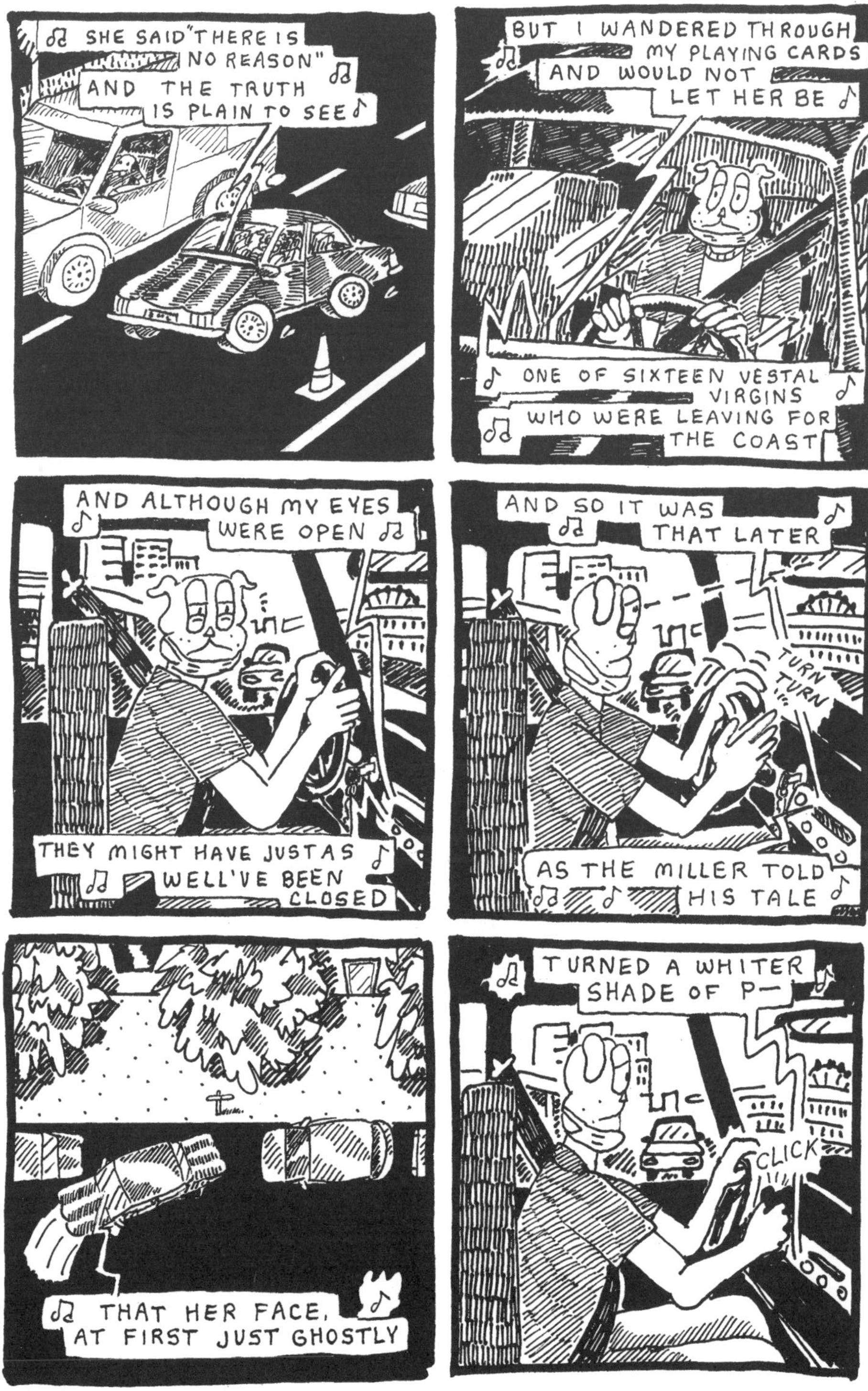
SHE SAID "THERE IS NO REASON"
AND THE TRUTH IS PLAIN TO SEE
BUT I WANDERED THROUGH MY PLAYING CARDS
AND WOULD NOT LET HER BE
ONE OF SIXTEEN VESTAL VIRGINS
WHO WERE LEAVING FOR THE COAST
AND ALTHOUGH MY EYES WERE OPEN
THEY MIGHT HAVE JUST AS WELL'VE BEEN CLOSED
AND SO IT WAS THAT LATER
TURN TURN
AS THE MILLER TOLD HIS TALE
THAT HER FACE, AT FIRST JUST GHOSTLY
TURNED A WHITER SHADE OF P—
CLICK

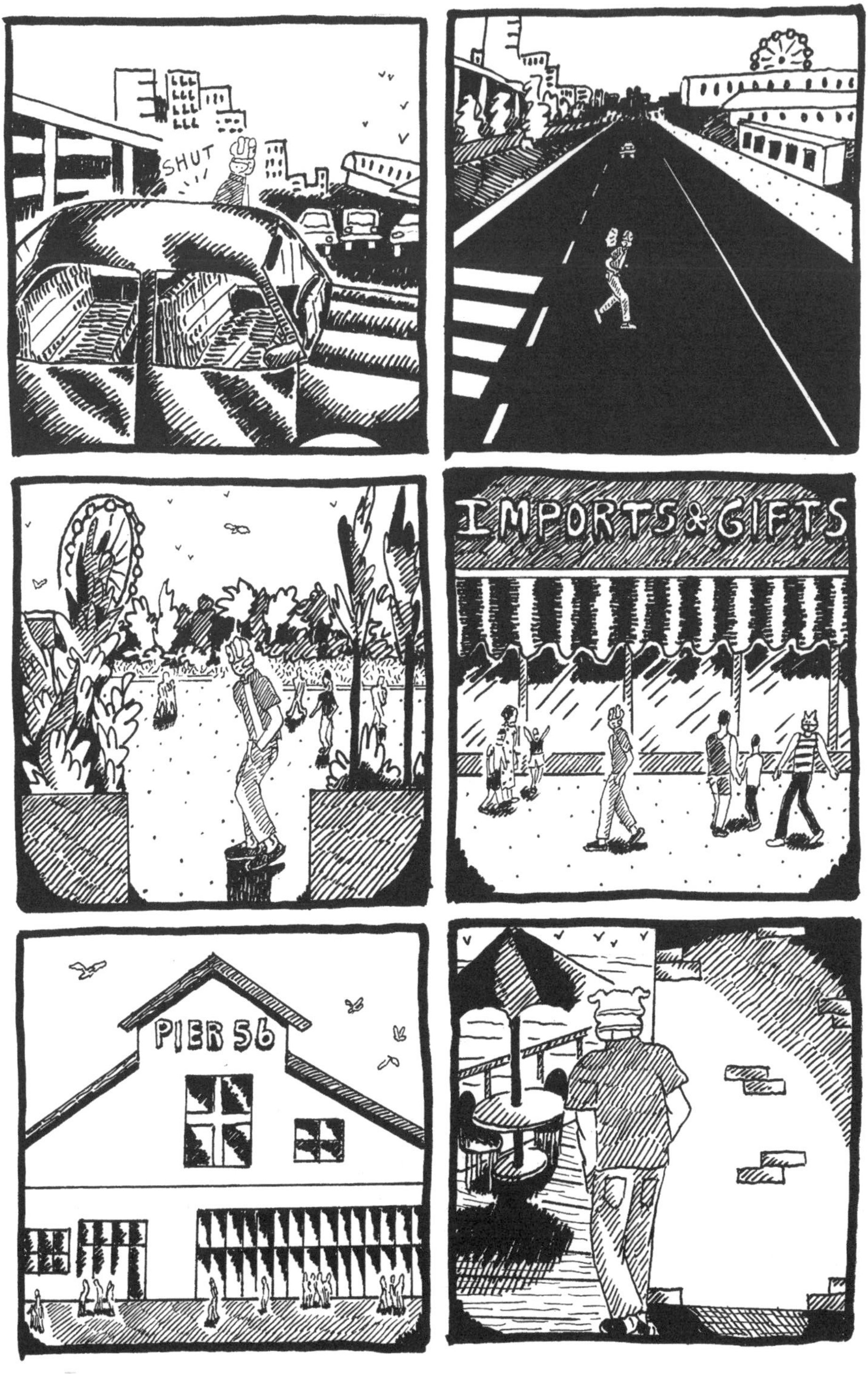
SHUT
IMPORTS & GIFTS
PIER 56

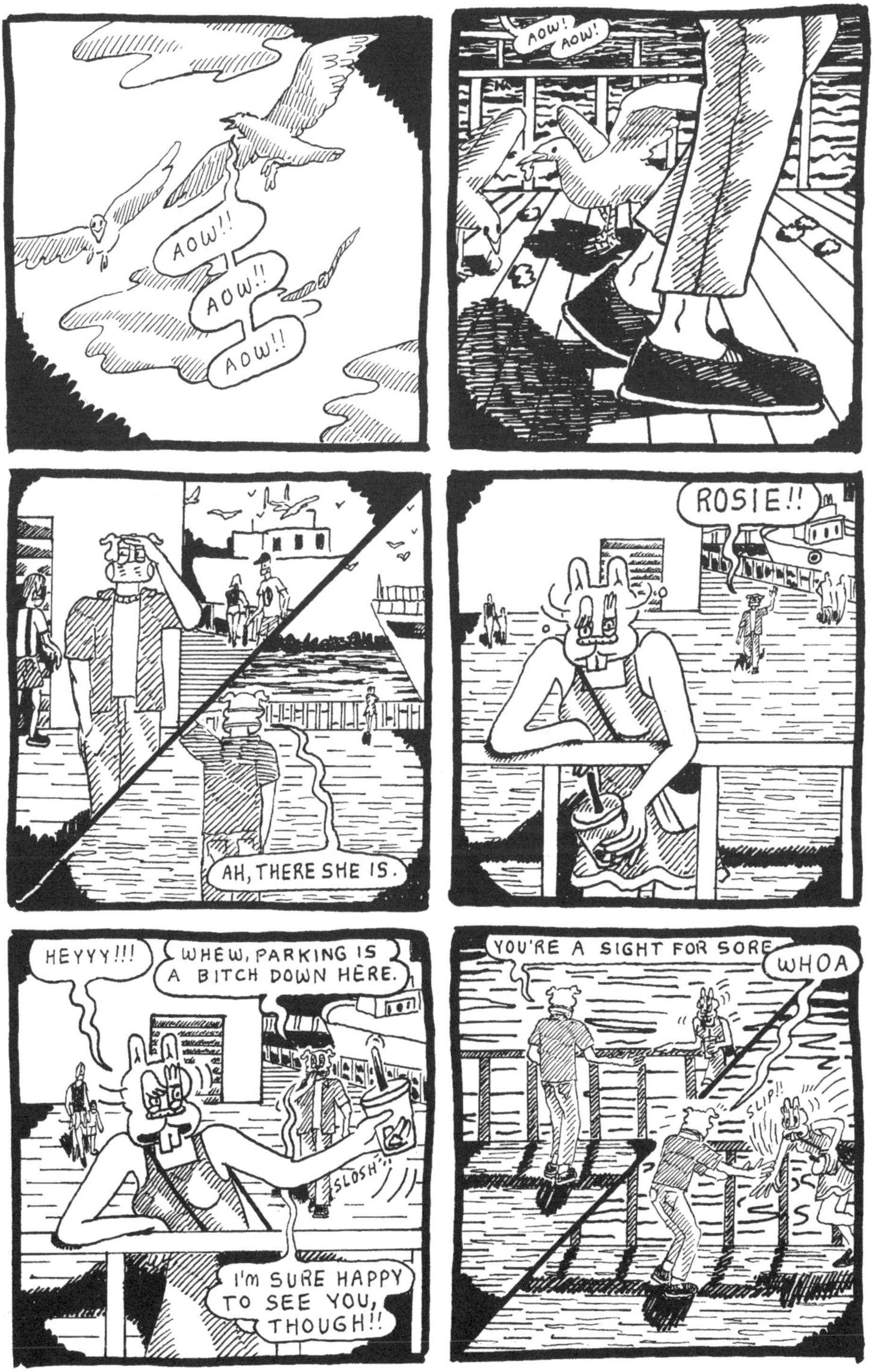
AOW!!
AOW!!
AOW!!
AOW!
AOW!
AH, THERE SHE IS.
ROSIE!!
HEYYY!!!
WHEW, PARKING IS A BITCH DOWN HERE.
SLOSH
I'm SURE HAPPY TO SEE YOU, THOUGH!!
YOU'RE A SIGHT FOR SORE
WHOA
SLIP!!

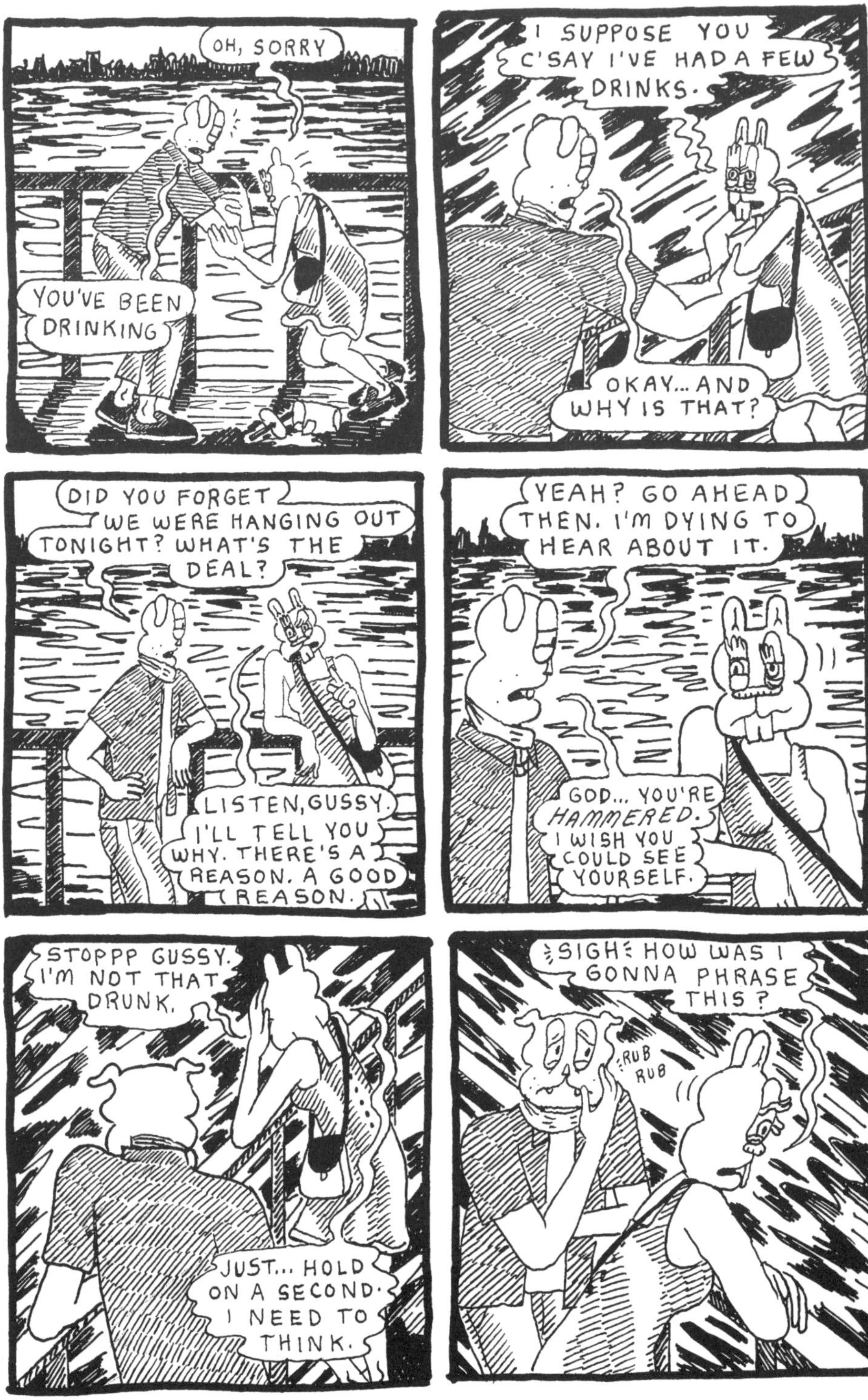
OH, SORRY
YOU'VE BEEN DRINKING
I SUPPOSE YOU C'SAY I'VE HAD A FEW DRINKS.
OKAY... AND WHY IS THAT?
DID YOU FORGET WE WERE HANGING OUT TONIGHT? WHAT'S THE DEAL?
LISTEN, GUSSY. I'LL TELL YOU WHY. THERE'S A REASON. A GOOD REASON.
YEAH? GO AHEAD THEN. I'M DYING TO HEAR ABOUT IT.
GOD... YOU'RE HAMMERED. I WISH YOU COULD SEE YOURSELF.
STOPPP GUSSY. I'M NOT THAT DRUNK.
JUST... HOLD ON A SECOND. I NEED TO THINK.
SIGH HOW WAS I GONNA PHRASE THIS?
RUB RUB

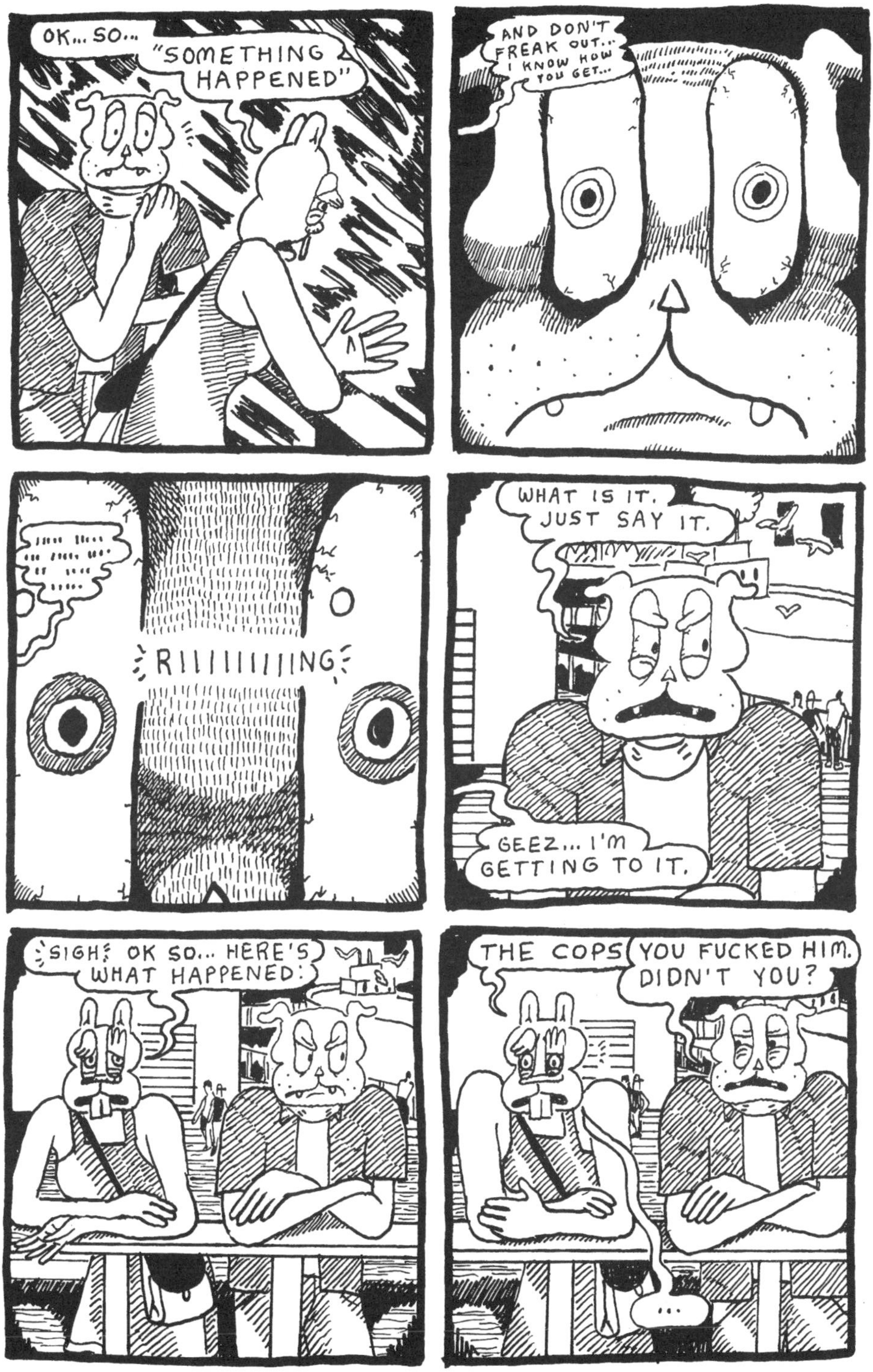
OK... SO...
"SOMETHING HAPPENED"
AND DON'T FREAK OUT... I KNOW HOW YOU GET...
RIIIIIIIIING
WHAT IS IT. JUST SAY IT.
GEEZ... I'M GETTING TO IT.
SIGH OK SO... HERE'S WHAT HAPPENED:
THE COPS
YOU FUCKED HIM. DIDN'T YOU?
...

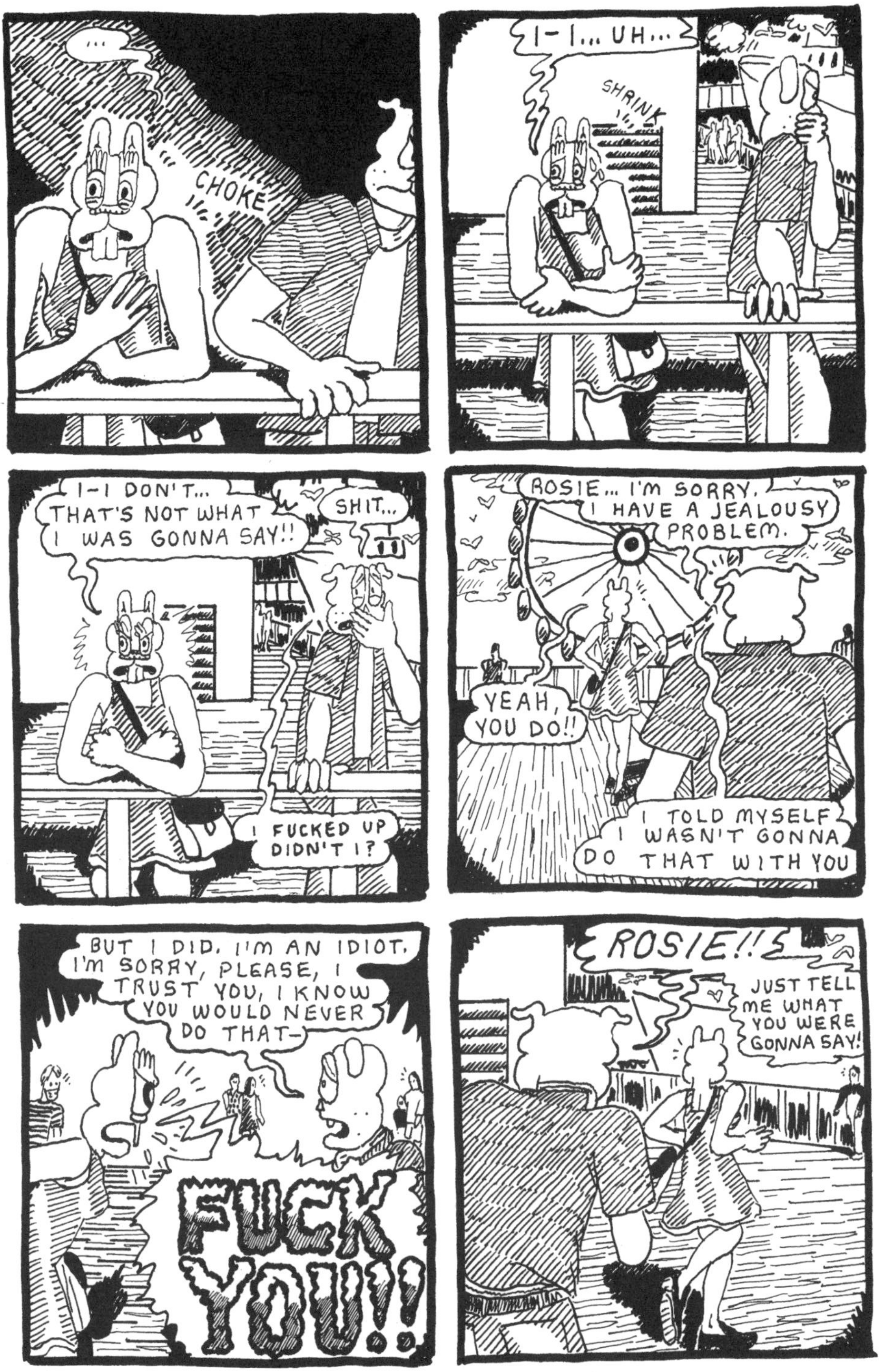
...
CHOKE
I-I... UH...
SHRINK
I-I DON'T... THAT'S NOT WHAT I WAS GONNA SAY!!
SHIT...
I FUCKED UP DIDN'T I?
ROSIE... I'M SORRY. I HAVE A JEALOUSY PROBLEM.
YEAH, YOU DO!!
I TOLD MYSELF I WASN'T GONNA DO THAT WITH YOU
BUT I DID. I'M AN IDIOT. I'M SORRY, PLEASE, I TRUST YOU, I KNOW YOU WOULD NEVER DO THAT-
FUCK YOU!!
ROSIE!!
JUST TELL ME WHAT YOU WERE GONNA SAY!

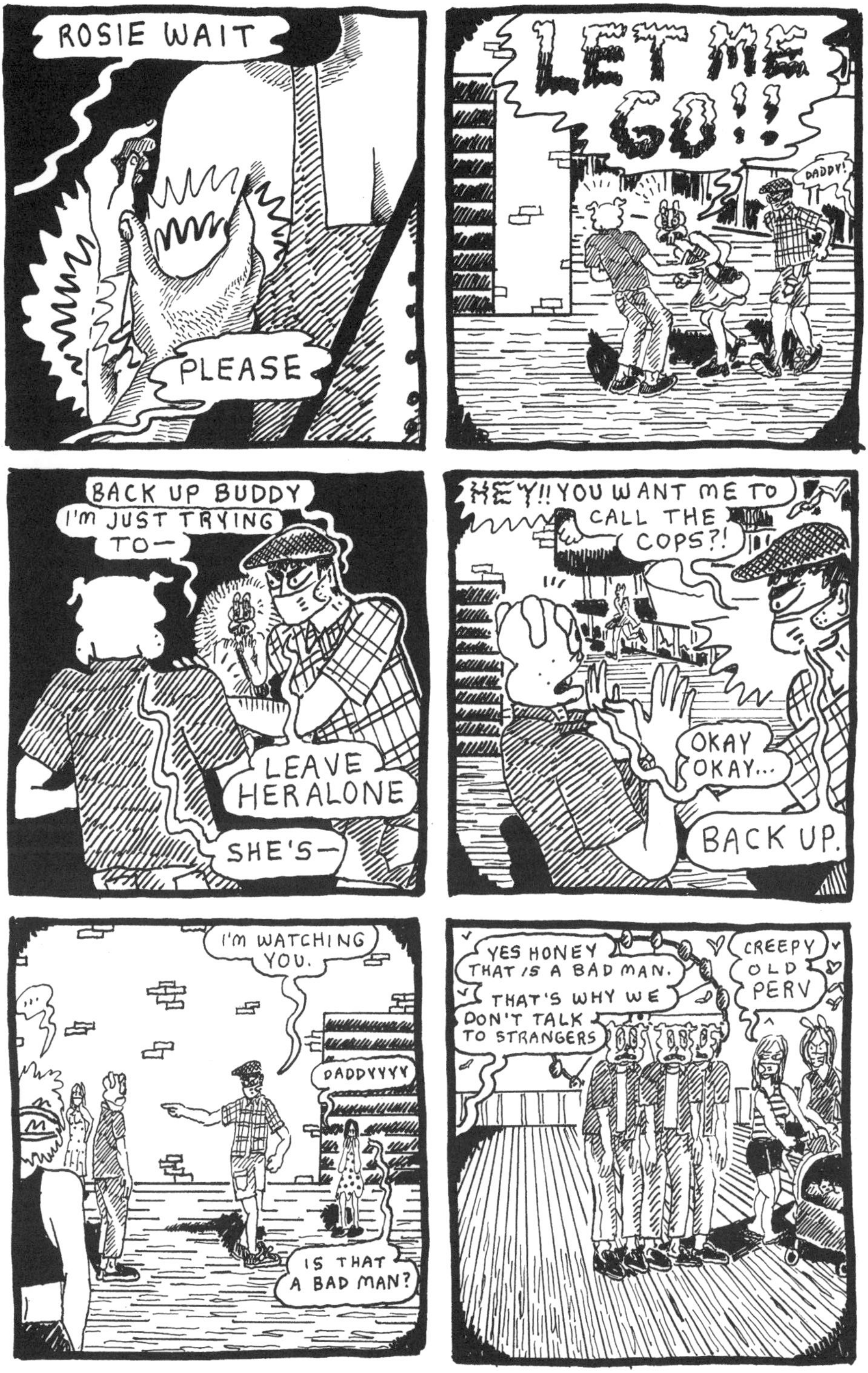
ROSIE WAIT
PLEASE
LET ME GO!!
DADDY!
BACK UP BUDDY
I'M JUST TRYING TO—
LEAVE HER ALONE
SHE'S—
HEY!! YOU WANT ME TO CALL THE COPS?!
OKAY OKAY...
BACK UP.
I'M WATCHING YOU.
DADDYYYY
IS THAT A BAD MAN?
YES HONEY THAT IS A BAD MAN.
THAT'S WHY WE DON'T TALK TO STRANGERS
CREEPY OLD PERV

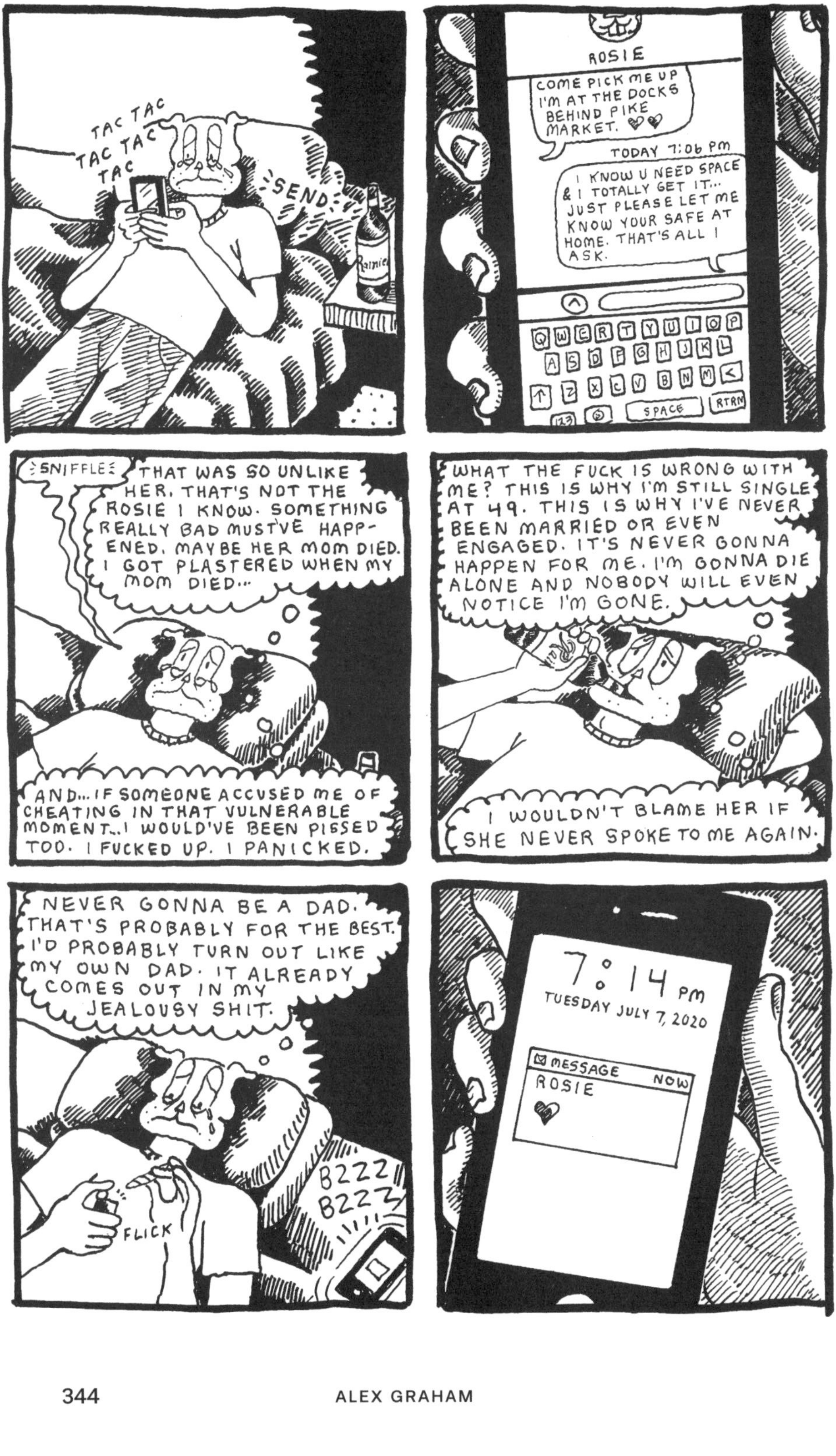
TAC TAC
TAC TAC
TAC
SEND
Rainier
ROSIE
COME PICK ME UP I'M AT THE DOCKS BEHIND PIKE MARKET.
TODAY 7:06 PM
I KNOW U NEED SPACE & I TOTALLY GET IT... JUST PLEASE LET ME KNOW YOUR SAFE AT HOME. THAT'S ALL I ASK.
Q W E R T Y U I O P
A S D F G H J K L
Z X C V B N M
123
SPACE
RTRN
SNIFFLE
THAT WAS SO UNLIKE HER. THAT'S NOT THE ROSIE I KNOW. SOMETHING REALLY BAD MUST'VE HAPPENED. MAYBE HER MOM DIED. I GOT PLASTERED WHEN MY MOM DIED...
AND... IF SOMEONE ACCUSED ME OF CHEATING IN THAT VULNERABLE MOMENT... I WOULD'VE BEEN PISSED TOO. I FUCKED UP. I PANICKED.
WHAT THE FUCK IS WRONG WITH ME? THIS IS WHY I'M STILL SINGLE AT 49. THIS IS WHY I'VE NEVER BEEN MARRIED OR EVEN ENGAGED. IT'S NEVER GONNA HAPPEN FOR ME. I'M GONNA DIE ALONE AND NOBODY WILL EVEN NOTICE I'M GONE.
I WOULDN'T BLAME HER IF SHE NEVER SPOKE TO ME AGAIN.
NEVER GONNA BE A DAD. THAT'S PROBABLY FOR THE BEST. I'D PROBABLY TURN OUT LIKE MY OWN DAD. IT ALREADY COMES OUT IN MY JEALOUSY SHIT.
FLICK
BZZZ
BZZZ
7:14 PM
TUESDAY JULY 7, 2020
MESSAGE
NOW
ROSIE

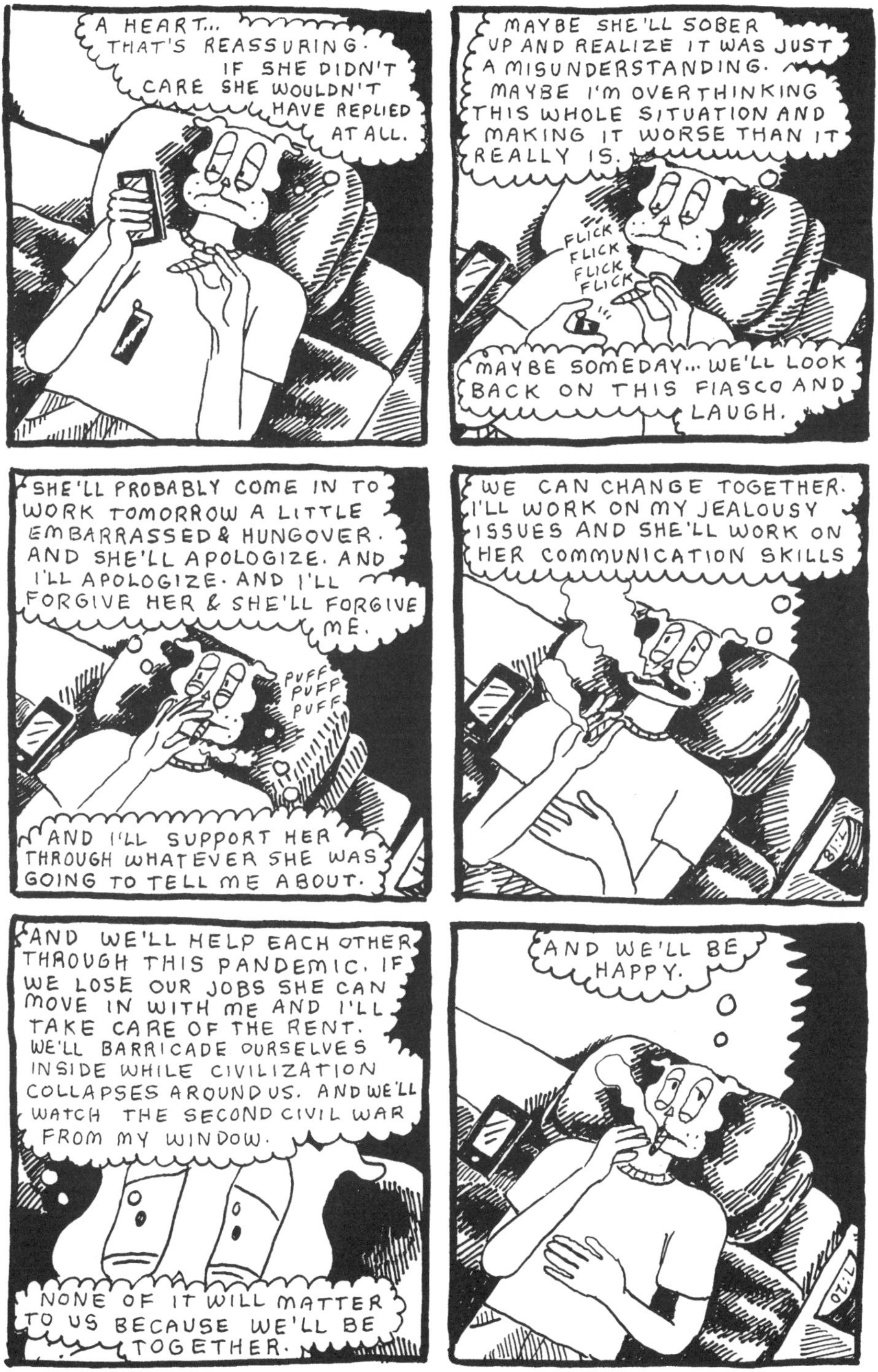
A HEART... THAT'S REASSURING. IF SHE DIDN'T CARE SHE WOULDN'T HAVE REPLIED AT ALL.
MAYBE SHE'LL SOBER UP AND REALIZE IT WAS JUST A MISUNDERSTANDING. MAYBE I'M OVERTHINKING THIS WHOLE SITUATION AND MAKING IT WORSE THAN IT REALLY IS.
FLICK FLICK FLICK FLICK
MAYBE SOMEDAY... WE'LL LOOK BACK ON THIS FIASCO AND LAUGH.
SHE'LL PROBABLY COME IN TO WORK TOMORROW A LITTLE EMBARRASSED & HUNGOVER. AND SHE'LL APOLOGIZE. AND I'LL APOLOGIZE. AND I'LL FORGIVE HER & SHE'LL FORGIVE ME.
PUFF PUFF PUFF
AND I'LL SUPPORT HER THROUGH WHATEVER SHE WAS GOING TO TELL ME ABOUT.
WE CAN CHANGE TOGETHER. I'LL WORK ON MY JEALOUSY ISSUES AND SHE'LL WORK ON HER COMMUNICATION SKILLS
1:18
AND WE'LL HELP EACH OTHER THROUGH THIS PANDEMIC. IF WE LOSE OUR JOBS SHE CAN MOVE IN WITH ME AND I'LL TAKE CARE OF THE RENT. WE'LL BARRICADE OURSELVES INSIDE WHILE CIVILIZATION COLLAPSES AROUND US. AND WE'LL WATCH THE SECOND CIVIL WAR FROM MY WINDOW.
NONE OF IT WILL MATTER TO US BECAUSE WE'LL BE TOGETHER.
AND WE'LL BE HAPPY.
1:20

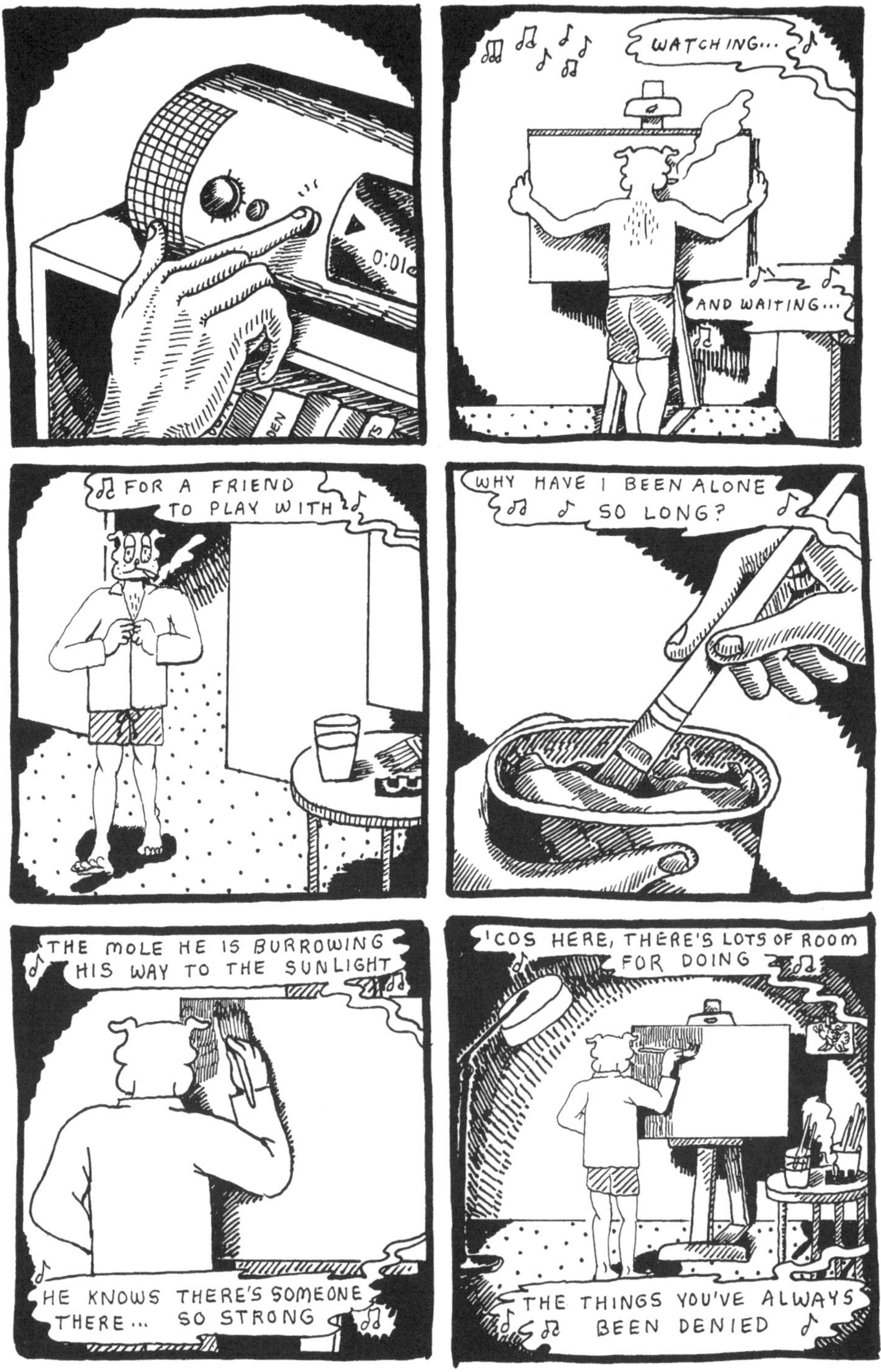
0:01
WATCHING...
AND WAITING...
FOR A FRIEND TO PLAY WITH
WHY HAVE I BEEN ALONE SO LONG?
THE MOLE HE IS BURROWING HIS WAY TO THE SUNLIGHT
HE KNOWS THERE'S SOMEONE THERE... SO STRONG
'COS HERE, THERE'S LOTS OF ROOM FOR DOING
THE THINGS YOU'VE ALWAYS BEEN DENIED

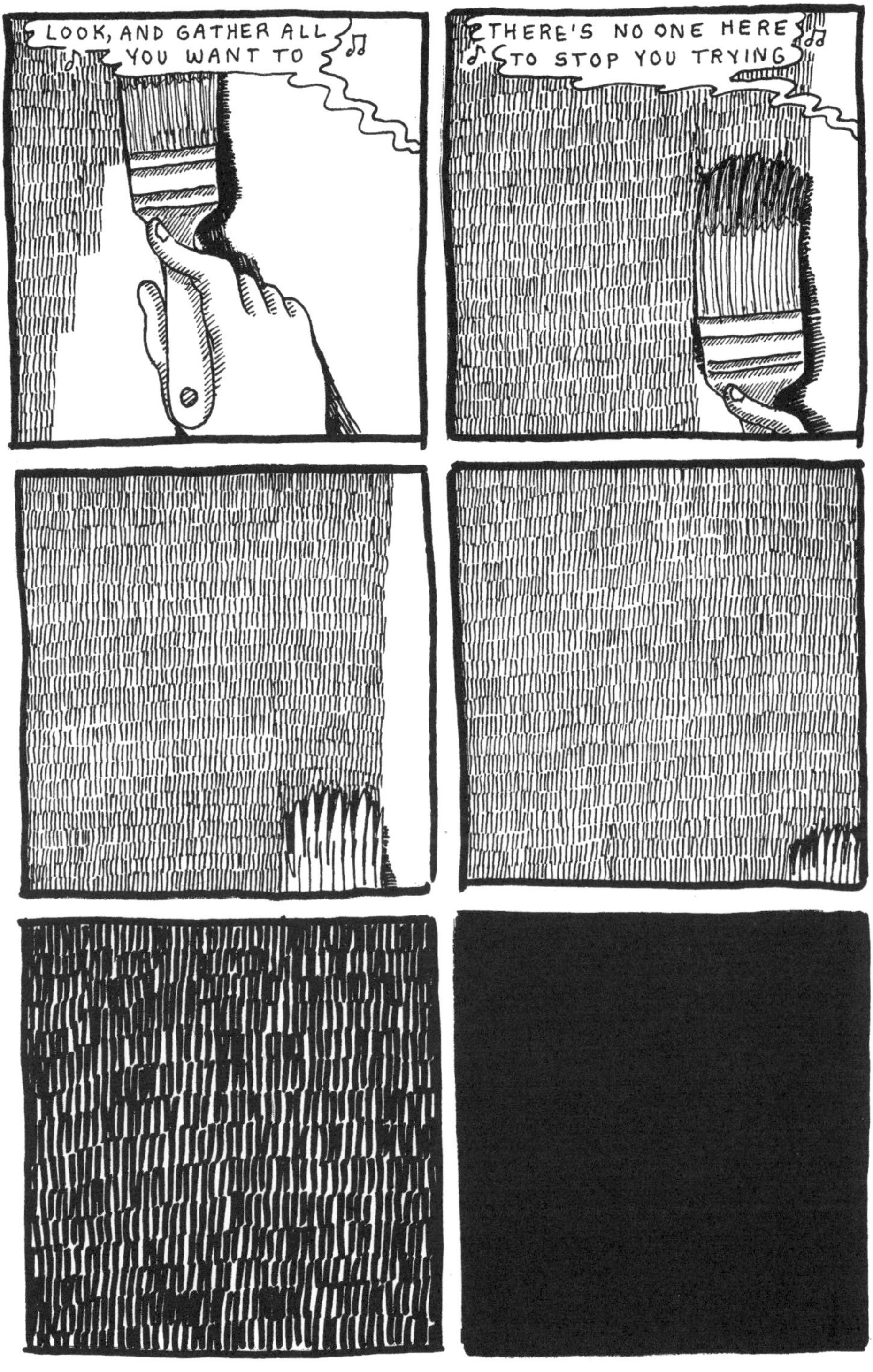
LOOK, AND GATHER ALL YOU WANT TO
THERE'S NO ONE HERE TO STOP YOU TRYING

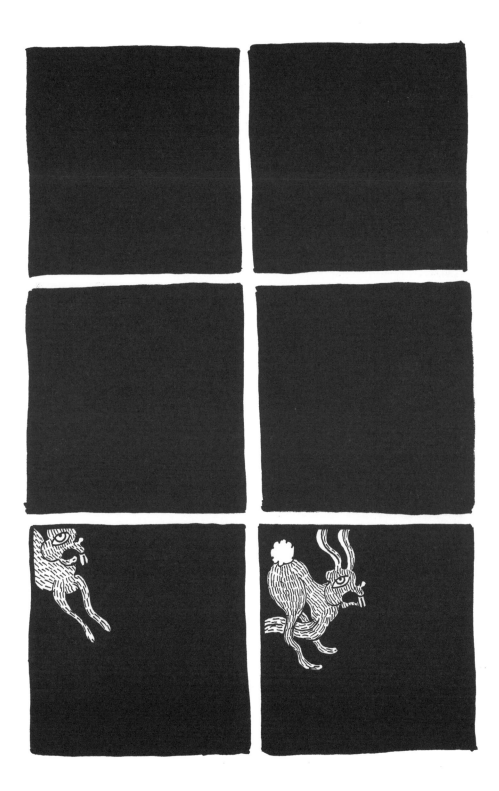

348   ALEX GRAHAM

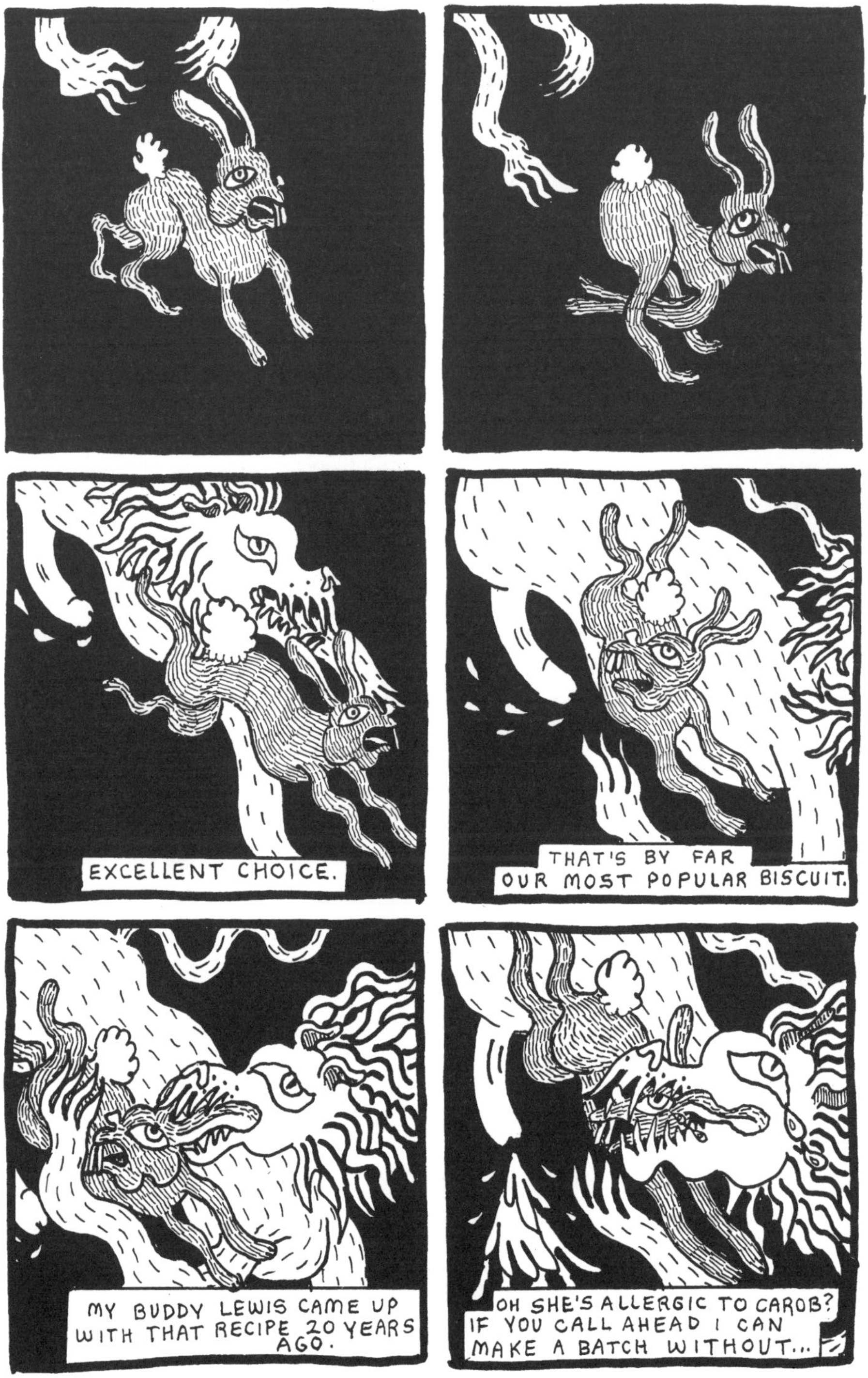
EXCELLENT CHOICE.
THAT'S BY FAR OUR MOST POPULAR BISCUIT.
MY BUDDY LEWIS CAME UP WITH THAT RECIPE 20 YEARS AGO.
OH SHE'S ALLERGIC TO CAROB? IF YOU CALL AHEAD I CAN MAKE A BATCH WITHOUT...

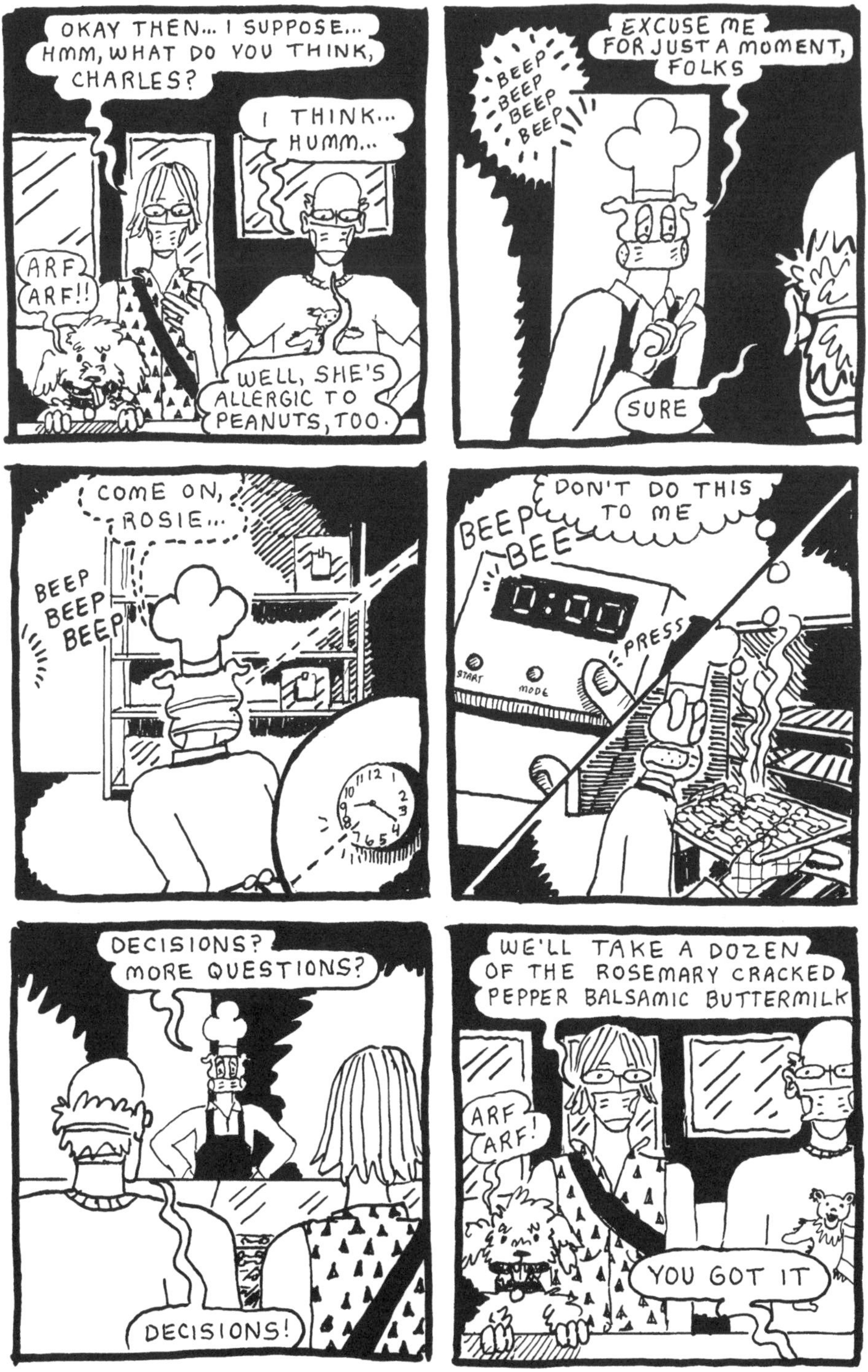
OKAY THEN... I SUPPOSE... HMM, WHAT DO YOU THINK, CHARLES?
I THINK... HUMM...
ARF ARF!!
WELL, SHE'S ALLERGIC TO PEANUTS, TOO.
BEEP BEEP BEEP BEEP
EXCUSE ME FOR JUST A MOMENT, FOLKS
SURE
COME ON, ROSIE...
BEEP BEEP BEEP
DON'T DO THIS TO ME
BEEP BEE
PRESS
START
MODE
DECISIONS? MORE QUESTIONS?
DECISIONS!
WE'LL TAKE A DOZEN OF THE ROSEMARY CRACKED PEPPER BALSAMIC BUTTERMILK
ARF ARF!
YOU GOT IT

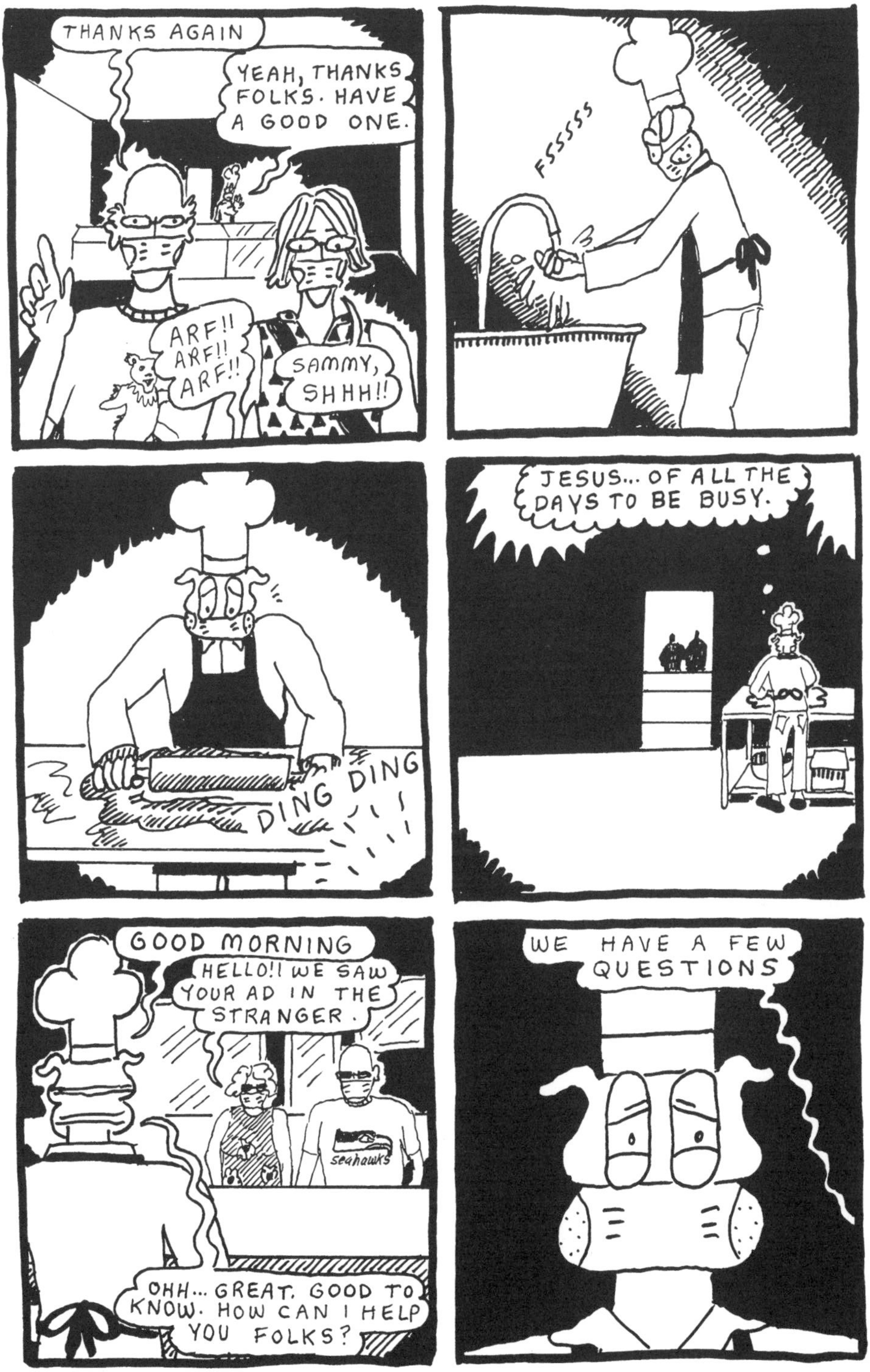
THANKS AGAIN
YEAH, THANKS FOLKS. HAVE A GOOD ONE.
ARF!! ARF!! ARF!!
SAMMY, SHHH!!
FSSSSS
DING DING
JESUS... OF ALL THE DAYS TO BE BUSY.
GOOD MORNING
HELLO!! WE SAW YOUR AD IN THE STRANGER.
OHH... GREAT. GOOD TO KNOW. HOW CAN I HELP YOU FOLKS?
seahawks
WE HAVE A FEW QUESTIONS

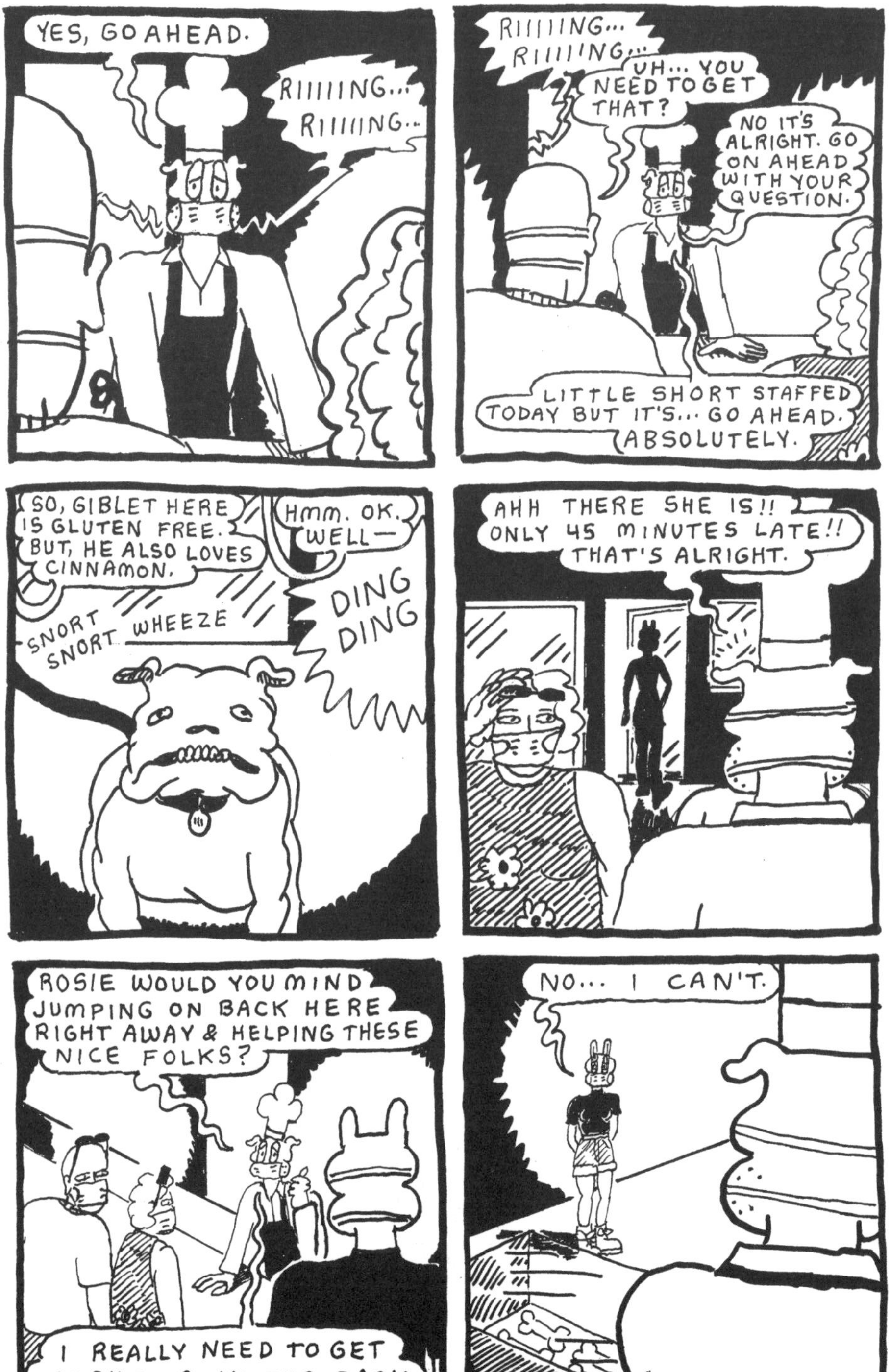
YES, GO AHEAD.
RIIIIING... RIIIIING..
RIIIIING... RIIIIING...
UH... YOU NEED TO GET THAT?
NO IT'S ALRIGHT. GO ON AHEAD WITH YOUR QUESTION.
LITTLE SHORT STAFFED TODAY BUT IT'S... GO AHEAD. ABSOLUTELY.
SO, GIBLET HERE IS GLUTEN FREE. BUT, HE ALSO LOVES CINNAMON.
HMM. OK. WELL—
SNORT SNORT WHEEZE
DING DING
AHH THERE SHE IS!! ONLY 45 MINUTES LATE!! THAT'S ALRIGHT.
ROSIE WOULD YOU MIND JUMPING ON BACK HERE RIGHT AWAY & HELPING THESE NICE FOLKS?
I REALLY NEED TO GET CAUGHT UP IN THE BACK.
NO... I CAN'T.

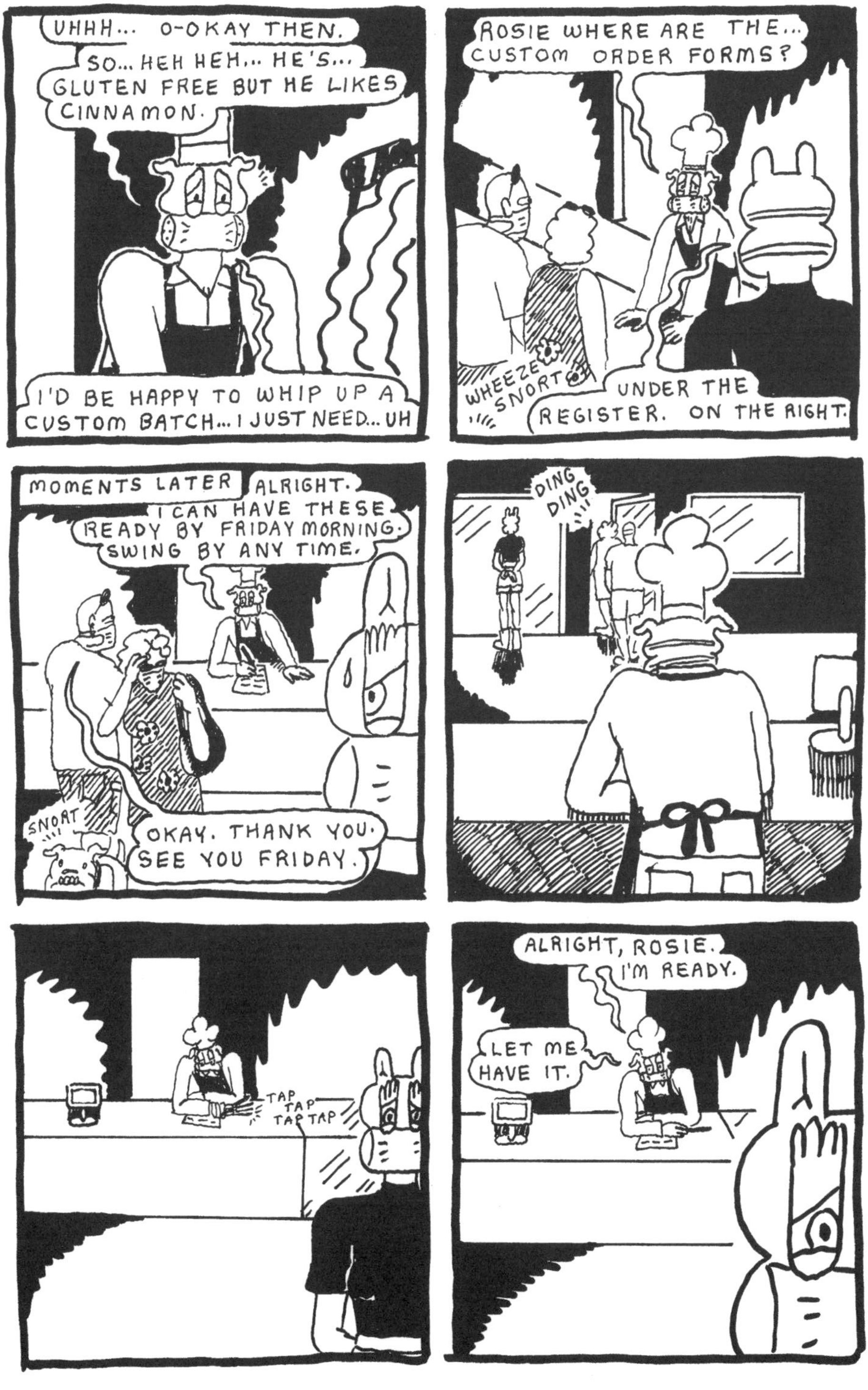
UHHH... O-OKAY THEN.
SO... HEH HEH... HE'S... GLUTEN FREE BUT HE LIKES CINNAMON.
I'D BE HAPPY TO WHIP UP A CUSTOM BATCH... I JUST NEED... UH
ROSIE WHERE ARE THE... CUSTOM ORDER FORMS?
WHEEZE SNORT
UNDER THE REGISTER. ON THE RIGHT.
MOMENTS LATER
ALRIGHT. I CAN HAVE THESE READY BY FRIDAY MORNING. SWING BY ANY TIME.
SNORT
OKAY. THANK YOU. SEE YOU FRIDAY.
DING DING
TAP TAP TAP TAP
ALRIGHT, ROSIE. I'M READY.
LET ME HAVE IT.

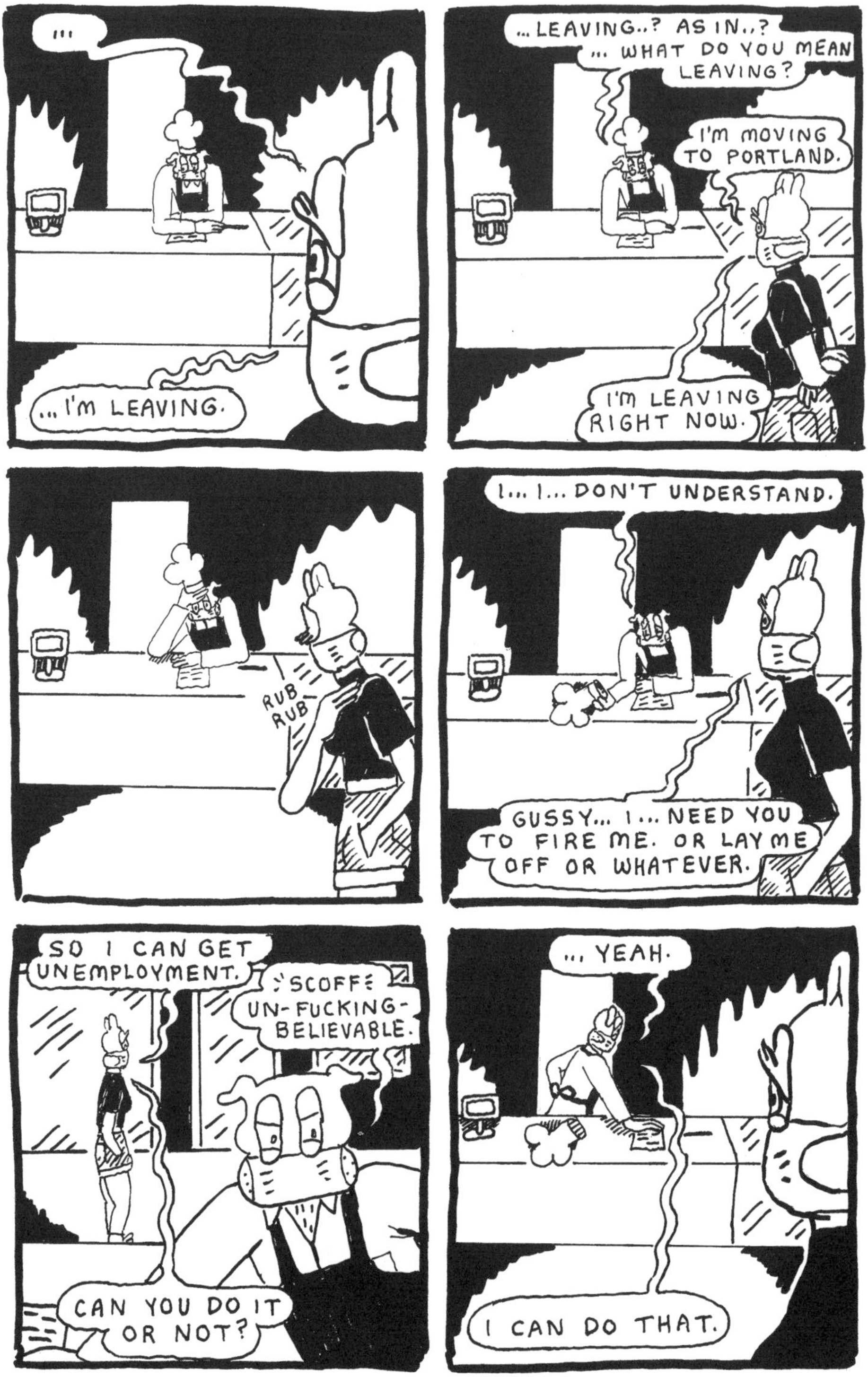
...
... I'M LEAVING.
... LEAVING..? AS IN..? ... WHAT DO YOU MEAN LEAVING?
I'M MOVING TO PORTLAND.
I'M LEAVING RIGHT NOW.
RUB RUB
I... I... DON'T UNDERSTAND.
GUSSY... I... NEED YOU TO FIRE ME. OR LAY ME OFF OR WHATEVER.
SO I CAN GET UNEMPLOYMENT.
SCOFF UN-FUCKING-BELIEVABLE.
CAN YOU DO IT OR NOT?
... YEAH.
I CAN DO THAT.

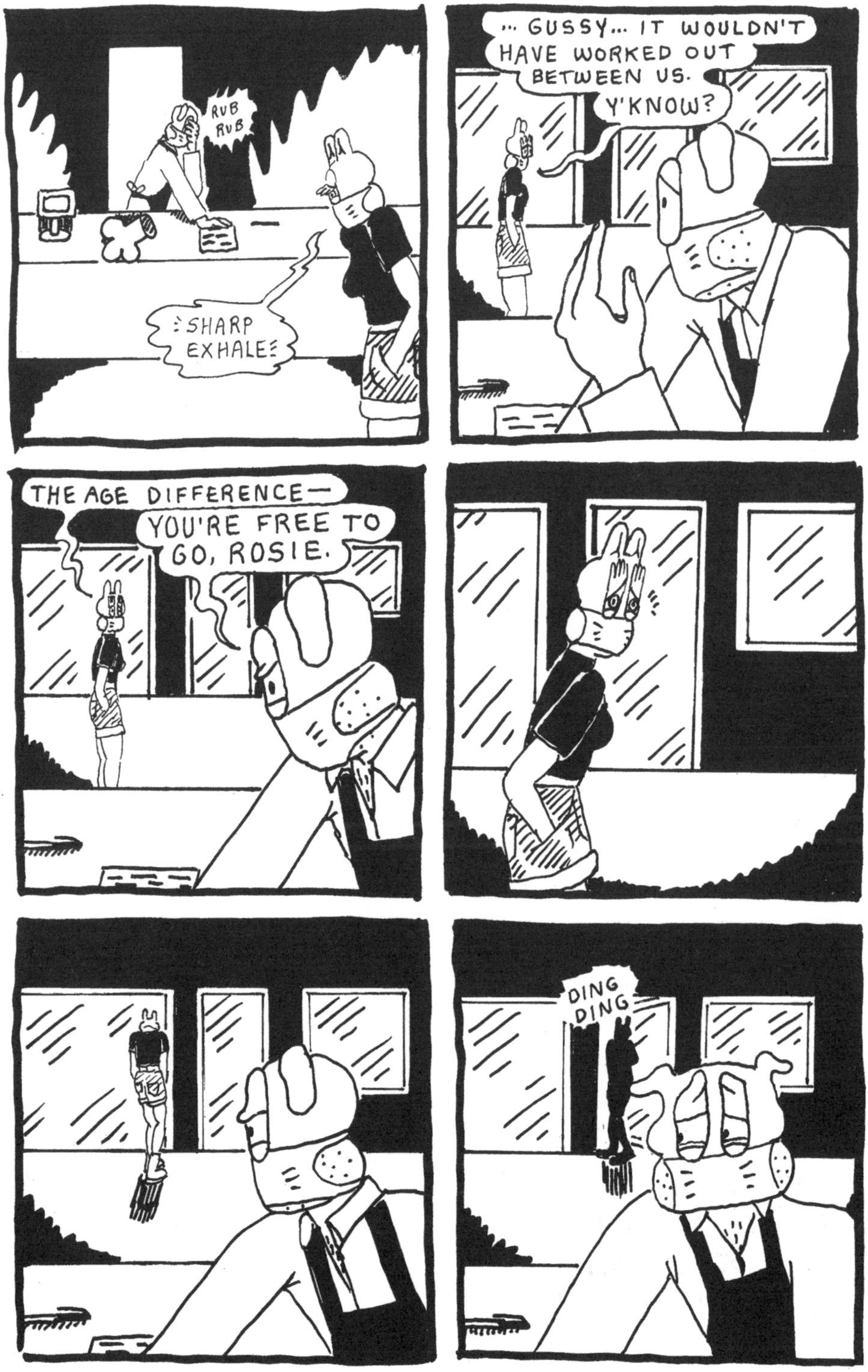
RUB RUB
SHARP EXHALE
... GUSSY... IT WOULDN'T HAVE WORKED OUT BETWEEN US.
Y'KNOW?
THE AGE DIFFERENCE—
YOU'RE FREE TO GO, ROSIE.
DING DING

SHUT
PULL
WHAT'D HE SAY?
WILL HE DO IT?
SOB SOB SOB
AW COME ON. THERE ARE PLENTY OF HOT *YOUNG* DUDES IN MY 'HOOD. DON'T CRY OVER THAT SCUMBAG.
RR-RRRR-R-R-RRA!!
DON'T CALL HIM THAT!!
BITCH, *YOU* CALLED HIM THAT LAST NIGHT ON THE PHONE. REMEMBER??
TURN TURN
SOB SOB *I'M* THE SCUMBAG, PETUNIA.
UM... NO YOU'RE NOT. YOU'RE *EMPOWERED*. YOU'RE A *QUEEN*. YOU KNOW WHAT YOU WANT... AND YOU GO FOR IT.
KRRRSH
NO MATTER WHAT IT TAKES.
AND NO MATTER WHO STANDS IN YOUR WAY.

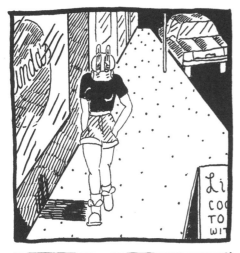

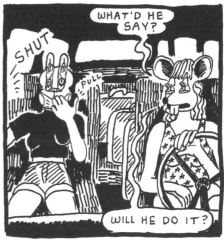

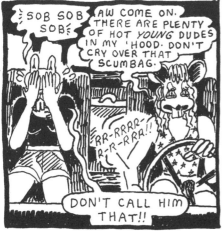

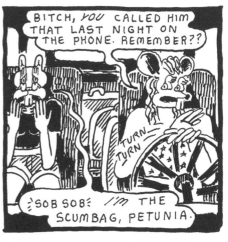

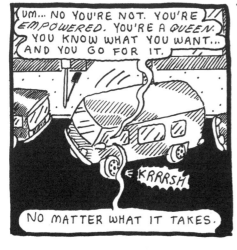

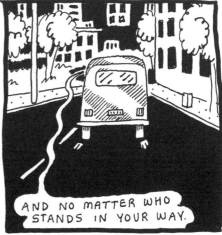

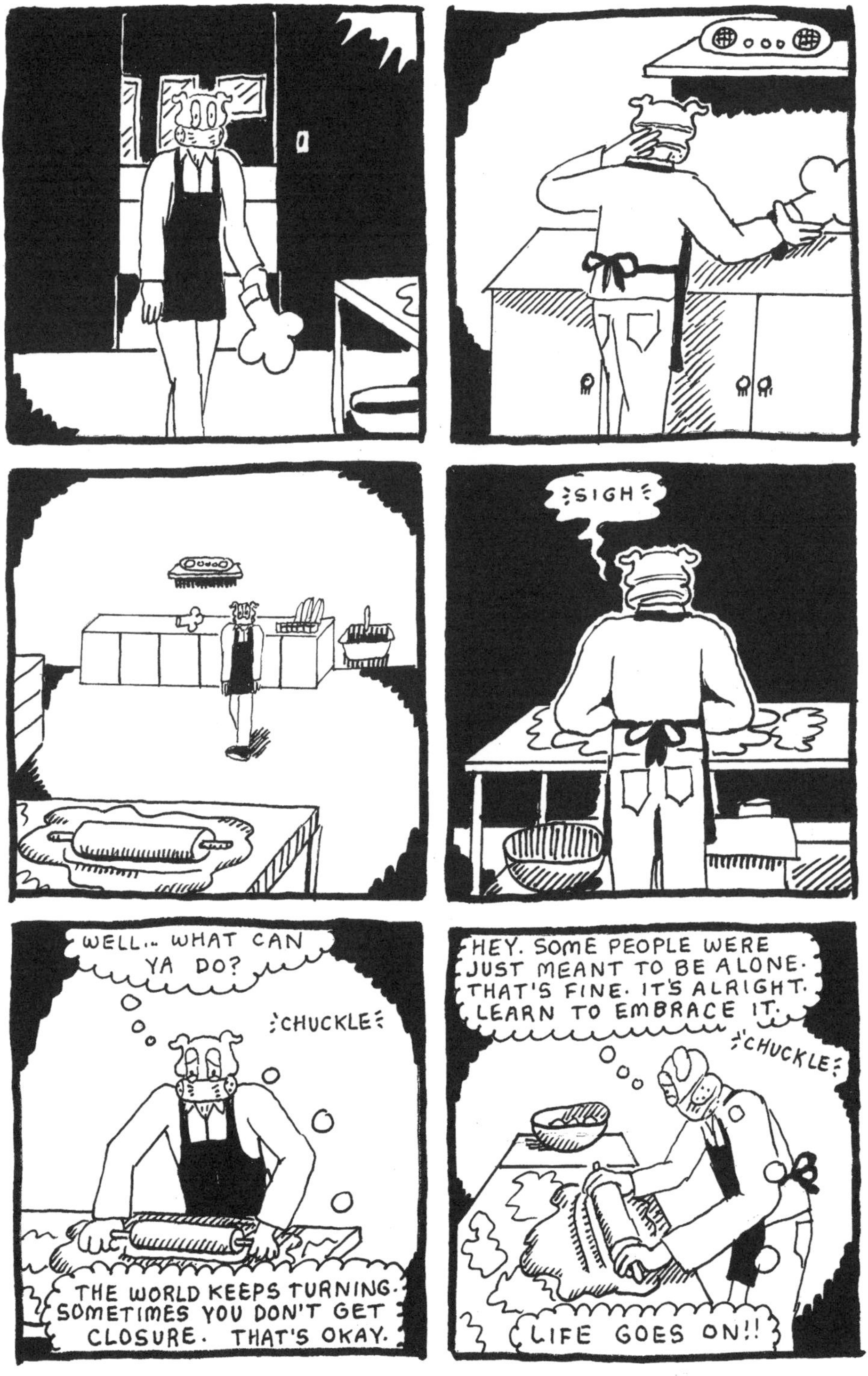
SIGH
WELL.. WHAT CAN YA DO?
CHUCKLE
THE WORLD KEEPS TURNING. SOMETIMES YOU DON'T GET CLOSURE. THAT'S OKAY.
HEY. SOME PEOPLE WERE JUST MEANT TO BE ALONE. THAT'S FINE. IT'S ALRIGHT. LEARN TO EMBRACE IT.
CHUCKLE
LIFE GOES ON!!

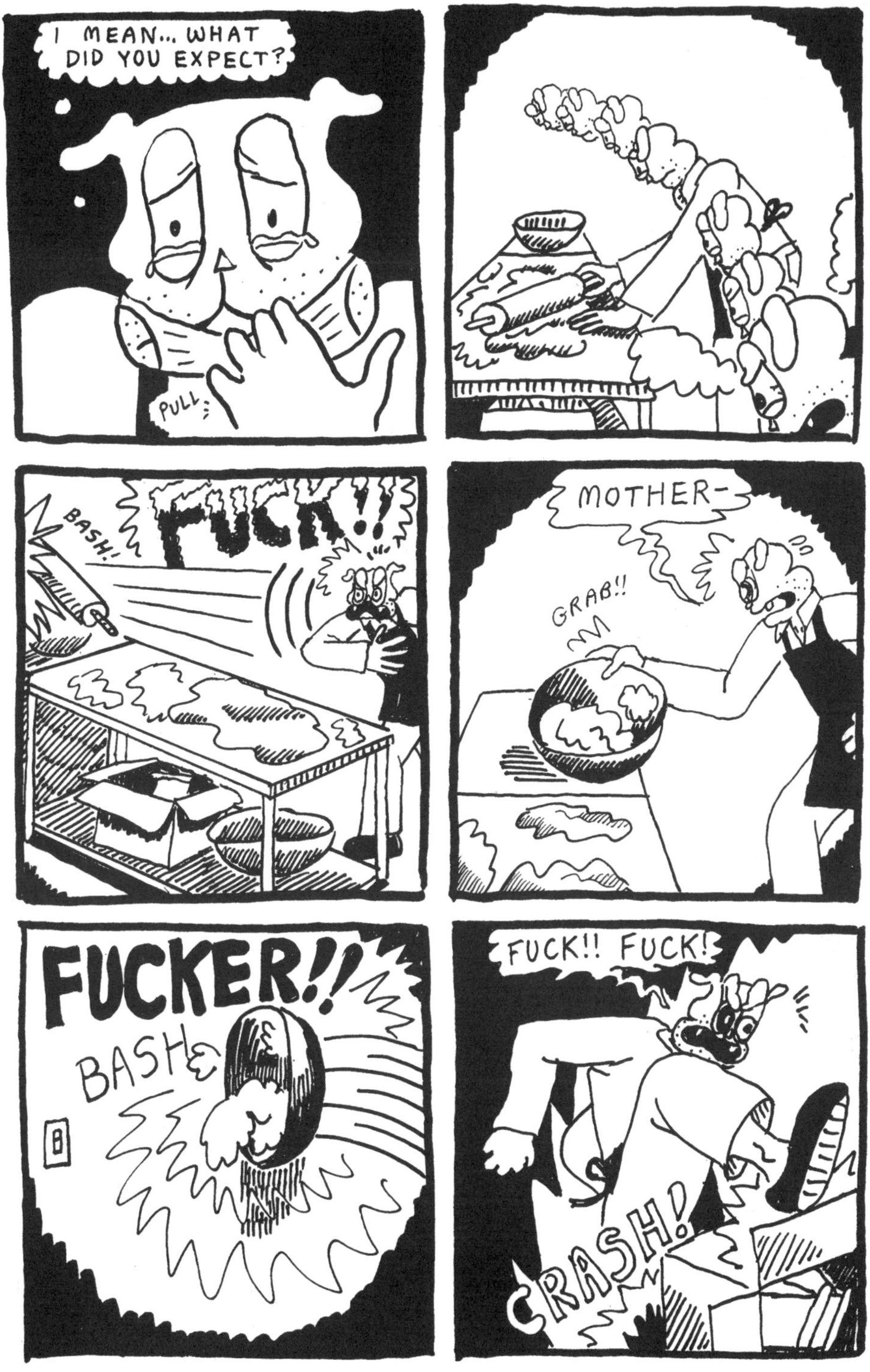
I MEAN... WHAT DID YOU EXPECT?
PULL
BASH!
FUCK!!
MOTHER-
GRAB!!
FUCKER!!
BASH
FUCK!! FUCK!
CRASH!

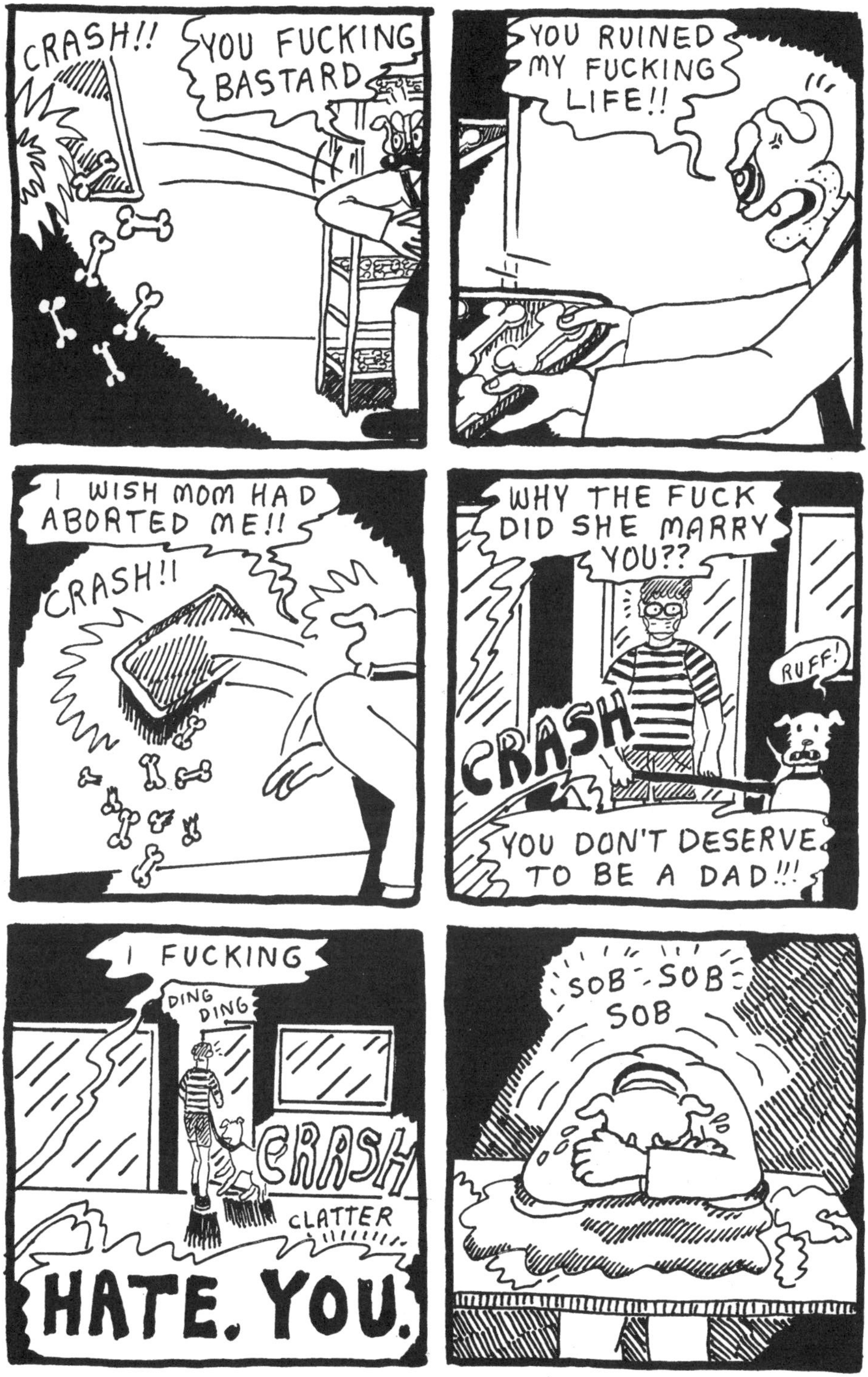
CRASH!!
YOU FUCKING BASTARD
YOU RUINED MY FUCKING LIFE!!
I WISH MOM HAD ABORTED ME!!
CRASH!!
WHY THE FUCK DID SHE MARRY YOU??
RUFF!
CRASH
YOU DON'T DESERVE TO BE A DAD!!!
I FUCKING
DING DING
CRASH
CLATTER
HATE. YOU.
SOB SOB SOB

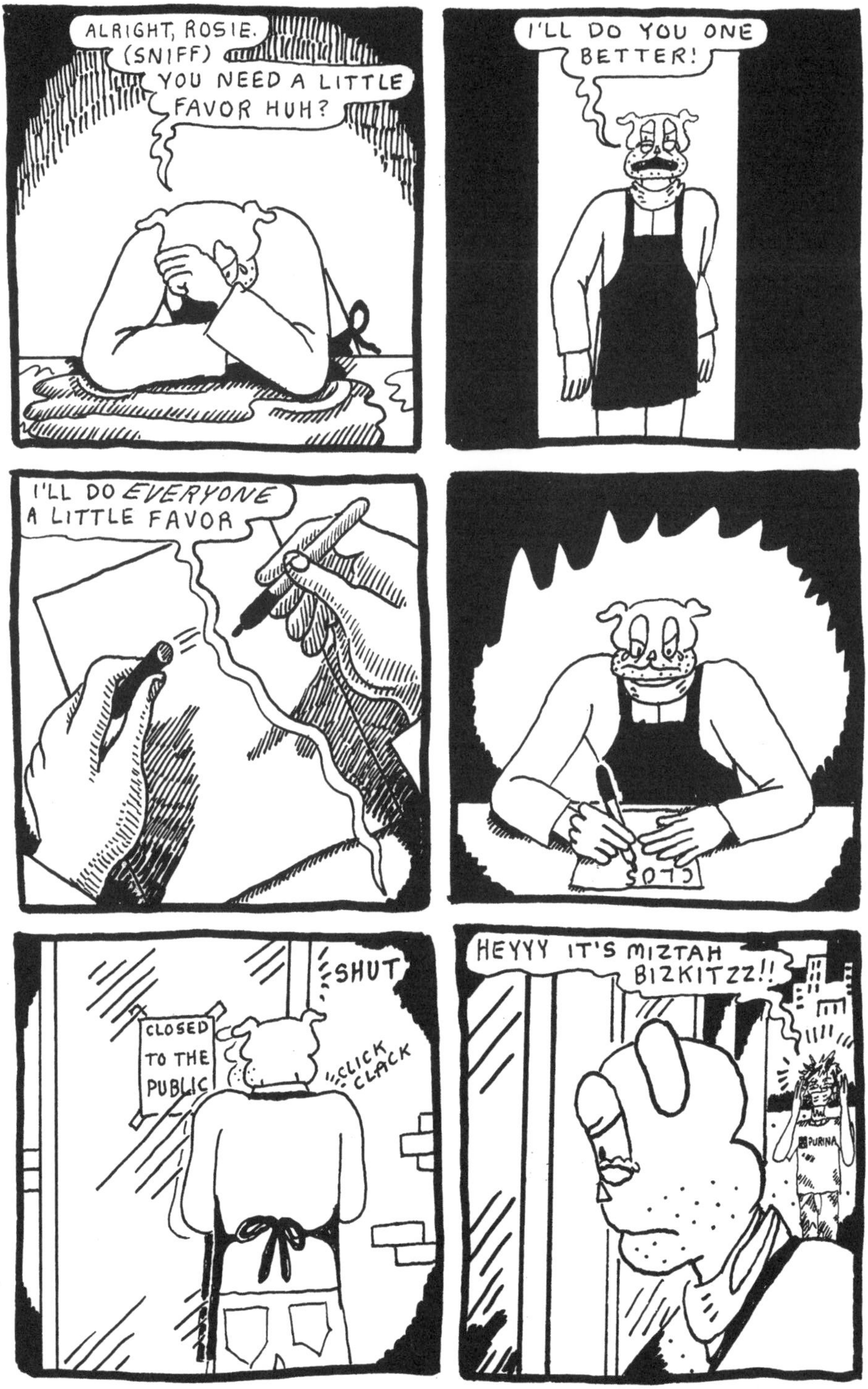
ALRIGHT, ROSIE. (SNIFF)
YOU NEED A LITTLE FAVOR HUH?
I'LL DO YOU ONE BETTER!
I'LL DO *EVERYONE* A LITTLE FAVOR
SHUT
CLOSED TO THE PUBLIC
CLICK CLACK
HEYYY IT'S MIZTAH BIZKITZZ!!
PURINA

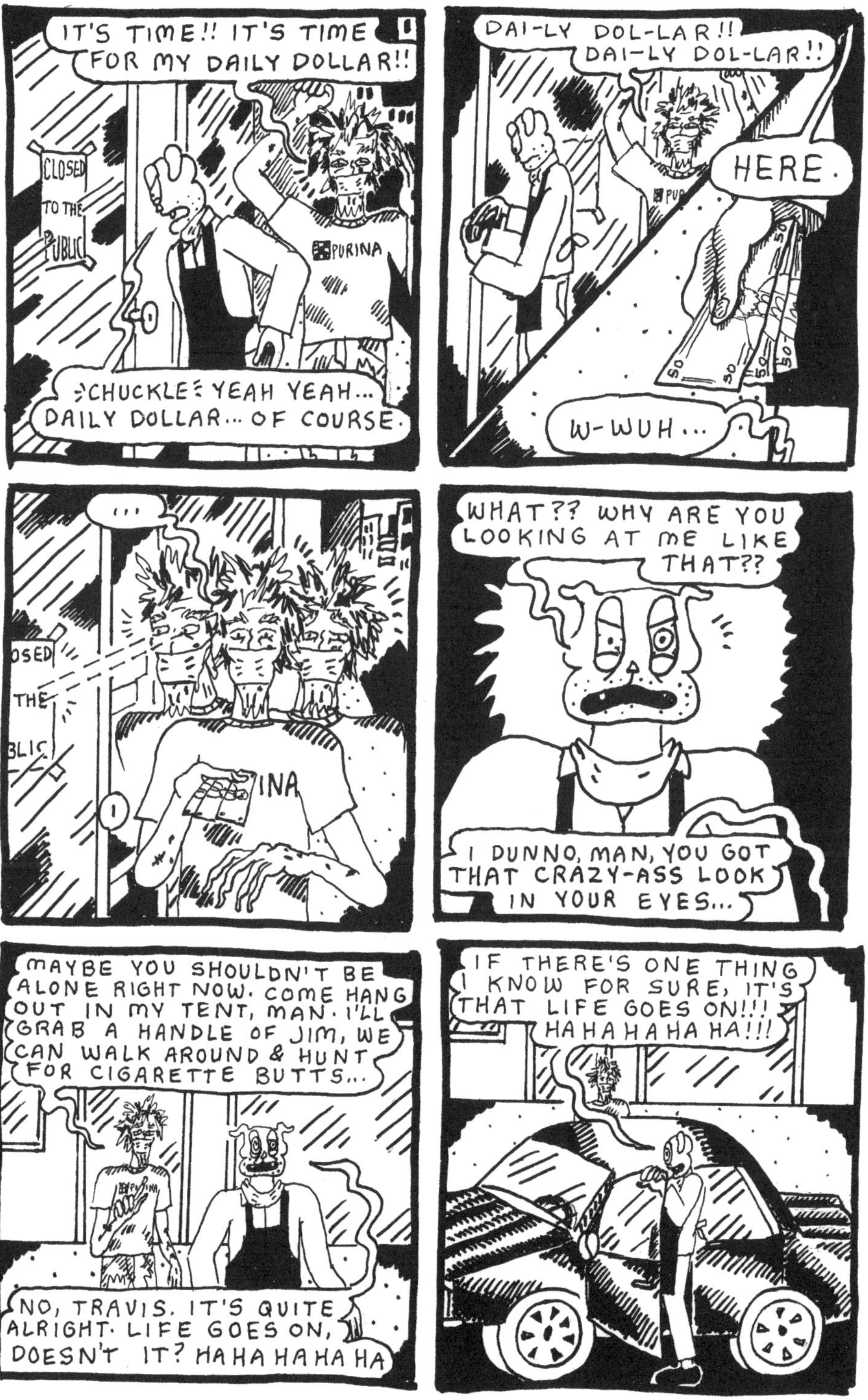
IT'S TIME!! IT'S TIME FOR MY DAILY DOLLAR!!
CLOSED TO THE PUBLIC
PURINA
:CHUCKLE: YEAH YEAH... DAILY DOLLAR... OF COURSE.
DAI-LY DOL-LAR!! DAI-LY DOL-LAR!!
HERE.
W-WUH...
...
WHAT?? WHY ARE YOU LOOKING AT ME LIKE THAT??
I DUNNO, MAN, YOU GOT THAT CRAZY-ASS LOOK IN YOUR EYES...
MAYBE YOU SHOULDN'T BE ALONE RIGHT NOW. COME HANG OUT IN MY TENT, MAN. I'LL GRAB A HANDLE OF JIM, WE CAN WALK AROUND & HUNT FOR CIGARETTE BUTTS...
NO, TRAVIS. IT'S QUITE ALRIGHT. LIFE GOES ON, DOESN'T IT? HA HA HA HA HA HA
IF THERE'S ONE THING I KNOW FOR SURE, IT'S THAT LIFE GOES ON!!! HA HA HA HA HA HA!!!

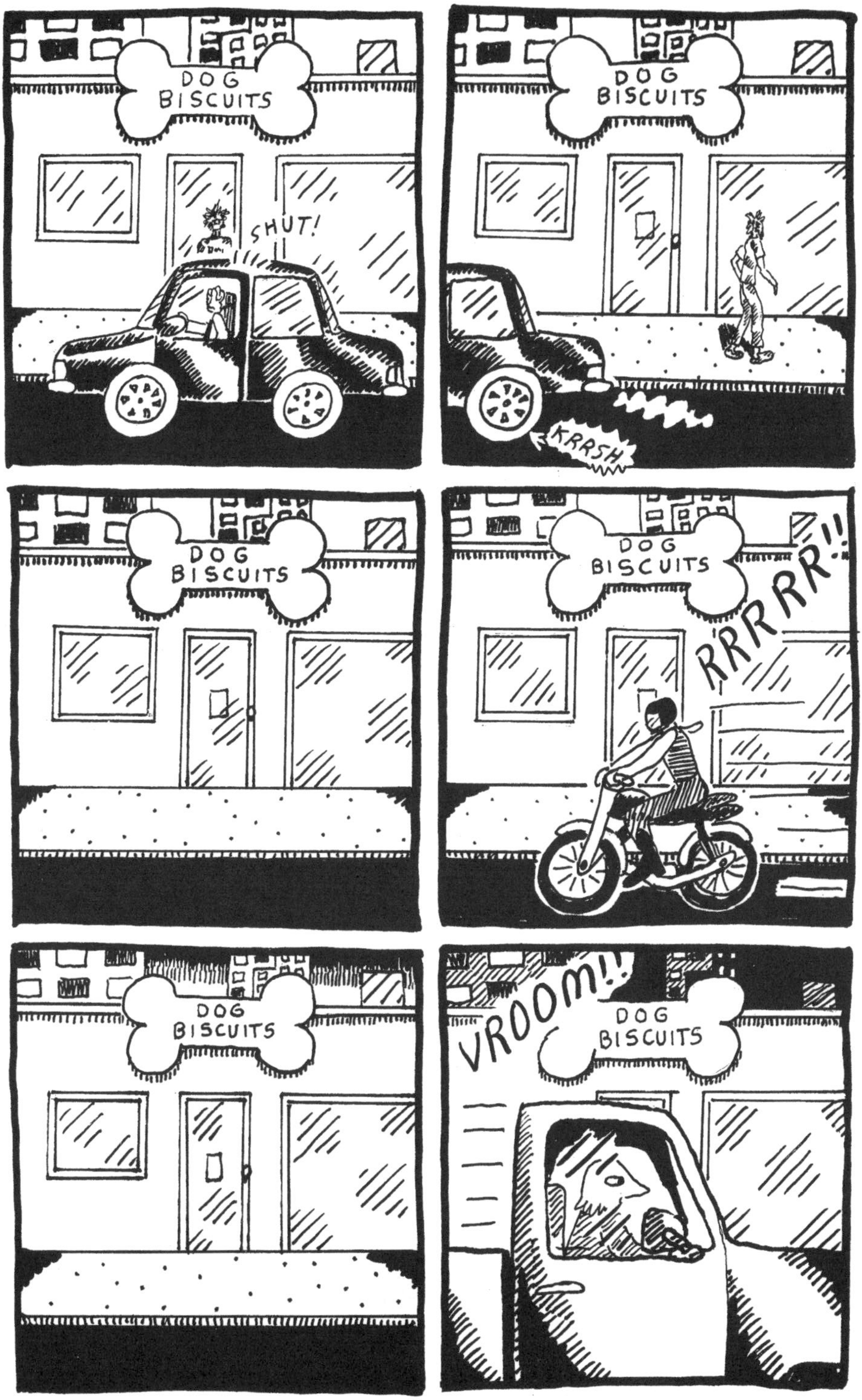
DOG BISCUITS
SHUT!
DOG BISCUITS
KRRSH
DOG BISCUITS
DOG BISCUITS
RRRRR!!
DOG BISCUITS
VROOM!!
DOG BISCUITS

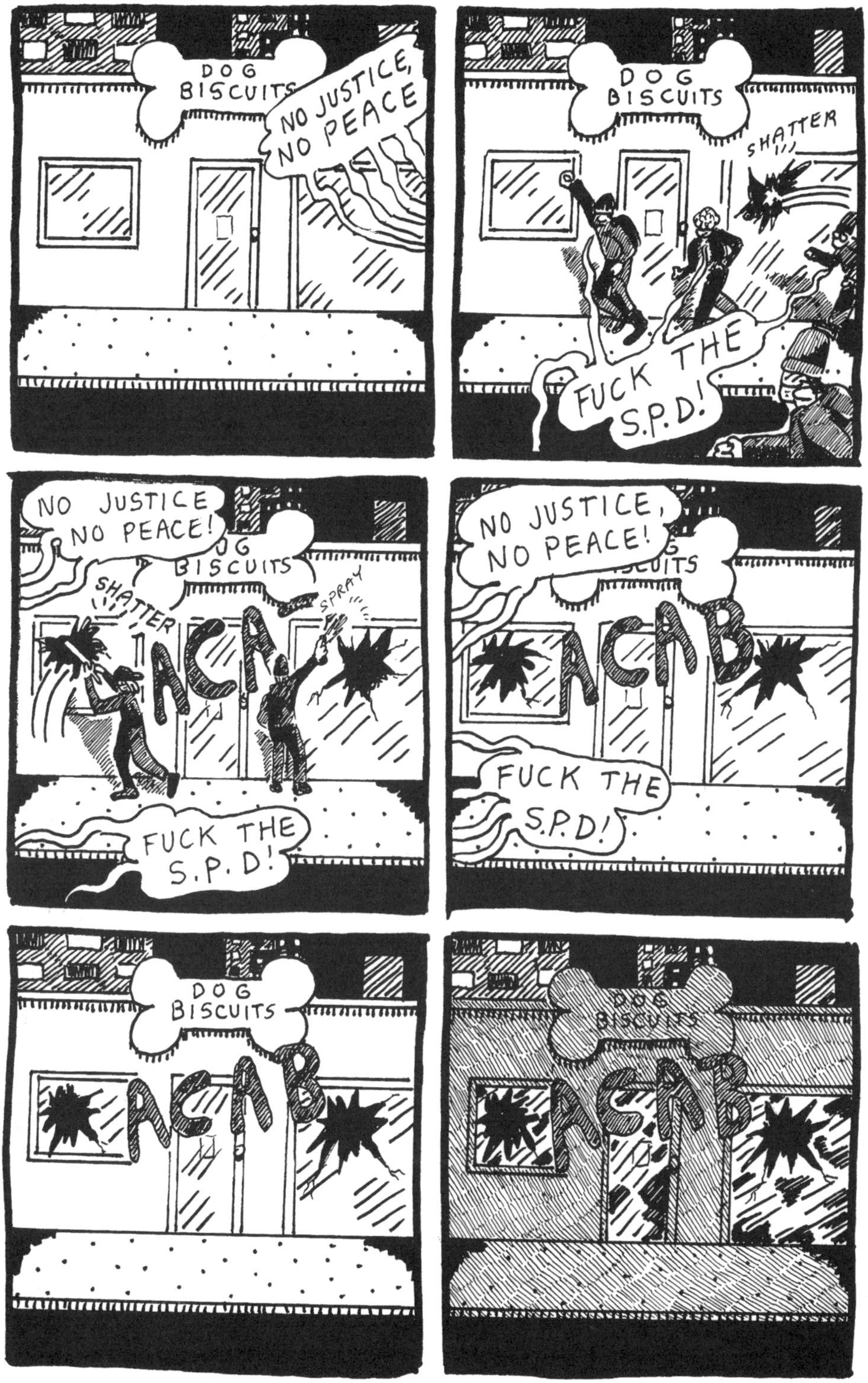
DOG BISCUITS
NO JUSTICE, NO PEACE
DOG BISCUITS
SHATTER
FUCK THE S.P.D!
NO JUSTICE NO PEACE!
BISCUITS
SHATTER
SPRAY
ACA
FUCK THE S.P.D!
NO JUSTICE, NO PEACE!
ACAB
FUCK THE S.P.D!
DOG BISCUITS
ACAB
DOG BISCUITS
ACAB

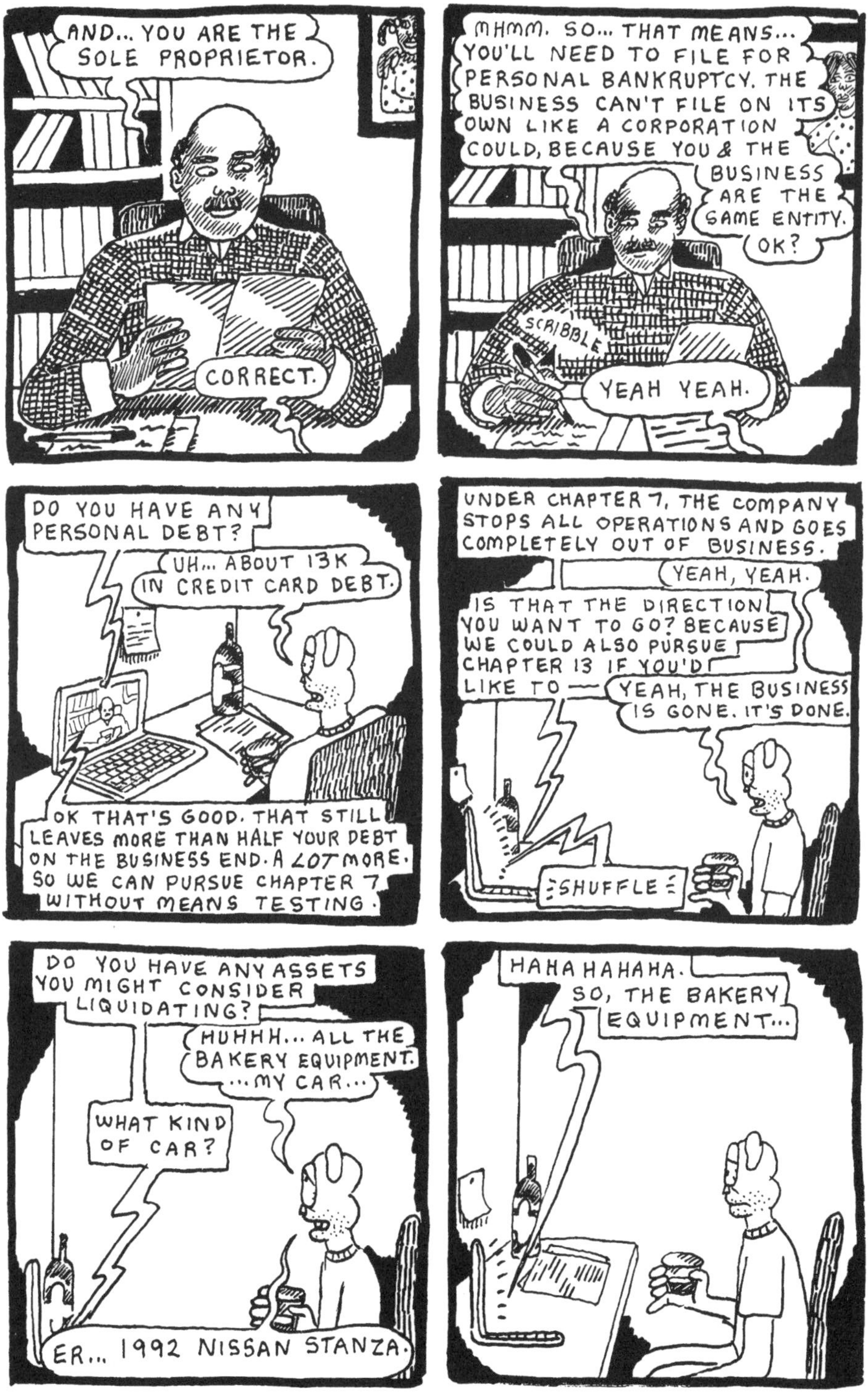
AND... YOU ARE THE SOLE PROPRIETOR.
CORRECT.
MHMM. SO... THAT MEANS... YOU'LL NEED TO FILE FOR PERSONAL BANKRUPTCY. THE BUSINESS CAN'T FILE ON ITS OWN LIKE A CORPORATION COULD, BECAUSE YOU & THE BUSINESS ARE THE SAME ENTITY. OK?
SCRIBBLE
YEAH YEAH.
DO YOU HAVE ANY PERSONAL DEBT?
UH... ABOUT 13K IN CREDIT CARD DEBT.
OK THAT'S GOOD. THAT STILL LEAVES MORE THAN HALF YOUR DEBT ON THE BUSINESS END. A LOT MORE. SO WE CAN PURSUE CHAPTER 7 WITHOUT MEANS TESTING.
UNDER CHAPTER 7, THE COMPANY STOPS ALL OPERATIONS AND GOES COMPLETELY OUT OF BUSINESS.
YEAH, YEAH.
IS THAT THE DIRECTION YOU WANT TO GO? BECAUSE WE COULD ALSO PURSUE CHAPTER 13 IF YOU'D LIKE TO —
YEAH, THE BUSINESS IS GONE. IT'S DONE.
SHUFFLE
DO YOU HAVE ANY ASSETS YOU MIGHT CONSIDER LIQUIDATING?
HUHHH... ALL THE BAKERY EQUIPMENT. ...MY CAR...
WHAT KIND OF CAR?
ER... 1992 NISSAN STANZA.
HAHA HAHAHA.
SO, THE BAKERY EQUIPMENT...

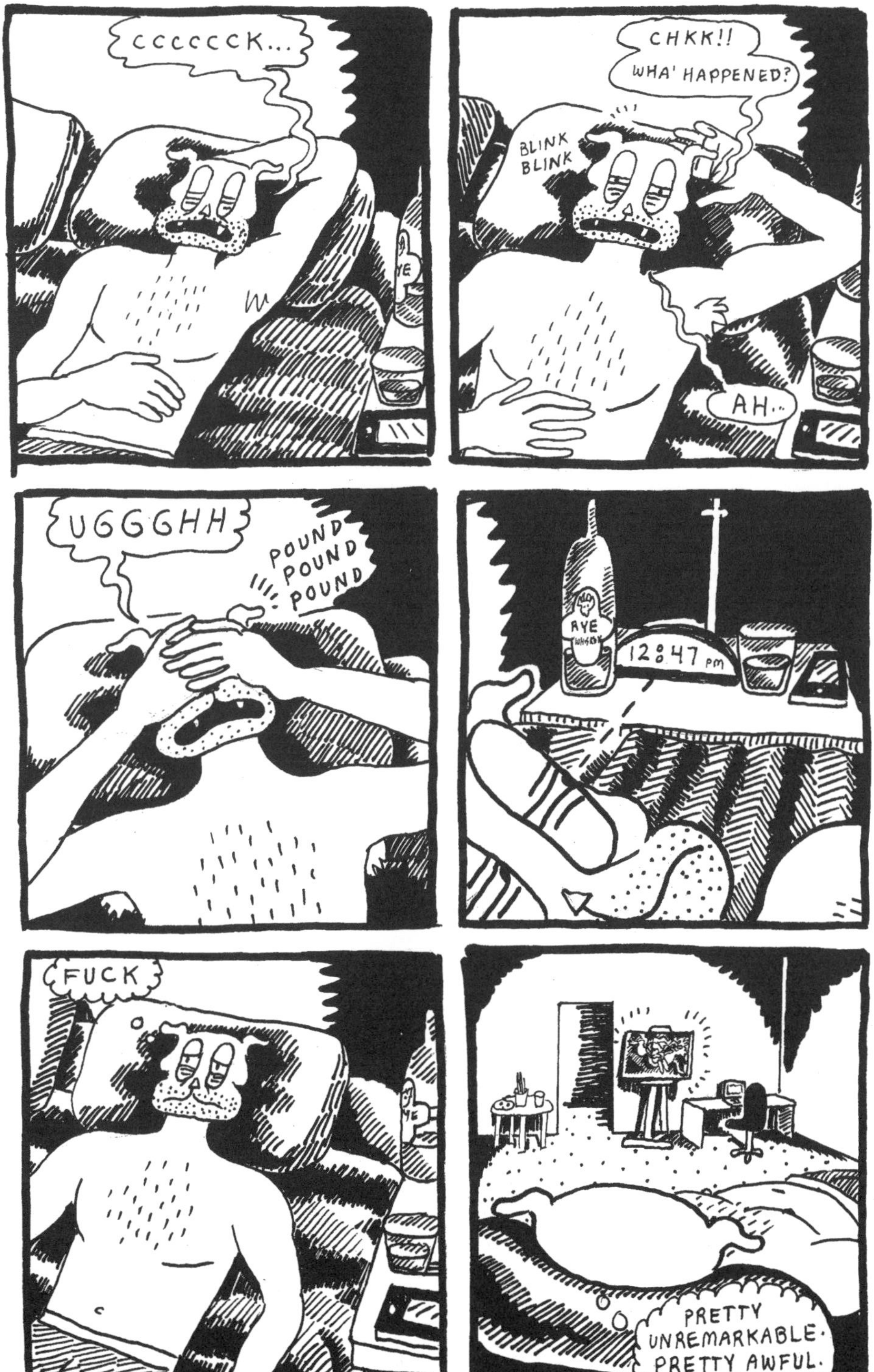
CCCCCCK...
CHKK!!
WHA' HAPPENED?
BLINK
BLINK
AH..
UGGGHH
POUND
POUND
POUND
RYE
12:47 pm
FUCK
PRETTY
UNREMARKABLE.
PRETTY AWFUL.

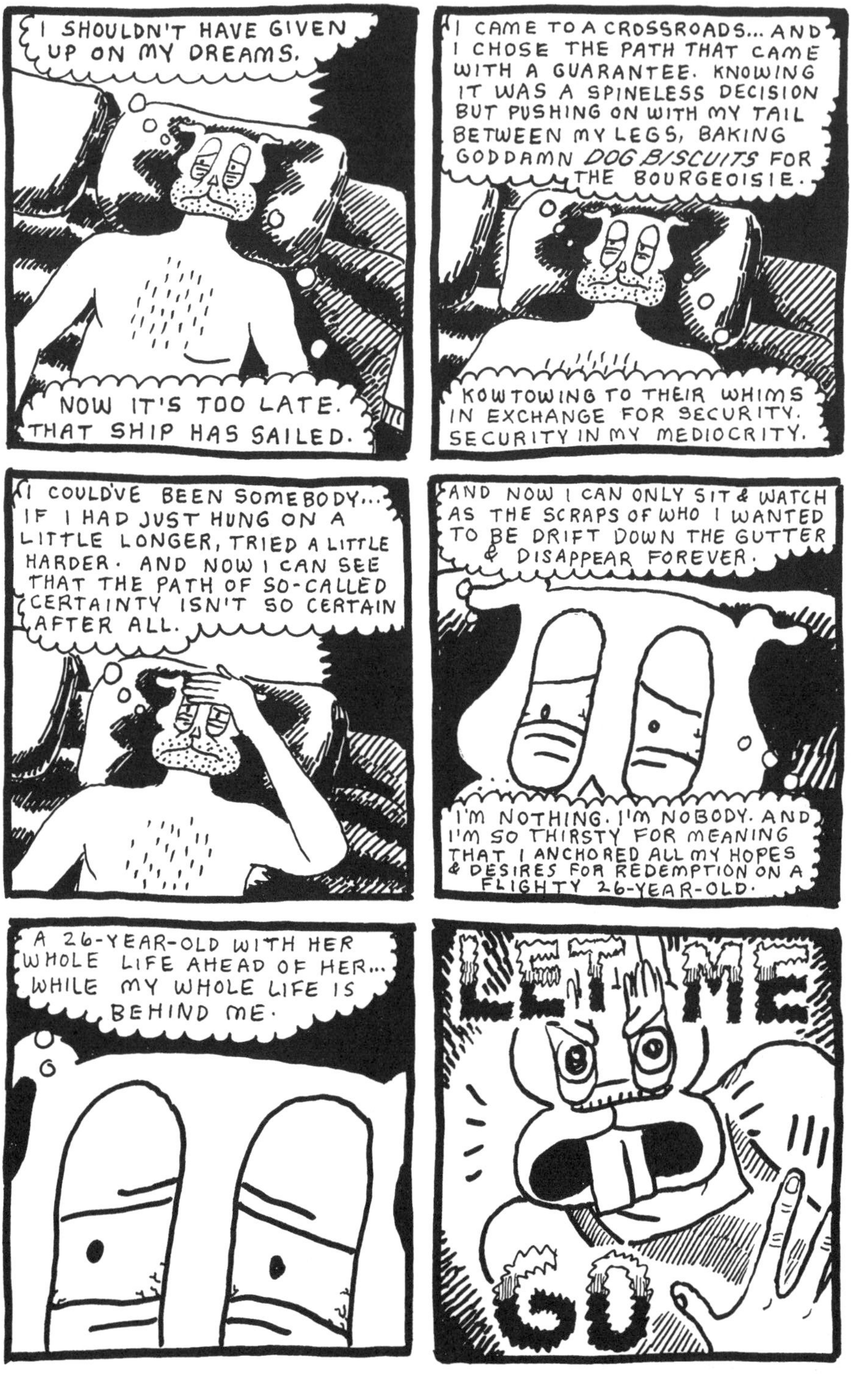
I SHOULDN'T HAVE GIVEN UP ON MY DREAMS.
NOW IT'S TOO LATE. THAT SHIP HAS SAILED.
I CAME TO A CROSSROADS... AND I CHOSE THE PATH THAT CAME WITH A GUARANTEE. KNOWING IT WAS A SPINELESS DECISION BUT PUSHING ON WITH MY TAIL BETWEEN MY LEGS, BAKING GODDAMN *DOG BISCUITS* FOR THE BOURGEOISIE.
KOWTOWING TO THEIR WHIMS IN EXCHANGE FOR SECURITY. SECURITY IN MY MEDIOCRITY.
I COULD'VE BEEN SOMEBODY... IF I HAD JUST HUNG ON A LITTLE LONGER, TRIED A LITTLE HARDER. AND NOW I CAN SEE THAT THE PATH OF SO-CALLED CERTAINTY ISN'T SO CERTAIN AFTER ALL.
AND NOW I CAN ONLY SIT & WATCH AS THE SCRAPS OF WHO I WANTED TO BE DRIFT DOWN THE GUTTER & DISAPPEAR FOREVER.
I'M NOTHING. I'M NOBODY. AND I'M SO THIRSTY FOR MEANING THAT I ANCHORED ALL MY HOPES & DESIRES FOR REDEMPTION ON A FLIGHTY 26-YEAR-OLD.
A 26-YEAR-OLD WITH HER WHOLE LIFE AHEAD OF HER... WHILE MY WHOLE LIFE IS BEHIND ME.
LET ME GO

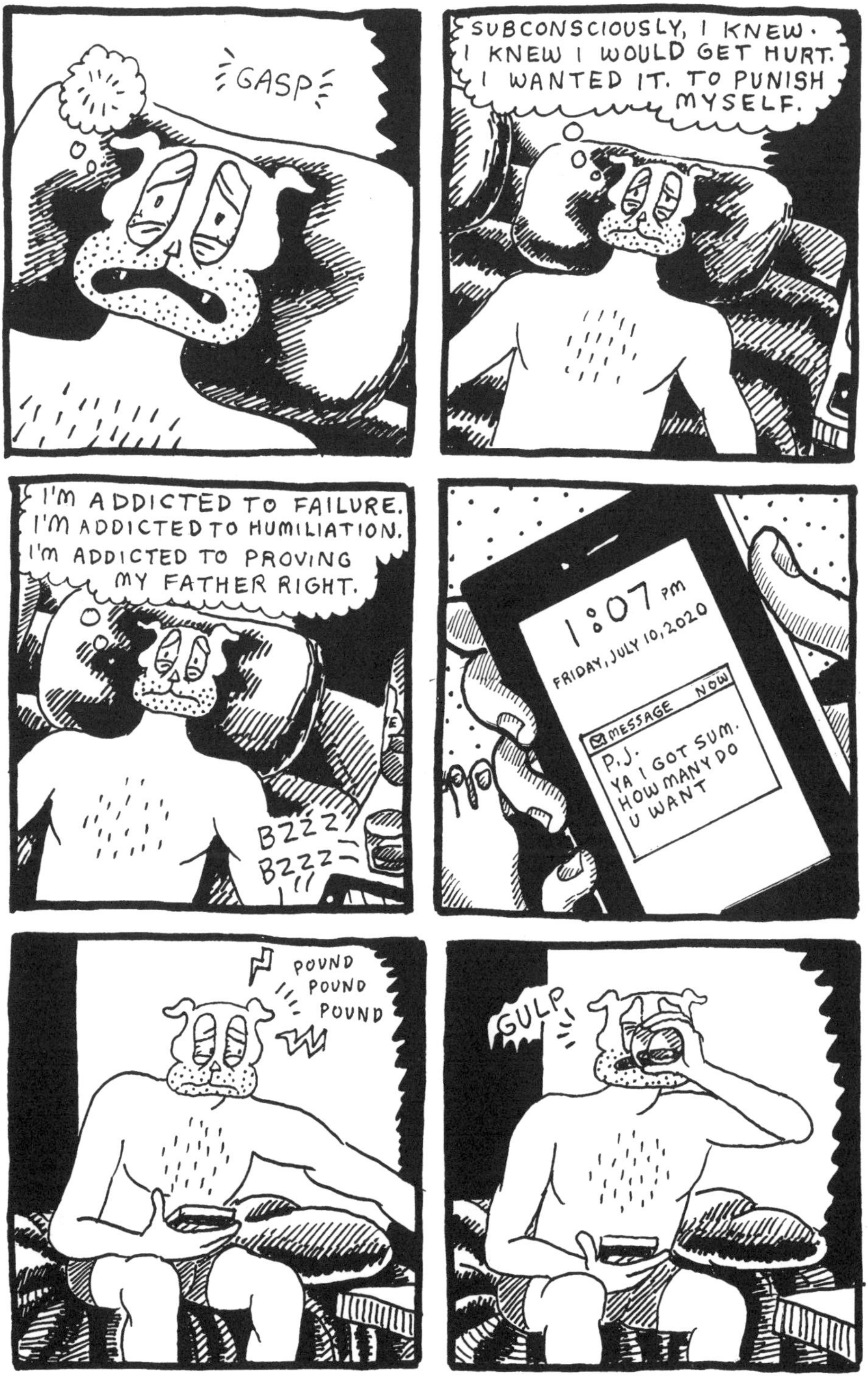
GASP
SUBCONSCIOUSLY, I KNEW. I KNEW I WOULD GET HURT. I WANTED IT. TO PUNISH MYSELF.
I'M ADDICTED TO FAILURE. I'M ADDICTED TO HUMILIATION. I'M ADDICTED TO PROVING MY FATHER RIGHT.
BZZZ BZZZ
1:07 pm
FRIDAY, JULY 10, 2020
MESSAGE NOW
P.J.
YA I GOT SUM. HOW MANY DO U WANT
POUND POUND POUND
GULP

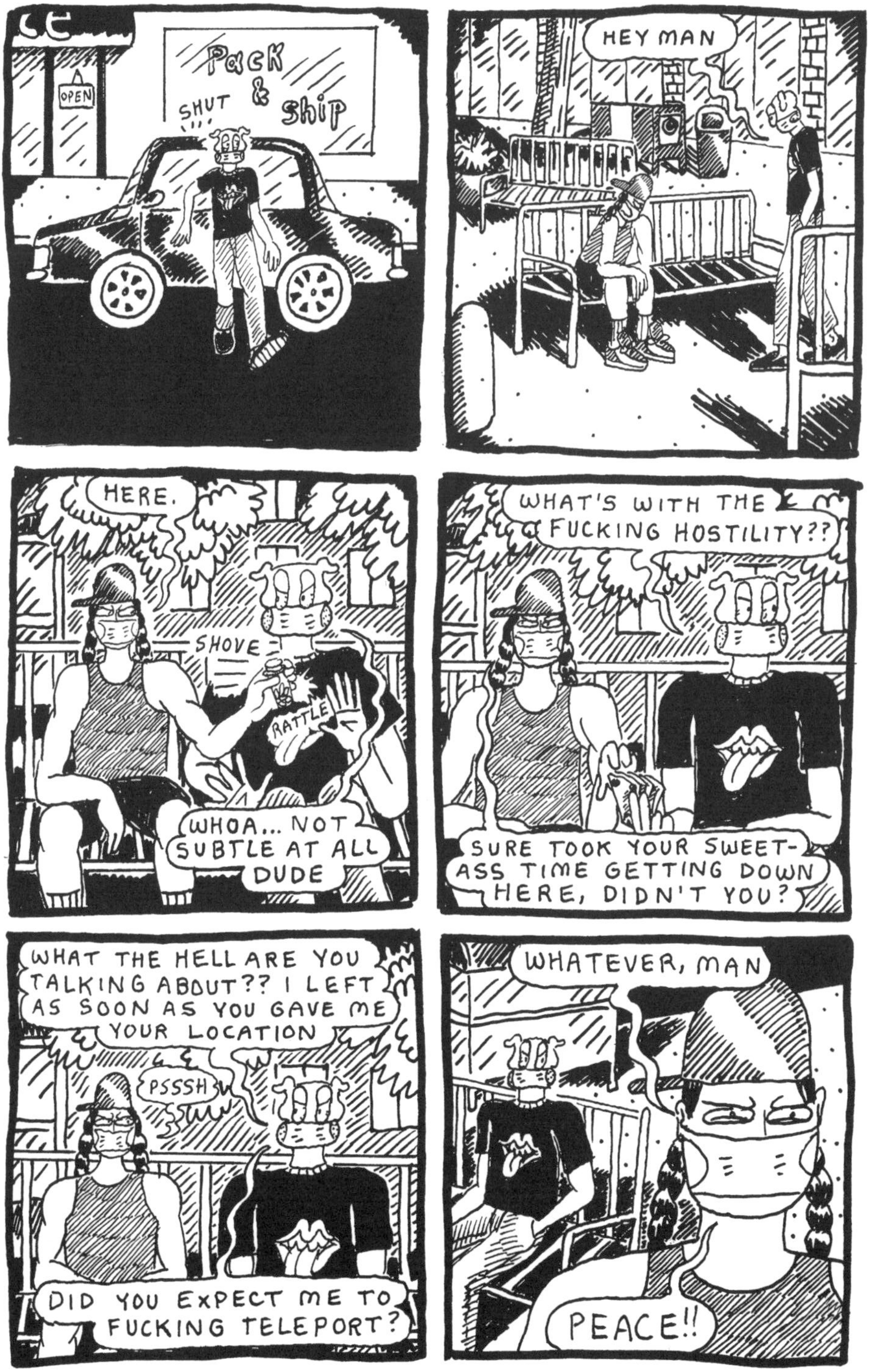
OPEN
Pack & Ship
SHUT
HEY MAN
HERE.
SHOVE
RATTLE
WHOA... NOT SUBTLE AT ALL DUDE
WHAT'S WITH THE FUCKING HOSTILITY??
SURE TOOK YOUR SWEET-ASS TIME GETTING DOWN HERE, DIDN'T YOU?
WHAT THE HELL ARE YOU TALKING ABOUT?? I LEFT AS SOON AS YOU GAVE ME YOUR LOCATION
PSSSH
DID YOU EXPECT ME TO FUCKING TELEPORT?
WHATEVER, MAN
PEACE!!

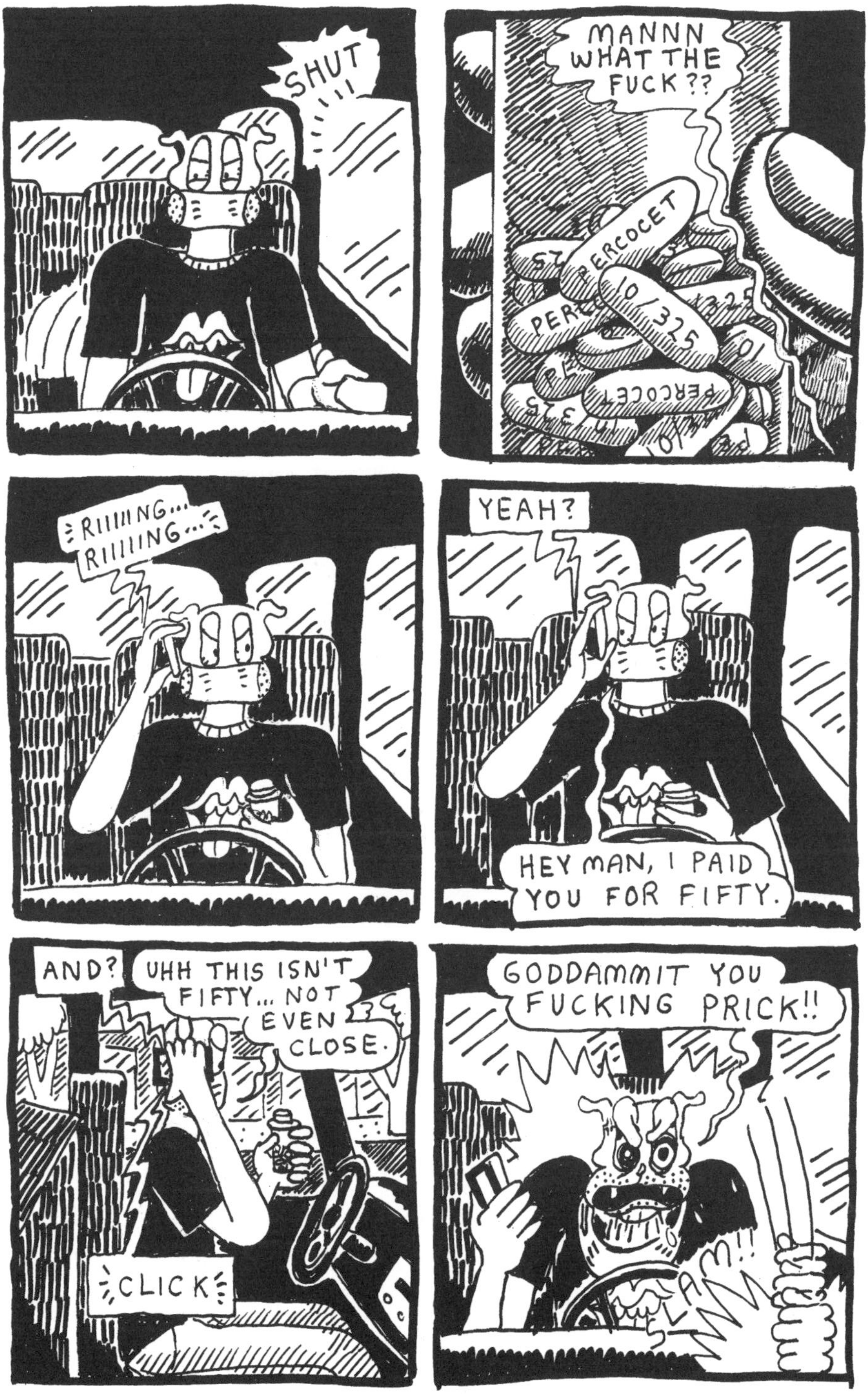
SHUT
MANNN WHAT THE FUCK??
PERCOCET
10/325
RIIIIING... RIIIIING...
YEAH?
HEY MAN, I PAID YOU FOR FIFTY.
AND?
UHH THIS ISN'T FIFTY... NOT EVEN CLOSE.
CLICK
GODDAMMIT YOU FUCKING PRICK!!
SLAM!!

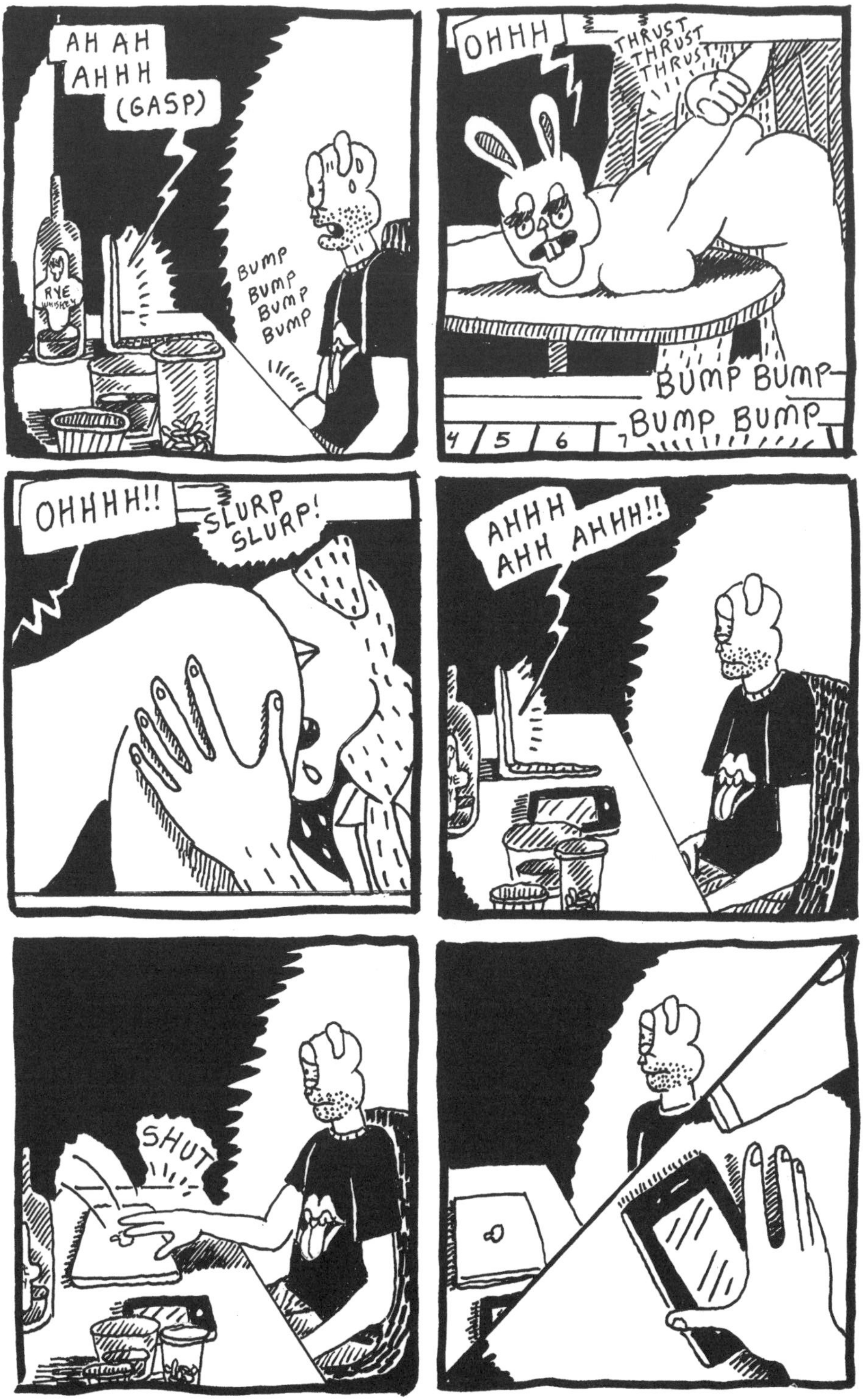
AH AH AHHH (GASP)
RYE WHISKEY
BUMP BUMP BUMP BUMP
OHHH
THRUST THRUST THRUST
BUMP BUMP BUMP BUMP
4 5 6 7
OHHHH!!
SLURP SLURP!
AHHH AHH AHHH!!
SHUT

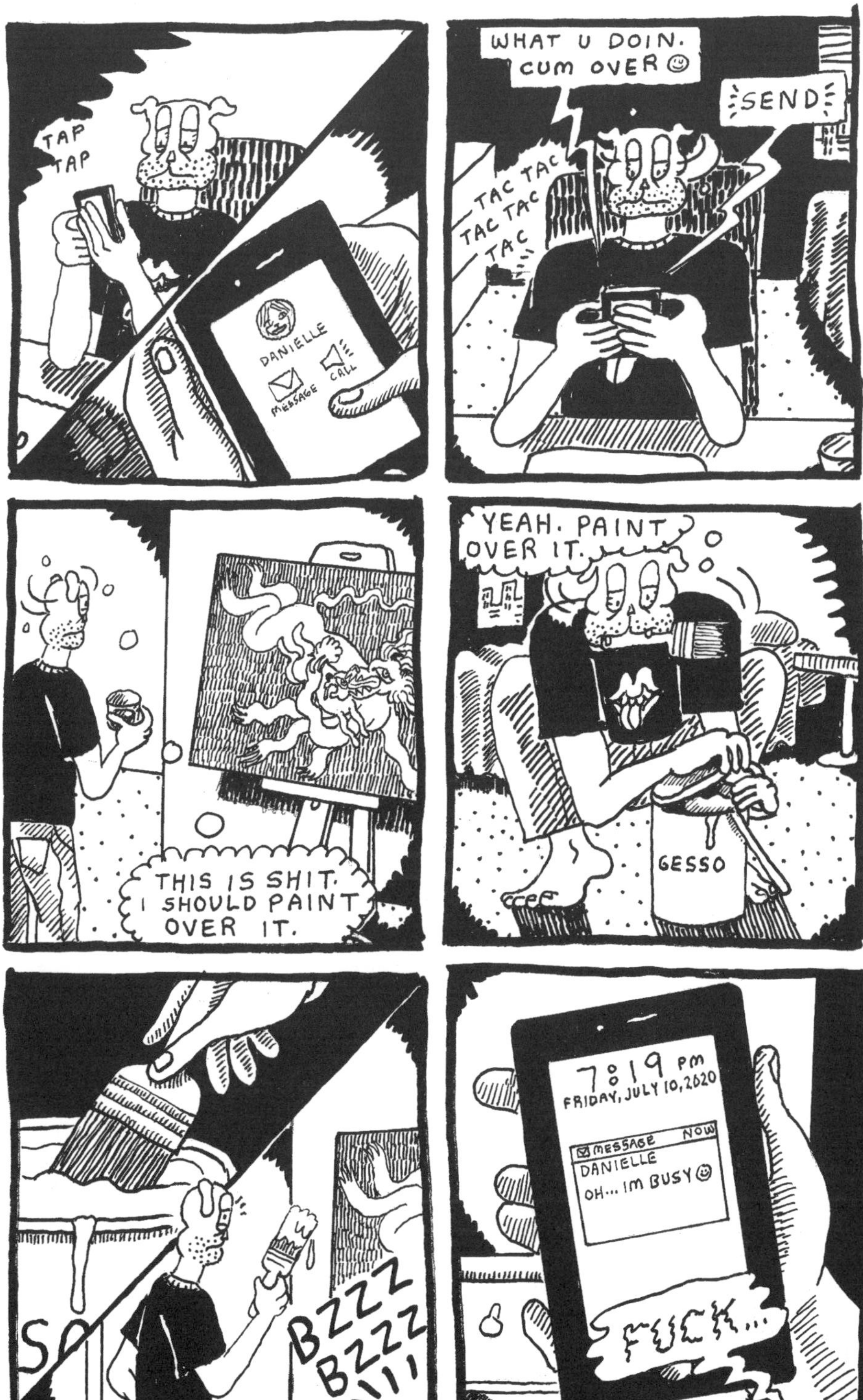
TAP
TAP
DANIELLE
MESSAGE
CALL
WHAT U DOIN.
CUM OVER ☺
SEND
TAC TAC
TAC TAC
TAC
THIS IS SHIT.
I SHOULD PAINT
OVER IT.
YEAH. PAINT
OVER IT.
GESSO
SO
BZZZ
BZZZ
7:19 pm
FRIDAY, JULY 10, 2020
MESSAGE NOW
DANIELLE
OH... IM BUSY ☺
FUCK...

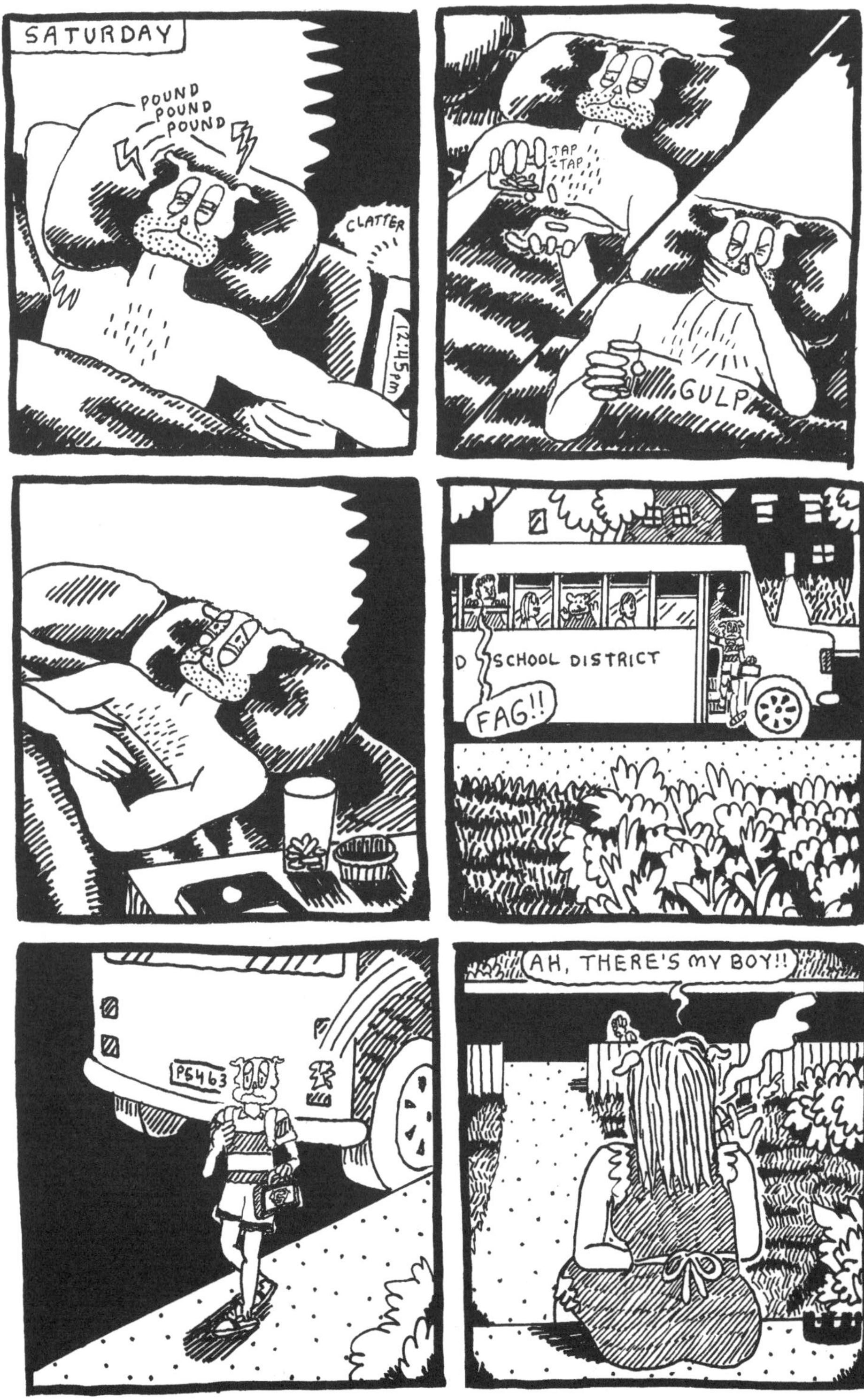
SATURDAY
POUND
POUND
POUND
CLATTER
12:45pm
TAP
TAP
GULP
SCHOOL DISTRICT
FAG!!
P5463
AH, THERE'S MY BOY!!

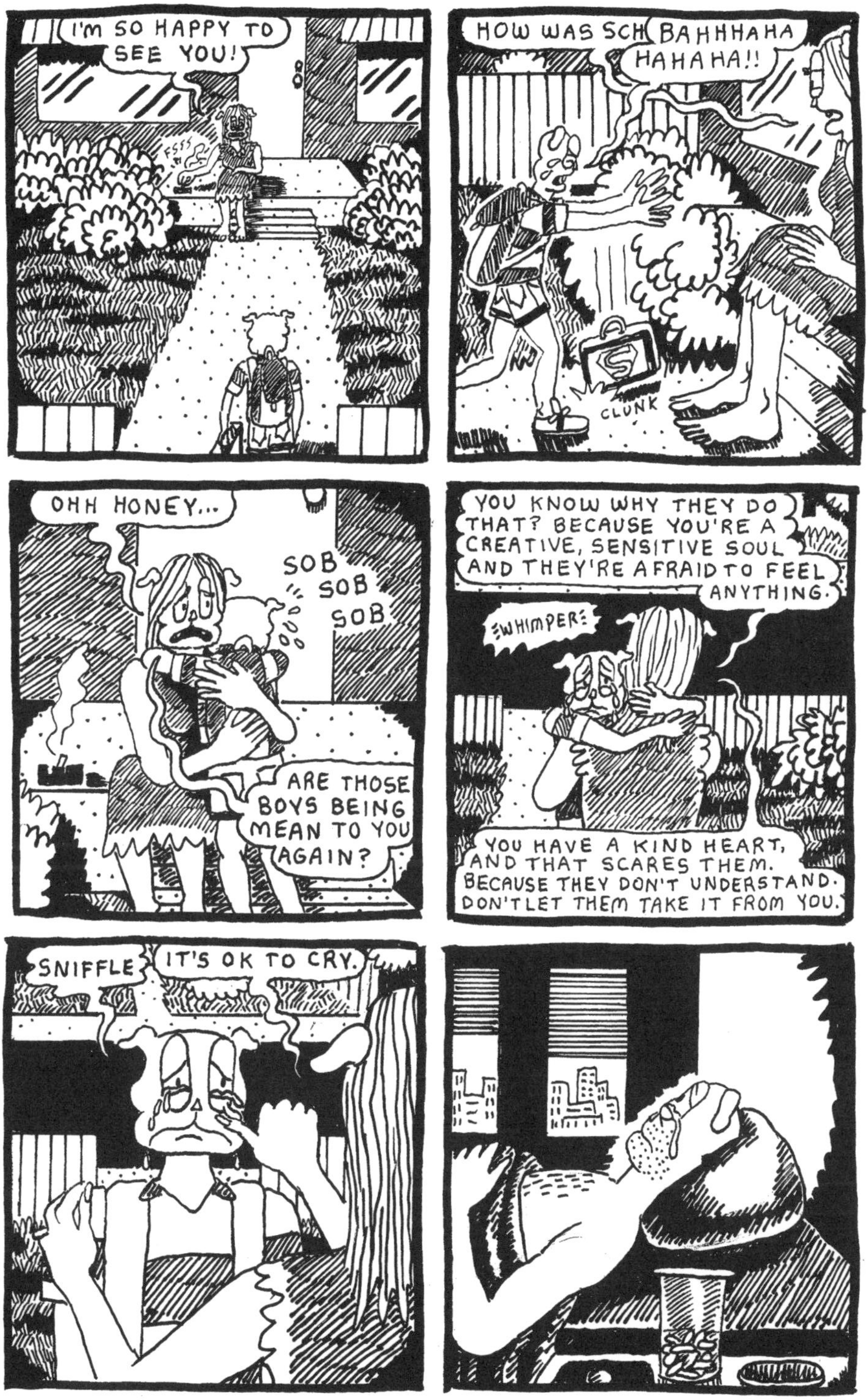
I'M SO HAPPY TO SEE YOU!
FSSS
HOW WAS SCH
BAHHHAHA HAHAHA!!
CLUNK
OHH HONEY...
SOB SOB SOB
ARE THOSE BOYS BEING MEAN TO YOU AGAIN?
YOU KNOW WHY THEY DO THAT? BECAUSE YOU'RE A CREATIVE, SENSITIVE SOUL AND THEY'RE AFRAID TO FEEL ANYTHING.
WHIMPER
YOU HAVE A KIND HEART, AND THAT SCARES THEM. BECAUSE THEY DON'T UNDERSTAND. DON'T LET THEM TAKE IT FROM YOU.
SNIFFLE
IT'S OK TO CRY.

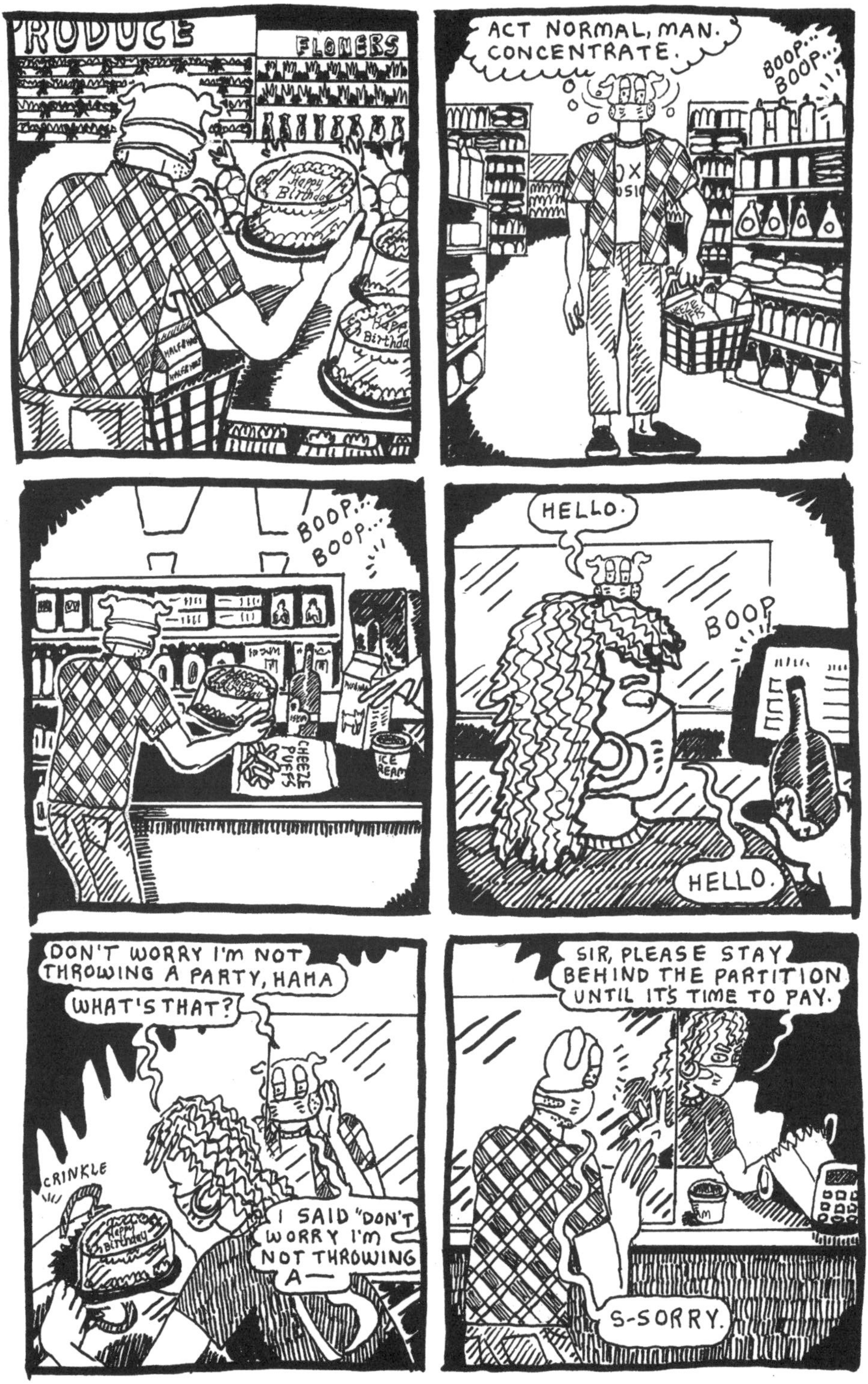
PRODUCE
FLOWERS
Happy Birthday
ACT NORMAL, MAN. CONCENTRATE.
BOOP... BOOP...
CHEEZE PUFFS
BOOP... BOOP...
CHEEZE PUFFS
ICE CREAM
HELLO.
BOOP
HELLO.
DON'T WORRY I'M NOT THROWING A PARTY, HAHA
WHAT'S THAT?
CRINKLE
Happy Birthday
I SAID "DON'T WORRY I'M NOT THROWING A—
SIR, PLEASE STAY BEHIND THE PARTITION UNTIL IT'S TIME TO PAY.
S-SORRY.

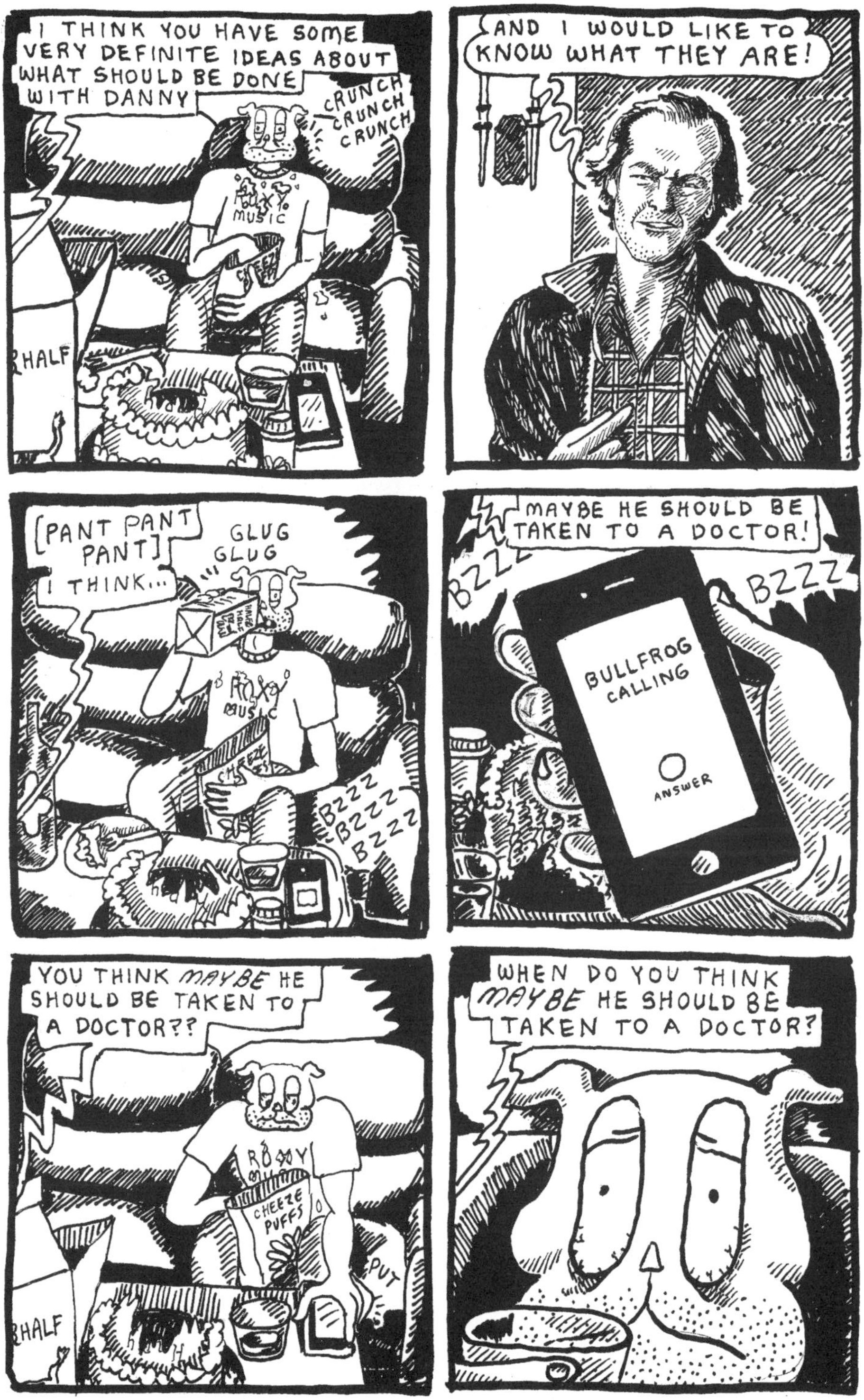
I THINK YOU HAVE SOME VERY DEFINITE IDEAS ABOUT WHAT SHOULD BE DONE WITH DANNY
CRUNCH CRUNCH CRUNCH
ROXY MUSIC
HALF
AND I WOULD LIKE TO KNOW WHAT THEY ARE!
[PANT PANT PANT] I THINK...
GLUG GLUG
ROXY MUSIC
BZZZ BZZZ BZZZ
MAYBE HE SHOULD BE TAKEN TO A DOCTOR!
BZZZ
BZZZ
BULLFROG CALLING
ANSWER
YOU THINK *MAYBE* HE SHOULD BE TAKEN TO A DOCTOR??
CHEEZE PUFFS
PUT
HALF
WHEN DO YOU THINK *MAYBE* HE SHOULD BE TAKEN TO A DOCTOR?

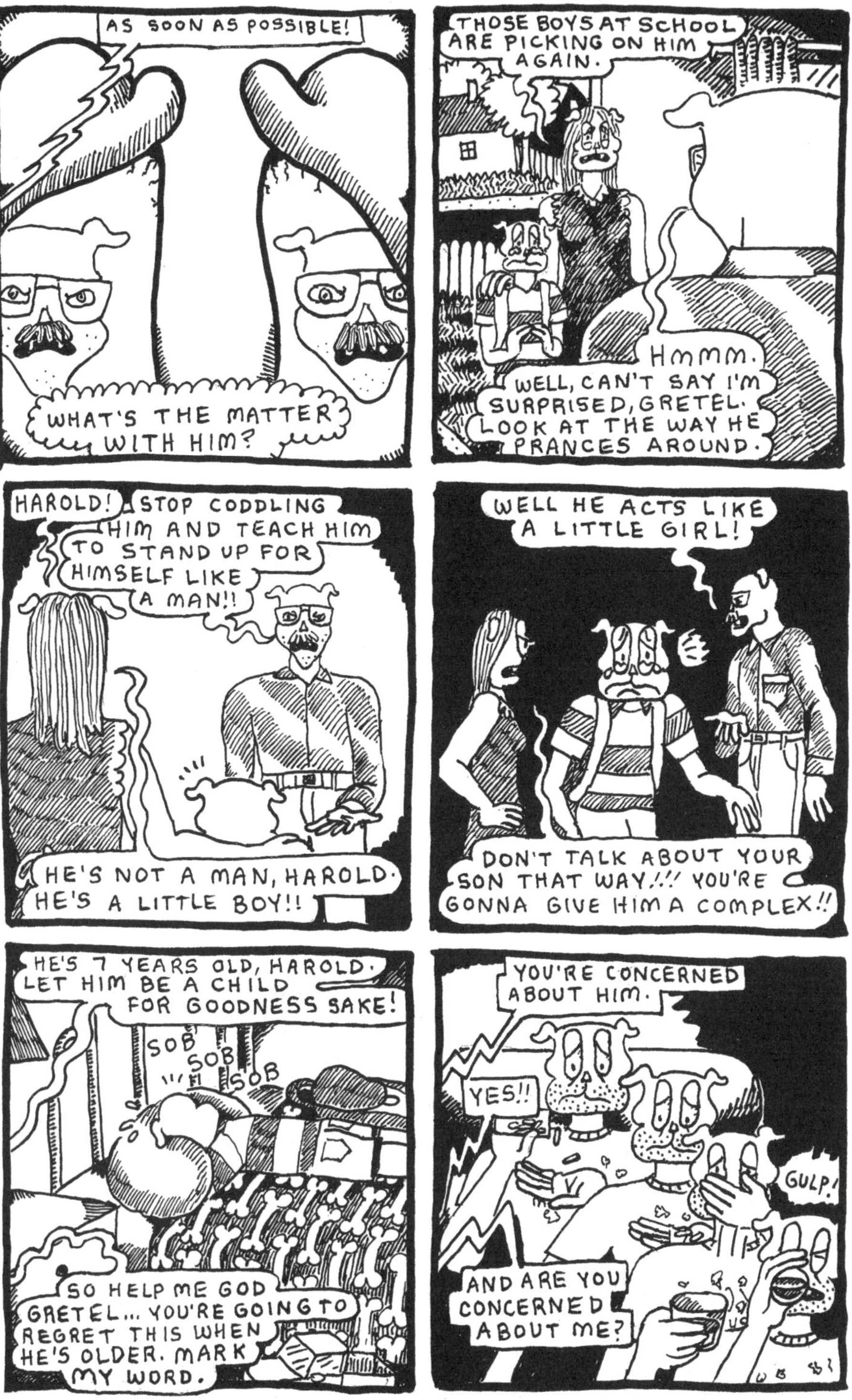
AS SOON AS POSSIBLE!
WHAT'S THE MATTER WITH HIM?
THOSE BOYS AT SCHOOL ARE PICKING ON HIM AGAIN.
HMMM.
WELL, CAN'T SAY I'M SURPRISED, GRETEL. LOOK AT THE WAY HE PRANCES AROUND.
HAROLD!
STOP CODDLING HIM AND TEACH HIM TO STAND UP FOR HIMSELF LIKE A MAN!!
HE'S NOT A MAN, HAROLD. HE'S A LITTLE BOY!!
WELL HE ACTS LIKE A LITTLE GIRL!
DON'T TALK ABOUT YOUR SON THAT WAY!!! YOU'RE GONNA GIVE HIM A COMPLEX!!
HE'S 7 YEARS OLD, HAROLD. LET HIM BE A CHILD FOR GOODNESS SAKE!
SOB
SOB
SOB
SO HELP ME GOD GRETEL... YOU'RE GOING TO REGRET THIS WHEN HE'S OLDER. MARK MY WORD.
YOU'RE CONCERNED ABOUT HIM.
YES!!
GULP!
AND ARE YOU CONCERNED ABOUT ME?

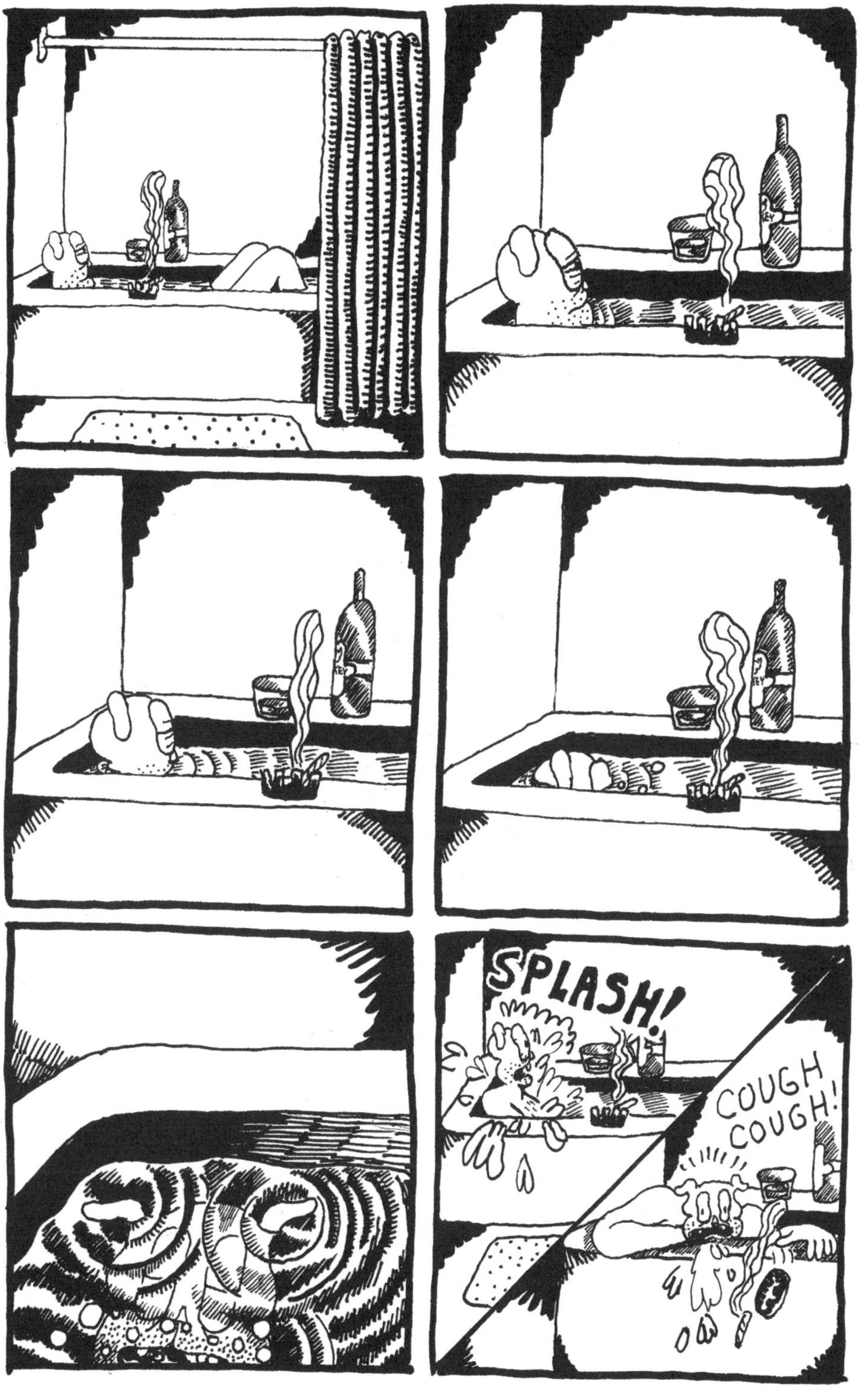
SPLASH!
COUGH COUGH!

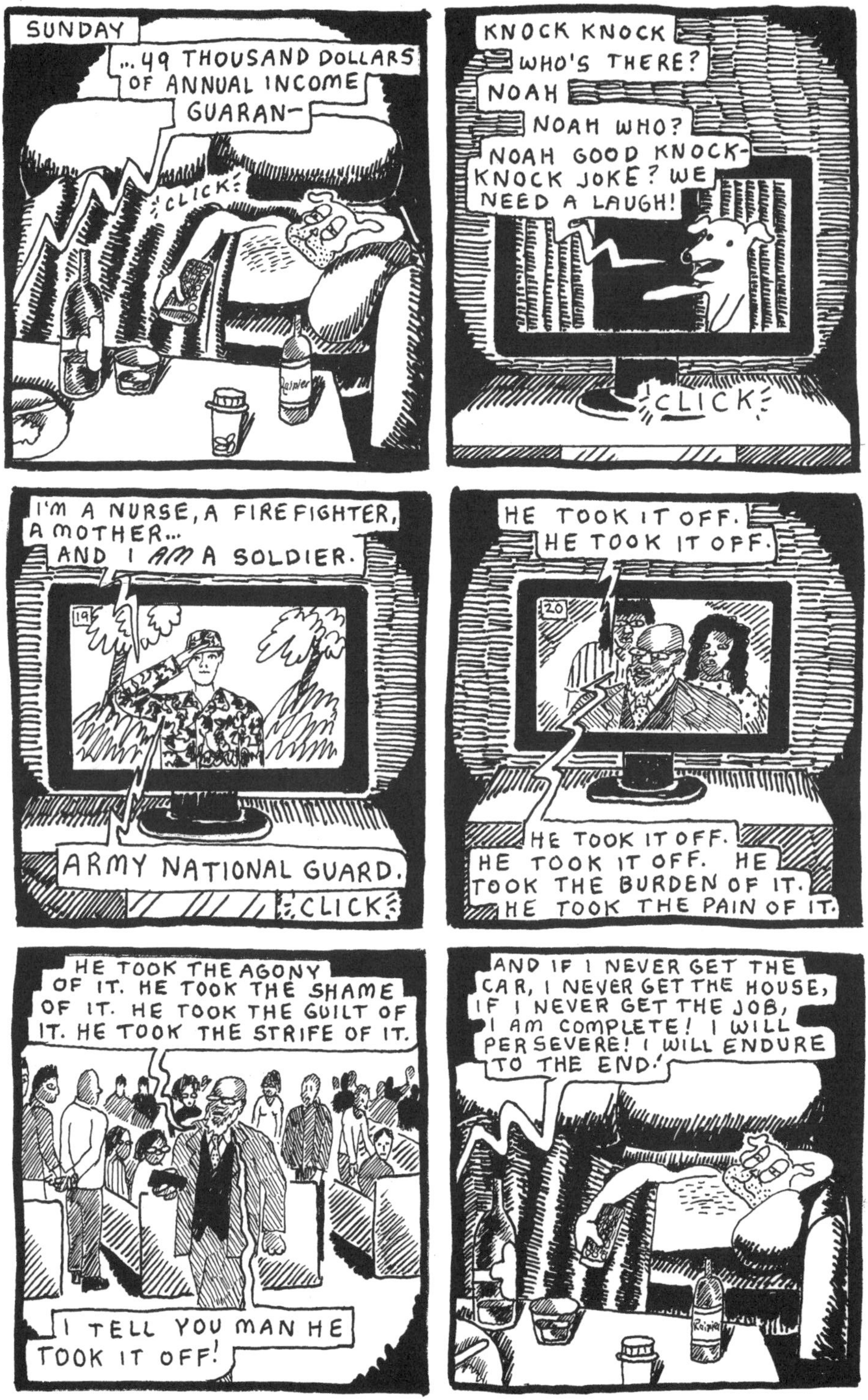
SUNDAY
...49 THOUSAND DOLLARS OF ANNUAL INCOME GUARAN-
CLICK
KNOCK KNOCK
WHO'S THERE?
NOAH
NOAH WHO?
NOAH GOOD KNOCK-KNOCK JOKE? WE NEED A LAUGH!
CLICK
I'M A NURSE, A FIREFIGHTER, A MOTHER... AND I AM A SOLDIER.
19
ARMY NATIONAL GUARD.
CLICK
HE TOOK IT OFF. HE TOOK IT OFF.
20
HE TOOK IT OFF. HE TOOK IT OFF. HE TOOK THE BURDEN OF IT. HE TOOK THE PAIN OF IT.
HE TOOK THE AGONY OF IT. HE TOOK THE SHAME OF IT. HE TOOK THE GUILT OF IT. HE TOOK THE STRIFE OF IT.
I TELL YOU MAN HE TOOK IT OFF!
AND IF I NEVER GET THE CAR, I NEVER GET THE HOUSE, IF I NEVER GET THE JOB, I AM COMPLETE! I WILL PERSEVERE! I WILL ENDURE TO THE END!

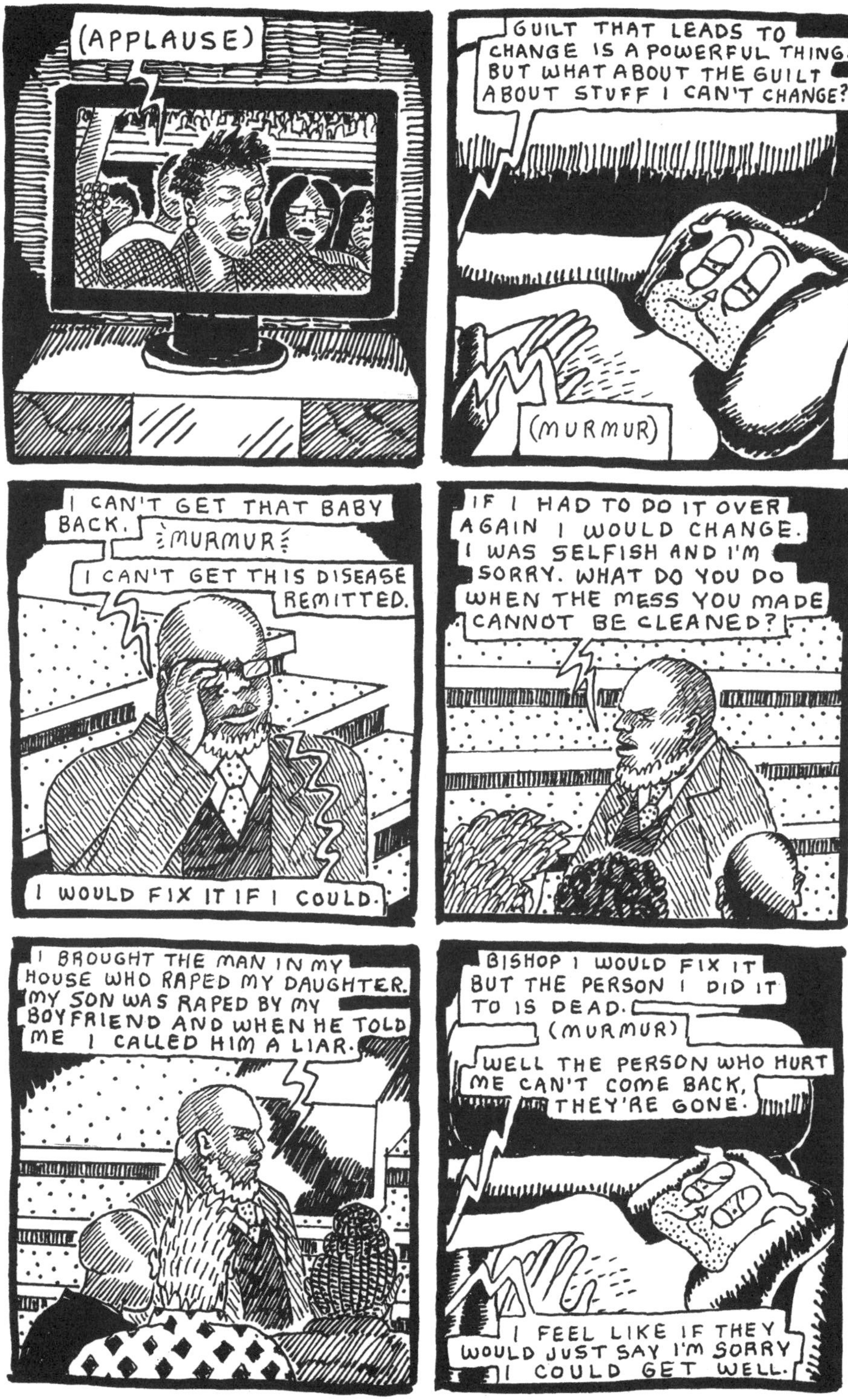
(APPLAUSE)
GUILT THAT LEADS TO CHANGE IS A POWERFUL THING. BUT WHAT ABOUT THE GUILT ABOUT STUFF I CAN'T CHANGE?
(MURMUR)
I CAN'T GET THAT BABY BACK.
MURMUR
I CAN'T GET THIS DISEASE REMITTED.
I WOULD FIX IT IF I COULD.
IF I HAD TO DO IT OVER AGAIN I WOULD CHANGE. I WAS SELFISH AND I'M SORRY. WHAT DO YOU DO WHEN THE MESS YOU MADE CANNOT BE CLEANED?
I BROUGHT THE MAN IN MY HOUSE WHO RAPED MY DAUGHTER. MY SON WAS RAPED BY MY BOYFRIEND AND WHEN HE TOLD ME I CALLED HIM A LIAR.
BISHOP I WOULD FIX IT BUT THE PERSON I DID IT TO IS DEAD.
(MURMUR)
WELL THE PERSON WHO HURT ME CAN'T COME BACK, THEY'RE GONE.
I FEEL LIKE IF THEY WOULD JUST SAY I'M SORRY I COULD GET WELL.

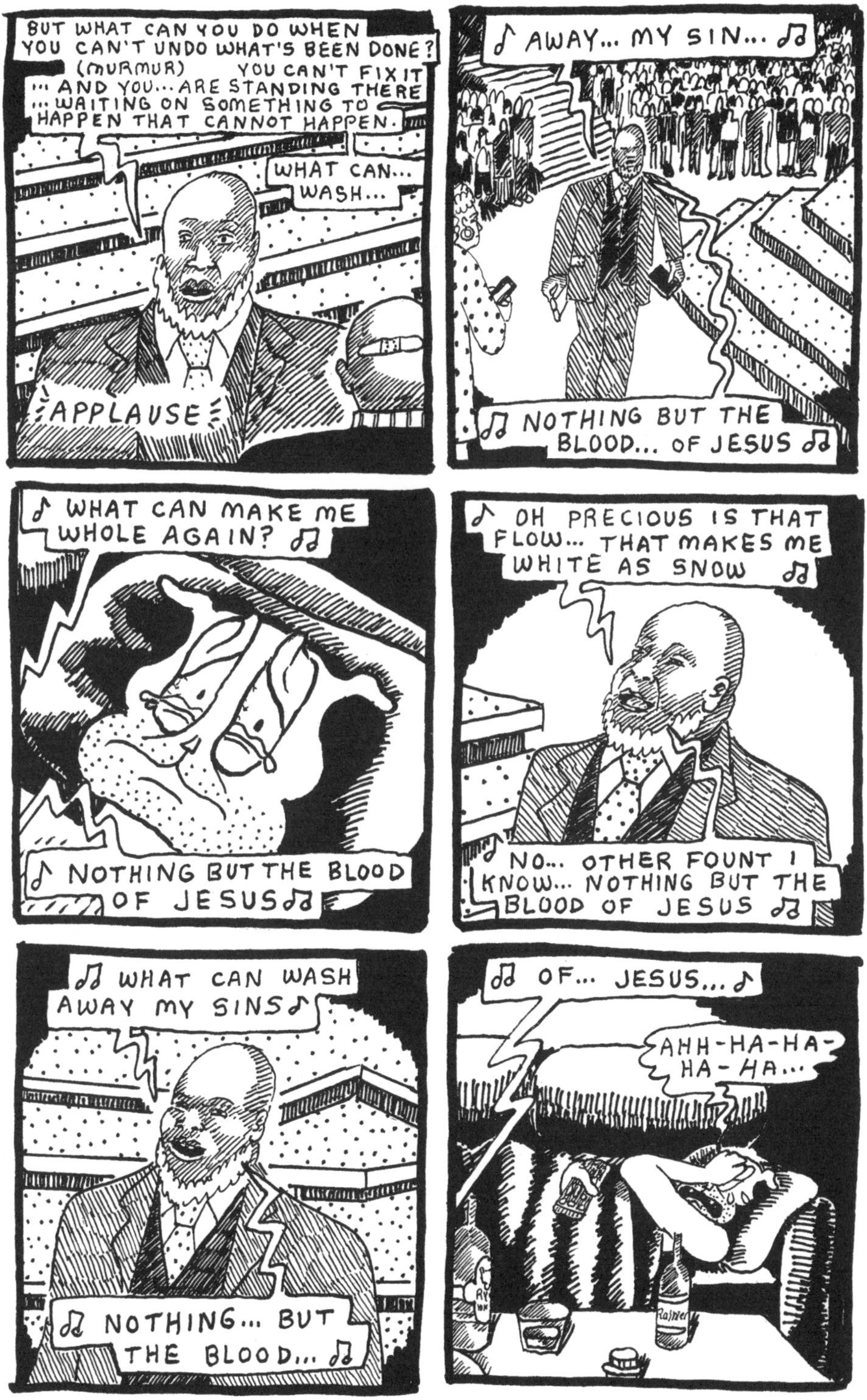
BUT WHAT CAN YOU DO WHEN YOU CAN'T UNDO WHAT'S BEEN DONE? (MURMUR) YOU CAN'T FIX IT ... AND YOU... ARE STANDING THERE ... WAITING ON SOMETHING TO HAPPEN THAT CANNOT HAPPEN.
WHAT CAN... WASH...
APPLAUSE
♪ AWAY... MY SIN... ♫
♫ NOTHING BUT THE BLOOD... OF JESUS ♫
♪ WHAT CAN MAKE ME WHOLE AGAIN? ♫
♪ NOTHING BUT THE BLOOD OF JESUS ♫
♪ OH PRECIOUS IS THAT FLOW... THAT MAKES ME WHITE AS SNOW ♫
♪ NO... OTHER FOUNT I KNOW... NOTHING BUT THE BLOOD OF JESUS ♫
♫ WHAT CAN WASH AWAY MY SINS ♪
♫ NOTHING... BUT THE BLOOD... ♫
♫ OF... JESUS... ♪
AHH-HA-HA-HA-HA...

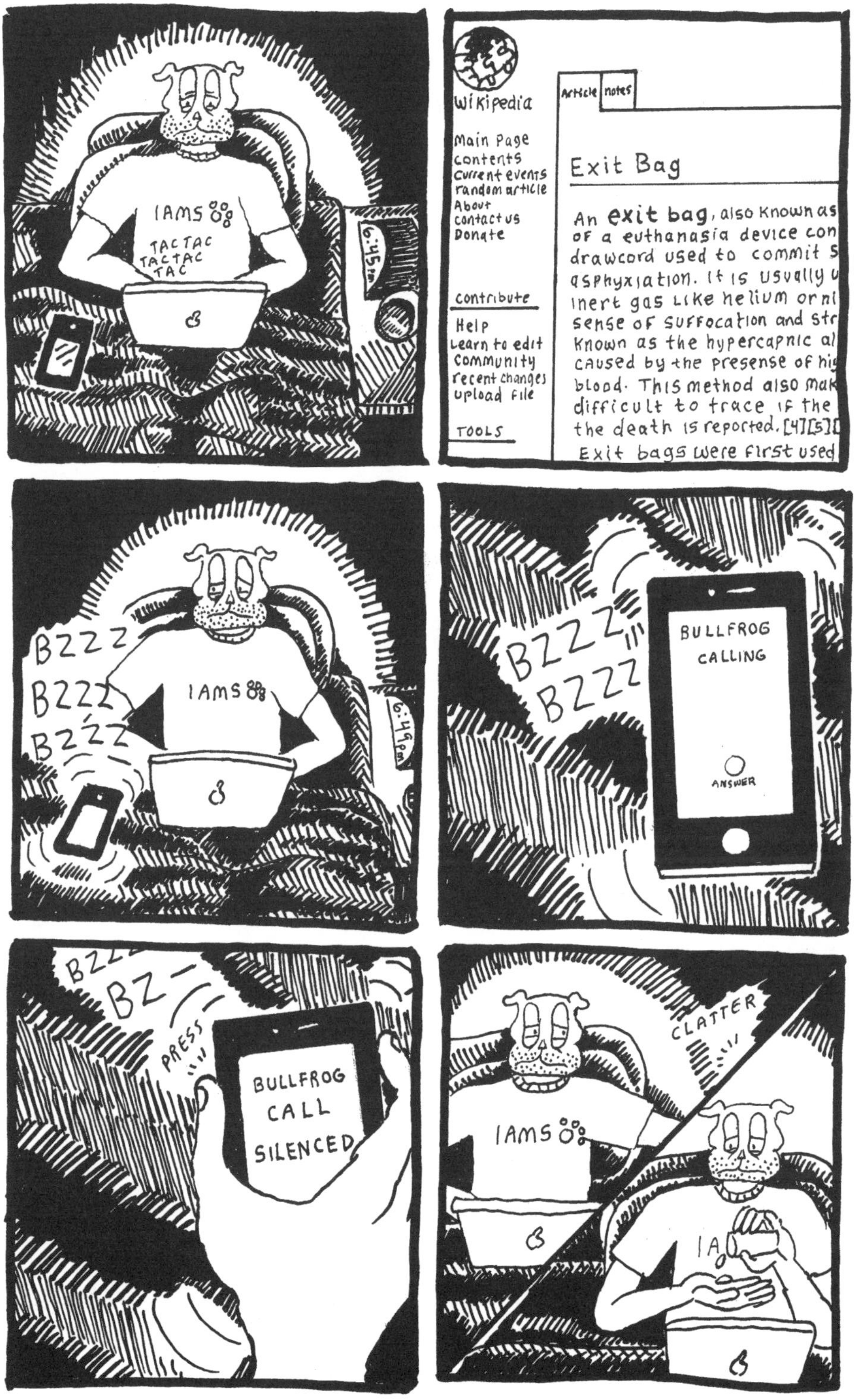
IAMS
TAC TAC TAC TAC TAC
6:45pm
Wikipedia
Main Page
contents
current events
random article
About
contact us
Donate
contribute
Help
Learn to edit
community
recent changes
upload file
TOOLS
Article
notes
Exit Bag
An exit bag, also known as
of a euthanasia device
drawcord used to commit
asphyxiation. It is usually
inert gas like helium or
sense of suffocation and
known as the hypercapnic
caused by the presense of
blood. This method also
difficult to trace if the
the death is reported. [4][5]
Exit bags were first used
BZZZ
BZZZ
BZZZ
IAMS
6:49pm
BZZZ
BZZZ
BULLFROG
CALLING
ANSWER
BZ
PRESS
BULLFROG
CALL
SILENCED
CLATTER
IAMS
IA

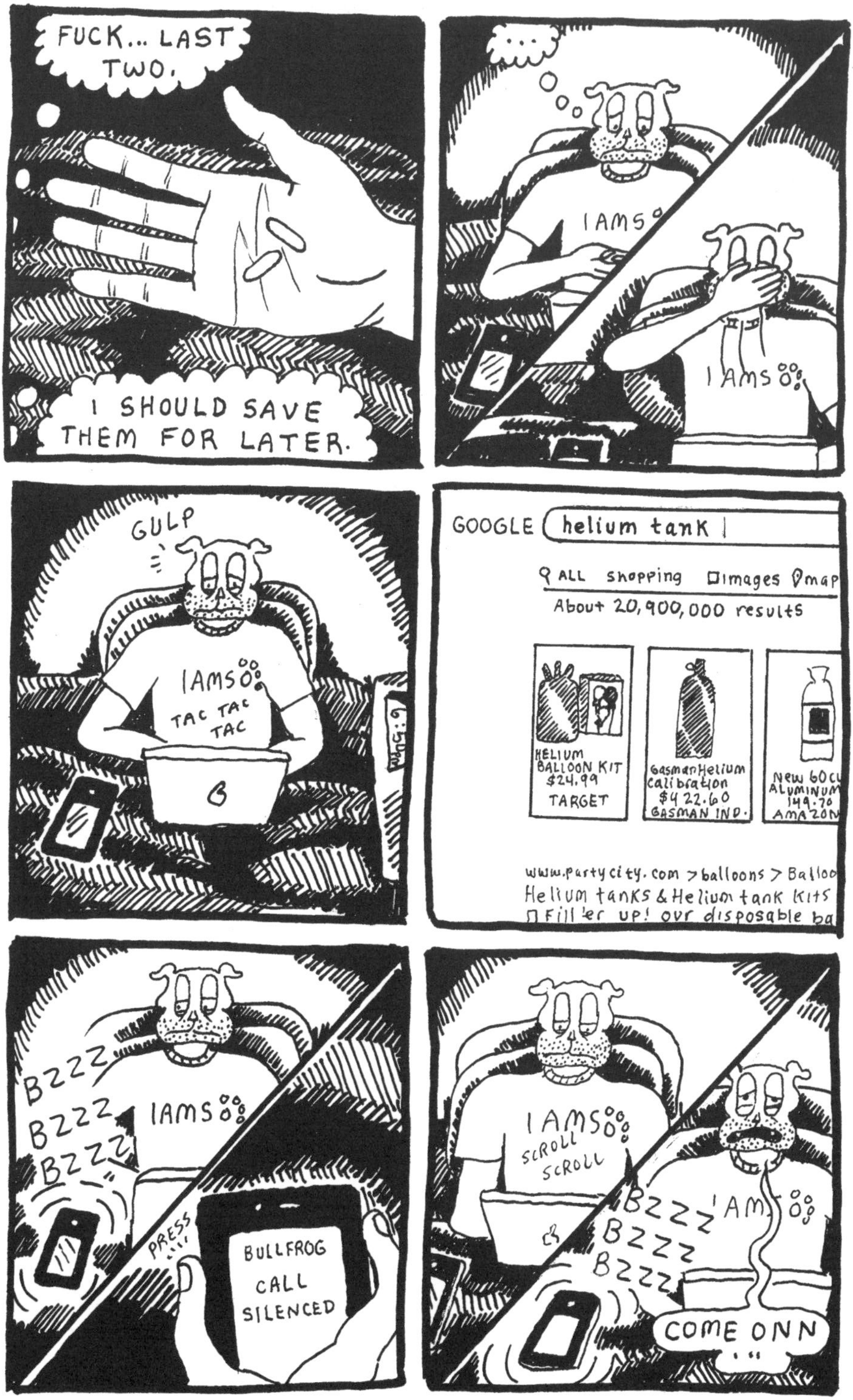
FUCK... LAST TWO.
I SHOULD SAVE THEM FOR LATER.
...
IAMS
IAMS
GULP
IAMS
TAC TAC TAC
GOOGLE
helium tank |
ALL
shopping
images
About 20,900,000 results
HELIUM BALLOON KIT $24.99
TARGET
GasmanHelium Calibration $422.60
GASMAN IND.
www.partycity.com > balloons > Balloo
Helium tanks & Helium tank kits
Fill 'er up! our disposable ba
BZZZ
BZZZ
BZZZ
IAMS
PRESS
BULLFROG CALL SILENCED
IAMS
SCROLL SCROLL
BZZZ
BZZZ
BZZZ
COME ONN
...

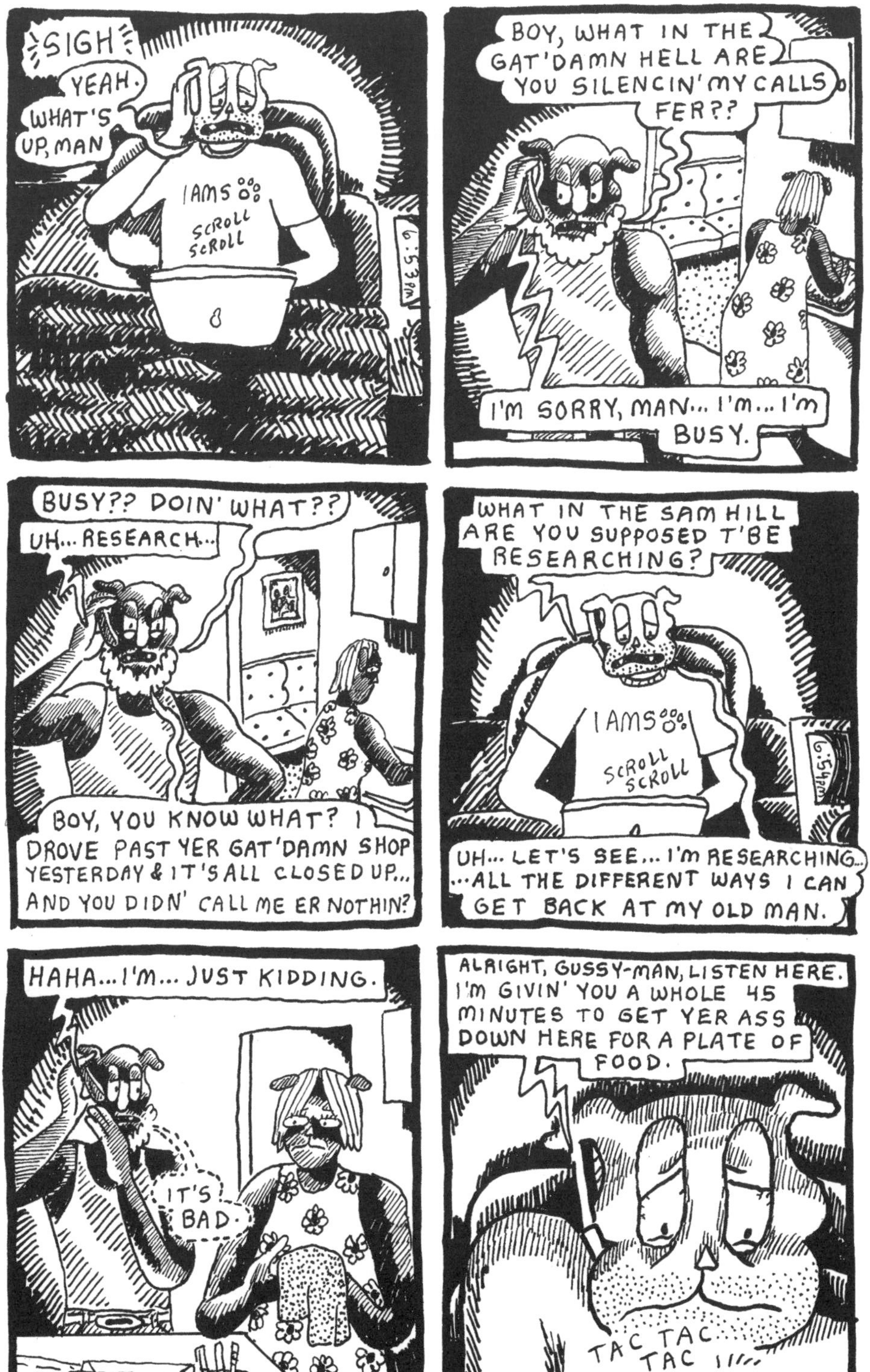
SIGH
YEAH.
WHAT'S UP, MAN
IAMS
SCROLL SCROLL
6:53PM
BOY, WHAT IN THE GAT'DAMN HELL ARE YOU SILENCIN' MY CALLS FER??
I'M SORRY, MAN... I'M... I'M BUSY.
BUSY?? DOIN' WHAT??
UH... RESEARCH...
BOY, YOU KNOW WHAT? I DROVE PAST YER GAT'DAMN SHOP YESTERDAY & IT'S ALL CLOSED UP... AND YOU DIDN' CALL ME ER NOTHIN?
WHAT IN THE SAM HILL ARE YOU SUPPOSED T'BE RESEARCHING?
IAMS
SCROLL SCROLL
6:54PM
UH... LET'S SEE... I'M RESEARCHING... ...ALL THE DIFFERENT WAYS I CAN GET BACK AT MY OLD MAN.
HAHA... I'M... JUST KIDDING.
IT'S BAD.
ALRIGHT, GUSSY-MAN, LISTEN HERE. I'M GIVIN' YOU A WHOLE 45 MINUTES TO GET YER ASS DOWN HERE FOR A PLATE OF FOOD.
TAC TAC TAC

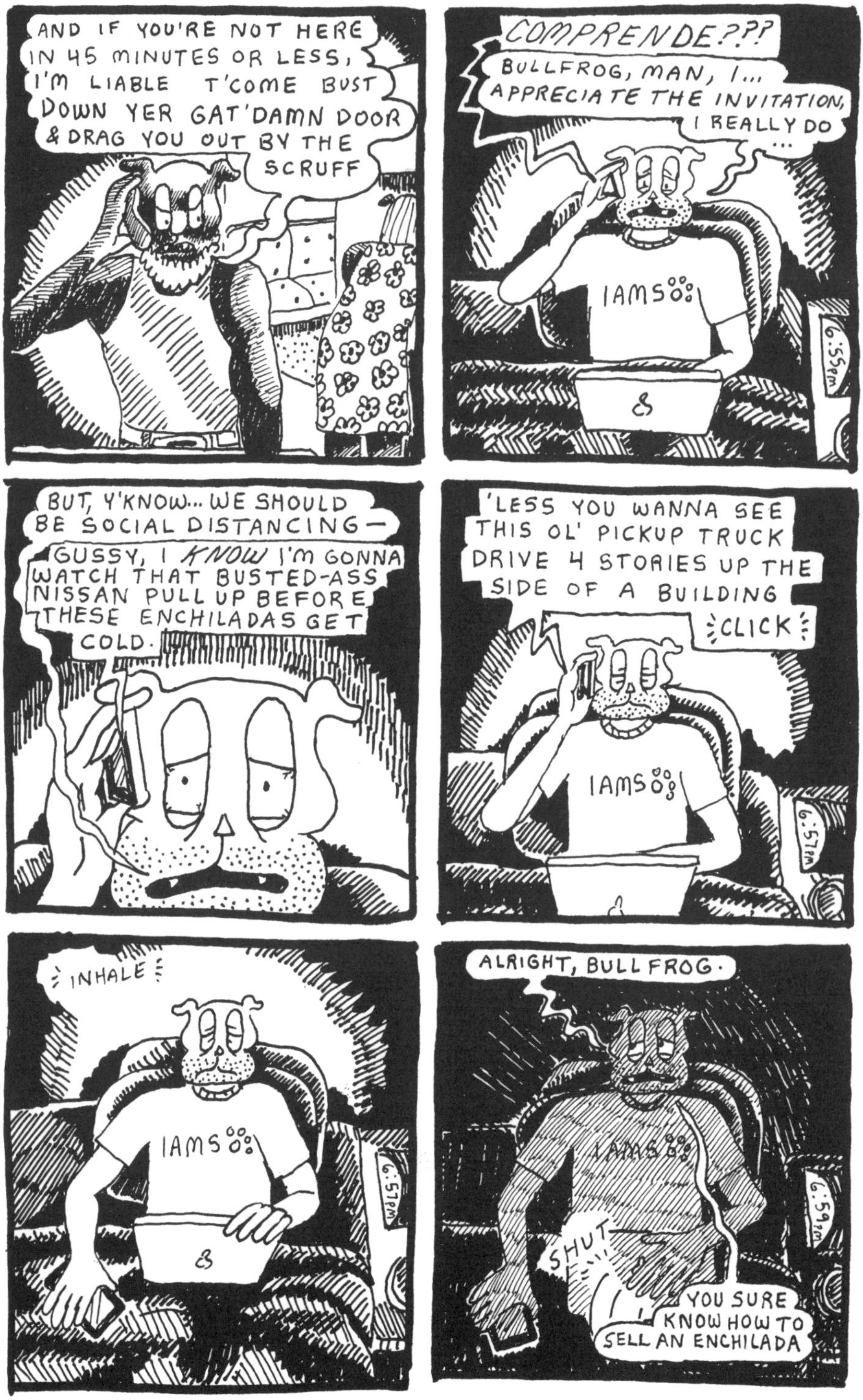
AND IF YOU'RE NOT HERE IN 45 MINUTES OR LESS, I'M LIABLE T'COME BUST DOWN YER GAT'DAMN DOOR & DRAG YOU OUT BY THE SCRUFF
COMPRENDE???
BULLFROG, MAN, I... APPRECIATE THE INVITATION, I REALLY DO ...
6:55PM
IAMS
BUT, Y'KNOW... WE SHOULD BE SOCIAL DISTANCING—
GUSSY, I KNOW I'M GONNA WATCH THAT BUSTED-ASS NISSAN PULL UP BEFORE THESE ENCHILADAS GET COLD.
'LESS YOU WANNA SEE THIS OL' PICKUP TRUCK DRIVE 4 STORIES UP THE SIDE OF A BUILDING
CLICK
IAMS
6:57PM
INHALE
IAMS
6:57PM
ALRIGHT, BULLFROG.
6:59PM
SHUT
YOU SURE KNOW HOW TO SELL AN ENCHILADA

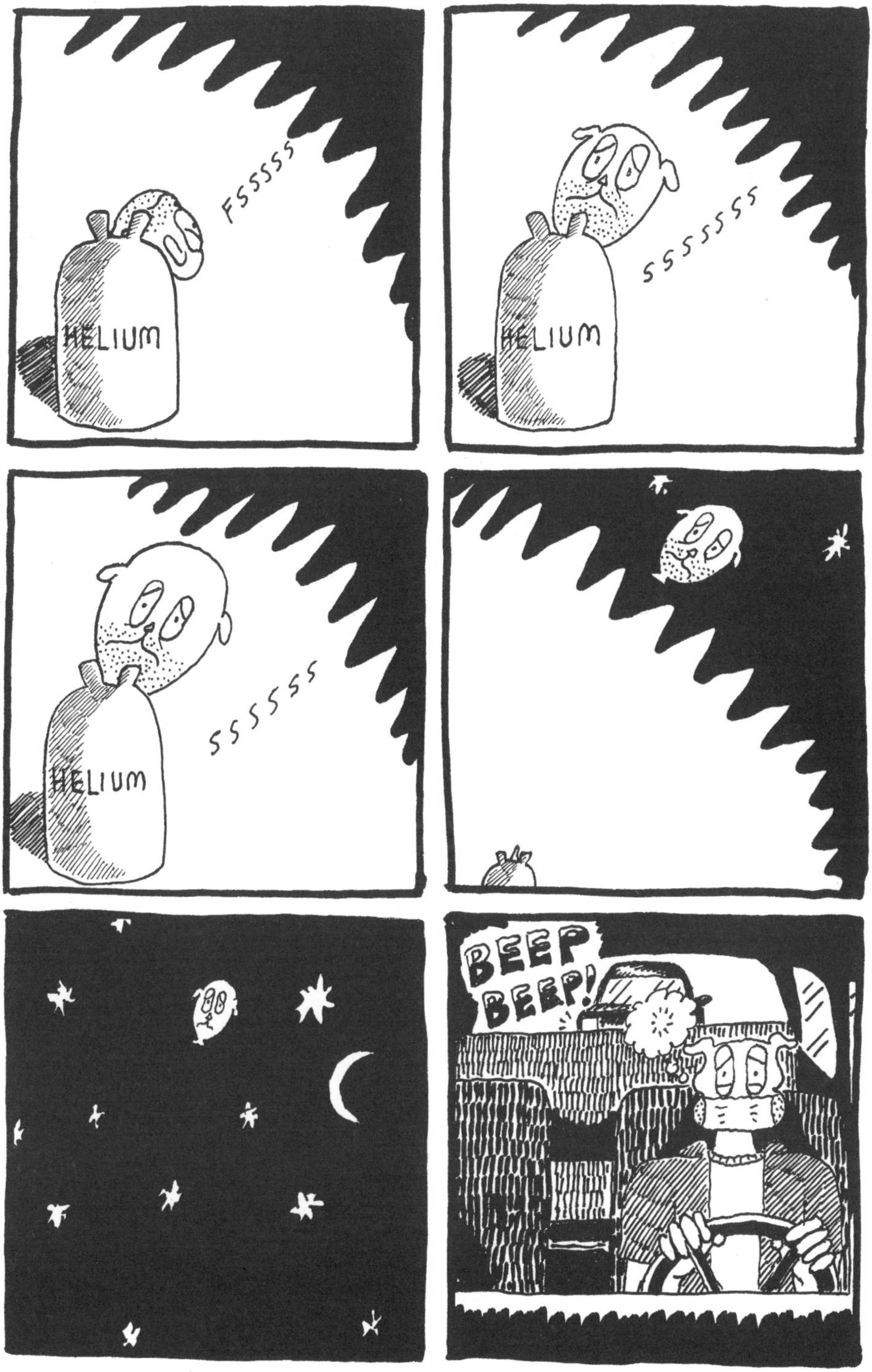
FSSSSS
SSSSSSSS
HELIUM
HELIUM
SSSSSS
HELIUM
BEEP BEEP!

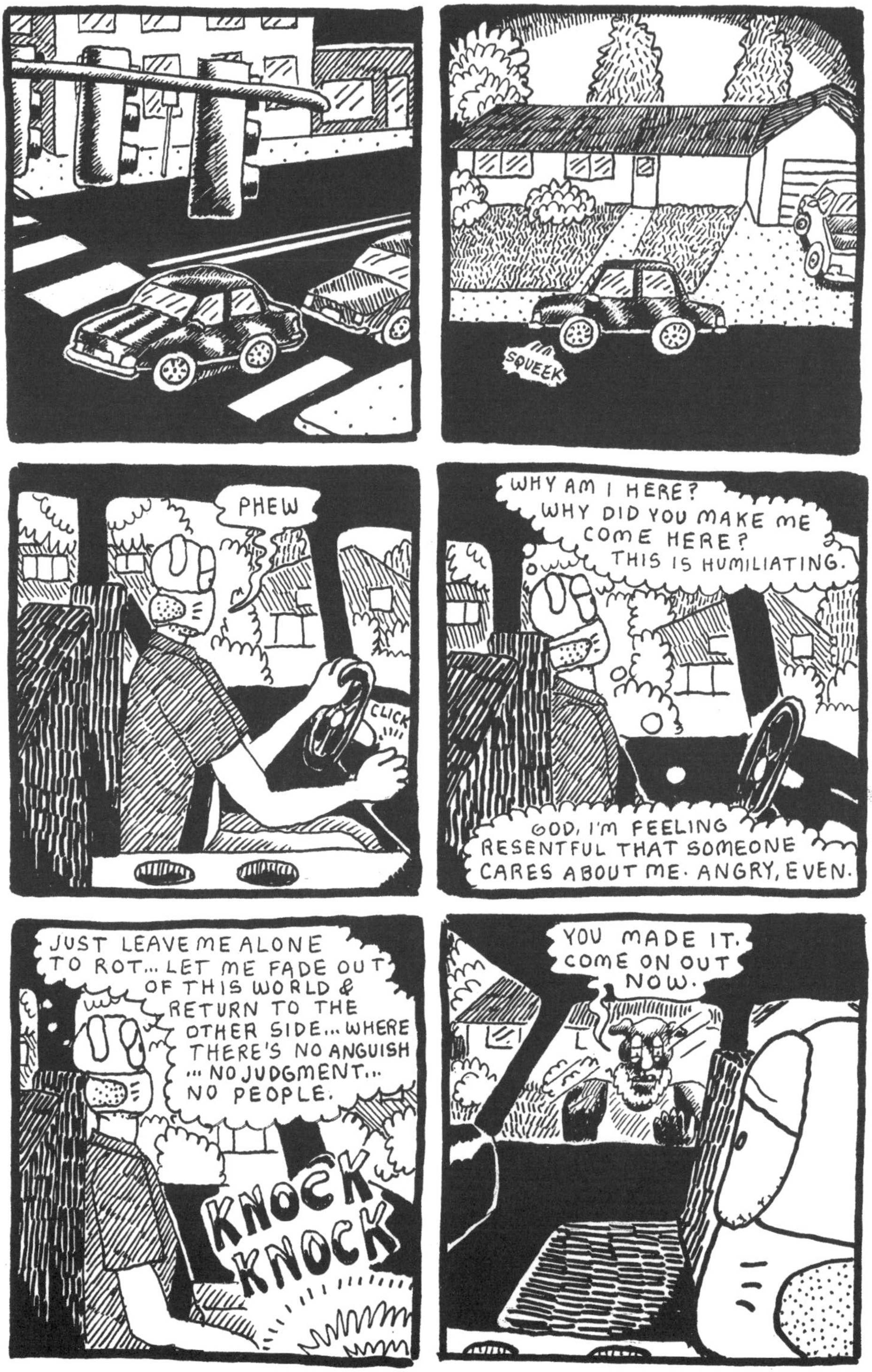
SQUEEK
PHEW
CLICK
WHY AM I HERE? WHY DID YOU MAKE ME COME HERE? THIS IS HUMILIATING.
GOD, I'M FEELING RESENTFUL THAT SOMEONE CARES ABOUT ME. ANGRY, EVEN.
JUST LEAVE ME ALONE TO ROT... LET ME FADE OUT OF THIS WORLD & RETURN TO THE OTHER SIDE... WHERE THERE'S NO ANGUISH ... NO JUDGMENT... NO PEOPLE.
KNOCK KNOCK
YOU MADE IT. COME ON OUT NOW.

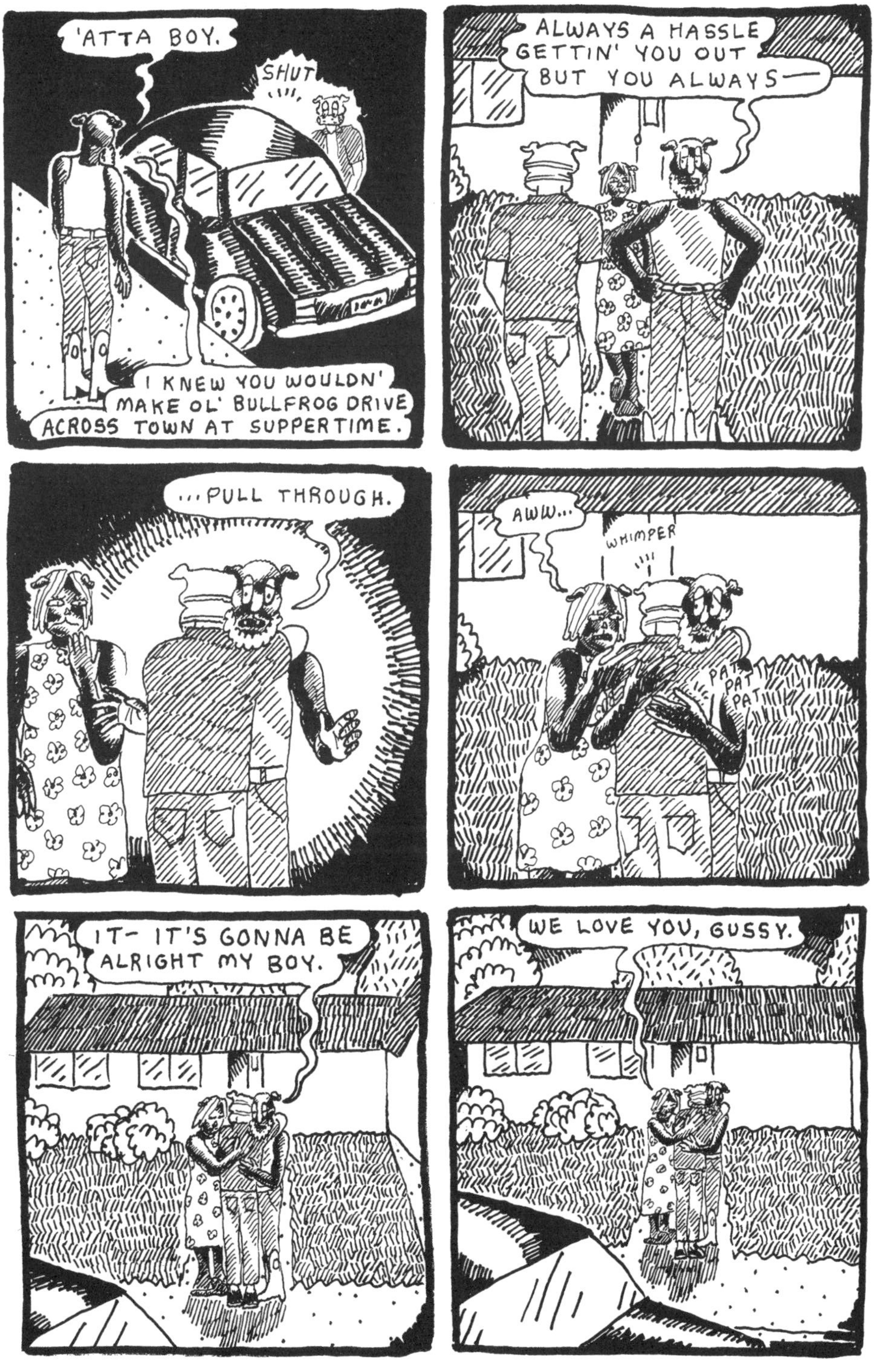
'ATTA BOY.
SHUT
I KNEW YOU WOULDN' MAKE OL' BULLFROG DRIVE ACROSS TOWN AT SUPPERTIME.
ALWAYS A HASSLE GETTIN' YOU OUT BUT YOU ALWAYS—
...PULL THROUGH.
AWW...
WHIMPER
PAT PAT PAT
IT- IT'S GONNA BE ALRIGHT MY BOY.
WE LOVE YOU, GUSSY.

"Life Goes On"

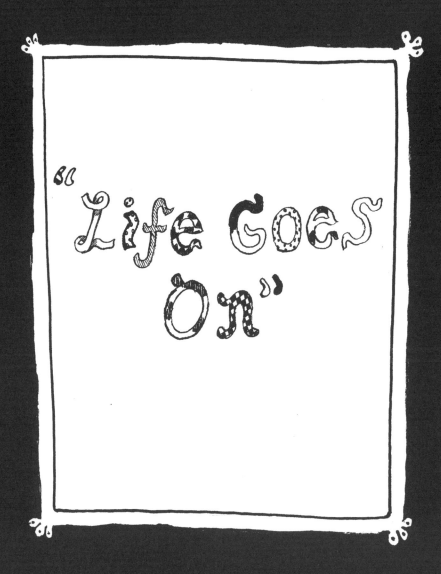

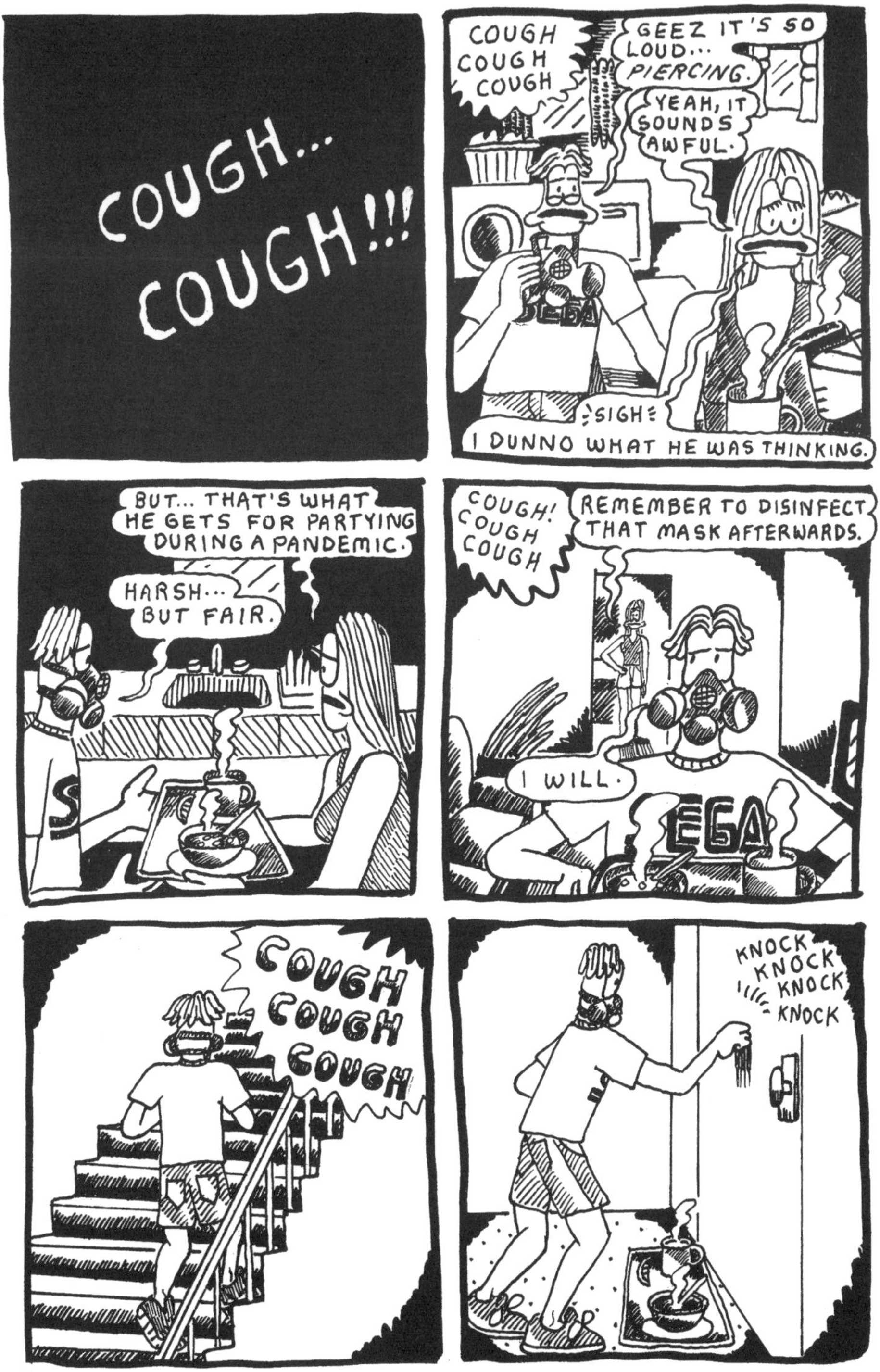
COUGH... COUGH!!!
COUGH COUGH COUGH
GEEZ IT'S SO LOUD... PIERCING.
YEAH, IT SOUNDS AWFUL.
SIGH
I DUNNO WHAT HE WAS THINKING.
BUT... THAT'S WHAT HE GETS FOR PARTYING DURING A PANDEMIC.
HARSH... BUT FAIR.
COUGH! COUGH COUGH
REMEMBER TO DISINFECT THAT MASK AFTERWARDS.
I WILL.
COUGH COUGH COUGH
KNOCK KNOCK KNOCK KNOCK

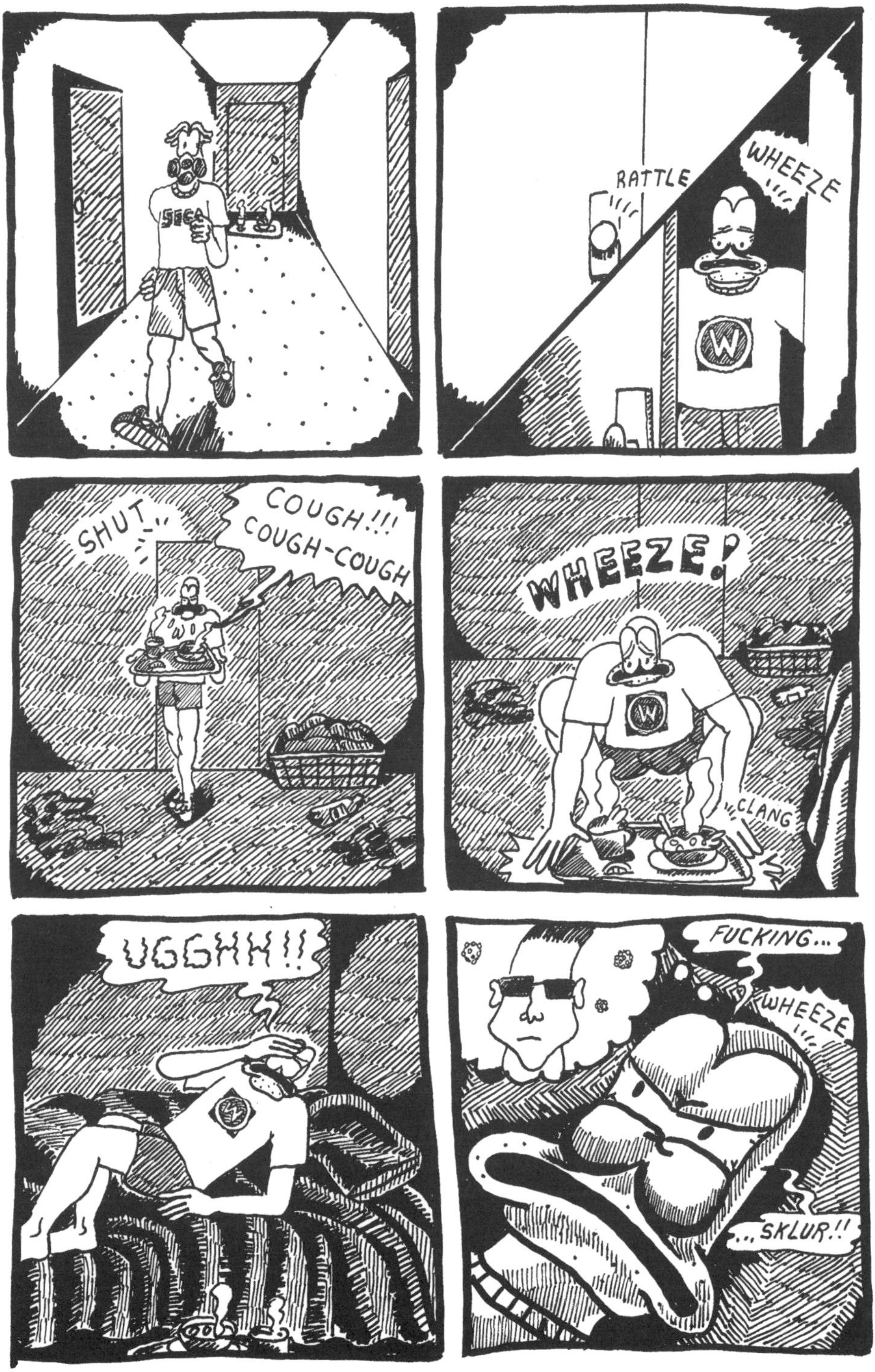
SEGA
RATTLE
WHEEZE
W
SHUT
COUGH!!!
COUGH-COUGH
W
WHEEZE!
W
CLANG
UGGHH!!
FUCKING...
WHEEZE
...SKLUR!!

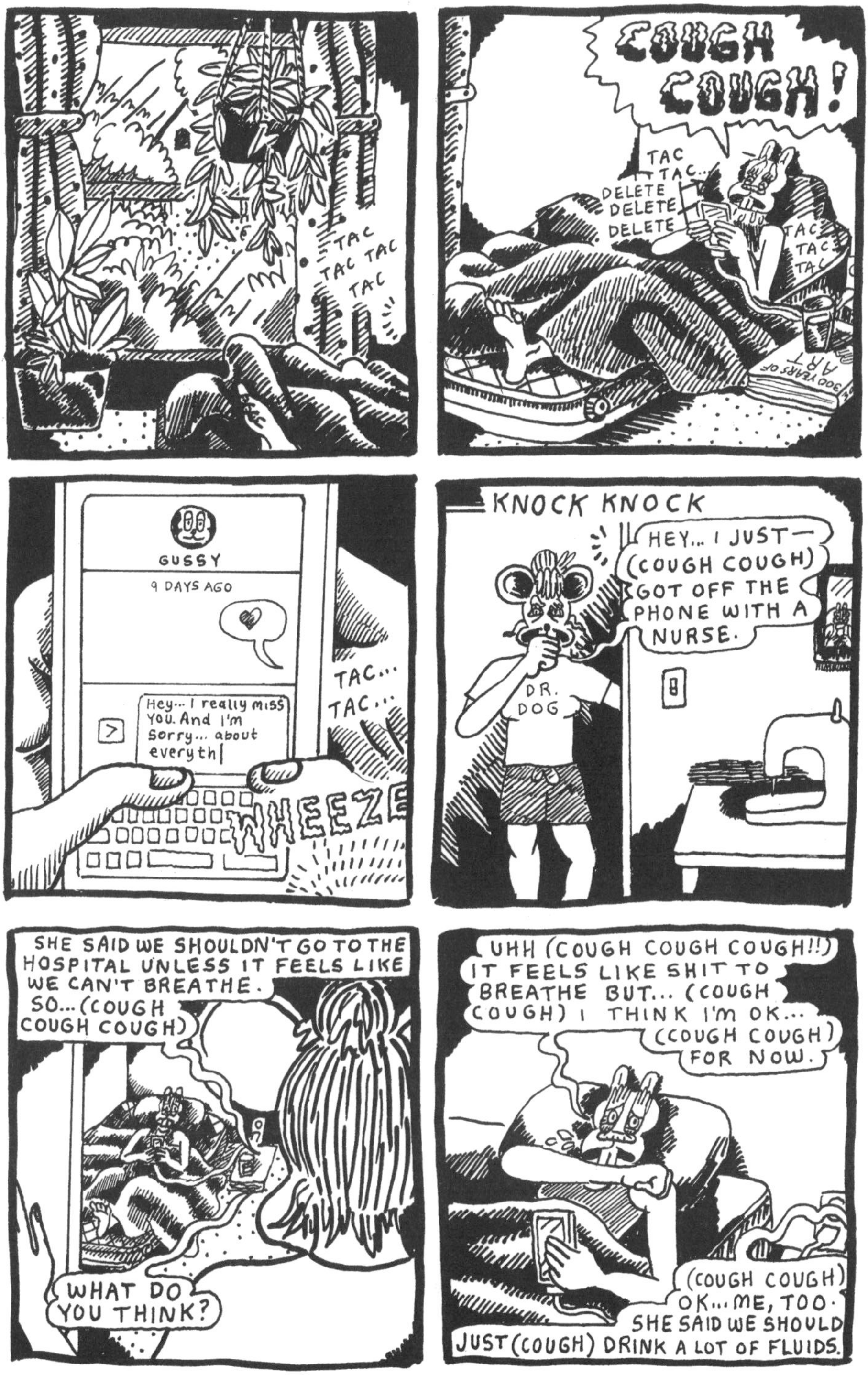
TAC
TAC TAC
TAC
COUGH COUGH!
TAC TAC...
DELETE DELETE DELETE
TAC TAC TAC
300 YEARS OF ART
GUSSY
9 DAYS AGO
Hey... I really miss you. And I'm sorry... about everyth
TAC... TAC...
WHEEZE
KNOCK KNOCK
HEY... I JUST— (COUGH COUGH) GOT OFF THE PHONE WITH A NURSE.
DR. DOG
SHE SAID WE SHOULDN'T GO TO THE HOSPITAL UNLESS IT FEELS LIKE WE CAN'T BREATHE. SO... (COUGH COUGH COUGH)
WHAT DO YOU THINK?
UHH (COUGH COUGH COUGH!!) IT FEELS LIKE SHIT TO BREATHE BUT... (COUGH COUGH) I THINK I'M OK... (COUGH COUGH) FOR NOW.
(COUGH COUGH) OK... ME, TOO. SHE SAID WE SHOULD JUST (COUGH) DRINK A LOT OF FLUIDS.

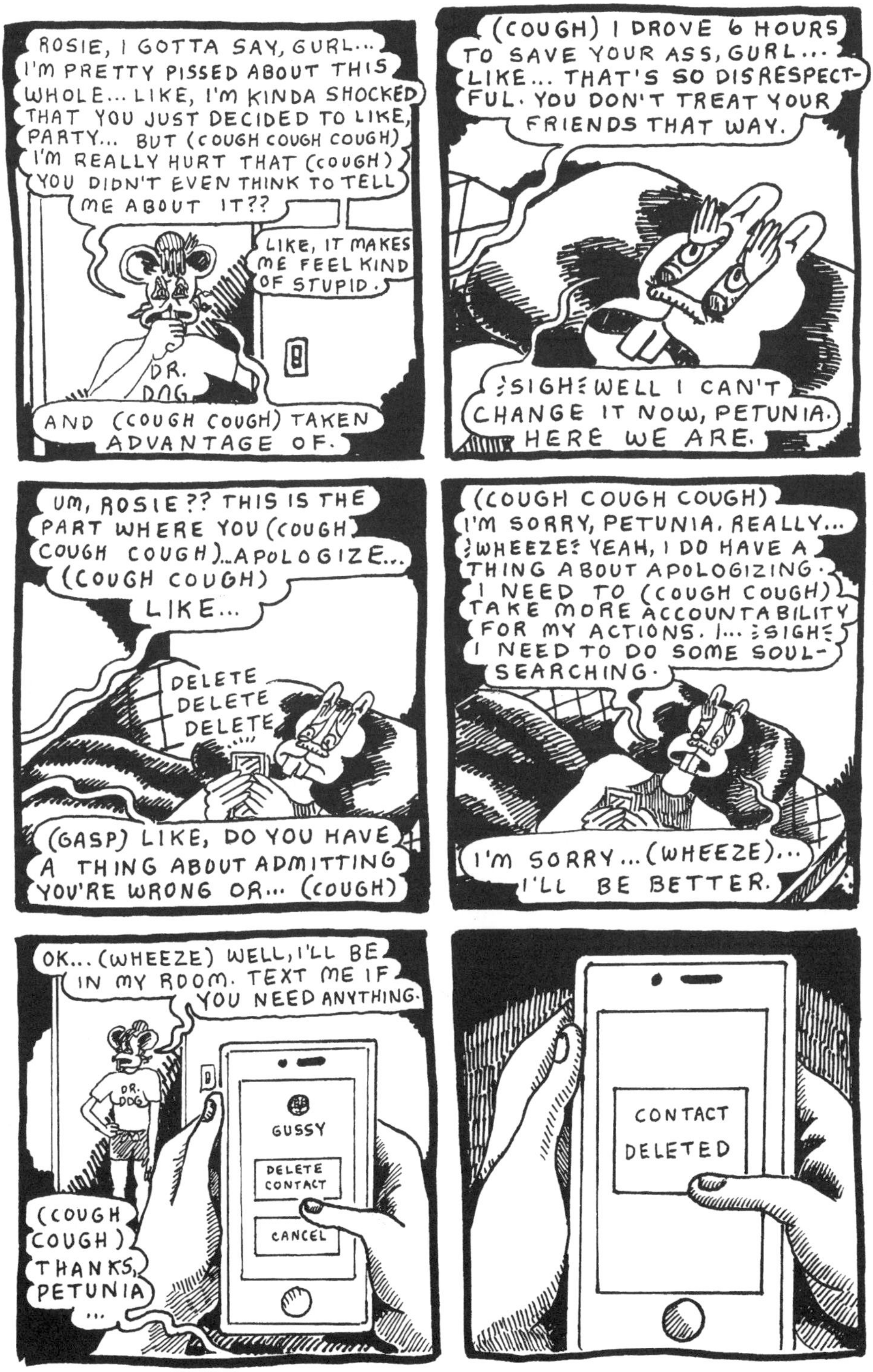
ROSIE, I GOTTA SAY, GURL... I'M PRETTY PISSED ABOUT THIS WHOLE... LIKE, I'M KINDA SHOCKED THAT YOU JUST DECIDED TO LIKE, PARTY... BUT (COUGH COUGH COUGH) I'M REALLY HURT THAT (COUGH) YOU DIDN'T EVEN THINK TO TELL ME ABOUT IT??
LIKE, IT MAKES ME FEEL KIND OF STUPID.
DR. DOG
AND (COUGH COUGH) TAKEN ADVANTAGE OF.
(COUGH) I DROVE 6 HOURS TO SAVE YOUR ASS, GURL... LIKE... THAT'S SO DISRESPECTFUL. YOU DON'T TREAT YOUR FRIENDS THAT WAY.
:SIGH: WELL I CAN'T CHANGE IT NOW, PETUNIA. HERE WE ARE.
UM, ROSIE?? THIS IS THE PART WHERE YOU (COUGH COUGH COUGH)...APOLOGIZE... (COUGH COUGH) LIKE...
DELETE DELETE DELETE
(GASP) LIKE, DO YOU HAVE A THING ABOUT ADMITTING YOU'RE WRONG OR... (COUGH)
(COUGH COUGH COUGH) I'M SORRY, PETUNIA. REALLY... :WHEEZE: YEAH, I DO HAVE A THING ABOUT APOLOGIZING. I NEED TO (COUGH COUGH) TAKE MORE ACCOUNTABILITY FOR MY ACTIONS. I... :SIGH: I NEED TO DO SOME SOUL-SEARCHING.
I'M SORRY...(WHEEZE)... I'LL BE BETTER.
OK... (WHEEZE) WELL, I'LL BE IN MY ROOM. TEXT ME IF YOU NEED ANYTHING.
DR. DOG
GUSSY
DELETE CONTACT
CANCEL
(COUGH COUGH) THANKS, PETUNIA...
CONTACT DELETED

...TANGENTIALLY, ACTRESS JENNIFER LOVE-HEWITT IS SEEKING A TEN MILLION DOLLAR SETTLEMENT FROM THE MUNICIPALITY... NEW COURT FILINGS IN THE CIVIL RIGHTS LAWSUIT BROUGHT BY LOVE-HEWITT AGAINST THE CITY OF SEATTLE CLAIM THAT HER SON WAS "UNLAWFULLY DETAINED AND BEATEN" BY TWO SEATTLE POLICE OFFICERS WHILE IN CUSTODY, AFTER BEING ARRESTED AT A PROTEST ON CAPITOL HILL.

3:04 PM

JENNIFER LOVE-HEWITT IS ONE OF A RECENT FLOOD OF LOS ANGELES-BASED CELEBRITIES TO CONTRACT COVID-19 FROM A YET-UNKNOWN "CELEBRITY SUPERSPREADER EVENT."

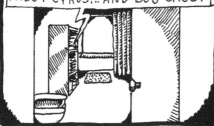

OTHER LOS ANGELES-BASED CELEBS WHO HAVE TESTED POSITIVE SINCE ATTENDING THIS UNKNOWN SUPERSPREADER EVENT INCLUDE MICK JAGGER, LADY GAGA, LIL NAS X, LANA DEL REY, ARIANA GRANDE, DOJA CAT, MEGAN THEE STALLION, MILEY CYRUS... AND BOB SAGET.

AND TRAGICALLY, TIMOTHÉE CHALAMET HAS PASSED AWAY AFTER CONTRACTING COVID AT THIS YET-UNKNOWN SUPERSPREADER EVENT, RENDERING HIM UNABLE TO PLAY BOB DYLAN IN THE UPCOMING BIOPIC DIRECTED BY JAMES MARIGOLD.

THE BIOPIC HAS BEEN CANCELLED.

CONSERVATIVE POLITICIAN HERMAN CAIN SEEMS TO BE RECOVERING SWIFTLY AFTER CONTRACTING THE VIRUS AT AN INDOOR TRUMP RALLY LAST MONTH...

"I FEEL LIKE A MILLION DAMN BUCKS" HE IS QUOTED AS SAYING.
THIS IS N.P.R. NEWS.

TAC TAC TAC TAC TAC

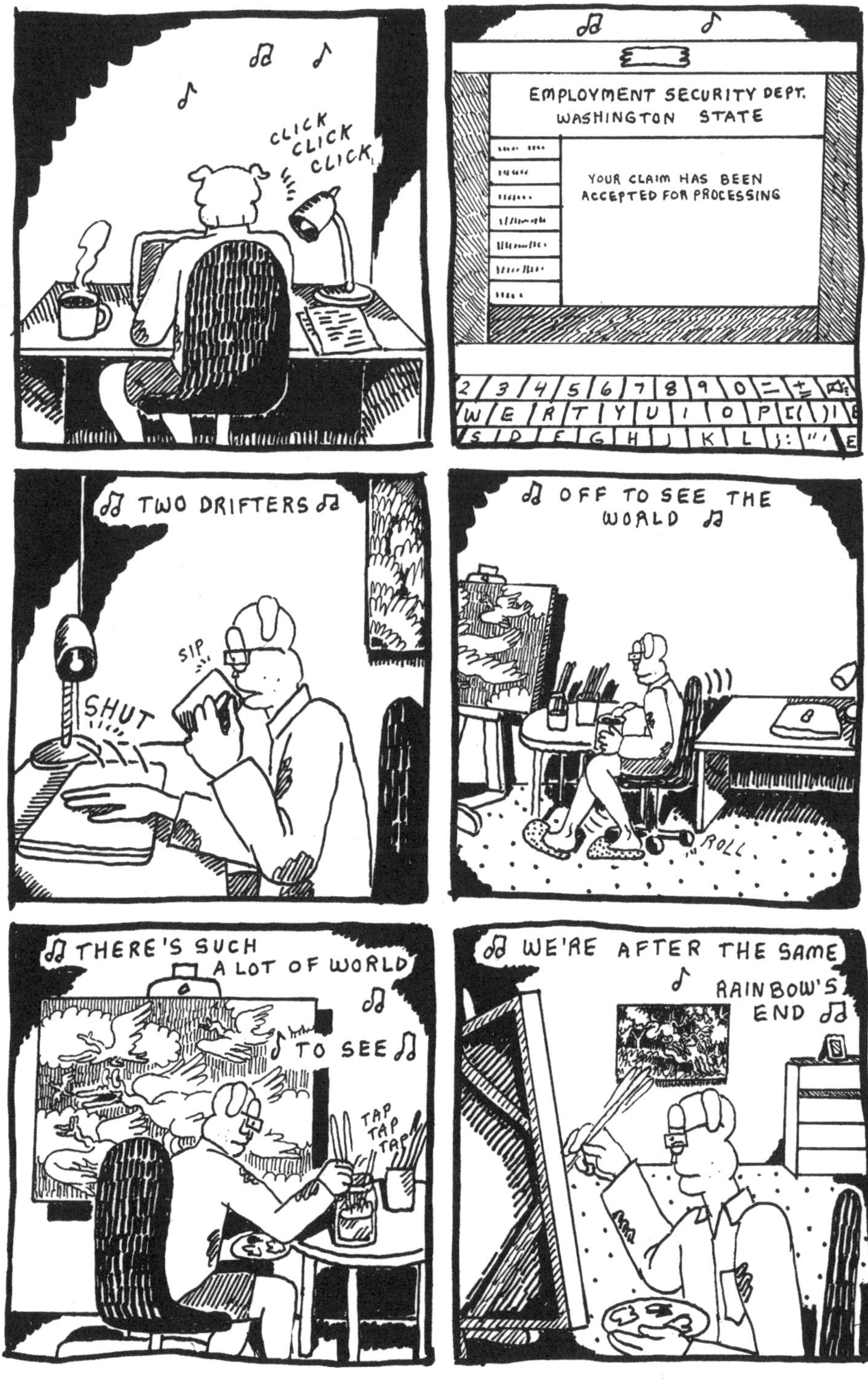
CLICK
CLICK
CLICK
EMPLOYMENT SECURITY DEPT.
WASHINGTON STATE
YOUR CLAIM HAS BEEN ACCEPTED FOR PROCESSING
TWO DRIFTERS
SIP
SHUT
OFF TO SEE THE WORLD
ROLL
THERE'S SUCH A LOT OF WORLD
TO SEE
TAP
TAP
TAP
WE'RE AFTER THE SAME
RAINBOW'S END

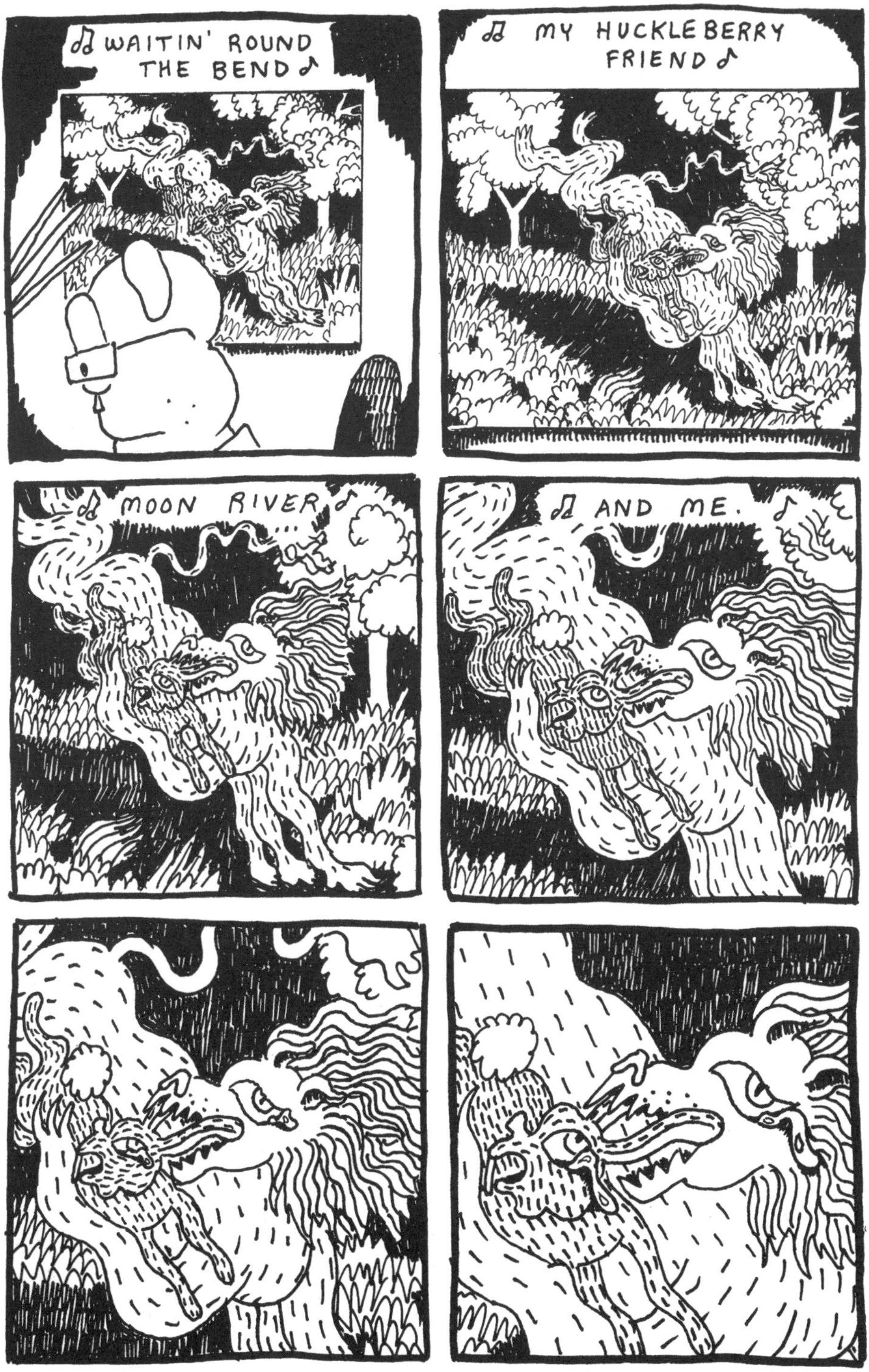
♫ WAITIN' ROUND THE BEND ♪
♫ MY HUCKLEBERRY FRIEND ♪
♫ MOON RIVER ♪
♫ AND ME. ♪

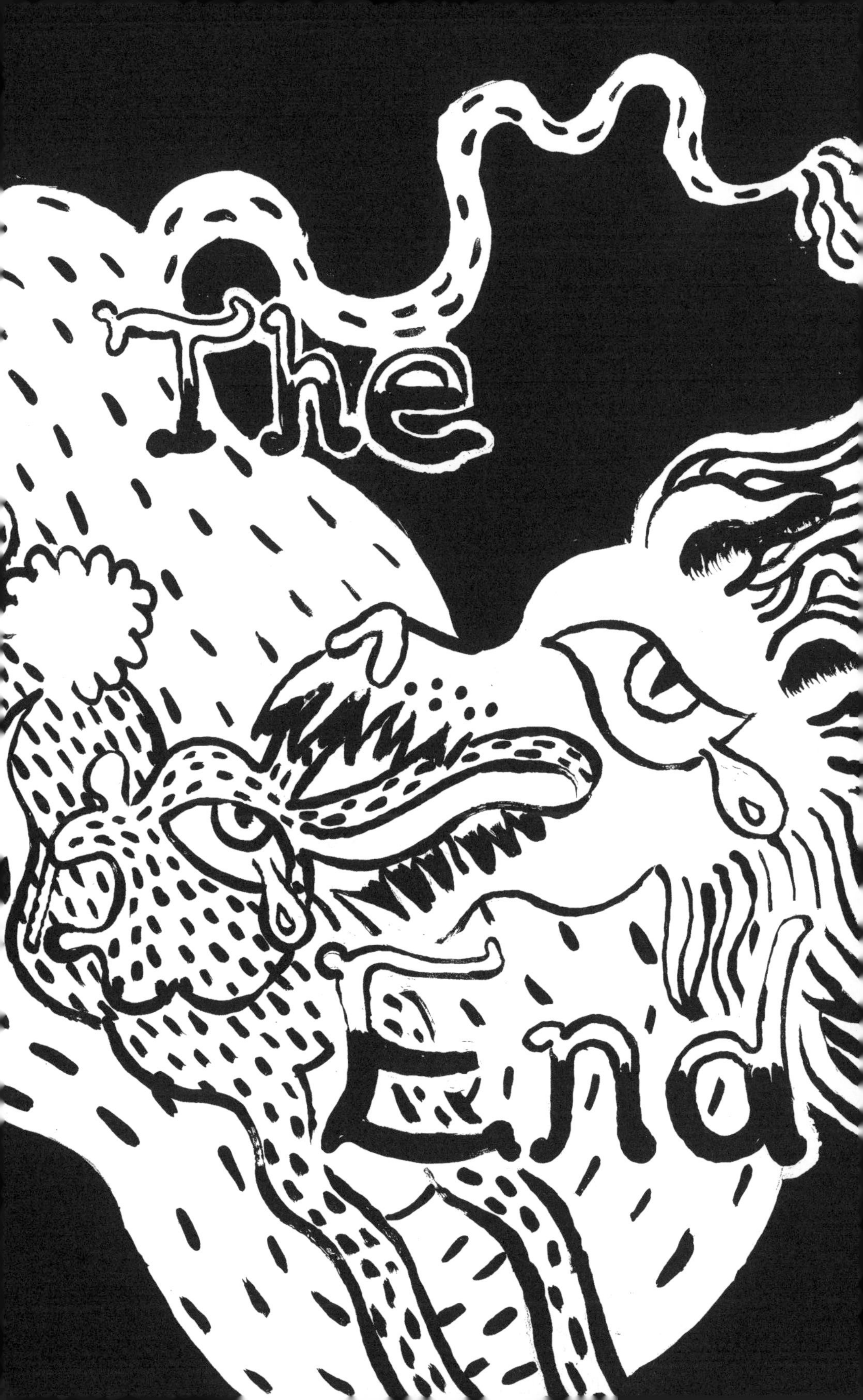
The
End

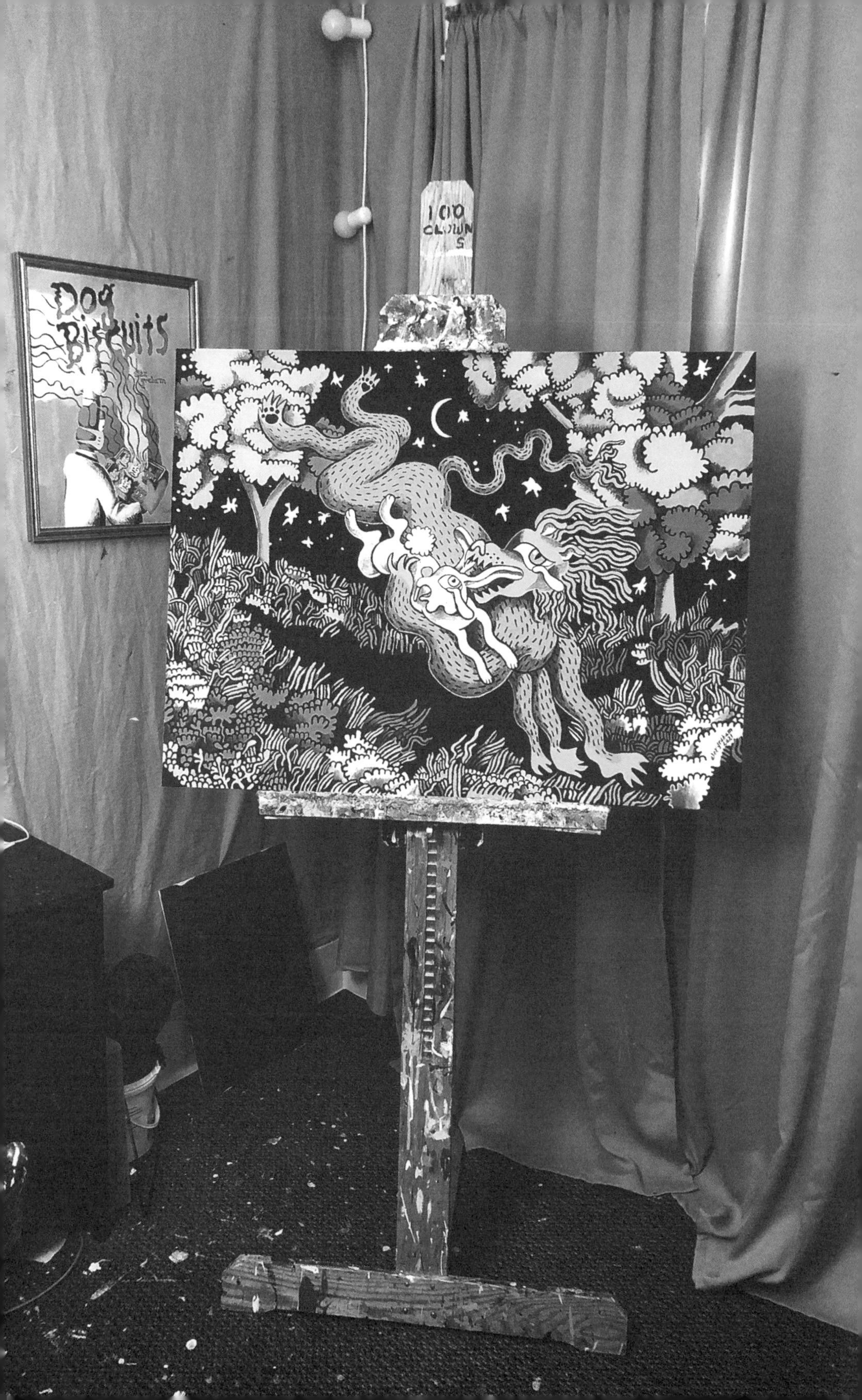
Dog Biscuits
100 CLOWNS

ALEX GRAHAM

IS A PAINTER & CARTOONIST
FROM DENVER, COLORADO, CURRENTLY
RESIDING IN SEATTLE, WASHINGTON.

alexNgraham.com

THE DOG BIS CUITS EX PERI ENCE

began drawing *Dog Biscuits* in June 2020, while sitting at the bar in the restaurant where I was an employee, after being hired back to fulfill the requirements of the pandemic loan our restaurant received. According to the loan, employees were required to clock in and be present for 40 hours a week, even though business was almost nonexistent due to the pandemic.

After weeks of sitting in silence at the bar reading books, scrolling... I decided to grab some printer paper from the office, drew the first page of *Dog Biscuits* (then untitled) with a sharpie, without any solid plans for a story, and casually posted it to Instagram thinking it would go unnoticed because of the sloppy drawing style and spontaneous, unchecked dialogue. But somehow, much to my surprise, people were hooked.

(Aside: I was furloughed again a few months later and started drawing *Dog Biscuits* from home for 6 to 8 hours a day.)

As the web comic gained more and more attention, thanks in part to Simon Hanselmann spreading the word, I started feeling myself mentally and emotionally preoccupied with the way commenters were reacting, not as readers of literature, but as judges presiding over private lives of my characters, and how quick they were to condemn the characters — especially the masculine ones — for even the most minor missteps.

If you were faithfully following along with the web comic, you might have witnessed several of my interjections, pleading with the audience not to violently heckle and wish death upon my characters, after which I always found myself embarrassed about having "given in" to the heckling.

About 150 pages into the comic, I decided to formally address these bizarre reactions beyond just replying and pleading via Instagram. I decided to eventually write an essay for the back of the book to address the public reception of *Dog Biscuits* as a daily webcomic, using actual quotes from the comment section as citations.

Foremost, I wanted to point out the bizarre ways social justice language skews the way we interpret and absorb fiction. But I also wanted to "stick it" to the most ridiculous and infuriating audience members.

By the time I had drawn the last page, however, I realized how ill the thought of reliving those emotions, and re-reading those comments for the purpose of writing this essay, made me feel.

When my friend Lane, who witnessed much of my frustrated reactions to audience members, heard that I was no longer intending to write the essay, they enthusiastically volunteered to do it, and I am so thankful because they really understood my intention and wrote it out beautifully.

—Alex Graham, 2021

EXIT DOG BIS CUITS

Constructive honesty is so scarce in the circulation of comic book stories in recent history, such that it's not outlandish to claim that it is entirely out of style. The exchange is in favor of unquestionable morality, the manifestation of fictive individu–als who are beyond reproach and devoid of personal history configuring tragedy as an Easy Bake Oven producing totally inoffensive, honest human beings. Our conception of a virtuous person, as portrayed in comics specifically, hedges around their perfect engagements with others, a refined temperament, and a holistic denial of hardship as something that can potentially make you more, rather than less, problematic. This is a fantasy and, moreover, a false construction. Privilege is effectively the ability to proceed through life unobstructed by personal history, or, at the very least, to only reckon with it on an immediate basis rather than bearing the weight of ingrained difficulty, immediate financial ruin, and the disastrous coping mechanisms that serve to make us less approachable. People, or at least actual living people, resist archetypal characterization, and these archetypal conceptions often lead us to meanness and insensitivity. *Dog Biscuits* is a genuine reflection on personal history and its social consequences. As a subject of its serialization on Instagram, this resulted in a varied set of reactions that can potentially be blamed on a misapprehension of its concept, an impatience with the necessity of portraying characters with genuine flaws, or a lurking jealousy inspired by Alex Graham's remarkable productivity and well-deserved public attention. It is also possible that the aggregate capacity for forgiveness in fictive popular media has grown especially thin as a consequence of the social conversation revolving around deplorable rich men doing deplorable things with virtually no consequences; resulting, unconvincingly, in a generation of narrative media that presents only virtue obscuring the immanent social relationships that exist in Actual Reality, which is obviously quite a bit more complicated.

The serialization of *Dog Biscuits* on Instagram generated a fair amount of propriety over the course of the narrative by the viewers. For those who weren't aware, each installment was well shared, well liked, and well engaged with, but many left comments to the effect of "This character makes me uncomfortable," or "This character is so *x*, I hate them," or "This makes me nervous," etc. This, I can only imagine, was infuriating. I do, however, think it makes a great deal of sense in the case of social platforms where people are given unlimited (if the comments are turned on) access to com-mentary when the fashionable *style* of commentary of the day is generally concerned with moral assessment. The comic was lightly controversial, and, in the moments where conflict was stressed (as is necessary both in real life and in the construction of a compelling piece of fiction), many of the commenters deigned to mistake the actions of fictional characters as the actions of real life persons to be cut-off and dispensed with because of their bad behavior. Again, everyone is entitled to this type of reaction. In fact, it's a reflection of Graham's good storytelling that people engaged with it so honestly, and candidly. That is, of course, a positive reading of the aggregate reaction. I couldn't help but feel that if Graham were more famous, had more books published, or had a bigger name in the cartooning world, people would by no means exert such a sense of ownership over her work, nor would they question her ability to construct a narrative that doesn't descend into garish edginess.

It was evident, in the comic's life on Instagram, that many commenters had a demonstrated lack of trust that Graham even understood the stakes of her own narrative, or the emotional intensity evident in the work itself. The scene where the Seattle Police raid Leroy and Rosie's apartment, destroying their property and physically abusing both, is an example of this relationship.

Many commenters spoke about how intense it was, but their approach in letting the artist know her scene was effectual was expressed as an inquiry into her own moral positioning, as if she couldn't comprehend it herself. This relationship of questioning, with the "correct" answer already in mind and an assumption that the creator, herself, is incorrect, prevailed especially strongly in situations where Rosie and Gussy interacted intimately. The audience, speaking generally, expressed that they knew where the story was going, and, albeit in good faith, assumed that the story was a polemic crafted intentionally to spite their values. As the story has now concluded, I can't imagine that very many people consider the age-gap relationship between Rosie and Gussy to be a success story. True to the social realism that governs most of the comic, the relationship falls apart on its own terms. Relative to their life experience the characters, authentically, give up on their relationship because of its inherent flaws. It plays itself.

Frankly I don't know the level of composition associated with the story, nor do I claim to know Alex Graham's process in creating *Dog Biscuits,* but watching the comic arrive at its conclusion demonstrated that her process was radically different than the understanding put forth by its viewers. The latent assumption I encountered is that the artist's role in constructing a story is to restrict and confine the actions of the personalities on display to a range of agency that is to be quickly restricted if it approaches anything resembling a flaw, and that flaws in characters are, themselves, mistakes on the part of the artist or reflections of the artist's poor morality. And at this point I'm not even sure if this is pessimism or naiveté. Frustratingly, I'm not sure if the audience is aware of the difference in this case, because the logical endpoint of what I apprehended was the frequent reaction to the comic was that a *good person* is someone who has no connection to reality. Someone who only feels altruistic pain in a manner that is extremely socially viable, and is wholly, constantly, concerned with the outcomes of their actions viewed within a scope of morality that is scarcely applicable to a real human being. In these terms a *good person* is someone who has never had to learn how to survive. The comic, however, restrains itself with internal moral diagnoses. The terms of the narrative even have the capacity for self-diagnosis insofar as the characters judge themselves, and frequently overestimate their own transgressions. Gussy is plagued with self-loathing, Leroy is caught in the stasis of chronic anxiety, Rosie traps herself in amorous relationships that she knows can't possibly work out for her, and Hissy realizes the superfluousness of his existence as a rich boy in a class society, albeit in what seems to be bad faith. All things considered, the characters are appropriately self-aware, perhaps too much so, but in a way that manages to be realistic and relatable relative to the cultural dialogue in which we currently exist.

After all, this is a comic that takes place in the era of COVID-19 and it addresses this both in the presentation of the circumstances and in the spectacle of its engagement. There are, of course, risks involved with socialization, and it would be simple to consider this in the metaphorical sense regarding these characters, but the hazards of romance, and the thorniness of social interaction are reflected in both the immanent content of the piece as well as in the aggregate social reaction to it. Abstracted from the liberation of social interaction we have all become critics, in both moral and aesthetic terms, in the only forum accessible to us on an immediate basis. As such, the spirit of social judgement pervades our interactions on the internet, as the genuine social reality is either totally obstructed or placed in a position of immediate physical peril; Leroy, Hissy, and Rosie do, ultimately, end up bedridden with COVID after attending a super-spreader that claims the life of Graham's fictionalized Timothée Chalamet. It's a joke in context, but the reinforcement of the reality of a deadly contagion as it both physically, mentally, and spiritually ravages the entire population of our country feels necessary. Nonetheless, the consequences of these interactions are balanced by their necessity in our lives. We need to see other people, and to find ourselves in our social environments to attempt to forget the mundane horrors of purpose and labor. Of course, there is the matter of responsibility, and these characters grapple with that as well. There's no correct answer to navigating any social reality in a person's life. Prescriptions and generalized conceptions of what is the *correct answer* point us in the direction to go, but ultimately compromises are made that aren't even consciously decided upon. Necessity creates complications and forces us to reconcile with them to ourselves and to those we are responsible to. That is too general but *Dog Biscuits* shows this in a specific location with specific elements to characters that act, speak, and think authentically. Watching this, in real time, over the course of my own reckoning with a totally unexpected global crisis, was humbling, illustrative, and, most importantly, true.

To me, *Dog Biscuits* is about forgiveness. Over the course of the narrative, the characters learn to forgive themselves, they learn to forgive others, and they learn what can't necessarily be forgiven. There is a demonstrated interest in constructing forgiveness as a form of salvation. The best example of this is Gussy, potentially the "main" character if there is one, who recovers his aspirations to be a painter in the story's conclusion. He quits lying to himself about who he wants to be and makes a bold choice that requires him to confront his self-doubt, his history of abuse, and the real possibility of failure. He has to forgive himself and move on. He finishes his painting. This reflects what I feel to be the "moral statement" of the work, if such a thing exists. Reflecting back to the matter of engagement, I found this, if not ironic, totally amusing from the perspective of an observer. The engagement pleaded and begged for a moral statement. Something grandiose and punitive that would show us all what these characters deserved for all their bad behavior, but the engagement never allowed for forgiveness. The conversation centered around punishment and not its opposite, for all its moral posturing the language of the internet lent itself most immediately to carceral logic. The stay of execution at the end of *Dog Biscuits* feels utterly miraculous and utterly true, because in life's lowest moments there is nothing but the nagging fantasy of termination, of ending things, of cutting them off and neglecting the viability of one's life. But it doesn't quite work out that way. This isn't a torture porn narrative, this is a story where characters try their best to be what they can be despite how achingly difficult it is to be. To live. To exist. It's fraught with complications, and disappointments, and, in these circumstances, the yawning dark of non-existence presents itself as comfort. With or without you, though, life moves on. It is you who has to make that life work; to make it something worth continuing.

For all the piss and vinegar generated from reading the comments and, frankly, from reading the comics — I believed in *Dog Biscuits*. The technical aspects are, of course, in all their right places. It's frequently funny, and excellently drawn, but you didn't need me to broach that. To me it was just *true*. It was outside of the conversation of making a "comic that works" or "a comic that appeals to all these readers" or "a relatable conversation relayed and reiterated, somehow arriving at inner peace". It wasn't cynical or snide or overblown. It was a comic that spoke to what I felt was real, and how I felt about what has happened to all of us during a pandemic. It was not a polemic, or an over justification of its own engagement with historical spectacle. It was a description of a situation with a cross-section of people who interacted. They had conversations, and that felt true. Such that the conversation around the conversation felt demonstrably untrue. It felt like a masquerade, and a persistent demonstration of moral superiority denying contingency. So, I am glad you are reading this in a context removed from that context. Without the background noise sputtering nonsense of morality vs. immorality as two diametrically opposed and permanent forces in the world. And, in the spirit of optimism, hopefully our social arrangement will be significantly altered such that reductions of this kind diminish in our newfound conviviality. At a bar, at a social event — fuck, at a comics convention — enjoying the company of other human faces with all the psychological advantages inherent in seeing someone's *actual* face. Hopefully this will be easier, and we won't hate each other so much. Hopefully when you read this you won't care about comments on Instagram. This is a book now, a historical object with tangible weight, and so it can be true, or untrue, to *you*, whenever, however *you* experience it. This isn't to say we should all buy each other a Coke, sing in perfect harmony, whatever: life will always be difficult, but you already knew that right?

—Lane Yates, 2021

GUSSY'S APARTMENT

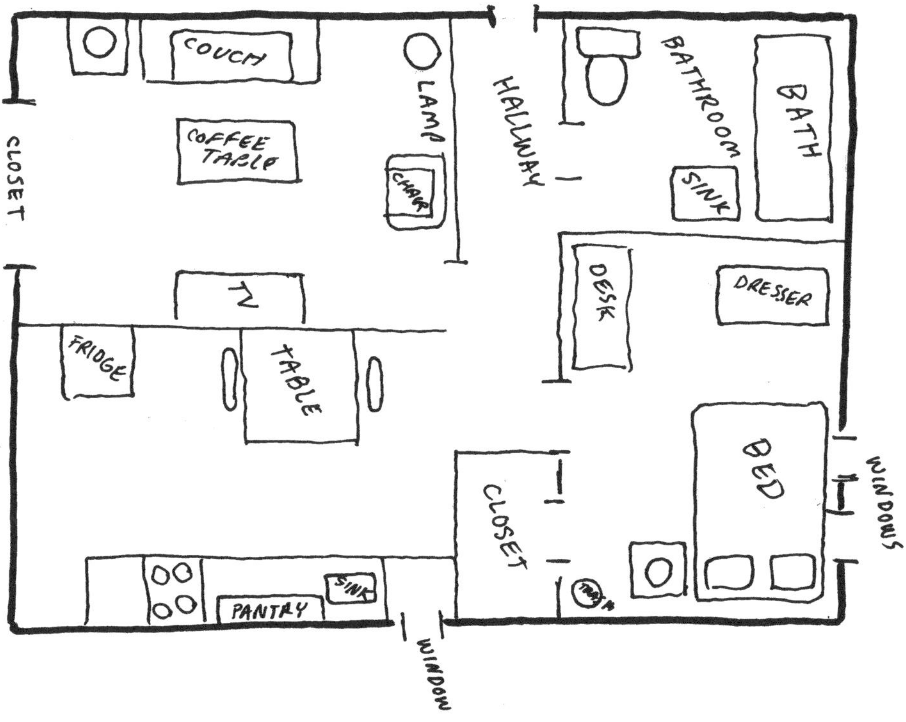
COUCH
LAMP
HALLWAY
BATHROOM
BATH
CLOSET
COFFEE TABLE
CHAIR
SINK
DESK
DRESSER
TV
FRIDGE
TABLE
BED
WINDOWS
CLOSET
SINK
PANTRY
WINDOW

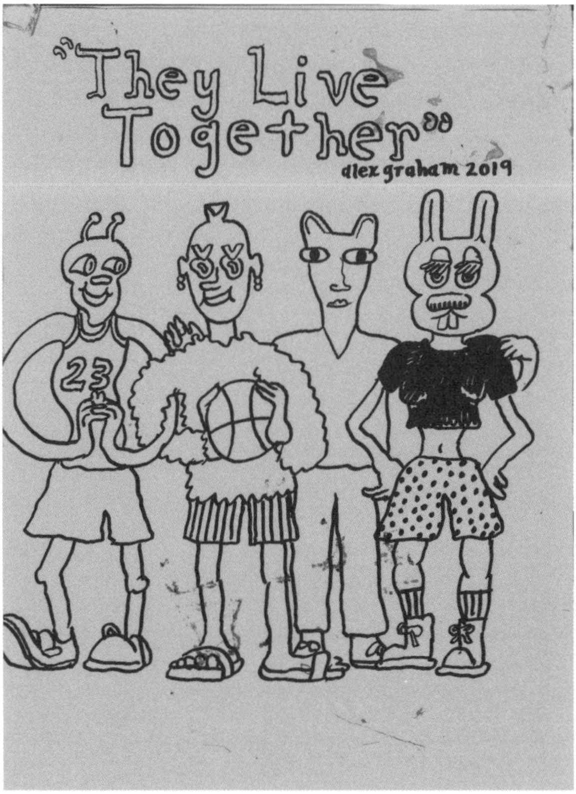
"They Live Together"
alex graham 2019
23

ABANDONED STORY/TITLE THAT
EVENTUALLY BECAME "DOG BISCUITS"

Thanks: Simon H., Brandon, Oliver, Skyler, Jason, Ben, Tyson, Valentina, Jean-marie, Lane Y.

This book is dedicated to Patrick, who patiently endured my insanity while I was working on this project, and was always available to proof-read or lend an ear. He also wrote the synopsis on the back of the book.

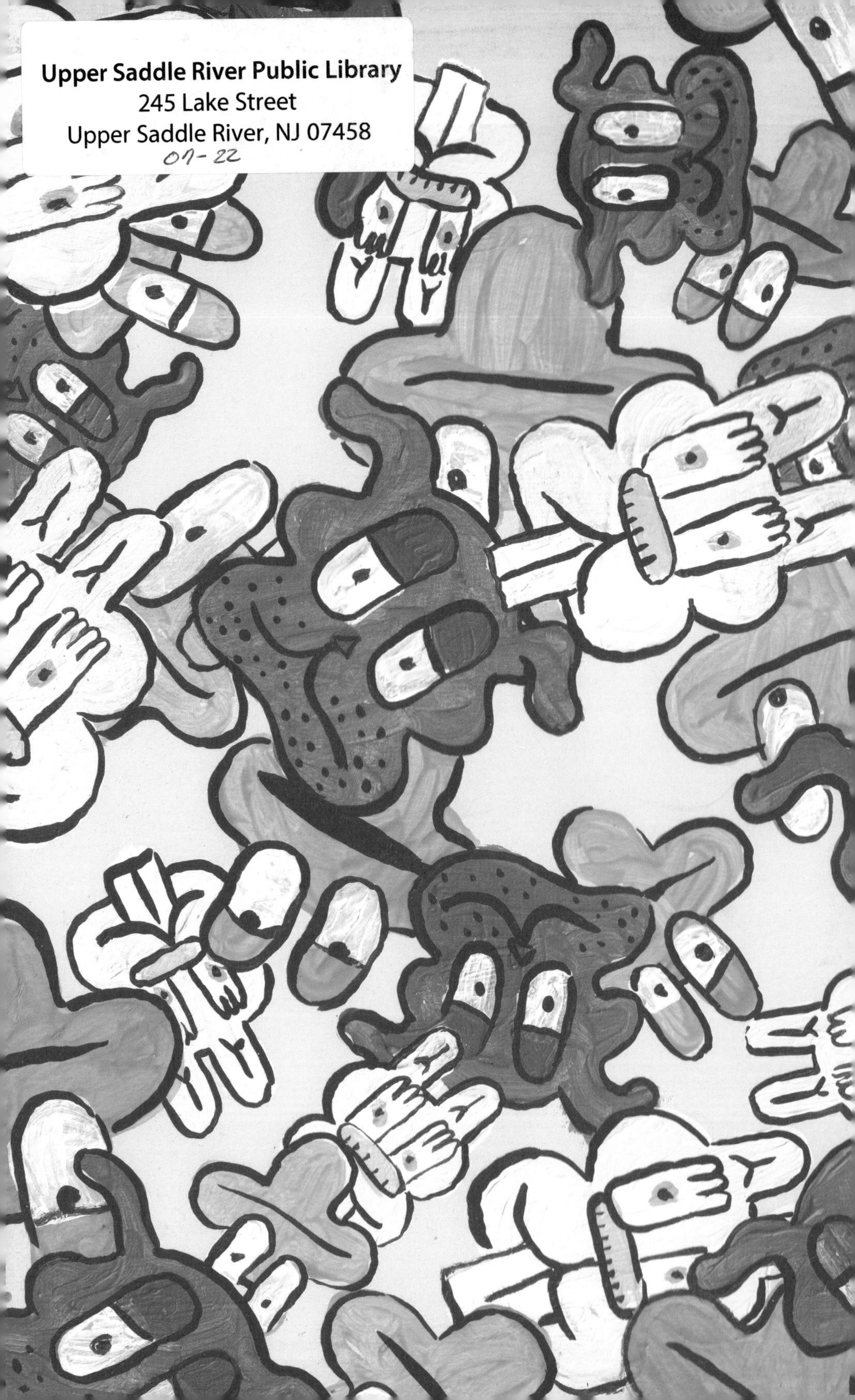